SOSE

Studies of Society & Environment

4

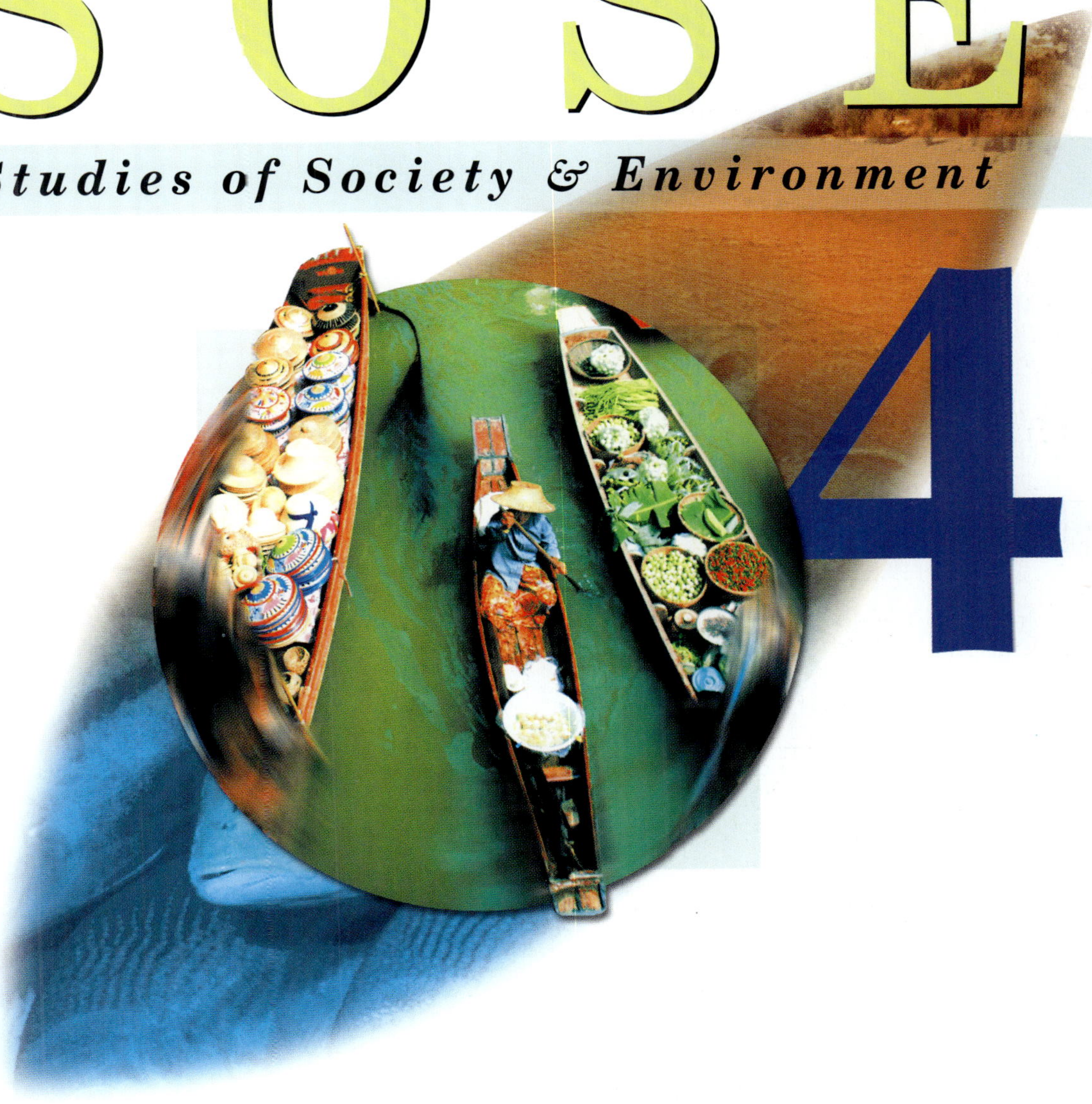

SECOND EDITION

jacaranda
jaconline.com.au

SOSE

Studies of Society & Environment

4

New for Level 6 of the Curriculum and Standards Framework II

Judy Mraz • Russell Ives • Jo Lamont
Megan Bourke • David Kronenberg
Mark Easton • Maureen Anderson

Contributing authors:
Anita Forsyth, Richard Morris

SECOND EDITION

Second edition published 2000 by
John Wiley & Sons Australia, Ltd
33 Park Road, Milton, Qld 4064

Offices also in Sydney and Melbourne

Typeset in 10.5/12 pt New Century

First edition 1998

National Library of Australia
Cataloguing-in-publication data

Jacaranda SOSE 4: studies of society & environment

2nd ed.
Includes index.
ISBN 0 7016 3488 X.

1. Social sciences — Australia — Juvenile literature.
2. Commerce — Australia — Juvenile literature.
3. Australia — History — Juvenile literature.
I. Mraz, Judy. II. Title: Studies of society and environment.

300.994

Cover images: Corbis (Uluru and fish) © 2000,
Digital Stock (floating market) © 2000

Maps supplied by MAPgraphics and
Ikon Computergraphics (Margaret Hastie)

Illustrated by Wendy Arthur, Paul Lennon, Miecke den Otter, Stephen Francis, Terry St Ledger, Craig Jackson, Steve Hunter and the John Wiley Art Department

Printed in Singapore

10 9 8 7 6 5 4 3

Contents

Acknowledgements

The publishers would like to thank the following authors for the use of material reproduced (with minor adaptations) from other Jacaranda textbooks.

• **Robert Engwerda**, from Jacaranda SOSE 4: spreads 1.1, 1.2, 1.3, 1.4, 1.5, 1.6, 1.7, 1.8, 1.9 • **Anne Lowe**, from *Retroactive 2*: spreads 4.7, 4.8, 4.9, 4.10, 5.1, 5.2 & 5.3 • **John Paine**, from *Geoactive 2*: spread 5.5 • **Alison Schlueter**, from *Legal Outcomes 1* • **Angelo Calandra,** from *SOSE 1*: spread 7.1 • Grace Ciavarella from SOSE 1: spread 7.1 • **Stephen Chapman**, from *Business Studies in Action HSC Course*: spread 8.2 • **Carolyn Harper**, from *Business Studies in Action HSC Course*: spread 8.6

The authors and publisher would like to thank the following copyright holders, organisations and individuals for permission to reproduce copyright material in this book.

Images

• Corbis: **cover** (Uluru and fish) © 2000, chapters 3, 4, 11, 12 & 13 background images, pp. **244** (left) © 1999, **310** (right)/Digital Stock ©1998, • Coo-ee Picture Library: source **5.11.2** (flag), • Digital Stock: **cover** (floating market) © 2000 • Australian War Memorial: pp. **2–3**, sources **1.1.1***, **1.2.1**, **1.3.1**, **1.4.2**/ Barbara Mobbs, **1.4.4**, **1.7.3**, **1.8.1**, **1.9.1**, **1.9.3**, pp. **50–51**, sources **3.3.2**, **3.4.4**, **3.5.7**, **3.5.9**, **3.6.3**, **3.6.4**, **3.7.2**, **3.8.4**, **3.9.3**, **3.9.7**, **3.10.2**, **4.9.2**, • Coo-ee Historical Picture Library: sources **1.2.5**, **1.8.2**, **2.1.1** (Woodrow Wilson), **2.7.1**, **2.11.2**, **3.4.3**, **3.8.1**, **3.10.4**, **4.5.3** • National Library of Australia, reproduced with permission **1.5.1**/Barbara Mobbs • Image Library, State Library of NSW: sources **1.6.1**, **1.6.2**, **3.9.4** • VISCOPY: pp. **24–5**, **2.7.6**/© Ludwig Hohlwein, 1935/Bild –Kunst. Licensed by VISCOPY, Sydney 2000 • © Solo Syndication: sources **2.1.3**, **2.7.3** • Topham Picturepoint: sources **2.2.1***, **2.2.2**, **2.7.5**, **2.8.2**, **2.10.2**, **4.4.5**, **4.4.9**, **4.6.6** • Allsport/Popperphoto: sources **2.3.3**, **2.9.3** • Herald & Weekly Times photographic collection: sources **2.5.1**, **2.5.3**, **3.2.1**, **4.8.2** • Fairfax Photo Library: sources **2.4.5**, **3.11.1**/The *Sydney Morning Herald*, **3.11.4**, **5.9.1** • © Newspix: sources **2.6.3**, **5.11.2** (right)/Tony Lewis, **5.11.2** (left)/Alan Pryke, **5.11.5**, pp. **152**, **232**, **272** (left)/Jeff Darmanin • photolibrary.com: sources **2.8.1**/Topham Picture Source, **3.2.3**/Hulton Getty, **3.11.2**/Hulton Deutsch, **4.2.3**/Topham Picturepoint, **4.3.1**/Hulton-Deutsch, **4.3.4**/Hulton-Deutsch **4.11.1**/NASA/Science Photo Library, pp. **247** (top right)/Martin King, **258**/Conor Caffrey/SPL, **272** (right)/Billy Hustace, **340**/Harvey Pincis, **346** (top)/Alain Evard, **348** (top)/Peter J. Robinson • Austral International: sources **2.9.1**/Rex Features, **4.5.2** • Australian Picture Library/D. McClenaghan: sources **3.3.5**, **4.10.2**/Popperfoto, source **5.5.6** (watch), p. **156**/J. Carnemolla • © Trish Anderson: sources **3.10.1**, **5.3.2** • Austral/Pictor Uniphoto: pp. **80–81** • AAP Photo Library: sources **4.6.3**, **4.10.1**, **5.3.3**/AP, **5.5.2**/Associated Press/Daimler Chrysler, **5.10.4**/AP, pp. **171**, **236** (right), **269** (bottom)/AP/Pavel Rahman, • Reproduced courtesy of *Punch*: sources **4.2.1**, **4.6.7**/Mansbridge, 'The Train Robbery', 18 January 1967, p. 73 • Courtesy Michael Eyre: source **4.7.3** • *The Australian*/News Ltd: source **4.7.4**, © *The Australian*, p. **221**/Mayu Kanamori • News Ltd: source **4.12.2** • Coo-ee Picture Library: sources **4.12.3**, **5.6.2***, **5.13.2**, pp. **195** (bottom), **261** • *Courier-Mail*: p. **110**/*Courier-Mail* 26 September 1982 • Fred Adler/Kino Studio: source **5.1.1** • Bruce Petty: source **5.1.2** • Peter Schrank: source **5.2.1** • Department of Immigration and Multicultural Affairs: source **5.2.2** • Ron Tandberg: source **5.4.1** • Michael Leunig/The *Age:* source **5.4.3** • Mediterranean Shipping Company: source **5.5.4**/John Paine • Jeffrey Bender: source **5.5.8** • Photo by Peter Dombrovskis: source **5.6.1**/© West Wind Press • A.N.T Photo Library: source **5.7.2**/Otto Rogge, pp. **262** (right)/Silvestris, **278–9**/Ken Griffiths, **280** (farm)/Natural Images, **280** (mine)/Otto Rogge, **281** (logging)/Rob Blakers, **281** (erosion)/Ted Mead, **281** (salinity)/Bill Bachman, **285**/ Ted Mead, **286**/Jan Taylor, **291**/Ken Griffiths, **294**/J.P. & E.S. Baker, **298–9**/Ted Mead, **303** (open forest)/J.P. & E.S. Baker, **303** (woodland)/Otto Rogge, **303** (closed forest)/Michael O'Connor, **304** (catchment)/Rob Blakers, **304** (fruits)/Jutta Hösel, **304** (soil conservation)/Fredy Mercay, **304** (possums)/D. Whitford, **305** (seeds)/Ford Kristo, Australia, **305** (hives)/Otto Rogge, **305** (research)/Fredy Mercay, **308** (cocoon)/Otto Rogge, **308** (feathertail glider)/C. & S. Pollit, **308** (seed)/Ralph & Daphne Keller, **308** (logging)/Fredy Mercay, **308** (woodchips)/Bill Bachman, **318** (both)/Grant Dixon • © Wildlight/Mark Lang: source **5.7.4** • The *Age*: sources **5.7.5**/Sandy Scheltema, source **5.8.1**/Jim McEwan, pp. **146–7***/John Wouldstra • Council for Aboriginal Reconciliation: source **5.10.5** • Cartoons by Peter Nicholson of The *Australian*, 38/8/99: source **5.10.7**, p. **324** • Auspic: source **5.11.3** • Photo courtesy Cummings collection, A/V archives, AIATSIS: source **5.13.3** • Ancient Art & Architecture Collection: p. **148** • Courtesy *The Mercury*, Hobart: p. **165** • © Photodisc 2000: pp. **166**, **174–5**, **180**, **181** (top) **195** (butcher), **205** (top), **215**, **222–3**, **224**, **228**, **229**, **238**, **252–3***, **256**, **305** (building), **323**, & background images for chapters 7, 8 & 9 • Mark Knight/*Sunday Herald-Sun*: p. **170** • Reproduced with the express consent of Go2Net, Inc., all rights reserved: p. **179** • DETYA: p. **181** (job guide) • Stock Photos/Paul Steele/TSM: p. **188** • Queensland Teachers Journal: p. **189** • The Photo Library — Sydney/Professional Sport International: pp. **209** (bottom)/Sipa Press, **246** • Dale Mann: pp. **192–3** • Image courtesy of McDonald's Australia: p. **195** (top) • Courtesy Coles Myer Ltd: p. **195** (centre left) • Courtesy *Dynamic Small Business* magazine: p. **197** • Used with permission of Trigger Brothers: pp. **198** (logo), **199** • Aaron Tait: pp. **200** (top & bottom), **208**, **209** (top), **218** • Target Australia: p. **200** (centre) • © *The Economist*, London, 21 August 1999: p. **202** • Amazon.com: p. **203** • Phantom Zone: p. **204** • APL/John Carnemolla: p. **205** (bottom) • The Coca-Cola Company: p. **206** • Courtesy of The Body Shop, www.thebodyshop.com.au: pp. **210** (logo and poster), **211** • Still Pictures: pp. **230**/Jorgen Shytte, **263**/Mark Edwards • Austral: pp. **244** (Simpsons), **274**/Pictor Uniphoto, **326**/Sygma/Thierry Prat, **339**/Sipa Press/E. Guner, **348** (bottom)/John Shelley • Bureau of Meteorology: p. **260** • Bill Leak of The *Australian*: p. **271** • photolibrary.com — Sydney: p. **273** (top) • Sporting Images: p. **273** (bottom) • © The *Sydney Morning Herald*: p. **277** (bottom) • Peter Connellan: p. **290** (left) • Conservation photography reproduced with permission of the Department of Natural Resources, Qld: p. **290** (right top, bottom) • Bill Twigg: page **293** • Main Camp Tea Tree Oil Ltd: p. **304** (medicinal) • Megan Bourke: p. **304** (recreation x 2) • Australian Paper: p. **305** (wood products) • Lochman Transparencies/Dennis Sarson: p. **313** • Rowan Reid: p. **322** • Image Bank/Guido Rossi: p. **330** • APL/UPPA: p. **335**

* Also used as background image in same chapter

Text

• Victorian Board of Studies, extracts from Curriculum and Standard Framework Statement II, SOSE Levels 5 and 6 Outcomes, reproduced with permission: pp. viii–x • Daniel Connell: sources **3.5.5**, **3.5.8**, • Commonwealth of Australia copyright, reproduced by permission: sources **4.7.5**, **4.12.2**, **4.12.4**, **5.1.3**, **5.12.3** and p. **191** • © The *Australian*, 3 March 1999: source **5.11.1** • Margaret Tucker: source **5.9.2** • Patrick Donovan is a journalist with The *Age* newspaper: p. **157** • Victorian Legal Aid: page **161** • Senator Natasha Stott Despoja: p. **171** • David Kelly & Professor Loane Skene, University of Melbourne: p. **173** • Courtesy of 'The Footy Show', Nine Network: pp. **184** (mock ad.), **185** (mock letter) • www.mycareer.com.au: p. **190** • Nike: pp. **246–9** • Bill Twigg: p. **293** • Landcare Australia: pp. **292**, **294**

Every effort has been made to trace the ownership of copyright material. Information that will enable the publisher to trace the copyright holders of sources 1.5.2, 1.5.3, 1.9.2, 2.6.1, 2.10.4, 2.11.3, 2.11.4, 3.5.4, 3.8.3, 3.9.1, 3.9.9, 3.10.3, 4.1.2, 4.4.2, 4.7.1, 4.8.1, 4.8.3, 4.10.3, 4.12.1, and images on pages 13, 14 (top) or to rectify any error or omission in subsequent reprints will be welcome. In such cases, please contact the Permission Section at John Wiley & Sons Australia, who will arrange for the payment of the usual fee.

Coverage of outcomes

	Learning outcomes	This is evident when the student is able to:	SOSE 3	SOSE 4
HISTORY	**H6.1** Describe the reasons for the colonisation of Australia.	• Examine the factors involved in the British colonisation of Australia.	**1.1, 1.2, 1.3, 1.4, 1.5, 1.6, 1.7, 1.11**	
		• Evaluate the impact of colonisation on Aboriginal and Torres Strait Islander communities.	**1.9, 1.10, 1.11, 1.12**	
		• Analyse any one particular social or political change in a colony and its impact on people.	**1.3, 1.4, 1.5, 1.8, 2.1, 2.2, 2.3**	
		• Describe the motives, values and events behind the move from a number of colonies to one nation.	**3.1, 3.2, 3.3, 3.4, 3.5, 3.6, 3.7, 3.8**	
	H6.2 Analyse the continuing significance of major events and ideas that shaped Australian society.	• Identify significant events and ideas which shaped Australian society, including Federation, World War I, the 1930s Depression, World War II and post-war migration.	**2.2, 2.5, 2.7, 3.8, 3.9, 4.1**	**1.1, 2.1, 2.2, 2.3, 2.4, 2.5, 2.6, 3.2, 3.3, 3.5, 3.6, 3.8, 3.9**
		• Analyse the events and ideas bringing about significant change.	**2.1, 2.4, 2.5, 2.8, 4.2, 4.8**	**1.2, 1.8, 2.6, 3.4, 3.9, 3.10, 4.7, 5.4**
		• Evaluate the contributions of key participants and leaders in these events.	**1.2, 1.7, 2.9, 2.10, 2.11**	**4.7, 4.8, 5.7**
		• Compare different perspectives about a significant event.	**1.9, 1.10, 2.6, 4.5**	**1.5, 3.5, 3.8, 4.8, 4.9, 5.7**
	H6.3 Analyse the campaign by Aboriginal and Torres Strait Islander communities for civil and political rights.	• Identify which civil and political rights were denied the Aboriginal and Torres Strait Islander communities.		**5.9**
		• Analyse the reasons why civil and political rights were denied to Aboriginal and Torres Strait Islander communities.		**5.9**
		• Outline the different ways in which the Aboriginal and Torres Strait Islander communities campaigned for civil and political rights.		**5.8, 5.10**
		• Evaluate the degree to which the Aboriginal and Torres Strait Islander communities have been successful in their campaigns.		**5.10, 5.13**
	H6.4 Analyse the impact of significant events and ideas in shaping world history in the twentieth century.	• Identify significant events and ideas that shaped world history in the twentieth century, including World War I, the Russian Revolution, the 1930s Depression, World War II, the Chinese Revolution and the Cold War and its aftermath.	**4.1, 4.3, 4.7, 4.9**	**1.1, 1.3, 1.7, 1.9, 2.1, 2.2, 2.3, 2.4, 2.7, 2.8, 2.9, 2.10, 3.1, 3.2, 3.3, 3.6, 3.7, 3.11, 4.1, 4.2, 4.3, 4.4, 4.5, 4.6**
		• Discuss the ideas and people associated with the events.	**4.4, 4.6**	**1.4, 1.6, 2.7, 2.9, 4.4, 4.11**
		• Evaluate the impact of the events and ideas on people, values and structures.	**4.1, 4.3, 4.5, 4.6, 4.8, 4.9**	**1.1, 1.3, 1.5, 1.6, 1.8, 1.9**
		• Analyse the ways in which a significant event has been represented in cultural forms.	**4.3, 4.5**	**1.3, 1.5, 2.7, 3.4, 4.4, 4.10**
	H6.5 Explain the key changes in social and political attitudes and values in modern Western society.	• Describe the ways in which significant events affected change in such areas as family structures, gender roles and work organisation.	**4.6, 4.8**	**1.6, 1.8, 3.4, 3.10**
		• Explain how the values of particular societies changed as a result of significant events.	**4.9**	**1.9, 4.6**
		• Examine the ways in which advances in technology affected other areas, such as health, medicine, transport and education.		**5.5, 5.13**
		• Evaluate the effect of significant events and ideas on groups.		**4.6, 5.5, 5.6, 5.13**

Coverage of outcomes *(continued)*

GEOGRAPHY

Learning outcomes	This is evident when the student is able to:	SOSE 3	SOSE 4
G6.1 Explain the processes and interactions between people and major natural systems.	• Describe the location and distribution of major natural systems.	6.1, 7.1, 7.2, 7.4, 7.5, 7.7, 8.1	10.1, 10.2, 10.4, 10.5, 10.6, 12.1, 12.2
	• Describe the processes that drive the major natural systems.	6.1, 6.2, 6.3, 6.4, 6.5, 7.3, 7.4, 7.7, 7.8, 7.10	10.1, 10.4, 10.5, 10.6, 11.3, 11.4
	• Analyse the impact of human activities on natural systems.	6.6, 6.7, 6.8, 7.5, 7.9	
	• Suggest strategies to manage the effects of human activities on natural systems.	6.9, 6.10, 7.6, 7.9	10.2, 12.5
G6.2 Evaluate how different factors affect the distribution and dynamics of human population.	• Identify a range of factors responsible for change to human populations.	5.1, 5.9	13.1, 13.2, 13.3, 13.4, 13.5
	• Apply relevant factors to explain the distribution pattern in human populations.	5.1, 5.2, 5.3, 5.8	13.1, 13.2, 13.3, 13.4, 13.5
	• Analyse relevant factors to describe the dynamics of change affecting human populations.	5.4, 5.5, 5.6, 5.7	13.2, 13.3, 13.4, 13.5, 13.8
	• Use current and historical data to predict future patterns in the distribution of human populations.	5.10	13.1, 13.2, 13.3, 13.4, 13.5, 13.8
G6.3 Predict the effects of resource development and use on a selected natural and human environment.	• Outline the relationship between current use of the environment and future availability of resources.	8.1, 8.2, 8.4	10.2, 10.3, 10.4, 10.5, 10.6, 10.7, 10.8, 11.1, 11.2, 11.3, 11.4, 11.6, 12.1, 12.3, 12.4, 13.6, 13.8
	• Describe the likely impact of resource development and use on a natural environment.	8.3, 8.5, 8.6	10.3, 10.4, 10.5, 10.6, 10.7, 10.8, 11.4, 11.5, 12.3, 12.8, 12.9, 13.6, 13.7
	• Suggest ways of sustainably developing a natural and human environment.	8.7, 8.8, 8.9, 8.10	10.3, 10.4, 10.5, 10.8, 11.5, 11.6, 11.7, 12.5, 12.6, 12.7, 13.6, 13.7
G6.4 Develop a comprehensive strategy to resolve an issue related to the use and management of a natural or human environment.	• Use a range of geographical media to describe the environment.		11.4, 12.2, 13.6
	• Evaluate the factors contributing to the development of an issue relating to the use and management of an environment.		10.8, 11.6, 11.7, 12.6, 13.5, 13.6, 13.7
	• Identify strategies formulated to address the issue.		10.8, 11.5, 11.7, 12.6, 12.8, 12.9, 13.5, 13.6, 13.7
	• Justify a strategy to manage the environment.		10.8, 12.7, 13.6, 13.7

ECONOMY AND SOCIETY

Learning outcomes	This is evident when the student is able to:	SOSE 3	SOSE 4
ES5.1 Analyse key features of Australia's political system at local, state and federal levels.	• Identify the key values of representative democracy, including participation, representation, rights and responsibilities.	10.1, 10.6, 10.10	
	• Describe key political structures, noting similarities and differences among the three levels of government.	10.2, 10.3, 10.4, 10.5	
	• Describe the role of key individuals and groups within the legislative and executive branches, including head of state, prime minister, premiers, the ministry, backbenchers, political parties and the role of the opposition.	10.5, 10.7	
	• Explain ways in which individuals and community groups can participate in political processes.	10.8, 10.9, 10.10	
ES5.2 Examine the origin of Australia's legal system and how Australian laws are made.	• Examine the origins and key values of Australia's legal system.		6.1, 6.4, 6.7
	• Describe key judicial and enforcement structures at federal, state and local levels.		6.2, 6.3, 6.5, 6.6
	• Explain how law-making processes allow for participation by active and informed citizens.		6.9
	• Investigate avenues of dispute resolution.		6.8

Coverage of outcomes (*continued*)

ECONOMY AND SOCIETY

Learning outcomes	This is evident when the student is able to:	SOSE 3	SOSE 4
ES5.3 Explain key factors that influence the Australian economy.	• Describe key factors that affect the economy, including sectors, factors of production, resource use, ownership and management, and types of business ownership models.	**9.1, 9.2, 9.4, 9.7, 9.12**	**9.6**
	• Analyse the role and impact of the government, individuals and organisations on economic activity, including how they interact to produce, market and consume goods.	**9.3, 9.5, 9.6, 9.12**	**9.3**
	• Examine the nature and importance of trade to the Australian economy.	**9.8, 9.12**	**9.4**
	• Identify key economic issues, such as inflation, availability of resources, and globalisation.	**9.9, 9.10, 9.11**	**9.6, 9.7, 9.8**
ES5.4 Identify and discuss factors that affect opportunities for current and future work.	• Analyse information on factors influencing current and future work.	**11.1, 11.2, 11.3, 11.4, 11.6**	
	• Examine the relationship between education, training and work opportunities.	**11.5**	
	• Investigate changes over time to work practices and work opportunities in a particular industry.	**11.5, 11.7**	
	• Discuss how technology has changed work, work environments and the way goods and services are produced.	**11.8**	**8.5**
ES6.1 Describe the management of the Australian economy in an international context.	• Examine how different types of economic system achieve economic development.		**9.1, 9.2, 9.9**
	• Discuss ways in which the government influences the development of the Australian economy.		**9.3, 9.9**
	• Identify examples of how international economic transactions, decisions and agreements affect the Australian economy and society.		**9.4, 9.5, 9.6, 9.9**
	• Discuss how contemporary issues related to global resource use and management affect the Australian economy.		**9.7, 9.8**
ES6.2 Analyse a proposed change in the law in Australia and explain the legal processes to implement the change.	• Describe a proposed change to the law in Australia.		
	• Analyse how individuals, groups, communities, legal and political institutions may be affected by a proposed change.		**6.10**
	• Explain different perspectives on a proposed change and the roles of individuals and groups in promoting or challenging the proposed change.		**6.9, 6.11**
	• Evaluate the effectiveness of the democratic processes in relation to political and legal issues in bringing about changes in the law.		**6.10**
ES6.3 Analyse vocational pathways and education and training requirements to develop possible career paths and work opportunities.	• Identify the education and training requirements and pathways for a selected range of occupations.		**7.2, 7.3**
	• Identify future job opportunities and predicted labour market changes in Australia.		**7.1**
	• Participate in and evaluate real or simulated job-seeking processes (résumé preparation, job application letter, portfolio presentation, response to selection criteria, interview participation).		**7.4, 7.5, 7.6**
	• Compare generic processes and skills valued in workplaces.		**7.7**
ES6.4 Demonstrate an understanding of personal and business financial management, and identify and apply enterprise skills and attributes.	• Describe different ways that individuals can successfully plan and manage personal finances.	**12.1, 12.2, 12.3, 12.4, 12.6, 12.7, 12.8, 12.9, 12.10, 12.11, 12.12**	
	• Examine the structures and financial management processes of business enterprises, including the identification of management skills.	**12.5**	**8.1, 8.2, 8.3, 8.4, 8.6, 8.8, 8.10, 8.11, 8.12, 8.13**
	• Identify enterprise attributes and skills, and describe how innovation and enterprise affect the economy and society.	**12.13**	**8.7, 8.9**
	• Plan and conduct a small-scale project that applies enterprise skills and attributes.	**12.13**	**8.14**

Introduction

The second edition of ***Jacaranda SOSE 4*** has been comprehensively revised for the SOSE key learning area of the new Curriculum and Standards Framework II (CSF II) and specifically addresses the new learning outcomes for the strands History, Geography, and Economy and Society. It has been updated to provide a comprehensive coverage of the CSF II curriculum focus statements for the strands, learning outcomes and performance indicators for level 6.

This edition has been updated in both content and activities in order to provide an excellent basis for classroom pedagogy and the delivery of a stimulating and comprehensive SOSE course in line with the CSF II.

HOW IS *JACARANDA SOSE 4* SECOND EDITION ORGANISED?

This text has been organised into three sections, representing the CSF II strands:

- History
- Geography
- Economy and Society.

Each of the 12 chapters covers the major knowledge and skills outcomes. Each chapter begins with a double-page opening spread incorporating an **introduction**, a **glossary** of key terms, and **learning outcomes**, which detail what students 'should know and be able to do' by the end of the chapter. All chapters are divided into two-page and four-page spreads for ease of student understanding and assessment.

ACTIVITIES

The activities have been designed in line with the **CSF II performance indicators** so that teachers can use them as a basis for assessing whether or not students have achieved the outcomes for level 6. Each spread in ***Jacaranda SOSE 4 Second Edition*** builds knowledge and skills by using interrelated inquiry-based learning activities. The activities are divided into the following categories: 'Check your understanding', 'Investigation' and 'Communication'. These learning activities allow teachers to use a variety of assessment techniques. **Check your understanding** activities are designed to allow students to check their understanding of the knowledge and concepts developed in the History, Geography, and Economy and Society strands. **Investigation** activities are designed to develop students' skills in researching, processing and interpreting data, such as source documents, maps and tables. Each Investigation activity has a sub-heading describing what students will be investigating. **Communication** activities are designed to develop students' skills in using written or graphic material from the book as well as presenting answers in a variety of formats (including posters; brochures; presentation of data in the form of tables, graphs, maps or statistics; story writing; and the use of technology such as PowerPoint).

MEETING THE OUTCOMES

At the end of each chapter is a set of activities for each CSF II outcome for History, Geography, and Economy and Society. Each activity enables students to consolidate their understanding and skills for each area of study and achieve the key CSF II outcomes. The structure of the 'Meeting the Outcomes' spread enables teachers to further assess and report on student achievement of the key CSF II outcomes. For each outcome, a **relevant performance indicator** has been included to help determine whether the outcome has been achieved.

Jacaranda SOSE 4 Second Edition has been written in a student-friendly format, using a clear, lively and colourful design. This edition continues to provide students and teachers with a course that is comprehensive, relevant and up to date — as well as stimulating and engaging.

CSF II LEVELS 5 5 6 6

Chapter

1

WORLD WAR I

INTRODUCTION

Federation was an important step in Australian independence. The Great War was even more significant. For the first time people had to rally behind their nation. They were no longer simply Victorians or Tasmanians. Out of the 'baptism of fire' that was World War I came a recognition that Australians were the equal of their British counterparts. They were tested in war and proven to be up to the task. On the home front, however, the war came at a terrible cost. The toll of 60 000 dead left scars that would never heal. Government management of the economy and society, and the conscription referenda, created deep divisions in Australia. Australia may have gone into the war an innocent, but it emerged from the conflict wounded but wiser.

Australian War Memorial
neg. no. H16130

LEARNING *outcomes*

- Analyse the continuing significance of major events and ideas which shaped Australian society.
- Analyse the impact of significant events and ideas in shaping world history in the twentieth century.

Glossary

Allies: Britain, British Empire, France, Russia and the nations allied with them in World War I
anti-authoritarian: opposed to those in authority
bonds: loans of money to the government at a fixed rate of interest
breadwinner: the main financial contributor to a household
capitalist: someone who benefits from ownership of property and resources
cavalry: soldiers on horseback
communist: one who supports a system where all of a country's resources are shared equally by all of its people
conscription: forced military service
Constantinople: Istanbul
deported: to be forcibly sent out of a country
dominions: lands ruled by a government
enlistment: joining armed forces
infantry: foot soldiers
interned: to be kept under guard in a specific area or place
Kaiser: German monarch
pacifist: person against war or violence of any kind
patriots: those with a great love for their country
propaganda: information used to persuade people to a particular point of view
revolution: overthrow of government
zeppelin: airship

AUGUST 1914

Defence was a focus of the early federal governments. A system of compulsory military training for youths was introduced in 1909 and amended in 1911 to include 'Junior Cadets', boys as young as 12.

'Boy conscription', as it became known, was not universally popular and there were many cases of boys being imprisoned for not completing the required 64 hours of drill each year. **Pacifist** and religious groups such as the Quakers were also opposed to the scheme. Despite these training schemes, the opening of the Royal Military College at Duntroon and the existence of the Australian navy, it is questionable whether Australia really was prepared for war when it did come in 1914.

ATTITUDES TO WAR

Attitudes toward war were also very different in 1914. Today, if a European war broke out, people would understand that it would mean untold death and destruction and misery for the lives of millions. But this was not the case in 1914. So far as most Australians were concerned at that time, war was usually glorious and heroic, over quickly and inevitably victorious for their 'side' — the British Empire. Furthermore, the great majority of Australians had little experience of war itself. About 2000 Australians had gone to New Zealand to fight in the Maori Wars during the 1860s; in 1885, 500 New South Welshmen fought in the Sudan with the British; and, in the Boer War of 1899–1902, some 16 000 Australian troops fought, suffering about 500 casualties. A scattering had travelled to China to help put down the Boxer Rebellion in 1900.

Source 1.1.2

Andrew Fisher, an Australian wartime prime minister, supports Britain (August 1914)

Turn your eyes to the European situation, and give the kindest feelings towards the mother country at this time . . . Australians will stand beside our own to help and defend her to our last man and our last shilling.

. . . That practical assistance should be given will be generally agreed. We are bound to the motherland by ties not so much of material interest as of kinship and of gratitude. For a century we have lived in freedom under Britain's protection . . .

Australia in 1914 was still very British. While most people were born in Australia, nearly 96 per cent could claim British ancestry. All the basic systems of education, law and government

Source 1.1.1

The New South Wales Mounted Rifles at the Orange River, South Africa, in 1901

(Australian War Memorial neg. no. A04337)

were founded on English models. Children in schools studied the heroic deeds of British military heroes. The main sports played were English. There was an almost universal belief in the superiority of the white, English race.

CAUSES OF WORLD WAR I

There was no single reason why European powers went to war in 1914. Since the second half of the 1800s there had been growing rivalry between countries over issues such as trade, colonial settlements and naval and military build-ups. Alliances and treaties signed between countries tended to put them into 'blocs' whereby the other countries within a bloc would be obliged to defend another in that bloc if it were threatened or attacked.

The assassination of the heir to the Austrian throne, the Archduke Franz Ferdinand, at Sarajevo on 28 June was the trigger that would plunge Europe into chaos. Source 1.1.3 is a brief timeline of events in 1914 after Ferdinand's death.

Activities

Investigation: *The road to war*

1. Look at source 1.1.1 and the text. In which war were these Australian soldiers fighting?
2. Would most Australians have known what war would be like in early 1914? Explain your answer.
3. Look at source 1.1.2.
   (a) Find three different terms used to describe Britain.
   (b) Why was Australia so closely linked to Britain?
4. Outline some of the main reasons for war breaking out in Europe in 1914.
5. Read source 1.1.3.
   (a) Work out which European countries fell into the two opposing blocs.
   (b) Show this in a simple sketch.
   (c) Discuss the advantages and disadvantages of being in an alliance with other countries and record these in your workbooks.
6. The extract in source 1.1.4 was written by a man whose son was imprisoned under the (Australian) *Defence Act*.
   (a) As an Australian living in June, 1914, write a letter to your local newspaper either in support of or opposition to F. J. Roberts' letter.
   (b) As a class, discuss how the arguments about military service might have changed after August, 1914.

Source 1.1.3

A war begins

Source 1.1.4

Conscientious objection

Dear Sir,

Finding I am unable to obtain justice from the Defence Department, I write earnestly appealing to you to kindly use your influence in connexion with the unjust treatment of our lad, who, through loyalty to his parents' views of Christian teaching, is undergoing solitary confinement in the cells at Queenscliff fortress.

Tom is a lad of 16, and was sent to Queenscliff on Wednesday last for 21 days, for refusing to train under the Defence Act. My wife and I are members of the Society of Friends, and hold strong convictions on this matter of militarism . . . He is locked in a cell 10 foot by 10 foot . . . It has no window, the light coming through a grating. He has a wooden stretcher, the mattress and blankets are taken away in the morning, and not brought back until dark. He has half an hour's exercise in the morning . . . is on half diet, has not been allowed to read, nor to write to his parents. . .

A letter written by F. J. Roberts, 10 June 1914, taken from *Commonwealth Parliamentary Debates*, vol. 74, pp. 2338–9.

RUSHING TO ENLIST

RESPONSE TO WAR

The announcement made by Prime Minister Cook, that Australia was following Britain into war, was met with enthusiasm and approval. Few people could have anticipated the horrors that were to follow. Crowds rushed newspaper offices hoping for news of the latest developments. Men swamped the **enlistment** offices, frightened that they might miss out on their chance to join a great adventure.

Some men were so concerned the war might be over before they became involved that they went to England and signed up there. But what motivated the keen response to war? By December, 52 000 men had joined up across all states. Training camps were set up in all the capital cities.

There was a great amount of general support for the war from all quarters. Newspapers unquestioningly supported Britain. Ministers in churches spoke from the pulpit about the need to defend the 'mother country' in her time of need.

Source 1.2.1

Outside a recruiting office, Melbourne
Australian War Memorial neg. no. A03406

Source 1.2.2

From a farm near Toowoomba

I was the oldest of six children in our family on a not too rich dairy farm near Toowoomba . . . in 1915 there was a severe drought and things were not too good on the farm and the only topic of talk was the war and it seemed the proper thing to do was enlist, however I think it was the spirit of adventure and seeing things that was the prime mover.

Quoted in J. N. I. Dawes and L. L. Robson, *Citizen to Soldier*, Melbourne University Press, Melbourne, 1977.

Source 1.2.3

Hard times

'One who knows' observed darkly, in regard to why they enlisted, I will sum it up in a few lines. Half of them were out of work, hungry, broke and sleeping out, it was a job for them, a feed and a tent to sleep in . . .

ibid.

Source 1.2.4

Mixed motives

To sum up my motives for enlisting, I would say:

1. **To a small degree a spirit of adventure and a desire to see other parts of the world.**
2. **A sense of duty to Australia, although not so significant as our country seemed so far away from hostilities.**
3. **To go along with my contemporaries and support one's comrades in the field.**
4. **To a greater extent possibly than the three previous motives was the desire to help the Motherland in her hour of need.**

ibid.

There was general outrage that a powerful country such as Germany had invaded a 'weak and defenceless' country such as Belgium. It was rumoured that the Germans slaughtered nuns, babies and kittens alike. There were also other pressures applied to coax men into enlisting when they were perhaps reluctant, especially after enlistment figures began to decline after mid-1915. Propaganda became an important tool of persuasion for both soldiers and civilians.

Source 1.2.5

Great War recruiting poster

WAR OVER BY CHRISTMAS?

When it became clear to everyone that the war wasn't going to be 'over by Christmas' and that great numbers of lives were being lost, enlistment figures slumped. The government put more resources into recruitment campaigns with mixed success. There was division in the community as 1915 dragged into 1916 and beyond. Why, it was thought, should some families sacrifice sons when others had contributed nothing?

There were also concerns about the impact of the war on the economy and the labour force. Talk of conscription in 1916 led some to argue that the war had become a '**capitalist's** war', in which rich industrialists were getting richer while living standards were falling for workers and their families.

The government's handling of the country was also under fire. People resented the strict censorship of newspapers and mail. New laws restricted political freedom. The government used non-union labour to break strikes. Unemployment was high. Only certain sections of the community seemed to be making sacrifices for the war effort.

Activities

Investigation: *Enlisting for duty*

1. What was the response by Australians to the prime minister's announcement that Australia was at war?
2. List the reasons for enlistment given in sources 1.2.2–1.2.4. What other reasons, not mentioned here, could you add to this list?
3. What conflicts were beginning to emerge in Australian society as the war continued?
4. Source 1.2.6 shows enlistment figures for the Great War. Study it and suggest reasons for:
   (a) sharp rises in mid-1915, January–February 1916 and October 1916
   (b) the general decline throughout the war.

Source 1.2.6

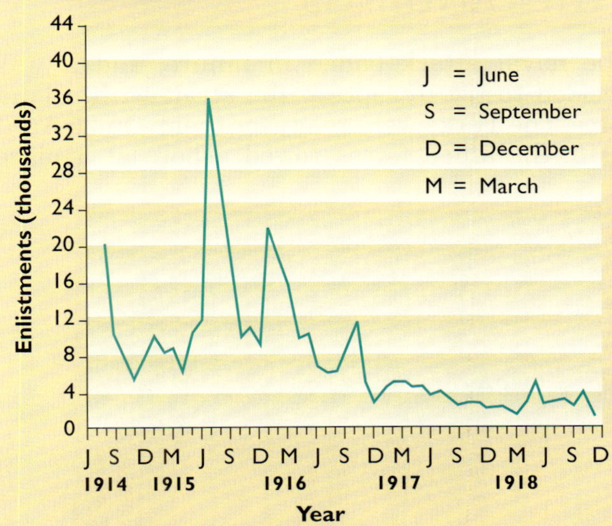

Enlistments in the AIF 1914–18

Source: Audio-visual Education Centre, Education Department of Victoria, Recruitment Slide Set.

Communication: *Recruitment posters*

1. What does source 1.2.5 tell you about the way Australia saw itself during the Great War? Discuss reasons for this.
2. Design your own poster encouraging people to be involved in the war effort. Discuss with fellow students which aspects to highlight in your design. On completion, display it to the class as a whole.

GALLIPOLI

THE CAMPAIGN

Australian troops, having completed their final training in Egypt and keen for action, were sent as part of a 70 000-strong Allied force to capture the city of **Constantinople** and the strategic Gallipoli Peninsula. The idea behind this campaign was to gain control of the passage of water known as the Dardanelles Strait so that supplies could be sent more easily to Russia. Knocking Turkey out of the war would also place more pressure on Germany.

The campaign was doomed. An earlier naval attempt to capture the strait in March 1915 ended badly when ships were sunk by mines. Turkish forts on the shores of the narrow strait also proved an obstacle.

THE LANDINGS

The naval attack ended in failure, and it was decided to try to capture the strait with a land force. The Turks were ready for them. On 25 April 1915, the allied forces rowed ashore at a place later called Anzac Cove where they met fierce initial resistance from waiting Turkish gunners who later retreated to await major reinforcements from the east. Headlines in the *Age* and the *Herald* reported the landings as a stunning triumph.

The British war correspondent Ellis Ashmead-Bartlett described the Australians as 'this race of athletes' and wrote, 'The Australians rose to the occasion. Not waiting for orders, or for the boats to reach the beach, they sprang into the sea . . . They lost some men but did not worry. In less than a quarter of an hour the Turks were out of their second position, either bayoneted or fleeing . . .' Reports that followed in the newspapers cemented these images of Gallipoli. King George V called the Australians 'worthy sons of the Empire'.

Censorship and the need to keep war morale high meant that these images were rarely challenged. But as time went on it became obvious that casualty rates were very high and that the campaign itself had not gone as well as it had been claimed.

The soldiers at Gallipoli suffered terrible conditions. The heat of summer meant shortages of

Source 1.3.1

Anzac Beach, Gallipoli
Australian War Memorial neg. no. C02145

water and millions of flies. Corpses were buried and uncovered by blasts from shells. In winter, freezing temperatures brought mud and ice. Thousands died of exposure and disease. Most Anzac troops fought with great courage under impossible conditions. In the end, British leaders were forced to admit that the campaign had met with defeat and ordered an evacuation of the Gallipoli Peninsula. The evacuation was probably the best planned and most successfully executed part of the whole campaign — all soldiers were evacuated without any loss of life.

THE ANZAC LEGEND

The Gallipoli experience is best remembered for the series of blunders that led to the unsuccessful campaign and because it created the 'Anzac legend' — the Australian soldier who came to be seen as the 'true Australian'. This legend grew out of the earlier 'bushman' stereotype and claims the typical Australian to be brave, resourceful, practical, loyal, independent and **anti-authoritarian**. Many Australians would argue that these qualities typify us today.

Activities

Communication: *Using maps*

1. Look at source 1.3.2 which shows a map of the Gallipoli area.
   (a) Why would it have been so difficult to capture Constantinople (now called Istanbul) by sea?
   (b) How would capturing the Gallipoli Peninsula have helped capture Constantinople?
   (c) What were the basic objectives of the Gallipoli campaign?

Source 1.3.2

Gallipoli and surrounding regions

2. As an Anzac being ferried to the beaches of Gallipoli on the morning of the first landings, describe the sights around you and your feelings as you approach land. What happens when the first shots ring out? What is your response when someone in the boat beside you is shot dead? You could also describe the confusion on the beach and your attempts to storm the hills and cliffs on shore.
3. Why might the opinions of British newspaper reporters and the British king be important to Australians in 1915? What does this tell us about Australians at this time?

Investigation: *The Anzac legend*

In a recent edition of *Australian Historical Studies*, historian Alistair Thomson wrote of the debate that flared between Australian and British war historians in 1927 over the conduct of Australians at Gallipoli. In 1927, Australians helped prevent the publication of an account of the campaign by a British staff officer, Cecil Aspinall-Oglander. Aspinall-Oglander claimed that 'the truth about the Australians has never yet been told and in its absence a myth has sprung up that the Anzac troops did magnificently against amazing odds'. He wrote that the landings on 25 April were initially fairly easy but that confusion reigned among the Australians when the Turks launched their attack. He added that the strain told on the Australians and that numbers of uninjured troops straggled away from the fighting and into the security of gullies at the rear of the battle.

1. In what ways do Aspinall-Oglander's comments challenge the Anzac legend?
2. Why might Australians in 1927 have wanted to stop these opinions from being published?
3. What influence might Aspinall-Oglander's own position have had on his views of the 25 April landings?
4. Discuss your response to **3** with the class. What do you think was the truth about the 25 April landings? Can one or the other or both versions of history be correct?
5. Discuss the representation of the typical Australian in 1915. Watch the film *Gallipoli* and think about how the main Australian characters are portrayed. How are people of other nationalities portrayed? What role do women play in the film? What does the film suggest about Australia's role in the war and, in particular, its relationship with Britain? In what ways would an Australian film of Gallipoli made in the 1920s be different?
6. Is there such a thing as a 'typical' Australian today? What qualities might such a person have? What impressions of Australians do people from other countries have? For instance, what kinds of images of Australians are conveyed by *Crocodile Dundee*? How would we describe the 'typical' American, Indian or German?

1.4 THE ENEMY WITHIN

GOVERNMENT REACTION

The Australian government gave itself increased powers in 1914 to manage the war effort and society. One dilemma was what to do about people of German, Austrian or Turkish background living in Australia. One section of the *War Precautions Act* introduced by the government is reproduced below.

Source 1.4.1

Dealing with the enemy

> 5. the Governor-General may by order published in the *Gazetteer* make provision for any matters which appear necessary or expedient with a view to public safety and the defence of the Commonwealth, and in particular —
>   (a) for prohibiting aliens, either generally or as regards specified places, and either absolutely or except under specified conditions and restrictions, from landing or embarking in the Commonwealth;
>   (b) for deporting aliens from the Commonwealth;
>   (c) for requiring aliens to reside and remain within certain places or districts;
>   (d) for prohibiting aliens from residing or remaining in any areas or districts;
>   (e) for requiring aliens residing in the Commonwealth to comply with such provisions as to registration, change of abode, travelling, trading or otherwise as are specified in the order;
>
> *Commonwealth Acts*, vol. xiii, 1914–15, no. 10.

It was thought that aliens living in Australia were a threat to our security and that strong measures were needed to keep them in check. As the war dragged on and **propaganda** increased, these foreigners also became more of a target — people upon whom Australian **patriots** could vent their anger. As the population tired of a war 16 000 kilometres away, it became necessary to push the idea of an 'enemy within' — enemy spies and agents under cover in Australia.

The idea of the 'enemy within' was a way of making sure that people realised that the threat of the enemy was right on their doorstep and not just on the other side of the world where it did not concern them.

Source 1.4.2

Ogre, by Norman Lindsay
Australian War Memorial neg. no. ARTV00078

Reactions against anything associated with Germany and those who were German-born were often extremely hostile.

German churches and schools were shut down and German place names were changed: German Creek became Empire Bay; Mueller Park became Kitchener Park. There were many other examples. Thousands of alien citizens were also **interned** and many were **deported** after the war had ended. According to the law, even if you were born in Australia but your parents or grandparents had come from Germany, you could in theory be interned. There were cases where

this happened. Many people with foreign surnames lost their jobs as fellow workers went on strike demanding that they be sacked. There is no doubt that most people discriminated against in this way had done nothing wrong. They, too, were victims of the war.

Source 1.4.3

German Australians

LOYALTY TO THE EMPIRE

FERVENT DECLARATIONS

HAMILTON, Thursday. About 350 Germans, residents of Hochkirch and district, assembled at the school hall, Hockkirch, on Wednesday night, to proclaim their loyalty to the British throne.

The meeting was called by the officials of the Lutheran Church, and was characterised by the greatest enthusiasm.

Pastor Kriewaldt, who was appointed chairman, said that they, as Australians, were part of the British Empire, and could not exist without the protection of the British flag.

Those of them who were Australians of German descent enjoyed the same privileges and protection as all other Australians.

It might seem that they would not be staunch supporters of the British flag.

They, however, desired not merely to be tolerated by their English-speaking fellow citizens, but to be regarded as such, and as staunch supporters of the Government of their adopted country, who honoured King George as their Sovereign liege and lord (applause) and who were prepared, if necessary, to sacrifice their goods and their lives for their country.

Argus, 7 August 1914.

Source 1.4.4

The internment camp at Holdsworthy, New South Wales, 1915 Australian War Memorial neg. no. H17352

Source 1.4.5

A sausage by any other name . . .

I asked for German sausage; the shop had none, but it did have Belgian sausage. As I was being served a lady in a fur coat waited with her dachsund on a lead. In came a couple of eighteen-year-olds and kicked the dog — 'horrible German dog' — and its owner could do nothing to protect it from patriotism.

Quoted in B. Lewis, *Our War: Australia During World War I*, Melbourne University Press, Melbourne, 1980.

Activities

Investigation: *German Australians*

1. Read source 1.4.1 again. What does the *War Precautions Act* allow the government to do to aliens?
2. Look at source 1.4.2. Describe the way that Germany is shown here. Why has Germany been drawn in this way?
3. Carefully read source 1.4.3.
   (a) How did the 350 German–Australians react to the announcement of World War I?
   (b) Why do you think their meeting was called by the officials of the Lutheran Church?
4. Observe source 1.4.4.
   (a) Why were people sent to these camps?
   (b) Which people were selected for internment and why?
   (c) Describe the conditions shown in the pictured internment camp.
5. In source 1.4.5 why has the name of 'German sausage' been changed to 'Belgian sausage'?
6. What might be indicated about Australian society in wartime when German breeds of dogs are kicked? Would this sort of behaviour be more or less likely to happen in peacetime? Explain.

Communication: *Writing from one perspective*

1. Prepare two posters, one representing an anti-German view and another representing the view of German–Australians.
2. Write a creative story based on the experiences of someone interned during the Great War. Use the information from this section as well as what you can discover through further research.
3. As a journalist working during the second half of the war, write a newspaper account detailing the experiences of an interned family.

CONSCRIPTION

By 1915, getting more Australian men to join the army to fight overseas had become an urgent problem in Australia. Enthusiasm for the war had declined as people realised that victory was not going to be either quick or easy. The belief in a 'victory by Christmas 1914' had not eventuated.

In January 1915, 10 225 men signed up for active service. By April in the same year, this had dropped alarmingly to 6000. News of the Gallipoli landing temporarily inspired confidence, and recruitment numbers rose. However, overall, not enough men were joining the army.

The Australian people had realised that war was not a game. However, the Australian government still had to keep its promise to Britain. The Australian prime minister, Billy Hughes, became convinced of the need for **conscription** — compulsory call-up of men for military service.

Source 1.5.2

'Propping up his throne'

Source 1.5.1

'Your turn next.'

Source 1.5.3

'Struth!'

Because he was certain that the Australian people would support him, Hughes decided to let Australians vote on conscription in a referendum. The vote was held in October 1916.

The referendum pushed people into the 'pro' or 'anti' camps. It was very difficult for people to remain indifferent or be 'fence-sitters'. Australia became a divided country over the conscription issue.

Besides posters and cartoons, songs, handbills and cards were also ways of spreading the message. Part of a popular anti-conscription song ran:

> *I didn't raise my son to be a soldier,*
> *I brought him up to be my pride and joy.*
> *Who dares to put a musket to his shoulder*
> *To kill some other mother's darling boy?*

Source 1.5.4

A popular handbill called 'The anti's creed'

I believe the man at the Front should be sacrificed.
I believe we should turn dog on them.
I believe that our women should betray the men who are fighting for them.
I believe in taking all the benefit and none of the risks.
I believe it was right to sink the *Lusitania*.
I believe in murder on the high seas.
I believe in the IWW.
I believe in Sinn Fein.
I believe that Britain should be crushed and humiliated.
I believe in the massacre of Belgian priests.
I believe in the murder of women and baby-killing.
I believe Nurse Cavell got her desserts.
I believe that treachery is a virtue.
I believe that disloyalty is true citizenship.
I believe that desertion is ennobling.
I believe in Considine, Fihelly, Ryan, Blackburn, Brookfield, Mannix and all their works.
I believe in egg power rather than man power.
I believe in holding up transports and hospital ships.
I believe in general strikes.
I believe in burning Australian haystacks.
I believe in mine-laying in Australian waters.
I believe in handing Australia over to Germany.
I believe I'm worm enough to vote No.
Those who DON'T believe in the above Creed will VOTE YES.

Approximately 2 300 000 Australians voted in the referendum which was defeated by 71 549 votes. A second referendum was held in December 1917 and was defeated by a bigger margin. After that, conscription wasn't seriously raised as an issue again during the Great War.

Source 1.5.5

The 1916 referendum

	Yes	No	Informal
New South Wales	356 802	474 523	27 038
Victoria	353 930	328 216	14 538
Queensland	144 017	157 049	7 596
South Australia	87 908	119 119	4 009
Western Australia	94 049	40 875	5 680
Tasmania	48 490	37 830	1 037
Territories	2 136	1 269	63
Commonwealth	**1 087 332**	**1 158 881**	**59 961**

Yes	1 087 332
No	1 158 881
Majority for No	71 549

Activities

Check your understanding

1. Why had enlistments for the army dropped by 1915?
2. What news helped increase enlistments?
3. What solution did Billy Hughes come up with?
4. Why did Hughes decide to let the people vote on conscription in a referendum?

Investigation: *The conscription issue*

1. From the information in this section and discussion with classmates and friends, draw a table showing arguments for and against conscription.
2. Which sources on these pages support conscription? Which ones are opposed to it?
3. Choose one source from sources 1.5.1–1.5.3 and detail the arguments it uses to support its case.
4. Read source 1.5.4. Who or what are the following: the *Lusitania*, the IWW, Sinn Fein, Nurse Cavell, Blackburn and Mannix? Which groups of people seem to be specifically attacked in this source?
5. What were the strengths and weaknesses of arguments put forward by both conscription groups? If you had to vote in 1916 and 1917 how would you have voted? If you had to vote on conscription today how might your vote be different and why? Discuss these issues as a class.

1.6

WOMEN'S ROLES

As large numbers of troops travelled overseas, a heavier burden fell on women at home. Some men used the war as a chance to escape their family responsibilities and fled, leaving women and children to fend for themselves. Fortunately the government made it compulsory for soldiers to set aside a percentage of their pay for their families. But with prices rising and wages staying more or less static, living conditions were often very difficult on the home front.

Despite the war causing great changes in society, women's roles did not change significantly. Men were still expected to be the '**breadwinner**' in the family and, if women did go into the work force, it was only for the duration of the war. Returning soldiers would then take 'their' jobs back.

Women had to accept mostly passive roles: supplying comforts to the troops at the front, prviding moral support for soldiers overseas and their families at home, joining voluntary groups and organisations that conducted home-front war work. Most of this work was unpaid and, just as there was pressure on eligible men to enlist, there was also pressure on women to participate in some visible war work.

But the war did allow many women opportunities, even if they were only temporary. About 10 000 women went into clerical positions and there was some work available in factories and business. There were also some jobs in the police force and on the land where there were shortages of labour after the drought of 1915 broke. Women were usually paid about half the male wage for their work. These rates of pay were based on the idea that only single women worked and therefore they had only themselves to support.

Probably the greatest area of female involvement during the war was in voluntary work. Women joined groups and organisations that carried out home-front war work. This involved packing parcels for the troops overseas, knitting clothes for them and raising money for the war effort.

Source 1.6.1

Women of the Cronulla Voluntary Aid Detachment fundraising in King Street on 30 November 1917

Not all women were happy accepting supporting roles. Many wanted to do much more. Groups such as the Australian Women's Service Corps were formed to:

> 'reinforce the men in the firing line by taking over the work mentioned on the membership forms ... (such as working as cooks, drivers and orderlies) ... or any other work the Defence Department may think advisable, thus releasing the able-bodied men who are now performing those duties to join the fighting units ...'

Many hundreds of women joined this group but their offers were never taken up.

The only women to have an active, frontline role in the war were the 2000 or so nurses who served overseas. Some female doctors had also volunteered for active service but were refused on the grounds that war conditions would be too terrible for them. Some of these women nonetheless enlisted for service in England.

There was also a lot of community pressure on women to encourage their husbands and sons to enlist. They would be accused of not doing their 'patriotic duty' if they did not. Women were also a focus of attention during the referendum debates, their votes giving them more real power than at any other stage during the war.

Because women were restricted in what they could do during the Great War, many felt the strain of the war years badly. Whereas having an active role and being fully involved in the war effort in a meaningful way would have given women a sense of purpose and cohesion, being restricted to secondary roles created frustration and anxiety. Women's fears were also played upon. The *Woman* magazine of 1 December 1917 reported:

> 'A message from Turin says that prior to the offensive against Italy, the German soldiers were incited by the distribution of a new hymn. A translation of part of the hymn is as follows:
>
> 'Sons of Germany
> Your great hour has come!
> Neither women nor children must be spared.
> For the children of the vanquished
> May some day vanquish yours.
> Forward! Shatter! Destroy! Thrust! Burn!
> Kill! Kill! KILL!'

Source 1.6.2

The blood vote

Activities

Investigation: *Women during WWI*

1. What new pressures did the war bring to women's lives?
2. What areas of the work force did women enter during the Great War?
3. Did women have the opportunity to contribute significantly to the war effort? Explain your answer.
4. Study source 1.6.1 and discuss the information it is presenting. What different sorts of roles are women occupying? Is this photograph representative of the role played by women in the Great War?
5. Read source 1.6.2 closely.
   (a) What is this poster trying to achieve?
   (b) Who is the 'conversation' in this poster between?
   (c) What tactics is the poster using to try to achieve its aims?

Communication: *Write a letter*

As a female during the Great War, write to a brother, son, husband or friend fighting overseas telling him what it is like living in Australia at this time. Describe the financial hardships, the trouble over the conscription debates, the work you are doing to help the war effort and your fears for the people fighting in Europe.

OR

You are a nurse serving in a field hospital. Describe the conditions in the hospital and your views on the war.

THE WESTERN FRONT

Germany's 'Schlieffen Plan' did not bring the hoped for victory over France. For the Schlieffen Plan to work, German troops had to pass through Belgium quickly and isolate France from British troops. The defeat of France would then allow Germany to concentrate its resources on Russia.

A slow rate of movement, resistance from French and Belgian troops and tiring German soldiers all meant the plan did not work effectively. To make things worse, on the Eastern Front the Russians were able to mobilise their troops more rapidly than expected. Germany found itself deadlocked on the Western Front and fighting a second war against Russia on the Eastern Front.

After the evacuation of Gallipoli, Australian troops joined other Allied forces in the huge stalemate of the Western Front. Dreams of early successes evaporated as both the Central Powers and the Allies dug in along a line extending from Belgium through France and finishing in the south of Germany. The romance and heroism associated with **cavalry** charges and lightning strikes by **infantry** disappeared with the onslaught of a new kind of warfare. In this new kind of war, technology became more important than human lives; mind-boggling numbers of men were sacrificed as the warring sides tried to gain an advantage. The invention of the machine gun meant that a well-positioned gunner could keep at bay or wipe out greater numbers of the enemy. Heavier bombardments of shells sent over long distances pummelled troops in their trenches. Lines of barbed wire slowed down any attempt to move men forward quickly. **Zeppelins**, aeroplanes and tanks added terrifyingly new and increasingly important dimensions to warfare.

Casualties were high on both sides. Between July and November, 1916, France and Britain lost 750 000 men along the Somme. On the ground, soldiers dug themselves into lines of trenches. The conditions here were no better and often worse than at Gallipoli. In the air, by 1917 the average length of survival of a front-line pilot was just two weeks. At sea, passenger and merchant ships were sunk with heavy loss of life.

Source 1.7.1

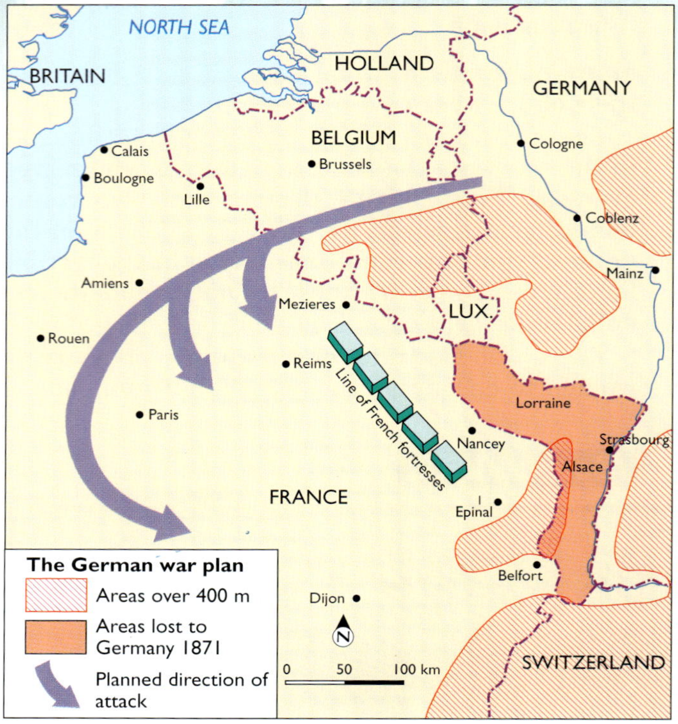

The Schlieffen Plan

Source 1.7.2

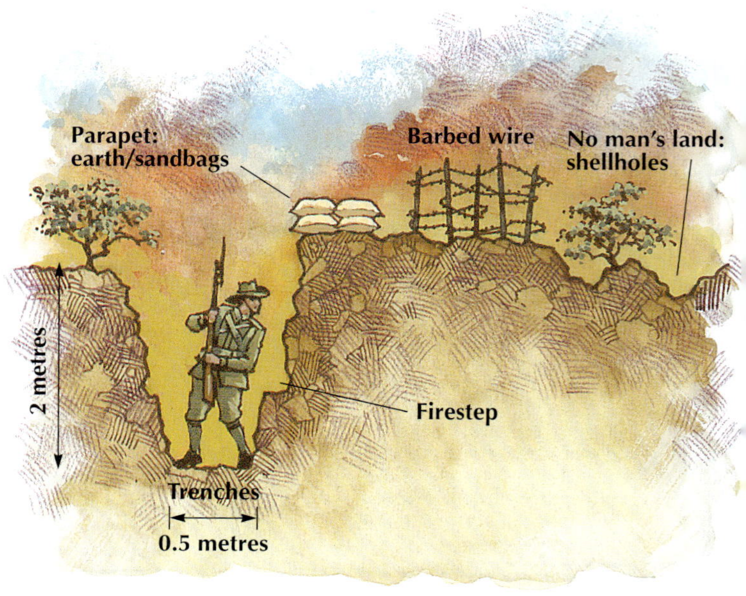

Cross-section view of a trench

Source 1.7.3

Ypres, Belgium, 1917 Australian War Memorial neg. no. E00977

The sinking of the *Lusitania* caused a massive outcry. In May 1915, a torpedo from the German submarine *U-20* sank the British Cunard ocean liner *Lusitania* with the loss of 1195 passengers and crew. Among the dead were 123 Americans. This was the first step involving the United States of America in World War I.

Source 1.7.4

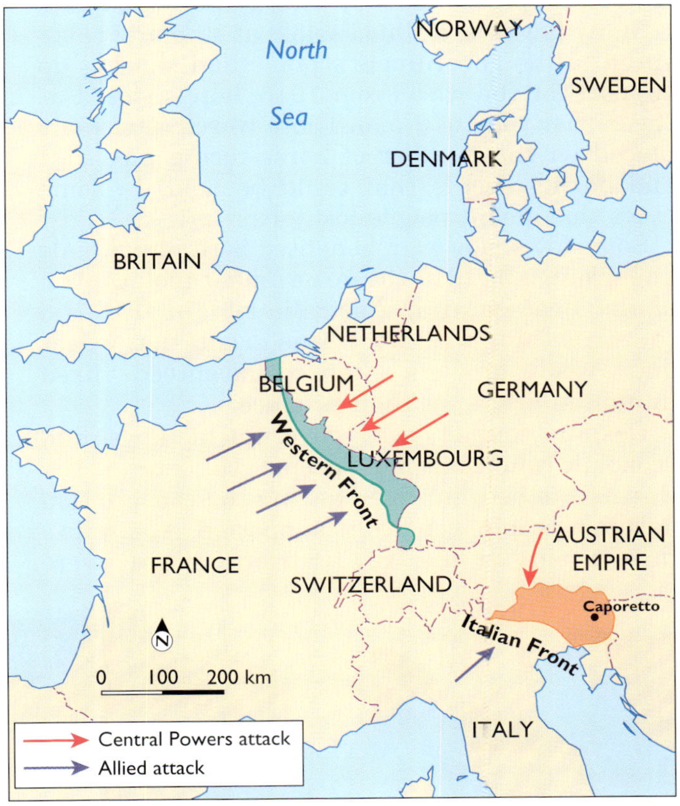

The Western Front

In 1917 the course of the war began to change. There was a **revolution** in Russia, and later that year the **communists** began to negotiate a peace plan with Germany. America entered the war on the side of the Allies, giving them a big boost in morale.

Early in 1918 the Germans began a major offensive on the Western Front. For a while they were successful, getting just 60 kilometres from Paris. But German progress was halted at the Second Battle of the Marne. The Germans were wearying and keeping up supplies and reinforcements was difficult. In mid-1918 fresh American troops arrived on the battlefront.

The Allied armies began counterattacking in August 1918. One by one the Germans began losing their allies. By the end of September Bulgaria had submitted, Turkish forces were on the run, and the last Austrian army was defeated. Recognising that it was pointless fighting on, the **Kaiser** fled to Holland on 9 November and the German government surrendered on the eleventh hour of the eleventh day of the eleventh month. The war was over.

Celebrations erupted all over the world. But the German military, like General Hindenburg, were bitter, believing that their politicians had stabbed them in the back. A young German soldier, Adolf Hitler, agreed with Hindenburg and vowed future revenge for the defeat cast upon Germany.

Activities

Check your understanding

Use the information from this section to complete the following sentences:

(a) The basic idea behind the Schlieffen Plan was to ________.

(b) This German plan did not work as well as anticipated because ________.

(c) Changing technology made the Great War different from previous wars in the following ways ________.

(d) Trench warfare is ________.

Investigation: *The defeat of the Germans*

1. Using source 1.7.3 and the text, explain what the impact of war might have been on the environment.
2. Sketch source 1.7.4 and, with information from the text, explain why the battle on the Western Front was a stalemate.
3. Explain why casualty rates were so high on all sides during the Great War.
4. Suggest the long-term and short-term reasons for the defeat of the Germans.
5. Why might the German military have been unhappy with their government's decision to surrender?
6. Find out about the following people and their role in the Great War: Marshal Foch, Manfred von Richthofen, Adolf Hitler, Winston Churchill, Woodrow Wilson, Admiral Jellicoe.

THE HOME FRONT

The war in Europe and Turkey had a tremendous impact, not only on the soldiers on active duty but also on those at home. In some ways it was worse for people at home because they felt powerless to change or influence events that were turning the world upside down.

As soon as war was declared in 1914, life in Australia changed. During the years of the Great War prices increased by almost 30 per cent. The most rapid rise occurred during the first year of the war when there was an increase of 12 per cent. States like Tasmania were hit hard. The *Trading With The Enemy Act* meant the loss of valuable exports. Germany was Tasmania's biggest importer of mineral ores. Those who made a living selling wallaby skins (and other animal skins) to Germany were also badly affected. Unemployment rose from 5.7 per cent in July 1914 to 13.1 per cent by January 1915.

Profiteering and panic-buying, as people feared shortages, sent the prices of food and groceries sky-rocketing. In Tasmania, prices rose 16.5 per cent in the first year of the war. Prime Minister Billy Hughes' refusal to hold a price-control referendum set a lot of people against the government. There were cries that the burden of war wasn't being spread equally among the population.

Unions pointed to the wages freeze imposed by wages boards in the first few years of the war. Workers were expected not to ask for increases in wages to keep up with the increased cost of living during a wartime. As the unions began to push for wage increases in 1915, they pointed to the war contractors, farmers and profiteers who were making a fortune from the war.

The federal government was introducing many new laws, however, which affected most Australians. Before the war, the state governments had been more important; but now, as the country and its economy had to be geared towards the war, the federal government became more important and powerful.

A lot of money had to be raised to support the war effort. Millions of pounds were borrowed from Britain; encouraging Australians to buy war bonds raised some money, but not enough. Income tax was thus introduced in 1915, with taxes on entertainment brought in during 1916. A wartime profits tax was introduced in 1917.

Many laws were aimed solely at stopping opposition to the government's plans and shoring up support for the war. From 1916, hotels closed at the earlier time of 6 p.m. There were restrictions placed on the number of horse-racing meetings and boxing events that could be held. In some cases this meant people lost jobs.

Some laws, however, benefited both individuals and groups. In 1915 the government took control of all wheat grown in Australia and, in 1916, did the same thing with wool. This meant that wheat and wool growers were guaranteed fixed minimum prices for their produce.

Despite conflict over government laws and economic conditions most people still believed the war had to be won. Even during the conscription debates people generally supported Australia's involvement in the war. Patriotic groups were

Source 1.8.1

Voluntary workers preparing parcels and clothes for the AIF
Australian War Memorial neg. no. J00346

Source 1.8.2

Images of children were used to encourage support for the war effort.

busy raising funds for the war at dances and public entertainments. Schoolchildren contributed by selling odds and ends — in the country it was often rabbits. Even if people didn't believe it was right to send men to fight overseas against their will, they did contribute to the war effort by putting their money into government **bonds** or through charity or war work.

Source 1.8.3

Some of the offences listed under the *War Precautions Act*

Tearing down recruiting posters
Failing to register as an alien
Being in unauthorised possession of wireless apparatus
Spreading a false rumour that a transport with Australian troops on board had been torpedoed
Wrongfully dyeing military overcoats
Exhibiting the red flag
Disturbing referendum meetings
Evasion of censorship of letters for enemy countries
Falsely representing to be returned soldiers

THE END OF WAR

When the war ended in 1918 Australians were relieved as much as happy. The conscription debates had divided Australia and the wounds created by this took decades to heal. The English had been set against the Irish, Catholic against Protestant, trade unionist against employer. Up until the 1960s, it was possible to read a job advertisement in a newspaper which included the line, 'Catholics need not apply'.

Australians wanted to quickly forget about the war and get on with the task of rebuilding their lives. With 60 000 soldiers dead and a great many more wounded, virtually every family in the country had been hit by the war in one way or another.

Activities

Investigation: *Life on the home front*

1. Using the information on these pages, set out what you believe were the positive and negative impacts of the war on Australians at home.
2. In what ways did the federal government become more important than the state governments during the Great War?
3. Hotels closing at 6 p.m. led to what was called the 'six o'clock swill'. What was this?
4. How would fixed prices for wheat and wool have helped growers?
5. What was the point of placing restrictions on sporting and entertainment events? Who would have supported these moves and who would have opposed them?
6. Could an Australian in 1916 have opposed conscription and still supported the war? Discuss this point as a class. Describe the different ways that people could express their support for the war.
7. What do you think about the line 'Catholics need not apply' at the bottom of job advertisements? Was this fair in the years after the war? Could you still print such a line in an advertisement today? Why or why not?
8. A Tasmanian calling himself 'Old Bark Stripper' wrote of 6 o'clock closing of hotels:

   > 'These same temperance people could carry a successful referendum for total prohibition, the doing away of smoking, the evil of young girls hanging around the streets at night, Sunday pictures, steamer excursions, picnics in the bush, eating too much, Tattersals and last but not least regulating the time we shall go to bed and the time we shall get up.'

   What point is 'Old Bark Stripper' making about the new law and the control of people's lives generally? Are any of the issues raised by him still relevant today?
9. Source 1.8.3 lists some offences under the *War Precautions Act*. Discuss these as a class and try to come to some agreement about whether these laws were justified or not.

THE WAR'S IMPACT

At the Versailles peace conference in 1919 Prime Minister Billy Hughes ruffled some British feathers when he insisted that Australia have its own voice at the conference. Britain had wanted to speak on behalf of all its **dominions**. At one point during the conference when American president Woodrow Wilson objected to a point Hughes had made, the Australian prime minister replied, 'Mr. President, I speak for 60 000 dead. How many do you speak for?' Wilson was not able to answer.

As a result of the Versailles conference Australia was given control of the former German colony in New Guinea — an important gain, in light of what was to follow in World War II. It was also given financial compensation, little of which was ever paid.

Hughes also featured in the defeat of Japan's quest to be considered in all respects equal to other nations, which perhaps in part explained Japan's attitude toward Australia during the early 1940s.

Source 1.9.1

Helping the wounded at Randwick Military Hospital, Sydney
Australian War Memorial neg. no. H16130

In human terms the war had been a disaster for Australia, as it was for all countries involved. About 65 per cent of those who served overseas were killed or wounded, the highest casualty rate among the **Allies**. Thousands were hospitalised on their return to Australia and some people never left the rehabilitation hospitals.

Society was also left deeply scarred by the war. Living standards had fallen and communities were divided over the conscription issue. Many people never recovered from having lost a family member or friend. There were cases where four members of the one family had been killed. Some of the soldiers had been older men. Some were as young as 16.

Political changes in Australia were brought on by the war. Billy Hughes became prime minister after the war had started. The party he led in 1915, the Labor Party, split the following year over the conscription issue when Hughes, and the more conservative members of his party, joined with the opposition Liberals to form the Nationalist Party.

The war provided some positive outcomes for Australians. Wheat farmers and wool growers benefited from government policies. The government set up a national shipping line and improved transport within the country. Communications also improved. The era of the aeroplane was beginning and Australians were being brought closer together. The BHP steelworks started in Newcastle in 1915 and industry in general developed as a result of the war, especially in areas such as the chemical and metal industries but also in areas such as textiles.

Although Australia had become a nation in 1901, it was really only the Great War which gave everyone a strong sense of being an Australian. While soldiers had identified with their battalions, they regarded themselves as Australians first and were proud of it.

Australians at home too had developed this same, strong sense of identity. Australia had become a proud member of the British Empire and, through its 'baptism of fire', had shown that it was able to stand on its own two feet.

Whether on the home front or the war front, Australians were determined to protect what they had built in Australia. A key belief was the dominance of their white race. During the conscription referenda the anti-conscriptionists had warned that conscription would lead to a flood of cheap 'coloured' labour which would undermine living standards. Most Australians were also unhappy with the alliance formed in 1902 between Great Britain and Japan. They feared for their own security, as the war had made them conscious of their own isolation. Australians may have liked to think that they treated all people as equals but there were many exceptions to their self-made rule.

Source 1.9.2

SHIPS THAT PASS IN THE NIGHT.

When Australia has been denuded of white men by Conscription, it will be necessary to import Chinese or colored labour to keep the industries going. A plentiful supply of such labour is already assured.—News item.

[Drawing by Rob Shaw of "Truth" Office, 244–46 Little Lonsdale-street, Melbourne.]

Ships that pass in the night

By the time the war ended, in 1918, Australia had changed markedly. The naive attitudes about war were gone forever and, when the next major war erupted two decades later there were few illusions about what that war might bring. After 1914, people were more cynical and disillusioned. The war had made a nation of Australia but it had also led to the senseless slaughter of a good part of an entire generation of young men.

Source 1.9.3

War is over. Australian War Memorial neg. no. J00350

Activities

Check your understanding

1. Why did Billy Hughes ruffle feathers at the Versailles conference?
2. How did the Great War establish an Australian identity?

Investigation: *A changing Australia*

1. Under the heading 'How The War Changed Australia' make a table which categorises these changes.

Area	Changes
Political Economic Social Cultural	

2. Across Australia there are thousands of memorials to our involvement in war. In some towns and suburbs, they take the form of statues. In other places, they might be memorial halls. Find your local war memorial and investigate when it was built, which war or wars it commemorates, the number of dead it is honouring and its main inscription. Write down and sketch any other information you feel is useful.

1.10 Meeting the outcomes

ANALYSE THE CONTINUING SIGNIFICANCE OF MAJOR EVENTS AND IDEAS WHICH SHAPED AUSTRALIAN SOCIETY.

Identify significant events and ideas which shaped Australian society.

Complete the paragraph below, filling in the gaps with words from the list provided.

While Australia became a federation in ________, it was the experience of the ________ which really made it a nation. Australians were ________ about the idea of war in 1914 but the war dragged on for years and changed the way they thought about it. Australians were proud of their achievements at ________ and on the ________ . But on the ________ there was conflict as debate raged about whether ________ should be introduced. In all, some ________ Australian soldiers were killed and over ________ wounded. Australia would never be the same again.

Word list
Gallipoli conscription 1901 Great War 150 000
home front excited 60 000 Western Front

Evaluate the contributions of key participants and leaders in these events.

1. Billy Hughes became a key figure in Australia during World War I. (1.5, 1.9)
   (a) Who was Billy Hughes?
   (b) With what key issue is he associated?
   (c) How successful was he with this issue?
   (d) Which two countries did he upset at the conference at Versailles and why?

Source 1.10.1

AIF troops, by occupation

Occupation	AIF embarked	Percentage of total embarked
Tradesmen	112 452	34.00
Labourers	99 252	30.00
Country callings	57 430	17.36
Clerical	24 346	7.36
Professional	15 719	4.75
Miscellaneous	12 878	3.89
Seafaring	6 562	1.98
Nurses	2 131	0.64
Total	330 770	99.98

Source: J. Bassett, *The Home Front 1914–1918*, Oxford University Press, Melbourne, 1983, p. 20.

2. Look carefully at source 1.10.1.
   (a) Which two occupations made up almost two-thirds of the AIF?
   (b) What sorts of jobs might be included in 'country callings'?
   (c) Looking at this table, would you say that all sections of the community appear to have contributed equally to the ranks of those who fought? Which groups might be over-represented? Which groups might be under-represented?
   (d) In what ways might you need to be careful when assessing information of this kind? How is the composition of the work force today different from that of 1914–1918?

Compare different perspectives about a significant event.

Outline the different reactions of Australian soldiers to the physical and emotional problems faced by them on the Western Front as shown in source 1.10.2.

Source 1.10.2

Conditions on the Western Front

Waiting for the attack:

The tension affected the men in different ways. I couldn't stop urinating, and we were all anxious for the barrage to begin. When it did begin, it seemed as if the earth opened up with a crash. The ground shook and trembled, and the concussion made our ears ring. It was impossible to hear ourselves speak to a man lying alongside. It is strange how men creep together for protection. Soon, instead of four paces interval between the men, we came down to lying alongside each other, and no motioning could make them move apart.

— unknown.

The effects of a shell attack:

All day long the ground rocked & swayed backwards & forwards from the concussion . . . [like] a well built haystack . . . swaying . . . about . . . men were driven stark staring mad & more than one of them rushed out of the trench over towards the Germans. Any amount of them could be seen crying & sobbing like children their nerves completely gone . . . we were nearly all in a state of silliness & half dazed, but still the Australians refused to give ground. Men were buried by the dozen, but were frantically dug out again some dead and some alive.

— Barwick, *D* IV, pp. 11–13 (24/7/16).

The mud:

. . . about the MUD here . . . on foot one has to go very cautiously. Last time we were here one of our officers rode into a Shell hole. His horse disappeared in the mud & he was only rescued with great difficulty. He had to be pulled out with ropes & in doing so they strained his internal organs . . .

— Gatliff, *L* 13/12/16.

Source 1.10.3

Forces of the British Empire in World War I, 1914–18

Population			Troops						Percentages	
	Year		Raised	Took the field	Killed and died of wounds	Wounded less died of wounds	Number reported prisoners	Total battle casualties	Troops took the field to population	Battle casualties to took the field
United Kingdom	1916	48 089 249	5 704 416	5 399 563	702 410	1 662 625	170 389	2 535 424	11.2	47.1
Canada	1917	8 361 000	628 964	422 405	56 625	149 732	3 729	210 086	5.0	49.7
Australia	1916	4 875 325	416 809	331 781	59 342	152 171	4 084	215 045	6.8	64.8
New Zealand	1916	1 099 449	128 525	98 950	16 654	41 317	530	58 501	8.9	58.6
South Africa	1916	6 685 827	136 070	136 070	6 928	11 444	228	18 600	2.0	13.6
Newfoundland	1918	254 587	11 922	10 619	1 195	2 314	152	3 661	4.2	34.5
India	1916	315 200 000	1 440 437	1 338 620	53 486	64 350	3 762	121 598	0.4	9.1
Fed. Malay States	1918	820 871	1 000	1 000	103	290	40	433	0.1	43.3
West Indies	1916	1 772 000	15 601	15 601	1 256	697	—	1 953	0.09	12.5
Ceylon	1918	4 686 383	2 182	2 182	333	437	—	770	—	35.3
Totals		391 844 691	8 485 926	7 756 791	897 780	2 085 377	182 914	3 166 071	8.3	47.4

Source: A. G. Butler (ed.), *Official History of the Australian Medical Services in the War of 1914–18*, vol. III, p. 880.

A salvo of shells landed near. I glanced up to try to locate the bursts by the flying mud, when I noticed that the whole side of the shell-slit was falling in ... It struck me in the act of rising and completely buried me. The weight on my tin hat pressed me down irresistably and forced my chin into my chest. After struggling a little I found that it only settled the earth closer around me. The brim of my hat kept the earth out of my nose, but the weight gradually forced it further down on my head, the head band gradually travelling down my nose and taking the skin with it ... The realization came of what was gradually but surely ending things. The soft earth at first yielded slightly to my struggles, but was slowly settling down and compressing under the weight above, so that the movement of my ribs was becoming more and more constricted. It was as though an iron band were tightening round my chest and preventing any movement. Then I heard the Sergeant Major speaking, and calling me, as though he were a long way off ... I heard him say, 'Good God, I believe the man's buried! Come here two men with shovels. Now gently — don't maim him.' At last the terrible weight was relieved, and they lifted me out and laid me on the floor of the trench.

— McInnis, *D* –/11/16.

Reactions of soldiers:

Many a man smiles when he is told he will never be able to fight again or that we won't be right again for some months. Its Blighty for a spell anyhow, and probably back to Australia again, he may casually remark. The fellows shake hands with and congratulate their mates and brothers when they find that they have a wound that . . . will most likely keep them away for a few months.

— Richards, *D* 30/7/16.

Source: B. Gammage, *The Broken Years*, Penguin, Victoria, 1975, pp. 162–91.

ANALYSE THE IMPACT OF SIGNIFICANT EVENTS AND IDEAS IN SHAPING WORLD HISTORY IN THE TWENTIETH CENTURY.

Evaluate the impact of the events and ideas on people, values and structures.

Source 1.10.3 shows the impact of the war on the countries of the British Empire.

(a) Which country sent the most troops to the war?
(b) Which country suffered the most casualties in terms of total battle casualties and percentage of casualties who took to the field?
(c) Suggest why Australia and New Zealand might have had such high casualty rates.
(d) What impact might these high casualty rates have had on those at home?

Some of the other 'discomforts' of life in the trenches:

We all have lice, . . . The big-wigs say we are 'pediculous' and that only means lousy. They're on us from head to foot. The German prisoners tell us they're all as bad . . . We had 2 flannel shirts and the one I was not wearing I washed. It was a frosty night and I hung it up and it was frozen so solid I hit it with a stick and the sound echoed off and icicles tinkled off and I thought 'that's the end of the people who have been living with me' but sure enough as soon as my body warmed up after I'd put it on me, out they came. You couldn't get rid of them. . . . There's no wound worse than trench feet. The ball of your foot swells up very painfully and red and it gives you no rest at nights.

— Richard Smith.

Source: P. Adam-Smith, *The ANZACS*, Thomas Nelson, Melbourne, 1978, p. 268.

Chapter 2

BETWEEN THE WARS

INTRODUCTION

The peace conference held at Versailles in 1919 satisfied the short-term anger of the victors but created other, more dangerous conflicts. Struggling to get back on its feet, a ruined Germany was torn by political conflict and economic problems. The Great Depression of 1929 would provide the perfect breeding ground for Adolf Hitler's extremist views.

The onset of the Great Depression in 1929 brought the hopes and aspirations of millions around the world to a crashing end. As unemployment numbers grew bigger by the day, governments, groups and individuals all sought solutions to the problem. Ironically, their solutions often worsened society's troubles.

Japan's military used the depression as a chance to spread its influence, and in 1937 embarked on a full-scale war with China in an attempt to secure natural resources to feed its growing manufacturing industry. China's ability to defend itself was weakened by civil war between the Kuomintang and the communists.

LEARNING *outcomes*

- Evaluate the impact of the Great Depression in Australia.
- Identify the ideas that shaped the growth of communism in China.
- Analyse the role of Adolf Hitler in the rise of the Nazis.
- Use political cartoons to understand issues behind significant events.
- Understand the reasons behind Japan's military growth.

GLOSSARY

abdicate: to give up the position of king or queen, or some other important power
Allies: Britain, British Empire, United States, Russia, Italy, France, Belgium
armistice: an agreement to stop fighting
Central Powers: Germany, Austria–Hungary, Turkey, Bulgaria
charter: document giving legal rights
communism: system of social organisation in which the community or state owns all property
coup: sudden takeover of government, usually by force
coupons: ticket or certificate that entitles the holder to something
default: fail to meet financial obligations
depot: central storehouse or collection point
dole: payment by a government to an unemployed person
Führer: tyrannical leader
Gestapo: secret police in Nazi Germany
infanticide: killing of babies or very young children
inflation: rise in prices and cost of living
latrines: toilets
means test: the evaluation of a person's or family's income in order to determine whether they qualify for a pension, allowance, benefit etc.
nationalism: great love for one's own country; national spirit or desire for national advancement
Reichstag: German parliament and building
SS: Nazi special police and Hitler's bodyguards
stormtroopers: the militant members of the Nazi Party who disrupted opponents' political rallies and who were active in promoting Nazi parades, rallies and the political murder of opponents; also known as 'brownshirts'
tariff: tax on imported goods
Wall Street: the financial centre of the United States in New York; alternative name for the New York Stock Exchange

2.1

THE TREATY OF VERSAILLES

At the end of the Great War, the victorious powers had to decide what to do about rebuilding Europe and making it safe for the future. They met at Versailles, just outside Paris, in January 1919 to work out a peace settlement. The defeated powers were not invited to the conference.

The four key players at the conference were Lloyd George of Britain, Clemenceau of France, Wilson of the United States of America and Orlando of Italy. Wilson put forward 14 points which he thought would bring lasting peace.

Although the terms proposed in Wilson's 14-point plan imposed certain penalties and restrictions on Germany, many people in France and Britain thought they were not tough enough. They were demanding that the conference 'make Germany pay'. Much of the war had been fought in France and Clemenceau wanted the Germans punished badly for inflicting such loss of life and physical damage on his country. The conference delegates were also keen to block any threatened expansion of Russian communism, which had become a political factor after the 1917 Russian Revolution.

At the end of the conference, German delegates were brought in to sign the treaty drawn up by the victors. Separate treaties dealt out punishments to the other defeated **Central Powers**.

The main outcomes of the Treaty of Versailles were:

(a) **Redistribution of territory**
- Germany lost Alsace-Lorraine to France.
- The new country of Poland was created in the east.
- Austria–Hungary and western Russia were divided up into new countries.
- Former German colonies were to be taken over by the League of Nations.
- Germany was forbidden union with Austria.

(b) **Reduction of Germany's fighting power**
- Germany's army was reduced to 100 000.
- Germany was allowed no planes, tanks or submarines and only six battleships.
- No German troops were allowed in the Rhineland.

(c) **Imposition of harsh conditions**
- Germany was to pay compensation to the **Allies** (6600 million pounds in 1921).
- Germany was forced to sign a 'war guilt' clause where it accepted blame for starting the Great War.

Source 2.1.1

Wilson's 14-point peace proposal

Woodrow Wilson

1. No more secret treaties.
2. The seas to be free to merchant ships at all times.
3. No restrictions on trade between countries.
4. Countries to reduce their armaments.
5. All claims to colonies to be treated in the interests of the people living there.
6. Russia to be free to choose her own system of government.
7. Belgium to be evacuated (freed of enemy presence).
8. Alsace-Lorraine to go back to France.
9. Italy's frontiers to be redrawn on the basis of nationality.
10. The peoples of the Austro-Hungarian Empire to be free.
11. The peoples in the Balkans should be free to form their own countries.
12. The peoples in the Turkish Empire should be free to form their own countries.
13. Poland to be 'recreated' and given access to the sea.
14. A League of Nations should be set up.

Many Germans were furious over what the treaty had imposed on them. Source 2.1.2 gives two views.

Source 2.1.2

German reaction to the Treaty of Versailles — two views

Today in the Hall of Mirrors of Versailles the disgraceful Treaty is being signed. Do not forget it! The German people will with unceasing labour press forward to reconquer the place among nations to which it is entitled. Then will come the vengeance for the shame of 1919.

Deutsche Zeitung

Only fools, liars and criminals could hope for mercy from the enemy. In these nights hatred grew in me, hatred for those responsible for the dead.

Adolf Hitler

Source 2.1.3

"PERHAPS IT WOULD GEE-UP BETTER IF WE LET IT TOUCH EARTH"

A British cartoon opposing the 'make Germany pay' policy

Source 2.1.4

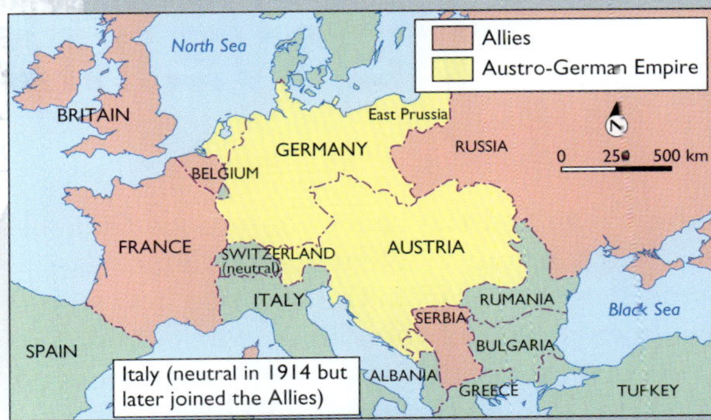

Europe in 1914

Europe in 1920

Activities

Communication: *Using visual resources*

1. Source 2.1.3 is a famous cartoon by the British cartoonist Low. Explain the points it is making about the Treaty of Versailles.
2. Study the two maps in source 2.1.4 and then answer the following questions.
   (a) Which new countries are shown in the 1920 map that do not appear in the 1914 map?
   (b) From what former countries or empires did these new countries appear?
   (c) Which country or countries appear to have lost most from the redrawing of territorial boundaries? Which gained most?
   (d) What problems might these changed political boundaries have caused subsequently?

Investigation: *The Treaty of Versailles*

Organise a role play that recreates the Treaty of Versailles conference. Groups of students will represent France, Britain, the United States and Italy respectively. Also include Germany so there is an opportunity to discuss Germany's point of view. Research the characters of the main players and investigate what each country had to gain or lose from the conference. Around a table, debate each country's case. Then vote on the conditions your treaty will contain. Remember that it does not have to be the same as the original treaty.

2.2

GERMANY – THE WEIMAR REPUBLIC

The Great War and the peace conference that followed it left Germany defeated and demoralised. How would it recover from the war and how would its people ever pay off their huge war debts?

On 9 November 1918 the Kaiser **abdicated** and fled to the Netherlands. Philipp Scheidemann of the Social Democratic Party declared from a window in the German parliament building (the **Reichstag**) that Germany was now a republic. Two days later, Germany had to sign an **armistice** with the Allies.

Political problems continued to worry the new German republic. Communist groups, including the Spartacus League, tried to set up a government like that in the Soviet Union. The Social Democrats used the army to squash opposition to the party, and in 1919 thousands of political opponents were killed, including the leaders of the Spartacus League.

Elections were held in 1919 but because of political demonstrations in Berlin the government met in the city of Weimar. A republic was declared with the chancellor made the head of the government, and the president the head of state. The latter would be elected every seven years and would become involved in day-to-day politics only in the event of a crisis. Then he would have wide powers, including being able to suspend the parliament and to call in the armed forces to restore 'public security and order'.

The spectre of the Treaty of Versailles continued to hang over the heads of Germans. Many still felt the government had betrayed the people by surrendering to the Allies, and there were attempts to overthrow the government. One notable attempt occurred in Munich in 1923 when a group led by Adolf Hitler attempted to seize power. The action failed and Hitler spent nine months in prison; however, he learnt a valuable lesson about how to gain control of power, and would not make the same mistake again.

The year 1923 was also a crucial turning point in other ways. French troops marched into the Ruhr region after Germany failed to meet its war reparation payments. The German economy collapsed and a period of extreme **inflation** resulted. People's lives were ruined as money became all but worthless. Sources 2.2.2 and 2.2.3 show some of the impacts of this runaway inflation.

Source 2.2.1

Street fighting in Berlin in 1919

THE STRESEMANN ERA

From late 1923, Germany began to work more closely with its former enemies. Gustav Stresemann was briefly made chancellor, and the war payments to the Allies were renegotiated. Stresemann was foreign minister from 1923 to 1929 and Germany's economic position improved during this period. The devalued former currency was replaced with the rentenmark. Investment money, much of it from the United States, financed growth in industry which reduced unemployment and encouraged exports. In 1926 Germany joined the League of Nations and it seemed that a lasting peace was becoming a reality.

The death of Stresemann in 1929 and the collapse of the New York Stock Exchange were to undo all the good work of the late 1920s.

Source 2.2.2

Stacks of money waiting to be paid out as wages in 1923

Source 2.2.3

Inflation levels in Germany in 1923

As soon as the factory gates opened and the workers streamed out, pay packets (often in old cigar boxes) in their hands, a kind of relay race began: the wives grabbed the money, rushed to the nearest shops, and bought food before prices went up again. Salaries always lagged behind; the employees on monthly pay were worse off than workers on weekly. People living on fixed incomes sank into deeper and deeper poverty.

A familiar sight in the streets were handcarts and laundry baskets full of paper money, being pushed or carried to or from the banks. It sometimes happened that thieves stole the baskets but tipped out the money and left it on the spot. There was a dry joke that spread through Germany: papering one's WC with banknotes. Some people made kites for their kids out of them.

E. Larsen, from R. Gibson & J. Nichol, *Germany*, Simon & Schuster Education, United Kingdom, 1992, p. 17.

Activities

Investigation: *Exploring the Weimar Republic*

1. Answer true or false for each of the following statements. Rewrite any incorrect sentences so that they are true.
   (a) The German republic was created after the Kaiser fled and the Social Democrats declared that Germany had become a republic.
   (b) All political groups cooperated to make the Weimar Republic a success.
   (c) Germans believed that the Treaty of Versailles was fair.
   (d) Hyper-inflation meant money lost most of its value.
   (e) Stresemann was able to improve Germany's economic situation during the late 1920s.
2. Refer to sources 2.2.1, 2.2.2 and 2.2.3 to answer the following questions.
   (a) What does source 2.2.1 tell you about the political climate in Berlin in 1919? Why were the opposing parties not able to sort out their differences by peaceful means?
   (b) What evidence is there in sources 2.2.2 and 2.2.3 that money was almost useless?
3. Discuss whether you think source 2.2.2 or 2.2.3 is the more reliable source of evidence. What are the advantages and limitations of graphic evidence as opposed to written evidence?

Communication: *Studying a table*

1. The following information shows the falling value of the mark in Germany in the early 1920s. In each case, the number of marks is equivalent to one United States dollar.

Date	Number of marks
January 1921	65
January 1922	192
January 1923	17 972
July 1923	353 412
August 1923	4 620 455
September 1923	98 860 000
October 1923	25 260 208 000
November 1923	4 200 000 000 000

   Discuss the causes of inflation and its negative impacts on a society. Does inflation have a positive impact on anyone? If so, who might have gained from this in Germany during the 1920s?
2. What is the inflation rate in Australia today? Why is it important for Australia that the rate be kept low?

THE GREAT DEPRESSION

For those who cared to look, there were already signs of a looming economic crisis in the United States by 1927. Some causes, such as over-borrowing by governments worldwide and by individuals, were long term. Others, such as overproduction of agricultural and rural goods and a decline in industries like the building industry, were more short term. The immediate spark for the beginning of the Great Depression was the collapse of the New York Stock Exchange on 24 October 1929.

THE WALL STREET CRASH

Through the 1920s the value of shares on the New York Stock Exchange had risen steadily, accelerating during 1928 and 1929. Source 2.3.1 shows the movement of share prices over the period from 1920 to 1932.

Many people believed that the share market was an easy way to make money. A share bought for 50 cents one year could be sold a year or two later at a good profit. Many people borrowed from banks so that they could invest in the share market, and while prices continued to rise people continued to make profits.

The problem was that the shares issued by a particular company were supposed to reflect the value of that company (that is, the total worth of its buildings, equipment and assets). Companies issued dividends or payments to shareholders based on company profits. When profits for many businesses began to decline after 1927, some people began to wonder whether the price of their shares was too high. Their increasing anxiety about the declining value of their shares forced many to consider selling them.

Black Thursday — 24 October 1929 — is remembered as the day the economic bubble burst, sending the world into a long depression. Earlier in the month, investors and speculators had begun to sell off stock, as they started to doubt the strength of the American economy. This selling pattern reached panic proportions on 24 October when 13 million shares were sold. Prices plummeted throughout the day as people off-loaded their shares for whatever price they could get. By the end of the day, the value of shares on the New York Stock Exchange had been destroyed as had the lives of thousands of investors, many of whom had borrowed to buy into the share market. The impact of the stock exchange collapse on the economy was immediate.

Source 2.3.1

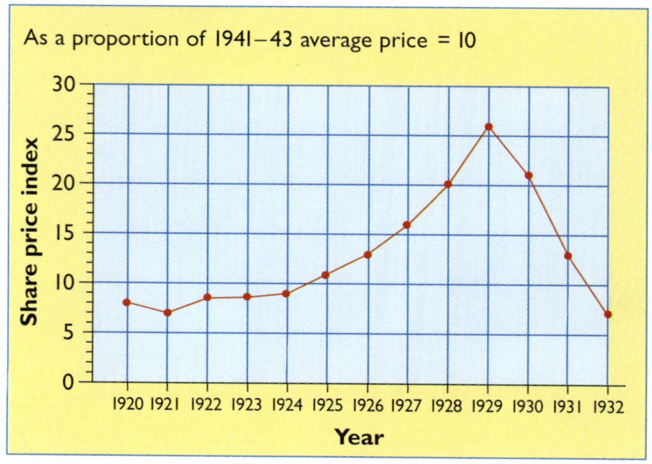

American share price index 1920–1932

GOVERNMENT REACTION

What the collapse of **Wall Street** signalled most was a loss of confidence in the economy. People suddenly stopped investing and spent only what they had to. Government and private projects ground to a halt as people everywhere waited to see in which direction the economy would head.

A halt to spending was probably the worst thing that could have happened. Less money circulating meant fewer jobs. In turn, fewer jobs meant fewer people spending money. This started a chain reaction that was very difficult to stop. (See source 2.3.2.)

Most governments around the world did not know what to do. The general reaction was to reduce spending by as much as possible. Those who kept their jobs often had their wages reduced. Those who relied on the sale of exports found themselves in serious trouble as demand for exports dried up. The high **tariff** walls that countries had built up during the 1920s to protect their own industries now meant even harder times for those countries that relied heavily on selling their goods to other nations. The cessation of investment overseas and the withdrawal of loan monies also contributed to the worldwide disaster.

Source 2.3.2

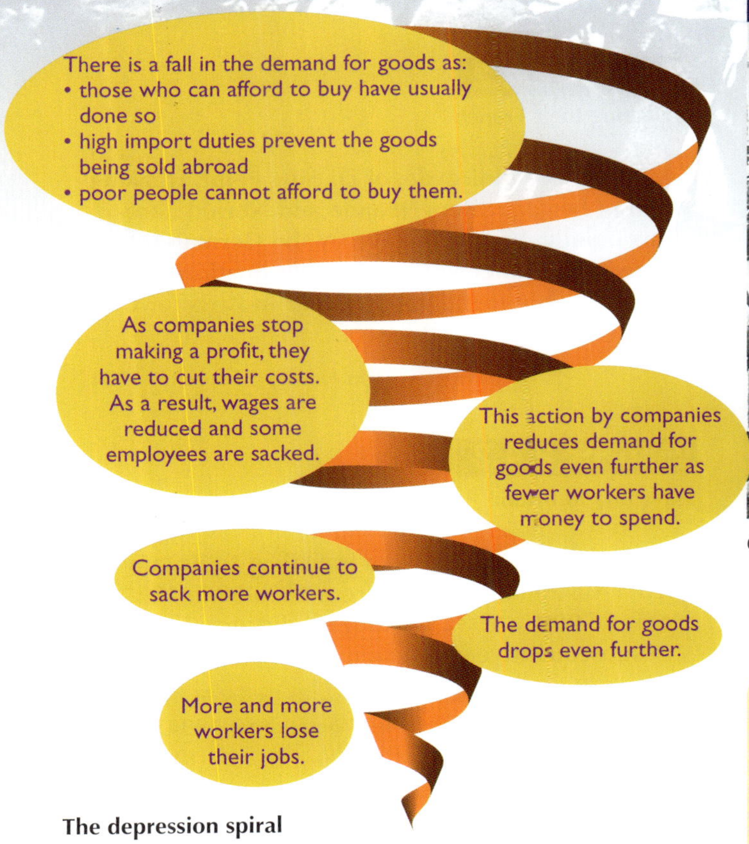

The depression spiral

THE UNEMPLOYED

Unemployment was the greatest tragedy caused by the Great Depression. Although the depression struck in 1929, its worst effects hit in about 1932. In that year unemployment was approximately 25 per cent in the United States, 32 per cent in Australia and over 40 per cent in Germany. Initially, there was little social welfare available to the unemployed, who had to rely on their savings if they had any, on selling off their possessions, or on charities. But soon even the charities could not cope.

Eventually, people who had money began to spend it on more than necessities. Governments, too, were forced to act to help the legion of unemployed and their families. Assistance sometimes came in the form of coupons or work relief, whereby men spent a certain number of days a week working on projects like road building and repair, or community work. Work relief restored some pride and provided some income, but it was neither full-time work nor a career. It was often an individual's own strength of character that got that person through the unemployment crisis. Ironically, it was only another world war which broke the high unemployment levels worldwide.

Source 2.3.3

Crowds gather on Wall Street on Black Thursday

Activities

Check your understanding

1. What were the underlying causes of the Great Depression?
2. What was the immediate cause of the Great Depression?
3. What happened on Black Thursday?
4. What impact did the Great Depression have on employment?
5. What help did the unemployed receive?

Investigation: *The Great Depression*

1. In your own words describe what you think an economic depression is. Compare your definition with those of your classmates. Is it possible to come to a single definition? Why or why not?
2. Draw a flow chart to show how a stop in spending started a chain reaction leading to depression.
3. What made the experience of unemployment so hard for people in the late 1920s and 1930s?
4. Consider source 2.3.1. By what percentage had shares risen over the period from 1920 to 1929? By what percentage had they fallen over the period from 1929 to 1932? What might these trends tell you about the real 'value' of shares in 1929?
5. Find out what happened to share prices in October 1987. What similarities and differences were there between the situations in 1929 and 1987? How might you account for these similarities and differences?

THE DEPRESSION IN AUSTRALIA

The worldwide economic depression hit Australia hard, as the country depended heavily on European and American prosperity. Prices for wool and wheat plummeted, governments cut spending, banks restricted loans, businesses cut wages or closed, and thousands were left with no work. As people's incomes fell they stopped spending, sending even more businesses into bankruptcy.

There are many common images that people today still have of the Depression. One is of a country where large numbers of Australians suffered badly, forced to line up outside soup kitchens for meals. Another image is of vast numbers of the homeless sleeping out in parks or under bridges. A further image shows a sick, dispirited population aimlessly shuffling along on a search for non-existent jobs. There are other images and perceptions too. But are these images of hard times accurate for everyone?

Study the following information and, as you read through and view it, judge for yourself the extent to which all Australians were affected by the Depression.

FACT*file*

At the exclusive Geelong Grammar School, the headmaster realised that students were ignorant of the poverty endured by families living just outside the school. To bridge the gap between rich and poor, he established an unemployed boys' club and technical training centre to provide free training for the poor.

Source 2.4.1

Trade union unemployment figures

Year	Percentage of work force unemployed
1929	11.1
1930	19.3
1931	27.4
1932	29.0
1933	25.1
1934	20.5
1935	16.5
1936	12.2
1937	9.3
1938	8.7
1939	9.7

Source 2.4.2

Perfecting their French

Mrs. Eustace Molroyde, of Darling Point, is taking two of her daughters (Joanne and Norah) abroad this month. They will leave by the German liner *Oder*, and France will be their destination. They will probably spend about a year in Paris for the girls to perfect their French.

The Home, 2 February 1931.

Source 2.4.3

Travelling to Britain

The number of passengers travelling to Britain from Australia decreased from 183 000 in 1927 to only 86 000 in 1932, although it did increase again in subsequent years.

J. Close, 'The Depression Decade' in *Issues in Australian History*, Longman Cheshire, Melbourne, 1990, p. 339.

FACT*file*

Research shows that some people, even though they suffered unemployment during the 1930s, look back on the Depression as a very happy period of their lives. People describe the solidarity among the poor, the sharing of resources and the improvised leisure and recreational activities.

Source 2.4.4

Australian families receiving aid 1932–39

Year	Number of families receiving aid
1932	673 840
1933	394 453
1934	171 505
1935	137 233
1936	138 309
1937	123 603
1938	118 569
1939	111 440

Source: Australian Bureau of Statistics, 1932–39.

Source 2.4.5

An unemployed family outside their improvised housing

FACT*file*

Between 1928 and 1934 the 'real' wage of the full-time worker rose by two per cent because prices of goods dropped more than wages did. Nevertheless, the fear of being reduced to part-time work or losing one's job completely meant that very few people felt secure in their employment.

Source 2.4.6

School lunches

We had lunch in a lunch-shed and if you had any food left over, you placed it on the lunch table. These children without lunches would stand quietly and unobtrusively in the background and, as the others put food on the table, they would move forward, take a sandwich or a piece of bread and move quickly away. An occasional thoughtless member of the well-fed would call out 'Susso! Susso!'

Reminiscences of the Great Depression, Audio Visual Education Centre, Education Department of Victoria, Study Print, no. 28, 1975.

Source 2.4.7

Shame

You fell into the habit of slouching, of putting your hands into your pockets and keeping them there, of glancing at people, furtively, ashamed of your secret, until you fancied that everyone eyed you with suspicion. You knew that your shabbiness betrayed you, it was apparent for all to see. You prayed for the winter evenings and kindly darkness. Darkness, poverty's cloak.

W. Greenwood, *Love on the Dole*, Jonathan Cape, London, 1956.

Activities

Investigation: *Images of the Great Depression*

1. What common images do we have of the Depression today? Discuss this as a class.
2. How have we come to have these images?
3. Is it fair to say that all Australians were affected by the Depression? Use evidence from sources 2.4.1 to 2.4.7 to support your answer.
4. When an economic depression strikes, people tend to stop spending, especially on non-essential items. Bearing this in mind, what sectors of the work force might have been hardest hit by the Depression and subsequently have experienced the highest unemployment rates?
5. People who are said to be 'underemployed', that is, people who work for two or three days a week instead of five, don't appear in unemployment figures. How might this influence the real unemployment figure?
6. The unemployment figure given in source 2.4.1 for 1932 is 29 per cent of the work force. Elsewhere the figure is given as 32 per cent, or even as high as 40 per cent. Provide a possible explanation for the differences in these figures. Source 2.4.1's caption will give you a clue.

Communication: *Class discussion*

There were many factors which influenced how an unemployed person coped with the experience of being unemployed. As a class, discuss the following factors:

- availability of work
- a person's attitude and expectations
- a person's experiences during the 1920s
- age and gender
- marital status
- number of dependants
- mortgages or other financial commitments
- investments
- ability to improvise.

What other factors might also have influenced a person's experiences during the 1930s?

THE AUSTRALIAN UNEMPLOYED

The most noticeable impact of the Depression was the number of breadwinners thrown out of work. However, what actually happened to people after they became unemployed was often less noticeable. Prior to the 1930s, people had been brought up to believe that only through work could a person be whole and worthwhile.

It was little wonder then that unemployment (or underemployment) came as a devastating blow to Australians. Some people refused to be beaten by it, others muddled along hoping that things would improve. And there were some, tragically, who gassed themselves in their kitchen ovens.

CHARITY

Before the 1930s there was no government scheme to help the unemployed. Only Queensland had a form of unemployment insurance.

Australians generally believed that people were responsible for looking after themselves. Unions opposed unemployment benefits because they believed that everyone had a right to a job, not the **dole**. Governments opposed benefits because of the cost but also because of the prevailing attitude that benefits would encourage people not to look for work and become 'bludgers'. If people found themselves out of work, they were supposed to have savings put aside for a 'rainy day'. Those who could not look after themselves would be given assistance by a charity like the Salvation Army or a local church group.

ATTITUDES TO UNEMPLOYMENT

The Depression had already struck with great force by late 1929, and individuals and governments seemed to hope that the whole problem would simply go away. But it didn't. Charitable organisations soon found that they could not cope with the deluge of people seeking help. Though people were powerless to solve the country's economic ills, the same attitudes and ideas about unemployment still lingered. Those dispensing charity often insisted on proof that the unemployed had no assets they might be able to spend or sell first. Charity was often dispensed with a superior attitude that left the recipient feeling isolated and humiliated. The Depression was no-one's fault, but the unemployed often felt as though it was theirs.

RELIEF WORK

When it became obvious that charitable and voluntary groups could no longer cope with the demands being made of them, the government was forced to step in. The unemployed and unions had also put pressure on the government by holding street marches and by signing petitions. At a time when the government was trying to cut costs everywhere it could, it claimed at first that it had no money for any assistance schemes. In the end it had no other choice than to help.

Source 2.5.1

Relief workers on the Yarra Boulevard, Melbourne, 1934

Source 2.5.2

'Ten ways to overcome failure'

Let Your New Year Resolutions Be That You Will Work Hard For Success

1. Let your courage overwhelm your fears.
2. Let concentration replace distraction.
3. Let self-knowledge take the place of ignorance of self.
4. Substitute worthwhile friends for unworthy associates.
5. Let definite purpose take the place of aimlessness.
6. Let thrift supplant extravagance.
7. Stand for high moral ideals.
8. Let cooperation take the place of independence.
9. Let noble motives supersede low purposes.
10. The look ahead should take the place of shortsightedness.

Sun News Pictorial, 1932.

The government's initial response was to provide food for the unemployed. By mid-1930 **depots** had been set up and food **coupons** were delivered to unemployed married men and their families. These coupons were then exchanged at local stores for groceries. This was called 'sustenance' ('the susso') or the 'dole'. No money was given as assistance, partly because it was thought the unemployed might not use the money responsibly — that is, they might spend it down at the pub or out at the racetrack.

In 1931 single people were given the dole at a lower rate than was given to married people. A strict **means test** was placed on families who were receiving assistance and, at times, families were investigated. This could mean strangers going through someone's house looking for evidence of assets.

During 1932 the Victorian State Government decided that people should work for the dole. Those people who refused to do so would lose their entitlements, even if working for the dole meant travelling long distances or performing work they were unsuited to. Relief work took many forms but was often linked to improving infrastructure like roads, bridges and public buildings. The work was paid work when the economy showed signs of improving. Preference was given to married men. Single men might get one day's work a week while married men might be offered three days' work.

Those who could not get any of this work still relied on food coupons. In Victoria, by the end of 1933, about 75 per cent of the unemployed were engaged in some form of relief work. However, unemployment rarely dropped below 10 per cent throughout the Depression decade.

Source 2.5.3

Relief workers

Activities

Investigation: *Relief from unemployment*

1. If people needed economic assistance before 1930, to whom could they turn?
2. What was the prevailing attitude in the 1930s about the importance of work? Have things changed today?
3. Construct a timeline which outlines the forms of assistance available to the unemployed.
4. What do sources 2.5.1 and 2.5.3 indicate about the types of relief work people could be expected to do? Would this work have suited everyone? Explain.
5. Re-read the text, paying special attention to source 2.5.2. Writing as an unemployed person, outline your feelings about the treatment of the unemployed and what it feels like to be without a job.
6. 'Work for the dole' schemes are still being discussed today. Set up a class discussion or debate which looks at this issue. Is it a more or less appropriate idea today than it was during the 1930s?

2.6

RESPONSES TO THE AUSTRALIAN CRISIS

After 13 years in the political wilderness the federal Australian Labor Party won office on 12 October 1929 with a landslide majority. Their celebrations were short-lived. Less than three weeks later the New York Stock Exchange collapsed and tore down international economies with it. Export prices plummeted. Unemployment soared. Australia, which had been reliant on export earnings and overseas borrowings, quickly felt the sting of the Depression.

The new government, inexperienced and wanting to keep faith with its voters, was reluctant to enforce any drastic measures. Military spending was cut, tariffs were raised and the export of gold was prohibited. As confusion increased and the distress of the unemployed worsened, Prime Minister Scullin began a 'Grow More Wheat' campaign to increase exports. Australia's situation did not improve.

THE BANK OF ENGLAND

One pressing problem was how to meet our loan commitments, most of which were owed to England and the United States. When the Commonwealth Bank could not reach agreement with the Bank of England over Australia's debts, two Bank of England representatives, Sir Otto Niemeyer and Professor T. Gregory, were sent to Australia. Scullin's invitation to them and their subsequent findings angered many Australians, in particular those connected with the labour movement. Niemeyer's advice was greeted with applause in some quarters and dismay in others. He claimed that Australia had been living beyond its means for too long and now had to tighten its belt, reduce its spending, pay off its overseas debt and balance its budget.

THE MELBOURNE AGREEMENT

As a result of the Bank of England's advice, the State premiers and the Federal Government came together in Melbourne in August 1930 to sign the 'Melbourne Agreement' whereby they agreed to cost-cutting measures. Under this plan the banks would provide finances for the government to meet its overseas debt commitments. It did not, however, solve the basic causes of the crisis. There was no job creation or benefits for the unemployed. On the contrary, the reduction in spending would mean that even more Australians would be put out of work.

Source 2.6.1

Niemeyer's visit to Australia, as portrayed by a cartoonist in 1930

THE LABOR PARTY SPLIT

Over the next 12 months there was furious debate about what would be the best way to tackle the economic crisis. Politics had as much to do with this debate as economics. The Labor Party began to split again, as it had done in 1916, when a small group of conservatives led by Joe Lyons and another group of radical Jack Lang supporters deserted the party. By November 1931 the Scullin Labor government would be brought down.

JACK LANG

Jack Lang was elected Premier of New South Wales for the second time in October 1930. He was either loved or hated depending on what side of politics a person came from. Lang considered himself a champion of the working class and poor. He was in deadly opposition to the conservative solutions of reduced spending and balanced budgets.

Source 2.6.3

Jack Lang, the 'Big Fella'

Source 2.6.2

Bank interest or relief?

> **If we spent three and a half million pounds overseas to meet interest payments we would have to stop issuing dole tickets. It was simply a question of whether the unemployed would be left to starve or whether the bond-holders went unpaid.**
>
> Jack Lang, New South Wales Premier

Lang argued that if England had been allowed to renegotiate its loans with the United States then Australia should have been allowed to do the same with England. He argued that Australia should not pay any interest on loans until this had been done. Money saved could then be spent on public works projects which would create employment. He also suggested that governments pay only three per cent interest on money borrowed by them within Australia. He formally presented his ideas at a Premiers' conference in February 1931. To use his own words, 'It was as though I had let a death adder loose in the room'. Lang was dismissed from office in May 1932 by the Governor of New South Wales for **defaulting** on interest payments on overseas loans.

THEODORE'S PLAN

During the same month that Lang was putting forward his ideas, the Labor Party's Treasurer, Edward Theodore, was also coming up with a plan. In the early months of 1931 Australia, and indeed the world, had still not come to grips with just how huge a problem was confronting them.

Theodore's plan, like Lang's, went against the conservative opinion of the day by advocating more spending. He said that 18 million pounds worth of new notes should be printed and circulated through the economy. Banks should expand the credit they were giving to business and for government public works. Prices of goods were to be returned to pre-Depression levels. But Theodore could not win the support of the banks and his plans were opposed by a hostile Senate.

THE PREMIERS' PLAN

While politicians were arguing, more and more people were being thrown out of work. The state of the economy was worsening and government income falling. The chairman of the Commonwealth Bank Board wrote to Theodore in April 1931 and told him that the bank had almost advanced as much money as it could to the government. In May a sub-committee of the Loan Council was set up to tackle the crisis. The committee released its report and, in June 1931, it was accepted by the premiers, the prime minister and his treasurer. It became known as the 'Premiers' Plan'. Its main features were:

- that the government had to meet all overseas debt repayments
- an increase in taxation
- a reduction in bank interest rates
- a reduction of 20 per cent on all adjustable government spending, including wages.

Unlike earlier plans and proposals, the Premiers' Plan was acted upon.

Activities

Investigation: *Government action*

1. What factors were always going to make it hard for the new Scullin government to govern in 1929?
2. Do you think Scullin's invitation to Niemeyer and Gregory was a wise one? Explain.
3. In table format set out the main features of the Melbourne Agreement, Lang's plan, Theodore's plan and the 'Premiers' Plan'. Include the main advantages and disadvantages of each of these approaches.
4. Why do you think the Premiers' Plan was the course of action that was finally followed? Do you think this was the correct policy to pursue? Why or why not?

THE RISE OF THE NAZIS

Germany's relative prosperity during the latter part of the 1920s meant that the National Socialist or 'Nazi' Party was not able to increase its power and influence as it would have liked. On his release from prison in 1924, Hitler resumed leadership of the party and set about reorganising it. He divided the party into units called 'gaue' or districts, and put each under the control of a Gauleiter appointed by himself. In this way, he hoped to spread his influence. After his failure in Munich, Hitler was determined to use the political process to his advantage to secure power. Once in a position of power, he could ignore the democratic system and do as he pleased.

Source 2.7.1

Adolf Hitler

THE GREAT DEPRESSION

While times remained good for most Germans, the Nazi Party held little sway, remaining as just one of the many political parties vying for people's votes. It was the collapse of the New York Stock Exchange in 1929 and the subsequent plunge of the world into an economic depression that gave the Nazis the crisis they needed.

The depression left millions of Germans unemployed as foreign investment money was withdrawn from Germany and export markets dried up. By 1932, the number of unemployed had risen from 2.8 million (in 1929) to over 6 million. Signs of social distress were everywhere. The streets were full of people wandering aimlessly looking for work that was not there. Shanty towns sprang up. Charities could not cope with the multitude who were seeking assistance. In their despair, people looked not only for solutions but also for something or someone to blame for their misery.

GERMANY'S VOTING SYSTEM

Germany had a government elected by proportional representation. Under this system, the total number of votes a party gets determines how many members of parliament it will have. Because there were many political parties in Germany, it was very difficult for a single party to gain a majority of seats in the parliament. Therefore, governments were made up of coalitions of different parties. Source 2.7.2 shows the position of the main political parties between 1928 and 1932. It is clear from this that before the Great Depression, the political influence of the Nazi Party was minimal.

Source 2.7.2

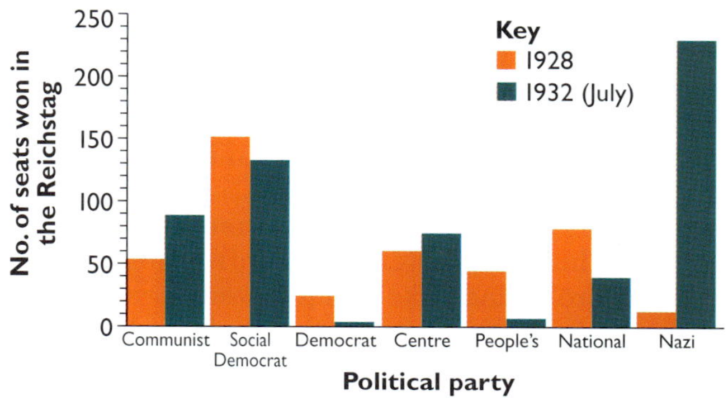

Influence of main political parties in Germany from 1928–32

HITLER'S VIEWS AND STRATEGIES

The dark years of economic chaos provided the perfect climate for the spread of Hitler's ideas which he had set out in the book *Mein Kampf* (My Struggle). He had written this book while in prison. In it, he argued that:

- to be a strong nation Germany had to be united under a strong leader
- struggle was the basis of history
- struggle occurred between different races, and the main struggle for Germany was with the Jewish race
- Germany had to have more land to safeguard itself if needed.

One of Hitler's skills was his ability to persuade others to accept his point of view. He was an exceptional public speaker, and carefully stage-managed his speeches to create maximum effect. They were as much about theatre as they were about public issues. He spoke of Germany's betrayal at Versailles and how a new 'reich' (or empire) would be created in Germany. Germany's enemies would be chased down and wiped out.

Source 2.7.3

THEY SALUTE WITH BOTH HANDS NOW.

***Evening Standard* cartoon by David Low, London, 3 July 1934**

THE NAZIS GAIN CONTROL

The economic crisis caused by the Great Depression put a severe strain on the government in 1930. Unable to get the parties to agree on how to solve the crisis, Chancellor Müller resigned in March of that year and was replaced by Chancellor Brüning. The chaos in the Reichstag continued and Article 48 of the Weimar Constitution was invoked, allowing the chancellor to rule by decree, that is, without the parliament.

By May 1932 President Hindenburg had been persuaded to dismiss Brüning, and von Papen became the new chancellor. A month earlier Hitler had run for the office of President against Hindenburg, but had failed.

The change of chancellor made little difference. At fresh elections in July 1932 the Nazis gained the largest number of seats, with 37 per cent of the vote. Hitler demanded that he become chancellor, but Hindenburg refused. The Nazis then brought a no-confidence motion against von Papen which succeeded. More elections were held in November 1932 and although the Nazis lost some ground, they remained the largest party in the Reichstag. After further manoeuvring, Hitler became chancellor in January 1933.

Despite its success, the Nazi Party still did not have full control of Germany. A new election was called for March 1933. The Nazis used propaganda to great effect, whipping up the German people's fear of communism. On the night of 27 February, the Reichstag building burnt to the ground and the communists were accused. A young Dutchman, Marinus Van der Lubbe was tried and executed. Hitler used the fire as an excuse to round up thousands of communists, convincing Hindenburg that the situation was serious enough to declare a state of emergency.

In the 1933 elections the Nazis gained 44 per cent of the vote. To gain the absolute control he wanted, Hitler first secured the support of the Nationalist Party (which won 8 per cent of the vote) and then did a deal with the Centre Party to give himself a two-thirds majority in the parliament. He took the opportunity to ban communist parliamentarians from taking up their seats under the emergency laws.

With his two-thirds majority Hitler was able to introduce an Enabling Act which let him make laws for four years without the consent of the Reichstag. By July 1933 Hitler had banned all political parties except the Nazi Party. To cement his position he arranged for the leaders of his own **stormtroopers** and other opponents to be killed so that he could win the support of the army. This massacre became known as the 'Night of the Long Knives'.

POLITICS, TERROR AND PROPAGANDA

When Hindenburg died in 1934, Hitler added the powers of the President to those of the Chancellor. He also added a new title — **Führer**.

These changes were to Hitler's benefit as democracy became almost non-existent. The army was reorganised into a new army, called the Wehrmacht, which, in effect, became part of the Nazi machine. In just a few years, the Nazis had taken control of all facets of life in Germany. Propaganda and terror were two of the key weapons they used.

THE POLICE STATE

Two groups were set up to make sure that opposition to the Nazis was destroyed. The first was the **SS** under the control of Heinrich Himmler. The SS consisted of three main sections: a group responsible for security; the 'death's head units', which were responsible for the concentration camps; and the Waffen SS, which was an elite band of highly trained troops within the armed forces.

The second organisation was the **Gestapo**. Set up by Hermann Goering in 1933, this group came under Reynhard Heydrich's command in 1936. Source 2.7.4 sums up the main role of the Gestapo.

Source 2.7.4

The political purpose of the Gestapo

> **Any attempt to gain recognition for, or even uphold, different ideas will be ruthlessly dealt with as the symptom of an illness which threatens the healthy unity of the state. To discover the enemies of the state, watch them and render them harmless at the right moment is the duty of a political police. In order to fulfil this duty, the political police must be free to use every means suited to achieve the desired end.**
>
> **Deputy Chief of the Gestapo, Werner Best (from Stephen Lee, *Nazi Germany*, Heinemann Educational Ltd, Oxford, 1989, p. 28.)**

These two groups ensured that there was little opposition to the Nazis. Joseph Goebbels' 'Ministry for People's Enlightenment and Propaganda' made sure there was strict censorship of the radio and press. Painters and writers had their works destroyed. Society moulded itself to be the way the Nazis wanted it to be.

HOUNDING THE ENEMY

Anyone who opposed the ideas and actions of the Nazis in any way was considered an enemy. But certain groups and races were singled out for special attention. Making a common enemy of certain groups bound the German population closer together and provided a visible enemy which Hitler could exploit. We have already read how he used communists as a way of increasing his own power and that of the Nazi party.

The Jewish people were a main focus of Nazi attention. Hitler believed in the superiority of the German 'race' and that all other 'races' were inferior. The Jews were particularly singled out as Hitler blamed them for Germany's misfortunes in the past. From 1933 Jewish shops were boycotted. In 1935, marriage between Jews and non-Jews was forbidden. Neither could Jews vote. In 1938 Jewish firms had to be specially registered and Jews had to carry identity cards and have only Jewish names. On 9 November 1938 over 7000 Jewish shops were systematically wrecked across Germany in incidents now known collectively as 'Kristallnacht' (the night of broken glass). Thirty-six Jews were murdered and more than 25 000 sent to concentration camps. Further victimisation of Jews occurred up until the outbreak of World War II.

Source 2.7.5

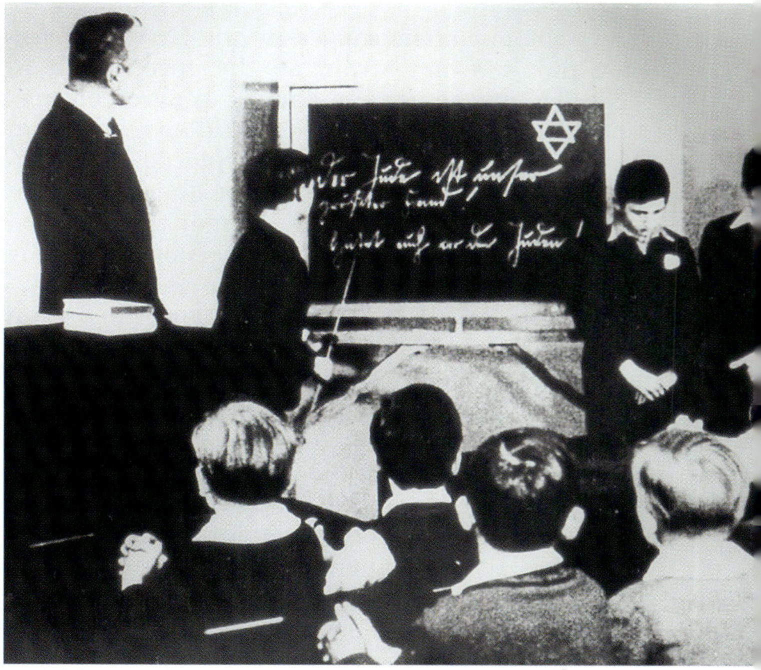

Jewish boys called to the front of the class. The writing on the board behind them reads: 'The Jew is our greatest enemy. Beware of the Jew'.

WOMEN AND CHILDREN

The vision for women in Germany was clearly spelt out by its leaders. Hitler commented: '[A] woman has her battlefield too; with each child that she brings into the world for the nation she is fighting her fight on behalf of the nation'. Goebbels put it even more simply: '[A] woman has the task of being beautiful and bringing children into the world'.

Children were considered to be a vital part of Germany's future success and so their indoctrination began early. By 1934 education was designed to spread the Nazi message. The Hitler Youth movement also gave boys and girls the opportunity to be part of a group actively working for the betterment of Germany. Before the age of 10 a boy could join the Pimpfen (Little Fellows), between 10 and 14 years the Jungvolk (Young Folk) and thereafter the Hitler Jugend (Hitler Youth). Girls between the ages of 10 and 14 could join the Jungmädel (Young Maidens) and those between 14 and 21 years the Bund Deutscher Mädel (League of German Maidens).

Source 2.7.6

A poster entitled 'World Meeting of Hitler Youth'

Activities

Communication: *Draw a timeline*

1. Make a timeline and include the events that correspond with these dates: May 1932, July 1932, November 1932, January 1933, March 1933, July 1933 and 1934.
2. Write a sentence or two on each of the following people: Hindenburg, Van der Lubbe, Himmler, Goering and Goebbels.
3. What were each of the following: *Mein Kampf*, Enabling Act, Night of the Long Knives, Gestapo, SS and Kristallnacht?
4. Why was it so difficult for one political party to have a majority in the Reichstag before 1933? How would this have influenced political stability and the running of the country? (See source 2.7.2.)
5. Look at source 2.7.3. What event is being referred to here? What is the cartoonist's attitude to this?
6. According to source 2.7.4, what were the aims of the Gestapo? In your own words, how would you describe this group?
7. What roles did the Nazis see for females (both women and girls)? In what ways were these roles different to the roles held by males?
8. 'To achieve political stability and unity in Germany certain groups had to become "sacrificial lambs".' Discuss this statement.
9. Working in small groups, research what life was like in Germany in the period leading up to World War II. Think about the rights that an ordinary citizen has today in Australia and compare these with the rights of citizens in Germany during the 1930s. Think, too, about the differences between Germans at this time — cultural, ethnic, gender and so on. Select a spokesperson to present your group's findings to the class.

Investigation: *Nazi Germany*

Hitler's attempt to grab power in 1923 failed. From prison he wrote: 'When I resume active work, it will be necessary to pursue a new policy. Instead of working to achieve power by an armed **coup**, we will have to hold our noses and enter the Reichstag against the Catholic and Marxist members. If outvoting them takes longer than outshooting them, at least the result will be guaranteed by their own constitution . . .'.

(a) Who did Hitler see as his enemies in the Reichstag?

(b) How did his failure in 1923 mark a change in tactics for gaining power?

(c) Why do you think Hitler's speeches were so successful in influencing the German people?

2.8

JAPAN IN THE 1920s AND 1930s

Under the Treaty of Versailles, Japan was given control of German colonies in the Pacific Ocean. But this gain for Japan was offset by European countries recommencing trade with Asia after the war. The Treaty of Versailles was also disappointing, even hurtful, for Japan when its attempts to have a clause acknowledging racial equality included in the **charter** of the League of Nations was defeated. Australia and the United States were instrumental in defeating this clause as they wanted to retain restrictive immigration policies.

In 1923 Japan was also rocked by natural disaster. A massive earthquake destroyed the Tokyo–Yokohama area, claiming over 100 000 lives, most being lost in fires that burned wildly after the earthquake.

Economic conditions remained hard for most people in Japan throughout the 1920s. Despite the fact that incredible progress had been made in modernising Japan, only about 16 per cent of the work force was employed in manufacturing. Conditions in factories were difficult and life was a grind for most, although some of the larger organisations were starting to introduce benefits like fringe benefits and bonuses for productivity — benefits which we recognise as a feature of Japanese industry today.

Source 2.8.1

Many occupations and industries in Japan were barely affected by modernisation.

GROWING NATIONALISM

While all men aged over 25 years had the right to vote by 1925, the police were actively used to stop socialist political agitation. As a result there was little opposition to the growing **nationalism** that would soon draw Japan into a disastrous war. The Americans had successfully forced Japan to limit its spending on its navy in 1921, but the military was already active in the Japanese parliament and beginning to exercise real power.

Many Japanese people were frustrated by their country's lack of economic progress and lack of empire. If only their country could reach and influence the huge markets in Asia, life in Japan would surely improve — or so the people thought.

THE GREAT DEPRESSION

Like Western countries, Japan was devastated by the onset of the Great Depression in 1929. The collapse of international trade combined with the tariff barriers put up by overseas countries slashed Japan's exports of manufactured goods by nearly 60 per cent. Half of Japan's factories had shut down by 1931. In the countryside things were no better.

Demand for rural produce fell as millions were thrown into unemployment. Some provinces suffered from widespread famine.

The economic crisis of the Great Depression created opportunities for the Nazis in Germany. In Japan, however, there was no single extreme right-wing party to gather the starving and disillusioned together; however, the military used the crisis as a chance to spread its influence. The civilian government in Japan, as elsewhere, was seemingly unable to find any answers to the economic depression, and more and more the military began to direct key aspects of Japanese policy. During the 1930s four of Japan's 10 prime ministers were high-ranking army officers.

Foreign expansion and a build-up of the armed forces created improved conditions in the Japanese economy. While governments in some countries tried to solve the depression by spending as little as possible, the Japanese government increased its spending dramatically from 1932. Political assassinations and support from extremist groups for the military added to the latter's strength.

THE MUKDEN INCIDENT

The civilian government was losing control over the army, which was increasingly asserting itself in pursuing the different interests of its many factions. Japan had extensive financial interests in China and Manchuria and had troops stationed there to protect its interests. Japan was, in fact, still waiting for a chance to seize greater control in China. The opportunity came when Japanese soldiers blew up a section of railway line near the town of Mukden and put the blame on the Chinese.

Without the Japanese Government's approval, the army used this incident as an excuse to take control of the region. It set up a 'puppet' government, with the last Chinese emperor 'Pu Yi' as Emperor. In reality, however, the Japanese were the rulers. Japan was soundly criticised by the League of Nations for this action, and consequently withdrew from the organisation. From now on, the military would be firmly in charge as Japan pursued a policy of foreign expansion.

Source 2.8.2

Japanese soldiers, with guns captured from the Chinese after the Mukden incident

THE LATE 1930s

Japan's economy grew strongly during the second half of the 1930s, especially in industries like ship building and steel manufacture. In 1937 Japan embarked on a full-scale war with China as it sought to create the empire it had dreamed of. China's rich mineral deposits made it an attractive target for Japan. The oil fields and rubber plantations further south would also be in the sights of the Japanese war machine by 1941.

Activities

Investigation: *Japanese expansion*

1. Examine the strength of each of the following arguments which Japan used to defend its foreign expansion activities.
   - It had to protect its economic interests in Asia. The civil war in China was a special concern.
   - It wanted to protect Asia from communism.
   - It wanted to prevent Asian nations from being exploited economically by Western powers.
   - It wanted to help Asian nations preserve their Asian heritages and prevent the spread of Western culture.
   - It had a duty to help support the growth of Asian nations. Under Japanese guidance these countries would work together in a mutually beneficial way.
   - It needed new 'living space' to support its growing economy and population.

   Now rank these arguments from the strongest to the weakest.
2. Historian Toyomasa Fuse argued in a 1975 issue of the *Journal of Asian and African Studies* (vol. 10, pp. 3–4) that rapid modernisation created psychological stress in the Japanese. As traditional society collapsed and people lived during times of rapid change and unplanned progress, the great stress this created led to a desire for aggressive military action outside Japan. What do you think of this argument?
3. Summarise what you think were the main reasons for Japan's desire for foreign expansion.

CHINA — THE RISE OF COMMUNISM

THE GREAT WAR

China entered the Great War in 1917 on the side of the Allies. Consequently, when the Treaty of Versailles gave German possessions in China to Japan, the Chinese felt betrayed. A huge demonstration in Beijing on 4 May 1919 (the May Fourth Movement) vented Chinese anger. Japanese goods were boycotted. In this atmosphere of unrest, new ideas were emerging.

COMMUNISM

During May 1920 the first communist group was set up in Shanghai and the Chinese Communist Party officially began the following year. A prominent member was an assistant librarian at Beijing University named Mao Zedong.

Communism in its simplest form is based on the idea that all people are equal and should have equal opportunities and rights in society. Modern communism, as it developed in Russia in 1917 and in China from 1920 onwards, drew its ideas from the writings of Karl Marx in particular.

Marx believed that human history was a struggle between the different classes in society. In essence, this was a struggle between classes that were wealthy and powerful and those that were not. He wrote that all societies travelled through three stages: the feudal stage, the capitalist stage and the communist stage. Communism, he believed, was the inevitable outcome for all societies.

Marx argued that a communist revolution would be led by the 'urban proletariat', that is, by factory and industrial workers, or the working class. As China had little industrialisation, Mao realised support for a revolution would have to come from elsewhere. 'Whoever wins the peasants will win China. Whoever solves the land question will win the peasants', he said.

Source 2.9.1

Mao Zedong, one of the original 57 members of the Communist Party, was undisputed leader of the party by 1935.

THE LONG MARCH

Chiang Kai-shek, leader of the Kuomintang party, ordered the slaughter of communists and their supporters before proclaiming government in 1928. The communists, with barely one-fifth of their number left, retreated to the countryside to regroup. Their main leaders, including Mao Zedong had survived. Between 1930 and 1934 the Kuomintang carried out five extermination campaigns against communists in the countryside. The first four campaigns failed to crush the communist guerillas. In the fifth campaign in 1934 Chiang Kai-shek sought advice from German officers sent by Hitler. He sealed off the communist-held territories. The communists decided to break the blockage and undertake a journey to Yenan — a trek of some 9600 kilometres — where they hoped to regroup. Some 87 000 marchers began the year-long trek. As few as 10 000 survived the journey.

THE RED ARMY

Mao and the communist Red Army fought both the Kuomintang and the Japanese during the 1920s and 1930s. Almost obliterated in the massacres of 1927 and along the tortuous route of the Long March, the Red Army was able to not only to regroup but also to build up its numbers and supporters. Source 2.9.2, which sets out the 'eight disciplinary rules' of the Red Army, suggests why the communists were able to gain this support.

Red Army soldiers were also taught to fight to the death against enemies, to help arm the peasants and to raise money to support the fight for control of China.

Many peasants were still suspicious of the Red Army, however, and Mao himself had noted in 1928 that some peasants kept their distance from the communists. Mao believed education was the key to winning their hearts and minds.

Source 2.9.2

The eight disciplinary rules of the Red Army

1. Replace all doors when you leave a house.*
2. Return and roll up the straw matting.
3. Be courteous and polite to the people and help them.
4. Return all borrowed articles.
5. Replace all damaged articles.
6. Be honest in all transactions with the peasants.
7. Pay for all articles purchased.
8. Be sanitary: establish latrines at a safe distance from people's houses.

*Wooden doors were hung on pegs. They could be easily removed, and sometimes served as beds.

LAND REFORM

Central to winning the support of the peasants and thus the revolution was land reform. Even though the communists did not complete their victory in the civil war against the Kuomintang until 1949, they did begin changing life in the provinces they controlled from the early 1930s.

Source 2.9.3

A landlord being tried by a court of peasants

Land was taken from wealthy landlords and divided up among peasants who did not have land. Many landlords were tried and executed for their treatment of peasants in the past. Peasants were also sometimes given loans or helped in other ways, such as by having their rents or taxes lowered. Engineers from the Red Army assisted peasants by making farming tools, and schools were set up.

WOMEN

Government of their regions by the communists also brought significant changes for women. Communism aimed to introduce equal rights for women, and, during the 1930s, moves to introduce these included the abolition of foot-binding, prostitution, **infanticide**, child slavery and the sale of women. Women's associations were also formed to protect women from the violence of men, especially their husbands.

Source 2.9.4

An American, Edgar Snow, visiting communist areas in China in 1939, wrote:

> To youths and women — for the Reds courted them first and last — they [the communists] opened up unheard-of vistas of new personal freedom and importance. Side by side with political reforms have gone economic and social changes. In the case of women the enforcement of laws like monogamy, freedom of marriage at the age of consent, free education, and suffrage at the age of eighteen, has won a surprising response. Many women have been elected to village and town councils, and large numbers of young girls carry serious political and military responsibilities.
>
> L. Wheeler Snow, *Edgar Snow's China*, Orbis Publishing, London, 1981, p. 174.

Activities

Investigation: *The concepts of communism*

1. In your own words explain Marx's basic ideas.
2. In what way did Mao Zedong adapt Marx's ideas?
3. What was the Long March?
4. What did Mao mean when he said, 'Whoever solves the land question will win the peasants'? Which source refers to this view?
5. Look at source 2.9.3
   (a) Who is the person kneeling on the ground?
   (b) Who are the group at the table?
   (c) To which group does the person holding the gun belong?
   (d) Draw a flow chart to show the connection between the three pictured groups.
6. List the changes that communism brought to the lives of peasant women. How significant were these changes?

JAPAN AND CHINA AT WAR

The Japanese takeover of Manchuria in 1931 raised another threat which became a nightmare reality for the Chinese in 1937 when the Japanese launched a full-scale invasion of China. Again, the communists had to join forces with the Kuomintang to fight the common enemy. But it was a very uneasy alliance. At times, there were two different wars in China during the 1930s: the war against Japan and the civil war.

Japan had set its sights on accessing China's vast natural resources long before it finally invaded in 1937. Japan needed the minerals and oil to fuel its rapidly expanding industries and armed forces. Just keeping its navy's ships going required enormous amounts of oil that Japan itself did not have.

The Japanese were merciless in their conquest of China. The ferocity of their destruction of Nanjing in 1937 stunned observers. Their slogan after 1941 of 'Kill all, destroy all, burn all' summed up their approach. They planned to terrorise the Chinese into submission. The following sources offer different perspectives on the Japanese invasion of China.

Source 2.10.1

Inflated national pride

Look at the map and note the smallness of Japan compared to China. Can anyone doubt that we shall triumph?

Chiang Kai-shek

Source 2.10.3

Maintaining peace and harmony in Asia

Japan's expansion into the Asiatic mainland has been motivated not only by the necessity to improve conditions at home, but also to forestall the danger of aggression from the continent, for the proximity of the Korean peninsula leaves Japan forever exposed to attacks from this direction ... The Oriental ideal of love, benevolence and mutual help condemns war for selfish ends. Japan's armament — always a 'divine sword that slays not' — is dedicated to the peace of East Asia and the welfare of the world ... Japan's advance, inspired by humanity, should not be confused with aggression for gain at the expense of other nations ... The Japanese nation is forced to destroy the anti-Japanese regime which refuses co-operation and rejects the Asiatic ideal ... Japanese expansion on the Asiatic continent is an inevitable development of history. But Japan desires neither conquest nor territory ... The Japanese ideal of 'one world, one household' as was stated by Emperor Jimmu, carries no thought of domination, but envisages universal concord on the basis of freedom and equality ... Japan is the pioneer of a new age; she is the hope of a new Asia.

Tatsuo Kawai, *The Goal of Japanese Expansion*, Hokoseido Press, Tokyo, 1938.

Source 2.10.2

Child in the wreckage of a Chinese railway station bombed by the Japanese

Source 2.10.4

Japanese poster encouraging trust in the Japanese

Source 2.10.5

Senseless destruction

> Sunkiang ... presented a scene of indescribable desolation and destruction. Acres of houses have been laid waste as a result of aerial bombing, and there is hardly a building left standing that has not been gutted by fire. Smouldering ruins and deserted streets presented an eerie spectacle, the only living creatures being dogs unnaturally fattened by feasting on corpses. In the whole of Sunkiang, which should contain a densely packed population of approximately 100 000, I saw only five Chinese ...
>
> A British journalist reporting in 1938 on a city 50 kilometres from Shanghai.

Source 2.10.6

Kuomintang tactics

> On 12 November 1938 the city of Changsa was in great part destroyed by fire, not started by the Japanese but by the Kuomintang themselves. In their stupid scorched earth policies they laid waste all about them ...
> In the spring the Yellow River dykes had been breached by order of Chiang Kai-shek to flood the land and stop the Japanese. It had not stopped them, though it did flood the land, and a million Chinese peasants were drowned.
>
> Han Suyin, *Birdless Summer*, Jonathan Cape.

Activities

Investigation: *Japanese expansion into China*

1. Which sources in this section give a positive view of the Japanese? Which are negative? How do you account for these different views of the Japanese in China?
2. What evidence is there in these sources to support the claim that the Japanese were merciless in their invasion of China? Use specific quotes and references to support your answer.
3. According to source 2.10.3, why did Japan 'expand' onto the Asian mainland? How convincing are the arguments put forward in this source? Examine them individually.
4. What methods did the Chinese use to resist the Japanese invasion? Were these methods always successful? Refer to specific sources in your answer.
5. How effective might the Chinese resistance to the Japanese have been given the conflict between the communists and the Kuomintang? Discuss.
6. Source 2.10.5 describes a ruined and empty city. What might have happened to the people of Sunkiang?
7. Working with a partner, write a newspaper article that describes the impact the Sino-Japanese war had on China. Imagine you are Australian reporters, based in China, and that you are writing for an Australian newspaper.

2.11 Meeting the outcomes

ANALYSE THE IMPACT OF SIGNIFICANT EVENTS AND IDEAS IN SHAPING WORLD HISTORY IN THE TWENTIETH CENTURY.

Identify significant events and ideas which shaped world history in the twentieth century.

1. Write a brief paragraph outlining who these people were and how they changed the course of history:
   - Gustav Stresemann
   - Adolf Hitler
   - Mao Zedong.
2. Place the following events in their correct sequence on a timeline for Germany.
   (a) Reichstag burns down.
   (b) Germany joins the League of Nations.
   (c) Hitler becomes President and Führer.
   (d) Treaty of Versailles punishes Germany for her involvement in World War I.
   (e) Hitler becomes chancellor.
   (f) Gustav Stresemann dies.
   (g) Hyper-inflation is recorded in Germany.
   (h) The Nazi Party gains the largest number of seats in the Reichstag.
   (i) The Enabling Act is introduced.
   (j) Hitler's first attempt to seize power fails in Munich.
   (k) The Great Depression begins.

Discuss the ideas and people associated with the events.

Study the following two sources and then answer the questions that follow.

Source 2.11.1

Hitler's view of the roles of men and women

> **Every child that a woman brings into the world is a battle, a battle waged for the existence of her people. Man and woman must therefore mutually value and respect each other when they see that each performs the task which Nature and Providence have ordained. And from this separation of the functions of each there will necessarily result this mutual respect. It is not true, as Jewish intellectuals assert, that respect depends upon the overlapping of the spheres of activity of the sexes: this respect demands that neither sex should try to do that which belongs to the other's sphere.**
>
> **N. H. Baynes (ed.), *The Speeches of Adolf Hitler*, Howard Fertig, New York, 1969, pp. 528–30.**

Source 2.11.2

Members of the League of German Girls

(a) What do the girls in source 2.11.2 appear to be doing?
(b) Are all the females in this photograph enthusiastically performing this role? How do you know?
(c) What views did Hitler have about men's and women's roles? What specific roles did Hitler believe women should perform?
(d) How might German women have responded to Nazi attitudes about the roles of women? In what ways might their public and private views on this have been different?

Source 2.11.3

CAPITALISM: 'You must work harder to produce more and fill up the shop with goods!'

WORKER: 'What's the use? I don't get enough wages to buy what's in the shop already!'

Cartoons are a valuable record of public opinion. This cartoon is from the *Australian Worker*, 26 March 1930.

Source 2.11.4

Jack Lang is depicted hanging onto the bull's tail in this *Bulletin* cartoon, 5 November 1930, commenting on solutions to the depressed economy.

Analyse the ways in which a significant event has been presented in cultural forms.

Look at the two cartoons on the right. In each case:
(a) identify the significant event it refers to
(b) identify any characters in the cartoon
(c) explain the point of the cartoon.

Chapter 3

AUSTRALIA AND WORLD WAR II

INTRODUCTION

During the first half of the twentieth century the world experienced two of the most destructive wars in human history. World War I and World War II resulted in the deaths of millions of people and the introduction of weapons of mass destruction. World War II was far more widespread than World War I. Many ordinary people were killed in their homes from bombing raids. Some were moved into camps where they were subjected to torture and cruelty. Most experienced the horror of modern war or were expected to participate in the war effort of their country. In Europe, Africa, Asia and the Pacific there was a terrible loss of life and human suffering in the years from 1939 to 1945. Australia also suffered in World War II although not as badly as some other parts of the world. Some of Australia's major towns and cities were attacked by Japanese aircraft and shelled by Japanese ships. In 1942, it was believed by most Australians that the country would be invaded by the Japanese. Men, women and children did what they could to achieve victory, either by joining the armed forces or helping to keep the armed forces supplied. Many of those who joined made the supreme sacrifice in an attempt to keep Australia a free country.

Australian troops parading through the streets of Sydney on their return from the Middle East in 1942
AWM — 026499

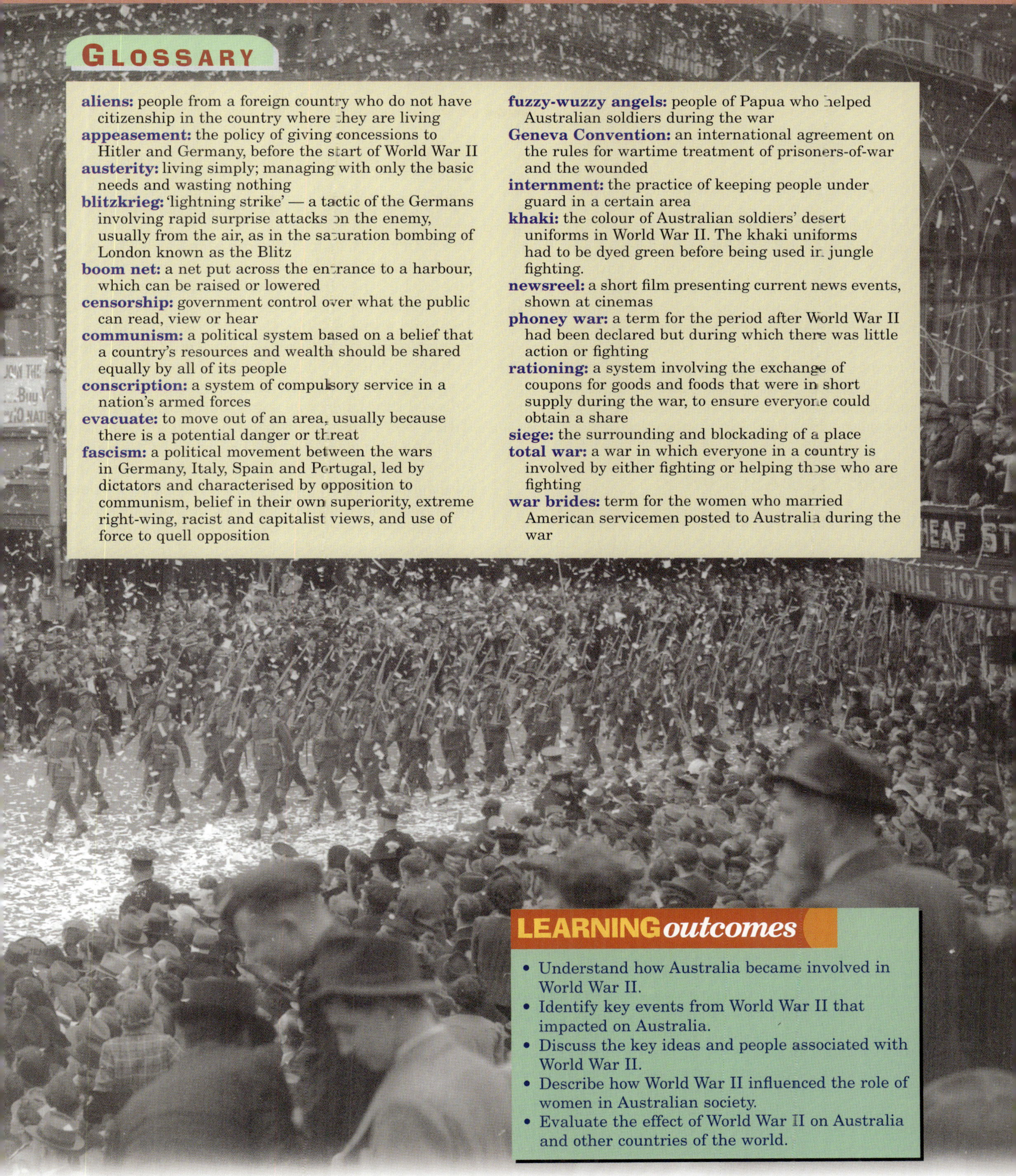

Glossary

aliens: people from a foreign country who do not have citizenship in the country where they are living

appeasement: the policy of giving concessions to Hitler and Germany, before the start of World War II

austerity: living simply; managing with only the basic needs and wasting nothing

blitzkrieg: 'lightning strike' — a tactic of the Germans involving rapid surprise attacks on the enemy, usually from the air, as in the saturation bombing of London known as the Blitz

boom net: a net put across the entrance to a harbour, which can be raised or lowered

censorship: government control over what the public can read, view or hear

communism: a political system based on a belief that a country's resources and wealth should be shared equally by all of its people

conscription: a system of compulsory service in a nation's armed forces

evacuate: to move out of an area, usually because there is a potential danger or threat

fascism: a political movement between the wars in Germany, Italy, Spain and Portugal, led by dictators and characterised by opposition to communism, belief in their own superiority, extreme right-wing, racist and capitalist views, and use of force to quell opposition

fuzzy-wuzzy angels: people of Papua who helped Australian soldiers during the war

Geneva Convention: an international agreement on the rules for wartime treatment of prisoners-of-war and the wounded

internment: the practice of keeping people under guard in a certain area

khaki: the colour of Australian soldiers' desert uniforms in World War II. The khaki uniforms had to be dyed green before being used in jungle fighting.

newsreel: a short film presenting current news events, shown at cinemas

phoney war: a term for the period after World War II had been declared but during which there was little action or fighting

rationing: a system involving the exchange of coupons for goods and foods that were in short supply during the war, to ensure everyone could obtain a share

siege: the surrounding and blockading of a place

total war: a war in which everyone in a country is involved by either fighting or helping those who are fighting

war brides: term for the women who married American servicemen posted to Australia during the war

LEARNING *outcomes*

- Understand how Australia became involved in World War II.
- Identify key events from World War II that impacted on Australia.
- Discuss the key ideas and people associated with World War II.
- Describe how World War II influenced the role of women in Australian society.
- Evaluate the effect of World War II on Australia and other countries of the world.

3.1

THE PATH TO WAR — ACTIONS OF THE WORLD POWERS

In the 1930s, the devastation of World War I was still fresh in people's minds. Most still believed that World War I had been 'the war to end all wars'. People did not want to fight again. While the western nations, including Australia, were also struggling to cope with the economic woes of the Great Depression, military dictators in Europe and Asia were expanding their countries' territory. Germany, led by Hitler, was conquering Europe; Italy, led by Mussolini, was conquering North Africa; and Japan, led by Hirohito, was conquering the Pacific. They did so by military power and by attacking weaker countries.

RISE OF FASCISM

Between the two world wars in Europe, the political movement known as **fascism** arose in Italy, Germany, Spain and Portugal. Fascists were characterised by:

- opposition to **communism**
- belief in the superiority of their own nation or race
- extreme right-wing, racist views
- use of force to quell opposition, often using the military or special police squads
- control by a dictator.

Britain and France hoped to gain Mussolini's support in opposing the increasingly aggressive tactics of Hitler in Germany. However, Mussolini had his own ambitions to expand his power and territory and, in 1935, invaded the North African state of Abyssinia. He aligned himself and his country with Germany and its fascist leader, Adolf Hitler. In 1936, Italy and Germany formed the Rome–Berlin Axis.

In 1936, General Franco, a Spanish fascist, led a military revolt against the Republican government of Spain, which had replaced the monarchy in 1931. Both Hitler and Mussolini supported Franco and supplied him with bombers, troops and transport aircraft. In response, over 40 000 people from 54 countries volunteered for the international brigades — including anti-fascists, unionists and students — and flocked to Spain to fight the spread of fascism. The international brigades left in 1938 when it became clear that the fascists were going to win. The Spanish Civil War came to an end on 28 March 1938.

POLICY OF APPEASEMENT

The policy of Britain and France towards Hitler in the 1930s became known as **appeasement**. This meant that they did not take direct action to stop his moves to take over other countries. His demands were discussed but little was done, as everyone hoped that another war could be avoided. Neither Britain nor France was financially prepared for a war in the 1930s. Some people believed that there was some justification for what Hitler was doing, on the grounds that Germany had been poorly treated by the Treaty of Versailles. Hitler's opposition to communism won him additional support and trust. The other leaders dealt with him on the assumption that he was a reasonable person who would keep his word.

Appeasement was still considered to be a workable policy in September 1938 when the leaders of Britain, France, Italy and Germany met to discuss the growing crisis. This culminated in the Munich Pact: an agreement signed by British Prime Minister Neville Chamberlain and Hitler, which gave Hitler his demands for territory in Czechoslovakia and lifted the threat of war in Europe.

Activities

Check your understanding

1. Draw up a table with three columns headed 'Germany, 'Italy' and 'Japan'. Using the information on this page, list the countries that each of these three had either attacked or occupied by the end of 1939.
2. Historians still debate whether appeasement was the most appropriate policy for Britain and France to follow. Why did they follow this policy? What was the alternative?

Communication: *Using sources*

Refer to source 3.1.1 and place the following events in the order in which they occurred:

- non-aggression pact between USSR and Germany
- USA imposes ban on exports of oil to Japan
- Munich Conference
- Germany's invasion of Poland
- Japanese attack on Pearl Harbor.

Great Britain
Leaders: Chamberlain (to 1940); Churchill (from 1940)
Government: Democracy
Actions
June 1935: Signs naval agreement with Germany
September 1938: Chamberlain tells people he has achieved 'Peace in our time' on his return from Munich Conference
31 March 1939: Guarantees assistance to Poland in case it is attacked
April 1939: Guarantees help to Greece if it is attacked
3 September 1939: Declares war on Germany
10 December 1940: Lends China £10 million and gives military assistance

France
Leaders: Blum (to 1938); Daladier (from 1938)
Government: Democracy
Actions
May 1935: Forms pact with USSR
April 1939: Guarantees assistance to Poland in case it is attacked
3 September 1939: Declares war on Germany

USSR
Leader: Stalin
Government: Communist
Actions
23 August 1939: Signs non-aggression pact with Germany

USA
Leader: Roosevelt
Government: Democracy
Actions
1935: American Neutrality Act passed
Early 1941: Lend-Lease introduced: materials loaned to countries whose survival was of benefit to the United States (Britain)
1 August 1941: Imposed a total oil embargo on exports to Japan
7 December 1941: Declares war on Japan, Germany and Italy

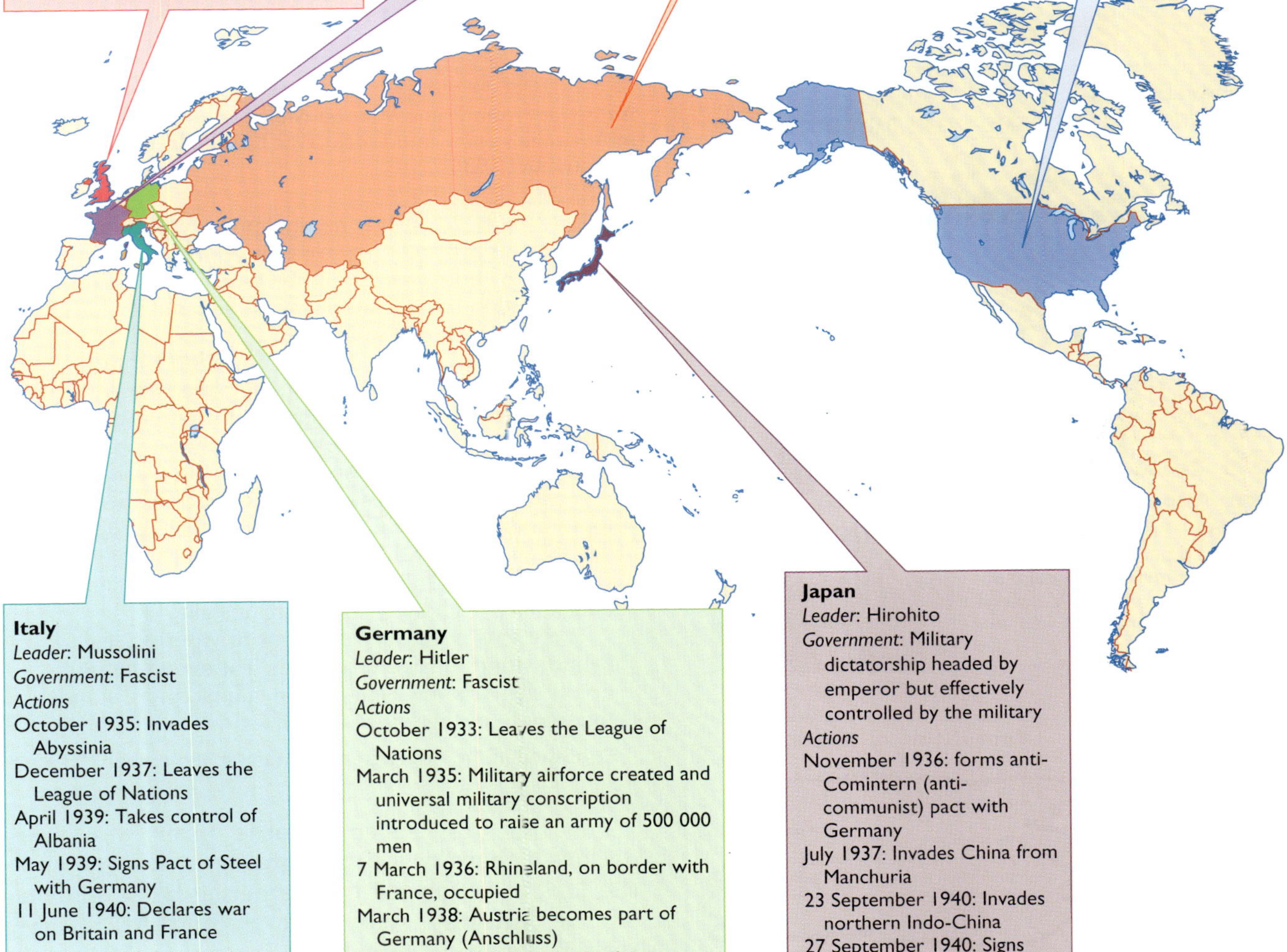

Italy
Leader: Mussolini
Government: Fascist
Actions
October 1935: Invades Abyssinia
December 1937: Leaves the League of Nations
April 1939: Takes control of Albania
May 1939: Signs Pact of Steel with Germany
11 June 1940: Declares war on Britain and France

Germany
Leader: Hitler
Government: Fascist
Actions
October 1933: Leaves the League of Nations
March 1935: Military airforce created and universal military conscription introduced to raise an army of 500 000 men
7 March 1936: Rhineland, on border with France, occupied
March 1938: Austria becomes part of Germany (Anschluss)
September 1938: Munich Conference: Britain, France, Italy and Germany agree that Germany can occupy part of Czechoslavakia
15 March 1939: Germans take over all of Czechoslavakia
1 September 1939: Germans attack Poland
June 1941: Germany invades USSR

Japan
Leader: Hirohito
Government: Military dictatorship headed by emperor but effectively controlled by the military
Actions
November 1936: forms anti-Comintern (anti-communist) pact with Germany
July 1937: Invades China from Manchuria
23 September 1940: Invades northern Indo-China
27 September 1940: Signs Tripartite Pact with Germany and Italy
July 1941: Invades southern Indo-China
7 December 1941: Attacks Pearl Harbor

Source 3.1.1

Actions of the major world powers that led to the outbreak and worsening of World War II

3.2

AUSTRALIA BECOMES INVOLVED

By 1939, the British and French were starting to see Hitler's real motive: German control of Europe. Poland asked Britain to assist it against the threat of German invasion. Britain announced that if Hitler went on to invade Poland, Britain would declare war on Germany. Hitler attacked Poland on 1 September 1939. Two days later, Britain honoured its pact and declared war on Germany. The Australian Prime Minister, Robert Menzies, then announced that Australia was also at war.

Source 3.2.1

DAVIS CUP PROSPECTS — Page 30

WEATHER FORECAST: Further Showers

AUSTRALIA'S LARGEST SALE—243,465 DAILY

The Sun NEWS-PICTORIAL

With Which Is Incorporated The Morning Post

No. 5287 | Registered at the G.P.O., Melbourne, for transmission by post as a newspaper | Melbourne: Saturday, September 2, 1939 (48 Pages and 8-Page Supplement) 1½d.

NAZIS START WAR

BRITAIN, FRANCE MOBILISE: POLES SEEK AID

Australian Associated Press

LONDON, Friday.—Britain and France to-day ordered a general mobilisation following the German invasion of Poland.

The King signed an order for a general call-up after the Privy Council had met this morning for 12 minutes.

A Polish official source informed United Press that Poland has invoked the military alliance with Britain and has asked her aid.

The French Premier conferred with the French war leaders. Subsequently Cabinet decided to put 6,000,000 men in the field.

German troops, converging on three fronts, have crossed all Polish frontiers.

Polish sources say that the Polish Army is falling back slowly on previously-prepared positions in Upper Silesia.

The Polish Embassy reports that many lives, including women and children, were lost in air raids on Warsaw. The British Embassy at Warsaw, however, reports that there had been no bombings there today.

Other Crisis News on Inside Pages

King George VI

First News of Fighting

URGENT PRESS W 632 SIDNEY 32/2 6-1 CHOE A A P

COMFULL MELBOURNE

NEW YORK 1 ST 2-20 AM AMPRESSES WARSAW STATES REPORTED WARSAW THAT KRAKOW KATOWICE TOZEN CZESTOCOOWA BOMBED GERMANOPLANES EARLY SMORNING FIGHTING REPORTED AT DANZIG WARSAW AWAKENED 0620 BY SIRENS AIRRAID AWAITED

THE CABLE MESSAGE which announced the beginning of hostilities between Germany and Poland. It came from an American source.

The front page of the Melbourne *Sun*, 2 September 1939, at the start of war in Europe

There were many Australians who believed that the war did not concern Australia and that we should not become involved. In 1938, the Australian Labor Party had even decided to oppose Australian involvement in any overseas conflicts. The reasons for this were varied. For example, some Australians felt that our relationship with Britain was becoming weaker, particularly after the events of the 1930s. Others did not want Australians to be involved again in the sorts of conditions that soldiers had endured in World War I. However, Prime Minister Menzies was pro-British and most Australians agreed with his belief that Australia should support Britain.

Source 3.2.2

An extract from Prime Minister Menzies' announcement of Australia's entry into World War II, broadcast on 3 September 1939

> Fellow Australians. It is my melancholy duty to inform you officially that, in consequence of the persistence by Germany in her invasion of Poland, Great Britain has declared war on her, and that, as a result, Australia is also at war . . .
>
> It may be taken that Hitler's ambition is not to unite all the German people under one rule, but to bring under that rule as many countries as can be subdued by force. If this is to go on, there can be no security in Europe and no peace for the world.
>
> A halt has been called. Force has had to be resorted to, to check force. The right of independent people to live their own lives, honest dealing, the peaceful settlement of differences, the honoring of international obligations — all these things are at stake.
>
> There was never any doubt as to where Great Britain stood in regard to them. There can be no doubt that where Great Britain stands, there stands the people of the entire British world.
>
> Published in the *Advertiser*, Adelaide, 4 September 1939.

For the first seven months after war was declared, there was little fighting in Europe and the lack of action led to this period being known as the '**phoney war**'. The Second AIF (Australian Imperial Force) was formed in 1939 but few Australians were interested in what was happening and the rate of enlistment was slow. The men who did join voluntarily were mainly:

- unemployed people who wanted a job
- people who wanted to help Britain
- sons of men who had fought at Gallipoli
- men who had served in World War I.

THE PACIFIC WAR BEGINS

World War II was extended to the Pacific and the United States became involved when, on Sunday, 7 December 1941, the Japanese attacked Pearl Harbor, the United States naval base in Hawaii. The Japanese attacked without warning and without having declared war on the United States. The United States Pacific fleet was nearly wiped out, but four of its aircraft carriers were out of the harbour at the time. This was very important later in the war. On 9 December 1941, after Japan had declared war on Britain and the Commonwealth, Australia's new Prime Minister, John Curtin, announced that Australia was at war with Japan.

Most people now realised Australia was in danger. It was even suggested that a line be drawn on a map from Brisbane to Adelaide, and that only places south of this 'Brisbane line' would be defended. Fortunately, the idea was rejected by the government.

Source 3.2.3

Japanese planes attacking Pearl Harbor, 7 December 1941. This photograph was taken from one of the planes.

Source 3.2.4

The Allied and Axis Powers and their leaders

Allied Powers		Axis Powers	
Country	**Leader**	**Country**	**Leader**
Australia	Curtin	Germany	Hitler
Britain	Churchill	Italy	Mussolini
USA	Roosevelt	Japan	Hirohito
Soviet Union	Stalin		

Source 3.2.5

How one newspaper told of the start of the Pacific war

JAPAN FIGHTING BRITAIN, U.S.

War Declared in Tokyo

SUDDEN TREACHEROUS BOMBING OF AIR AND NAVAL BASES IN HAWAII

American Fleet Goes To Sea: Naval Action Rumored

Australian Associated Press

WASHINGTON, Sunday — Japan has declared war on Britain and the United States.

Imperial Headquarters in Tokyo announced at 6 a.m. today that Japan had entered a state of war with the United States and Britain in the Western Pacific as from dawn today. The Premier (General Tao) held a 20-minute Cabinet meeting at 7 a.m. The Foreign Minister (Mr Togo) then summoned the British and American Ambassadors.

Following swiftly on news of the Japanese action against Britain and the United States, the Netherlands East Indies declared itself at war with Japan. General mobilisation was ordered, and the Government invited the Royal Air Force to station planes at strategic points in the Indies. Canada also declared war on Japan.

Hostilities broke out early today, when sudden and treacherous attacks were made by Japanese aircraft on American naval and air bases in Hawaii.

Simultaneously Japanese Marines took over the waterfront of the International Settlement at Shanghai. The British gunboat Peterel (310 tons, complement 55) was sunk at Shanghai.

The Japanese Domei (official) newsagency announced in Tokyo that naval operations were in progress off Hawaii, with at least one Japanese aircraft carrier in action against Pearl Harbor, the U.S. naval base in the island of Oahu, Hawaii. It said that Japanese bombers raided Honolulu at 7.35 a.m., Hawaii time. Later it was reported that a naval battle was in progress in the Western Pacific between Japanese and British and American units.

The United States Fleet steamed out of Pearl Harbor tonight.

***Herald*, 8 December 1941**

Activities

Check your understanding

1. Which country invaded Poland in 1939?
2. What was the 'phoney war'?
3. Why were the Japanese so successful in their attack on Pearl Harbor?

Investigation: *The start of WWII*

1. What do sources 3.2.1 and 3.2.2 reveal about Australia's relations with Britain and the reasons for Australia's involvement in World War II?
2. Compare the newspaper account of the outbreak of war in Europe and the Pacific as shown in sources 3.2.2 and 3.2.5. Which source appeals more to the emotions? Quote four examples that support your opinion.
3. Carefully read source 3.2.5. Which other places did Japan attack apart from Pearl Harbor? What evidence is there that the Japanese were well prepared for war?
4. Research the Japanese attack on Pearl Harbor. Write a report for US President Roosevelt, outlining why the United States suffered such heavy losses.
5. Prepare a 25-word news flash announcing the outbreak of war in either Europe or the Pacific.

FIGHTING, BY LAND, SEA AND AIR

The Second AIF (Australian Imperial Force) left Australia in January 1940 and joined the fighting in the Mediterranean, the Middle East and North Africa. When Italy invaded Egypt in September 1940, the Australian 6th Division forced them back. The Australians were then sent to Greece. Here, Germany had control of the skies and its planes attacked soldiers, cities and supply ships. The Australians were forced to **evacuate** to the nearby island of Crete. The Germans attacked the island using parachute troops to overcome opposition, and many Australians were killed or captured.

Source 3.3.1

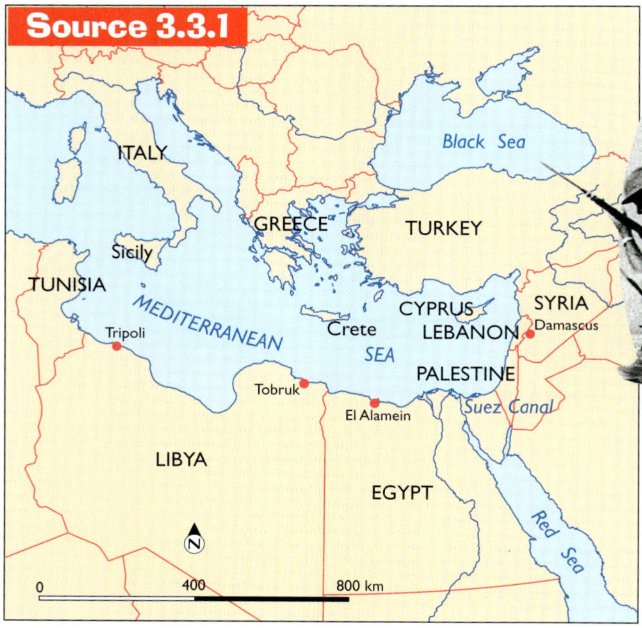

The areas in which Australians fought in the Mediterranean, the Middle East and North Africa

By the end of 1940, Germany's position was strong and Hitler's tactic of **blitzkrieg** was a great success — it took him only six weeks to take control of France (World War I had taken four years to end). With Europe now under German control, the Australian 7th Division was sent to fight against the Vichy French in Syria, where, in a five-week campaign, 1500 Australians were killed.

One of the most famous events of the north African campaign was the **siege** of the town of Tobruk. The town was cut off by the German general Rommel. There were 15 000 Australians of the 9th Division in the town and their only supply route was by sea. Despite attacks from dive bombers, tanks and infantry, the defenders — Australian, Polish, Indian and British soldiers — held on for eight months, from 11 April to 10 December 1941. The Germans called them the 'Rats of Tobruk', which the Australians considered a mark of respect. Late in 1941, a British counter-attack forced the Germans to lift their siege.

Source 3.3.2

Australian soldiers in action in North Africa during World War II
AWM — 010580

Source 3.3.3

An Australian soldier's description of conditions in Tobruk

> **Dust storms, heat, fleas, flies, sleepless nights, when the earth shook with the roar of the enemy's fury, daring raids into no man's land through mine fields and barbed wire, scorching day after day in the front line, where no man dared stand upright, but crouched behind a knee-high protection of rocks — all these things had been the lot of the defenders of Tobruk.**
>
> ***Age*, 24 November 1941.**

From October to November 1942, the 9th Division of the AIF fought at the Battle of El Alamein, where the Germans were finally defeated by the Allies and forced to leave North Africa. The British commander, General Montgomery, expressed admiration for the Australian soldiers for their determination in appalling conditions, saying that 'we could not have won the battle in twelve days without that magnificent 9th Australian Division'.

The Royal Australian Navy (RAN) fought several battles in the Mediterranean Sea. When the Japanese entered the war, many Australian ships came back to fight in the Pacific. They helped protect troop and supply ships from attack and were under frequent attack themselves from enemy planes, submarines and ships. Losses and damage were severe at the height of the Pacific War.

Australian aircrews from the Royal Australian Air Force (RAAF) went to Britain and Canada for training at the outbreak of the war. They then helped to defend England against Germany during the Battle of Britain from July to October 1940. Later, these men served on British planes which bombed German cities such as Cologne and Dusseldorf. RAAF members also served in Crete, Greece, France, Italy and North Africa.

In the Pacific, the RAAF helped the Allied soldiers by bombing enemy positions and reinforcements. They operated from bases in northern Australia, escorting convoys and attacking Japanese planes that were trying to bomb Australian cities.

Source 3.3.4

Some of Australia's ships lost in World War II

HMAS *Sydney*	A cruiser. Sank the Italian cruiser *Bartolomeo Colleoni* in the Mediterranean Sea (19 July 1940) but was damaged and disappeared after fighting the German raider *Kormoran* off the coast of Western Australia (19 November 1941). No trace has ever been found of the *Sydney* or any of its 645 crew members (see page 79).
HMAS *Parramatta*	Torpedoed off Tobruk (17 November 1942). Only 20 men survived.
HMAS *Nestor*	Sunk after a fight with German aircraft in the Mediterranean (June 1942).
HMAS *Australia*	A cruiser. Fought in the Battle of the Coral Sea (May 1942) but was then damaged in the Philippines when a Japanese kamikaze pilot scored a direct hit (21 October 1944).
HMAS *Perth*	Cruiser. Sunk in the Sunda Strait during the Battle of the Java Sea (1 March 1942). 883 men were reported missing.
HMAS *Canberra*	A cruiser. Sunk during a night action off the Solomon Islands in the Pacific. 84 men were killed (9 August 1942).

Source 3.3.5

Most of the planes flown in the Pacific War were American-built Kittyhawks, which were well suited for ground attacks and were a match for the Japanese Zeros.

Activities

Check your understanding

1. How were the Germans able to capture Greece and Crete so quickly?
2. What happened to Australian troops in Greece?
3. Why is the siege of Tobruk an important event for Australians?
4. How did the RAN and the RAAF help defeat the Japanese?

Communication: *Using a range of presentation styles*

1. List five points that can be observed about the soldiers' uniforms shown in source 3.3.2.
2. What evidence is there in source 3.3.2 to support what is said in source 3.3.3?
3. Draw a timeline showing when the Australian ships listed in source 3.3.4 were involved in World War II.
4. Conduct an imaginary interview with an Australian soldier at Tobruk. Start by asking why he is proud to be called one of the 'Rats of Tobruk'. Working with a partner, present your interview to the class.

WOMEN IN THE FORCES

Soon after the outbreak of World War II, Australian women showed that they were determined to contribute actively to the war effort. As in World War I, women initially faced opposition from government and military leaders who were reluctant to allow them into battle zones. Women were mainly trained as nurses, drivers, signallers and motor mechanics. The Voluntary Aid Detachments (VADs) — groups of unpaid nursing assistants that had been formed in World War I — were re-formed after the outbreak of war to assist in Australian military hospitals.

The Women's Australian National Service was established in 1940 to coordinate the many groups of women who wanted a more significant role in the forces.

It soon became clear that Australia's involvement in the war was increasing and more troops would be needed overseas. In 1941, the government announced that women would be allowed to enrol in the armed forces, but only nurses would serve overseas and in battle zones. The main women's branches of the armed services were as follows:

- the Women's Royal Australian Naval Service (WRANS), formed in 1941. The Naval Board were reluctant to accept women and the WRANS faced a lot of opposition. They were never allowed to go to sea during the war and had to be content mainly with communications work, such as operating telegraph and signals stations, code work and interpreting.
- the Women's Australian Auxiliary Air Force (WAAAF). Recruitment began in 1941 and had reached 43 600 by the end of the war. The WAAAF allowed women to carry out such duties as radio communications and mechanical repairs, which left men free for active service.
- the Australian Women's Army Service (AWAS), also formed in 1941. The women of the AWAS were fully enlisted into the service and were trained in transport, communications, maintenance and to go into battle if Australia was attacked. These women were not enlisted to replace men — they were additional to them and were expected to serve their country fully. Over 20 000 women joined the AWAS in two years.
- the Nursing Corps. The Australian Army Medical Women's Service (AAMWS) was formed in December 1942 and 10 000 nurses joined, many of whom were already working as Voluntary Aids (VAs). The Australian Army Nursing Service (AANS) enlisted another 3500. Nurses served in every theatre of war, including overseas postings to Britain, Greece, North Africa, Malaya and Papua. They were sent to hospital aid posts in whatever area the men were fighting and served on hospital ships and transport vessels.

By the end of the war, more than 65 000 women had joined one of the forces. Thousands more Australian women were involved in supporting the war effort at home, undertaking heavy factory work, farm labouring, rural postings organised by the Land Army, and all manner of roles that were previously seen as the domain of men (see section 3.10, pages 74–5.)

Source 3.4.1

A newspaper report announcing the decision of the RAAF to enrol women

About 250 qualified women wireless and teleprinter operators will be enrolled immediately to fill RAAF ground staff vacancies.

Mr McEwen, Air Minister, said yesterday that the women would be enrolled until they could be replaced by qualified men. Fighting in the air, on land and at sea had demanded the services of so many skilled radio men that war cabinet had considered it necessary to enrol women . . .

Argus, 26 February 1941.

Source 3.4.2

Vivian Bullwinkel describes how some of the Australian nurses felt about their role in the war.

. . . We went away and none of us anticipated anything happening to us because it had never happened to nurses before. You were relatively protected, and away from the enemy. We went away because we wanted to nurse the troops. We felt we had the ability to do it . . . When things began to get serious — the enemy started coming into the thing — we still accepted the fact that we had volunteered to go and nurse these fellows, and that they deserved the best we could give them . . . There was never any thought about being sorry about having enlisted. In fact when we first went to Malaya everybody was terribly upset, because they wanted to go to the Middle East because that was where the action was.

From an interview on 13 November 1991, quoted in G. Hunter-Payne, *On the Duckboards: Experiences of the Other Side of War*, Allen & Unwin, Sydney, 1995, pp. 43–44.

Source 3.4.3

A poster designed to enlist women into the AWAS

SINKING OF THE *CENTAUR*

Hundreds of nurses served on transport vessels and hospital ships during the war. Hospital ships bore the Red Cross sign to indicate they carried wounded soldiers and their carers. These ships were not supposed to be attacked. Australians were shocked on 14 May 1943 when news came through that the hospital ship *Centaur* had been sunk by a Japanese submarine off the Queensland coast. The attack took place at 4 a.m. without any warning. As the ship caught fire and sank, people were thrown into the sea which was covered in hot oil — many burned to death or suffocated. Of the 332 people on board, 299 died, including 11 nurses and 18 doctors.

The survivors spent up to 36 hours on rafts or wreckage. They were thirsty and had to beat off sharks with pieces of wreckage. There was very little food — they shared scraps that were salvaged such as a lick of meat extract, milk tablets and prunes. The only nurse to survive was Sister Eleanor Savage of Gordon. She took control of the survivors on one raft, even though in pain herself, and helped them until they were rescued. The sinking of this hospital ship caused outrage in Australia and made people even more determined to defeat Japan.

Source 3.4.4

A poster encouraging Australians to increase their war efforts to 'avenge the nurses' who were killed when the hospital ship *Centaur* was sunk by a Japanese torpedo on 14 May 1943

Artist unknown. *Work, Save, Fight* 1943–45
Lithograph 50.2 × 63 cm AWM — ARTV09088

Activities

Check your understanding

1. What roles did women perform in World War II?
2. Why was the sinking of the *Centaur* an important event?

Investigation: *Women in the forces*

1. According to source 3.4.1, why did the RAAF find it necessary to enrol women?
2. According to Vivian Bullwinkel (source 3.4.2), what did the Australian nurses think about the dangers involved in their war roles?
3. In source 3.4.3, what is offered to women to attract them to the AWAS?
4. What was the purpose of the poster in source 3.4.4?

AUSTRALIA STANDS ALONE, 1942

The Japanese attack on Pearl Harbor was followed by attacks on Burma, Borneo, the Dutch East Indies (Indonesia), Malaya and other parts of South-East Asia. The island of Singapore was strategically important for the British and Allied forces in South Asia at the start of 1942. It was the location of Britain's naval base for the defence of the Far East and Australian troops were posted there in support of the British effort. Singapore appeared to be a stronghold whose coastlines could always be defended from invasion. So long as Britain maintained its presence there and continued to defend the island and the seas around it, Australia felt protected.

Source 3.5.1

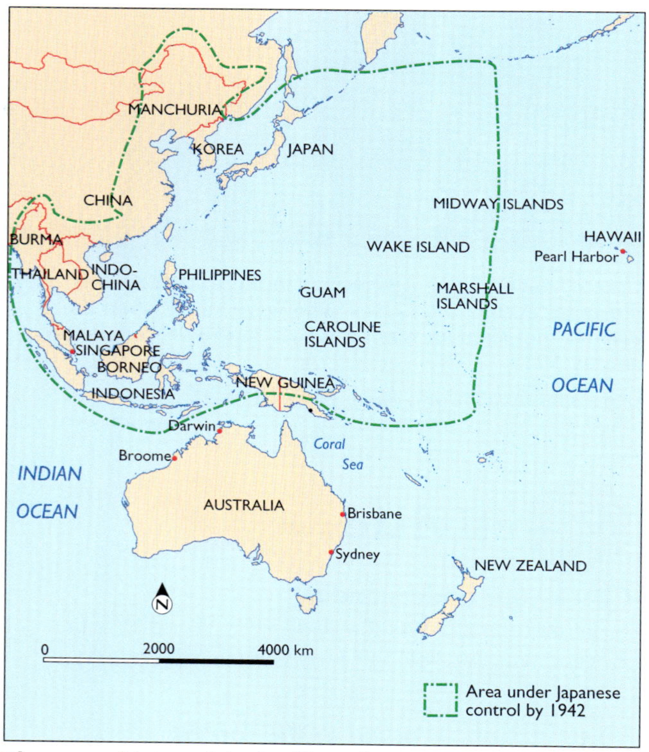

The areas of Asia and the Pacific under Japanese control by 1942

THE FALL OF SINGAPORE

On 10 December 1941, two British warships, the *Repulse* and the *Prince of Wales*, were sunk by Japanese bombers off the coast of Malaya. This was a serious blow for Britain and its naval strength. Singapore's defences were severely weakened and there was increasing concern in Australia.

At the end of December 1941, Prime Minister Curtin appealed to the United States for help with defence.

Source 3.5.2

Extract from an announcement by the Prime Minister, John Curtin, that Australia would look to the United States for help with defence

> [The] United States and Australia must have the fullest say in the direction of the [Pacific] fighting plan . . . I make it quite clear that Australia looks to America free of any pangs as to our traditional links or kinship with the United Kingdom. We know the problems the United Kingdom faces. We know the constant threat of invasion . . . but we know too that Australia can go, and Britain can still hold on . . . We are therefore determined that Australia shall not go and we shall exert all our energies towards the shaping of a plan, with the United States as its keystone, which will give our country confidence of being able to hold out until the tide of battle swings against the enemy.
>
> *Herald*, 27 December 1941.

An attack on Singapore was expected to come from the sea. There were no permanent defences on the landward side and Singapore's big guns pointed towards the ocean and couldn't be turned around. The Japanese advance continued by land and the troops moved quickly down the Malay Peninsula, many on bicycles.

Allied troops, including the soldiers of the Australian 8th Division, tried valiantly to hold back the Japanese advance, but were forced down the peninsula and across to Singapore. Japanese air attacks devastated Singapore and Allied resistance was ineffective against the Japanese troops who crossed over the strait from Malaya by boat. On 15 February 1942, Singapore was captured; around 85 000 Allied troops surrendered, including 15 000 Australians of the 8th Division. Many became prisoners of war and died of starvation and ill-treatment in Japanese prisoner-of-war camps (see pages 66 and 67).

For Australians, the fall of Singapore was a serious development in the war. For the first time, Australia was alone and defenceless. Curtin called on all Australians to focus their efforts on the war that was now on their doorstep.

Source 3.5.3

The Prime Minister, John Curtin, describes what he expected of Australian citizens after the fall of Singapore.

> ... For Australia our utmost, which means everything we have and everything that belongs to us, must now be mobilised.
> ...The protection of this country is no longer that of a contribution to a world at war but the resistance to an enemy threatening to invade our own shore.
> ... It is now work or fight as we have never worked or fought before.
> ... The hours previously devoted to sport and leisure must now be given to the duties of war. Every citizen has a parallel duty to that of the man in the fighting forces.
> ... And brains and brawn are demanded in every place of war endeavour. We have to pep up the production of every essential requirement.
>
> *West Australian*, 17 February 1942.

DARWIN ATTACKED

The fears of Australians were realised when the disaster at Singapore was followed by a Japanese bombing raid on Darwin. The ships and airfield at Darwin were the Japanese targets — they needed to destroy these so they could invade New Guinea and then Australia. On 19 February 1942, in the first enemy attack on Australian soil, Darwin was bombed by 93 Japanese planes. About midday on the same day, 54 Japanese bombers attacked Darwin's RAAF base. In both raids, 243 people were killed and hundreds were injured. Most of these were civilians. Damage to the town and ships in the harbour, including a hospital ship, was extensive. To avoid panic among the Australian people, the government stated that only 15 people had been killed and 24 wounded.

Source 3.5.4

'Long-distance thinking'

A cartoon from the *Daily Telegraph*, 1942

Over the next two years, Darwin was attacked at least 58 times. The town of Broome, and ships in the Torres Strait, were also attacked. Even Qantas aircraft were shot down by Japanese planes.

In March 1942, the American base in the Philippines was under threat from the Japanese. The United States President, Franklin D. Roosevelt, ordered his Commander in the Pacific, General Douglas MacArthur, to move his headquarters to Sydney. Australians welcomed this as a sign of American commitment to defend Australia.

Source 3.5.5

Les Barnett, an air force electrician, describes the Japanese attack on Darwin on 19 February 1942.

> They were making unusual sounds and going at odd speeds. Then we saw Kittyhawks flying close to the runway and other planes coming down and machine-gunning them, and hitting them. There were explosions and aircraft crashing. We started to think this is fair dinkum! Out the other end of the building, looking south we could see all these aircraft coming in at low level. They were divebombing and machine-gunning the shipping in the harbour.
>
> Outside our block there was an air raid trench and we jumped in. There were bombs dropping all around us and you could see the machine-gun bullets running up the fibro walls and through the roofs. We had our rifles and tin hats and some of us did try to shoot the Jap planes but it was impossible. You think you can do these things but you can't. They were that fast, zooming down and past you. I didn't think about dying, I just thought about getting out of the way. Everyone was cursing the Jap! We were going to get them one way or another, but it was hopeless.
>
> Quoted in Daniel Connell, *The War at Home*, Australian Broadcasting Corporation, Crows Nest, 1988, p. 44.

BATTLE OF THE CORAL SEA

Up until May 1942, Japan enjoyed victories in South-East Asia. Its troops and supplies were now stretched over a wide area of control, but the advance continued. The next aim of the Japanese was to capture and occupy Port Moresby in Papua New Guinea. From there they could launch attacks on Townsville and other Australian cities, or even invade northern Australia. For Australia, the Battle of the Coral Sea in early May 1942 was the most important battle ever fought because it forced the Japanese invasion fleet to turn back.

Two United States aircraft carriers, which had been away at sea when the Japanese attacked Pearl Harbor, played an important role in the Battle of the Coral Sea. Most of the naval battles fought in the Pacific involved aeroplanes attacking ships, so aircraft carriers were very important. They could get the planes close enough to the enemy ships to sink them. At the Battle of the Coral Sea, planes from the American aircraft carriers USS *Lexington* and USS *Yorktown* sank and damaged many Japanese ships.

The Americans were supported by HMAS *Australia* and bombers that took off from bases in north Queensland. The battle lasted from 4 to 8 May. Even though the *Lexington* was sunk and the *Yorktown* and *Australia* were damaged, the Japanese retreated. This was the first defeat for the Japanese at sea. When they were also defeated at the Battle of Midway from 5 to 7 June 1942, it was clear that they were starting to lose control of the Pacific waters.

ATTACK ON SYDNEY

Despite the Japanese fleet's retreat after the Battle of the Coral Sea, Japanese bombers and submarines were still attacking Australia. Barbed wire was placed on beaches to stop any possible invasion and everyone had to practise what to do in case of an air raid.

Japanese submarines were very busy off Sydney during May and June 1942. A **boom net** was even placed across Sydney Harbour to stop submarines getting in.

Early on Saturday 30 May 1942, a Japanese seaplane flew down Sydney Harbour past the Harbour Bridge and back out to its mother submarine. No-one fired at it and it was able to note where the important warships were. On Sunday night, 31 May 1942 three Japanese midget submarines entered Sydney Harbour. Each submarine had two crew members and a torpedo. One of the submarines was caught in the boom net but the other two followed a Manly ferry into the harbour.

People only realised that Sydney was being attacked when the crew caught in the boom net blew themselves up to avoid capture. One of the remaining submarines was sunk but the third fired its torpedo at the USS *Chicago*. It missed but hit the *Kuttabul* and nineteen sailors were killed.

One week later, on 7 June 1942, Sydney was attacked by a Japanese submarine off the coast. Ten shells were fired and four exploded in the Bondi area. Newcastle was also shelled by Japanese submarines. Now Australians knew what it was like to be involved in **total war**

Source 3.5.6

An Australian newspaper report of the Battle of the Coral Sea

JAP FLEET BEATEN OFF

Invasion Armada Smashed In Coral Sea Battle

A Japanese invasion fleet has been repulsed in the great sea and air battle fought in the Coral Sea, off the Queensland coast.

Naval action has been broken off temporarily, but Allied bombers, with undiminished ferocity, are still pounding the scattered enemy armada as it speeds north.

This dramatic news came in a special General Headquarters communique and despatches from correspondents of "The Sunday Sun" late yesterday.

First round in the Battle of the Pacific has ended in a decisive Allied victory, is the view of informed, but official observers.

"A full-scale attempt by Japan to invade Australia has been turned aside," says Norman Stockton, our war correspondent at an advanced Allied base.

"For four days, the stark reality of invasion threatened Australia. The menace has temporarily receded, but it is still present," adds Stockton warningly.

This is where the battle was fought (M = miles)

THE JAPS LOST —

2 Aircraft Carriers Sunk

1 9000-ton Seaplane Tender badly damaged

2 Heavy Cruisers One sunk, one badly damaged

4 Gunboats sunk

2 Light Cruisers One sunk, one badly damaged

1 Supply Vessel sunk

9 Destroyers sunk

1 Cargo Vessel badly damaged

Enemy Losses — 18 Ships Sunk, 4 Damaged

Source 3.5.7

One of the Japanese midget submarines which was sunk in Sydney Harbour in 1942 AWM — 012723

Source 3.5.8

Judith Hunt recalls the evening when, as a nine-year-old girl, her home in Bellevue Hill, Sydney, was shelled by the Japanese.

> One of my aunts had been repairing an old wireless and as I was sleeping I was dreaming about it. Suddenly I heard a long low whistling sound, then another and another, and then the most enormous explosion. The next thing I remember was my mother lying on top of me. Then she pulled me under the bed. My grandmother was in the room behind ours. Fortunately she also crawled under her bed because the brick wall beside her collapsed. It fell straight across her bed. Afterwards you could see the imprint of her head on the pillow with the bricks all around.
>
> Quoted in Daniel Connell, *The War at Home*, ABC, Crows Nest, 1988, pp. 66–7.

Source 3.5.9

AWM — 012594

The damage to a home after the Japanese shelling of Sydney

Activities

Check your understanding

1. Who was Australia's Prime Minister in December 1941? Which country did he turn to for help? Why?
2. Why was the fall of Singapore such a significant event for Australians?
3. When in 1942, and for what reasons, was Darwin bombed?
4. Why was the Battle of the Coral Sea a turning point in World War II?
5. How did Japanese midget submarines enter Sydney Harbour in 1942 and for what reason?

Investigation: *The war comes to Australia*

1. Using source 3.5.1 and the text, explain why Singapore was considered as Australia's last line of defence.
2. Explain in your own words what Curtin is saying in source 3.5.2 about Australia's links with Britain and the United States of America.
3. From source 3.5.3, list, in note form, what John Curtin believed Australians should do as a result of the fall of Singapore.
4. Identify the people shown in source 3.5.4. What point is the cartoonist making?
5. Referring to source 3.5.6, answer true or false to the following questions about the Battle of the Coral Sea.
   (a) The battle was fought closer to Australia than New Guinea.
   (b) The Japanese were going to invade Australia
   (c) The battle lasted seven days.
   (d) Two Japanese aircraft carriers were sunk.
   (e) The Japanese turned back after the battle.
6. Suggest why the submarine shown in source 3.5.7 was recovered from the harbour floor.
7. Referring to the sources, explain why the attack on Sydney was such a cause for concern.

Communication: *Different presentation styles*

1. Debate whether the fall of Singapore or the attack on Darwin was the greater threat to Australia.
2. Create headlines, news articles and drawings for the front page of a newspaper the day after either the Japanese midget submarine attack on Sydney or the shelling of Sydney.
3. Imagine you are a crew member of the midget submarine which has not been found. Give your version of what happened.
4. Research and prepare a report for the Allies about the battles of Midway and Guadalcanal. Include a map of the area and a summary of the fighting. Mention its significance to the course of the Pacific War.

KOKODA AND MILNE BAY, 1942

THE KOKODA TRACK

Although Japan's sea and air strength was severely weakened after the Battle of the Coral Sea, its forces were determined to capture Port Moresby. On 21 July 1942, Japanese troops landed at Buna and Gona on the north coast of New Guinea. They planned to cross to Port Moresby by land. The route would take them over the Owen Stanley Range, along a narrow, rugged track through dense jungle, swift flowing rivers and steep mountains up to 2200 metres high. Machinery was useless and supplies had to be brought up by hand or by aeroplane.

Source 3.6.1

The Kokoda Track

Australian conscripts from the AMF were sent to stop the Japanese. At the start they were hopelessly outnumbered and had little equipment. Even their **khaki** uniforms were the wrong colour for jungle fighting and had to be dyed green. However, they were helped by the local people of Papua, who the Australians called '**fuzzy-wuzzy angels**'. These locals would bring supplies up the track and take wounded men back for medical help. Many Australians owed their lives to these people.

FACT*file*

As well as New Guinea, Australian troops served on other islands to the north from 1942–5, striving to repel the Japanese forces. The local people of islands such as Java, Ambon and Timor, like the 'fuzzy-wuzzy angels' of Papua, assisted the Australians in many ways, and firm friendships and ties were formed. The significance of these ties was recalled over 50 years later when the East Timorese voted for independence and Australian troops led the United Nations peacekeeping force onto the island.

Despite all the difficulties, the Australians were able to prevent the Japanese reaching their objective of Port Moresby. The Australians made the Japanese fight for every centimetre of jungle. On 29 July 1942 the Australians were forced to retreat from a small town called Kokoda, and on 11 August the airfield there fell into Japanese hands. On 17 September 1942, the Japanese reached Ioribaiwa Ridge. In the distance they could see Port Moresby, which was only fifty kilometres away, but on 25 September they were forced back by Australian troops.

Source 3.6.2

An Australian soldier describes conditions on the Kokoda Track

We were greatly outnumbered, nevertheless we held our ground for two and a half days before we were obliged to withdraw, because we were cut off from all supplies of food and ammunition.

So began our fortnight of starvation. I was one of a party of considerable size, who were cut off in the dense jungle for fourteen long weary days without food.

All I had to eat for the first ten days was one tin of bully beef, one packet of hard biscuits, half pound dehydrated ration and a little chocolate ration.

. . . When we were permitted to light a fire, it was often too wet, as it rains up here every day and every night. We would be wet through and have to sleep in wet clothes, and would we shiver! . . . All we had to sleep in was a holey ground sheet. The ground up in the jungle is never dry, and smells terribly, the leaves and trees are simply rotten through no sun ever penetrating the thick foliage.

The Australian troops, which included those who had returned from the Middle East, quickly drove the Japanese back along the Owen Stanley Track to Kokoda (on 2 November) and on 16 November Australian and United States troops began attacking Buna and Gona. Gona fell to the Allies on 1 December and a month later Buna was captured (2 January).

Source 3.6.3

A photograph showing how difficult it was to move supplies along the Kokoda Track AWM — 054746

The fighting around Buna and Gona was very fierce as the Japanese believed it was an honour to die for their Emperor (Hirohito). Some would even booby-trap themselves with grenades that would kill themselves and any Australians who took them prisoner.

Although conditions in the jungle were terrible, the Australians never gave up. They were fighting to defend Australia, which was only 800 kilometres away.

MILNE BAY

While the Australians were busy trying to stop the Japanese crossing the Owen Stanley Range, the Japanese decided to capture the newly built Allied airfields at Milne Bay on Papua/New Guinea's eastern coast. The Japanese could then use the bay as a base for their ships and aircraft and attack Port Moresby from two sides. Japanese troops landed at Milne Bay on 25 August 1942.

The Australian troops were untrained in jungle warfare and many had never fought before. However, they were helped by the RAAF planes which destroyed several Japanese landing barges. After days of bitter fighting in mud and rain the Australians successfully defended the airfields and forced the Japanese to retreat (6 September 1942). This was the first defeat of the Japanese on land in the Pacific and it destroyed the belief that the Japanese were unbeatable in jungle fighting. It was a great morale boost for the troops and for the people back home. The Australian victory on the Kokoda Track was Japan's second defeat on land and marked the start of the Japanese retreat in the Pacific. Although the last pockets of resistance were not wiped out until the war ended, the threat of Japanese invasion was over for Australia.

Source 3.6.4

Conditions in Milne Bay, New Guinea, for Australian soldiers in 1942 AWM — 013339

Activities

Check your understanding

1. Why did Australian troops fight in Papua/New Guinea?
2. How well prepared were the Australians for jungle fighting?
3. Why was fighting around Buna and Gona so fierce?
4. How important was the Papua/New Guinea campaign for Australia's security?

Investigation: *Conditions in PNG*

Using the text and sources 3.6.2, 3.6.3 and 3.6.4, describe the difficulties encountered by the soldiers in the jungles of Papua/New Guinea, along the Kokoda Track and at Milne Bay.

3.7

PRISONERS' EXPERIENCES

International rules for the treatment and protection of prisoners in wartime were laid down by the **Geneva Convention**. In spite of this, many terrible things were done to people during the war, including Australian military and civilian prisoners.

The Japanese believed that soldiers should die for their country and their emperor rather than surrender. People who surrendered were thought to be cowards. Prisoners of war in Japanese camps were treated badly, partly because of this attitude. They were made to work very long hours without proper food or medical supplies and many Australians died in the camps. Of the 22 000 Australians captured when Singapore was taken by the Japanese in 1942, around 8000 died, either in prisons such as Changi and Outram Road or in prisoner-of-war camps. During the attack, patients in hospital were bayoneted and nurses were raped and killed. Ships attempting to evacuate civilian women and children were torpedoed and sunk. People thrown from sinking ships or crew from planes that had been shot down were either machine-gunned in the water or left to die.

FACT*file*

In Europe, the Nazis, led by Hitler, tried to wipe out the Jewish race. In a process that became known as the 'Holocaust', the Nazis took Jewish people into concentration camps, where they carried out experiments on them. Nearly six million Jews were killed by the Germans, many by gas poisoning. For ordinary people, resistance to the Germans was also severely punished. The German Secret Police (SS) tortured and killed many people when trying to obtain information from them.

As the war neared its end, the Japanese had little food to feed themselves, so they took their prisoners — men, women and children — on long marches of thousands of kilometres, finding food in the villages they passed through. The prisoners who failed to keep up were killed along the way. In Borneo, 1800 Australian POWs began a death march. Only six survived. Just before the final Japanese surrender, many Australian prisoners who had survived the camps were murdered and buried in mass graves so they would not be able to identify their captors.

Source 3.7.1

Map showing places where Australians were held by the Japanese, 1943

Source 3.7.2

A photograph of Australians held prisoner in a Japanese camp, 1945

AWM — 019199

After the war, many of those responsible for war crimes were put on trial and executed when found guilty. However, many evaded capture and are still being sought.

Source 3.7.3

A newspaper account of conditions for Australians in a Japanese prison camp, 1945

During the past six months the Japanese High Command in the Philippines has insisted that it does not recognise any form of international law, although the Japanese Premier told America in 1942 that Japan would honour the Geneva Convention. [Convention on the Treatment of Prisoners of War].

In the camps, men, women and children, including the aged and sick, were supplied with less than 900 calories per person per day, although 1700 are required to keep a sleeping person healthy. Everyone in the camp suffered from malnutrition and because of the lack of protein they were not able to control urination.

During the penultimate six months of our internment, rations were reduced to six ounces of corn and rice per person per day, plus 150 kilos of soya bean meal. There were virtually no vegetables, except those grown by the internees, and absolutely no fruit, no meat, and no fish. We were supplied with a pinch of salt.

According to the Japanese Army there is no such thing as an internee, and all enemy non-combatants, whether adult or baby, are prisoners of war. Persons over 10 years of age are classed as adults; under 10 they are children and entitled to only a half ration.

The rations were cut with each successive American victory.

Sydney Morning Herald, 6 February 1945.

Source 3.7.4

An account of the experience of survivors from the *Vyner Brooke*, one of the ships sunk by Japanese bombers on 13 February 1942 while evacuating nurses and civilians out of Singapore

The *Vyner Brooke* suffered a direct hit ... Ten miles out to sea from Bangka Island she sank, rapidly ... The survivors tried to group together. Some made for the lighthouse visible on the island ... it was obvious [to] those gathered on the beach that they would have to surrender to the Japanese who had taken the island ... The nurses sent the civilian women and children on ahead, remaining with the wounded on the beach. When the Japanese arrived, they marched the men around the corner of the beachhead, returning minutes later with bloodstained bayonets. The Australian nurses were then forced into the water and shot from behind. Only one, Staff Nurse Vivian Bullwinkel, survived the shooting. That is how we know about it ... the bullet that struck her passed through her side just below waist level. After many days of living in the jungle ... and caring for the only male survivor, Private Kingsley, the two ... once more surrendered to the Japanese. This time they were taken into custody. Kingsley later died, but Bullwinkel survived and was reunited with thirty-one of her colleagues ... [who became] prisoners of the Japanese on Bangka Island, together with hundreds of other women and men.

The men were separated almost immediately. The women were to be moved many times during the next three and a half years, spending most of their time at Palembang in Sumatra. The Japanese refused to recognise the Australian nurses as military personnel ... they received no Red Cross parcels and were not permitted to write home for eighteen months, or receive mail ... through it all they retained dignity, close friendships, an ability to cope and adapt to their new environment ... the last few months were very hard ... eight of the women died in those final months ...

G. Hunter-Payne, quoted in *On the Duckboards: Experiences of the Other Side of War*, Allen & Unwin, Sydney, 1995, pp. 44–6.

Activities

Check your understanding

1. How did the Germans and Japanese treat people who were captured during the war?
2. What belief did the Japanese hold that might have led them to treat prisoners badly?
3. What steps did the Japanese captors take to avoid being punished for their actions?

Investigation: *The treatment of prisoners*

1. Using the map in source 3.7.1, list the places where Japanese prison camps were set up. Why were some of the actual locations unknown?
2. Why were photographs such as the one in source 3.7.2 taken? Why are they a valuable source of information for historians?
3. How does the account in source 3.7.3 support what is shown in the photograph?
4. What evidence is presented in source 3.7.4 of Japanese mistreatment of prisoners?

Communication: *Researching prisoners of war*

1. Find out about some of the common diseases that affected prisoners of war and how the diseases are treated today.
2. Do you believe that those responsible for the mistreatment of Allied prisoners should be punished today if caught?
3. Write an essay on the following topic: 'Historians must make sure the stories of people's experiences during World War II are never forgotten, in order to prevent such terrible things from ever happening again'.
4. Imagine you are a prisoner of war who has survived the camp. Write a letter to a member of your family telling them that you are safe.
5. Watch the video *Paradise Road* and present a review of this video to the class.

CONTROLS AT HOME — CONSCRIPTION AND CENSORSHIP

World War II was the first truly total war; in other words, everyone — not just those involved in the actual fighting — was contributing in some way to the war effort. In Australia, the government took control of ordinary people's lives. There were restrictions on what people could say, write and do — everyone was expected to contribute to the war and the defeat of Japan and Germany.

Source 3.8.1

A recruitment poster for World War II, published in 1942

CONSCRIPTION

Soon after war broke out in Europe, the Australian government decided to introduce **conscription** for the defence of Australia and her territories. Australia already had a militia of about 80 000 men who were immediately called up. Compulsory military training of 20-year-old single men was introduced in October 1939. This was opposed by the trade unions and members of the Labor Party but the Prime Minister, Robert Menzies, believed that it was fair: other militia members had to give up their jobs so these men should as well. Australia then had two armies:

- the Second AIF which was made up of volunteers for overseas service
- the AMF which was made up of conscripts. These conscripts were trained to defend Australia and could not be sent outside Australia or its overseas territories (Papua, for example).

In 1941, as the possibility of war with Japan increased, the Australian government made all men, when they turned 18, register for possible service. The upper limit was increased to 33 years. Early in 1942 these young men were called up into the army. They were given from one to three months training and then sent to Papua, which was an Australian territory at this time, to try and stop the advance of the Japanese. The conscripts managed to slow the Japanese advance (see section 3.7, page 66) and then, with the help of the AIF troops who had just returned from the Middle East, drove the Japanese back. For the rest of the war, AIF and AMF battalions fought side by side. Most conscripts joined the AIF when they turned 19. In January 1943, the area to which conscripts could be sent was expanded to include the entire island of New Guinea and the islands of Bougainville, New Britain and New Ireland. For the first time, Australian conscripts were sent to fight outside Australian territory.

Also in 1943, the *Defence Act* was altered to allow women to be conscripted into the auxiliary forces (see page 58) because not enough were volunteering.

CENSORSHIP

Within days of the Australian declaration of war against Germany, the Australian government introduced **censorship** of news on radio and in the press and these restrictions applied for the rest of the war. Overseas communications by telegraph, telephone and post could also be censored and the radio telephone services to Britain and New Zealand were stopped. The *National Security Act* (Cwlth), passed on 7 September 1939, also gave the government a wide range of powers to deal with enemy **aliens**, which Prime Minister Menzies believed would 'promote the security of Australia'.

A Department of Information was set up and, for the next six years, Australians were told only what the government wanted them to know. The powers to control the press were extended in July 1940. From then, the government could have the final say about the 'position, space or time allotted to any item published, broadcast or exhibited' in any newspaper or magazine, or on radio and at the cinema. The government believed that this would prevent misleading and untruthful stories being circulated which could weaken Australian morale. Many people believed that, by censoring the press, Australia would become no different from the countries that it was fighting against, which also controlled what could or could not be printed or heard.

Source 3.8.2

Prime Minister Menzies gives his reasons for introducing censorship, 7 September 1939.

I agree in advance that we must preserve Australia — that is why I have introduced this bill — but we must also preserve liberalism of thought in Australia; we must preserve as much freedom of thought and action as is consistent with the safety of the country. I agree with what the leader of the Opposition (Mr Curtin) said, that we may reach a point where the safety of the country may require that Jones or Brown should be stopped from doing something or saying something; but in every case, the real test should be, 'Is this related to the safety of the country?' — not, 'Is this a golden opportunity to suppress the opinions of someone who does not agree with me?' . . . I have no hesitation whatever in asking Parliament to do now what it did 25 years ago; that is, to arm the government with the authority necessary to carry on this struggle, which may become a very grim struggle even for Australia before we are much older.

Commonwealth Parliamentary Debates, House of Representatives, 7 September 1939, vol. 161, pp. 163–5.

Source 3.8.3

A poster from the early years of World War II demonstrating that the security of Australia was everyone's responsibility

During the war, censorship was firmly applied. The government warned people not to gossip or spread information. Personal letters from servicemen and women to family and friends in Australia were heavily censored. Servicemen and women were not allowed to keep personal diaries in case the enemy obtained and used them for information. Letters could not include details of when ships were sailing or the numbers, locations, movements and destinations of troops.

Source 3.8.4

Mail being censored during World War II

Newsreels also presented a positive view of the war effort and victories were celebrated while most losses were only briefly mentioned.

The truth about such events as the sinking of HMAS *Sydney* (see page 79) the bombing of Darwin, the conditions experienced in the jungles of New Guinea and the treatment of Australian prisoners of war only became widely known after the war ended. Historians are still searching for evidence to help understand many of the events that occurred. Some official documents are so 'top-secret' that they may never be read.

Activities

Check your understanding

1. What changes were made during the war to the method of conscription?
2. What types of news media were censored during World War II?
3. Why did some people oppose censorship?

Communication: *Propaganda*

1. What does source 3.8.1 suggest as a reason for volunteering to join the AIF?
2. What reasons does Menzies give in source 3.8.2 for his belief that censorship is necessary?
3. What kinds of information do you think the government was concerned about that led it to distribute posters such as source 3.8.3?

Investigation: *Conscription*

John Curtin was an opponent of conscription during World War I. Find out why he changed his mind about conscription in World War II. Write a paragraph either supporting or opposing his action.

SUPPORTING AND DEFENDING THE NATION AT HOME

Everyone living in Australia was affected in some way by the war. Life changed in many ways for the people at home and there were many hardships. There was constant concern about loved ones who were involved in the fighting and there were difficulties in coping with shortages of food and everyday goods. Generally, however, people supported the Prime Minister, John Curtin, and appreciated the need to cooperate in the war effort for Australia and the free world.

Australia was an important base in the Pacific area, for defence installations such as airfields, training camps, repair facilities, weapons storage sites and hospitals. As the threat of Japanese invasion increased, many measures were taken at home to defend Australia's shores and cities.

RATIONING AND AUSTERITY

Most goods were in short supply during the war and substantial supplies of food and clothing were needed for the troops so they could continue fighting. A system of **rationing** was introduced by the government and this restricted the quantity and types of goods that people could buy. Every household was given a ration book and goods such as clothing, tea, sugar, meat and butter could only be bought if the correct coupons were presented. In August 1942, Prime Minister Curtin called for a 'season of **austerity**' and asked Australians to 'deprive themselves of every selfish, comfortable habit'.

People would often swap coupons with neighbours for goods which they wanted. Meat was in such short supply that in 1944 the meat ration was only one to two kilograms per person per week. Petrol was also rationed.

Source 3.9.1

HER LETTER TO HER SOLDIER

'Milk's rationed, meat's dear. I can't buy fish or fruit and the bakers are on strike. Wish we were with you!'

A cartoon from the *Bulletin*, 24 March 1943

Source 3.9.2

Unice Atwell, a child during the war years in Charters Towers, Queensland, describes some of the ways families coped with rationing

> **Mothers . . . cut adult garments down to make children's, and there was even more handing-down to younger brothers, sisters, even cousins, than before . . .**
>
> **Silk, most of which had come from China and Japan before the war, was now very scarce, and far too valuable [for parachute making] to be used for making ladies' stockings. In those pre-nylon days, this meant that stockings all but disappeared. Since being caught without your stockings on was then more or less equal to being caught starkers these days, this was a serious problem for many women. Some overcame it by applying leg make-up . . . Stockings in those days had a seam down the back, so this too had to be painted on . . .**
>
> **Cars began to appear with charcoal-fuelled gas producers, or with gigantic bags of town gas on top of them. As tea substitutes, newspapers suggested tea-tree . . . maidenhair fern, red clover blossom and lucerne.**
>
> Unice Atwell, *Growing up in the 40s*, Kangaroo Press, Sydney, 1983, pp. 45–7.

FACT*file*

- Australians became very inventive. Some made clothes out of flour bags, and jewellery from bread dough. There was little elastic available, so underwear had to be done up with string or rope.
- Saturday race meetings were banned until November 1943.
- People had to sell their property, such as cars, to the government when told to do so.

DRILLS AND PRECAUTIONS

After the attack on Pearl Harbor, precautions against air-raids became a fact of life in Australian towns and cities. Air-raid trenches were dug and shelters were built in playgrounds, parks and backyards. Adults and schoolchildren were drilled in air-raid and evacuation procedures at the sound of the wailing siren. Home defence groups were formed, which included the appointment of air-raid precaution (ARP) wardens who practised bomb removal and monitored other security measures.

Source 3.9.3

A photograph from the early 1940s showing air-raid precaution wardens practising bomb removal, while curious locals look on
AWM — 027451

Source 3.9.4

A photograph of kindergarten children in Sydney, in 1941, practising air-raid drill. The headgear was designed to muffle the sound of explosions, protect their teeth and prevent them from biting their tongues.

Examples of defence precautions included the following:

- beaches were spread with barbed-wire, apart from a path to the water that was locked at night; guards patrolled the beaches
- windows in towns and cities had to be blacked out to prevent enemy planes seeing lights from the air and the ARPs would go around checking that residents were complying
- street lights were reduced: in Sydney, every second light had the globe removed
- street signs, railway station names and signs naming towns were taken down to confuse the enemy
- every building with more than 130 people working in it had to have an air-raid shelter.

Source 3.9.5

A photograph of an air-raid shelter built by an Australian family, c. 1940

FACT*file*

Other defence precautions included:

- Every Australian over 14 had to have an identity card and people could be asked to show their card at any time, such as in the street, at the movies or in a restaurant.
- Newspapers were censored and could give only the most basic information on what was happening in the war. All mail to and from overseas countries was also censored (see page 69).
- People living in Australia who had come originally from the enemy countries of Germany, Italy and Japan were arrested and confined temporarily to *internment* camps, as a security precaution against possible spying activities.

CHILDREN AND SCHOOLS

World War II was also a difficult time for children. Some children didn't see their father for long periods of time and others would never see their father again. Other children were evacuated from England to Australia or from cities to country towns. Some pets had to be put down because of the lack of food caused by rationing. Schoolchildren contributed to the war effort by collecting rubber, paper and saucepans. Even empty zinc-lined toothpaste tubes were taken to school for scrap metal collections. There were also strict rules about wasting paper.

Schools were very different from today. Many teachers left their jobs to join up. The return to school at the beginning of 1942 had to be delayed for two weeks while trenches were dug in all the school grounds. Pupils were taught the procedure for moving into the trenches, which were about one metre deep and often poorly drained. Air-raid drills were held regularly and children had to take their own air-raid bag to school containing specific items for emergency use (see source 3.9.4).

Source 3.9.6

John Spencer, a schoolboy during the war, recalls the regular air-raid drills.

> **Every child had to carry across his or her shoulder a small calico bag, usually made by the mother, in which had to be a set of earplugs, a clothes peg, a number of bandages and some dehydrated food, usually in Aspro-sized pellets. These bags were not to be opened except during the regular drills, which we had every day.**
>
> **A particular type of bell ring meant that everyone should evacuate the building. Each class would evacuate [to the trenches] in order in our classes and in pairs.**
>
> **. . . We used to practise this and it was considered deadly serious. What they didn't do, of course, was put in a drainage system so when we had the normal Sydney rain the trenches were about three feet deep in water. We just had to wait till it drained away before we could have air raid drill again.**
>
> **Quoted in Daniel Connell, *The War at Home*, ABC, Crows Nest, NSW, 1988, p. 35.**

ABORIGINES AND TORRES STRAIT ISLANDERS

Aborigines were not eligible for conscription because they were not classed as citizens. Some military generals also doubted the loyalty of the Aborigines, and thought that those who lived in

Source 3.9.7

Recycling was very important for the war effort. In this photograph, boy scouts are collecting used rubber tyres and lengths of hose. AWM — 042773

northern Australia would give the Japanese invaders information, so a decision was made to move the Aborigines south. Despite these and other prejudices against them, many Aborigines joined the Second AIF and made valuable contributions to the defence of Australia.

About 3000 Aborigines had served in the armed forces by the end of the war. Other Aborigines helped in the building of airfields. Some were formed into guerilla units to help prevent a Japanese invasion of the north.

The experiences of Aboriginal diggers varied. Some, especially at first, were faced with discrimination, given menial tasks and were paid much less than non-Aboriginal soldiers. Respect for their special skills and endurance increased as the war progressed.

In contrast, Torres Strait Islanders were encouraged to fight against the Japanese and some special units were formed, such as the Torres Strait Defence Force. Aborigines like Reg Saunders gained promotion and Leonard Waters was able to become a fighter pilot for the RAAF.

'OVERPAID, OVERSEXED, OVER HERE'

In March 1942, the United States General Douglas MacArthur arrived in Australia and the continent became a base for troops fighting in the Pacific. By September 1943, there were 120 000 Americans in Australia. At first, the Americans were welcomed but trouble soon broke out, especially between the troops. There were many reasons for this. For example, the Americans:

- were paid twice as much as the Australian soldiers
- did not have to pay taxes on goods

- were able to impress Australian girls, as their uniforms were smarter
- could pay more for luxuries such as chocolates and stockings, so the prices went up even higher.

Source 3.9.8

A Charters Towers resident describes the arrival of the Americans.

The Americans were an absolute sensation from their very first day in town. Everybody hurried up town just to look at them, almost as if they were from another planet ... Instead of crumpled serge tunics and baggy trousers like the Australians, the Americans wore neatly pressed drill shirts and ties and trousers ... jaunty little forage caps [and] ... instead of cloddhopper boots, they wore shiny black shoes.

They had the charm of the exotic about them, called the local mothers 'Ma'am', and had about twice the spending power of the Australian troops, plus such wonders as Coca-Cola and American cigarettes. Some of them found the system of pounds, shillings and pence just too complicated, and would offer a handful of notes and coins, trusting the recipient to take only the correct amount, a trust not always justified.

The general impression about the Americans, among Australian males of all ages, and among the females who were either too young or too old to benefit from their presence, came to be summed up in the expression 'over-paid, over-sexed and over here'.

In spite of these feelings, the Towers did its best to make all soldiers welcome, both Australian and American. Most nights the streets, pubs, cafes, picture theatres and dance halls were full of them. Two halls in the town were turned into clubs, and people often brought soldiers home for a meal, a drink and a talk.

Unice Atwell, *Growing Up in the 40s*, Kangaroo Press, Sydney, 1983, pp. 40–1.

Trouble between the troops occasionally led to brawls. The most famous was the Battle of Brisbane. It began on 26 November 1942 when Australians were refused entry to an American entertainment centre. An Australian soldier was shot dead and, for the next three days, Australian and American troops fought each other in the streets. A similar brawl in Melbourne between 2000 men stopped traffic for an hour.

By late 1944, most of the Americans had left Australia. Many Australian women had married Americans but they were not allowed to live in America until after the war. They became known as **war brides**.

The influence of the Americans on Australian society was felt in many ways. They brought new ideas and attitudes that sometimes challenged the traditional British ways. Many Australians began to see themselves as Australians, not simply as British subjects.

Source 3.9.9

Many Australians were sad to see the Americans leave Australia, as this *Bulletin* cartoon from the mid-1940s shows.

Activities

Check your understanding

1. List ten restrictions placed on the lives of ordinary Australians during the World War II. For each restriction, suggest a reason why it was necessary.
2. How were children in Australia affected by World War II?
3. What part did Aboriginal and Torres Strait Islanders play in the defence of Australia?
4. Why were the Americans popular with many Australians in the 1940s?
5. What were the main reasons for conflict between Australian and American soldiers?

Investigation: *The home front*

1. What does source 3.9.1 reveal about life in Australia during World War II? What additional information does 3.9.2 provide? Which of the two sources is the most valuable for historians?
2. Use source 3.9.3 to write a brief description of the method of removing bombs.
3. Use sources 3.9.4, 3.9.6 and 3.9.7 to write a summary of how children were affected by the war.
4. Using sources 3.9.8 and 3.9.9, list the people who benefited most from the presence of the Americans and those who would be unhappy about them leaving. Suggest reasons why each may have felt this way.
5. Write a diary entry for a school student, including details of some of the unusual aspects of life in the war years.
6. As a class, research how World War II affected your local area and make a video. Include interviews with people who lived in the area and the reminders of war still present in the area.

3.10

WORKING ROLES — CHANGES FOR WOMEN

Industries and employment in Australia became focused on the war effort. Everyone was expected to work hard and the government was strict on those who didn't. In 1942, the government appointed a Director of Manpower to ensure that the Australian labour force was being used effectively to meet the wartime needs.

Source 3.10.1

Strictness and discipline applied in the workplace as well as in the forces, as suggested in this cartoon from the *Australian Women's Weekly* from the early 1940s.

The system of conscription took away the males who were fit and who were not working in an 'essential industry'; that is, one that was vital to the war effort. On 6 March 1942, the upper age limit for conscription was increased to 45 for married men and 60 for single men. As more men left for active duty, Australian industry suffered a shortage of workers and the government called on women to enter the work force.

FACT*file*

- During the war, people were not allowed to change their jobs without permission, and school-leavers could be told what job they must go to.
- Many of the older conscripted men worked in the Civil Construction Corps (CCC) and built airfields and other installations or worked in munitions factories.

Women in their thousands — married as well as single — took on work roles that were traditionally men's, and thus they kept Australia's industries running and producing. During the course of the war, women made up about 40 per cent of the work force in munitions factories. Others worked in the aircraft and shipbuilding industries, doing mechanical and maintenance work.

Women received training in operating machinery and worked in conditions that were very different from their traditional roles as housewives and mothers. By October 1942, over half a million women were employed in industry. Their working hours were long and the workload in war-related industries was heavy. Most also had the added responsibility of managing the household and looking after children.

Source 3.10.2

A photograph showing a woman checking and counting bullets in a munitions factory during the war. AWM — 007731

Women entered a range of other occupations and became, for example, tram conductors, bus drivers, taxi drivers, security guards, mail deliverers, bread carters and meter readers. Women showed that they could handle all manner of jobs that were outside their traditional sphere and many hoped that these roles would continue to be open to them when the war ended. However, there were concerns among trade unionists that because the women were paid lower wages than men, employers would try to keep them after the war and men would lose their jobs. Although women's efforts were acknowledged as being vital to the nation while the men were away, it was clear that they were considered as a 'reserve' labour force and were expected to be housewives and mothers again when the men returned.

THE LAND ARMY

Australia's farmers also found themselves with insufficient workers to keep up food production. To meet this need, the government called on women to join the Australian Women's Land Army. It was established in July 1942 and over 3000 women volunteered over the next three years. They were sent to work in country areas, harvesting cotton and fruit and working in the dairy, sheep and poultry industries. Many farmers thought, initially, that women would not cope with the heavy farm work, but soon they had nothing but praise for the hard-working Land Army women.

Source 3.10.3

An extract from Esme Corcoran's account of her time with the Land Army

When I was 17 I volunteered for the Land Army ... my first job was working on a dairy farm and vegetable garden for three months, then a wheat farm ... I was put to work chopping mallee stumps and grubbing out bushes, [then] working a team of eight horses pulling a combine ...

We girls in the Land Army were better off than most other people as all our clothes were provided. Also, because I was on a farm I had plenty of butter, milk, eggs and meat, so I was able to send my ration coupons down to my mother. She was very grateful because all those things were in such short supply.

Looking back, I am glad we learned the hard way. My generation was taught to work at a very young age. We had to live without depending on lots of support.

***Australian* magazine, 26–27 August 1989.**

Source 3.10.4

A member of the Land Army is illustrated on this cover of the *Australian Women's Weekly*, 31 May 1941.

Source 3.10.5

Australian average weekly wages in shillings (s) and pence (d) — male and female

	Wages				
	Males		Females		Female % of male rate
Year	s	d	s	d	
1939	95	3	52	8	**55.3**
1940	98	1	54	3	**55.3**
1941	104	3	58	2	**55.8**
1942	115	8	64	4	**55.6**
1943	119	5	68	4	**57.2**
1944	119	6	71	11	**60.2**
1945	120	4	72	0	**59.8**

S. J. Butlin and C. B. Schedvin, *War Economy 1941–45*, Australian War Memorial, Canberra, 1977, p. 561.

Activities

Check your understanding

1. List the difficulties faced by women working in Australia during World War II.
2. How did women's roles change during the war?
3. What happened when the men returned from the war? How do you think many women felt about this?

Investigation: *The changing role of women*

1. How realistic do you think the illustration of the Land Army worker is in source 3.10.4? (Consider the description in source 3.10.3 of the type of work the women carried out.)
2. Examine the table of average weekly earnings in the war years (source 3.10.5). Write a paragraph describing the trend in the figures as the war progressed, and comment on the differences between male and female wages.

Communication: *Preparing a speech*

Prepare a speech that you might deliver to a group of women who have worked in the war industries, either supporting or opposing their desire to be allowed to keep working after the war. Present your speech to the class.

VICTORY IN EUROPE, VICTORY IN THE PACIFIC

During the final years of World War II most attention was on winning the war in Europe against Germany. On D-Day, 6 June 1944, Allied forces invaded France. In less than a year, on 8 May 1945, Germany surrendered. Australians were happy to hear this news but they still had the war against Japan to win.

In the Pacific, General MacArthur began a policy of 'island-hopping'. He knew it would take a long time to capture each Japanese occupied island so he decided to attack only the important ones, using United States troops. Bases could then be established close to Japan to allow large-scale bombing raids on Japanese cities. Australian troops were to continue clearing the Japanese from areas such as New Guinea, New Britain, Bougainville and Borneo.

Many Australians felt that this policy was a waste of Australian lives and many resented MacArthur's use of United States troops, instead of Australians, to island-hop. John Curtin wrote to MacArthur in February 1945, asking for a greater attacking role for Australians. Curtin was very ill at the time and died on 5 July 1945, six weeks before the war ended in the Pacific.

The Allies realised that it was going to cost many lives to invade Japan. Attacks on Iwo Jima and Okinawa had been very costly and they knew that the Japanese would fight to the death.

Source 3.11.1

Prime Minister John Curtin and General Douglas MacArthur

THE ATOMIC BOMB

Both Germany and the United States had been working on a secret weapon to end the war. The United States won the race. The atomic bomb was first tested in New Mexico and then used against two Japanese cities:

- 6 August 1945 — Hiroshima— 70 000 killed
- 9 August 1945 — Nagasaki — 40 000 killed.

Source 3.11.2

Hiroshima after the atomic bomb exploded (1945). A single bomb wiped out 10 square kilometres.

Japan still refused to surrender. The Japanese wanted their Emperor to remain as their leader. With the Soviet Union threatening to attack Japan from the west, the Japanese finally surrendered unconditionally to the United States on 15 August 1945. At 9.30 a.m. (EST) the new Australian Prime Minister, Ben Chifley, announced the war was finished. More than one million people went into the streets for a day of celebration.

Source 3.11.3

JAPAN CAPITULATES

DELIRIOUS JOY IN AUSTRALIA

PLANS FOR SURRENDER

GENERAL DOUGLAS MacARTHUR, who has been appointed Supreme Commander of the Allied Forces of Occupation in Japan.

The announcement yesterday morning that Japan had capitulated was received with delirious joy by the peoples of the United Nations.

Cease fire in the Pacific was ordered by the Allies at 9.15 a.m. yesterday.

In Sydney immense crowds took part in scenes of unprecedented emotion and gaiety.

Events of Historic Day

Major events yesterday were:—

9 a.m. (Sydney time), British Prime Minister, Mr. Attlee, and President Truman announce Japanese surrender.

9.15 a.m., Admiral Nimitz orders cease fire.

11.25 a.m. Japanese ordered to give cease-fire order and send emissaries to General MacArthur, Supreme Allied Commander.

11.55 a.m., Tokyo announces Japanese Cabinet has resigned, and War Minister, General Anami, committed hara-kiri.

1 p.m., Japanese planes shot down when they approach U.S. Fleet.

4.45 p.m., General MacArthur orders Japanese to cease hostilities immediately and send representatives to Manila for instructions. Also orders Japanese Government to place radio stations at his continuous disposal for orders.

The *Sydney Morning Herald* announces peace (1945)

Source 3.11.4

A photograph of the celebrations in Sydney when it was announced that the war with Japan was over

World War II changed Australia in many important ways. It was no longer a country that did as Britain told it to do. Women had worked in factories to keep the troops supplied and had been given freedom and responsibilities that they did not want to give up now that the war was over. Australia had been united for the first time and the States had worked together for a common purpose.

Activities

Check your understanding

1. How were the Allies able to defeat both Germany and Japan?
2. What was the policy of 'island-hopping'? Why did many Australians oppose this policy?
3. Why was it decided to use atomic weapons against the Japanese?
4. Why was VJ Day of greater significance than VE Day for Australians?

Communication: *Using a range of sources*

1. How did each of the men in source 3.11.1 help defend Australia in World War II?
2. What does source 3.11.2 reveal about the destructive power of the first atomic bomb?
3. Compare the article in source 3.11.3 with source 3.2.1 (page 54). What does this suggest about how Australia had changed as a result of World War II?

3.12 Meeting the outcomes

ANALYSE THE CONTINUING SIGNIFICANCE OF MAJOR EVENTS AND IDEAS WHICH SHAPED AUSTRALIAN SOCIETY.

Compare different perspectives about a significant event.

It can be difficult for historians to uncover the truth about what happened in an event, especially when there is little evidence on which to base conclusions. The sinking of HMAS *Sydney* in World War II was an event that shocked the country, yet its loss is still as mysterious as it was in 1941. The 7000-tonne ship and 645 men simply disappeared without a trace. The only eyewitness accounts were from the crew of the German ship *Kormoran*, which attacked the *Sydney* without warning. More Australian men died in this one event than in the entire Vietnam War.

Source 3.12.1

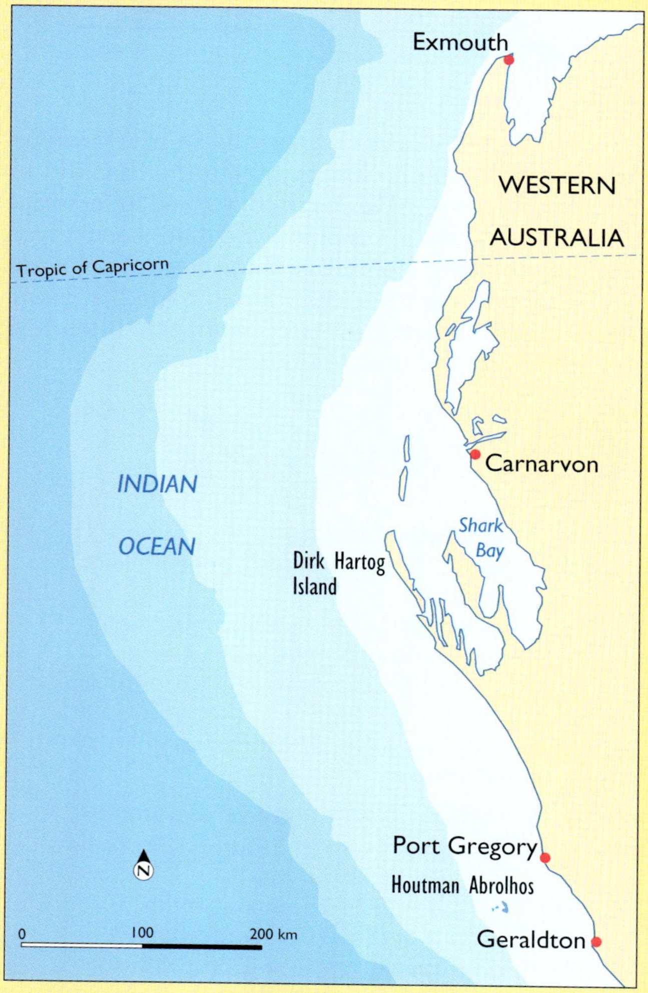

A map of the area off the coast of Western Australia in which HMAS *Sydney* went missing

The statements in source 3.12.2 are related to the sinking of the HMAS *Sydney*. Read them and complete the following activities in an effort to decide what really happened.

1. Draw up a table with three columns headed 'Definitely true', Possibly true' and 'Uncertain'. In groups, summarise each statement in source 3.12.2 and enter it into one of the three columns according to your opinion of its truth or otherwise.
2. Report your group findings to the class.
3. As a class, discuss the possible reasons why no trace was found of the *Sydney* or its crew.
4. As a group, use the Internet to locate additional information about the sinking of HMAS *Sydney*. Present a summary of this research to the class. This additional information can be word-processed and distributed to class members.
5. Write a feature article for publication giving your opinion of what happened to HMAS *Sydney*. Remember to use the evidence to support your opinion.

ANALYSE THE IMPACT OF SIGNIFICANT EVENTS AND IDEAS IN SHAPING WORLD HISTORY IN THE TWENTIETH CENTURY.

Evaluate the impact of the events and ideas on people, values and structures.

Look at source 3.12.3.

(a) What does the map show?
(b) What events took place in concentration camps?
(c) How many Jews died in Europe during World War II?
(d) Why did the Germans target Jews? (2.7)
(e) What impact do you think the German extermination of Jews has had on:
  - the Jewish population today
  - the German population today.
(f) What was the process of extermination called? (3.7)
(g) Compare the treatment of Jews in concentration camps to Australians in prisoner-of-war camps. (3.7)

EXPLAIN THE KEY CHANGES IN SOCIAL AND POLITICAL ATTITUDES AND VALUES IN MODERN WESTERN SOCIETY.

Describe the ways in which significant events affected change in such areas as family structures, gender roles and work organisation.

Reread spreads 3.4 and 3.10.

(a) Make a list of the industries and occupations in which women worked during World War II.
(b) Draw up a chart with three columns to show the difference in women's work in Australia before 1939, during World War II and today.
(c) Explain the changes that have occurred for women between 1939 and the present day, and evaluate the significance of World War II in effecting these changes.

Source 3.12.2

Twenty statements about the sinking of HMAS *Sydney*

1. HMAS *Sydney* was a cruiser, *Kormoran* merely a raider.
2. *Sydney* had thicker armour than *Kormoran* and its guns had a longer range.
3. On the afternoon of 19 November 1941, HMAS *Sydney* approached the *Kormoran* off Shark Bay.
4. The *Kormoran* was disguised as a Dutch ship. Its guns and torpedo launchers were camouflaged.
5. According to some Germans, the *Sydney* was originally at battle stations then its crew relaxed and the *Kormoran* was told to proceed.
6. Some believe HMAS *Sydney* was going to board *Kormoran* and came too close.
7. HMAS *Sydney* asked for a secret identification signal.
8. *Kormoran* launched a torpedo and starting firing. HMAS *Sydney* returned fire and both ships were badly damaged.
9. Captain Detmers of the *Kormoran* abandoned his ship and charges were set to sink it. He last saw HMAS *Sydney* on fire and heading for the horizon. Then it disappeared. He made no attempt to look for survivors. He also believed that the fire had reached the magazine, then the ship blew up and sank. None of the other Germans reported hearing an explosion.
10. People at Yallabathra, near Port Gregory, reported hearing explosions and seeing flashes off the coast on a night in late November about midnight. Fifteen visitors to Dirk Hartog Island on 19 November reported seeing a ship heading south at high speed at 1000 hours.
11. The *Sydney* disappeared 18 days before the Japanese attack on Pearl Harbor.
12. Many believe a Japanese submarine sank the HMAS *Sydney*. There was a rumour that survivors were being held in Japan.
13. Reports of a possible distress signal from the HMAS *Sydney* were not followed up. There is no surviving record of these calls.
14. Air and sea search for HMAS *Sydney* began on 24 November, five days after sinking. Many Germans had already been rescued. Search was called off on 29 November. No trace was found of any survivors or the ship, except for an empty Carley life-float damaged by gunfire.
15. According to some, the *Cape Otway* found bodies in the water but was told to leave the area immediately. Its logs for the period are missing.
16. On 1 December, the Prime Minister officially announced the loss of HMAS *Sydney*.
17. For the previous 12 days there was strict secrecy, with 11 censorship notices preventing publication of any details.
18. Three hundred and fifteen members of *Kormoran* were rescued. Their story is the basis of the official account of what happened.
19. A Carley life-float was found off Christmas Island, to the north-west of Australia, on 6 February 1942, possibly from HMAS *Sydney*.
20. Many of the files related to this event were classified *not to be released for 75 years* when the war ended.

Source 3.12.3

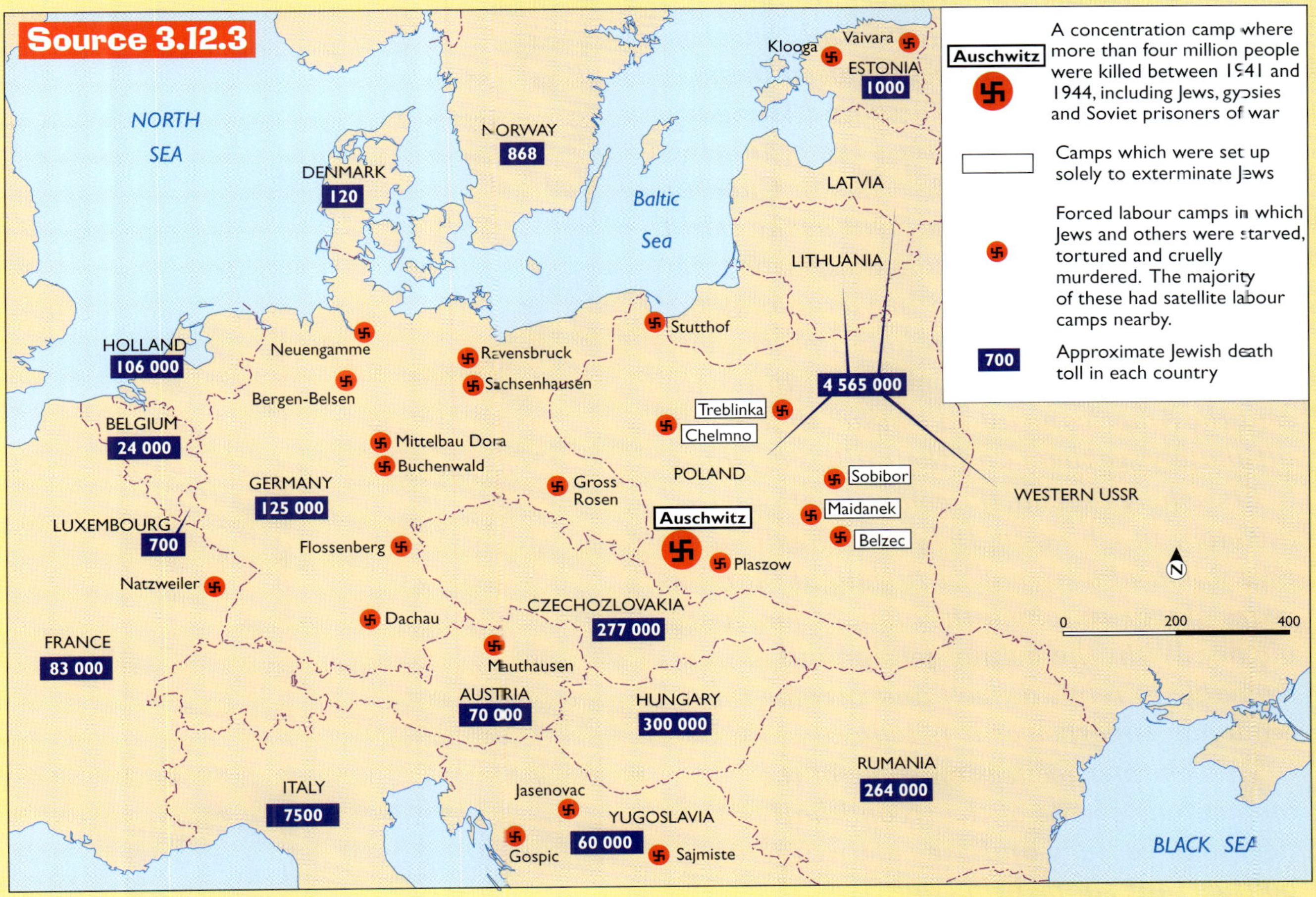

The concentration camps in Europe

Chapter

4

THE WORLD SINCE 1945

LEARNING outcomes

- Describe the issues behind the Cold War.
- Discuss the ideas and people associated with the Chinese revolution.
- Examine how the Vietnam conflict shaped change in the world.
- Understand the impact communism had on Western values.
- Analyse the effect the Vietnam War had on political and social groups.
- Describe advances in technology that influenced relations between superpowers.

INTRODUCTION

World War II both scarred and shaped the modern world. Communist Russia re-emerged as a major power and, together with the United States, drew new battlelines in the communist/capitalist conflict. These two countries dominated international politics over the next 40 years and concerns about the balance of power between them spilled over into Berlin, Korea and Hungary. The postwar era also marked the beginning of the nuclear age and the crisis in Cuba in 1962 was as close to nuclear war as the world has come. The end of the colonial period after World War II was evident in Vietnam as the French lost their former colonial possession. Fears about spreading communist influence sent the Americans into a conflict that would ultimately see them and their allies defeated.

Elsewhere in Asia, the communists secured a victory in China in 1949 and the decades that followed were no less turbulent than the years of war in which they fought for this victory. With the help of foreign aid, Japan was able to rebuild itself and become the economic superpower it is today.

This chapter focuses on some of the momentous events of the second half of the twentieth century and the vastly different politics that shaped this age.

GLOSSARY

ANZUS: a cooperative alliance between Australia, New Zealand and the United States
capitalist: describes a system in which the means of production, distribution and exchange are privately owned and organised
Cold War: serious economic and political conflict between nations, stopping just short of military action
communes: large-scale cooperatives, averaging 5000 families, in which all resources are shared
conscription: compulsory enrolment in the armed forces
cooperatives: groups of mutual-aid teams working together and sharing resources with the cooperative owning the land

coup: a sudden takeover of government, often illegally or by force
Cultural Revolution: a movement in China beginning in 1966 which claimed to preserve and reinforce the basic principles of communism
defoliation: the complete loss of leaves from trees or other vegetation
domino theory: the theory that a communist takeover in one South-East Asian country would lead to similar takeovers in neighbouring countries
establishment: a constituted order or system
feudalism: system of peasants working the land with landowners obtaining maximum benefit from the labour of the peasants
guerillas: small, independent group of soldiers who engage in surprise raids
imperialism: system where one country dominates another, either by holding it as a colony or, indirectly, by military or economic influence
indigenous: native to a particular area or country
Iron Curtain: the name given in the Cold War period to the ideological division between communist countries in eastern Europe and non-communist countries to their west
Marshall Plan: American economic aid plan introduced in 1947; designed to assist Europe's recovery from World War II and to prevent the spread of communism
mutual-aid teams: Chinese peasants sharing farming resources
napalm: substance mixed with petrol and used in fire bombs; inflicts terrible burns
nationalise: to bring under public ownership or government control
North Atlantic Treaty Organisation: 1949 military alliance originally linking a group of Western European countries with the United States and Canada
pacifist: someone who opposes all war or violence
poll tax: tax placed on a household
Red Guard: student military groups active during the Chinese Cultural Revolution
SEATO: a former defence alliance of anti-communist nations, founded in 1954
Truman Doctrine (1947): President Truman's American policy of containing the spread of communism; formed the basis of US foreign policy in the Cold War period
United Nations: an international association of countries formed in 1945 to promote international peace and cooperation
Viet Cong: members of the communist National Front for the Liberation of South Vietnam
Viet Minh: nationalist guerilla group which fought French colonial rule in Vietnam
Warsaw Pact: former military alliance of Eastern European, communist nations, organised by the Soviet Union and set up in 1955

CARVING UP EUROPE

YALTA AND POTSDAM

In February 1945 Churchill, Stalin and Roosevelt met at Yalta in the Crimea to begin discussion and negotiation on the fate of Europe after the war. By this time it was already clear that Germany would be defeated. What was on the leaders' minds had more to do with preserving their own interests through the years ahead.

A number of important decisions were made at Yalta. Not surprisingly, one was that the Nazi power structure was to be dismantled and its leaders made to face court. Germany would also have to pay huge reparations for war damage, half of which would go to Russia. Stalin agreed that, three months after the end of the war in Europe, Russia would declare war on Japan.

Germany's fate was also decided. It would be carved into four zones, one 'quarter' each controlled by the United States, Russia, Britain and France respectively. Berlin, deep in the Russian zone, would also be divided into sectors controlled by the four powers. It was also agreed that a **United Nations** organisation be set up to replace the old League of Nations.

In July, as the Americans were testing their new nuclear weapon in the New Mexico desert, representatives of the big three powers met again at Potsdam near Berlin. Stalin already had a determined plan to occupy Poland and the United States, and Britain seemed powerless to stop him. (Since the Yalta conference Roosevelt had died, to be replaced by Truman; Churchill had lost power in Britain and was replaced by Attlee.) German-speaking people living in Poland, Czechoslovakia and Hungary were to be 'transferred' to Germany.

Central to the tensions between Russia, the United States and Britain were their vastly different political and economic systems (see source 4.1.2).

Source 4.1.2

French cartoon of Stalin

Source 4.1.1

Communism versus Capitalism

Some features of the theory of communism

- developed from the ideas of Karl Marx
- one political party with leader elected by the party
- government owns all land, industry and businesses
- all goods and services shared equally by the people
- no private ownership of property
- government controls the media
- religion banned

Some features of the theory of capitalism

- minimum government interference in the economy
- private ownership of land, industry and businesses
- people have the right to work and use their money as they wish
- people responsible for managing their own lives
- system based on supply of and demand for goods and services, which sets prices

THE BEGINNINGS OF THE SUPERPOWERS

In reality it is difficult to find countries which represent a 'pure' form of communism or capitalism. Even in Australia today, for example, governments are expected to play a major role in providing for the welfare of their citizens.

However, after the end of World War II, Russia and her wartime allies saw each other in simple 'black and white' terms. Communism was good or evil, depending on which side of the fence you were on; the same applied to capitalist countries. These contrasting views were fostered by the political parties in each country, through propaganda in the press and on radio, and by organisations such as churches.

It was in this climate of hostility and suspicion that the boundaries of Europe were being re-drawn yet again.

THE IRON CURTAIN

Russia had suffered badly from invasion in the past and Stalin wanted to make sure such devastation never happened again. Twenty million Russian soldiers and civilians had perished during the war and the only way to protect Russia in future was by the establishment of a 'buffer' zone between Russia and Western Europe.

To America and her friends, however, this was not so much a buffer zone as an attempted communist takeover of Europe. Half of Germany had been given over to communism. The Russian Government also had encouraged and helped the rise of communist governments in a number of Eastern European countries. Speaking as a visitor to the United States in 1946, Churchill commented, 'From Stettin in the Baltic, to Trieste, in the Adriatic, an **Iron Curtain** has descended across the continent . . .'

By 1948, Eastern Europe had come under the control of Stalin's government. Yugoslavia was also a communist republic but, under the leadership of wartime resistance hero Tito, had remained independent of Russia, despite Russia's attempts to bring her into the fold.

Source 4.1.3

An 'Iron Curtain' is drawn across Europe

CONTAINMENT

Britain and France were still recovering from the war and it was only the United States which could exert any significant influence over Europe. The presence of active communist parties in Western Europe created fears that further communist inroads into Europe were likely. Alarmed at this possibility, President Truman, in March 1947, announced a new American policy of containment. Communism would be checked in its existing borders and would not be allowed to spread to other countries. This policy, known as the **Truman Doctrine**, has influenced American foreign policy to this day.

Activities

Check your understanding

1. What decisions were made on the future of Europe at Yalta and Potsdam? Were there any similarities with the Treaty of Versailles?
2. In your own words, describe the basic differences between communism and capitalism.
3. What was the 'Iron Curtain'?
4. What was the Truman Doctrine?
5. Investigate how Eastern European countries came to be under communist control.

Communication: *Using a range of sources*

1. Refer to source 4.1.1. Debate the advantages and disadvantages of communism and capitalism. Is one system 'better' than the other?
2. Look at source 4.1.2.
   (a) Who are the four figures in the background?
   (b) What message is the cartoonist conveying?
   (c) What is the French position in this matter?
3. Refer to source 4.1.3. How did Europe become divided according to the type of political system?

CONFLICTS OF THE COLD WAR

The '**Cold War**' refers to the hostilities between the Soviet Union (the union of Russia and its Eastern European allies) and the United States after World War II. While no direct fighting took place between these two superpowers, there were a number of conflicts and wars which did erupt as a result of political differences.

THE MARSHALL PLAN

The years immediately after the war were difficult ones for Europe. Much of Western Europe was still in ruins. Both Europeans and Americans feared that the poverty and hardship faced by people in Western Europe might push them into the arms of the communists. To counter this, in 1947, the Americans introduced to Europe a program of economic aid called the **Marshall Plan**. In return for billions of dollars worth of aid the Americans would be allowed to build military bases in Europe. Countries receiving aid would also be expected to buy American products and allow American investment in their countries. The slide of Czechoslovakia into the communist camp in February 1948 persuaded the United States Congress, at first inclined to block the plan, to allow the aid to proceed.

CRISIS IN BERLIN

Berlin, divided between the powers and sitting in the middle of Soviet-controlled East Germany, remained a perceived threat to the Russians. In an attempt to force the Americans, British and French to leave their zones, the Russians threw a blockade around West Berlin. On 24 June, 1948, all road, water and rail links between West Germany and Berlin were cut by the Soviets.

A number of options were open to the United States as the Truman Doctrine was put to the test for the first time. In the end, the US decided to airlift massive quantities of essential supplies into West Berlin. The United States, Canada and Western European countries also decided to form a military alliance, the **North Atlantic Treaty Organisation** (NATO). The blockade was to continue for 318 days before the Russians ended it. West Berlin remained free of communist rule.

Source 4.2.1

'Come on Sam! It's up to us again.'

Cartoon from *Punch*, October 1947

Source 4.2.2

Defence and cooperation

> The Parties agree that an armed attack against one or more of them in Europe or North America shall be considered an attack against them all; and consequently they agree that, if such an armed attack occurs, each of them ... will assist the Party or Parties so attacked by taking forthwith, individually and in concert with the other parties, such action as it deems necessary, including the use of armed force.
>
> Part of NATO's founding agreement, 4 April 1949.

KOREA

When news came in September 1949 that the Russians had developed their own nuclear bomb, fears of war increased. China also became communist in 1949 as Mao Zedong's forces triumphed over the Nationalists, who fled to Taiwan.

Korea had been split at the end of World War II when defeated Japanese forces had surrendered to Russian forces in the north and American forces in the south. A communist government emerged in the north, a non-communist one in the south.

On 25 June, 1950, war erupted when North Korean troops crossed the border to invade South Korea. At the urging of the United States the United Nations agreed to send forces to support South Korea. Sixteen non-communist countries joined the UN effort but American forces provided the bulk of opposition to the Soviet-backed North Koreans.

Source 4.2.3

The American battleship *New Jersey* off the coast of Korea

With great support from the UN troops, the South Koreans managed to push the North Koreans back north of the border. This in turn brought Chinese troops — 'volunteers' — into the war. With these additional troops the war ground to a stalemate. An armistice was signed in July 1953 but it didn't resolve the tensions between the two parts of Korea.

WARSAW PACT

In May 1955 a military alliance, the **Warsaw Pact**, was formed between communist countries.

Source 4.2.4

The Communist alliance

> **In accordance with the pact of friendship, co-operation and mutual assistance between the People's Republic of Albania, the Hungarian People's Republic, the USSR and the Czechoslovak Republic, the states have decided to set up a unified command of armed forces . . .**
>
> **Warsaw Pact document.**

FACT*file*

In the *Communist Manifesto* (1848), German philosopher Karl Marx had argued for a communist political system that would provide everyone with an equal share of their country's wealth. Marx believed that these communist societies would be formed after revolutions overthrew the capitalist world.

Activities

Investigation: *Cold War*

1. What does the term 'Cold War' mean?
2. Source 4.2.1 shows a British–American view of the Marshall Plan. What point of view is the cartoonist putting forward?
3. In 1953 the world seemed to be falling into two camps: communist and non-communist.
   (a) Who was to blame for increasing tensions and conflict?
   (b) Who benefited from tensions and conflict in Berlin and Korea? Who lost?
4. Refer to pages from sections 4.1 and 4.2 to create a timeline of key events in the Cold War. Add to it as you learn more about this superpower conflict.

THE WORLD ON THE BRINK — CUBA, 1962

The 1950s were a time of much uncertainty and tension — in Europe especially, but throughout the world as well. After the Korean war the arms race sped up. Both the Soviet Union and the United States vied to have the most powerful, destructive weapons available. The Americans exploded a test hydrogen bomb in 1952. The Russians followed in 1953. Spying became a lucrative and a dangerous business. Nuclear weapons were made to fly over longer and longer distances.

The space race became a part of superpower competition. In 1957 the Russians put a satellite, *Sputnik 1*, into space. In 1962, they were also the first to put a man into space (the astronaut Yuri Gargarin). The Americans resolved that they would surpass the Russians and be the first to put a man on the moon.

THE HUNGARIAN UPRISING

Suspicions and hostilities increased through the 1950s as countries cemented themselves into the two superpower camps. Stalin's death in 1953 brought hopes for a thaw in the Cold War as the new Russian leader, Premier Nikita Khrushchev, spoke of 'peaceful co-existence'. Encouraged by a seeming softening of its hard-line attitudes, in 1956 the Eastern European 'satellite' country of Hungary rebelled against its Russian master. The Hungarians had hoped for more political freedom and more control of their own economy. Instead, 6000 Russian tanks trampled the country into submission. Over 30 000 Hungarians were killed and 180 000 more fled the country. The outside world gave no assistance to Hungary.

THE BERLIN WALL

In 1961 the East German Government suddenly closed the border between East and West Berlin. East Berliners found themselves trapped in their city. The wall that was built between the two halves of the city became a visible reminder of the barrier between the two political systems.

CUBA

In 1959 a revolution in Cuba led by Fidel Castro, his brother Raul and Che Guevara succeeded in overthrowing the corrupt government of dictator Fulgencio Batista. But this was less a triumph of communist revolution than a triumph of the disillusioned urban and rural poor (in a country that was relatively prosperous) over a repressive regime. At first Castro had no clear communist agenda for Cuba.

Americans had large economic interests in Cuba, especially in the sugar industry. After Fidel Castro became leader he announced plans to **nationalise** companies owned by foreigners. When Americans began to boycott Cuban products, Cuba began trading with the Russians. The United States discovered that an ally of the Russians, now itself a communist country, was sitting uncomfortably close. In April 1961, an American-backed plan to overthrow the Castro government failed miserably at the Bay of Pigs, and relations between the US and Cuba deteriorated further.

THE CUBAN MISSILE CRISIS

In October 1962, photographs taken from American U2 spy planes showed Soviet missile bases being built on Cuba.

The United States and, in particular, young president John Kennedy were faced with a crisis. What could they do? Possible solutions to the threat were discussed. They could:

(a) do nothing
(b) launch a nuclear strike on the missile sites
(c) bomb the missile sites with conventional weapons
(d) invade Cuba with armed forces
(e) enforce a naval blockade of Cuba, not allowing any more missiles and military equipment onto Cuban soil.

As Russian ships steamed toward Cuba, the US chose to enforce a naval blockade of its neighbour and let through only ships not carrying 'offensive weapons'. Khrushchev wrote a first letter to Kennedy on 26 October.

Source 4.3.1

U2 photograph of part of Cuban missile base

Source 4.3.2

Khruschev to Kennedy

> **If assurances were given that the President of the United States would not participate in an attack on Cuba and the blockade were lifted, then the question of the removal or the destruction of the missile sites in Cuba would then be an entirely different question ...**
>
> **Part of Khrushchev's letter, 26 October 1962.**

A second letter followed the next morning.

Source 4.3.3

The second letter

> **All countries want to relieve themselves from danger. But how can we, the Soviet Union and our government, assess your actions which, in effect, mean that you have surrounded the Soviet Union with military bases ... Your rockets are stationed in Britain and in Italy and pointed at us. Your rockets are stationed in Turkey. You are worried over Cuba. You say that it worries you because it lies at a distance of ninety miles across the sea from the shores of the United States. However, Turkey lies next to us.**
>
> **Khrushchev in letter to Kennedy, 27 October 1962.**

On advice from Robert Kennedy (who was the US Attorney-General at the time), the President decided to respond to the first letter with its offer of a solution and ignore the second. The Americans would promise not to invade Cuba and lift its blockade if the Russians agreed to remove their missiles from Cuba and not install any more. The following day Khrushchev wrote that he had 'given a new order to dismantle those arms which you have described as offensive, to crate them, and return them to the Soviet Union'. The Cuban Missile Crisis was over.

For ten days the world had believed itself on the brink of a nuclear war. Some positives did emerge, however. After the crisis the Americans and Russians agreed to keep in closer contact; a 'hot line' was set up. Nuclear arms control talks also began.

Source 4.3.4

Laden with missiles, a Soviet ship turns home

Activities

Investigation: *Cuban missile crisis*

1. How did the Hungarian uprising of 1956 and the erection of the Berlin Wall add to superpower tensions?
2. Look carefully at source 4.3.1.
   (a) Who took the photographs?
   (b) What do the photographs show?
   (c) Why did this discovery cause a crisis to occur?
   (d) How are sources 4.3.1 and 4.3.4 linked?
3. Why did the Russians send missiles to Cuba? Why did the United States see this as a threat?
4. Complete the following table using points (a) to (e) from page 86.

American solutions to the missile crisis

Option	Advantages	Disadvantages
Do nothing		

5. Why was the missile crisis world-threatening?
6. What solution to the crisis did the Russians suggest?
7. Why did Kennedy respond to Khrushchev's first letter and not his second?
8. Investigate one of these topics: the nuclear arms race; the space race; the Hungarian Uprising; the Berlin Wall; the Bay of Pigs invasion.

4.4

THE CHINESE REVOLUTION

On 1 October 1949, Mao Zedong proclaimed the People's Republic of China. In his victory speech, Mao declared that 'Our nation will never again be an insulted nation'. The Chinese people had very high expectations of their new government. They wanted peace, a fair standard of living and a united country in which they could take price.

The communist victory in China in 1949 did not mean the end of change or conflict in that country. Despite the hopes that people had for peace and prosperity, the task of rebuilding the country after years of war was always going to be difficult. Industry had been ruined. Unemployment was high. Agriculture, the lifeblood of China, had been severely disrupted. While the communists' political opponents had been sent fleeing to Taiwan, there would always be some ongoing opposition as Mao Zedong himself had already acknowledged.

Source 4.4.1

Democracy and dictatorship

> **Democracy is practised by the people. The people enjoy the rights of freedom of speech, freedom to meet together, the right to form associations and so on. The right to vote belongs only to the people and not to the reactionaries. There is democracy for the people and dictatorship for the reactionaries. This is the People's Democratic Dictatorship.**
>
> **Mao Zedong.**

Here Mao had skirted around the central problem facing China. How could a country with a vast population (that was growing at the rate of about 15 million a year when the communists took over) be managed? How many freedoms could be allowed? How many restrictions would be placed on people for the greater good of the country?

LAND REFORM

In the countryside, the communists encouraged peasants to claim land once it had been 'liberated' from the old landowners. Landlords and their families were often put on trial in what were little more than 'kangaroo courts'; several million were executed for their crimes, real or imaginary. Others of the landlord class were sent to prison or to camps to be 're-educated'. A lucky percentage were allowed to remain in their villages but were usually stripped of most land and property.

Receiving land for the first time did not necessarily solve peasants' problems. With no money, and often no equipment or livestock, peasants had to pool their resources in **mutual-aid teams**. There still remained some exploitation of poorer peasants by wealthier ones, however. For example, charges were made for the 'loan' of equipment.

Source 4.4.2

A 1950 poster — peasants putting their former landlord on trial

ENEMIES HUNTED DOWN

By 1951 the old landowning class had been removed as a threat to the government. New laws were promoted throughout the country. In theory, women were now equal and infanticide was banned, as was the selling of females. Divorce was made easier. When China became involved in the Korean War there were great suspicions about 'enemies of the people'. Propaganda became even more important to the government as these 'enemies' began to be hunted down. Mao's thoughts and writings were spread through the country to be memorised and acted upon.

THE FIVE YEAR PLAN

Shortly after the communist victory in 1949, the Chinese had turned to the Russians for help in developing their country. With the aid of 10 000 skilled Russian workers the Chinese embarked on their first Five Year Plan, an ambitious project designed to increase China's industrial output. This plan began in 1953 but the plan's targets were announced only in 1955. Source 4 4.3 shows figures provided by the Chinese Government.

Source 4.4.3

Industrial production under the first Five Year Plan

Product	1952	1957 (planned)	1957 (achieved)
Coal (million tons)	63.5	113	124
Pig-iron (million tons)	1.9	4.7	5.86
Steel (million tons)	1.35	4.12	5.24
Chemical fertiliser (thousand tons)	194	570	740
Machine-tools (pieces)	13 734	37 192	80 000 (1958)
Crude oil (million tons)	0.44	2	1.42
Cement (million tons)	2.6	6	4.65
Electric power (thousand million kilowatts)	7.26	15.9	19.1

Reforms were also continuing in the countryside. The revolution had given millions of peasants their own land for the first time, many working together for mutual benefit (though this had happened in the past too). The communist government was still concerned about the question of land. It instructed mutual-aid teams to work together in **cooperatives**

Source 4.4.4

Land reform

> **This is China's position. There is a large population with not enough land being farmed. Natural disasters and farming methods are backward. As a result, although land reform had greatly helped the lives of the peasants, many still face hardship. Only a small number of peasants are well off. Some poor peasants have been forced to sell up in order to survive. They now have to work as labourers again. So there is a great need to increase the numbers of cooperatives.**
>
> **Mao Zedong, July 1955.**

Under this land reform a crucial change happened. Now the cooperative, rather than the peasant, owned the land. Toward the end of 1956, most of the 300 million who had been given land in 1950 were again without land.

THE HUNDRED FLOWERS

The changes in industry and agriculture caused tensions in China. In 1956 Mao announced that he wanted to improve communism, and therefore society, in China. He wanted to use the method of 'unity-criticism-unity' whereby people would be encouraged to speak their minds so that better ways could be found of doing things. 'Let a hundred flowers bloom', he said.

Criticism came freely. Wall posters appeared and newspapers printed stories which criticised the Communist Party. Students protested in some cities. Mao and other communist officials seemed surprised by the extent of the criticism. Soon the communists were cracking down on their critics. The press was censored again, people were sent off for 're-education' and others lost their jobs. Today, historians still argue about the real purpose of the 'Hundred Flowers'.

THE GREAT LEAP FORWARD

In 1958 China began its second Five Year Plan While China would continue to industrialise, the focus of the plan, China's great resource, its

Source 4.4.5

Poster encouraging communal effort

peasant population, would be harnessed into a system of industrial and agricultural production as never before.

Groups of villages were organised into **communes**. These communes varied in size but an average one might contain about 5000 families. Everything was owned by the commune, nothing by the individual. By the end of 1958 about 700 million had been organised into over 26 000 communes. Peasants in communes worked as an army might, with teams responsible for various tasks. The commune was also closely linked to the Communist Party and propaganda played an important part in getting people to work hard.

The energies of rural workers were often diverted into industrial production. People were encouraged to make steel in 'backyard' furnaces. Villages melted down scrap metal, cooking utensils and whatever else they could lay their hands on. The problem with this was that about 3 million of the 11 million tonnes of steel made in this way was useless for industrial use and had itself to be rejected as scrap. The steel-making and related work had also taken workers away from growing food and agriculture suffered as a result.

Three bitter years

China suffered very badly, in particular between 1959 and 1961. The Great Leap Forward had set unrealistic agricultural and industrial targets and the momentum of the revolution began to stall from exhaustion and misguided economic objectives.

Severe food shortages ocurred in 1959, their impact worsened by floods and droughts. The weather was even worse in 1960 and large-scale famine occurred, killing up to 10 million people. Food rationing was introduced and the Great Leap Forward was officially abandoned in 1960.

Source 4.4.6

Famine

It was in 1960 that all China fell on hard times. I was almost seven. Rice, cooking oil and soya beans were strictly rationed. Meat, eggs, flour and sugar disappeared completely. The cost of fresh vegetables went out of sight . . . One day Father came home very quiet and depressed . . . Finally he told us that at a commune in Hengyang District to the south, nearly a whole production team had died of hunger, and there was no-one left with enough strength to bury the bodies. They were still lying scattered about in the fields from which they had been trying to pull up enough food to stay alive.

A peasant's account, in C. K. Macdonald, *Modern China*, Basil Blackwell, 1985, p. 45.

THE CULTURAL REVOLUTION

Between 1962 and 1966 China's leaders argued about China's economic direction. Moderates now controlled the government after the failed Great Leap Forward but Mao was still very influential with the people. In 1966 he launched the **Cultural Revolution**, which he argued would bring people back to the true values of communism.

What it brought to China was chaos on an almost unprecedented scale. Mao had the support of the four-million strong People's Liberation Army and students were organised into military groups called the **Red Guard**. The aim of the Cultural Revolution was to 'purify' communism and rid China of all 'capitalist, Western and reactionary influences'. Mao encouraged the Red Guards as they rampaged through China. Schools and colleges were shut down so curriculums could be rewritten, their teachers often publicly humiliated and even murdered. Factories shut down as workers began marches. Buildings were wrecked and the economic life of the country destroyed. Hundreds of thousands were killed as, by 1967, law and order broke down completely, with the Red Guards doing as they pleased. China slid closer to civil war when rival Red Guard factions began fighting each other.

Source 4.4.7

The Red Guards

> **I followed some people into a school and peered into rooms where a rival group of Red Guards were being beaten with leather belts. The Rebels' hatred frightened me. Some of the prisoners seemed nearly dead and were bleeding badly. That summer things got even worse in Changsha. The Rebels began fighting among themselves. Those who had once been friends became deadly enemies and the streets of Changsha ran with blood. The Cultural Revolution no longer had anything to do with the crack down on people who were against communism. That had been forgotten. A civil war was going on with each side claiming to love Chairman Mao more than the other.**
>
> Liang Heng, in C. K. Macdonald, *Modern China*, Basil Blackwell, 1985, p. 51.

Source 4.4.8

Quotations from Mao were ever present during the Cultural Revolution.

Because of the damage the Cultural Revolution was causing China and because he had succeeded in his objective of regaining complete power, Mao began trying to reel back the Cultural Revolution during late 1967. By 1969 the Cultural Revolution was over.

Source 4.4.9

Red Guards putting up posters during the Cultural Revolution

Activities

Investigation: *Reforms in China*

1. What did 'land reform' in China mean after 1949 and how did attitudes towards ownership of the land change up to the late 1960s?
2. What do you think the word 'reactionary' might have meant during this period? Why might people have been described in this way? Who might have suffered most from this?
3. What different reasons could you give for Mao Zedong starting the 'Hundred Flowers' campaign? What is the most likely explanation? Why?
4. What did the two Five Year Plans hope to achieve for China? Which one appeared to be the most successful? What questions might you ask yourself about the evidence contained in source 4.4.3? How useful is it as evidence?
5. Why do you think the Great Leap Forward ended in failure? Try to suggest as many reasons as you can.
6. What was the Cultural Revolution and what was its impact on China? How might it still be influencing China today?
7. As a class, discuss the advantages and disadvantages of private, collective and government ownership of land. What are the differences between these systems of ownership? Which system or systems might encourage the most productive use of land and why?

VIETNAM — THE HISTORICAL BACKGROUND

The people of Vietnam have a long and proud history of resisting invasion of their country. As a powerful neighbour, the Chinese overran Vietnam in 111 BC. For the next thousand years the Chinese had to quell many unsuccessful rebellions — until 939 AD, when the Vietnamese were finally able to win back control of their country. Then it became the turn of the Vietnamese to resist further attempts by the Chinese at re-conquering Vietnam.

THE FRENCH

In the sixteenth and seventeenth centuries European powers like Britain and Spain began sailing to Asia. There was intense competition as they fought to establish their own trading posts and colonies there. India was an early target for the Portuguese and British. Then the Spanish claimed the Philippines in 1564. The Dutch exerted control over Indonesia in the early 1600s. Militarily superior, the European powers all staked their claims in India and Asia, despite resistance from **indigenous** peoples.

Perhaps surprisingly, little trading had occurred between European countries and Vietnam until the French arrived in the nineteenth century. In 1858 the French began their assault on the coastal city of Da Nang. By the following year they had captured Saigon and, in 1882, Hanoi. The French also took control of Cambodia and Laos.

In French Indochina, and particularly in Vietnam, old systems and traditions were overturned in order to secure French profit and control. The local people were 'assimilated' into French cultural systems and the area was organised and developed for exploitation by French business interests. Heavy taxes were imposed on the Vietnamese peope, and plantations of rubber, silk, cotton, coffee and tea replaced subsistence agriculture. This caused dislocation, debt and starvation amongst the largely peasant, agricultural, rural population.

NATIONALISM

Vietnamese rebellion and guerilla activity against the French was primarily concerned with returning Vietnam to its rightful owners. But the overthrow of the Russian Government in 1917 and the growing communist support throughout Europe meant that new ideas were filtering into Asia as well. Many political parties were formed in Vietnam. Prominent leaders included Ho Chi Minh who founded the Communist Party of Indo-China in 1929, and Nguyen Thai Hoc who led the Vietnamese Nationalist Party.

Source 4.5.1

The aims of the Communist Party of Indo-China, as set out at their first conference

1. To overthrow French **imperialism**, **feudalism** and the reactionary Vietnamese capitalist class.
2. To make Indo-China completely independent.
3. To establish a worker-peasant and soldier government.
4. To confiscate the banks and other enterprises belonging to the imperialists and put them under the control of the worker-peasant and soldier government.
5. To confiscate all of the plantations and property belonging to the imperialists and the Vietnamese reactionary capitalist class and distribute them to poor peasants.
6. To implement the eight hour working day.
7. To abolish public loans and **poll tax**. To waive unjust taxes hitting the poor people.
8. To bring back all freedom to the masses.
9. To carry out universal education.
10. To implement equality between man and woman.

Ho Chi Minh, *Ho Chi Minh on Revolution*, edited and with an introduction by Bernard B. Fall, New York, 1967, p. 129.

As leader of the Communist Party, Ho actively spread the communist ideology which promoted the power of the working class, centralised control and abolition of private ownership. The French felt threatened, hunting down and killing leaders of both communists and nationalists, including Nguyen Thai Hoc. Heavy weapons and aerial bombardment were deployed to try to force the Vietnamese into submission.

WORLD WAR II

When Japan entered the war it quickly overcame the French in Vietnam. Now the Vietnamese nationalists had a new oppressor, a new enemy to fight. During this war both nationalist and communist forces gathered strength. The Americans gave the Viet Minh (as the communist forces were called) a small amount of assistance against the Japanese. The nationalists' and the communists' fighting ability won the admiration of even their enemies. The Japanese defeat in 1945 gave the Viet Minh the opportunity to seize control of the country. On 2 September 1945, the new President of the Democratic Republic of Vietnam, Ho Chi Minh, announced his country's independence. Aided by the British who were disarming the Japanese in the south, the French began to re-establish themselves in Vietnam.

Source 4.5.2

Ho Chi Minh

Source 4.5.3

The colonial past: Saigon's Roman Catholic Cathedral in 1935

WAR WITH THE FRENCH

The French tried to restore the colonial presence they had enjoyed before the war but too much had changed. The Viet Minh under Ho Chi Minh were firmly entrenched in the north. Many nationalists who wanted neither French nor communist rule were killed or intimidated. A bitter nine-year war resulted. China assisted the Viet Minh to expand communism and the United States assisted the French to contain it. In the end, with help from China's military advisers and equipment, the Viet Minh was able to claim victory in 1954 after 8000 French lives were lost in a disastrous battle at Dien Bien Phu. At a meeting of the major powers at Geneva in Switzerland it was decided to divide Vietnam into two, with the north becoming a communist republic under Ho Chi Minh and the south a republic under the nationalist Ngo Dinh Diem. Elections to reunite the country were proposed for 1956, but never took place.

Activities

Investigation: *Competing interests*

1. Write a few sentences describing how the Vietnamese resisted invasion of their country by the Chinese, the Japanese and the French.
2. Suggest reasons why China and France would have wanted to gain control of Indo-China. What valuable resources come from that region today? Use an atlas or library references to help you.
3. Judging by sources 4.5.1 and 4.5.3, what might have been some of the aspects of French rule that the Vietnamese disliked or hated most?
4. The Americans gave the Viet Minh aid during the war against Japan. Why did they then turn against them when they fought the French after 1945?
5. Give detailed reasons why the Vietnamese were able to defeat the French by 1954. You will need to use other sources to do this. You could explore the Internet or watch a documentary like *The 10 000 Day War.*
6. Create your own 'manifesto' for the Communist Party of Indo-China. Use source 4.5.1 but select six key points only, and rewrite them in your own words.

THE VIETNAM WAR

After World War II the US wanted to create a **capitalist** world, where countries would evolve in a way that was beneficial to American interests. America was committed to fighting communism wherever it might be. Its credibility as a world power and the tapping of necessary resources such as rubber, tin and oil were the prime concerns of American foreign policy. In the years 1953–1962, the US was giving substantial aid to Indo-china, but also to Turkey, Greece, Spain, South Korea, Taiwan and Pakistan. It was indeed a far-flung net.

While the communists took control of the north in the 1954 division of Vietnam, the south became a republic under the nationalist and Catholic Ngo Dinh Diem. The United States supported Diem because they thought he would provide strong opposition to the communists. By this time the Americans had developed their '**domino theory**' that if one country fell to communism so would others. Diem announced that South Vietnam would have nothing to do with the proposed elections because he could not be guaranteed that the north would provide fair elections. This may not have been the only reason, however. The Chinese and Soviets supported Ho Chi Minh to expand communism, while the United States supported Diem to defend against it.

Source 4.6.1

The 'domino theory'

Source 4.6.2

The 1956 elections

> **On the basis of the evidence we have at this early date, however, we believe a favourable development of the situation in South Vietnam is unlikely . . . It is even possible that at some point during the next two years the South Vietnam Government could be taken over by elements that would seek unification with the Viet Minh in the North even at the expense of Communist domination. Even if the scheduled elections were held in July 1956, and if the Viet Minh do not prejudice its political prospects, the Viet Minh will almost certainly win.**
>
> US Government National Intelligence estimate, 3 August 1954, US–Vietnam Relations, Book 10.

OPPOSITION TO DIEM

While communist propaganda portrayed Ho as the beloved 'Uncle Ho' in the north, Diem was unpopular in the south. Ho organised the communists who had remained in the south after the war with France into the National Front for the Liberation of South Vietnam. Its members were called the **Viet Cong** and they fought Diem after the cancellation of the elections.

Diem resisted land reform attempts, as well as Buddhist criticism of his regime. He cracked down ruthlessly on his opponents, using a police force headed by his brother, Ngo Dinh Nhu. Widespread corruption was reported by western reporters who were allowed to operate in the south only.

Demonstrations and spectacular protests (see source 5.17) against Diem's government gathered pace. The Viet Cong operated mostly in rural areas as a guerilla force. They worked under commanders sent from the north by Ho and fought alongside the north's regular army divisions.

The United States had hoped to support the Diem regime by providing only political and economic help. However, as they perceived the situation worsening, they increased the number of 'military advisers' they were sending to South Vietnam. By 1963, the US had over 16 000 troops stationed there. In 1967, there were also 170 000 Chinese soldiers as well as many Soviet troops in the north.

Source 4.6.3

A Buddhist monk burns himself to death in protest against Diem's government.

DIEM ASSASSINATED

By 1963 the United States Government was also losing patience with Diem. President Kennedy was open in his criticism of Diem and, on 1 November, Diem was murdered in a **coup** staged by South Vietnamese army officers. His downfall resulted from popular discontent with his policies, particularly 'strategic hamlets' as well as the communists' destabilisation campaigns.

Source 4.6.4

Forced evacuation

[The American plan] forced the evacuation of the people in certain parts of the countryside into fortified villages which were defensible. In a Vietnamese context the village, the people living in the village and on the produce of the land were inextricably entwined ... the plan ... displaced too many people, creating disorientation among the peasants and a decided disinclination to support those who moved them out of their traditional homes ... this scheme did more to undermine Diem's and therefore the Americans' position than any other.

A. Bullock (ed.), *History of the 20th Century*, Phoebus, 1976, p. 469.

John F. Kennedy too was assassinated, just three weeks after Diem's death. The South then went through frequent changes of government, further destabilising it. At the same time, Chinese troops and supplies also increased. The new American president, Lyndon Johnson, committed more troops to Vietnam.

Source 4.6.5

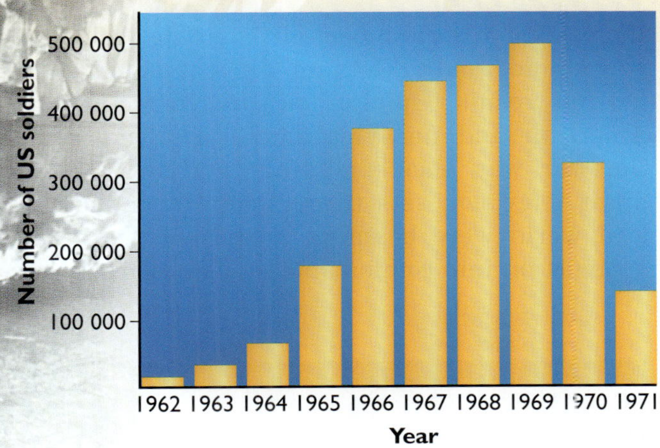

Number of US troops in Vietnam 1962–71

P. Fisher, *The Great Power Conflict after 1945*, p. 47.

THE WAR ESCALATES

The Johnson government stepped up its involvement with large-scale bombing raids from the air and with South Vietnamese forces conducted search-and-destroy missions on the ground. Meanwhile, China and the Soviet Union continued to provide personnel and equipment assistance to North Vietnam.

Supplies, many from China and the Soviet Union, were laboriously carted south through the 'Ho Chi Minh Trail'. Its incursion into Laos' and Cambodia's lands brought these countries into the conflict. The Viet Cong dug in; extensive tunnel networks underground provided safety from air strikes. Guerillas struck in unpredictable ways. Many American and South Vietnamese soldiers were killed by guerillas posing as civilians, and many innocent civilians thought to be guerillas were killed. Their frustration grew. The late 1960s were marked by atrocities from both sides. At the village of My Lai in March 1968, Lieutenant William Calley led a slaughter of between 300 and 500 unarmed civilians. The Viet Cong massacred the villagers of Dak Son, burning more than 200 alive in huts with flamethrowers and shooting the survivors. While both sides were told to 'win the hearts and minds' of the people, the use of indiscriminate killings, booby traps, **napalm** and chemical warfare meant that constant terror ruled the lives of most civilians.

CHANGING OPINIONS

Increasing the number of bombing raids on North and South Vietnam did not achieve the desired result. Opinion on the correctness of American and non-Vietnamese involvement in the war was also beginning to change. Every night television sets throughout the industrialised world were beaming images of death and destruction into comfortable lounge rooms. Many people later claimed that television lost the Vietnam War for America. In American and Australian streets (Australia had entered the war as a US ally in 1965), huge crowds of protesters and demonstrators argued against conscription as foreign interference which killed young Americans and Australians. Others argued that the spread of communist dictatorships was a threat to the free world.

THE TET OFFENSIVE

In February 1968, the communists arranged a ceasefire for the Vietnamese Tet, or New Year holiday, then ignored it and launched a massive offensive which caught the south off-guard. For a while, the communists controlled large numbers of villages and towns in South Vietnam and even briefly occupied the American Embassy in Saigon.

The South Vietnamese–American coalition was able to recapture all lost territory over the following weeks and inflict severe losses on the communists. But American propaganda that victory was almost won was exposed for the myth it was. Protests increased. Meanwhile American, Australian and Chinese servicemen continued to be killed.

In his 1964 election campaign Johnson had spoken of building a 'Great Society'. The resources being poured into Vietnam had diverted attention away from domestic issues. A demonstration in 1970 by students at Kent State University, Ohio, saw four students killed and many others wounded by the National Guard. America had run off the rails, people observed with disgust, when it began killing its own. Others claimed America had already been doing that for a long time in Vietnam.

Source 4.6.6

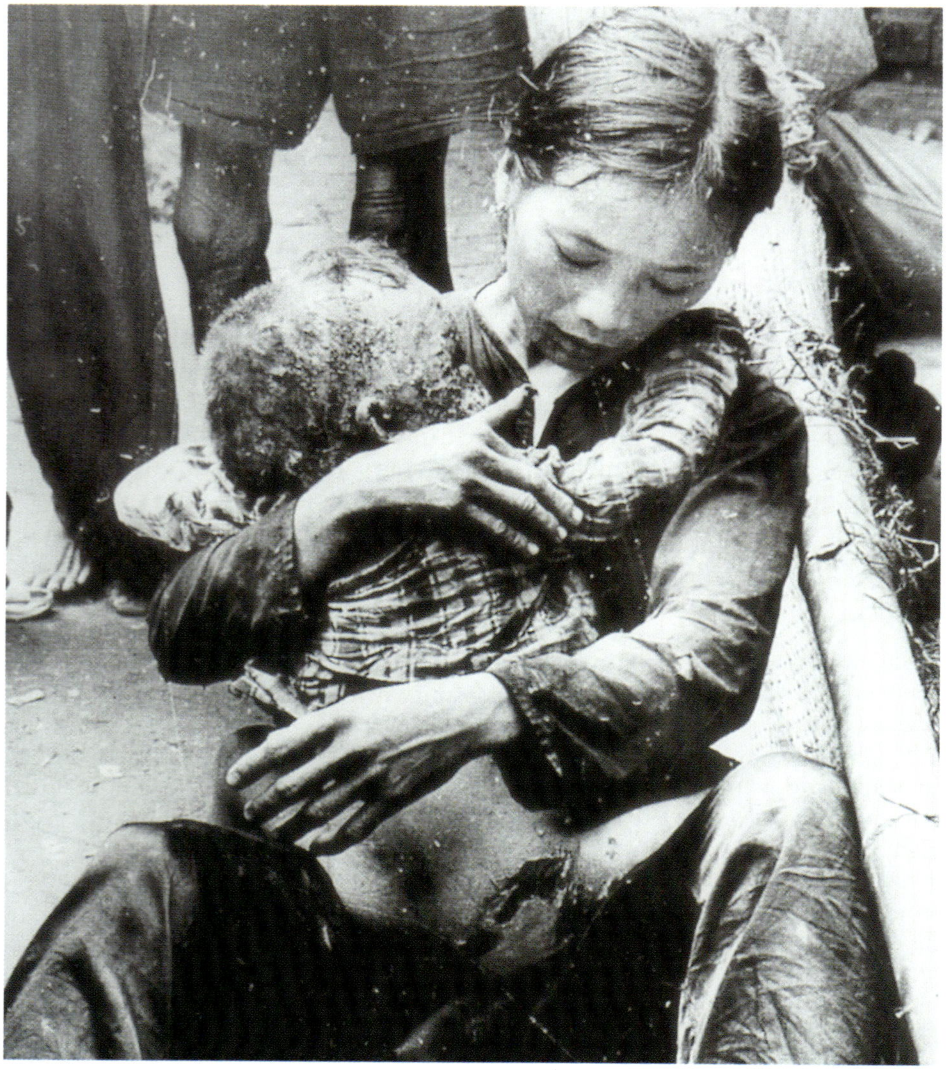

A young boy burnt in a napalm attack

Source 4.6.7

Cartoon on Johnson's 'Great Society' and Vietnam

Punch, January 1967.

PEACE TALKS

The announcement of peace talks first came in 1968 just before Johnson left the presidential office. Johnson did not seek re-election in the 1968 American presidential elections. The Vietnam War had dug his political grave. His successor, Richard Nixon, on the one hand claimed to be pushing for the peace process; on the other, he continued saturation bombing raids on North Vietnam and other targets including Cambodia. The war spread to Cambodia as the communist Khmer Rouge fought the American-backed Lon Nol government.

Despite the signing of a peace treaty in Paris in 1973, the war continued. But the Americans had lost the will to fight and they began to withdraw from Vietnam. On 30 April 1975, North Vietnamese troops entered Saigon as the defenders scrambled to leave. Two million people fled Vietnam and about one million people were put into re-education camps where many died.

Activities

Investigation: *America and Vietnam*

1. Explain the 'domino theory' and why the United States became involved in the war in Vietnam.
2. Write a few lines explaining the role played in the Vietnam war by each of the following:
   Ngo Dinh Diem
   Viet Minh
   National Liberation Front
   Lyndon Johnson.
3. What reasons does source 4.6.2 offer for the South Vietnamese refusal to be involved in elections after the defeat of the French? What do you think of these reasons?
4. Explain Diem's unpopularity and Ho's popularity.
5. In your own words describe the purposes of the 'strategic hamlet' policy. (Refer to source 5.18). What do you think are the negative and positive aspects of it? What might have been the outcomes of this plan?
6. Explain what source 4.6.7 is showing. Is there any evidence in the other sources in this section that might support or contradict the cartoonist's attitude?
7. Why were America, China and the Soviet Union involved in the war between North and South Vietnam? What are some reasons against such involvement? Why hasn't the communist expansion called the 'domino theory' continued? Discuss.
8. What basic military tactics were used by the Americans and communists during the war? What comment can you make about the effectiveness of these tactics?
9. Individually rank in order of importance the reasons for the communist victory in Vietnam. Then compare your reasons with those of your classmates. Is it possible to say that there were key reasons behind the American defeat?

Communication: *Looking at films*

There are numerous documentaries, films and web sites on the Vietnam War. Watch the film *Platoon* or browse the web.

- What are the key issues covered?
- Can you see any anti-war or pro-defence bias of the producers?
- How are the South and North Vietnamese and foreigners portrayed?
- What went on in Vietnam immediately after the war?

WHY DID AUSTRALIANS FIGHT IN VIETNAM?

From 1962 until 1972 Australia was involved in the war in Vietnam. Approximately 47 000 Australian men and a large number of women served there. The decision to commit troops to the conflict centred on the fear of communism. The North Korean invasion of South Korea in 1950 had been viewed as a communist threat to democracy. Australia's commitment of troops to the United States and United Nations forces fighting in Korea was a stand against Chinese communism as it thrust southwards. The United States was also a powerful ally, providing Australia with protection in case of attack. Led by Prime Minister Robert Menzies, the conservative politicians built a more secure position for Australia 'under the US wing'. The two main alliance agreements establishing Australian security were:

- *the* **ANZUS** *Agreement of 1951*. Australia, New Zealand and the United States agreed to come to one another's aid in the event of attack.
- *the* **SEATO** *Treaty of 1954*. The South-East Asia Collective Defence Treaty provided for defensive action to be taken in the event of an attack on the United States, Britain, France, Australia, New Zealand, Thailand or Pakistan. South Vietnam, Cambodia and Laos were also guaranteed protection under the treaty's security arrangements.

The Korean War had reinforced the sense of a massive, powerful communist system but had also been a big step in securing a firm alliance for Australia with the United States.

Source 4.7.1

'At the Quartermaster's Store'.

Opposition to Australian involvement in Korea was expressed in cartoons like this in the *Bulletin*, 1950. The Prime Minister, Robert Menzies, is depicted as having given all our supplies to the United States.

Source 4.7.2

Menzies explains the Australian government's position on Australia's involvement in the Korean conflict.

> **We are for peace. We do not understand aggression, but we will resist it with all we have and are. We are, with all our imperfections, a Christian nation, believing in man's brotherhood, anxious to live at peace with our neighbours . . . We do not seek to tell another country how to live or how it shall govern itself. We intervene in no domestic dispute. But just as we seek the deep still waters of universal peace, so we know from bitter experience that the waves of war sweep right around the world.**
>
> R. G. Menzies quoted in P. Joske, *Sir Robert Menzies 1894–1978; A New Informal Memoir*, Angus & Robertson, Sydney, 1978, p. 27.

In 1951, Menzies had warned Australians to be prepared for a war against Soviet communists within three years. In August of that year, compulsory military training and universal **conscription** were introduced. The possibility of communism spreading to Australia from Asia was regarded with increasing seriousness as political change came to the region. In 1955, Australian troops were sent to Malaya to assist the British against communist guerilla forces. In March 1960, President Sukarno claimed Dutch-controlled western Papua New Guinea for Indonesia. Strong communist influences in the Indonesian government gave rise to a sense of threat and communist aggression close to Australian territory.

The outbreak of war in Vietnam was seen as further communist aggression. It was a conflict similar to that in Korea from 1950 to 1953. A country divided between communist north and capitalist south had been brought to civil war.

Australia feared the domino effect, so the decision to send Australian troops to fight in Vietnam was not surprising given the belief that 'the takeover of South Vietnam would be a direct military threat to Australia'.

Source 4.7.3

'Oh, we're here because we were invited—how about you?'

President Sukarno is portrayed as an intruder in Malaysia in this cartoon in the *Sydney Morning Herald*, 21 April 1964.

Source 4.7.4

THE AUSTRALIAN

OVER 65,000 COPIES SOLD DAILY

WE SAY

SEE PAGE 8

MENZIES SAYS IT – WE FIGHT IN VIETNAM

First Battalion to be flown out

DRAFTEES MAY HAVE TO GO, TOO

THANKS FROM LBJ

MOVES TOWARDS AGREEMENT

The war yesterday

HALF-FULL HOUSE HEARS NEWS

BOOST TO SEATO

LATE NEWS

The front page of the *Australian*, 30 April 1965

Source 4.7.5

On 29 April 1965 Prime Minister Robert Menzies announces Australian involvement in Vietnam.

There can be no doubt of the gravity of the situation in South Vietnam. There is ample evidence to show that with the support of the North Vietnamese and other Communist powers, the Viet Cong has been preparing on a more substantial scale than hitherto insurgency action to destroy South Vietnamese Government control, and to disrupt by violence the life of the local people ... We have not, of course, come to this decision without the closest attention to the question of defence priorities. We do not and must not overlook the point that our alliances, as well as providing guarantees and assurances for our security, make demands upon us ... Assessing all this, it is our judgement that the decision to commit a battalion in South Vietnam represents the most useful additional contribution which we can make to the defence of the region at this time. The takeover of South Vietnam would be a direct military threat to Australia ...

***Commonwealth Parliamentary Debates,* House of Representatives, 29 April 1965, vol. 45, pp. 1060–1.**

Activities

Check your understanding

1. When was Australia involved in the war in Vietnam?
2. What were the two main alliance agreements that established Australian security?
3. What did Menzies believe Australia would have to face in the 1950s?
4. Why was Australia concerned about developments in Indonesia?
5. What was the similarity between the conflict in Vietnam and the conflict in Korea?

Investigation: *Using a range of sources*

1. A quartermaster is an army officer in charge of rations, clothes etc. What does source 4.7.1 suggest about our relationship with America?
2. How does the Prime Minister's speech in source 4.7.2 seek to justify Australian troops being sent to Korea?
3. How does source 4.7.3 contrast the Australian military presence in Malaysia with that of Indonesia?
4. In 1965, the Prime Minister had to convince Australians that troops should be sent overseas. Using sources 4.7.4 and 4.7.5, explain the argument presented by Menzies for sending Australian troops to Vietnam.
5. Use the information from the text, sources and your own library research to write an essay that answers the question: How did Australia respond to the Cold War?

'SAVE OUR SONS' — CONSCRIPTION AND ANTI-WAR PROTESTS

Debate about the wisdom of our involvement in Vietnam raged from the day that the government announced Australia's commitment to the war effort. As the years passed, the nation grew more divided between the anti-war movement and government supporters. Australia's anti-war movement was strongly connected to protests against conscription, or 'National Service' as it was called. In the years since Australia's Federation, conscription had existed in some form for 42 years.

Conscription was a controversial issue during World War I and continued to arouse passions during the height of the Vietnam War. In 1950, Menzies had introduced a limited form of conscription requiring three months of full-time training and home service. This system was abandoned in 1958, only to be reintroduced in 1964. When they reached their 20th birthday, all males had to register for National Service. Conscripts were chosen by a birth date lottery to serve for a period of two years. Men in this age bracket had approximately a one in ten chance of being selected.

In 1966, the Prime Minister, Harold Holt, announced that conscripts would be sent to fight in Vietnam. This was the first time conscripts had been sent to fight overseas during peacetime. In May 1966, the first conscripted soldier was killed in action. Early protests against conscription had come from religious groups and members of the Australian Communist Party. Conscription soon became a focus of the anti-war movement, with protest organisations urging men to not register and to resist the call-up, or 'draft'. Under particular conditions, exemptions from National Service could be granted. If a person could prove he was a **pacifist** he could lodge a conscientious objection to service. The consequence for others who refused to be conscripted was a two-year jail sentence.

Over the period of the Vietnam War, a wide range of groups organised protests against the continuation of the conflict. Youth Against Conscription and Save Our Sons were formed in 1964. While still a minority movement, the protest against the war in Vietnam became more

Source 4.8.1

An interview with one of the founding members of Save Our Sons, Jean McLean, shows how and why the protest movement grew in Australia.

I convened the first meeting of SOS ... The issue of being against the war came later. These [women] were mainly against conscription as such ... Our aims were that we were against conscription for overseas service ... SOS was mainly a women's group ... at its height we had 500 people on our mailing list in Victoria and we had many more supporters ... Some joined because they were politically aware, some because they were worried about their sons, and there were some like me with very young children but who objected to the whole idea of conscription ... Every month we were at the barracks. We had to get there at some ungodly hour like 5 a.m. for the intakes, and then we'd march around with our flag and wearing 'Save Our Sons' sashes. We got continuous coverage in the media for eight years for doing that.

Our first arrest was under By-law 418. This was at the Richmond barracks and occurred because we were becoming effective ... By-law 418 was a Melbourne City Council by-law which said you weren't allowed to hand out printed information on the street. It had been on the statute books for a hundred years and nobody had ever been arrested under it. They started with us. We used to stand in protest at the City Square after our monthly meetings, and they started arresting us there for handing out leaflets in the street. Of my twenty-seven arrests altogether, about seventeen of them were for breaking By-law 418. We just kept on and on making our protest, and they kept on arresting us.

My other ten arrests were for things like filling in false registration forms which we would do outside the post office every intake when people had to register. We even had a 'Fill a Falsi' party here one night which Channel 7 and Channel 9 covered while we all sat here filling in false forms. By-law 418 was in the end repealed. This was a campaign that we stuck to, refusing to budge on and we won it.

Interview with Jean McLean, in B. Gilligan, *The Struggle for Freedom*, McGraw-Hill, Sydney 1997.

extreme and widespread after the 1966 election and the return of the Liberal Party/Country Party coalition to power. The Labor leader, Arthur Calwell, continued to voice his party's opposition to Australia's involvement in Vietnam. By 1967, the Monash University Labor Club was collecting money for the North Vietnamese war effort and burning draft registration cards had become common. The government took a tough stand on people avoiding the draft and this increased popular protest. Draft resister support groups were established and a lively 'Don't register' campaign was begun. Anger over conscription was rapidly turning into disillusionment with the nature of the war in Vietnam and Australia's continued commitment to it.

Source 4.8.2

Save Our Sons was an early protest group representing a broad section of the Australian public.

Source 4.8.3

'Mum!! Where did you spring from?!'

This Rigby cartoon in the *Daily Mirror*, 1966, supported the view that National Service was a valuable and character-building experience for young Australian men.

Activities

Check your understanding

1. What was National Service and how was it connected to the anti-war movement?
2. How were conscripts chosen?
3. What happened to those who refused conscription?
4. What sort of protest groups emerged in the 1960s?

Investigation: *Protesting against war*

1. (a) Using source 4.8.1, identify the activities in which the Save Our Sons group participated.
   (b) What would have been the aim of their protest and how effective do you think it would have been?
2. What does source 4.8.2 indicate about the membership of the anti-war and anti-conscription groups of the 1960s? (Comment on the sex, age group and dress of the protesters.)
3. (a) How has the Rigby cartoon (source 4.8.3) portrayed the young Australian servicemen?
   (b) Using source 4.8.3 as evidence, explain what you think the cartoonist's attitude to conscription and the SOS would have been.

Researching and communicating: *Designing cartoons*

Cartoons were widely used by both pro- and anti-war groups during the Vietnam War. Imagine you have been appointed as a newspaper cartoonist. Design a series of cartoons expressing how different groups of Australians felt about our involvement in Vietnam. You will need to use the library to find a broader range of such cartoons to help you with your ideas.

THE VOICE OF THE VIETNAM VETERAN

On 3 October 1987, the 'Welcome Home' parade for Vietnam veterans took place in Sydney. The welfare of the veterans had been ignored after 1972 and so the parade was a long overdue recognition of their service to Australia. Many of the soldiers who fought in Vietnam had experienced difficulties settling back into civilian life, for a range of reasons.

- Vietnam veterans had come home to hostility rather than to expressions of gratitude.
- Many veterans were left untreated for 'post-traumatic stress disorder' (known as 'battle fatigue' in previous wars).
- Drugs had been widely available in Vietnam and so some veterans had developed drug-related illnesses.
- Many veterans were exposed to dangerous chemicals in the **defoliation** campaign, leading to serious medical problems.

Source 4.9.1

Vietnam veterans had reported a wide range of well-documented illnesses by the 1970s.

> **I've got rashes under the arms, groin. I get headaches all the time ... Flashes of temper. It's like a boiler without a pressure-release valve. It builds up and builds up until it explodes ... I explode. I can't mix with people. I've got no sex drive ... I was married twice. My first wife had quite a few miscarriages ... I used to pick on the kids, isolate myself from their lives, behave irrationally until it got to a stage where they just couldn't take anymore. Unfortunately I realised the problem just a little too late.**
>
> Ron Witty, quoted in S. Rintoul, *Ashes of Vietnam: Australian Voices*, Heinemann, Melbourne, 1987, p. 208.

Australia had been unwilling to deal with the problems of these returned soldiers of an unpopular war. In 1980, the Vietnam Veterans' Association of Australia was established to lobby governments for financial compensation and political recognition for its members. Veterans were reporting various disabilities but were still receiving no government support from the Department of Veterans' Affairs.

'Agent Orange' was the most commonly used chemical mixture in Vietnam for defoliation. It was absorbed by the leaves of plants and would enter the water system. By 1967, an estimated 20 per cent of jungles, 36 per cent of mangroves and 42 per cent of food crops had been destroyed in Vietnam. The main aim of this defoliation was to deprive the Viet Cong **guerillas** of cover. The RAAF also sprayed the Australian bases three times every week with various insecticides. In the late 1970s, Agent Orange was linked with three possible disabilities: cancer, birth abnormalities and toxic brain dysfunction.

The Vietnam Veterans' Association put pressure on the Federal Government to establish an inquiry into Agent Orange. In 1983, the Hawke Labor Government appointed a royal commission to investigate the effects of the chemical agents used in Vietnam. After hearing from the veterans, the government, the chemical companies and the scientists, the commission released its findings. It reported that there was insufficient evidence to prove that the veterans' disabilities were caused by chemical defoliation. The commission did, however, find that the war had left veterans with significant psychological problems entitling them to government financial assistance.

Source 4.9.2

AWM — COA/66/0877/VN

Photograph taken in 1966 of Australian soldiers helping their wounded comrade during the Vietnam War

For the following nine years, the veterans lobbied to have the findings of the Evatt Commission overturned. In October 1994, the Labor government finally acknowledged Agent Orange as the direct cause of cancer and other illness suffered by the Vietnam veterans. American veterans were also successful in their legal action

Source 4.9.3

In 1994, the McLennan Report cited medical evidence supporting the claim that Agent Orange was responsible for the serious health problems veterans suffered.

Vietnam vets hail cancer decision

by Ebru Yaman and Cameron Stewart

Vietnam veterans yesterday applauded the Federal Government's landmark decision to accept a link between Agent Orange and cancer but said more needed to be done to recognise other war-related cancers.

The Government has announced it will accept the findings of an independent medical study which found clear links between a range of cancers and exposure to herbicides such as Agent Orange.

The decision, revealed exclusively in *The Australian* yesterday, is a key breakthrough in the 25-year battle by the Vietnam veterans to obtain government recognition of the cancer-producing effects of Agent Orange.

The move means more than 600 cancer-stricken Vietnam veterans will be eligible for disability payments within twelve months at an estimated cost to the Government of about $4 million.

The president of the Vietnam Veterans Association of Australia, Mr John Printz, described the decision as a major victory.

'It is a very positive development for veterans, many of whom have had to suffer the turmoil, the strain and the stress of trying to obtain compensation for their disabilities . . . they were kicked in the guts for years about (Agent Orange),' Mr Printz said . . .

The Minister for Veterans Affairs, Mr Sciacca said veterans would be able to lodge compensation claims within months for the effects of exposure to herbicides.

He did not expect a flood of claims but would not care if 'thousands' of people sought compensation because it was important that all veterans received a fair deal.

A spokeswoman for Mr Sciacca said widows of Vietnam veterans who died of the nominated cancers would be eligible for a widow's pension if their former spouse had been exposed to herbicides in Vietnam.

The Government's decision to recognise the link between cancer and Agent Orange overturns the findings of the 1985 royal commission which concluded that Agent Orange was not a reason for the unusually high cancer rates among veterans.

The decision to recognise a link follows the Government's acceptance of the findings of an independent Australian report written by Professor Robert MacLennan, of the Queensland Institute for Medical Research, and Professor Peter Smith, of the Royal Children's Hospital in Melbourne . . .

'This is not only a matter for justice. It is and has been a matter of life and death for these "forgotten veterans", the RSL's acting president, Mr John Bailey said.

A Melbourne solicitor and Vietnam veteran who specialises in veterans' compensation claims, Mr Geoffrey Tobin, said the Federal Government's admission of the cancer link was like 'the end of the war'.

'In the 70s everyone said we were looking for an excuse to answer our own inadequacies. The Government denied there was an increase of cancer in Vietnam veterans,' Mr Tobin said . . .

'If we had had this admission 10 years ago, the pain and anger some of these blokes feel would have been a lot less,' he said.

'If it had been earlier I really believe we would have saved the lives of some of the 2000 Australian Vietnam veterans who have committed suicide.'

Weekend Australian, 8–9 October 1994, p. 4.

against seven chemical companies. A multimillion-dollar American fund was then established to help veterans and their families.

The work of the Vietnam Veterans' Association in gaining recognition for returned soldiers is an example of how citizens of a democracy can directly influence government. Veterans felt their particular needs and wishes were being ignored by successive Australian governments. The Veterans' Association is an 'interest group' established to influence government decisions, not to form a government.

Activities

Check your understanding

1. Why has the experience of many Vietnam veterans been so difficult?
2. Why was the Vietnam Veterans' Association established?
3. What is Agent Orange?
4. How successful has the Association been in securing recognition for the plight of its members?

Investigation: *Vietnam veterans*

1. In what ways would the medical problems described in source 4.9.1 have an impact on a veteran's family life?
2. Look at source 4.9.2. What qualities can you see in these men and what difficulties do you think they would have faced?
3. Read the source 4.9.3 account of the McLennan Report. In what way did this report establish the success of the Vietnam Veterans' Association as an 'interest group'.
4. There are many occasions when ordinary people feel that direct involvement and action is necessary to influence or change government decisions. The work of the Vietnam Veterans' Association is a clear example of this.

   Research and write a report of 600–800 words about the work and achievements of the Vietnam Veterans' Association. Your report should discuss what the objectives of the association were, how the association gathered support and used the media, and what the outcome of the work of this interest group has been.

THE MUSIC OF PROTEST

The 1960s were turbulent times. It is often referred to as the 'youth decade', as the young questioned their parent's values and ideas and challenged their government. The tension and conflict within society was nowhere more evident than at the time of the war in Vietnam. With the cultural barriers broken in the 1950s, many young Australians now identified with the values, politics and culture of the United States.

The United States of the 1960s was a country of civil rights movements, women's liberation, concern for the environment, and the growth of political awareness. Opposition to the war in Vietnam had been strong from the beginning, particularly on university campuses. The serious issues and emotions of the time were expressed through the protest music of this 'flower power' generation. Bob Dylan's 'The Times They Are a Changin' became the protest anthem for a generation that had found many causes for which to fight.

Bob Dylan, an American folk singer, played for the first time in public at the Gaslight café in Greenwich Village, New York, in 1961. Within a few years he had captured a huge audience with his songs of protest and anger about the major issues of the 1960s. His songs' strong political messages expressed the sense of youthful alienation from the **establishment**. For example, his song 'A Hard Rain's a Gonna Fall' dealt with the threat of nuclear war.

By the mid-1960s the American 'hippy' movement was carrying the social protest message all over the world. Born in San Francisco, the movement rejected the conventional values and lifestyle of the adult generation. Hippies wore flowers in their hair and colourful clothes from around the world. They preached peace, love and understanding and turned to Eastern philosophy for their spiritual guidance. As in the United States, the Australian hippies were usually from middle-class, well-educated backgrounds. Their beliefs were a reaction to the brutality of the war in Vietnam.

FACT*file*

The largest gathering of young people in the twentieth century occurred on a farm at Woodstock, New York State, in the United States. It was a music festival attended by over 400 000 people and it took place over three days in 1969. Despite the heavy rain and poor organisation it featured the 'Who's Who' of the rock generation and has come to represent the 1960s American youth culture.

Source 4.10.1

Bob Dylan, 1969, Isle of Wight
AP XEN NY329

Source 4.10.2

The stage musical *Hair* followed the story of a young man conscripted to fight in Vietnam. This extremely successful musical also came to represent much of the culture of the 1960s, dealing with a wide range of issues including censorship, nudity, drug taking and the hippie experience.

Source 4.10.3

'The step's the same, on the moon or a mine . . .'

The cartoonist Rigby summed up a decade of conflict and change when he commented, in the *Daily Mirror*, 1969, on Neil Armstrong becoming the first man to walk on the moon.

The popular culture of the 1960s had a profound effect on Australia. Community attitudes were more tolerant of individual self-expression by the 1970s. People had been exposed to a broader range of ideas about personal freedom and fulfilment. Some Australians chose alternative lifestyles at places such as Nimbin, in northern New South Wales. The 1960s experience left most people with an understanding of some of the less competitive ways of living, learning and working.

As the 1960s came to a close, the world watched in amazement as American astronauts walked on the moon. It was an event witnessed by millions of people on their television screens. In 1964, Canadian academic Marshall McLuhan had predicted that satellite communications would shrink the world into one large global village where television would dominate as the means of communication. By the 1970s, we were watching remote events as if they were happening in our own part of the world. American television broke through Australia's sense of geographic isolation. With America's mass communications, trade, financial investment, politics and popular culture, we had entered the modern, post-war world.

Activities

Check your understanding

1. Why was the 1960s often referred to as the 'youth decade'?
2. Why did Bob Dylan become an important figure in the protest movement?
3. Why was the 'hippy' movement such a break with conventional society?
4. How did Woodstock become more than just a rock concert in the minds of the 1960s generation?
5. Mass communication has had a powerful effect on the post–World War II world. How can its importance be explained?

Investigation: *The 1960s*

1. The singer and songwriter Bob Dylan became a leader of the 1960s protest movement. Look at source 4.10.1 and explain how Dylan represented the image of 1960s youth.
2. The American musical *Hair* had a long run in Australia. How are the values and culture of the American hippy movement evident in the clothing and body language shown in source 4.10.2?
3. Look at sources 4.10.1 and 4.10.2, and explain how you think Australian parents in the 1960s would have reacted to the new ideas, values and fashion.
4. In what way did the Rigby cartoon in source 4.10.3 attempt to draw Australia's attention to the conflict and change of the 1960s?
5. Go to your library to locate more information about the music and fashion of the 1960s. Write an essay on the topic, 'In what ways did American music and fashion influence social change in Australian society'?
6. Locate some more of the music produced by the moratorium generation of musicians. Design a CD cover for a collection of protest songs from the 1960s.

THE FIRST MOON LANDING — A SMALL STEP AND A GIANT LEAP

THE SPACE RACE

In the 1960s, space exploration was dominated by the efforts of American and Soviet astronauts and their governments. For the United States and the Soviet Union, this was another aspect of the competition to be the world superpower. Each was determined to show the world that it was the leader in space exploration and achievement.

It seemed for some years that the Soviet Union was winning. In October 1957, it launched the first artificial satellite, *Sputnik 1*. Less than a month later, *Sputnik 2* went into orbit carrying Laika, a dog, who went down in history as the first living space traveller. In 1959, the Soviet Union launched *Luna 1*, the first spacecraft to leave the Earth's gravity. On 12 April 1961, Yuri Gagarin in his spacecraft *Vostok 1*, became the first human in space. Valentina Tereshkova became the first woman in space when she orbited the Earth 48 times in *Vostok 6* in June 1963. In 1966, *Luna 9* became the first craft to land on the moon and send back pictures of its surface.

The United States responded to these achievements with increased spending on space projects and the establishment of NASA (National Aeronautics and Space Administration). On 31 January 1958, the United States launched its first satellite, *Explorer 1*. This was followed in March 1958 by the *Vanguard 1* satellite, which found that the Earth was not round but pear-shaped. The voyage of the spacecraft *Mercury*, on 5 May 1961, made Alan Shepard the first American astronaut to travel into space. On 25 May 1961, the American president at the time, John F. Kennedy, made a public commitment to land an American on the moon by 1970.

The American public reacted with excitement and enthusiasm for this idea. Project Apollo, as it came to be known, would prove American leadership in space technology. In the mid 1960s, American satellites sent back detailed pictures of the moon's surface. On 24 and 25 December 1968, *Apollo 8* orbited the moon and then returned successfully to Earth. Early in 1969, *Apollo 9* tested the lunar module in orbit around the Earth and *Apollo 10* tested descent by going down to only 15 kilometres above the moon's surface. The stage was set to fulfil the commitment which Kennedy had made eight years earlier.

Source 4.11.1

Photograph showing Buzz Aldrin on the moon next to the *Apollo 11* lunar module, *Eagle*

THE *EAGLE* HAS LANDED

Apollo 11 took off from the Kennedy Space Center in Florida at 9.32 a.m. on 16 July 1969. The crew comprised Neil Armstrong (commander), Edwin 'Buzz' Aldrin (lunar module pilot) and Michael Collins (the command module pilot). Their task was to land on the moon, collect samples from its surface and return safely.

On 20 July 1969 the *Apollo 11* lunar module, *Eagle*, with Armstrong and Aldrin aboard, slowly descended towards the moon's surface. At 4.18 p.m. EST it touched down in a large crater called the Sea of Tranquillity. The lunar commander, Neil Armstrong, radioed back to Earth 'The Eagle has landed'. At the same time, Michael Collins orbited overhead in the Apollo command module which was to take the crew back to Earth.

Around the world people watched these events on television and waited for the moment when the first human would step onto the moon's surface. A few hours later, Commander Neil Armstrong climbed down the module ladder to the moon below saying the now famous words, 'That's one small step for man, one giant leap for mankind'.

Over the next 22 hours, Armstrong and Aldrin planted a US flag, collected samples of soil and rock, set up scientific experiments and walked and jumped in gravity that has only one-sixth the strength of the Earth's gravity. On 21 July, they returned to the command module for the journey back to Earth with its pilot, Collins. The three astronauts became international heroes, in demand as guest speakers and as the focus of parades celebrating their achievement.

THE LEGACY

The 1969 moon landing established the United States as the most technologically advanced nation in the world. For the first time people saw what their planet looked like from a distance. This helped to make people more interested in protecting its environment for their own benefit and the benefit of future generations.

Over the next three and a half years, there were five more US landing missions on the moon, each of which spent more time there. Astronauts collected soil and rock samples from different areas, took photographs, set up more experiments to learn about the moon's environment and drove around the moon's surface in a Moonrover.

Humans remain fascinated with their solar system and its universe. The old rivalry between the United States and the former Soviet Union (now the CIS) has been replaced by a new era of cooperation, with astronauts from each nation meeting together in space and working together on scientific experiments. In the 1990s, astronauts made frequent trips on the US space shuttle to spend time living and working with astronauts on the Russian space station *Mir* — the Russian word for 'world' or 'peace'.

FACT*file*

- Project Apollo cost US$25.4 billion (close to $100 billion in today's money).
- As the moon has no rain and no wind, the footprints which Armstrong and Aldrin left in the lunar soil should remain there for millions of years.

Activities

Check your understanding

1. Create a timeline to show the main developments in space exploration in the period 1958–69. List the US events on one side and the Soviet Union's on the other.
2. What kinds of rivalry existed between the former Soviet Union and the United States during this time?
3. Why were people so excited by the thought of a human landing on the moon?
4. What did Neil Armstrong mean when he spoke of 'one small step . . . one giant leap'? (*Note*: Armstrong's intention had been to say 'a man'.)
5. Why would many people today criticise Neil Armstrong's choice of the words 'man' and 'mankind'? What does this indicate about how attitudes have changed since 1969?
6. In what ways were the responses to the moon landing different from the responses to Copernicus' announcement of a heliocentric solar system? What does this tell us about differences in the experiences and attitudes of people in the sixteenth century compared to the experiences and attitudes of people in the twentieth century?

Communication: *Thought bubbles*

Look at the photograph in source 4.11.1. Create a thought bubble to indicate what Buzz Aldrin might have felt at this moment in his life.

Investigation: *Further research*

1. Use an atlas (and human help if necessary) to locate the splashdown area for the return of *Apollo II*. It was at 13° 19′ N and 169° 9′ W at 12.50 p.m. on 24 July 1969.
2. Find out the name used to describe the period of competition between the former Soviet Union and the United States.

4.12 Meeting the outcomes

ANALYSE THE IMPACT OF SIGNIFICANT EVENTS AND IDEAS IN SHAPING WORLD HISTORY IN THE TWENTIETH CENTURY.

Identify significant events and ideas which shaped world history in the twentieth century.

Fill in the gaps in these sentences on Vietnam using the words from the list.

(a) The __________ were the first Europeans to begin trading actively in Vietnam.

(b) By __________, most of Vietnam had come under the colonial rule of the French.

(c) The Vietnamese had for centuries used __________ tactics to fight foreign invaders.

(d) The Communist Party of Indo-China was established in 1930 by __________.

(e) During World War II the Vietnamese had to fight a new enemy — __________.

(f) After World War II, the Vietnamese overcame the French in a decisive battle at __________.

(g) The United States became involved in Vietnam because it feared the spread of __________.

(h) After the Americans began to withdraw from Vietnam the communist forces defeated the South Vietnamese army and claimed total victory in __________.

Communism, Ho Chi Minh, 1882, 1975, Dien Bien Phu, Japan, guerilla, French.

EXPLAIN THE KEY CHANGES IN SOCIAL AND POLITICAL ATTITUDES AND VALUES IN MODERN WESTERN SOCIETY.

Explain how the values of particular societies changed as a result of significant events.

1. What was the Truman Doctrine in response to? (4.1)
2. How did the Cold War divide the world in two? (4.2)
3. Look at the cartoon opposite.
   (a) What do you think the spider represents?
   (b) What is the significance of the web?
   (c) What does this cartoon say about Australian values in the 1950s?
4. How did American society change in the 1960s? (4.10)

Examine the ways in which advances in technology affected other areas, such as health, medicine, transport, education.

1. What role did technology play in the Cold War? (4.3)
2. In what way did changes to communications technology change Australia in the 1970s? (4.10)
3. Why did the USA and USSR undertake a space race during the late 1950s and the 1960s? (4.11)
4. Does this rivalry exist today? (4.11)

Source 4.12.1

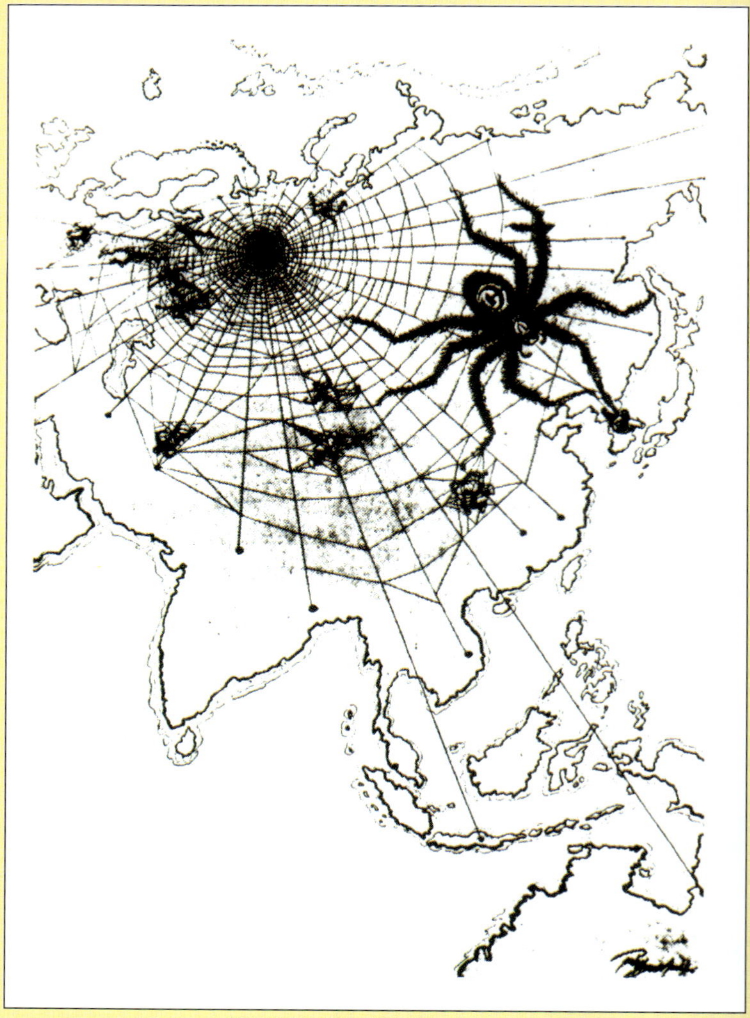

'The Spreading Web'

An image of the growing power of communism spreading across the world, from the *Bulletin*, July 1950

Evaluate the effect of significant events and ideas on groups.

Look carefully at the sources that follow to complete the following paragraphs:

(a) It is 1965 and I am the Australian Prime Minister. I have just ordered that the first battalion of soldiers be sent to Vietnam. I have done this because . . .

(b) I am the leader of the Labor Party, the Opposition to the government in 1965. I don't believe the decision to send troops to Vietnam is a wise one. I think this because . . .

(c) I am a university student involved in a march against the Vietnam war. I have friends who have been conscripted. I am against the whole idea of conscription because . . .

Source 4.12.2

On 29 April 1965 Prime Minister Robert Menzies announces Australian involvement in Vietnam.

There can be no doubt of the gravity of the situation in South Vietnam. There is ample evidence to show that with the support of the North Vietnamese and other Communist powers, the Viet Cong has been preparing on a more substantial scale than hitherto insurgency action to destroy South Vietnamese Government control, and to disrupt by violence the life of the local people ... We have not, of course, come to this decision without the closest attention to the question of defence priorities. We do not and must not overlook the point that our alliances, as well as providing guarantees and assurances for our security, make demands upon us ... Assessing all this, it is our judgement that the decision to commit a battalion in South Vietnam represents the most useful additional contribution which we can make to the defence of the region at this time. The takeover of South Vietnam would be a direct military threat to Australia ...

Commonwealth Parliamentary Debates, House of Representatives, 29 April 1965, vol. 45, pp. 1060–1.

Source 4.12.4

Opposition Labor Party leader Arthur Calwell's response, explaining why Australia should not be in Vietnam

We do not think it is a wise decision. We do not think it is a timely decision. We do not think it is a right decision. We do not think it will help the fight against Communism. On the contrary, we believe it will harm that fight in the long term. We do not believe it will promote the welfare of the people of Vietnam. On the contrary, we believe it will prolong and deepen the suffering of that unhappy people so that Australia's very name may become a term of reproach among them ... the Government's decision rests on three false assumptions: an erroneous view of the nature of the war in Vietnam; a failure to understand the nature of the communist challenge; and a false notion as to the interests of America and her allies ... Australia's aim should have been to help end the war, not extend it. We have now lost all power to help end it ...

Commonwealth Parliamentary Debates, House of Representatives, 4 May 1965, vol. 46, pp. 1102–7.

Source 4.12.3

Vietnam Moratorium march in Melbourne, May 1972

Chapter 5

KEY ISSUES FOR MODERN AUSTRALIA

LEARNING *outcomes*

- Describe change in modern Australian society.
- Appreciate that Australia is now a multicultural society.
- Discover how technology has affected transport.
- Analyse how significant events such as the Franklin Dam proposal affected groups in Australia.
- Identify why Aboriginal and Torres Strait Islander communities were denied basic rights.
- Examine how Aboriginal and Torres Strait Islander communities fought for rights.

INTRODUCTION

*Australia in the late twentieth century was a very different nation from the one that emerged as a **federation** in 1901. In 1901, Australia was characterised by a predominantly Anglo-Celtic culture: close ties with Britain, the 'mother country', strong religious allegiances and divisions, a **Eurocentric** outlook, and a desire to be 'white'. Popular images of the time focused on 'typical' Australians as bush-dwellers who were resourceful, independent — and good mates.*

By the late twentieth century, Australians found themselves living in an age of uncertainty. A gender revolution had redefined the roles and responsibilities of men and women, and information technology was making dramatic changes to people's lives. New social, economic, political and cultural bonds had been established with the world beyond Britain.

Australians sought to define their cultural identity, their spiritual and ethical values and to determine the type of government best suited to their society. They debated whether to become a republic or remain a constitutional monarchy.

By the late 1990s, Australia was showing itself willing to face some of the issues which it had avoided for nearly 200 years — reconciliation between indigenous and non-indigenous Australians and a realistic appraisal of its position within the Asia–Pacific region.

GLOSSARY

autonomy: self-government, independence
charter: a written document of rights and privileges
commercial: to do with commerce, business
compensation: the task of making up for some misfortune or wrongdoing
conservation: the process of preserving something either by keeping it in its existing state, restoring it to its original state or adapting it to a new use which still protects its cultural significance
Constitution: the document that specifies the powers, duties and procedures of the Commonwealth Parliament
constitutional monarchy: a form of government which has a hereditary ruler as its head of state and where the powers of that ruler are limited by the rules of the nation's constitution
democracy: a government ruled by the people through those they have elected to represent them
digitisation: conversion of analog information into digital form
diplomacy: official government negotiations between countries
download: to transfer data from one computer to another
egalitarianism: a belief in equality for all people
Eurocentric: seeing Europe as providing the cultural focus
federation: a system where powers and responsibilities are shared between a central national government and state governments
Federation: the uniting of the six self-governing colonies of Australia to form a union of states under a central government on 1 January 1901
green bans: the refusal of building workers to engage in work that would result in the destruction of property judged to be of historical or environmental significance
head of state: the person who is the nation's ceremonial leader. This person can be given power to make independent political decisions or may have no political power at all.
heritage: all things which we have inherited from previous generations and which we value, including the events, traditions, influences and experiences that have shaped our present reality
honours system: the civil and military awards of honours and ranks approved by the sovereign
indigenous: the term used to describe the 'first peoples' of a particular country. Since the 1980s the federal government has defined Australia's indigenous peoples as 'a person of Aboriginal or Torres Strait Islander descent who identifies as Aboriginal or Torres Strait Islander and is accepted by the community with which he or she is associated'.
land rights: indigenous peoples' claims to land they occupy or used to occupy
Mabo: the short name for the High Court case *Mabo and Others v. the State of Queensland* (1992)
multicultural: a term that describes a society made up of peoples of different cultural and racial backgrounds
native title: a legal right to land based on recognition of indigenous peoples' traditional and spiritual ownership of it dating back to when their ancestors first came to the land
parliamentary government: system of government in which citizens elect representatives to parliament
piecework rates: payment based on how many pieces of work are produced; usually a fixed amount per item
pluralist society: society that is diverse in nature and membership
poverty line: the lowest level of income at which people can maintain an adequate standard of living
reconciliation: bringing cooperation and harmony to groups who have opposed one another
referendum: a vote in which the people are asked whether they agree to a proposed law or change to a law. In Australia, there must be a referendum before any change to the Commonwealth Constitution.
representative democracy: a political system with a government which rules on behalf of the people and which is formed from an elected parliament
republic: a democracy in which the head of state is appointed or elected, rather than inheriting that position
sacred site: a site that is important to the spiritual or cultural beliefs of indigenous peoples
self-determination: the right of a group to choose and control its destiny and development
Stolen Generation: the name given to the victims of the practice of forcibly removing Aboriginal and Torres Strait Islander children from their parents and families
***terra nullius*:** Latin term meaning 'the land of no-one'. According to eighteenth century law, a land which had no owner could be lawfully taken over by the people of another land.
tradition: a belief or custom that has been handed down through generations
treaty: a written document explaining the terms of agreement reached between two groups with regard to friendship, military alliance, a trading relationship or some other factor

5.1 DEVELOPING A MULTICULTURAL SOCIETY

In 1901, 'Australia for the white man' was a commonly heard slogan. Seventy years later, Australia opened its doors to migrants from all ethnic and racial groups and so brought an end to what was commonly called the White Australia Policy. This policy had been a humiliation to Asians and a source of conflict between Australia and its neighbours. It had also been a barrier to our full participation in the trade, politics and culture of our region.

By the 1970s, Australia no longer saw itself as white and British. The national anthem was changed from 'God Save the Queen' to 'Advance Australia Fair'; the British **honours system** was replaced with an Australian honours system and the term 'British subject' was dropped from the Australian passport. In forging this new image, the government was declaring Australia to be multiracial and **multicultural**. It was official recognition of the great post-war migration to Australia from different parts of Europe, the Middle East, South America and Asia. This immigration program had transformed a thinly populated and isolated Australia into a culturally diverse society. By the 1970s, Australia was a nation in which more than a third of its inhabitants were born overseas or were the children of those born overseas. Australians living in the major cities could enjoy films and live entertainment from many different parts of the world, join in festivals of other cultures and eat styles of food from all over the world. Australians from very different cultural and racial backgrounds also shared the pleasure of traditional Australian events like the Melbourne Cup and football grand finals.

In 1977 a **charter** for multicultural Australia was drawn up. This charter identified three basic principles necessary to multiculturalism:

- economic efficiency— the need to maintain and develop the skills and talents of all Australians regardless of their background
- cultural identity — the right of all to express and share their cultural heritage, language and religion
- equality of opportunity — the right of all to equality of treatment and the removal of barriers of race, ethnicity, culture, religion, language, gender or place of birth.

In 1988, Prime Minister Bob Hawke launched the Year of Citizenship. At the launching ceremony, two people were granted the two millionth Australian citizenship. They were Nigel Stoker, a Scotsman who had arrived in Australia in 1984, and Ngoc Anh Nguyen, a Vietnamese medical science student who had arrived as a Vietnamese refugee in 1981. They had been chosen as symbols of our successful and multicultural Australia.

Source 5.1.1

Chinese New Year being celebrated with a dragon dance in Melbourne

Source 5.1.2

In 1987 the Australian government established a committee to look at how future immigration programs could best strengthen our economy and cultural life. The committee was headed by Dr Stephen Fitzgerald. The committee's recommendations received humorous comments in the media.

Activities

Check your understanding

1. In what ways did the Australian image change during the 1970s?
2. Put into your own words the principles identified in 1977 as necessary for multiculturalism.
3. Why do you think Nigel Stoker and Ngoc Anh Nguyen were regarded as symbols of a successful and multicultural Australia?

Communication: *Using images to make a point*

1. Source 5.1.1 captures the popular image of multiculturalism. What other symbols of multiculturalism can you think of in Australia's daily life?
2. Source 5.1.2 is a humorous look at the findings of the Fitzgerald Committee. The committee was set up to examine the relationship between immigration and the social, cultural and economic development of Australia. What comment is the cartoonist making about the committee's recommendations?
3. Source 5.1.3 emphasises the importance of skills as a major consideration in selecting migrants to Australia. Do you think source 5.1.2 is a fair picture of the report's recommendations?
4. Using the recommendations from the report *Immigration: A Commitment to Australia* design your own poster advertising Australia's immigration program to suitable candidates overseas.

Investigation: *Researching migrant groups*

1. Investigate any migrant services in your local community. Gather information about the services available and set up a classroom display.
2. Invite an ethnic community leader to your school to speak to your class about the migrant experience of life in Australia and attitudes towards multiculturalism. Conduct a class brainstorm to help develop prepared questions for your guest.

Source 5.1.3

A summary of some of the main Fitzgerald Report recommendations

- **The existing immigration policy of non-discrimination on grounds of national or ethnic origin, race, sex and religion must continue to be asserted.**
- **150 000 immigrants a year be accepted for the period 1988–89 to 1990–91, and until the Government assesses that it has the program right, more substantial increases should not be contemplated.**
- **The immigration program consist of three categories: Family Migration, Refugee and Humanitarian, and Open.**
- **In the Open category an order of merit approach to immigrant selection be used, taking only the top point scorers from around the world.**
- **The selection of immigrants in the Open category should be based on seven groups of factors, in the following priority order:**
  (1) labour market skills;
  (2) entrepreneurship and special talents;
  (3) age;
  (4) language capacity (with English seen as a priority);
  (5) family support links already in Australia;
  (6) other links with Australia; and
  (7) skills and attributes of spouse.
- **Family Migration be expanded to cover grandparents of Australian citizens. Refugee and Special Humanitarian program to remain at 10 per cent of intake.**
- **Australia gradually disengage itself from Indo-chinese refugee settlement, in line with the diminishing number of refugees.**
- **More emphasis be placed on the value of citizenship, with some consideration given to restricting benefits to non-citizens.**
- **Sponsorship of immigrants be limited to Australian citizens except in the case of spouses, dependent children or refugees.**

***Immigration: A Commitment to Australia*, Committee to Advise on Australia's Immigration Policies, 1988.**

MIGRANTS FROM ASIA — REFUGEES AND NON-REFUGEES

Source 5.2.1

This 1990s cartoon graphically illustrates the impact of economic ruin, war and population growth.

With the end of World War II, the Labor government Minister for Immigration, Arthur Calwell, declared that Australia's first priority was to increase the population. A planned immigration scheme was seen as a way of providing Australia with better defence and more substantial economic growth through a larger work force. During the following 25 years, nearly two million migrants from Britain and Europe came to Australia. In 1973, the Australian immigration policy that used a person's race as part of the selection process ended. With the White Australia Policy dismantled, a planned immigration program from Asia could begin.

Australia's involvement with Asia can be traced back to the days of the early European occupation of this land. After World War II, our relationship with Asia broadened to include a whole range of areas such as trade, investment, education, **diplomacy** and defence. The greatest test of Australia's relationship with Asia was the war in Vietnam. With the 1975 fall of South Vietnam's government in Saigon, the movement of refugees became a major political and humanitarian issue. Australia played an important role in the resettling of Indo-chinese refugees after the Vietnam War. By the end of the 1980s, nearly two million refugees from the Indo-chinese region had fled their war-torn countries. Over 120 000 of them had made their new home in Australia.

Source 5.2.2

Refugees from Vietnam endured life-threatening sea voyages to finally make their way to Australia. These people were rescued in the South China Sea.

The Vietnamese and Cambodian refugees arrived in Australia in much the same way that refugees from the previous war had. Most had been forced to leave all their possessions behind and had been forced to migrate because of politics and the destruction of their homes. Roughly 80 per cent of all the Vietnamese and Cambodians who arrived during these years were refugees who had come to Australia as 'boat people' or through the refugee camps in South-East Asia. The refugees were often of ethnic Chinese descent and feared persecution because of their religious or political beliefs. They had often undertaken perilous sea voyages in overcrowded and unseaworthy boats, facing storms, pirate attacks and starvation on their voyages.

By the end of the 1980s, over 20 per cent of Australia's non-refugee intake of migrants was from Asia. The Australian government encouraged migration from Asia because of the business opportunities it created. Because Asian migration was making Australia more ethnically diverse, this sparked community debate about the future and the benefits of multiculturalism. After World War II the influx of southern European migrants, such as the Greeks and Italians, had altered the character of

Australian society. By 1992 Asian immigrants and their descendants made up 3.5 per cent of the Australian population. The ability of Australians to accept another wave of migration and even greater cultural diversity was questioned.

Source 5.2.3

Refugees often arrived in Australia with little idea of where they were going or what they would find.

I was in the camp over four months. I didn't know anything about Australia except I knew about kangaroos and crocodile. I find out about Australia after I meet the government official. They very friendly.

When I leave the island for a camp in Kuala Lumpur, I know I will go to Australia. They got a small library. I look for the books about Australia but can only find out about New South Wales and about the famous Sydney Opera House.

Then after one month I got listed. I feel the freedom. They got a Boeing 707 for the people travelling from Malaysia to Australia ... Oh, my face shining from tears because I'm very happy.

H. Martin, *Angels and Arrogant Gods: Migration Officers and Migrants Reminisce 1945–85*, AGPS, pp. 105–6.

Source 5.2.4

Journalist John Masanauskas looks at Australia's migrant and refugee intake in 1990 in a global context.

... Consider ... a request by the Soviet Union to resettle in Western Europe two million people living in radiation-contaminated land around Chernobyl — site of the world's worst nuclear power accident.

Suddenly, the prospect of dealing with a couple of hundred Cambodians is looking good. And even 20 000 Chinese students, many of whom are already integrated into Australian life, seem a drop in the ocean compared with the millions of people displaced around the world.

It is the view of Alan Matheson, ethnic liaison officer with the ACTU, that Australia can no longer make immigration and refugee decisions without heeding developments in the rest of the world. According to the latest data, the world has 15 million official refugees, six million people in refugee-like situations and another 18 million displaced within their own countries.

'I think one thing that Europe and North America have discovered is that no country can make isolated decisions,' said Mr Matheson, 'that no country is an island any longer and that it doesn't really matter whether you're a physical island or not.'

Age, 2 July 1990.

Throughout the 1990s, migration remained widely discussed (as, for example, in source 5.2.4). The debate grew to include such issues as overall population targets for our fragile Australian environment, the particular skills we most want in our migrants, the level of English competence required and the balance between family reunion and skills. Whether they be skilled workers, refugees or professionals, approximately half of Australia's migrant intake today come from Asia. Migrants settle in all parts of Australia and take their place in our **pluralist society**.

Activities

Check your understanding

1. Why did Australia establish a planned immigration scheme at the end of World War II?
2. How did Australia's relations with Asia alter after the end of World War II?
3. What was one of the major issues confronting the world when the war in Vietnam came to an end?
4. Who were the 'boat people' and why is their story so important to Australia?
5. How has the nature of Australian society changed in the post-war world?

Investigation: *Immigration*

1. What impression of immigration does source 5.2.1 provide?
2. Write a caption to accompany source 5.2.2 that would help create an appreciation of the humanitarian issues that relate to immigration.
3. Using source 5.2.3 as your evidence, explain in a paragraph what the common image of Australia was to many refugee settlers.
4. Read source 5.2.4, then briefly explain why decisions about refugees must take into account global problems.
5. Imagine Arthur Calwell has asked you to design posters to educate Australians about the value of immigration for Australia's future. Have a class discussion on the different angles you could look at and then design a series of promotional posters that will help the 1950s immigration program gain acceptance.
6. Draw a map that shows the places of origin of Australia's migrant populations from Asia. You could begin with the gold rush Chinese and move through to the refugee camps that were set up after the Vietnam War and to the business migrants of today.
7. As a class, discuss the concepts of multiculturalism and democracy. Debate the topic that: 'Multiculturalism has made Australia a truly democratic nation.'

INDONESIA AND TIMOR — RELATIONS WITH OUR NEAREST NEIGHBOUR

Source 5.3.1

The Indonesian national emblem. The shield carries the five principles of Indonesian government known as 'pancasila'.

Australia's complex relationship with Asia can be better understood by examining more closely our relations with Indonesia. The islands of Indonesia are home to 180 million people. Indonesia is the world's single biggest Islamic nation but has as many as 250 different languages. Six hundred years ago, the biggest religions in Indonesia were Buddhism and Hinduism, and the influence of these beliefs can still be seen in many aspects of Indonesian culture today. At its closest point, Indonesia is only 150 kilometres from Australian territory and yet we are nations far removed from each other in history and culture.

In the struggle for independence, Indonesian nationalists were supported by private Australian citizens and the Chifley Labor government. When the Dutch finally withdrew from Indonesia in 1949, a Western style of **parliamentary government** was established. This democratic system failed 10 years later when the Indonesian President, Sukarno, took on the position of the commander of the armed forces and the political head of state. The President was given the power to make laws in Indonesia without the approval of the Parliament. This stirred the Australian fear of the 'yellow peril' descending from the north. Australia's foreign policy had to face the challenge of dealing with a potentially hostile and powerful neighbour whose system of government differed from our own. The Australian sense of insecurity increased when Indonesian paratroopers landed in West Irian in 1962, and conflict between Malaysia and Indonesia erupted in 1963.

Source 5.3.2

A cartoon from the *Courier-Mail*, 19 August 1958, illustrating Australia's fears of Indonesian territorial expansion

THE INVASION OF EAST TIMOR

Civil war broke out in the Portuguese colony of Timor when Portugal abandoned her responsibilities and quickly withdrew from the territory in 1972. Indonesia argued that East Timor was too small to exist as an independent nation and so should join Indonesia. Indonesia was prepared to use force to take the territory and so, in 1975, it moved over 3000 troops in. By December, the East Timorese capital of Dili fell to the Indonesians. The report of five Australian journalists killed in the Timorese town of Balibo during the invasion alarmed the public and strained the Australian and Indonesian relationship. By 1976 about 40 000 Indonesian troops occupied East Timor.

The Australian government largely accepted the invasion of East Timor by Indonesia. By 1978, Australia publicly acknowledged the reality of Indonesian control over the Timorese because maintaining good diplomatic relations with Indonesia was the highest priority. Humanitarian issues nevertheless remained a concern, and the

Australian government continued to express regret that the Timorese had no choice in their destiny. In November 1991 the brutality of the Indonesian control of East Timor was once again brought to public attention. Indonesian troops were filmed shooting unarmed demonstrators in a cemetery in the Timorese capital of Dili. An estimated 200 to 300 Timorese were killed, with many more injured. The Indonesian government argued that the soldiers had been provoked during rioting. After an international outcry, the Indonesian government held an official inquiry into the Dili massacre. The following trials resulted in the short imprisonment of several junior Indonesian officers and life sentences for the Timorese found guilty of organising the protest march.

Source 5.3.3

Pro-independence East Timorese demonstrating in the weeks before the referendum on 30 August 1999, in which they would vote for the future of their country.

INDONESIA'S FUTURE?

In December of 1998, the Indonesian President B. J. Habibie had agreed to allow an act of **self-determination** in Timor. He declared the act would finally provide the Timorese with the opportunity to choose between **autonomy** (but remaining part of Indonesia) or complete independence from Indonesia through a United Nations supervised vote. On 30 August 1999, the 450 000 registered voters of Timor used the power of the polling booth to decide their future and voted for independence from Indonesia. Under the supervision of the United Nations, the people of East Timor have been pledged a free **democracy** within two or three years.

The leader of the East Timorese independence movement, Xanana Gusmao, described 1999 as a year of extremes for his people. It was a year of great joy on the day of the ballot proclaiming independence, and a time of grief at the loss of life that followed. 1999 remains a year that marked the determination of the East Timorese people to vote for an independent future.

Since gaining independence, Indonesia's history has been dramatic and troubled. It continues to face the challenge of raising general living standards in a poor nation with a very large population. Throughout the crises and despite the differences, successive Australian governments have tried to maintain **commercial** and cultural links with Indonesia because we recognise the importance of the country to our own future security and prosperity.

Activities

Check your understanding

1. Briefly explain some of the characteristics of the Indonesian nation.
2. How did Australia show support for the Indonesian nationalist movement?
3. How can you account for insecurity in Australia's diplomatic relationship with Indonesia?
4. Why has the fate of East Timor remained such an important human rights issue in the Asian region?
5. Why is 30 August 1999 an important date for Indonesia and the East Timorese?

Communication: *Analysing visual resources*

1. Source 5.3.1 features the garuda bird. In the ancient Ramayana story of the Hindu religion, the garuda helped to return a good king to the throne. Read the explanations of the symbols in the source, then explain what hopes for Indonesia were being expressed by the nationalists who designed the emblem.
2. How did source 5.3.2 express Australia's fear of Indonesia in 1958?
3. How would you describe the people shown in source 5.3.3? What clues are there about their degree of wealth and their ethnic origin?

Investigation: *Researching a troubled region*

1. Restoring a peaceful way of life to East Timor remains one of the biggest challenges to our region. Events move quickly in Indonesia and they are given wide coverage in our media. Compile a timeline of the major political and news events in our immediate region over the last 30 years.
2. The territory shown in source 5.3.2 is today a part of Indonesia and is known as Irian Jaya, or West Irian. Imagine you are an Australian journalist asked to write a cover story on the troubles of Irian Jaya. Research and write on its history between the 1960s, the 'Act of Free Choice', and the present day.
3. Imagine you are one of the main players in the modern story of East Timor: Bishop Carlos Belo, Xanana Gusmao, Jose Ramos Horta, Dr B. J. Habibie, Eurico Guterres or General Wiranto. Write a letter to the editor of an Australian newspaper explaining what your hopes are for your people's future and what Australia's role should be.

5.4

EGALITARIANISM — THE DREAM OF A 'LEVEL PLAYING FIELD'

The United Nations' Development Report of 1999 ranked Canada first and Australia seventh in terms of the quality of life that nations could offer their people. Australia was seen by many as the 'lucky country', where people could achieve on the basis of merit rather than on social or economic position, and where there was a 'level playing field', with equality of opportunity for all. Australians wanted to believe that their nation was an **egalitarian** one — although they did not have to look far to see that it was not.

SOME ARE MORE EQUAL THAN OTHERS . . .

In the late 1990s, the distribution of wealth within Australian society was one of the most *unequal* among all the nations of the developed world.

- Ten per cent of Australia's population controlled up to 50 per cent of its economic resources.
- Fifty per cent of Australians controlled more than 95 per cent of the nation's wealth.
- Up to 15 per cent of the Australian community lived below the **poverty line**.

Prime Minister Bob Hawke's 1987 promise that 'no Australian child would live in poverty by 1990' showed little chance of being fulfilled by the end of the century. Results of a 1999 survey conducted by Professor Bob Gregory at the University of Canberra indicated that one in five children had experienced life in a household with *no* breadwinner.

Source 5.4.1

Ron Tandberg's cartoon comment on poverty

WHAT HAPPENED TO THE 'WORKING MAN'S PARADISE'?

The almost full employment that Australians enjoyed from the late 1940s until the early 1970s no longer existed by the end of the century. In 1999, the average unemployment rate was 7.4 per cent, with many unemployed never having had a job. Increasing numbers of Australians were in part-time or casual employment. While part-time work benefited students and people with other responsibilities, it created a large gap in the incomes of those who needed full-time work to fund their living expenses. As full-time work and job opportunities decreased, some saw a place in the work force as the prize in a ruthless competition between different groups. With reductions in staff numbers throughout the public and private sectors, those in full-time, paid work had to work longer hours. The problem seemed to be one of unequal distribution of work rather than a genuinely depressed economy.

Source 5.4.2

An extract from a 1997 article on the changing face of work

A revolution in the nation's workplace

by Helen Trinca

The story of work in the 1990s is a story of contrasts — the full-timers versus the part-timers; the core workers versus the peripheral staff called in when they are needed; contract workers versus the rest; those working too much and those not working at all; the men falling off the work wagon and the women clambering on any which way they can; young people desperately seeking jobs and older people asked to retire early to give them a go . . .

Researchers Geoff Mulgan and Charles Leadbeater at the Demos think-tank in London wrote recently: 'Even those in the very best jobs realise that something is badly awry in a labour market that leaves a widening divide between those forced into the idleness of unemployment and those stressed by high-paid, high-pressure jobs; between work-rich families which bring home several incomes and families without work which survive on a mixture of welfare benefits and, in many cases, on undeclared cash in hand payments for odd jobs and petty crime' . . .

Sydney Morning Herald, 20 October 1997.

STICKY FLOORS AND GLASS CEILINGS

By the twentieth century's end, women were still fighting for equality in the work force. Many had the double burden of unpaid domestic labour and a job in the paid work force. Others found that their household responsibilities limited their opportunities for seeking paid employment. As a result, women were often financially dependent on someone else and less likely than men to be able to purchase property, generate retirement savings and accumulate long-service leave. A 1999 survey revealed that women had invested only a third of what men had in superannuation.

In the mid 1990s, the Australian work force had the highest level of segregation into 'male' and 'female' jobs of any nation in the developed world. With 'men's work' valued more highly than 'women's work', Australian women had fewer opportunities to reach the levels of pay that men did. Women spoke of 'sticky floors' which kept them from advancing in their careers and 'glass ceilings', through which they could see (but not attain) the upper management positions dominated by men. For **indigenous** and migrant women, there was the 'glass door' which served as a barrier to entry into any junior management roles. Those paid **piecework rates** struggled to gain the protection and benefits offered within the regular work force.

Source 5.4.3
Cartoon by Michael Leunig published in the *Sydney Morning Herald*, 25 May 1995

CITY VERSUS COUNTRY

About one-third of Australia's population lives in country areas. A Human Rights and Equal Opportunity Commission (HREOC) inquiry in the late 1990s found that their quality of life was often markedly inferior to that of city dwellers. Rural Australians experienced hardships resulting from remoteness, a downturn in the rural economy and problems caused by droughts and floods. In New South Wales, where most rural townships have less than 4000 people, employment opportunities were fewer and people experienced longer periods of unemployment than urban Australians did. Around 43 per cent of rural workers were unemployed and nearly half of these were under 25 years of age.

Poverty in rural areas was also higher than the national average. In New South Wales overall, 13 per cent of households could be classified as poor, whereas the figure for rural New South Wales varied from 18 per cent to 24 per cent. Health care was at crisis point because most doctors preferred to work in cities. On average, urban Australians had more than twice the number of doctors available to them than rural Australians had. Some country towns had no doctor at all. Over 150 000 rural Australians lacked running water in their homes.

TOWARDS EGALITARIANISM?

Australia in the late twentieth century may not have been an egalitarian society but it was one in which people were willing to identify the barriers to equality and try to remove them. Government inquiries and the work of individuals and interest groups highlighted problem areas. Anti-discrimination legislation at both state and federal level had made it illegal to discriminate on the grounds of race, sex, marital status, disability and age. Ordinary Australians increasingly questioned whether the status quo gave others a 'fair go'.

Activities

Investigation: *An egalitarian society*

1. In your own words, explain the meaning of the terms 'egalitarianism', 'level playing field' and 'poverty line'.
2. List five pieces of evidence to support the view that Australian society is not egalitarian.
3. What developments in Australian life suggested progress towards egalitarianism in the Australian community?
4. In your own words, identify the problems of the 1990s work force outlined in source 5.4.2. What aspects of the workplace do the London researchers see as undermining egalitarianism?

Communication: *Studying political cartoons*

1. Who do the people in source 5.4.1 represent? Who are they looking for? What 'landmarks' do they use to guide their search? What is the message Tandberg wants to get across in this cartoon?
2. Explain the meaning of source 5.4.3.

5.5

TRANSPORT AND COMMUNICATION TRENDS

Technology is the application of science to industry. Improvements in technology involve the application of scientific discoveries in actually producing new goods and services and/or more goods and services. The twentieth century will be remembered as the century of greatest technological change. Enormous advancements were made — from the novelty of the first forms of motorised transport to the communications links that allow people across the world to interact in 'virtual space' in a fraction of a second. We will look at some of the important trends that have made their impact on communities on a regional and global scale.

Source 5.5.1

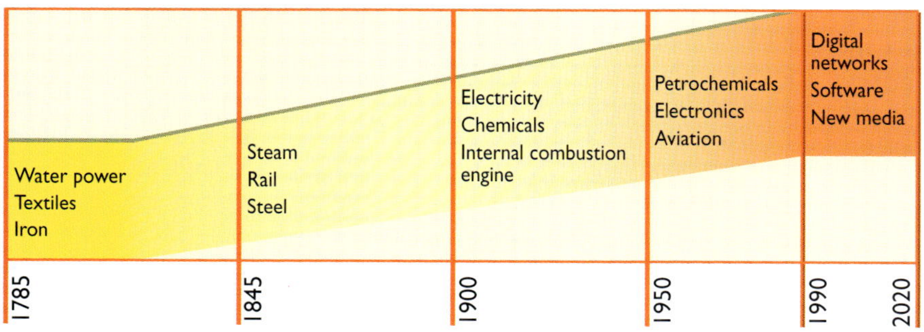

The timeline shows the approximate times when major technological innovations had a strong influence on economic growth. Older technologies did not disappear with time. They were improved on, but were gradually less important than the new technologies.

THE AGE OF THE MOTOR CAR

The United States led the field in transport technologies in the nineteenth century with the development of the motor car. In 1895, one-third of all the cars registered in the state of Michigan, USA, were battery operated, one-third steam powered and one-third had internal combustion engines using petrol as a fuel. Within 20 years, the steam and electric cars had all but disappeared and the petrol-powered Model-T Ford was by far the most popular car.

The twentieth century was the age of the motor car, powered by the internal combustion engine and using petrol as its primary fuel. At the close of the twentieth century, four major forces were influencing the issue of the type of fuel that would provide power for personal transportation in the new century. They were:

- a possible decline in oil supplies
- the threat of global warming
- urban pollution
- urban congestion.

It is expected that petrol-powered cars will continue well into the twenty-first century, but battery-powered electric cars could become a real alternative, especially for shorter trips in urban areas.

Source 5.5.2

DaimlerChrysler's NECAR 45 is one of several fuel-cell electric powered vehicles being developed. It could be in production by 2004. The fuel cell car produces energy through a chemical reaction of hydrogen and oxygen and it emits nothing more than steam.

Source 5.5.3

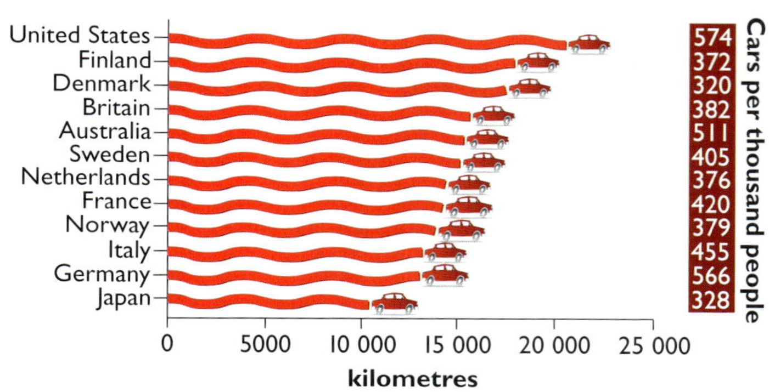

Car usage in selected countries in 1993 (kilometres per car per year) (*Source*: adapted from International Energy Studies, Lawrence Berkeley Laboratory, California)

TRAINS AND CHANGING TECHNOLOGY

Trains revolutionised long distance transport during the nineteenth century and continue to play a role into the twenty-first century. Train technology has shifted from steam to electric powered. Train technology plays three major roles:

- on a local scale, underground railways provide mass transit systems in large cities, such as Paris, Shanghai, London, New York and Tokyo
- on a national and continental scale, trains move freight and bulk long distances, for example, coal transport in central Queensland
- high speed trains make overland travel between major centres almost as fast as airline flights, for example, the Shinkansen (bullet trains) which travel at around 270–300 km/h between major cities in Japan.

OCEAN SHIPPING — A CHANGING FOCUS

Boats have been an important form of transport for thousands of years. The development of air travel lessened their importance as a means of transport for passengers but cruise ships are still popular for holidays. Most of the ships that travel the oceans today are either fishing or naval vessels or are transporting goods and bulk freight between countries. In the latter part of the twentieth century, two major technologies transformed shipping, making it more efficient and cheaper:

- the development of supertankers for bulk cargoes such as oil and wheat
- the development of containerisation (unitised traffic) in which goods are packed into containers of a specified size at the factory, taken by train or truck to the port and easily and quickly loaded by specialised cranes.

Source 5.5.4

A container ship at Port Botany in Sydney

AEROPLANES: CONQUERING DISTANCE

Even though there were aeroplanes flying in the early twentieth century, they only became important as a transport technology with the development of the jet engine and wide-bodied jets. These could carry large numbers of people very quickly to different locations around the world. With the widespread use of the Boeing 747 in the 1970s, there were associated improvements in:

- radar and other navigational technologies
- computers to control air traffic
- airport terminal technology.

By 1999 technological advances had reduced airline passenger costs in real terms by more than 70 per cent compared with 1950 costs. The development of fast air transport technologies significantly reduced Australia's isolation, bringing all of the world's major cities closer — to within a day or less in travelling time.

Source 5.5.5

The 'kangaroo route' — then and now

In December 1947, Qantas began flying the longest airline route in the world, known as the 'kangaroo route' from Sydney to London. The journey took close to 94 hours with about 56 hours of actual flying time. There were overnight stops and landings at Darwin, Singapore, Calcutta, Karachi, Cairo, Castel Benito and sometimes Rome. The Constellation carried 28 passengers plus crew at a cruising speed of 480 kilometres per hour. The trip was for first class passengers only and cost £525, about nine times as much as the first class fare in today's terms. Today the flight from Sydney to London takes 24 hours and there is only one stop. The Boeing 747-438 carries nearly 400 passengers at a cruising speed of 920 kilometres per hour and at a fraction of the cost of the 1947 trip.

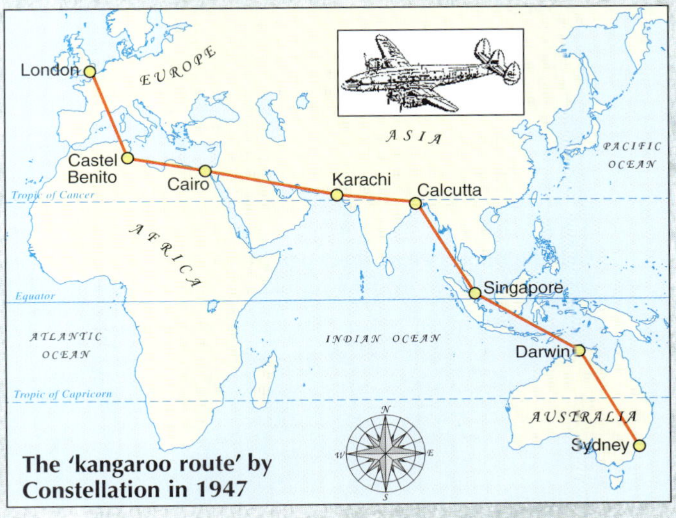

The 'kangaroo route' by Constellation in 1947

TELECOMMUNICATIONS AND THE DEATH OF DISTANCE

Traditionally, the further apart people have been, the longer it has taken for information to be passed between them. However, physical distance is of little relevance today for the communication and information flows that pass between countries and communities around the world. When European settlement began in Australia, communications to and from England took many months by sea and Australians felt isolated from the rest of the world. Later, air transport allowed letters to be carried overseas in a matter of days — yet now we refer to this as 'snail mail'. The recent startling changes in communication technologies and the onset of the 'Information Age' has ended Australia's isolation from the rest of the world.

Alexander Graham Bell, who invented the telephone in 1876, would never have imagined today's world of mobile phones, satellites, fibre optic cables and the Internet. The death of distance was truly signalled when the first satellite went into orbit in 1957. Satellites provided the technology that enabled the transmission of messages across the world, via space, in a fraction of a second and for a fraction of the cost of previous methods. By the 1970s, satellites made cheap international telephone calls a reality and television transmissions could be sent directly to almost anywhere in the world.

Source 5.5.6

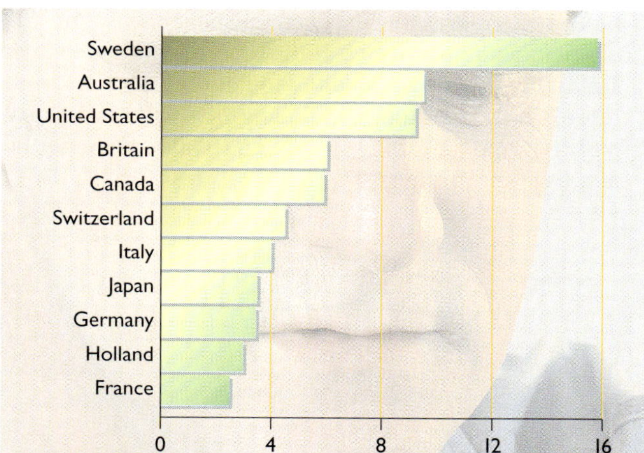

Cellular phone subscribers per 100 people, 1 January 1995
(*Source*: adapted from FT Mobile Communications, OECD)

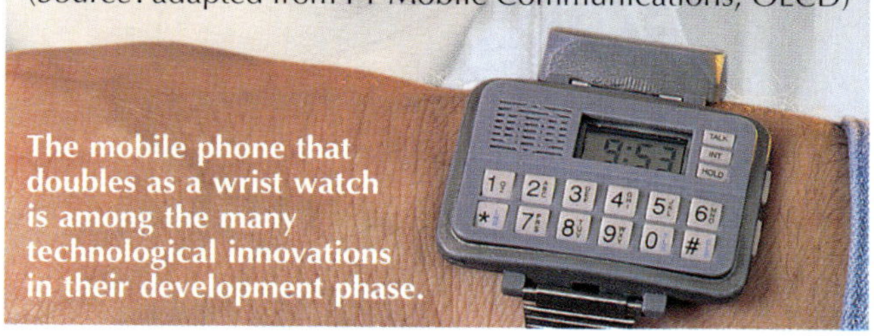

The mobile phone that doubles as a wrist watch is among the many technological innovations in their development phase.

FACT*file*

- Over 90 per cent of Internet users are in North America and Western Europe.
- Nearly 50 countries have fewer than one telephone line per 100 people.

COMPUTERS BECOME COMMUNICATORS

When computers were first used in the 1950s they were large — some occupying the whole floor of a building — and very expensive. Now some modern computers are small enough to fit in the palm of the hand. They are powerful and relatively cheap. The computer has enabled the breakthroughs in communications, printing, photography and sound to be brought together. High quality information and images can be sent directly down the phone line via modems. With **digitisation**, anything from a rock concert to a newspaper article can be received on a personal computer or television. The global communications system can now deliver audio, visual and text information through the Internet.

The Internet is a worldwide connection of computer networks organised to facilitate the sharing of information. There is a vast array of information available on the Internet in the form of text, graphics, sound, video or multimedia files.

Source 5.5.7

The modern Internet developed over five main stages.

- **The Internet had its origins in the 1960s when its precursor was developed by the United States Government Advanced Research Projects and the National Physical Lab in Britain. The original network, ARPANET, had only four users.**
- **In 1987 NFSnet was established by the US National Science Foundation to cater for academic institutions and military researchers. It was connected to a similar network by the NASA space centre in Houston.**
- **In 1989 the World Wide Web was developed by a Swiss scientist at the European Centre for Particle Research. He was looking for a new way of organising on-line scientific data.**
- **In 1993 an American wrote a program called MOSAIC which used a system to link text, images, sound and video. This Hypertext system eventually became Netscape, a program used by many on the Web.**
- **In 1995 the US government pulled out of its ownership of much of the system and enabled it to be operated by private corporations.**

Source 5.5.8

Tuvalu and the Internet

In 1995 the small Pacific nation of Tuvalu learned that the body that allocates Internet domain sites had assigned Tuvalu the letters .tv (Australia has .au), and that media corporations highly value these letters. Tuvalu is located 1000 kilometres north of Fiji and has a total land area of only 26 square kilometres. It is a poor, developing economy with a population of 10 000. The country has few natural resources. Its main potential resource is its large fishing grounds.

In 1998 Tuvalu signed an agreement with a media company resulting in an upfront payment of around $10 million (roughly equal to Tuvalu's annual GDP), regular payments each year and a share of the company. The future is looking more promising for the people of Tuvalu with the opportunity of additional income to develop resources such as the fishing grounds. However, there is another potential problem. The highest point in Tuvalu is less than 4.5 metres above sea level. Serious global warming and a rise in sea levels could destroy the island nation.

Tuvalu's size, location and lack of natural resources place large constraints on its economic development. The majority of the population (about 80 per cent) is engaged in fishing and agriculture.

The following are the main features of the Internet today:

1. *World Wide Web* (WWW) — a collection of files from all over the world, linked together so they are accessible to other users. The Web can be used to search for and **download** information, copy and print out images, send and receive text, images and sound and publish information in the form of Web pages.
2. *E-mail* or electronic mail is a message from one Internet user to another or to a mailing list of other users and can include 'attachments' such as documents and images.
3. *Newsgroups* — a method of receiving and communicating information about a specific topic, similar to a noticeboard. Any user who subscribes to the newsgroup can read or post messages.

Activities

Investigation: *Communication technology*

1. What are the major forces at work which could limit the use of petrol-powered vehicles into the twenty-first century?
2. Examine source 5.5.3.
   (a) Where does Australia rank in car usage compared with other major users?
   (b) Rank the countries in the table according to cars per thousand people. Present this information in a bar graph.
   (c) Which country do you think would use the most petrol in a year? Why?
3. In a paragraph, describe the major roles played by trains in modern transport systems.
4. Which technologies enabled aeroplanes to play an important part in modern transport systems?
5. There has been a regional and global trend towards faster and more reliable transport. Imagine it is the year 2020. Write a half-page description of the transport technologies that might be used.
6. Why has the computer been so important in the development of modern communications?
7. What is the Internet? Describe the development of the Internet.
8. What happened that has the potential to turn Tuvalu from a poor, developing economy into a much more prosperous one?
9. Draw a mind map to express your ideas on the advantages of modern technology and communications.
10. Working with a partner or in teams, make a list of ways in which modern communication technologies affect our daily lives. Using the list, prepare a report to be presented to the class.
11. Imagine you are a reporter writing a story on 'how modern communications have changed people's lives in the last twenty years'. Interview two older members of your family (at least 40 years old) or friends to gain their ideas on the topic. Share your findings with the class.

5.6

THE FRANKLIN — COMPETING VALUES

Political action to save important features of the physical, built and cultural environments had become quite common in Australia by the 1980s. Protesters often used the tactics developed during the **green bans** in the 1970s.

Concern with Australia's **heritage** grew into concern for the preservation of the world's natural and cultural heritage. In 1974, Australia signed the international Convention Concerning the Protection of the World Cultural and Natural Heritage. This convention created the World Heritage Commission. By signing the convention, Australia was expressing its commitment to identifying, conserving and protecting areas of 'outstanding universal value' within Australia's natural and cultural heritage. Countries that signed the convention were expected to make their own laws to put this into practice.

Source 5.6.1

The Franklin River — part of the area nominated for inclusion on the World Heritage List

THE FRANKLIN DAM ISSUE

In December 1982, the World Heritage Committee accepted the Australian federal government's nomination of the Western Tasmanian National Parks for entry into the World Heritage List. Before the parks could be listed, the Tasmanian government intervened by passing the *Gordon River Hydro-Electric Power Development Act 1982* (Tas.). The Act allowed the Tasmanian Hydro-Electric Commission (HEC) to construct a dam on the Franklin River within the nominated heritage area. This would assist the HEC in supplying Tasmania's electricity.

Environmentalists throughout Australia began protesting against the Tasmanian government's actions. They were angry that the government did not seem to value Tasmania's environmental heritage and because the HEC had made its decision without any discussion with the local community.

The Tasmanian Wilderness Society campaigned to increase public awareness of the beauty of the proposed heritage area. It informed people of the negative impact that excavation, building work and ongoing use of the dam would have on this unique wilderness. It also used photographs such as source 5.6.1 to show the public what would be lost if the dam went ahead. There were already at least 20 dams in Tasmania. The area that would be flooded to create the Franklin Dam contained caves that had been used by Aboriginal people for thousands of years and were therefore of significant cultural value.

Early in 1983, the Wilderness Society led a blockade of the proposed construction site. More than 2000 people took part in this action and 1400 of them were arrested. The demonstration was important in making politicians aware that environmental issues could not be ignored and that people expected our laws to protect the environment when necessary.

CONFLICT OVER POWERS

When the Labor Party won the federal election in March 1983, it came to government with a commitment to prevent the construction of the Franklin Dam. The Tasmanian Premier, Robin Grey, requested the new Prime Minister, Bob Hawke, to withdraw the federal government's nomination of the area for inclusion in the World Heritage List. The federal government responded by taking action to honour its election promise.

Source 5.6.2

Protesters blockading the site of the proposed construction of the Franklin Dam

First, the federal government used the existing *National Parks and Wildlife Conservation Act 1975* (Cwlth) to prevent any work occurring on the dam without its approval. Second, the government passed the *World Heritage Properties Conservation Act 1983*. This Act classified the whole area as 'natural heritage' and some of the areas closest to the site as 'cultural heritage' as well. The heritage classification of these areas meant that they could not be built on.

The Tasmanian government claimed that by passing this legislation, the federal government was acting outside the powers it had under the **Constitution**. The premier of Tasmania said that the decision to build a dam came under State powers, not Commonwealth powers, and that therefore Tasmania's own law — the *Gordon River Hydro-Electric Power Development Act 1982* (Tas.) — was valid and should prevail. This situation led to a High Court challenge.

COMMONWEALTH v. *TASMANIA* (1983): THE *FRANKLIN DAM CASE*

The Commonwealth Constitution places federal government law above state government law where both governments have laws about the same issue and where both have acted within the powers available to them under the Constitution. The Constitution requires that any disagreement over powers be decided by the High Court. In the case that became known as the *Franklin Dam Case*, the federal government had to prove that it had the power to make the laws it had made to prevent construction of the Franklin Dam. It claimed that the Constitution gave it three powers which applied in this case:

- the external affairs power which enabled the federal government to override state law in order to fulfil Australia's international obligation as a signatory to the Convention Concerning the Protection of the World Cultural and Natural Heritage
- the federal government power to make laws in relation to 'trading corporations' formed within Australia. The Commonwealth said that the HEC was a trading corporation wanting to build a dam so it could sell electricity to the people of Tasmania.
- the federal government's power to make law for 'people of any race for whom it is deemed to make special laws'. This meant that it had the power to make laws to protect the cultural heritage of Aboriginal people.

The Tasmanian government and the HEC argued that:

- the federal government had no reason to use its external affairs power because the World Heritage Commission had not put Australia under any *obligation* to make laws for these particular areas
- there was no justification for special use of the 'race' power because the Aboriginal caves were not of 'outstanding *universal* significance', they were only of significance to people within Australia.

The High Court judges decided by a 4–3 majority that the Commonwealth did have the power to pass laws preventing the construction of the dam. The majority decision accepted all three of the federal government's arguments.

Activities

Check your understanding

1. What convention did Australia sign in 1974, and what commitment did it make by doing so?
2. Explain how and why the federal and Tasmanian governments came into conflict over the Franklin Dam.
3. What actions did people take to help preserve the natural heritage of the Franklin Dam area?
4. Why did the issue have to be decided by the High Court, and what did it decide?

Communication: *Using photographs*

Use sources 5.6.1 and 5.6.2 to illustrate a paragraph of 15 to 20 lines in which you explain:

(a) the heritage value of the area shown

(b) what people have done to help conserve this heritage.

ULURU, KAKADU AND ECHOES OF THE DREAMING

Aboriginal Australians are the legally recognised owners of two of Australia's most significant national parks: Uluru–Kata Tjuta National Park and Kakadu National Park. Their continuing residence in these areas is an extension of one of the longest cultural traditions in human history and is therefore a very important part of Australia's heritage. Uluru–Kata Tjuta National Park and Kakadu National Park are on the World Heritage List for both their cultural and natural heritage values.

ULURU

Uluru is the largest monolith in the world. Scientists believe it began to form about 550 million years ago. Today it covers an area of about 3.3 square kilometres and is 348 metres high. The distance around its base is about nine kilometres. Uluru is an important part of Australia's heritage because of its unique physical impact on the landscape, its significant role in the Dreamtime (Tjukurpa) of the traditional owners, and its popularity as a tourist destination for thousands of visitors each year from within Australia and from overseas. As well as being on the World Heritage List, Uluru is listed as a Biosphere Reserve under the UNESCO Man and the Biosphere program.

FACT*file*

- Since its inception in 1972, the World Heritage Commission has placed 582 sites in 114 countries on its World Heritage List. These sites include the Pyramids (Egypt), the Taj Mahal (India), Notre Dame Cathedral (France), the Great Barrier Reef (Australia) and the interior of the Great Mosque (Spain).
- Many countries have only one site that has been classified as being of 'world heritage' value. Australia has 13 sites on the World Heritage List and possibly another 12 that are worthy of nomination.

Source 5.7.1

Australia's World Heritage sites

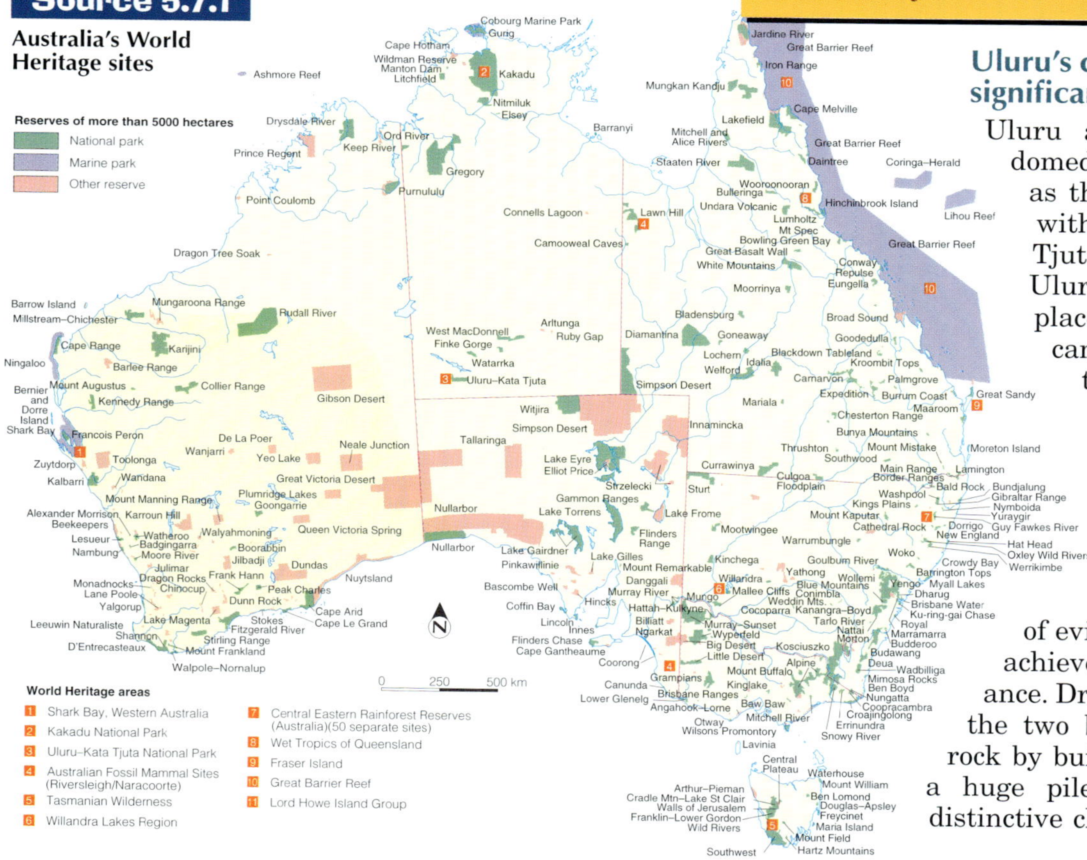

Uluru's cultural and religious significance

Uluru and Kata Tjuta (the domed rocks formerly known as the Olgas) are included within the Uluru–Kata Tjuta National Park. Uluru is a **sacred site**, a place of spiritual significance as a focal point in the landscape created by ancestral beings during the Dreamtime. Uluru's waterholes, cliff faces and caves all have special meaning and provide a record of evidence of how the land achieved its present appearance. Dreamtime stories tell of the two boys who created the rock by building up and shaping a huge pile of wet earth. The distinctive channels, which can be seen on the southern side of Uluru, were created by the action of the two boys sliding down the mud pile on their stomachs. The activities of other ancestral beings — Kuniya (the python woman), Kurpany (the devil dingo), Liru (poisonous snakes) and Lungkata (the blue-tongue lizard) — helped create some of the other natural features of the rock.

Source 5.7.2

The southern side of Uluru with the deep rock channels; Dreamtime stories tell of their creation by two boys sliding down the huge pile of wet earth they had made

Source 5.7.3

Extract from an article by Catharine Lumby

... the Rock isn't a tourist attraction which lets you off lightly. You don't amble up to it, ice-cream in hand and pat its side. You stand there with your mouth hanging open like an extra in a *Godzilla* remake. (I even switched off my mobile phone.)

Uluru's power isn't simply a function of its sheer physical beauty and size. It's rooted in something less tangible — in the way it occupies time and space, in the shock of seeing a spectacularly timeless edifice in the middle of nowhere.

It's only when you walk around the base, look at the rock paintings and notice the sacred sites, that an entirely different history comes into view. A view you certainly get if you climb to the top. Most tourists who go to Uluru know that Aboriginal people consider the Rock sacred in some way. But too few learn why. The proof is that, despite copious signs and locally available literature asking people not to climb, hundreds do every day.

In a booklet available on arrival at the Rock, the local Aboriginal people, the Anangu, tell the story of the Mala people who came to Uluru to perform a religious ceremony. The Mala men climbed to the northern end of the Rock to plant a ceremonial pole. When visitors climb the Rock today they are walking right over the tracks of these spiritual ancestors.

It's true that the Anangu haven't banned climbing. But it's also fairly obvious why — to do so would be a publicity disaster for Aboriginal ownership and joint management of the park.

Critics of so-called political correctness, of course, will be quick to sneer at mobile-phone wielding city chicks ostentatiously 'respecting' Aboriginal culture.

And perhaps they've got a point. I don't know any more about the Anangu's Tjukurpa (Aboriginal law) than I do about papal encyclicals. But I do know I wouldn't enter a Catholic church in a bikini and start lip-synching to Abba during Mass.

The mania for hiking up Uluru is a form of anti-social climbing in more ways than one. It's not only an affront to local Aboriginal people, it's a failure to grapple with the contemporary significance of Uluru itself. The Rock, like many Australians today, is symbolically situated between two points of view. On one side, there are those who believe that reconciliation with Aboriginal people is crucial to the future of Australia, and, on the other, there are those who think the process has gone far enough, or perhaps too far ...

Uluru is an icon of many conflicting themes in Australian history. It symbolises Aboriginal culture, European colonisation and a recent fragile but productive model of both groups working together. Anglo-Australians are free to treat the Rock as a monument to European exploration — as a place to get to the top of quickly. But if you walk around its perimeter you find yourself somewhere far more rewarding. Somewhere between a Rock and a better place for all Australians.

Sydney Morning Herald, 31 July 1998.

Management and ownership

In 1985, the federal government returned Uluru to its traditional owners, the Pitjantjatjara and the Yankunytjatjara peoples of central Australia. Since then they have leased it back to the Director of National Parks and Wildlife. The National Park is jointly managed by its traditional owners and the Australian National Parks and Wildlife Service (ANPWS) through a board of management chaired by Mr Yami Lester.

KAKADU

Kakadu National Park, in the wet-dry tropics of the Northern Territory, is Australia's largest national park (20 000 square kilometres). It incorporates wetlands, four major river systems, woodland plains, rainforest, hill country, elevated rocky outcrops and a large variety of plants and animals, including crocodiles. Kakadu's underlying formations date back 2000 million years. Its flood plains, created after sea levels began to stabilise about 6000 years ago, are relatively young.

Aboriginal Australians have lived in Kakadu for over 50 000 years. Their understanding of Kakadu's many landforms and changing seasons and their care of its environment are recorded in rock art, in the stories of the Dreamtime and in their continuing involvement in the management of this area. Kakadu National Park was inscribed on the World Heritage List for its natural and cultural values. Kakadu lies within the Northern Land Council's (NLC) area of responsibility. Its traditional owners lease it to the Australian Nature Conservation Agency (ANCA) and it is jointly managed by ANCA and tribal elders.

Source 5.7.4

Part of the Kakadu National Park

Conflicting land uses at Kakadu

It took ten years of planning (1965–75) before a formal proposal was made to create a national park in the Alligator Rivers (Kakadu) region of the Northern Territory. In the meantime, the federal government issued licences to allow companies to explore for minerals in most of the proposed park. Experts identified three major deposits of uranium: at Ranger, at Koongarra and at Jabiluka, which holds the world's largest uranium deposit.

The *Aboriginal Land Rights (Northern Territory) Act 1976* enabled the Mirrar people to claim traditional land in the Alligator Rivers region. The Director of the Australian National Parks and Wildlife Service now leases from them the 20 000 square kilometres of land which comprise Kakadu National Park and, as part of the agreement, has made a commitment to manage the park in accordance with the highest international **conservation** standards.

Ranger, Jabiluka and Koongarra were excluded from the National Park even though they were within its boundaries. Mining began at Ranger in 1980. By late 1982, mining companies had federal government approval and agreements from the Northern Lands Council, representing the traditional owners, to allow mining at Jabiluka. Government approval was withdrawn under the Labor government from 1983 to 1996 but mining became an issue again under the Liberal Party/National Party Coalition government.

Conservation groups have opposed uranium mining in the Kakadu area from the very beginning because of the threat it poses to Kakadu's natural environment. Traditional owners could see the financial benefits of mining, but were also concerned about its effects on the land. When agreements were renegotiated in 1998, Yvonne Margarula, the Mirrar senior traditional owner who had inherited the 1982 Jabiluka lease, opposed it but some of the other tribal elders were in favour of continued mining.

In 1998, a UNESCO team reported that mining at Jabiluka would threaten the World Heritage values of Kakadu National Park. The Australian government spent $1 million publicising its pro-mining stance and was successful. When UNESCO met in Paris on 13 July 1999, the majority of its 21-nation committee found that Kakadu was not 'in danger' from mining at Jabiluka.

Source 5.7.5

Jacqui Katona and Yvonne Margarula at a press conference to talk about a protest being launched against the Jabiluka uranium mine

Activities

Check your understanding

1. Who are the owners of the Uluru–Kata Tjuta National Park and Kakadu National Park?
2. What is meant by 'cultural and natural heritage'? Why are Uluru and Kakadu important to Australia's cultural and natural heritage?
3. Explain why many people believe that Kakadu is under threat.

Investigation: *Heritage and cultural values*

1. Use information from sources 5.7.2 and 5.7.3 to write a 10- to 15-line description of the heritage values of Uluru.
2. In source 5.7.3, what does Catharine Lumby mean when she talks about the 'contemporary significance' of Uluru? What problem for Uluru's heritage does Catharine Lumby identify?
3. List the natural heritage values you can identify in the photograph of Kakadu shown in source 5.7.4.
4. Discuss or debate the following viewpoint: 'That uranium mining at Jabiluka poses a serious threat to the conservation of Kakadu National Park'.

MERIAM, MYTHS AND MABO

In 1982, Eddie Koiki Mabo (1936–92), Father David Passi (an Anglican minister), James Rice, Sam Passi and Celia Salee took the **land rights** issue all the way to the High Court of Australia. They wanted legal recognition of their ownership rights over particular plots of land on Mer (Murray) Island in the Torres Strait. The High Court's decision in *Mabo and Others v. The State of Queensland* (1992) was a major turning point in the history of land rights claims for Australia's indigenous peoples.

Source 5.8.1

Eddie Mabo

THE BACKGROUND TO THE CASE

Captain James Cook said that Australia belonged to no-one when he laid claim to its east coast on behalf of Britain in 1770. According to eighteenth century law, a land which had no owner could be lawfully taken over by the people of another land. Following the arrival of the First Fleet in 1788, Australia's east coast became 'Crown' land — land claimed in the name of the reigning sovereign and his or her governments. No consideration was given to the land rights of Australia's indigenous peoples. Gradually, governments claimed more land and either kept it, leased it to others, gave it away or sold it. The Queensland government took over the Torres Strait Islands in 1879. The Meriam Islanders continued to live on their island and carry out their traditional way of life there.

THE *MABO CASE* AND THE HIGH COURT DECISION

In the late 1970s, the Queensland government began to deny some of the Meriam Islanders the use of their lands. In 1982, Eddie Mabo led a group of them in a court case challenging the government's right to do this. They claimed that the indigenous peoples living on Mer Island owned that land because their families had lived there since 'time immemorial' (further back than anyone could remember). After losing their case in the Queensland Supreme Court, they appealed to the High Court of Australia. On 3 June 1992, the High Court handed down its historic decision on the case which Eddie Mabo had brought against Queensland. This case came to be known simply as **Mabo**.

Source 5.8.2

Summary of the High Court decision on Mabo

The High Court decided:

- in favour of the Meriam Islanders and against the state of Queensland
- that *native title* to land had existed before 1788 and might still be in existence on land which had never been sold or given away
- that for native title to continue to exist, the land would have to have been continuously lived on by indigenous families and their descendants since 1788. The people would have to have continued traditional customs.
- that on land which had been legally granted or sold by governments to someone else for their exclusive use, native title had ceased to exist.

Source 5.8.3

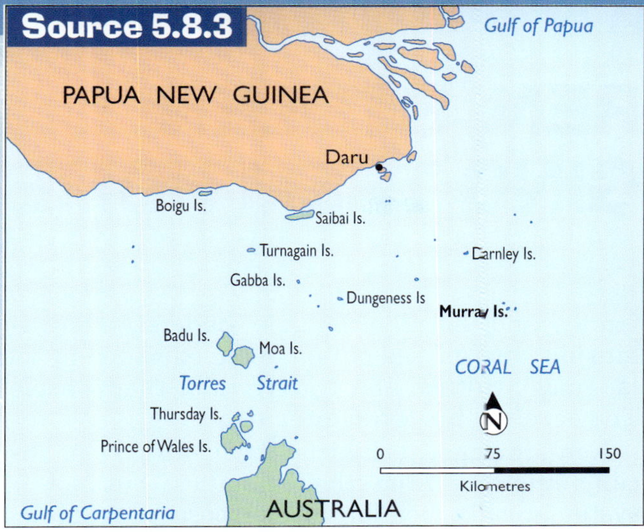

Location of Mer (Murray) Island

The Mabo judgement was important for all Australians because it overturned the legal fiction that Australia had been ***terra nullius*** ('land belonging to no-one') when the British took possession of it in 1788. This was an important step towards reconciliation. The High Court recognised that Aboriginal and Torres Strait Islander peoples were the original owners of Australia and that some of these peoples might still retain native title of land. In other words, native title was not granted by the government. It existed as a result of indigenous peoples' customary law — the legal system which had existed in Australia in 1788. The High Court did not decide whether or not native title could still exist on land which had been leased to pastoralists on a long-term basis but which they did not actually own.

Some Australians worried that they might lose their suburban backyards but there was no basis for this in the Mabo decision, which provided limited opportunities for small numbers of indigenous peoples to claim the ongoing existence of native title.

THE *NATIVE TITLE ACT*

On 22 December, 1993, after eighteen months of discussion and debate with government and community groups, the federal parliament passed the Native Title Bill, which was its response to the Mabo decision. The main features of this law were:

- recognition of existing land rights for all owners of freehold property, and land rights also for many people who held pastoral or other leases
- the requirement that native title claims be supported by proof of continued association with the land claimed
- provision for claims to be heard by state tribunals or through the Federal Court
- financial assistance to claimants, to farmers and to indigenous peoples whose land had been taken but who could not claim land under the terms of the Act.

However, like the High Court's 1992 decision, the government's *Native Title Act 1993* (Cwlth) did not provide any answers on the question of whether native title could still exist on land which governments had leased to pastoralists. This was the issue considered in the *Wik Case* of 1997 (see section 12.8).

State and Commonwealth legislation and the establishment of funds for land purchase have resulted in about 15 per cent of Australia being recognised as indigenous peoples' land. Much of this land is in semi-desert areas and of marginal economic value. In New South Wales and Victoria, the two States where most indigenous Australians live, the *Native Title Act 1993* offered little likelihood of successful native claims.

FACT*file*

Eddie Mabo died in early 1992. He was posthumously (after death) named Australian of the Year by the *Australian* newspaper on 26 January 1993. He is now buried on Mer.

Activities

Check your understanding

1. Name the people who joined Eddie Mabo in his fight against the Queensland government.
2. How did the British act in the eighteenth century in regard to land which indigenous people owned?
3. What were the Meriam Islanders' reasons for taking the Queensland government to court?
4. What aspects of the *Native Title Act*:
   (a) created certainty for Australian landholders?
   (b) provided help to some groups?
5. What question had still not been answered by the *Native Title Act*?

Investigation: *Land rights*

1. Write three facts about the man shown in source 5.8.1 to explain why he is important to Australian history.
2. What was important about the High Court's decision in Mabo? Use source 5.8.2 to explain, in a paragraph, why very few people would be able to claim land as a result of the Mabo decision.
3. Devise three to five questions to find out what other people know about the Mabo decision. Use your questions to survey between five and ten people and discuss your findings with the class.

5.9

STOLEN CHILDREN, STOLEN IDENTITIES — BRINGING THEM HOME

For most Australians, the family unit is where people should be cared for, protected and educated in the behaviour and customs of their society and culture. In Aboriginal and Torres Strait Islander families, feelings of kinship are also important. Kinship involves special bonds that link an individual to the extended family group. It includes an understanding of the value of sharing and being able to rely on the support of family members and those who understand the Dreamtime and other important features of spiritual life. Kinship also involves respect for elders who pass on the important **traditions**, values and stories within indigenous culture and who serve as role models for younger members.

The practice of separating indigenous children from their families existed from the earliest years of the British colony and continued officially until 1969. By the late 1980s, there were more than 100 000 people of Aboriginal and Torres Strait Islander descent who had lost their links with family and land, lost their understanding of kinship, and missed out on being educated in the language, culture and traditions of their people. They are the **Stolen Generation**.

Non-indigenous children have also been forcibly removed from their families, but not so systematically, not for the purpose of removing them from their culture and traditions and not with the hope that their parents' unique culture and identity would die out.

In 1995, the Human Rights and Equal Opportunity Commission (HREOC) began a national inquiry into the separation of Aboriginal and Torres Strait Islander children from their families. The Commission released its report, *Bringing Them Home* in 1997. The report summarised the rationale behind the policy, its negative impact, and the continuing feelings of grief and loss which individuals and communities experienced while trying to gain some sense of identity.

HREOC found that forcibly removing children from their parents went against Australia's own legal standards, its international human rights obligations and the values held by many Australians at the time. Governments did not recognise indigenous parents as having any rights with regard to their children and did not consider a child's right to grow up within his or her own family. Parents had no right of appeal against a decision to take their children. By continuing to approve the forcible removal of indigenous children 'to another group', Australia was breaking its commitment to the UN Convention on the Prevention and Punishment of the Crime of Genocide, which it had signed in 1949. The convention defines the forcible removal of children 'to another group' as genocide (that is, the policy of destroying a culture).

The motives for taking the children were underpinned by racism. Those who took children 'for their own good' assumed that their own families could not properly care for them or felt that they were saving them from sub-standard and impoverished living conditions. They believed that indigenous culture had nothing worthwhile to offer when compared to European culture. Government bodies and welfare organisations failed to consider that it might have been better to improve indigenous peoples' poor living conditions rather than deprive their children of their own family and culture.

Source 5.9.1

The late actor and businessman Burnum Burnum was removed from his family when he was five months old and spent the next 16 years in a boys' home.

STOLEN LIVES, LIMITED OPPORTUNITIES

The stolen children did not usually move on to a better life. Many were sent to do farm work or taken to institutions to be trained as domestic servants for white families. Little was done to ensure that they received a thorough education. Within families and institutions alike, children were in danger of physical and sexual abuse and exploitation as cheap labour. Many never received the wages which their employers claimed had been banked on their behalf.

Source 5.9.2

The personal tragedy of the Stolen Generation from the autobiography of Margaret Tucker

> **All my mother could say was, 'Oh, no, not my Baby, please let me have her. I will look after her.'**
>
> **As that policeman walked up the hospital path to get my little sister, May and Myrtle and I sobbed quietly. Mother got out of the car and stood waiting with a hopeless look. Her tears had run dry I guess. I thought to myself, I will gladly go, if they will only leave Geraldine with Mother.**
>
> **'Mrs Clements, you can have your little girl. She left the hospital this morning,' said the policeman.**
>
> **Mother simply took that policeman's hand and kissed it and said, 'Thank you, thank you.'**
>
> **Then we were taken to the police station, where the policeman no doubt had to report. Mother followed him, thinking she could beg once more for us, only to rush out when she heard the car start up. My last memory of her for many years was her waving pathetically, as we waved back and called out goodbye to her, but we were too far away for her to hear us.**
>
> **I heard years later how after watching us go out of her life, she wandered away from the police station three miles along the road leading out of the town to Moonahculla. She was worn out, with no food or money, her apron still on. She wandered off the road to rest in the long grass under a tree. That is where old Uncle and Aunt found her the next day.**
>
> **Margaret Tucker, *If Everyone Cared*, Grosvenor, Melbourne, 1983, pp. 93–4.**

Most children were removed because of their skin colour rather than for their wellbeing. It was assumed that lighter-skinned children could more easily be assimilated into the non-indigenous community, where they would acquire new cultural values and identities. They were given new, non-indigenous names, punished for using their own language or for continuing their cultural traditions, and encouraged to fear and look down upon the culture they had been forced to abandon. Those who were brought up in loving environments still experienced a sense of loss.

BEING SORRY

It would not be possible to make up for what had been lost by indigenous peoples as a result of the forced removal of their children. The HREOC Inquiry did make some suggestions, including an apology from the institutions that had been involved in taking children; assistance to indigenous peoples to help them reunite with their families and regain their cultural identities; public recognition of past injustices through education and a National Sorry Day; and the establishment of a national compensation fund.

The report was accompanied by renewed discussion within the Australian community of what the historian Geoffrey Blainey and, later, Prime Minister John Howard have labelled a 'black armband' view of history. Most state parliaments passed formal motions of apology to the 'stolen children'. The federal government, under Prime Minister John Howard, did not apologise (although two years later it did express 'regret' for past injustices). The federal government did pledge $63 million towards the implementation of the other HREOC suggestions. This did not include a **compensation** fund.

Activities

Check your understanding

1. What role does the family usually serve in the upbringing of children?
2. What additional role did traditional Aboriginal and Torres Strait Islander families perform?
3. Who produced the report *Bringing Them Home* and what was it about?
4. How were indigenous children often treated following their removal from their families?
5. What were the main recommendations of the report and what has been the response to it?

Communication: *Analysing sources*

1. What does source 5.9.2 show about the impact of the forced removal of indigenous children from their families?
2. What do you think should be done to redress the injustices suffered by the Stolen Generation?

TOWARDS RECONCILIATION?

Non-indigenous Australians have frequently had a poor understanding of the experiences of Aboriginal and Torres Strait Islander peoples. Indigenous Australians frequently struggle to survive in a society in which they have a low social status and where they encounter constant negativity and even hostility. **Reconciliation** is a process aimed at improving relationships between indigenous and non-indigenous Australians. It includes a recognition of past injustices and an understanding of how relationships between indigenous and non-indigenous Australians have been shaped by past events, policies and attitudes. The achievement of a cooperative and harmonious relationship between indigenous and non-indigenous Australians is an important step in Australia's development towards mature nationhood. The federal government identified reconciliation as an important goal for the period leading to the centenary of Australian Federation in 2001.

THE COUNCIL FOR ABORIGINAL RECONCILIATION

The *Council for Reconciliation Act* was passed unanimously by federal parliament on 2 September 1991. It established a 25-member council with representatives from Aboriginal and Torres Strait Islander groups as well as from industry, agriculture, the union movement, employers, the media and the major political parties.

Source 5.10.1

The vision statement formulated by the Council for Aboriginal Reconciliation

> **A united Australia which respects this land of ours, values the Aboriginal and Torres Strait Islander heritage and provides justice and equity for all.**

In its desire to achieve harmony within Australian society, the Council aims to have all Australians recognise that its indigenous peoples were the original owners of the land; that they have suffered ongoing social and economic disadvantage as a result of having their land taken from them; and that this has resulted in indigenous peoples missing many of the benefits of life that other Australians take for granted.

Source 5.10.2

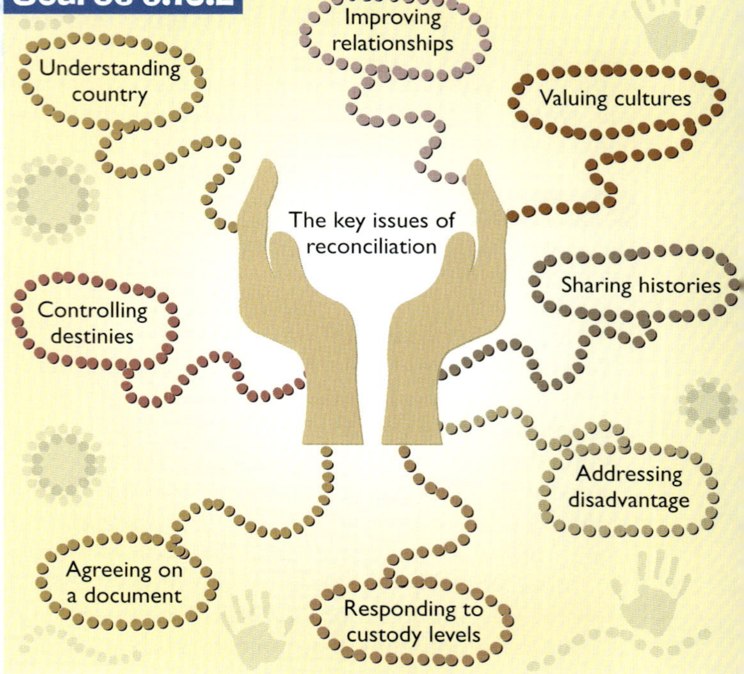

Mind map showing the key issues to be addressed in the reconciliation process as identified by the Council for Aboriginal Reconciliation

THE RECONCILIATION PROCESS

The 1967 referendum result, which meant Aboriginal and Torres Strait Islander peoples could be counted in the Australian census and that the federal government could make laws for them, was an important early step towards reconciliation. Land rights legislation in the 1970s and the *Racial Discrimination Act 1975* (Cwlth) helped continue this process. From the 1970s onwards, non-indigenous Australians have shown themselves increasingly aware of the importance of protecting the Australian landscape and environment and have joined with indigenous peoples in fighting to protect areas such as Kakadu from the potentially destructive processes of the mining industry. Exhibitions like those in the Yiribana section of the Art Gallery of New South Wales, and concerts from groups like Yothu Yindi have helped to breach the divide between indigenous and non-indigenous cultures.

Former Prime Minister Paul Keating took another step towards reconciliation in the 'Redfern speech', which he delivered at Redfern on 10 December 1992. In it, he acknowledged both the past injustices towards indigenous peoples and the fact that all Australians were in some way degraded by these injustices. The Mabo decision and *Native Title Act 1993* (Cwlth) were important in further recognising land rights and in providing funds for indigenous peoples to regain land. The strong support of 1800 participants at the Australian Reconciliation Convention in 1997 showed that reconciliation was a goal which many Australians had come to value.

Source 5.10.3

An extract from the speech of former Prime Minister Paul Keating at Redfern on 10 December 1992. The Redfern speech marked the beginning of the International Year of the World's Indigenous Peoples.

> It begins ... with an act of recognition. Recognition that it was we who did the dispossessing.
> We took the traditional lands and smashed the traditional way of life. We brought the diseases. The alcohol. We committed the murders. We took the children from their mothers. We practised discrimination and exclusion ...
> We failed to ask — how would I feel if this were done to me?
> As a consequence, we failed to see that what we were doing degraded all of us.

At the same time, there have always been threats to the reconciliation process. Mining companies and some state governments have often shown little appreciation of indigenous land rights and even less concern for the protection of sacred sites. Many non-indigenous Australians have been more concerned with what government assistance indigenous peoples were receiving than how and why they came to need it in the first place. In September 1996, Pauline Hanson, the independent member of Parliament for the Queensland seat of Oxley, gave her maiden speech in the House of Representatives. In it, she outlined her view that Asian migrants were 'swamping' the country and that they and indigenous Australians were receiving too many privileges. This view was supported by a number of Australians, often those whose own lives had been made harder by unemployment and tough living conditions. In 1997, she established the political party One Nation on the basis of these ideas. Even though the information put out by One Nation was frequently incorrect, it stirred up a lot of support for racist and discriminatory practices.

THE WIK DECISION

Australia appeared to be turning into a nation divided over the issue of race. In the midst of this, in December 1996, the High Court handed down its decision in the case brought to it by the Wik people of Cape York in northern Queensland. In *The Wik Peoples v. The State of Queensland and Others* (1996), the Wik people argued that native title rights continued on Crown land which had been leased to pastoralists. This was the issue which had not been sorted out by either the Mabo decision or by the *Native Title Act*. The High Court decided in the *Wik Case* (a) that native title continued in Queensland even on land which the government had leased to pastoralists and (b) that native title rights and the rights of the leaseholder existed concurrently (at the same time). The High Court also said that if there was any conflict, during the term of the lease, between how the two groups wanted to use the land, then native titleholders' 'rights and interests must yield to that extent to the rights of the leaseholders'. The Wik people celebrated the decision as one which strengthened native title claims and meant that pastoral leases did not extinguish native title for all time.

Many individuals and groups from the mining and pastoral industries were angered by the Wik decision and demanded that the federal government act to extinguish native title rights completely. The Queensland government responded by issuing titles and leases without following the provisions of the *Native Title Act*. The Prime Minister, John Howard, put forward a 'ten-point plan', which he claimed was a compromise. He expressed concern that the court had given too much to indigenous Australians and said his plan would 'return the pendulum to the centre'.

The Ten-Point Plan allowed for the approval of the Queensland government's actions; for some leases to give the leaseholder 'exclusive' use of the land; for local councils or state governments to put electricity or power services on land as a way of extinguishing native title; and for native title to be extinguished even after the lease had expired. In some cases indigenous peoples could continue to use their traditional lands if they could prove they had access to them (not easy if the pastoralist locked them out). The plan allowed for negotiation over mining exploration and mining work to be negotiated only by means of a one-stage agreement. It offered state governments the opportunity to acquire land for development which they intended to share with private companies. The plan addressed some of the problems of the *Native Title Act* which had made it too easy to register a native title claim even if it was unlikely to succeed, but it also weakened recognition of indigenous peoples' spiritual and cultural links with land. The final point seemed to put in place a time limit after which no native title claims could be made at all.

Members of opposition parties, religious leaders, academics, human rights activists and many members of the Australian public viewed the Ten-Point Plan as a racist proposal and did not hesitate to say so. A number of lawyers pointed out that if it became law, the plan might be challenged in the High Court for going against the *Racial Discrimination Act 1975* (Cwlth) or against the Constitution. The 1967 referendum had allowed the federal government to make laws for Australia's indigenous peoples. This 'race power' amendment to the Constitution has generally been taken to mean law-making for the *benefit* of indigenous peoples, whereas the Ten-Point Plan was not beneficial to them. Others questioned whether the Constitution gave the federal government the power to allow state governments to declare some land grants available for pastoralists' exclusive use. Some federal government MPs, like Warren Entsch, responded to such criticisms by calling on the public to boycott churches which had expressed their disapproval of the plan.

The Ten-Point Plan was incorporated into the Native Title (Amendment) Bill, which was passed in the House of Representatives and sent to the Senate with only minor amendments in late 1997. On 8 July 1998, after over a hundred hours of debate, the Native Title Amendment Bill was passed by the Senate. The final Act resulted from 400 pages of amendments to the original Bill. The requirement that a native title claimant needed to prove an ongoing relationship with the land was replaced by a requirement of proof that the claimant's *parents* had had an ongoing relationship with the land. The Act increased state and territory governments' powers over native title claims. Indigenous peoples would be allowed to negotiate with companies wanting to mine resources on native title land but not to negotiate with pastoral leaseholders who might want to change the usage of land.

WHERE TO NOW?

By the end of the twentieth century, governments, community groups and individuals had established a basis for reconciliation. Many non-indigenous Australians refused to accept misinformation about indigenous peoples and the conditions of their lives and eagerly sought accurate information on how historical events and issues have shaped the relationship between the two groups. This attitude was reflected in talk of 'Australian reconciliation' rather than 'Aboriginal reconciliation' and in surveys which show strong concern about race relationships and support for some form of **treaty**.

Source 5.10.4

The 'sea of hands' planted outside Parliament House in November 1997 during a demonstration over Wik, showing support for Aborigines

Source 5.10.5

Survey results from the research project entitled 'Unfinished Business' conducted in 1996 on behalf of the Council for Aboriginal Reconciliation

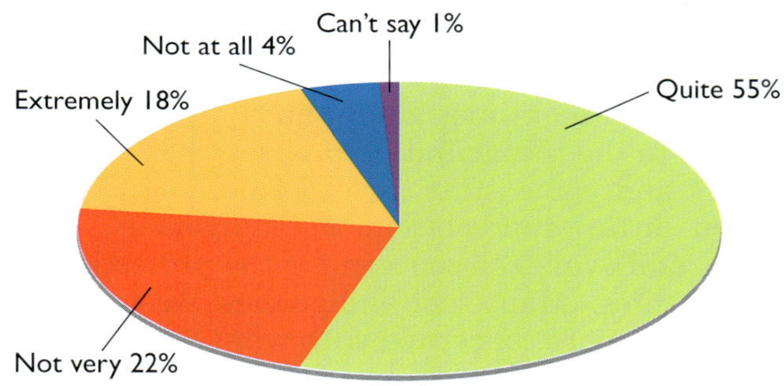

(a) Pie graph showing the extent of community concerns about improving relationships

Type of agreement	Support
Agreement at a national level which acknowledges that Aboriginal people were here before European settlement	75%
Regional agreements between people such as farmers and miners and indigenous communities	69%
Local agreements with indigenous communities about delivery of services such as health, housing and education	80%

(b) The percentage of support for three possible types of agreement

On 25 August 1999, 250 Aboriginal Australians crowded the Senate to hear the maiden speech of the first Aborigine to be elected to the Senate in 28 years. When Democrat Senator Aden Ridgeway gave this speech, many Australians hoped that the prime minister would respond to his call for an expression of regret for the injustices endured by indigenous Australians. Prime Minister Howard responded the following day.

Source 5.10.6

An extract from the motion passed by Parliament on 26 August 1999

> **I move that this House:**
> **(e) acknowledge that the mistreatment of many indigenous Australians over a significant period represents the most blemished chapter in our national history;**
> **(f) expresses its deep and sincere regret that indigenous Australians suffered injustices under the practices of past generations, and for the hurt and trauma that many indigenous people continue to feel as a consequence of those practices.**

While the Council for Aboriginal Reconciliation planned its final major public event in Sydney for May 2000, many Australians felt the absence of positive government enthusiasm for the process. Reconciliation awaits the achievement of justice with regard to indigenous land rights and of equity with other Australians in health, living conditions, education and employment.

Source 5.10.7

Cartoon by Nicholson published in the *Australian* on 30 August 1999

Activities

Check your understanding

1. What is meant by 'reconciliation' and why is it important?
2. List two positive steps toward reconciliation and two threats to its achievement.
3. What were the main features of the High Court's Wik decision?
4. In what ways did the proposed Ten-Point Plan undermine the Wik decision?
5. Why could a law based on the Ten-Point Plan be challenged in the High Court?

Investigation: *Aboriginal reconciliation*

1. Draw up two columns with the headings 'Plus' and 'Minus'. Use these to create a balance sheet to record the events and attitudes which have helped or hindered Australia's progress towards reconciliation. Decide how many points, between 1 and 5, each of these is worth. Add up your totals and use this as a guide in judging how well Australia is doing. Use your information to complete a paragraph of 10–15 lines which begins, 'Australia's goal of achieving reconciliation by 2001 . . .'
2. What vision of reconciliation is outlined in source 5.10.1?
3. Based on the knowledge you have of Australia's indigenous peoples, what do you think is meant by each of the issues identified in source 5.10.2?
4. Which of the reconciliation issues in source 5.10.3 did Paul Keating address in his Redfern speech (source 5.10.3)?
5. What does source 5.10.5 indicate about how Australians feel about reconciliation?
6. Is there a difference between the expression of 'regret' in source 5.10.6 and an 'apology'? Give reasons for your answer.
7. What is the message Nicholson was trying to express in source 5.10.7?
8. The *Hindmarsh Island Bridge Case* (*Kartinyeri v. The Commonwealth* (1998)) also played a role in the reconciliation process. What was the case about? What were the viewpoints of the different individuals and groups involved? What did the High Court decide? How did you think the court's decision would have affected the issues which must be resolved for reconciliation to occur? Present your findings to the class in the form of a news report suitable for presentation on television, radio or in a newspaper.

5.11

REPUBLICAN DEBATE — A NEW VISION IN DEFINING AUSTRALIA

The idea of a **republic** as a form of government goes back to views expressed by philosophers in ancient Greece and ancient Rome. Republicanism has had a long history in Australia too, and there have been many views on what the term actually meant. Some people say that indigenous Australians lived in a form of republic before the arrival of the British in 1788. In early nineteenth century Australia, talk of a republic involved discussion of separate Australian parliaments rather than a break with the monarchy. In 1880, the bushranger Ned Kelly and his gang talked of creating the Republic of North East Victoria, which would be completely free of British control. In the late nineteenth century, pro-Republicans were divided between those who hoped to gain a nation that would give all its citizens an equal share of the nation's wealth and those who associated the idea of a republic with nationalism and the preservation of a 'white' Australia.

The achievement of **Federation** in 1901 began a long period in which republicanism appeared to have died as an issue. Australians enjoyed a sense of independence at the same time as fighting two world wars along with Britain. Some Australians associated breaking with the monarchy as a communist idea and found that unacceptable. The republican issue began to revive in the early to mid 1960s through the writings of pro-republicans like Geoffrey Dutton and Donald Horne. The controversy surrounding the 1975 dismissal of the Whitlam government led to increased discussion of the issue and in 1977 Geoffrey Dutton published *Republican Australia*, containing essays giving the arguments for and against change.

THE REPUBLICAN ISSUE IN THE 1990s

With Federation and **representative democracy** forming the basic framework of Australia's political system, having a hereditary monarch as our head of state was the only thing that would have to change if Australia wanted to become a republic. Most Australians continued to support the British monarch as our **head of state** until the 1990s. The republican issue revived in the early 1990s with the establishment of two groups with opposing views on this issue. The Australian

Source 5.11.1

Percentage of Australians in favour of a republic — 1987–99

ARE YOU IN FAVOUR OF AUSTRALIA BECOMING A REPUBLIC?

	1999		1997			1995	1994	1993		1992	1991	1987
	Feb.	Jan.	Dec.	Sept.	June	June	Dec.	Nov.	July	May	June	Oct.
Strongly in favour	30	29	32	33	27	28	26	22	25	22	20	
Partly in favour	21	19	19	21	22	22	21	17	21	19	14	
Total in favour	51	48	51	54	49	60	47	39	46	41	34	21
Partly against	13	15	15	15	14	15	14	14	14	14	14	
Strongly against	20	20	20	15	16	20	23	30	22	31	38	
Total against	33	35	35	30	30	35	37	44	36	45	52	64
Uncommitted	16	17	14	16	21	15	16	17	18	14	14	15

From surveys conducted by Newspoll and reproduced from the *Australian*, 3 March 1999

Republican Movement (ARM) was formed in 1991 under the leadership of Malcolm Turnbull and former New South Wales Premier Neville Wran. Its main goal was to have an Australian as the nation's head of state rather than a foreigner who lived primarily in England. Australians for a Constitutional Monarchy (ACM) was formed in 1992 with Lloyd Waddy as convenor and Kerry Jones as executive director. Their goal was to convince Australians to retain the existing system.

In 1993, the Prime Minister, Paul Keating, formed a committee to investigate the 'minimal constitutional changes' needed to make Australia a republic while retaining the present system of government. In October 1993, the committee issued its report, *An Australian Republic*, and the following year the Opposition leader, Alexander Downer, suggested holding a people's convention to investigate the key issues further.

In June 1995, Keating announced his goal that Australia should become a republic with an Australian head of state. He hoped that this could be achieved by the time Sydney hosted the Olympic Games in 2000 or, otherwise, by the time of the centenary of Federation on 1 January 2001. An opinion poll taken not long afterwards showed that only 35 per cent of Australians supported the idea of keeping a **constitutional monarchy** as their form of government. The issue of Australia as a republic was back on the national agenda and the idea of an Australian republic was becoming linked to Australia's identity as a nation.

Keating's Labor government lost the 1996 election. The new Howard government decided to implement a suggestion put forward by its Foreign Minister, Alexander Downer. It would hold a constitutional convention to discuss the issues involved in Australia becoming a republic.

THE CONSTITUTIONAL CONVENTION

In November and December 1997, 45.3 per cent of eligible voters participated in a voluntary postal vote to elect half the delegates to a Constitutional

Source 5.11.2

The leaders of the two main groups in the republican debate; Kerry Jones of ACM (left) and Malcolm Turnbull of the ARM (right)

Source 5.11.3

The delegates to the Constitutional Convention of 2–13 February 1998

Convention. The remainder of the delegates were appointed by the government. Two-thirds of the elected delegates were pro-republican. From 2 February to 13 February 1998, 152 delegates attended the Constitutional Convention at Old Parliament House in Canberra. Under the joint chairmanship of former National Party leader Ian Sinclair and ALP President Barry Jones, the convention had to consider three issues:

- whether or not Australia should become a republic
- if 'yes', what model of a republic should be put to voters
- the time frame for change.

The Liberal Party/National Party coalition government, under pro-monarchist Prime Minister John Howard, promised that if there was majority support for the idea of a republic, then a **referendum** would put the question to the people.

The convention revealed strong support for a republic but there was considerable disagreement among pro-republicans about the method of choosing the head of state. At the time of the convention, over half the republican supporters favoured a head of state being chosen by direct election by the Australian public. The ARM argued strongly in favour of a head of state being chosen by a parliamentary majority of two-thirds or more. It believed that a direct election of the head of state would result in election campaigns and that candidates for the position would inevitably be linked to political parties. Election by parliament would make the position less politicised and make it more likely that the most able person would be chosen even if that person was not initially well known to the public.

THE MODEL CHOSEN

The delegates discussed four main models for the way an Australian republic could work. After much debate, they voted for their preferred model. The majority of votes supported the bipartisan appointment of the president model. Supporters of the ARM were especially thrilled with this result and looked forward to the referendum, which would put the question to the Australian people.

Source 5.11.4

Candidates must be Australian citizens who agree to being nominated.

→

All members of the Australian community can nominate candidates who will be considered by a committee.

→

The Prime Minister selects one nominee on the basis of the committee's report. This choice must be seconded by the leader of the Opposition and receive the approval of two-thirds of a joint sitting of both houses of parliament.

→

The person chosen as president has a 5-year term of office and the same powers as the Governor-General. The Prime Minister could remove the President but would have to gain House of Representatives approval of this action within 30 days. Non-approval by the lower house would be equivalent to a vote of no confidence in the Prime Minister.

Flow chart showing the main features of the bipartisan appointment of the president model

Source 5.11.5

Two emotional republican delegates following the decision that the question of a republic would be put to the people

Activities

Check your understanding

1. What different ideas did nineteenth century Australians have about the meaning of the word 'republic'?
2. How did attitudes towards republicanism change after Federation?
3. Name two events of the 1970s that stimulated renewed interest in the republican issue.
4. What signs were there in the 1990s that the republican issue had again caught the public interest?
5. What was the purpose of the January 1998 Constitutional Convention?
6. What issue created the most disagreement among the delegates?
7. Create a time chart showing key events and dates in the 1990s republican movement.

Communication: *Using a range of data*

1. Based on the information provided in source 5.11.1:
   (a) when were Australians least interested in becoming a republic?
   (b) what two pieces of evidence indicate that Australians' views had changed markedly by 1999?
   (c) what viewpoint has hardly changed over the period 1987–99?
2. The nineteenth and twentieth centuries both ended with conventions to consider Australia's Constitution. Look at the photograph of the 1998 Constitutional Convention (source 5.11.3). What would have been the main differences between the types of people who gathered to discuss constitutional issues in the late 1800s compared with those who did so in the late 1900s? What social changes in the years in between would explain these differences?
3. How does the model shown in source 5.11.4:
   (a) provide for public involvement in the choice of a President and
   (b) provide protection against the wrongful use of the Prime Minister's power?
   (c) What could future students of the republican issue learn from source 5.11.5?

THE REFERENDUM AND BEYOND

Australians have traditionally been reluctant to vote for change, perhaps because they have not fully understood the issues and perhaps because of lack of interest. Since Federation in 1901, only eight out of 42 proposals for constitutional change have been accepted by the people. On this basis, a 'yes' vote seemed unlikely. Anecdotal evidence indicated that Australians believed that a republic was inevitable even if they were not ready to vote in its favour in 1999. In the final weeks preceding the 6 November vote, the Australian Electoral Commission (AEC) provided for people's democratic rights by issuing every voter with a booklet

Source 5.12.1

A summary of the official 'yes' case from the ARM web site at www.republic.org.au/yescase.html

- Australia's future would best be served by having an Australian head of state, chosen on merit and able to represent the values underpinning the Australian identity.
- Australia's interests as a mature, independent and multicultural nation are no longer served by having the British monarch as head of state.
- Replacing the British monarch with an Australian head of state would symbolise and affirm Australia's independence as a nation.
- Proposed changes to the Constitution are minor and maintain the democratic rights of all Australians.
- Voting for an Australian head of state would not change the flag, the national anthem, the number of public holidays, our friendly links with Britain or our membership of the Commonwealth and would not give a president any more powers than those now held by the Governor-General.
- The position of President under the republican model would be the same in power and role as that of the Governor-General and therefore quite different to those of the United States President.
- The system for appointing a President will be more democratic and open than the current system of appointment of a Governor-General. Any Australian could put forward a nomination and the decision-making process would involve people from all sides of politics. A president could be appointed only after gaining the support of the Prime Minister and the leader of the Opposition, and gaining the approval of two-thirds of the two houses of federal parliament. This would provide protection against someone becoming President on the basis of money, influence or political loyalties and would ensure that the person chosen was above party politics and able to serve as a force uniting all Australians.
- Changing to a republic is important but it does not require any major change to Australia's system of government.

Source 5.12.2

A summary of the official 'no' case from the ACM web site at www.norepublic.com.au

- The Prime Minister could dismiss the President for no reason. The President would be the Prime Minister's puppet and unable to fulfil a role as an independent umpire in relation to the Constitution.
- The proposed model does not allow for a President directly elected by the people and therefore is undemocratic and would result in a President chosen by political deal-makers.
- 'If it ain't broke don't fix it'. The current system works well, provides political stability and has evolved to a stage where the Governor-General really is Australia's head of state.
- The proposed Bill would require 69 changes to the Constitution and no one knows how these would affect the Australian political system.
- The republican debate has divided Australians and the model put forward is not even supported by all republicans.
- Australia is already independent and our legal links with Britain were removed under the terms of the 1986 *Australia Act*.
- Becoming a republic will not improve trade, the economy or Australia's security.
- A Prime Minister could give a President a job for life.
- The nominations committee will be made up of politicians, who will work in secret and give the impression that the public's views will be considered.
- A politician could resign from his or her party and then become President.

outlining the official 'yes' and 'no' cases and the proposed changes to the Constitution, and showing sample ballot papers. The information was also available on audio cassette and disk and in braille, large print and through interpreting services for people speaking languages other than English.

Source 5.12.3

SAMPLE

AUSTRALIA

Commonwealth of Australia

BALLOT PAPER

Referendum on proposed Constitution alteration

DIRECTIONS TO VOTER

Write YES or NO in the spaces provided opposite the question set out below

A PROPOSED LAW: To alter the Constitution to establish the Commonwealth of Australia as a republic with the Queen and Governor-General being replaced by a President appointed by a two-thirds majority of the members of the Commonwealth Parliament.

DO YOU APPROVE THIS PROPOSED ALTERATION?

WRITE "YES" OR "NO"

Australian Electoral Commission **AEC**

Helping you have your say.

Sample ballot paper on the republican question from the Australian Electoral Commission

Source 5.12.4

An example of the proposed changes to Section 37 of the Australian Constitution. The proposed changes included one change of the word 'Queen' to 'President', 15 changes of the words 'Governor-General' to 'President' and the deletion of the words 'by the Queen' in another section.

> **37 Resignation of member**
> **A member may by writing addressed to the Speaker, or to the ~~Governor-General~~ President if there is no Speaker or if the Speaker is absent from the Commonwealth, resign his place, which thereupon shall become vacant.**

The referendum was defeated. The majority of Australians voted against it, with Victoria being the only state to vote in its favour. The reason for the referendum's defeat was not that the majority of Australians were pro-monarchy — they were not. The referendum was defeated because many republicans voted 'no'. They feared that without a direct election they would only gain what the ACM called a 'politician's republic'. It was unlikely that the issue would go away, but it would have to be decided by Australians in the next millennium.

Activities

Check your understanding

1. Why is it difficult for referenda to succeed in Australia?
2. What assistance did the AEC provide to Australian voters prior to the November 6 vote? Why did it do this?
3. Why was the referendum defeated?

Investigation: *The quest for a republic*

1. What advantages of Australia as a republic/constitutional monarchy are highlighted in sources 5.12.1 and 5.12.2? Which of the arguments either address or encourage fears among the general public?
2. What four pieces of information are provided in source 5.12.1? What information might the ARM and the ACM have preferred to include or delete? Give reasons for your answer.
3. Why was the change shown in source 5.12.4 necessary if Australia was to become a republic?
4. Use the sources and other information available in the text to conduct an open forum with students representing each of the two main viewpoints and the rest of the class asking them questions.
5. Use the information available in the text and sources to make up your own mind on the referendum question. Conduct a secret ballot within your class to see how it would have decided this issue.

5.13 Meeting the outcomes

EXPLAIN THE KEY CHANGES IN SOCIAL AND POLITICAL ATTITUDES AND VALUES IN MODERN WESTERN SOCIETY.

Examine the ways in which advances in technology affected other areas, such as health, medicine, transport, education.

1. What was the kangaroo route and how have changes in technology altered it? (5.5)
2. How have technological advances affected airline passenger costs? (5.5)
3. In what ways has technology contributed to the death of distance? (5.5)

Evaluate the effect of significant events and ideas on groups.

What impact did the Franklin Dam issue have on the following groups? (5.6)

(a) Australian government
(b) Tasmanian government
(c) Tasmanian Hydro-electric Commission
(d) Tasmanian Wilderness Society

ANALYSE THE MOVEMENT OF ABORIGINAL AND TORRES STRAIT ISLANDER COMMUNITIES FOR CIVIL AND POLITICAL RIGHTS.

Identify which civil and political rights were denied the Aboriginal and Torres Strait Islander communities.

1. Match the term in the left-hand column with its definition from the right-hand column:

A. discrimination	A. the act of removal of someone's property
B. dispossession	B. the act of bringing people into closer understanding of one another
C. exploitation	C. land which has no owner
D. indigenous	D. the act of treating individuals or groups differently according to sex, race, culture etc.
E. land rights	E. an agreement
F. native title	F. control over one's own life
G. reconciliation	G. land ownership based on traditional laws
H. self-determination	H. the rights of indigenous people to possess land
I. *terra nullius*	I. the first inhabitants of a particular country
J. treaty	J. taking advantage of others

2. Refer to source 5.13.1 to respond to the following questions:
   (a) Write a paragraph to summarise the results of these statistics.
   (b) Which state or territory was least discriminatory towards Aboriginal people in 1962?
   (c) Compare the lifestyle of Aborigines living in New South Wales and Queensland in 1962.

Source 5.13.1

Rights 'enjoyed' by Aborigines on settlements and reserves in 1962

	NSW	VIC.	SA	WA	NT	QLD
Voting rights (State)	Y	Y	Y	N	Y	N
Marry freely	Y	Y	Y	N	N	N
Control own children	Y	Y	N	N	N	N
Move freely	Y	N	N	N	N	N
Own property freely	Y	N	Y	N	N	N
Receive award wages	Y	N	N	N	N	N
Alcohol allowed	N	N	N	N	N	N

B. Attwood and A. Markus, *The 1967 Referendum, or when Aborigines didn't get the Vote*, AIATSIS, Canberra, 1997, p. 13.

Outline the different ways in which the Aboriginal and Torres Strait Islander communities campaigned for civil and political rights.

1. What action did Eddie Mabo take to improve Aboriginal and Torres Strait Islander rights? (5.8)
2. What was the result of his actions? (5.8)
3. What action did the Wik people take? (5.10)
4. What decision was made in the Wik case and how did it eventually change? (5.10)

Evaluate the degree to which the Aboriginal and Torres Strait Islander communities have been successful in their campaign.

1. What action occurred in 1985 to recognise Aboriginal land rights claims? (5.7)
2. Why do you think traditional owners of the land consider it so important that their land is returned?
3. Observe source 5.13.2.
   (a) What do you think the two men are holding in their raised hands?
   (b) Which groups do you think the two men represent?
   (c) What is the significance of the poster and the t-shirts?
   (d) What parts of the photograph suggest that this was an important occasion?

Source 5.13.2

The official ceremony to mark the return of Uluru to its traditional owners in November, 1985

Analyse the reasons why civil and political rights were denied to Aboriginal and Torres Strait Islander communities.

1. Who are the Stolen Generation?
2. How long did the practice of separating indigenous children from their families go on? (5.9)
3. Why were children removed from their parents?
4. Look carefully at source 5.13.3 and answer the following questions:
   (a) Explain how the children might have come to live in the children's home.
   (b) What types of work and study might they have been expected to do there?
   (c) What benefits were the Aboriginal children supposed to have gained by being removed?
   (d) What aspects of life did these children miss out on in their new homes?

Source 5.13.3

Inside the Retta Dixon Aboriginal children's home in the 1960s

Chapter

6

LIVING WITH THE LAW

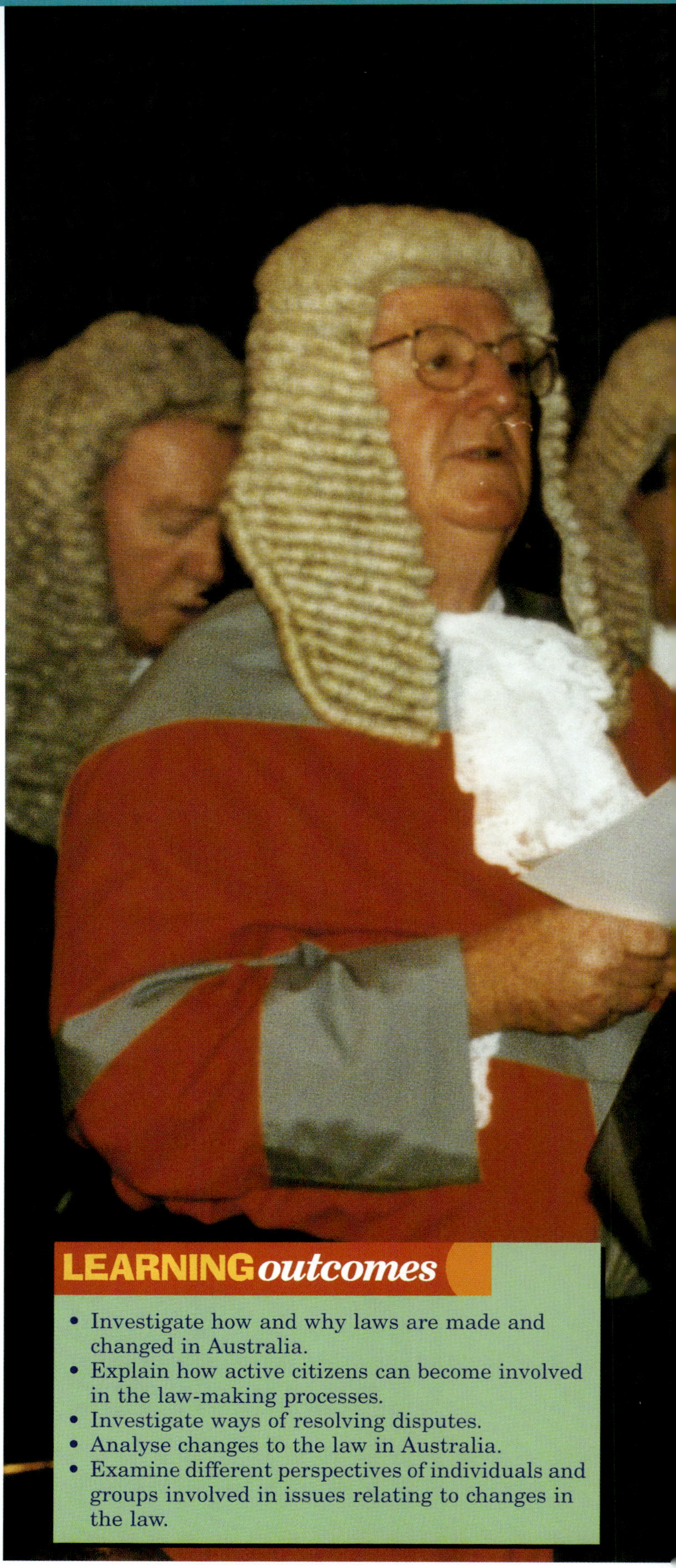

INTRODUCTION

Our society is constantly changing. Just think of the differences between the life of your grandparents and the life you lead today. Our world is much faster than your grandparents could have predicted, with fast computers, fast cars, fast foods and kinds of technology that were the subject of science fiction just decades ago. As the pace of our society changes, so do the values that society upholds.

As our life becomes faster and more complex, the laws that determine how we relate to each other must also change if they are to remain relevant. Laws that become irrelevant are often not obeyed.

In this chapter we will look at the way laws are altered to deal with the changes that occur in society. Sometimes the law changes in anticipation of events and sometimes it changes in response to events that have already taken place.

We will also look at some of the people who administer the law and we will consider your rights if you find yourself involved in the legal system. We will also look at some of the different types of law that exist in our society.

LEARNING *outcomes*

- Investigate how and why laws are made and changed in Australia.
- Explain how active citizens can become involved in the law-making processes.
- Investigate ways of resolving disputes.
- Analyse changes to the law in Australia.
- Examine different perspectives of individuals and groups involved in issues relating to changes in the law.

Glossary

amnesty: an officially declared period of time during which a particular law is not enforced
autopsy: the physical examination of a dead body by a coroner in order to determine the cause of death
civil law: the laws of a country that relate to private matters
cloning: the process of producing an organism identical to the organism or cell from which it has been derived
common law: unwritten laws that were developed by judges in the court system and based on precedent
defendant: the person in a civil or criminal action who is brought to trial by the actions of the plaintiff (civil) or the prosecutor (criminal)
hierarchy: a system in which things are in a graded order, with more power or importance at the top
indictable offence: serious criminal matter that can be tried in the County Court or the Supreme Court
injury: a loss suffered as a result of someone's actions, the injury being physical, psychological, real or assumed
judge: a trained legal professional who presides over trials in the County Court and above to ensure that the correct legal process is followed
jurisdiction: the extent or area of judicial authority
jury: a panel of ordinary people who hear the evidence presented in a trial and deliver a verdict based on this evidence
law: a standard or rule that all in society are expected to uphold and which is administered and enforced by the police and courts respectively
legal precedent: a legal decision which sets a pattern for future similar cases
lobby group: a political group which tries to influence decisions made by parliaments and ministers; for example, the gun lobby or animal rights lobby
plaintiff: the person in a civil action who has been wronged and wishes to pursue the issue through legal processes
prosecutor: the person in a criminal action who brings the case to trial and who represents the Crown
psychologist: a person who is trained to study all facets of human behaviour
statute law: law established by legislation; law that is passed by parliament
summary offence: a minor criminal matter that will be tried in the Magistrate's Court
tort: a civil wrong
trial: the final part of the legal process that determines whether someone committed an illegal act in a criminal case or caused another person to suffer a loss in a civil matter
verdict: a judgement or decision made by a jury

THE ORIGINS OF LAW

King Hammurabi, who lived in Sumeria by the rivers of Babylon around 2000 BC, was one of the earliest rulers to have a written legal code. He ordered a stone pillar, two metres high, on which he wrote over 280 **laws** for his loyal followers to obey. Some of these are listed below.

Law 161 If a man accuse another, but cannot offer proof, then he shall die.

Law 162 If a man assists a slave to escape, then he shall die.

Law 163 If a son strikes his father, then he shall lose his fingers.

Law 164 If a woman has not been a careful wife and belittles her husband, then she shall be thrown in the river.

Law 165 If a man destroy an eye of another, they shall destroy his eye.

Shamash, the god of peace, handing Hammurabi the laws of Babylon

Other societies' laws related to their cultures. In many communities, these were based on religion. The Jewish nation obeyed the ten commandments and the laws of the Torah, while the Muslims followed the Five Pillars of Islam. In Australia today, we would generally regard these religious laws as moral laws that are not necessarily enforced by the legal system. In other parts of the world, however, religious laws are the very foundation and fabric of society.

In Australia prior to the arrival of the Europeans in 1788, law existed as traditional Aboriginal law. This law was orally passed from one generation to the next, and was administered by councils of elders. A typical form of punishment was to banish an offender from the group.

When the English arrived in Australia, they brought with them their own legal system. Consequently, Australia's legal system is now very similar to that of England.

ENGLISH LAW

English law began as tribal law or customs which were appropriate to the particular people they affected. These customs became accepted throughout most English communities by being incorporated into the decisions of the regularly visiting court of the king. These unwritten laws, which were based on custom and precedent, now form the branch of law we call **common law**.

Henry II was the first English king to make a lasting impact on our laws. He organised his own advisers to tour the countryside and hear cases in his name. This process established some degree of 'commonness' about the laws of England.

Henry also decided that **trial** by ordeal was not the fairest way to administer justice. One example of a trial by ordeal was for an accused to carry a red-hot stone in his or her bare hands for a distance. The person's guilt or innocence was then determined by how quickly the hands healed. Henry II introduced a system of trial by **jury** to replace this ordeal. Initially, the jury was fined if the **judge** disapproved of the **verdict**, or it was locked up without any food or drink while it considered its verdict. By the latter part of the last century, however, we had learned to treat our jurors with more care.

Trial by ordeal: would justice have prevailed?

Over time, many of the law-making powers of the monarch, enforceable through the courts, came to belong to parliament. Today our courts have the right to make laws through common law while each level of parliament is also empowered to make laws. Thus any Bill that passes through parliament and is signed by the Governor-General (if federal) or the Governor (if state) becomes an Act (or statute) that is enforceable. All the Acts of parliament, both state and federal, form our **statute law**. Statute law and common law together form the laws of our country.

In our society, statute law will always prevail over common law and no court has the power to change it. However the courts are often asked to interpret or explain the meaning of the law, and in this way they can influence the way the law is practised.

Activities

Investigation: *Ancient laws*

1. Having read some of the laws of Hammurabi (opposite) what do you imagine Sumerian society was like?
2. Suggest laws that King Hammurabi might introduce today to cater for the following incidents:
   (a) bank robbery
   (b) failing to stop at a red light
   (c) polluting the atmosphere
   (d) arson (deliberate burning of building or property).
3. List any similarities between Hammurabi's laws and those of Moses (The Ten Commandments) and Mohammed (The Five Pillars of Islam).
4. List any differences between Hammurabi's laws and those of Moses and Mohammed, and explain why these differences might occur.
5. Which of the laws of Hammurabi, Moses and Mohammed would we still uphold today? Which laws do you feel are closest to the way that we write our laws? Explain.
6. Which of these ancient laws would you interpret as moral laws rather than community laws? Justify your point of view.

Common and statute law

1. Do you think that common law is well named? Explain.
2. Imagine that you are an adviser in Henry's court. Justify, to another person playing the role of Henry, the continued use of trial by ordeal rather than the new idea of trial by jury.
3. In a short paragraph, define the term 'jury'.
4. Was trial by jury a fair system before the late 1800s? Explain.
5. Discuss how statute law differs from common law.
6. Laws do need to adapt to changing values in society. Would common law or statute law be the more flexible? Discuss your point of view.

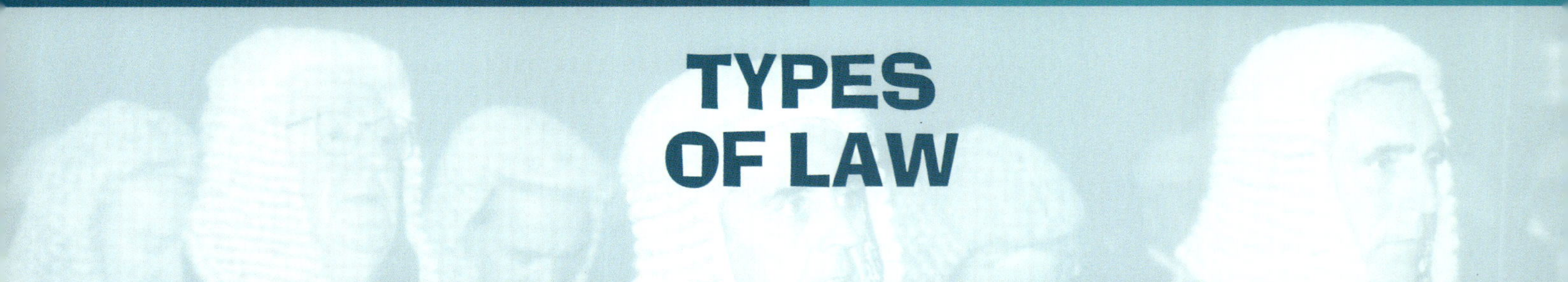

6.2 TYPES OF LAW

In all societies people have rights, but they are also responsible for respecting others' rights. Children and teenagers have a number of rights within the home environment. These rights are often laid down in laws made by the Commonwealth or are established by **legal precedent** in court cases. These rights are designed to protect you, a child, from being abused within the home. If a person's rights are infringed, then they can expect the law to offer some degree of protection, either through the criminal code or through civil action.

CRIMES

Criminal acts can be broadly classified into six types.

1. Acts against a person. Manslaughter and assault are examples here.
2. Acts against property. Theft and vandalism are two such acts.
3. Acts that are immoral. Incest is an act that is unacceptable on moral grounds.
4. Acts against the state itself. Treason (for example, stealing state secrets) is fairly rare.
5. Acts against the legal system. Lying in court, or perjury, is one example that is not too uncommon.
6. Acts that breach a regulation or a council by-law. Parking infringements and general traffic offences are obvious examples.

The various types of crime and the punishments imposed are described in the *Crimes Act* of each State.

TORTS

Civil law has come to us through common law, sometimes known as case law. One kind of breach of civil law is called a **tort**. This is a French word meaning 'a civil wrong'. Torts are of four broad types.

1. Negligence. A person can sue another person for not taking enough care to prevent an **injury**. Perhaps poor medical advice was given or a hole in the ground was left uncovered.
2. Nuisance. A person who prevents another from enjoying his or her own property is said to be causing a nuisance. A neighbour's loud music at 2.00 a.m. is an example of a nuisance.
3. Defamation. This occurs when someone makes untrue or harmful comments about another person. Slander involves a spoken comment while libel involves printed or taped comments.
4. Trespass. If someone interferes with another's land (by being on it without permission); interferes with their person (by threatening them or restraining them); or interferes with another's property (by touching or causing damage), they are trespassing.

In all these instances, the person who is wronged — the **plaintiff** — will usually seek monetary compensation or damages from the **defendant**. This may involve millions of dollars or just a few hundred.

Unlike crimes, torts do not involve the police.

Activities

Communication: *Analysing a cartoon*

1. From the cartoon opposite, select three incidents punishable by criminal law.
2. List all the examples of civil actions that you can find in the picture and classify them into the four types.
3. Crimes against property usually involve taking property with the intention of not returning it. This is referred to as theft.
   (a) An offence more serious than theft is robbery. What element in robbery makes it a more serious offence?
   (b) Burglary involves the intention to steal by entering a property uninvited. What do you think 'aggravated burglary' might involve? Should this be a more serious crime?

Investigation: *Analysing crimes*

Consider the following cases. Decide whether each involves a criminal action, a civil action (or maybe both) or no action at all. State which area of law may be involved, and why.

1. Fred is talking to Bob over the back fence about his tomatoes and calls him a silly old fool. No-one else hears the comment.
2. Phil is found asleep in the driver's seat of his parked car by a police patrol. He had been drinking heavily.
3. Masako holds a black belt in karate. When stopped by a would-be mugger who was intent on robbery, she kicked the robber and broke his arm.
4. Petros likes to take a shortcut to work by cutting through Karen's vacant corner block of land. He has been doing this for over five years.
5. Wayne is a spectator at the football. On seeing a bad error of judgement by umpire Thompson, he is abusive and rude towards Thompson in a loud and clear voice.
6. Daniel gets involved in an argument with Martin. He becomes so angry that he threatens to punch Martin on the nose. Martin believes that he means it.
7. After being booked by the police for dangerous driving, Jane forgets to respond to the summons to attend the court to explain her actions.
8. While digging a garden in her backyard, Rachel breaks a waterpipe and floods Mrs Paizes's henhouse next door, drowning her prize rooster.
9. Nick, a financial adviser, recommended that Mr Wilson buy shares in PQR Investments. Mr Wilson did, and lost his money when the company collapsed.
10. Nerida's house has been burgled several times. She sets a trap and shoots Tom as he enters with the intent to burgle again.
11. Choose a partner and, over a week, collect all the newspaper articles you can on criminal issues while your partner collects all reports of civil cases. Prepare a report outlining the legal differences and similarities between the two types of legal action.

THE COURT HIERARCHY

If you break a minor rule at school your 'guilt' and 'punishment' will probably be determined by your class teacher. If your offence is more serious, perhaps your level coordinator will deal with the matter. Finally, if you commit a major breach of a school rule you will find yourself staring at the carpet in the principal's office. The court system in each state operates under a similar structure.

Within each state there are three levels of court, each with its own area of jurisdiction (control or authority). The higher level courts generally deal with the more serious or important cases. Each court can hear both civil and criminal cases.

As we move up the court **hierarchy**, each court can hear appeals from the court immediately below it. Appeals are allowed where one of the parties involved objects to:

- the decision
- the law used to make that decision; or
- the penalty imposed by a lower court.

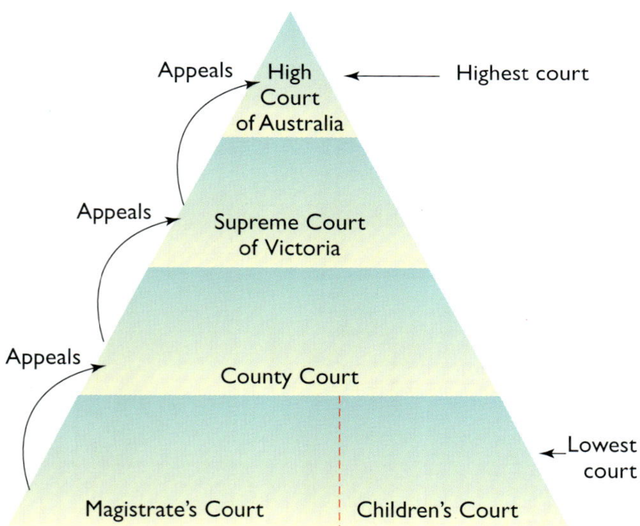

Hierarchy of courts in Victoria

In Australia, each state has its own names for the different courts, but the structure is much the same. The Magistrate's Court, as well as hearing minor criminal cases, conducts committal proceedings. These proceedings decide whether, in a serious criminal case, there is enough evidence for the case to go to trial in the County Court or the Supreme Court. If there is not enough evidence, the matter will be dismissed, thus saving the higher courts much valuable time. In civil cases, it is the amount of damages being sought by the plaintiff that determines which court hears the case. The higher the damages, the higher the court.

A problem facing all courts, but particularly the higher courts, is the cost of a trial. The further up we go in the hierarchy, the more expensive the trials become. Cases in the Supreme Court, for instance, cost the state a huge amount of money, and may cost the defendant or plaintiff well over $5000 per day in legal fees.

Full bench of the High Court

PRECEDENT

Another aspect of the court hierarchy is that decisions made in a higher court are binding, and must be followed by lower courts in cases that involve similar circumstances. This is part of 'the doctrine of precedent' and creates a degree of consistency in court decisions. The doctrine of precedent is therefore the basis for 'judge-made law', which we call common law.

The case of the itchy underpants

In 1936, Dr Grant of Adelaide bought a pair of knitted underpants from a menswear shop. After wearing these underpants as recommended by the manufacturer, Australian Knitting Mills, he developed a severe itch, which caused him great discomfort and distress.

At this time, there was no legislation which stated that a manufacturer must make sure that its products were fit for their intended use. Dr Grant sued the manufacturer of the underpants for compensation for his suffering, relying on a decision made in a previous case in a higher court. This case, called *Donoghue v. Stevenson* (1932), concerned a woman who discovered half a snail at the bottom of a soft drink bottle from which she had drunk. She was violently ill and suffered great nervous shock. She successfully sued the manufacturer of the soft drink for injuries. Where, after all, was the other half of the snail?

Activities

Communication: *Analysing a hierarchy diagram*

1. Which court can hear appeals from Supreme Court cases?
2. In what types of case might a person seek an appeal?
3. What barriers are there to people appealing to the Supreme and High courts?
4. Decide which court would hear the following cases.
   (a) Children sue Kanoo Foods Ltd for causing their father's death after he ate some food that contained the salmonella bacteria.
   (b) A car driver challenges a speeding ticket issued to her.
   (c) An arsonist is on trial for deliberately setting light to several neighbourhood hedges and fences.
   (d) A youth appeals against a conviction in the Magistrate's Court for car theft.
5. Draw a discipline hierarchy for your school, similar to that of the courts on the opposite page.

Investigation: *Court action*

1. Think of an action that is subject to both criminal and civil action. Write up a list of such cases.
2. Juries are:
   - not used in criminal trials in the Magistrate's Court but employed in the County and Supreme courts
   - used in civil cases in the County and Supreme courts only if the two parties agree to their use
   - never used in trials of appeal in any court.
3. The legal terms 'jury', 'jurisdiction' and 'jurisprudence' all have a common theme. Investigate the origin of each word and explain the legal implications of each.
4. Justify and explain why each of these might be so.
   (a) Carefully read the information about poor Dr Grant.
   (b) Explain how precedent may work in his favour.
   (c) Why might the court in Grant's case be bound by the decision of the *Donoghue v. Stevenson* case? After all, they are about different things — snails and underpants.
   (d) In what circumstances might the court not be bound by a previous decision?
5. Prepare a class discussion, the topic being: 'Courts should determine all cases on their merit and should not have to follow precedent'.

WHO'S WHO IN COURT

If you visit a court of law in Australia — as you are entitled to do at any time — you will see many people at work, each with specific roles to play.

The judge

'I am trained in the law and worked as a barrister before I was appointed as a judge. I work as a judge in the County Court, while good friends of mine are Justices in the Supreme Court. We all wear wigs and gowns in court and are addressed as "Your Honour". My job is to make sure that the trial follows correct legal procedure and to clarify any points of law that may arise.

In all criminal cases, a jury decides whether a person is guilty or not, even if I disagree with their decision. If a defendant is found guilty, I decide on the type and length of sentence in a criminal case. In a civil case, the jury determines what damages are awarded.'

The magistrate

'I preside over the lower court. I do not wear a wig or a gown but I am a qualified legal practitioner. I hold a law degree and I practised as a barrister before being appointed as a magistrate.

I decide in minor criminal cases whether someone is guilty or not, as there are no juries in my court. I administer the punishment following the guidelines in the *Crimes Act*. I also decide in civil cases who is liable and how much compensation may be paid in damages.

In my court, I am addressed as "Your Worship". Whereas I work in the Magistrate's Court, colleagues of mine are involved in the Children's Court and the Coroner's Court.'

The prosecutor

'The **prosecutor's** role in criminal trials is to convince the jury that a person is guilty. All cases are now handled by the Director of Public Prosecutions (DPP). I happen to be a member of the police force but my job is also done by other qualified practitioners with the DPP. I am trained in the law, and I present the Crown's case. All criminal cases are referred to as "R. v. ——", where R. is the Crown (the Queen, or State), who represents all society.

In civil matters, a solicitor or barrister will act on behalf of the plaintiff. They will attempt to prove their client's case and ensure the client receives compensation.'

- A Judge
- B Judge's associate
- C Court reporter (not in all courts)
- D Witness
- E Tipstaff
- F Jurors
- G Media and police
- H Prison officer
- I Accused
- J Counsel for the defence
- K Prosecutor

Counsel for the defence

‘I have a law degree and I am employed by the accused to represent him or her in court. I present my client's defence against the charges made by the prosecution. If my client pleads guilty at the start of the case, I speak on behalf of my client to try to lessen the punishment.

In civil cases, I also present my client's case and defend him or her against the claims made by the plaintiff. If I am successful in doing this, my client will not be liable for any damages.

Once I have enough experience, I hope to become a Queen's Counsel (sometimes called a QC, or a "silk"), which is the highest level of barrister.’

Legal practitioner

‘Today in Victoria I am called a "legal practitioner". I used to be called a "solicitor" before the *Legal Practice Act* was brought into effect. Clients who have a legal problem come to me to sort it out. This may include assisting in drawing up contracts, advising on conveyancing or on buying property, helping clients in a legal dispute with their neighbours, or any number of other legal problems individuals or businesses get themselves into. I am the first legal reference point and often the last. Although, as a law graduate, I may represent my clients in the lower courts, I usually work in tandem with barristers. I brief barristers on cases, giving them all the information they need, and I suggest how they might argue their cases in court. The barristers and I are an effective team, with the barrister presenting the case while I do much of the groundwork of looking up procedural rules and legislation and noting important precedents that might help our case. If you need a lawyer, you have to come and see me first.’

The juror

‘I had never served on a jury before. I was selected for jury duty last year, when my name was chosen from the electoral roll. As a jury member, I was one of a group of citizens who decided on a verdict in a specific case. Being a pilot, I could have been excused, but I chose to serve. Others who can be excused include teachers, nurses and firemen. A number of other citizens are disqualified from or ineligible for jury duty. These include people who:

- have been in jail in the last ten years
- work in the legal system
- are unable to read or speak English
- are over 65 years of age
- are pregnant.

I was told that a Parliamentary Law Reform Committee is looking at the way juries operate, including reassessing those who should be disqualified and excused. I could give them a few ideas. I certainly earned my $32 a day, as I and 11 others had to reach a majority decision (11:1) in a manslaughter case. If it had been a murder case, we would have had to reach a unanimous decision. A friend of mine once served on a civil jury in a case that went on for months. He helped determine the thousands of dollars damages that were awarded.’

Tipstaff

‘Tipstaffs are employed in both the Supreme and the County courts. I help with security of the court, I give the oath to all witnesses and I keep in order any members of the public who are visiting the court.’

Judge's associate

‘I am a trained lawyer, and assist the judge in and out of the courtroom. I ensure that all the paperwork is done and I help the judge wherever I can. I administer any bonds or fines that the judge orders and explain these to the accused wherever I can.’

Court reporter

‘In the recent past I used to record, by shorthand or shorthand machine, every word that was spoken during a trial in both the County and the Supreme courts . . . and I mean every word. Nowadays, most courtrooms have their own recording room and our task now is to transfer the recorded evidence into hard copy. This is a little more impersonal, but more efficient and accurate.’

Activities

Check your understanding

1. What is the difference between the following pairs:
   (a) judge and magistrate?
   (b) solicitor and barrister?
   (c) defendant and plaintiff?
   (d) sentence and damages?
2. In a criminal case, how many people are on a jury? What decisions do the jury and the judge make in these matters?

Investigation: *An organised talk*

As a group, either invite a member of the legal profession to your school to talk to your group, or visit a court.

6.5

THE ROLE OF THE POLICE

When we talk of the police, we often picture police officers simply patrolling in the 'divvy' van. As important as these officers are in making us all feel secure and protected, there is much more to police operation than police patrols. Several different sections of the police force can be involved in any single investigation.

Homicide squad

This squad investigates all murders across the State. It works in teams of five members and examines all murders or suspicious deaths, police shootings, deaths in custody or any event like a bushfire that causes a large loss of human life.

Forensic science laboratory

This has two broad purposes: firstly, to assist in police investigations by examining physical evidence either at the crime scene or in the laboratory; and, secondly, to provide evidence of their investigations in court.

The forensic laboratory has three main tasks:

- to analyse and identify substances such as drugs
- to identify the amount or type of a substance present, such as alcohol in blood, or to identify blood grouping or semen for murder, assaults or rape cases
- to compare items such as footprints, documents or writing (in fraud or extortion), paints, metals, fibres, bullets, gunshot residues, blood groups and soils for burglaries, rapes, hit and run accidents and murders.

An important division of the laboratory is the photography section. This is responsible for the photography of crime scenes and any victims. They are also involved in surveillance photography.

The Institute of Forensic Pathology is closely associated with the Coroner's Court and conducts **autopsies** in order to assist the coroner in determining the cause of death.

General duties officers

These are the police that are most apparent to us, as we see them patrolling their areas on foot or in patrol cars. Their role is to prevent crime and respond to any cries for help from the community. Such officers work out of local stations and some of their many duties are to:

- investigate crimes in their area, prosecute offenders and give evidence in court
- investigate the causes of accidents and unnatural deaths.

Criminal Investigation Branch (CIB)

This is composed of police officers who have completed a special two-year training program. All members of this group have investigative skills and training in law. They are responsible for conducting investigations into crimes by accumulating evidence, assisted by other specialist branches.

Specialised squads

There are several specialised squads such as the Search and Rescue Squad, the Drug Squad, the Rape Squad and the Dog Squad, all of which help to carry out the important responsibilities of the police in our community.

Activities

Investigation: *Understanding the role of the police*

1. Imagine you are an officer investigating the deaths described in the article below.
   (a) Outline how you think the events took place.
   (b) What evidence would you need to prove your case?
2. Which branches of the police force are mentioned in the article? Describe the role each played in the investigation.
3. From your reading of the article, explain the role of the coroner.
4. Collect news articles that highlight the many roles played by the police in our community. Pool your articles with others to make a comprehensive list of all these roles.
5. 'Police are the enforcers of law in our society and should not be bound by these very laws.' Discuss the idea that there may be instances where the police should not be bound by the laws of our society.

Communication: *Using and displaying data*

1. Examine the figures in the following table. Calculate and graph the ratio of police to population and comment on the trends.

	Police numbers	Population (Victoria)
1989	9148	4315200
1992	9883	4330000
1994	9794	4473600
1995	10016	4496300

2. Design a recruitment poster for the police force. Emphasise particularly the variety of roles that police play in our community and highlight the qualities that you think an effective police officer should have.

New evidence reopens riddle of 1984 killing

By PATRICK DONOVAN — court reporter

A new inquiry will be held into the 1984 death of a Mansfield woman shot twice in the head, after a second autopsy revealed she could not have committed suicide.

In the Supreme Court yesterday, Justice David Harper granted an application by the Attorney-General to quash the 1985 coroner's open finding and to order a fresh inquest.

Mr Gavin Silbert, for the Attorney-General, told the court that after a fresh investigation, Detective Inspector Paul Newman, from the homicide squad, had concluded the open finding into the death of Jennifer Ruth Tanner was made in error. Mr Silbert said the present investigation by the homicide squad had uncovered serious anomalies surrounding Mrs Tanner's death.

He said the investigation had produced strong evidence disproving the alibi of Mrs Tanner's brother-in-law, Detective Sergeant Dennis Tanner, who was one of the suspects.

'In my professional opinion the original inquiry into the death of the deceased was insufficiently carried out, as a result of which the coroner was led into error,' Detective Inspector Newman said, in a statement tendered in court. 'In my view the investigations now establish that the deceased was murdered and it is desirable in the interests of justice that another inquest be held.'

Mr Silbert said Mrs Tanner's body had been exhumed and tests revealed new evidence that, if available at the time, would have seen a different finding returned by the coroner.

Professor Stephen Cordner, head of the Victorian Institute of Forensic Pathology, concluded Mrs Tanner could not have caused her own death, Mr Silbert said. The death was investigated by police as a suicide and not as a homicide. He said the scene was never investigated, no ballistics were carried out and the autopsy was unsatisfactory.

He said the remains of a second body, transvestite Ms Adele Baily, had been found in a disused mine shaft near Mrs Tanner's property in July last year. He said common factors surrounding the death of Ms Baily and Mrs Tanner led to the homicide squad re-opening the investigation into Mrs Tanner's death.

In his affidavit, Detective Inspector Newman said on Wednesday 14 November 1984 Mr Laurence Tanner arrived home at Springfield, Maroondah Highway, Bonnie Doon, about 10.30pm to find his wife dead in the lounge room.

She was covered in blood and had Mr Tanner's Brno .22 bolt action rifle between her legs. She had four gunshot wounds — two to the forehead and one to each hand. No suicide note was found.

A friend, Angela McCormack, said she spoke to Mrs Tanner about 9pm on the day she died. She said Mrs Tanner had been cheerful and showed no signs of depression. Dr Geoffrey Patience, who had treated Mrs Tanner since 1982, said at no time had Mrs Tanner's demeanor suggested she was depressed or suicidal.

Local police from Mansfield were called. Senior Constable William Kerr described the scene to Detective Sergeant Welsh, in charge of Alexandra CIB, who determined death was caused by suicide. No photographs were taken.

The autopsy was performed by Dr Peter Dyte on 16 November 1984 at Goulburn Valley Base Hospital in Shepparton. He found that death was due to gunshot wounds to the head which caused gross cerebral contusion. He was unable to give evidence at the inquest because he was suffering from a terminal illness.

A specialist pathologist, Dr Terry Schultz, gave evidence that contradicted Dr Dyte's findings. He said while it was possible the wounds could have been self inflicted, it was likely Mrs Tanner would have lost consciousness after the first wound to the head.

In handing down his finding in December 1985, the coroner, Mr Hugh Adams, was scathing of the police investigation and indicated there were issues surrounding the death that gave rise to suspicion. He said the death had not been properly investigated, and the investigation slanted towards a situation of self-inflicted injuries when what appeared on the surface to be a non-suspicious matter may not have been so.

Age, 20 December 1996.

6.6

CRIME AND PUNISHMENT

There are two ways that you may find yourself in legal trouble. You may have broken a law and thus be involved in a criminal process. Alternatively, you may have infringed someone's rights and thus be caught up in a civil action.

THE CRIMINAL MAZE

A crime is an act that is harmful or potentially harmful to an individual and to society, and that will be punished by society. This covers actions from murder to traffic offences.

The type of offence committed will determine the court in which you will appear. **Indictable offences** are serious offences that are tried before a judge and jury in a higher court after a preliminary hearing in a lower court has accepted that there is enough evidence to justify the trial. A **summary offence** is a less serious offence, which is tried in the lower court by a magistrate, with no jury.

Procedures

1. After committing an offence, you may receive a caution — if you are lucky. This may be an informal caution ('Drive carefully next time, driver!') or a formal caution, where a warning notice is given to you. Young offenders often receive a formal warning by a police sergeant, who warns them in front of their parents. No legal action follows a warning, as long as you do not re-offend for five years.
2. On-the-spot fines are issued mainly for traffic offences. The offender must pay the fine by a specified date or be summonsed to court. Most people pay up-front.
3. A summons is issued if a magistrate agrees that the police have enough evidence against someone to justify an appearance in court. It is assumed that the alleged offender will attend court as 'invited', so summonses are usually issued only for minor offences.
4. A magistrate or judge can instruct the police, by means of a warrant, to bring someone before the court. The person may have failed to respond to a summons or may be a serious offender who does not wish to attend voluntarily.
5. If someone is caught 'red-handed', he or she can, of course, be arrested without a warrant. It would be impractical not to arrest a bank robber running from a 'bank job' simply because all the paperwork was incomplete.

After the arrest

Our criminal system operates on two principles.

1. The prosecution must prove beyond reasonable doubt that you committed an offence.
2. You are presumed innocent unless proven otherwise.

Therefore, between your arrest and your trial, it is your basic right to be released from custody. You may seek bail from a court; this means that you promise to appear before the court for your trial and if you do not, you forfeit a predetermined sum of money. If, however, you are deemed to be dangerous to society, you will not be granted bail and you will be held in 'remand' until your trial.

THE CIVIL MAZE

Civil procedures are different from criminal procedures because there are no police involved, since no-one has committed a crime.

Imagine your rights have been infringed in some way. What steps might you take to right the wrong?

1. Discuss the matter with the person who has harmed you. Will he or she do anything about it?
2. Visit your solicitor. Will you take legal action? What will you gain if you win?
3. Issue a writ of complaint to the defendant and outline the compensation you expect.
4. You may receive a counterclaim (the defendant states you caused him or her a loss); or a notice of defence (stating that the defendant will contest your claim).
5. At the discovery stage all documents to be used as evidence by both parties are swapped.
6. At the interrogatory stage the parties swap relevant questions and answers.
7. At the pre-trial conference you and the defendant try to reach agreement before trial.
8. At the trial you try to prove 'beyond the balance of probability' that the defendant is responsible for your losses.

Activities

Check your understanding

1. Explain the difference between the following pairs of words:
   - indictable offence and summary offence
   - summons and warrant
   - bail and remand.
2. In civil law, what is a writ of complaint?
3. Prepare a leaflet highlighting the differences between civil and criminal procedures.

Communication: *Working with news articles*

1. Read the article '$500 000 for dying woman' carefully.
   (a) What clues indicate that this issue is a civil matter?
   (b) Outline the procedures that would have led to the trial.
   (c) Explain the terms 'negligent' and 'damages'.
   (d) Imagine that you are Justice Bell. Justify your decision to award damages of $524 377.
2. Describe what you think occurs pre-trial that would explain why 75 per cent of civil cases do not end up in court.

$500 000 for dying woman

A WOMAN dying of breast cancer who was told she was too young for a mammogram was yesterday awarded more than $500 000 damages.

Kathryn Ann Curtin, now 32, said outside the NSW Supreme Court she hoped her experience would serve as a lesson to others.

'I don't have any bitterness at all; that wouldn't do me any good,' she said.

'I hope that this case hasn't been in vain and that doctors take note that cancer is not as discriminating as some doctors are about age.'

Ms Curtin, of Neutral Bay on Sydney's lower north shore, has breast cancer and a life expectancy of one year.

The court accepted Ms Curtin's account that she complained of lumpiness in her left breast during a June 1994 consultation with general practitioner Dr Louise Holliday.

She said Dr Holliday told her it was common for girls of her age to have hormone imbalance and it was probably just fibrous and 'not to worry about it'.

She claimed Dr Holliday said Ms Curtin was only 29, but if she was 50 'I would be going to get a mammogram as fast as my legs could carry me'.

Acting Justice Hubert Bell found Dr Holliday and endocrinologist Phillip Clifton-Bligh — who began seeing Ms Curtin for skin problems in March 1992 — negligent and ordered they pay a total of $524 377 damages.

A claim against Dr Maree Farley, a colleague of Dr Holliday at her Sydney practice, failed.

'Had she been diagnosed when she should have been, she would probably not have to die of cancer,' Justice Bell said.

During a March 1994 consultation with Dr Clifton-Bligh, Ms Curtin said there was a lump in her left breast, but he described it as a 'lobularity' and considered it 'normal'.

It was not until January this year, at the urging of a friend, she went to a different doctor and was diagnosed with cancer.

'It is . . . probable that had investigations been performed in 1994, the cancerous — or pre-cancerous — cells would have been discovered,' Justice Bell said.

'Had they been discovered, then successful treatment was probable.'

Ms Curtin planned to go to a clinic in Germany for further treatment, but Justice Bell said, even so, the remainder of her life would be 'progressively more painful, both physically and emotionally'.

He received expert medical opinion during the civil action and concluded that, irrespective of whether there was an indication of cancer, prudent doctors should refer patients with persistent lumps in their breasts for further checks.

AAP *Herald-Sun*, 18 December 1996.

THE RIGHTS OF THE INDIVIDUAL

In the area of criminal liability, you have different rights according to your age. A child under the age of ten is not considered by the law to be capable of understanding the difference between right and wrong and, therefore cannot be made liable for any wrongful actions. Between the ages of 10 and 14 the police must prove that you knew you were doing the wrong thing, and over the age of 14 you are legally accountable for your actions.

'Hello! My name is Charlie. I've just turned 15 and I live in Worralong with my parents and my sister and go to Worralong Secondary College. My mates Gino and Andy talked me into breaking into someone's Commodore and taking it for a spin onto the golf course last Thursday night. They saw the cop car and took off on foot. They were smarter than me. I was caught running from the car I had dumped at the golf course. Terrific! I'd broken into the car by smashing the passenger window with my hand. When I reached in and unlocked the car I cut my hand. Blood went everywhere, all over the wheel as I was trying to steer.'

'Constable Thomas, 26302, Worralong Police Station here. On the night of Thursday, 15 January, I was patrolling in the divisional van with Senior Constable Harris, when I saw what I knew to be a stolen Commodore parked at the golf course. I saw the defendant, Charles Sutcliffe, running away from the vehicle into the golf course. I arrested him after a brief chase and asked him to accompany me to the station.

I informed Charlie of his rights and cautioned him, saying that anything he told me could be used in evidence and I told him he was under arrest for suspected theft of a motor vehicle. We then returned to the police station. As I could not contact his parents to participate in the interview, I arranged for Alice Wright, a local youth worker to be present at the interview to act as an independent party. I asked Charlie who was in the car with him and where he took the car from, but he only gave me his name and address, and answered 'no comment' to my other questions. How frustrating!

Prior to the interview I searched Sutcliffe's person at the station, but found nothing of significance. After the interview I arranged for fingerprinting and a photograph to be taken, but he was aware of his rights and he refused both these procedures. I couldn't even get a sample from him for DNA testing, to match his blood with the blood on the steering wheel in the stolen Commodore. I am going to make an application to a magistrate for a court order to obtain a sample of his blood. This is known as a forensic procedure.

Based on the evidence I charged him with unlawful use of a motor vehicle and wilful damage. The evidence in my case will get a lot stronger if the result of the DNA blood match (if allowed to be taken by the magistrate) is the same as Charlie's.'

'Stipendiary Magistrate Enrico from the Worralong Children's Court here. Charles Sutcliffe, aged 15 years, of Worralong, appeared before my court last week charged with theft of a motor vehicle. Sutcliffe pleaded guilty, so the police prosecutor stated that the police would not proceed with the DNA application. Sutcliffe's teacher from school gave character evidence that convinced me that Sutcliffe is basically a good kid who sometimes gets led astray by his friends.

I decided not to fine or convict Sutcliffe, and obviously a jail sentence was entirely inappropriate. I could have let him off with a good behaviour order but there has been a spate of car thefts in the area of late, which has worried me. I thus put Charlie on a community service order without conviction.

Charlie won't have a criminal record, but I did warn him that next time he won't get off quite so lightly.'

Activities

Investigation: *Exploring legal rights*

1. What rights does Charlie have?
   (a) *Arrest.* Did the police inform Charlie that he was under arrest and why they were arresting him? Why is this important?
   (b) *Caution.* Did the police warn Charlie that he was not obliged to say anything? Did they allow him to contact someone to tell them where he was?
   (c) *Questioning.* Did the police retain Charlie for only a 'reasonable time'? What do you think a 'reasonable time' might be? Charlie being under 17, was someone else asked to attend his interview? Who may attend and why is it important that they do?
   (d) *Printing.* Was Charlie fingerprinted? Why is this only possible with an order from the Children's Court?
2. Is it possible for the police to issue a warning to a first-time juvenile offender of a minor offence and not follow up criminal procedures? Explain why this may not have occurred in Charlie's case.
3. The magistrate stated that a good behaviour order was inappropriate. What did she mean?
4. If Charlie reoffends and doesn't 'get off so lightly', what may that involve?

Further research into rights

In pairs, search the Internet for the pages of Amnesty International. Make a list of countries that do not recognise, to the extent that Australia does, the rights of people who have been arrested. Describe the difficulties faced by individuals as a result, and describe your findings to the class.

Communication: *Preparing visual displays*

1. Create a poster that will explain to other students their basic legal rights. Place it on a noticeboard.
2. After some investigation, draw up a table that compares the rights of the child in criminal proceedings to those of an adult. Explain all the similarities and differences.

Police questioning

Speaking to your family, lawyer and independent persons

If the police have arrested you or taken you into custody, they must allow you to:
- telephone a friend or relative. If you are under 17 the police must allow you to do this in private, and
- telephone a lawyer from a private space and to get legal advice.

The only times the police don't have to allow this is if they believe that during this time:
- someone else involved in the crime might get away
- some evidence may be lost or tampered with
- other people may be in danger, or
- it is a drink driving matter.

While you are waiting to speak to your family, lawyer or independent person, you should refuse to answer any questions after giving your name and address.

If you are under 17, the police must arrange for an independent person to be present during any formal questioning. The independent person can be a parent, family member, friend or other person independent from police. You, or the police, can suggest who you would like to act as the independent person. If an independent person is not present during questioning, the information you provide cannot be used as evidence in court.

Police caution

The police caution is recorded on tape at the beginning of a formal interview. Before the police can start asking you questions they must give you a 'caution' about your rights.

The caution used by police in a formal interview is:

'I must inform you that you are not obliged to say or do anything but anything you say or do may be given in evidence. Do you understand that?

I must also inform you of the following rights:
- You may communicate with or attempt to communicate with a friend or a relative to inform that person of your whereabouts.
- You may communicate with or attempt to communicate with a legal practitioner.'

These rights are for your protection. You must tell the police if you wish to exercise them. You should do this as soon as the police caution you. Do not wait. It is in your best interests to exercise these rights. Police must let you do these things if you ask.

Tape recorded interviews

If you are charged with an indictable (serious) offence, the police must tape record the caution they give you about your rights. The police must also tape record any questions they ask you and your answers if they want to use this information in court.

Anything you say before tape recording begins cannot usually be used as evidence in court. To use what you say as evidence, the police will often question you about your earlier statements once the tape starts. You can deny these earlier statements on the tape or say 'no comment'. If you agree on tape about what you said earlier, then it can be used as evidence.

Remember: refusing to answer just some questions will not help your case. If you choose to say 'no comment' you should do so to all questions.

The police must give you a copy of the taped record of interview. The tape is important for your lawyer — don't lose it.

Note: In summary (minor) offences, like loitering, or drunk in a public place, the police do not have to tape what you say for it to be used as evidence against you.

Fingerprinting

15 years and older

You have to give your fingerprints to the police if they believe you committed an offence in most situations, other than certain minor offences (e.g. jaywalking and littering).

If you refuse to give your fingerprints, the police can use reasonable force to get them. Note: reasonable force means the police may physically restrain you and take your fingerprints.

The police must first tell you, in language you understand:
- why your fingerprints are needed,
- the offence you are believed to have committed or have been charged with, and
- that the fingerprints may be used as evidence in court.

If you are 15 or 16, then your parents, guardian or an independent person must also be present when the police request is made and when your fingerprints are taken.

10 to 14 years old

If the police want to fingerprint a young person between 10 and 14 they **must** get the consent of the parents or guardian and young person.

You do not have to give your consent.

If the parents, guardian or young person refuse consent, the police have to get permission from the Children's Court to take your fingerprints.

Extract from *Police Powers: Your Rights*, Victoria Legal Aid, 2000.

DO WE HAVE TO GO TO COURT?

Not all legal matters are handled by the formal courts. In Victoria, many disputes — between individuals, between individuals and organisations, and between the government and its citizens — are dealt with by the Victorian Civil and Administrative Tribunal (VCAT). This less formalised arrangement prevents relatively minor matters from taking up court time and saves all parties considerable time and money.

The VCAT has two divisions — the Civil Division and the Administrative Division, each of which contains a number of lists (or specialist areas). The Administrative Division deals primarily with disputes between the government and its citizens. Three of the lists within the Civil Division are discussed in this spread.

THE CIVIL CLAIMS LIST

Jurisdiction

The Civil Claims List has the **jurisdiction** to hear claims up to an unlimited amount by any person against any other person, be they a private consumer, trader or professional person such as a doctor. Some time limits may apply.

Procedure

Claimants must complete an application form, and generally the process does not cost anything. In the application, the claimant lists the disputing parties and the amount claimed, and describes the history of the dispute. Relevant supporting documentation is also provided.

The hearing

The other party is sent a copy of the claim, and all parties are advised of the time and place of the hearing. Before the hearing, a VCAT referee will try to help the disputing parties settle their disagreement (that is, try to conciliate the dispute). If this fails, the disputing parties present their case at a formal hearing under oath. Witnesses and documentation can be produced by both parties.

The order

If the referee cannot help the parties conciliate their dispute during the hearing, he or she will determine (arbitrate) the matter and issue an order. This order is enforceable by the successful party. The referee's decision is binding on both parties, although a right of appeal to the Supreme Court is available. Failure to carry out an order is a serious offence.

THE RESIDENTIAL TENANCIES LIST

Jurisdiction

Any dispute between a tenant and a property owner over bonds, repairs, rentals and the like up to $10 000 in value can be heard before the Residential Tenancies List. Either party in the dispute may make a claim.

Procedure

To obtain a hearing, the tenant or the owner must complete an application form and lodge it with the Registrar, attaching any relevant documentation. An application fee of $25 is payable.

The hearing

Parties are encouraged to settle their own case first. This may involve seeking help from a tenancy advice service. Failing this, an open and informal hearing is held before a Tribunal member who decides on the dispute. Parties can have legal representation only in certain circumstances.

The order

Decisions made by the Tribunal are final and binding. If people wish to appeal a point of law, they can do so before the Supreme Court.

THE EQUAL OPPORTUNITY COMMISSION AND THE ANTI-DISCRIMINATION LIST

Jurisdiction

Anyone who believes they have been discriminated against on the basis of sex, skin colour, religion, size, appearance, disability or age can lodge a complaint with the Equal Opportunity Commission.

Procedure

Those with a grievance must apply in writing to the Equal Opportunity Commission, outlining the details of the grievance.

The hearing

A Commission employee, called a conciliator, will discuss the case with the person lodging the grievance and the other party involved. The conciliator will try to help the parties reach a satisfactory agreement. If this fails, the case will be heard before a decision-maker from the Anti-Discrimination List in an open, informal hearing. The decision-maker may call for witnesses to appear and for other documentation. The parties are not encouraged to have legal representation.

The order

The order of the decision-maker may include payment of compensation to the person determined as the victim, or a direction that discriminating practices cease immediately. The decision made is binding on both parties, although the right to appeal to the Supreme Court does exist.

THE OMBUDSMAN

The ombudsman is an independent investigator appointed by the state government but who acts independently of that government. People may write to the ombudsman to complain about the way in which the government — at any level — may have acted or made decisions, and the ombudsman must respond to these complaints. Usually the ombudsman will investigate your complaint only after you have unsuccessfully tried to resolve the problem with the relevant government body. The investigation by the ombudsman is free and confidential.

There is no formal hearing, but investigators assisting the ombudsman will examine the issue through letters, interviews and telephone calls. After assessing whether your complaint is justified, the investigators will make recommendations to settle the issue. The ombudsman then informs the government body of these recommendations. Although the recommendations are not strictly enforceable, they are usually adopted because the position of ombudsman is highly respected by the community.

OTHER BODIES

Other bodies that are able to resolve disputes are the Crimes Compensation Tribunal, the Transport Accident Commission and the Administrative Appeals Tribunal, and many other bodies that exist outside the formal court hierarchy.

Activities

Investigation: *Selecting the right body*

1. Outline the similarities and differences in the operation of the different review agencies discussed here. What might be the reasons for this?
2. Which body would deal with the following problems?
   (a) You are rejected as a part-time sales assistant as the employer says that your hair is too long.
   (b) You are a public servant and are refused a retirement package others are receiving because of a procedural technicality.
   (c) As the owner of a rented premises, you have given adequate notice of eviction to the tenants, but they refuse to leave the property.
   (d) You collect antique furniture and a dealer offers to sell you a bookcase she states is Edwardian and worth $2000. You buy it only to discover that it is not what she claimed.
3. In a small group, create a role play involving one of the agencies described here and act out the difference between the two terms 'arbitration' and 'conciliation'.

CHANGING THE LAW — THE PORT ARTHUR MASSACRE

Public opinion is a strong force in changing laws. Following the horrific slaughter of innocent victims in the Port Arthur massacre, public outcry against gun ownership forced the federal and state governments to reassess their laws in this area. Individuals, associations and political groups hotly debated the issue, and the state governments were left to decide on the most appropriate changes to legislation.

On a relaxing summer's day at the busy Port Arthur tourist site in Tasmania, a lone gunman went crazy and started to shoot and threaten people at random, with no obvious reason for doing so. Why this place? Why this time? Why those people? After 24 hours of horror, 35 innocent people had died and many others had been physically or emotionally scarred for life. Why this happened is the concern of criminal **psychologists**. The consequence of this event, from the legal point of view, is ours.

In all states, the laws relating to guns at the time of the shooting basically allowed anyone with a shooter's licence to own and carry many types of weapons, including some types of semi-automatic weapons. This was the type of gun used at Port Arthur. A semi-automatic weapon is any weapon that will automatically load a bullet into the breech every time the trigger is pulled. An automatic weapon will fire rounds continuously when the trigger is pulled and will do so until the trigger is released.

After two mass shootings in Melbourne (Hoddle Street and Queen Street) and the Strathfield massacre in Sydney, there was a groundswell of community support to limit the availability of guns. The 1996 slaughter of schoolchildren in Dunblane, Scotland, added support to community views. Following the Port Arthur shootings, the federal and state governments moved to change the law in relation to firearm ownership.

32 die in massacre

Hunt for more bodies as Tasmania siege goes on

At least 32 people are dead and 18 injured — some critically — after a lone gunman fired on children, tourists, staff and local residents at the historic Tasmanian settlement of Port Arthur yesterday.

Last night the young man responsible for Australia's worst mass shooting — described as a 'surfie-looking fellow' — was threatening to take even more victims. Police, who know his identity, said they understood he was intellectually disabled.

Early this morning he was holed up in nearby Seascape guesthouse with three hostages, including owners David and Sally Martin, as police used a secure telephone line to negotiate an end to the siege. He was firing randomly at those seeking to talk him out of the cottage — and [to prevent] any more killing. He is believed to be from Copping, a small town 50 kilometres east of Hobart.

The Prime Minister, Mr Howard, led a chorus of horror when he issued a statement deploring the 'tragic mass murder'.

Those killed are believed to include two Canadians and two Tasmanians. The rest were from mainland Australia.

The Port Arthur Massacre — as it will surely become known — began about 1.30 p.m. yesterday when the gunman wandered into a cafe at the convict-turned-tourist precinct, pulled a weapon from his tennis bag and started firing.

He had earlier driven to the settlement. As he entered the tourist cafe he talked 'quite lucidly', according to witnesses.

'He said "there are a lot of WASPS (white Anglo-Saxon Protestants) around today, there aren't many Japs, are there?"' recalled one witness. Then the killing began.

'He wasn't going bang bang bang bang — it was bang and then he'd pick someone else out and line them up and shoot them,' witness Phillip Milburn told ABC radio.

As dozens lay dead or dying, the gunman moved to the nearby Fox and Hounds Hotel where he continued his ghastly spree, before taking refuge in Seascape's attic rooms, about four kilometres north of Port Arthur.

The dead

Those killed include two Canadians, tourists of Asian origin and two Tasmanians. The rest were from mainland Australia.

The 18 injured were from the US, Canada and Australia. Eight were from Victoria, three from Tasmania, three from NSW and two from South Australia.

Age, 29 April 1996.

Shooters urged to fight MPs on gun laws

By MURRAY MOTTRAM and GEOFF STRONG

GUN lobby leaders yesterday urged tens of thousands of shooters rallying outside State Parliament to take their fight against strict new gun laws into the political arena.

The president of the Sporting Shooters Association, Mr Ted Drane, told the crowd, estimated by police at 70 000, that gun owners would have to elect their own MPs to State and Federal Parliaments to stop erosion of shooters' rights.

Rally organisers claimed the crowd, which took 30 minutes to pass Flinders Street Station, reached 150 000

The independent federal MP for Kalgoorlie, Mr Graeme Campbell, who told the crowd the new gun laws were part of an attack on basic freedoms, is expected to launch a new political movement today.

After the rally he said there was a vacuum in political representation for rural people and those who believed in individualism.

He condemned the Prime Minister, Mr John Howard, for introducing the laws without consulting shooters.

Mr Drane also castigated the Premier, Mr Jeff Kennett, and his National Party colleagues for supporting the national ban on automatic and semi-automatic guns.

'We are not guilty for what happened in Tasmania,' he said. 'We have been sentenced, convicted and the penalty imposed and there appears to be nothing we can do about it.

'Well, we are going to oppose it. We are going to have a go at the ballot box and we're going to tell the National Party they're a pack of dogs . . . they don't believe in these laws but they are sitting in there now looking at all these people wondering what the hell they're going to do about it.'

Mr Drane urged the crowd to support Mr Campbell's new political movement.

The chairman of the Shooters Party in Victoria, Mr Neville Sayers, said it appeared Mr Howard had taken the Port Arthur massacre as an opportunity to adopt 'draconian' gun laws pushed through United Nations forums by countries such as Colombia and Japan.

All speakers claimed the media were responsible for creating hysteria after the Tasmanian tragedy and for portraying gun owners as potential criminals.

The overwhelmingly male crowd was well organised, the only sour note coming after the rally when Gun Control Australia representatives taking a petition in the Bourke Street Mall claimed they were jostled and their petitions defaced by people leaving the march.

Earlier, in Spring Street, the anti-gun protesters staged a commemoration for the 35 people killed at Port Arthur five weeks ago. Police ordered them to disperse before the marchers arrived.

Shooting groups in the march had come from as far as Mallacoota, Warracknabeal and Echuca. Their banners included 'Honest Shooters Have Rights Too', 'Legalise Marijuana, Ban Guns. What a Joke'.

The procession marched to Parliament House and observed one minute's silence for the victims of Port Arthur.

Pro and anti-gun demonstrators clashed in Brisbane yesterday and the gun lobby is planning a demonstration in Adelaide today.

An anti-gun rally will be held in Melbourne today at the Treasury Gardens at 1.30pm.

Sunday Age, 2 June 1996.

STATE AND FEDERAL POWERS

Since the laws regarding firearms are basically the responsibility of the states, the federal government could only encourage and advise the states. By its constitutional limitations, it could not impose a law in this area without state approval.

A meeting of the police ministers from all the states agreed to establish a policy that banned all semi-automatic firearms. Using federal funds, they arranged a buy-back scheme whereby the current owners of the now banned guns would hand in their weapons to the authorities in return for monetary compensation. Anyone owning such a weapon, licensed or not, was required by law to surrender it. In Victoria, an **amnesty** was proclaimed, allowing anyone with an illegal gun to still claim the compensation.

Changing the culture

The Firearms Bill 1996 was later put through the Victorian state parliament in direct support of the federal *National Firearms Act*, which provided money to the states for the 'buy-back' program by temporarily increasing the Medicare Levy. This state Act not only reinforced attempts to control the ownership of semi-automatics, but also established government laws to control the storage, licensing, and purchase of all types of guns and the training of gun users. Other states enacted similar laws in a deliberate policy to unify and strengthen state gun laws.

The attitude of society towards the ownership of guns became an issue during this process. Many in the community came to accept that in Australia, unlike the United States, there is no fundamental right to carry arms. A licence to own a gun, like that to drive a car, is a privilege and thus carries a

Victoria 'satisfied' with gun outcome

by FARAH FAROUQUE and NICOLE BRADY

The Victorian Police Minister, Mr McGrath, last night said he was 'reasonably satisfied' with the outcome of the national gun summit.

Mr McGrath, who was seeking to soften the Commonwealth's minimum position of a virtual ban on automatic and semi-automatic weapons, embraced an exemption that will allow farmers to have access to some low-powered semi-automatic weapons.

This will mean that farmers can continue to have access to some self-loading .22 guns and self-loading and pump-action shotguns if they can satisfy police that they have a genuine need for them.

'I am reasonably satisfied with the result,' Mr McGrath said.

'[The exemption] goes a fair way toward alleviating some of the problems that could have been associated with farming practices. There is a very stringent requirement on those farmers to secure that permit arrangement. It's for 12 months and renewable if they can justify it to police.'

The issue was a sticking point for Victoria earlier in the week, with Mr McGrath resolving to argue that low-velocity semi-automatics should be left out of the general ban.

The Premier, Mr Kennett, last night welcomed the outcome, describing it as historic. He said yesterday's result was positive and should be welcomed by most Australians.

'The states, territories and the Commonwealth have acted cooperatively, swiftly, with common sense and in good faith to draw up some of the toughest gun laws anywhere in the world,' Mr Kennett said.

'Today's decisions have been taken in the best interests of all Australians as part of an effort to increase safety for all members of the community.

'All governments, on behalf of their respective communities, attended today's meeting with the purpose of achieving strict, national, uniform gun laws and that's precisely what has been achieved.'

Mr Kennett said that while there had been a substantial advance 'from where we were in Victoria', the state already had the best rules concerning the control of firearms.

The federal Attorney-General, Mr Williams, who chaired yesterday's meeting, said last night that every minister at the meeting had 'one thing in mind' and that was to come away with the consensus that had been reached.

'The people of Australia have expressed their opinion very firmly and we've acted on it,' he said.

Victoria's police chief commissioner, Mr Neil Comrie, who travelled with Mr McGrath to Canberra, also embraced the plan as an 'outstanding achievement'. 'It's a day that will go down in Victoria's history as a victory for the community over the minority,' he said.

The shadow attorney-general, Senator Bolkus, vowed to continue bipartisan support of this issue.

'The Opposition will give the Prime Minister its full support in implementing these measures so that Australians get the gun laws we need,' he said. Senator Bolkus added that the onus was now on the states and territories 'to deliver on their promises'.

Age, 11 May 1996.

responsibility. Such a privilege can also be removed. The law had to respond to changing community views, but not everyone in the community agreed. Future elections will no doubt demonstrate the support for different points of view in the community.

Firearm use in crime

In Victoria in 1995:

- 100 deaths were caused by firearms
- firearms were used in 27 per cent of attempted murders
- firearms were used in 18 per cent of murders
- 74 per cent of all homicides occurred in the home and 25 per cent of these involved firearms
- 80 per cent of suicides involved firearms.

Throughout Australia:

- firearms were used in 13 per cent of armed robberies
- about 4 million firearms were privately owned in 1995
- in a house where a gun is kept, it is 50 times more likely to kill a family member than an intruder
- of the 116 people killed in massacres since 1987, 74 per cent of deaths involved semi-automatic firearms.

Comparison of firearm-related homicides as a percentage of total homicides

Year	Australia	England	USA
1988	31.4	7.9	60.6
1990	20.4	10.4	64.3
1992	30.2	8.8	68.2
1994	23.7	9.3	70.0

Source: Information Victoria Factsheet, 13 August 1996.

Activities

Investigation: *Comparing points of view*

1. Read the article '32 die in massacre'.
   (a) Why do you think there was such an anti-gun outcry from the public following the massacre?
   (b) What other incidents have also been responsible for public movements against guns?
   (c) What was the law relating to gun ownership at the time of the Port Arthur shootings?
   (d) Is gun ownership a state or federal matter?
2. Read the article 'Shooters urged to fight MPs on gun laws'.
   (a) The Sporting Shooters Association (a **lobby group**) claim a crowd of 150 000. The police claim 70 000. How can there be such a difference?
   (b) What are the various means used by people mentioned in this article to express their disagreement with government? Which of these would be most effective?
   (c) What arguments are put forward by the Gun Lobby to support its point of view?
   (d) What evidence is there that others in the community oppose the views of the Gun Lobby?
3. Explain clearly the difference between a privilege and a right. Make a list of each of these that you may have under the law.
4. Read the article 'Victoria "satisfied" with gun outcome'.
   (a) Describe the outcome of the national gun summit. Why would the Victorian Police Minister be satisfied with this outcome?
   (b) Imagine that you are the federal Attorney-General. Write your closing speech to the summit, covering how the summit was arranged and its achievements.
   (c) Who are the 'minority' Neil Comrie refers to? Should the community always win over the minority? Explain your point of view.
   (d) Senator Bolkus talks of 'bipartisan support'. To what is he referring?
5. Examine the table (above) carefully.
   (a) Present this information as a graph.
   (b) Use your graph and other information to present a case in support of an anti-gun lobby group.
   (c) As a class, debate the statement: 'It is the right of every individual to own a gun, which thus makes gun control through state legislation unnecessary and undemocratic'.

Communication: *Creating a visual display*

Consider a law that is currently being debated by the community in your state. Draw up a poster that clearly describes:

- the issue
- the various groups involved in the debate
- the arguments presented by interest groups to support their claim
- the methods used by those involved in the debate
- the likely outcome.

6.10

CHANGING THE LAW — CHILD ABUSE

All children have a right not to be abused. Abuse covers the following areas:

- assault, which includes hitting, bashing and sexual assault
- ill treatment of a child
- exposing or subjecting a child to behaviour that mentally harms the child
- failure to protect or care for a child.

There have been many instances where the rights of citizens have been violated. How does society protect children from this kind of abuse, and at what point should we intervene? Are our standards as a society changing for better or worse?

During the 1980s, Victoria's child protection laws and services were constantly criticised. Several government reports and media exposure of the child protection system uncovered gaps in the service where children in need of protection were being failed and, in some cases, dying as a result. Pressure to amend the system was applied; however, successive governments had not modified the system.

In September 1990 a two-year-old boy named Daniel Valerio died as a result of abuse. He was certainly not the first child to die from physical abuse and it was not the first case of its type to make news headlines; however, his death and the circumstances surrounding it stirred up an emotional public response that eventually brought about a change in the law.

Daniel's death appeared to act as a catalyst for change. The circumstances of his death and the fact that Daniel had been seen by 22 different professionals in his short life, yet he still died, horrified many people.

The case created a very strong and vocal public response. Media coverage of the issue and the trial of Paul Aiton, who was sentenced to 22 years imprisonment, was extensive. Professional and community groups as well as individuals became involved in a public debate, using forums such as talkback radio and newspapers for the airing of their views. The *Herald Sun* organised a public forum called 'Save Our Children', where various speakers addressed the audience on the need for mandatory reporting to be introduced in the state.

CONFLICTING ATTITUDES

Some of the people and organisations in favour of mandatory reporting included the Royal Children's Hospital, the Community Policing Squad, Justice Fogerty, the state Opposition and the Victorian Society for the Prevention of Child Abuse and Neglect. Other groups, although not necessarily against mandatory reporting, raised concerns about how the change would be funded and managed. These groups included the Children's Welfare Association of Victoria, the Victorian Council for Civil Liberties and the Australian Medical Association.

PARLIAMENT'S RESPONSE

It is an important function of parliament that it is able to respond to community values and opinions. Politicians need to be responsive to community opinion as they realise that they may lose their seat in parliament if they are not. The public response and debate in relation to the Valerio case put significant pressure on parliament, in particular the Liberal government in power at the time to act.

The call for change in relation to Victoria's child protection laws was not new. There had been several parliamentary and government inquiries into child protection services during the 1980s. The Carney report in 1985 highlighted flaws in the system and in 1988 Mr Justice Fogerty, a highly respected Family Court judge, was asked to review child services. These inquiries resulted in changes to procedures and increases in funding, but there was no move towards the introduction of mandatory reporting.

However, this time the added influence of public opinion increased the pressure on the government to act. In early 1993 Justice Fogerty was again asked to investigate Victoria's child protection system. In March 1993 a government committee was formed to investigate the introduction of mandatory reporting legislation.

Finally, due to the overwhelming public support, in June 1993 the Victorian government passed legislation in the form of the *Children and*

Young Persons (Further Amendment) Act 1993 (Vic.). The amendment had the effect of compelling certain professional groups in the community to report cases of sexual or physical abuse.

Arguments for and against the introduction of mandatory reporting

For	Against
• The state has responsibility for the protection of children. • Children's rights are more important than the privacy of the family. • Professionals will find the decision to report easier knowing they are compelled to do it. • It will increase community awareness of the problem and promote more voluntary reporting. • It will promote educational awareness and therefore increase detection rates. • Children need to have their rights upheld.	• It will lead to an increase in unsubstantiated reports. • It will leave a stigma on those wrongly accused. • It will cause unnecessary intrusion into children's and their families' lives. • Mandatory reporting does not necessarily mean effective services. • Parents will be scared of taking injured children to doctors due to fear of being reported. • The system will not be able to cope due to over-reporting by professionals fearful of prosecution.

Section 4 of the *Children and Young Persons (Further Amendment) Act 1993*, now states

> in the course of practising his or her profession or carrying out the duties of his or her office, position or employment as described ... forms the belief on reasonable grounds that a child is in need of protection ... must notify the Secretary of that belief and of the reasonable grounds for it as soon as practicable.

Section 4, subsection 1(c) sets out the 11 categories of professionals compelled to report abuse and s4, ss 1(a) the penalties for not doing so.

The categories of professionals compelled to report abuse are:

- registered, legally qualified medical practitioners
- registered and probationary psychologists
- people registered under Part II of the *Nurses Act 1958*
- registered teachers
- head teachers or principals of state schools
- proprietors and qualified employees of children's services centre
- qualified people working in the health, education, community and welfare services
- youth and childcare workers
- members of the police force
- probation officers
- youth parole officers
- members of prescribed classes of persons.

Activities

Investigation: *Child abuse*

1. Explain the different types of abuse which come under the term 'child' abuse.
2. How is child abuse generally reported?
3. Do you think child abuse is easy to detect? Why?
4. Who is responsible for protecting the rights of an abused child?

Changes to the law

1. What was the public response to the Daniel Valerio case?
2. What impact did the public response have on parliament?
3. What change to the law was made as a result of the Daniel Valerio case?
4. Read the following scenarios and for each situation decide the following:
   - What type of abuse is it?
   - Would you report the abuse to the authorities? Why/why not?
   - If the abuse should be reported, who would you report it to and why?

   (a) You witness a mother giving her child a hard smack in the supermarket carpark.

   (b) You are aware that your neighbours leave their four-year-old son alone in the house for more than an hour each Friday night.

   (c) Your best friend confides in you that she has been sexually abused by her stepbrother since she was 10 years old.

   (d) You are changing for Physical Education when you notice what look like cigarette burns on the shoulder of the girl next to you. She quickly covers them over when she sees you looking.

   (e) It is late at night when you hear muffled sobbing outside. Upon investigation you discover the girl from next door sheltering in your carport. She explains that she has been locked out because of an argument with her mother. It is the second time that it has happened.

   (f) You earn money selling cosmetics in your local area. At one house you notice that the toddler appears very quiet and withdrawn. On another occasion you notice some fading bruises shaped like finger marks on his arm.

CHANGES IN THE LAW – HUMAN CLONING

At the moment there appears to be almost universal public and political rejection of scientists cloning human beings. **Cloning** is the reproduction of a cell or organism with the same genetic makeup as another cell or organism. However, as we have seen with the development of IVF and research on human DNA, science has a habit of outstripping public opinion and the law.

Cloning is not new. Experiments involving plants and animal embryos have been performed for years. However, experiments involving human beings have never been tried or thought possible until 'Dolly' the first cloned sheep was born on July 5, 1996. Dolly was the first clone of an adult mammal ever born. Cloning of embryos had been possible for many years but, for the first time, an adult cell had been used with success. Some scientists are optimistic that human cloning will occur in the near future, although this had led to vigorous discussion about whether human cloning should ever be legally allowed.

Researchers in the United States of America have successfully grown human embryonic stem cells in culture. These stem cells form all the other cells of the body and in future may be used to grow new cells to replace old ones. However, forming human embryonic stem cells is illegal in Victoria, Western Australia and South Australia.

ON HUMAN CLONING

A Position Statement

Australian Academy of Science, 4 February 1999

Speculation in the popular press about selfish or compassionate reproductive cloning of humans has tended to obscure the real scientific challenges in capturing this advance in knowledge for therepeutic cloning, for the benefit of mankind. Cloning techniques may one day revolutionise medical treatment of damaged tissues and organs, should it become possible to use human adult cells as the starting material for growth of new tissues. At present, one human organ, skin, can be grown in the laboratory to provide self-compatible skin grafts for burns victims. The possibility of growing other self-compatible cells, such as nerve cells for patients with spinal injuries or muscle cells for heart atttack victims, could one day be a reality, albeit within an unknown time frame.

The Council of the Australian Academy of Science, in accord with international opinion, considers that reproductive cloning to produce human fetuses is unethical and unsafe and should be prohibited. However, human cells, whether derived from cloning techniques, from human embryonic stem (ES) cells, or from primordial germ (reproductive) cells should not be precluded from use in approved research activities in cellular and developmental biology. In Australia at present, production of human ES cells would be approved only in exceptional circumstances under National Health and Medical Research Council (NHMRC) Ethical Guidelines, originally prepared to ensure ethical practices in in vitro fertilisation (IVF) clinics. For Australia to participate fully and capture benefits from recent progress in cloning research, it is necessary to revise the 1996 NHMRC Ethical Guidelines on Assisted Reproductive Technology and repeal restrictive legislation in some States.

Dolly the cloned sheep with first lamb, Bonnie

Activities

Investigation: *Law changes and cloning*

1. Outline and evaluate the concerns of Senator Stott Despoja.
2. What do you think the senator means when she says, 'so that we are not caught out with horror scenarios'?
3. Senator Stott Despoja says that human reproductive cloning 'is abhorrent and attacks the very foundations of what it is to be human'. What is her concern here?
4. What is the view of the Council of the Australian Academy of Science (CAAS) regarding reproductive cloning to produce human fetuses?
5. What human cloning is already taking place in Australia?
6. What human cloning is already taking place in the United States of America?
7. What legal action does CAAS suggest take place?
8. Conduct a survey on whether people support human reproductive cloning or cloning techniques to repair damaged tissues or organs.
9. What are the arguments for and against human cloning? Write your response in a two-column table.

Senator Natasha Stott Despoja

Australian Democrats

Science and Technology Spokesperson

Senate expresses concerns about human cloning

The Australian Democrats are relieved the Senate supported a motion today urging the Government to take measures to ensure human reproductive cloning is banned in Australia, the Australian Democrats' Consumer Affairs spokesperson, Senator Natasha Stott Despoja, said today.

Senator Stott Despoja's expression of concern is about the advertisement in the 23 March 1998 edition of the *Australian Financial Review* (page 24), offering funding for human cloning research.

'Human reproductive cloning should not be allowed in Australia. It is abhorrent and attacks the very foundations of what it is to be human,' said Senator Stott Despoja.

'The Government's commitment not to financially support human reproductive cloning does not go far enough. This advertisement shows the shortcomings of the Government's stance, and highlights the need for Government leadership on this issue to make sure human reproductive cloning is banned.

'I have attempted to get an informed and inclusive debate about genetic technologies in the Parliament, and have been stalled by the old parties. Genetic technology is, and will continue to have a significant impact on our lives, and we need to make sure we have examined the issues. The time for this debate is now.

'I have introduced a Private Members Bill, the *Genetic Privacy and Non-Discrimination Bill*, which addresses the other significant issues of how we collect, store and analyse genetic information. We need to debate these issues now so that we are not caught out with horror scenarios.

'I look forward to the Government taking measures to ban human reproductive cloning and promote an informed debate about genetic technologies,' said Senator Stott Despoja.

Media release,
3 May 1998.

6.12 Meeting the outcomes

EXAMINE THE ORIGIN OF AUSTRALIA'S LEGAL SYSTEM AND HOW AUSTRALIAN LAWS ARE MADE.

Examine the origins and key values of Australia's legal system.

1. Who were Australia's first law makers? (6.1)
2. On which system is Australia's legal system based? (6.1)
3. What is the difference between common and statute law? (6.1)

Investigate how and why laws are made and changed in Australia, including the role of the Constitution, parliaments and the courts.

Look at the cartoon below to answer the following questions.

(a) Why are laws needed? (6.2)
(b) Select three incidents punishable by civil law. (6.2)
(c) Who makes our laws?
(d) Who interprets our laws? (6.3)

Describe key judicial and enforcement structures at federal, state and local levels.

Imagine you are a police officer who arrives at this scene shown in the cartoon above. (6.7)

(a) Write a report about one incident using the following terms:
   - defendant
   - arrested
   - interviewed.
(b) In which court would the case be heard and why? (6.3)

Explain how law-making processes allow for participation by active and informed citizens.

1. What is the role of a juror? (6.4)
2. List three types of citizens that cannot perform jury duty. (6.4)
3. What vote is required by juries in murder cases? (6.4)
4. How were individuals and community groups active in changes to child abuse laws in Victoria? (6.10)

ANALYSE A PROPOSED CHANGE IN THE LAW IN AUSTRALIA AND EXPLAIN THE LEGAL PROCESSES TO IMPLEMENT THE CHANGE.

Describe a proposed change to the law in Australia.

1. What issue is the focus of the article about the Andrews Act?
2. List three other issues affected or soon to be affected by changes to the law.

Analyse how individuals, groups, communities, legal and political institutions may be affected by a proposed change.

1. List the groups that could be affected by changes to euthanasia laws?
2. Which groups were affected by changes to gun laws? (6.9)

Explain different perspectives on a proposed change and the roles of individuals and groups in promoting or challenging the proposed change.

1. Who are the authors of the euthanasia article?
2. Do you think they support or disagree with the Andrews Act?
3. What position does the Australian Academy of Science take on human cloning? Why do you think they have taken this position? (6.11)
4. Which groups were in favour of mandatory reporting of child abuse in Victoria? (6.10)

Evaluate the effectiveness of the democratic process in relation to political and legal issues in bringing about changes in the law.

1. What do you think the aim of the Andrews Act was?
2. Do the authors of the article think that the Andrews act will be successful in achieving these aims?
3. In what way was mandatory reporting of child abuse in Victoria a victory for community values and opinions?

Andrews act will end up a pyrrhic victory

The NT's euthanasia law would not have opened the floodgates, write DAVID KELLY and LOANE SKENE.

The proponents of the Andrews act are no doubt congratulating themselves for overturning the Northern Territory's euthanasia legislation. But it will prove to be no more than a pyrrhic victory.

The Andrews act reinstates the common law by overriding the Rights of the Terminally Ill Act (NT). But that will not stop euthanasia. The common law itself allows for assistance in dying in many of the cases covered by the Northern Territory act. Moreover, it allows that assistance in certain circumstances where the NT act did not.

And it offers far less protection than that act did against 'assistance' being given against a patient's wishes.

The common law allows a doctor to give a lethal dose of a drug to a terminally ill patient if two conditions are met. First, the dose must be necessary to relieve severe pain. Second, the doctor's primary intention must be to stop the pain rather than to cause the death. If these conditions are met, the doctor commits no criminal offence.

A doctor who wants to meet a patient's request for assistance in dying can satisfy the common-law conditions relatively easily. The first is met by focusing on the relief of pain rather than on the inevitable consequences of relieving it. In that case, the doctor can validly claim to have had the primary intention of relieving the pain, not killing the patient.

The second condition is met because, when a terminally ill (but not mentally ill) patient is begging for assistance in dying, that necessarily involves the person suffering from severe psychological pain that can be relieved only by the giving of the assistance sought.

Of course, some people may say that a lethal dose is never necessary because the pain can be effectively relieved by putting the patient into a virtual coma.

But a doctor would then be faced with a hopeless choice between artificially prolonging the comatose patient's life with intravenous fluids, or denying the patient sustenance and starving him or her to death. We do not believe that judges and juries will impose such a barbarous choice on doctors.

The common law allows assistance in circumstances where the NT act did not.

Despite the hysteria it aroused, the NT act did not open the floodgates to euthanasia. In fact, it closed off some gates open at common law.

First, it was restricted to patients who were both adult and competent — that is, mentally and physically capable of making the request. It excluded people who were, because of illness or accident, incapable of making the request. Neither restriction is recognised under common law.

Second, the NT act did not allow assistance in dying to be given to people who were suffering psychological pain alone. The bill was amended in its passage through the NT Parliament to require severe 'pain of suffering'. 'Distress' was not to be enough. Again, the common law contains no such limitation. It is the intensity of the pain that counts, not its category.

The common law offers far less protection than the act against 'assistance' being given against a patient's wishes. The only plausible argument against allowing assistance in dying is the risk of abuse. Regrettably, the common law is hopelessly defective here. The NT act, on the other hand, contained stringent safeguards.

First, the treating doctor could not act alone. The opinions of a specialist in the terminally ill patient's illness (diagnosis and prognosis) and of a psychiatrist (the absence of a treatable clinical depression) were also required.

First, the treating doctor could not act alone. The opinions of a specialist in the terminally ill patient's illness (diagnosis and prognosis) and of a psychiatrist (the absence of a treatable clinical depression) were also required.

Second, the patient had to sign a prescribed request form after being fully informed about diagnosis, prognosis and methods of treatment. The patient's signature had to be witnessed by the treating doctor and another independent doctor.

The latter had to be satisfied that the patient was competent, that the request had been made freely and after due consideration, and that all procedures had been followed.

Third, the treating doctor had to be there when the dose was administered, had to keep extensive records about the death and the procedures, and had to report the death to the coroner.

The common law, on the other hand, imposes no procedural requirements to minimise the risk that the patient is no longer able to consent, or consents without being properly informed or under some form of coercion, or the risk that the doctor's diagnosis is mistaken, or that alternative treatments have been overlooked.

There is no audit trail at all. As the particular patient is now dead, the doctor is in a commanding position to assert what happened. In the absence of other evidence, the doctor's assertions are impossible to rebut.

These, then, are the reasons why the Andrews act is a pyrrhic victory for its proponents. They have not put an end to euthanasia. It will be practised increasingly, in the NT and elsewhere, by doctors who feel morally and professionally bound to assist, and who are courageous enough to risk prosecution.

The common law will increasingly recognise the propriety of giving assistance in dying — and in circumstances far wider than the NT act allowed. Regrettably, there will be far less protection against abuse than the NT act would have provided. A pyrrhic victory, indeed.

David Kelly is a former chairman of the Victorian Law Reform Commission. Loane Skene is associate professor of law at Melbourne University.

Age, 26 March 1997.

Chapter 7

LEARNING *outcomes*

- Identify the education and training requirements for particular occupations.
- Investigate and participate in the job-seeking process.
- Identify the skills valued in workplaces.
- Identify future job opportunities in Australia.

CAREERS AND WORK

INTRODUCTION

The world beyond school requires us to equip ourselves with a number of skills. Outside school, life revolves around work. Once you are eligible for employment you are part of the ***labour force****. Some of you may already be employed in a part-time job and be part of this labour force; others may be waiting until they leave school.*

Getting a job usually requires a lot of preparation. You need to compile a history of your life and present it in the form of a curriculum vitae, and you may also have to participate in an interview.

Once you are employed in a job, there are many things to learn and understand. You have to learn not only the skills you need to perform the job, but how to read an employment contract, which you may be required to sign. To protect your rights as a worker, you may need to call upon the services of a trade union.

This is an exciting time of your life, as you embark on a career and experience many changes. It is important that you begin to plan for this phase in your life now.

GLOSSARY

apprenticeship: training and education for practical jobs such as plumbing and carpentry
arbitration: the process of hearing and settling a dispute
Australian Industrial Relations Commission (AIRC): a tribunal which hears cases between employers and unions. Their decision is binding on the parties.
award: minimum work conditions which are set down in law
bachelor: a three-year degree completed at a university
blue collar: relating to industrial workers
certificate: education for practical jobs
cadetship: professional job training in a full-time job with time to attend university
closed shop: an industry or work site where the employer could only call on a certain union to supply labour
conciliation: to bring together two or more parties in agreement
curriculum vitae: a résumé
diploma: a two-year course
employee: a person who is hired to work for another
employee agreement: a document that sets out the terms of your employment
employer: a person or firm that employs workers
ergonomically: to do with the engineering aspects of the connection between human workers and their working environment
formal: following established forms
industrial relations: the relationship between employers and employees
interview: a meeting in which an employer talks to you to see if you are suitable for a job
labour force: people aged 15 and over who are either employed or unemployed
negotiation: the process of working with another party in order to reach an agreement
pay slip: official record of a person's income details for a week, fortnight or month
referee: a person who vouches for your character or work performance
reference: a written letter about a person's work performance or character
résumé: a formal record of your personal information and work and education history
strike: the withdrawal of labour for a set amount of time, as a form of protest
TAFE: Technical and Further Education. A large education centre which offers VCE, certificates and diplomas
trade union: an organisation of employees, formed to help and protect each other and deal with employers
white collar: relating to workers in professional or clerical positions (who traditionally wear a suit, white collar and tie)

7.1

DIFFERENT WORK FOR DIFFERENT PEOPLE

There are many thousands of jobs people can choose from and they all require different levels of interest and skill. For example, if you have an interest in the 'outdoors', you might be a person who likes to work in the open, mainly outdoors, close to nature. There are many occupations that suit people interested in the outdoors — a gardener or a park ranger are just two examples.

People choose particular occupations based on other interests such as:

- Artistic — designing and creating objects of art, music or architecture
- Clerical — writing letters, organising and recording business information
- Engineering — designing or constructing machines, tools and technical equipment
- Personal contact — meeting, talking and discussing problems with people
- Scientific — undertaking research and experiments
- Manual and practical — working with the hands, using special tools
- Medical — working with people to cure physical or mental disabilities.

CLASSIFYING DIFFERENT TYPES OF WORK

How many different types of work are there? As you would guess, there are thousands. However, to make things easier, occupations throughout Australia can be grouped into eight main classifications of work. This helps us to distinguish one type of work from another. These eight classifications are listed in the table below.

Each of these eight classifications of work has hundreds of different occupations. The ones shown on the left are just a few examples. These classifications of work also have varying levels of status and prestige. Different people would regard some jobs as having more status than others.

EDUCATION AND WORK OPPORTUNITIES

The ever-changing nature of work is having an effect on young people's employment strategies. For many jobs, specific post-secondary qualifications are important. In fact the government predicts that professional occupations are likely to grow at a faster rate than other types of occupations, at least until 2001.

Students who leave school and do not progress to tertiary education can determine their chances of finding a job by examining recent trends in the labour market. These students could carefully consider the performance of industries that employ large numbers of school-leavers, and look at trends in apprenticeship and traineeship opportunities.

Classification of work	Examples of occupations	Classification of work	Examples of occupations
1. Managers/ administrators	farm manager, sales manager	5. Clerks	telephonist, typist, filing clerk
2. Professionals	engineer, doctor, teacher	6. Salespersons and personnel services	cashier, sales assistant
3. Paraprofessionals	medical officer, police, nurse	7. Plant and machine operators	rail driver, machine operator
4. Tradespersons	plumber, fitter and turner, plasterer	8. Labourers	cleaner, construction worker

Jobs of the future

Best prospects

- Computer programmer systems administrator/ analyst
- PC user support
- Desktop publisher
- Physiotherapist
- Medical imaging therapist
- Speech pathologist
- Occupational therapist
- Rehabilitation counsellor
- Chef/cook
- Hotel/motel/restaurant manager and front office clerk
- Tour guide
- Childcare worker/ coordinator
- Security officer and guard
- Fitness instructor
- Statistician and actuary

Worst prospects

- Gunsmith
- Milk deliverer/vendor
- Footwear pattern cutter, machinist, designer, clicker
- Electrical fitter
- Metal product/business machine operator

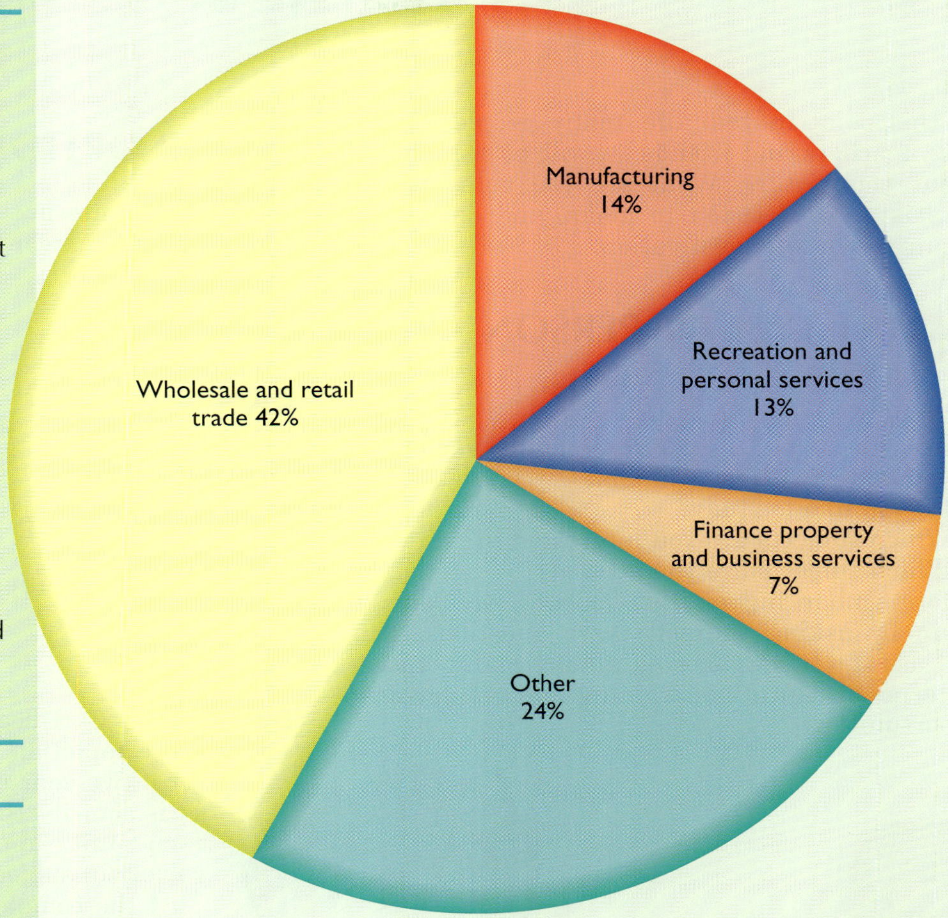

Source: School leavers are more likely to enter particular industries. (ABS, Transition from Education to Work, Cat. No. 6227.0) and from *Herald-Sun* 17/12/97 article by Karen Collier.

Activities

Communication: *Analysing a pie chart*

Carefully study the pie chart and complete the following questions.

(a) Which category of employment has the best prospects for future employment?

(b) Would you classify this industry as a **blue-collar** or **white-collar** occupation?

(c) List two manufacturing jobs that have the worst prospects for jobs in the future.

(d) Why is employment in manufacturing not predicted to grow as fast as other jobs?

Investigation: *Researching in newspapers*

Look up the employment section of a major newspaper. Find six occupation titles that fit each of these classifications of work:

- managers/administrators
- professionals
- tradespersons
- labourers
- salespersons
- plant and machine operators

Copy your answers into your workbook. Here is an example: professionals — mechanical engineer.

PATHWAYS IN LIFE

At this point in your life, many people — parents, teachers and friends — will be asking you about your future. What are you going to be? This is a big decision to make, and one which requires a lot of investigation.

WHAT TYPE OF PERSON ARE YOU?

1. What are your interests?
2. Are you a good thinker/problem solver or are you better with your hands?
3. Do you like to study?
4. Which subjects are you interested in?
5. Which subjects are you good at?

Before embarking on this journey, you should begin by asking yourself these questions. This will assist you in choosing among many choices in terms of education, training and employment opportunities.

YOUR OPTIONS

Some of the alternatives you have, which will take you to the career of your choice include:

1. **Education** —
   - VCE
   - **TAFE**
   - university
2. **Training** —
   - on the job
   - **cadetships**
   - work experience
   - **apprenticeship**
3. **Jobs** —
   - work opportunities

1. Education

VCE

The Victorian Certificate of Education is gained by the completion of a set number of units over a two-year period. You are required to satisfactorily cover a set of outcomes for each unit. You may choose among a variety of subjects offered by your school.

At the completion of your VCE studies, you will receive an ENTER score. This score is used to measure your place in university courses. The higher the score, the more options are available to you. Each university publishes their entry scores annually.

TAFE

Technical and Further Education courses offer training for many different career areas. They cater for people with all levels of education. The areas of study available can be as varied as tourism, business studies, visual arts and plumbing.

TAFEs offer **diplomas** and advanced diplomas for students who have completed Year 12. They also offer **certificates** with levels from I to IV. To gain entry into a certificate you must have completed Year 10.

You should go to the institution to receive more information relating to the types of courses available and the fees and charges associated with this type of education.

University

University is more than just a stepping stone between school and work — it is a new and challenging world in its own right. Universities are huge places, often with between 5000 and 10 000 students. There are limited rules, as students are treated as adults who are responsible for their own learning. There is usually no supervision of lecture attendance and, while tutorial involvement may count towards your assessment, there may be no 'roll-call'.

At the beginning of your first year at university, you may have the option of attending an orientation week, during which time you can participate in activities and meet your teachers and tutors.

Most university courses are taught through lectures and tutorials. At a lecture you will be in a large group of students taking your own notes from the speaker. Tutorials are small group classes which extend the information acquired from lectures or from the reading assigned to the course. You are expected to contribute to general discussions and this may form part of your assessment.

When you begin your **bachelor** degree you are known as an 'undergraduate'. Bachelor degrees are offered at pass and honours level. At some tertiary institutions, honours work is available after first year and involves undertaking extra study and classes. At other institutions, honours are achieved by completing an extra year at university. In both systems, however, you must be 'invited' to do honours, and must achieve and maintain high standards in your work and examination results.

At your formal graduation ceremony you become a 'graduate'. Any university course you then proceed to do is known as post-graduate study.

Most universities conduct open days, where interested students are welcome to go to the university and find out information about different courses. These are generally conducted in the second half of the year.

2. Training

Some schools conduct a work experience program where students are encouraged to seek temporary employment at a firm to gain an insight into that particular field of work.

If you take on an apprenticeship you will learn about your job as you work with your **employer**. On particular days, and some evenings you will be required to attend classes at a TAFE college.

Some professions, such as accounting, offer cadetships. A cadetship is where a company employs you and gives you time to attend university where you complete your degree in accounting. This is a great way to become trained and educated in this field of work, because you have permanent employment.

3. Jobs

To help direct you towards the right job, here are some suggestions:

- talk to people
- attend open days
- check the newspapers for vacancies
- consider a variety of options
- do some homework — find out about the industry.

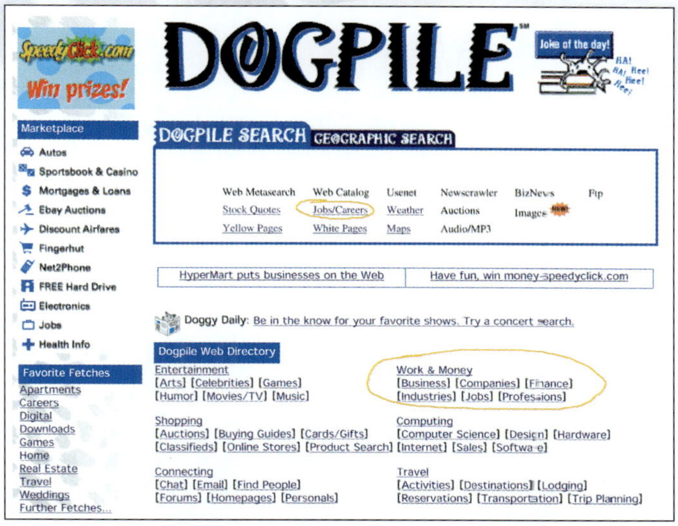

Search engines like this one can help you to find out about jobs.

Activities

Investigation: *Finding the right career*

1. (a) Design a poster which describes the person you are. Use figure one as a guide to give you suggestions on different areas to include on your poster.
   (b) Prepare an introduction to the class for the person sitting next to you. Cover their interests, subjects taken at school, their goals in life, including the area of work, and how they plan to achieve these goals.
2. Explain the difference between:
   (a) VCE and TAFE
   (b) TAFE and university
   (c) Apprenticeship and work experience.
3. How does university differ from school life? Prepare a list of strategies for university survival.
4. Using search engines (such as the one above), outline the procedure for achieving a career as:
   (a) an engineer (b) a plumber.
   Note: To do this you will need to outline the education requirements, and where the study may be undertaken and the details of the work opportunity.
   Find out if these careers are in a jobs growth area.

SO YOU WANT TO BE A . . .?

CARPENTER — DANIEL THEWMA

'I always enjoyed working with wood at school, and after completing Year 11 and receiving an offer to do an apprenticeship with a builder I decided to follow this path in life. After a two-month trial I decided that this was the job for me. I have to attend school at the Newport TAFE one week per month to complete both theory and practical lessons, as well as work with my boss. I pay a levy to attend TAFE which is tax deductible, and when I complete my three years of work experience and blocks of subjects, I will have a Certificate in Carpentry.

This job is very satisfying. I can always see a result at the end of the day, and I really feel as though I have accomplished something that takes a lot of thought and physical exertion. This physical exertion, along with the long hours per day, is a difficult part of this type of work.

My ambition in life is to have a business of my own called A1 Constructions. I really want to succeed in life and I know that with hard work and determination I can earn a lot of money and have a satisfying job.

To help me establish the skills that I will need to run my own business I will have to do some further study. The Master Builders Association (MBA) provides courses which teach builders the skills to run their own business.

I am confident that when I have my own business I will take on an apprentice. I want to give someone a chance, just like I had. I will ensure that I treat them fairly and guide them in the right direction so that they can have a successful career. I hope that I will have a good relationship with my apprentice and be able to refer jobs to them if I am too busy.

I am enjoying my life at present. I have eight months of my apprenticeship to finish, and I am about to work for a new builder. I am excited about this position because I will be responsible for building units from start to finish. My only regret so far has been my unwillingness to fully apply myself at the beginning of my apprenticeship. I worked with another guy my age, and we tended to chat and play around a lot. However, I am learning from my mistakes and I am confident that the future looks bright.'

HOTEL MANAGER — NORIZMAH AHMAD MORSHIDI

Exciting jobs, exotic locations, interesting people — the Tourism and Hospitality Industry can be glamorous, up-market and plain hard work.

In Australia it is estimated to be the fastest growing industry, contributing significantly to the economy.

Norizmah loves to work with people. She is a social person who always finds it satisfying to please other people and to have a lot of contact with people. Norizmah decided to get involved in Tourism and Hospitality in Year 10, where she had work experience at the Grand Hyatt Hotel.

'This industry is huge, and there are many opportunities. You can plan a career in the same part of the industry — from kitchen hand to chef to hotel manager.'

Norizmah is a hotel manager at the Rydges Hotel in Exhibition Street, Melbourne. A keen traveller, Norizmah decided to go overseas after completing her VCE. She satisfactorily completed accounting, economics, English, biology and general mathematics. After a year travelling Europe and Asia, Norizmah reinforced her desire to work in an area where she would have lots of contact with people, and keep her interest in overseas travel.

Norizmah decided to complete her degree in Sydney at the International College of Tourism and Hotel Management. She studied for three years and completed a Bachelor of Business Hospitality and Tourism degree. Norizmah explains the detail of the course below:

'The first year provides a grounding in hotel operations, concentrating on practical skills, food and beverage operations, kitchen, etc. It also includes computer training and business communications, and management skills. The second year embraces the complexities of hotel management and administration, human resource management, accounting, and leadership. The final year continues to develop and consolidate business skills, market and human resource planning.'

I am delighted with my career. I have moved back to Melbourne, but I plan to stay here for only a few years before going back to Europe where I hope to work in a hotel.'

Activities

Investigation: *Finding out more*

1. Invite your careers teacher to speak to the class about differing career choices.
2. (a) List four types of apprenticeships not discussed in this section which can be completed by students.
   (b) Investigate fully the requirements to satisfactorily complete an apprenticeship.
3. Identify the steps taken by Daniel to become a carpenter.
4. (a) What steps has Norizmah taken to become a Hotel Manager?
   (b) Suggest some other avenues Norizmah's career can take in the hospitality field.
5. Write a response to the following statement:

   'In today's society, we must equip ourselves for more than one career in our lifetime.'

   Expand your response by doing some research on this topic. Ask your careers teacher, parents and friends for advice.

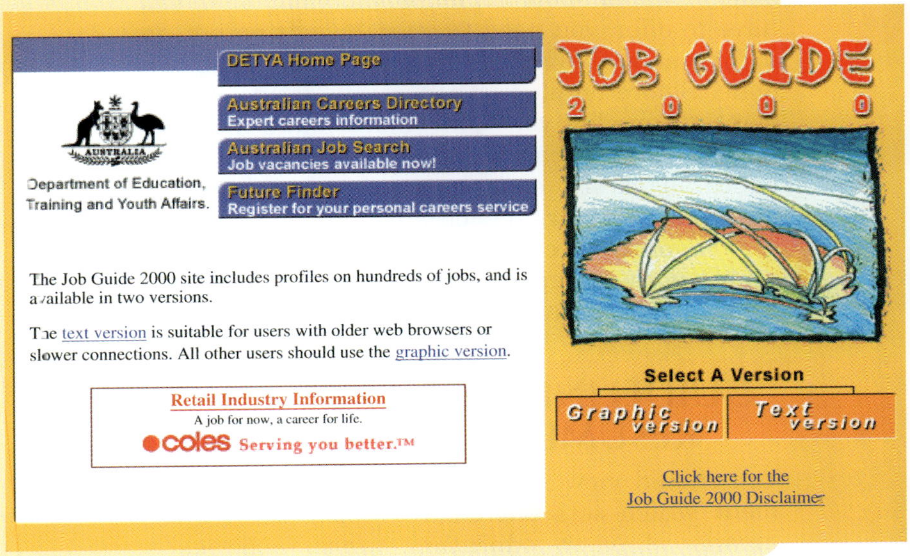

7.4

PROMOTING YOURSELF

Have you ever tried to advertise yourself? How would you go about doing it? With a television or newspaper advertisement? Or is a billboard with your photograph on it more your style?

In order to show an employer what it is you have to offer, you need to start by setting out, in a **formal** way, who you are and what you have done. Before employers can really decide if they want to employ you, they must make sense of who they are dealing with; for example, what education, work experience, personal interests and characteristics do you have?

A **résumé**, or **curriculum vitae** (often called a CV), is the accepted way of setting out the key aspects of your background.

GUIDELINES FOR PREPARING RÉSUMÉS

You should view your résumé as a formal document which sets out clearly and concisely the details of your education, work experience, extra-curricular activities and, in most cases, details of your referees. Remember the following points about style.

- Maintain a formal style. The style of your curriculum vitae should reflect its role as a formal document.
- Make it easy on the eye. The visual appearance of your résumé has to be very simple. Clearly label all sections, allow plenty of space between them, and keep a simple structure within each section so that it is easy to see the main areas.
- Keep it short. One to two pages is enough. There is no need to include everything you have ever done.
- Put your most recent details first. For example, show details of your current work experience first, then your previous job and so on.
- On a separate page, at the back of your CV, you can add more detailed information.

You should update your CV regularly so that the most recent information and results are included.

The elements shown on the opposite page are essential in a curriculum vitae.

Activities

Investigation: *Gathering information*

1. What is the difference between a reference and a referee?
2. Find two suitable referees for yourself. List their contact details.
3. Collect information on education, work, certificates, school reports and so on.

Communication: *Promoting yourself*

1. Prepare a one-minute oral presentation to the class about yourself. You could include your hobbies, sporting achievements, school achievements, likes and dislikes.
2. Prepare notes on your work experience, paying particular attention to achievements, good qualities, and the details of the work you have performed. Produce a draft of your curriculum vitae.
3. Use a computer to neatly present your curriculum vitae. Have a classmate check your presentation.

CURRICULUM VITAE

1. Personal details about yourself. Include name, address, telephone number, date and place of birth and nationality, or permanent resident status.

PERSONAL DETAILS

Name:	Chun Tse Ming
Address:	456 Ballarat Rd Sunshine Victoria 3030
Telephone:	(03) 9311 3719
Date of birth:	27 May 1983
Nationality:	Australian

2. Education. Include secondary education. Give details of your most recent results. This will eventually include secondary and tertiary education where relevant.

EDUCATION

Secondary — Braybrook College, Completed Year 10 1997

English	A
Commerce	A
Maths	B
Science	B
Indonesian	A
Art	C+
Technology	B

3. Work experience. List all your jobs in reverse order, with your most recent workplace first.

WORK EXPERIENCE

November 2000	Bakers Delight, salesperson
January 2000	McDonald's, kitchen hand, salesperson
September 2000	Awarded employee of the month, February 2000

4. Interests and activities. Do not underestimate the importance of these. They give an employer an idea of who you are, beyond the more formal elements of your background.

EXTRA-CURRICULAR INTERESTS AND ACTIVITIES

School	Member of school band, playing piano Class captain 1998 and 1999
Other	Tennis coach for the Braybrook under 10s Tennis player, Braybrook Tennis Club Pianist for local church Bushwalking, reading, computers

5. **Referees** and **references**. A reference is a letter which is written about you by someone who knows you well or for whom you have worked. It identifies the type of person you are, or describes your work performance in previous jobs. If you cannot get someone to write a reference for you, then you could ask the person to be a referee. A prospective employer will phone your referee and ask questions about your work performance. Provide at least two referees in your résumé.

REFEREES

Dr Russell Watson	Rev. C. Leadbetter	Ms Vivien Li
Maths Coordinator	Sunshine Anglican Church	Year 10 Coordinator
Braybrook College	Northumberland Rd	Braybrook College
Braybrook	Sunshine	Braybrook
Victoria 30.9	Victoria 3020	Victoria 3019
(03) 9312 4585	(03) 9311 4009	(03) 9312 4585

APPLYING FOR A JOB

After completing your curriculum vitae, you are now ready to apply for a job. The first step may be to respond to an advertisement by phoning the business, then writing a letter of application. After you have successfully contacted the business, you may then be asked for an **interview**. Here are some tips to help you on your way.

A BASIC APPLICATION LETTER

If applications in response to an advertisement are to be made in writing, get in first.

1. Ring the company and get some background information.
2. Find out details of the position available and the qualifications and qualities that are required. For example, what is the specific nature of the work? What type of personal qualities are they looking for?

Once you have the information you need, you are ready to prepare your letter of application. The following points will help you.

- ***Keep the structure simple.*** The first paragraph explains that you are applying for a particular position in response to an advertisement. It may also briefly indicate who and what you are. The second and third paragraphs set out the qualifications and skills which you have to offer (according to what the employer wants.) It may also include the reasons that you are interested in the position — your commitment to the job can be important in showing you are really motivated. The final paragraph must sign off in a positive way.
- ***Make your letter look impressive.*** The success of your application letter should create a very positive impression. It should therefore look businesslike — and that means typed. The term 'apply in writing' does not mean that your letters should be handwritten. Don't indent each new paragraph, use full block style.
- ***Avoid business jargon.*** Use simple, natural language, rather than business jargon. Carefully check your spelling, grammar and punctuation, and have someone else check it, too. Don't use slang.
- ***Keep it brief.*** Employers do not have the time to read through long, rambling letters. They are more likely to be interested in someone who can write clearly and concisely, and you cannot hold their interest for more than a page. Include your curriculum vitae with your letter.

Below is an example of a job advertisement, and opposite is a letter responding to the advertisement. Of course, this is a mock advertisement and letter, but it does provide an example for you to consider.

POSITIONS VACANT

The Footy Show

Position available

Co-host on the popular evening television show, 'The Footy Show'

Must have previous experience and good communication skills.

Please write to Eddie McGuire, care of Channel 9, and outline your ideas for the role of co-host.

Salary negotiable.

Activities

Investigation: *Analysing an application letter*

1. Refer to the mock advertisement and letter of application for 'The Footy Show'.
2. Identify the various parts of the letter.
3. What key information did the advertisement say should be in the letter?
4. Did Sam cover the important information? Where is this located?
5. List the areas which Sam covered well in his letter.
6. Identify the areas that Sam could improve on, and suggest improvements.
7. What do you think of the way Sam has sold himself? Is he overconfident? How should Sam express himself?

Mr Sam Newman
30 Geelong Street
SOUTH RIVER VIC 3000

15 March 2000

Mr Eddie McGuire
Program Writer of 'The Footy Show'
Channel 9
PO Box 999999
RICHMOND VIC 3121

Dear Mr McGuire,

I am writing in response to the advertisement in the *Age* newspaper dated 13 March 2000, for the position of co-host on 'The Footy Show'.

With experience in the television industry, a thorough knowledge of football and excellent interpersonal skills, I know I would be a suitable applicant for this position. My career began as a football player with the Geelong Football Club, where I was the star player. I retired from the game and took a position on a Sunday Sports program with Channel 7, where I was on a panel with a number of other ex-players. I gained this position because of my reputation as an excellent reporter with a thorough understanding of Australian Rules Football. It was on this show that I further refined my interviewing and questioning skills to the high standard they are today. I was definitely the best reporter on the show.

I am well known for my sense of humour and my interest in other people. I get along with people from many different backgrounds, states and nations. I encourage people to view their opinions and I have a unique style.

When I am appointed to the position of co-host, I would like to star in a segment in which people in the street are interviewed about their likes and dislikes in Australian Rules Football. I am available for an interview at any time. Please find enclosed my curriculum vitae.

Yours sincerely,

Sam Newman

Sam Newman

Communication: *Writing an application letter*

1. Write a letter of application to one of the advertisers on the right. Use a computer to produce your final version.
2. Design your own standard letter of application. This should include the main body of the letter and your address. The information which would need to be regularly changed is the date, the person the letter is addressed to, and key information relevant to the particular position.

THE MELBOURNE EXAMINER — Wednesday 18 March 2000

Employment

SALES ASSISTANT. Part time position available. Responsible, enthusiastic person to work in a take-away food shop. Apply in writing to The Manager, Fine Fast Food, 88 Main Road, Richmond 3121.

STOREPERSON. We need a storeperson to help assist in the effective operation of our busy store. Duties include packing of deliveries, clerical work and dealing with freight companies. Computer literacy is essential. Must be self-motivated and able to work alone. Fax résumé to The Accountant 9471 0000.

PERSONAL ASSISTANT ...

TRAINEE SALES MANAGERS

Newly opened branch office requires four people to train and develop in all aspects of sales, marketing and management.
If you have ability and good communication skills we will offer a comprehensive training program with an opening to management level for the right people.
Send written details to:
Recruitment Manager
GPO Box 5555
Melbourne 3001

LABOURER. CASUAL. Experienced in demolition ... have own ...

PERSONAL ASSISTANT. Your key responsibility will be to assist the Directors in sales and retail in achieving business objectives. This will involve presentations, typing documents and compiling reports. You will also be responsible for organising sales conferences, sourcing venues and negotiating rates. You must have skills in MS Office, 80 wpm typing and a self-motivated, conscientious attitude. This is a fast-moving, team-orientated environment. *Please call Joanne Jones on 9777 7070 or fax résumés to 9777 7171.*

SECRETARY. For large ...

FLORIST

Part-time, becoming full-time with an early May start.
Experience preferred but not essential.
Exciting new premises in the heart of St. Kilda.
Please forward résumé to:
Director
Jennifer's
Flower House
PO Box 2
Port Melbourne 3207
Ph 9646 0101 or
015 888 888

SHOP ASSISTANT. Experienced person required for busy ...

INTERVIEW TECHNIQUES

So, you've written your CV and you have seen the perfect job. One that you know you can do well. Contacting the business is an important step and must be executed with precision to ensure you get that job.

TELEPHONE TECHNIQUES

You have found a job advertisement that you are interested in, and the advertisement asks you to telephone. Phone up without delay, since the employer may stop taking calls after a certain number of people have applied. Get in early. Remember, first impressions are always lasting.

Before you get on the telephone, make a list of the further details you need. Also have available:

- your education results
- your recent employment details
- your diary or schedule for the week, so you can make an appointment for an interview
- pen and paper at your fingertips.

Speak clearly, watch your language, use whole words, not 'dunno' or 's'pose so'. Introduce yourself, specify the position you would like to apply for and where and when it was advertised.

Be prepared to sell yourself. You need to be able to stand out from other people. If asked for background information about yourself, do so in a concise manner. Use a summary of your sales pitch, which you should have in writing in front of you.

INTERVIEW TECHNIQUES

Going to a job interview requires some preparation. It is not enough to just turn up to the interview on time. It is important that you are fully prepared, that you have paid careful attention to your appearance and to the impression you are going to make. Avoid the following mistakes.

Being late for the interview or arriving at the last minute

Having an appearance that is all wrong

Showing an obvious lack of confidence

Not having much to say, not asking questions

Displaying a lack of knowledge about the job you are applying for or about the employer

Make sure that you find out about the position you are applying for, and that you have some knowledge about the firm you wish to work for. You must also be quietly confident, but not over confident. Your approach and manner has to be that of someone who believes they have something to offer and knows what that is. Your task is to convey this clearly to the employer.

If you know what to expect in an interview, you are less likely to be flustered. The structure of an interview generally follows this pattern:

1. preliminary discussion — the warm-up phase
2. obtaining information about the applicant
3. giving information about the position and the organisation
4. opportunity to ask your questions
5. concluding discussion — winding-up phase.

SUGGESTIONS FOR A SUCCESSFUL INTERVIEW

1. Participate. No one is going to offer a job to someone who sits there and contributes little to the conversation.
2. Watch your use of language.
3. Smile — but make a joke only if appropriate.
4. Take a copy of your CV into the interview, along with any other relevant documents such as a copy of final school results.
5. Any good sales pitch ends with a summary and reinforcement of its main points. You may be given the opportunity to make some final comments and you must use the opportunity to leave a firm and positive impression of what you have to offer.

   Also use this time to ask questions about the position and about the firm you wish to work for
6. Practise your interview techniques with a friend or member of your family.

Activities

Investigation: *Planning for an interview*

1. Identify the key points to remember when:
   (a) undertaking a telephone interview
   (b) participating in a personal interview.
2. From the interview situations shown in the cartoons:
   (a) identify the interview mistakes
   (b) suggest what the person should have done in each case.
3. Choose an advertisement of your choice from the paper and prepare a letter and preparation notes for an interview.

Communication: *Conducting an interview*

1. In small groups, look at the advertisements shown on page 185. Interview each other for the positions as though you were conducting a telephone interview.
2. In groups of three, conduct interviews in which two people interview the third person for a job. The person to be interviewed should decide on a particular job that interests him or her. The interviewers should also prepare for their roles by listing some questions they wish to ask the applicant.

   Swap roles so that each member gets a chance to be interviewed.

ON THE JOB

RIGHTS AND RESPONSIBILITIES

Once you begin working, you have many rights, and you have responsibilities to your employer. It is important that you are aware of these. As an **employee** you will be expected to:

- attend work regularly and punctually
- provide a fair day's work, as outlined in your job specification
- behave in a way that supports the 'culture' of the workplace
- obey the rules of the workplace and the laws of society.

In return you can expect from your new employer:

- a fair and just workplace and financial reward
- safe working conditions
- a safe and **ergonomically** sound workplace
- benefits such as sick leave and annual leave, which are standard in Australian workplaces.

Training

Some workplaces train you when you start your employment; this is often called 'on-the-job training'. This may involve going to special training sessions or being supervised by a more experienced employee in your first few months of work.

Many workplaces also train their staff so that they can perform more than one job. For example, Hoyts Cinemas train all their staff in each area of operation, including 'candy bar' service, ticket selling and ushering. This is sometimes called 'multiskilling'.

You may find that once you commence a job, you can continue with further education, funded by your employer. This brings added skills and expertise into your workplace and may enhance your chances of promotion in the future.

Money

You may be paid in cash but this is becoming very rare today. It is more common to be paid by cheque or by direct transfer into your bank account. Regardless of the way you are paid, you will receive a **pay slip** which outlines the details of your pay, tax deductions, leave entitlements and so on.

Employee agreements

The new way of having your conditions of employment set out is an **employee agreement**. It is a formal document that sets out the terms of your employment and the relationship between you and your employer.

Awards were introduced by the government; they set out the minimum standards between employers and employees. Now, employment agreements set these standards and conditions. The conditions may include the following:

- rates of pay
- hours of work
- promotion procedures
- grievances and appeals procedures
- termination procedures
- leave procedures.

WHAT ARE TRADE UNIONS?

A **trade union** is an organisation which looks after workers in a particular job or industry. People who do similar work may join a union so that the union can protect their working conditions, such as wage levels and safety. Members pay a fee to finance the union's operation.

Members of a union may meet to discuss an issue of concern to them.

Unions generally aim to:

- protect the interests of union members; for example, by increasing their pay rates
- improve the working conditions of members; for example, by monitoring health and safety
- ensure the fair treatment of employees at work; for example, by preventing unfair dismissals
- promote quality of life for all; for example, by limiting work hours.

You should be under no obligation to join a union when you commence work at a new job. In the 1980s, when membership of unions was high, people were often put under pressure to join a union. A **closed shop** was an industry or work site where the employer could only call on a certain union to supply labour.

In order to achieve the best outcome for its members in the case of a dispute, unions may go through the following procedures.

Negotiation. The first step is usually for the employer to meet with the employee (or, in a larger dispute, with employee representatives) and discuss the dispute in order to find a solution. This requires both parties to negotiate their differences until they reach an agreement, which may require both parties to compromise.

Conciliation. This is a formal process in which an independent third party listens to the problem. The employer presents their case to the conciliator, and so too does the union. The conciliator helps to solve the problem.

Arbitration. Where a dispute is still unresolved, the case may go to arbitration. This is the same process as conciliation, except that the decision made by the arbitrator (the person hearing the case) is binding, and therefore must be obeyed by both the union and the employer. While arbitration is still in existence, there are moves by the government to eliminate this process.

Strikes. When a union votes to strike it is taking direct action against employers by withdrawing its labour. This usually receives a lot of media attention. A strike is usually an option of last resort for a union. Nobody likes strikes. For the workers, it means a day (or longer) without a wage. For the employers it means they lose a day's production.

Employees can be ordered back to work while on strike by the **Australian Industrial Relations Commission (AIRC)**. If the employees refuse they can be fined (up to $10 000).

There has been an enormous amount of change in **industrial relations** law. The government has endeavoured to give the employer more power and control over its employees. This is designed to save employers money, and to limit the power unions and employees can have.

Activities

Check your understanding

1. Why would businesses continually train their staff? What benefits are there to the employee and the employer?
2. Identify the purpose of an employment contract.
3. Explain the use of awards for employees and employers.
4. What is the role of a union in the workplace?
5. How do unions go about achieving their aims?

Investigation: *Employment relations*

1. Collect articles from newspapers showing union activity in the last year. Bring the articles to class, summarise them, and present the summary to the class for class discussion.
2. As a class, discuss the question 'Would you join a union?'
3. In small groups, design an employment agreement for a casual job at McDonald's. Identify the minimum conditions you would need in your employee agreement.
4. In small groups, discuss the advantages and disadvantages of union membership. Summarise these points in a table.
5. Debate: Unions have no role in the workplace of the twenty-first century.

7.8 Meeting the outcomes

ANALYSE VOCATIONAL PATHWAYS AND EDUCATION AND TRAINING REQUIREMENTS TO DEVELOP POSSIBLE CAREER PATHS AND WORK OPPORTUNITIES.

Identify the education and training requirements and pathways for a selected range of occupations.

1. Look at the information from the Department of Education, Training and Youth Affairs on page 191.
   (a) What are the secondary education requirements for a position as hotel/motel manager?
   (b) List three different types of on-the-job training that you would expect to undertake as a trainee hotel/motel manager.
   (c) List three different degree courses on offer for hotel/motel managers.
2. Visit the Department of Education, Training and Youth Affairs Web site, other careers Web sites, or contact your Vocational Education Teacher.
   (a) Select two possible job areas in which you would like to become involved.What are the secondary education requirements for the positions?
   (b) What on-the-job training would you expect to undertake?
   (c) What courses are on offer for this career path?

Identify future job opportunities and predicted labour market changes in Australia.

1. List three of the best job prospects for school leavers in the near future. (7.1)
2. List three of the worst job prospects for school leavers in the near future. (7.1)
3. What impact is technology having on future job prospects? (7.1)

Participate in and evaluate real or simulated job-seeking processes.

1. Look at the advertisement for the positions of management trainees at The Pancake Parlour (opposite) from www.mycareer.com.au.
   (a) List the top three qualities that you think the employer will be looking for.
   (b) What experience might be relevant to highlight on a curriculum vitae?
2. Visit www.mycareer.com.au, other career Web sites, or look at the classified pages of the newspaper to select a position that could reasonably apply for in the next few years.
   (a) Identify courses that you may need to undertake for the position.
   (b) Prepare your own curriculum vitae and application for the position.
   (c) List five questions that you would expect to be asked in an interview for the position.

Compare generic processes and skills valued in workplaces.

1. Rank the following work skills in order of importance.
   Punctuality
   Diligence
   Adaptability
   Honesty
   Computer literacy
   Teamwork
2. Which of the qualities in question one would be most highly regarded by the employers of The Pancake Parlour (see advertisement below)?
3. Give yourself a rating out of 10 for each of the qualities outlined in question one.
4. Select one quality from the list and explain why it is so important in a work environment.

MANAGEMENT TRAINEES

The Pancake Parlour restaurants, Doncaster and Northland are currently seeking career-minded people who are wanting to work in the hospitality industry. Must be friendly and hardworking, willing to work a mixture of shifts, including days, nights and weekends. Experience not necessary but must be enthusiastic to learn and give 100pc. We will provide full on-the-job training with the view of training to our management team.

Previous experience in the industry would be an asset, but not essential as the successful applicants will be trained in all facets of the restaurant business.

This is a ground floor opportunity to join a successful Australian company with 35 years history.

Please send your résumé by Friday 31 March:

Attention Sara Giansiracusa,
The Pancake Parlour,
Shop C35, Upper Level, 2 Murray Road,
Northland SC, Preston East 3072.

Management trainee positions also available at our Bourke St, Chadstone and Doncaster restaurants. For these positions please send your résumé by March 31:

Attn Nicki Lumb, Lovely Pancakes,
11th Floor,
180 Russell St Melbourne 3000

Hotel/Motel Manager

Description

Hotel/motel managers generally work long, irregular hours including evenings, weekends and public holidays. They have a high level of contact with the public. They may have to deal with difficult guests and be on call if major problems arise.

Hotel/motel managers may work in privately owned hotels or motels or they may be employed by companies which operate a chain of businesses. Self-employment is possible through the purchase of small motels or management rights for larger properties. In large establishments, people have specialised in one or two areas, for example, rooms division or food and beverage. However, increasingly managers are expected to be skilled in all areas and may perform the following tasks:

- plan, direct and coordinate the service of accounting, food and beverages, guest services, maintenance, staff development, and sales and marketing
- assign tasks and priorities, coordinate resources, develop business plans and marketing strategy
- undertake facility management tasks such as building management including building costs, rents, maintenance, lighting, power, heating, air conditioning, floorings and furniture
- control capital and operational expenditure
- ensure all government health, industrial safety and licensing regulations are followed
- carry out marketing and sales activities for rooms, conventions, banquets and conferences
- prepare reports
- ensure work conditions comply with regulations
- manage the security of the hotel and its staff
- publicise the hotel/motel through public relations activities in the local business community.

Personal Requirements

- good organisational skills
- good communication skills
- an outgoing personality and an ability to deal with a range of people
- leadership skills
- good computer skills
- a capacity for hard work
- flexibility

Education and Training

There are no specified educational requirements for entry, however, formal training and operational experience are becoming increasingly important. Training in this field has traditionally been on-the-job and many large hotels conduct in-house training programs and provide on-the-job training.

There are now nationally accredited qualifications from Certificate I through to Advanced Diploma, to meet the training needs of people working in the tourism and hospitality industries from operational levels through to management. Qualifications from Certificate IV upward include the skills needed to work in supervisory or management positions. Considerable workplace experience is also needed to be an effective supervisor or manager. Skills can be learnt on the job and/or through formal training provided by registered training organisations, including TAFE. Degree courses are also available from tertiary institutions.

Entry to courses generally requires satisfactory completion of the VCE. Prerequisite subjects, particularly English and maths, are also required for some courses. Alternative entry may be available for these courses. Contact the institutions for details.

Degree Courses

La Trobe University — Albury–Wodonga and Shepparton campuses:

- Bachelor of Business (Hospitality Management), 3 years full time or equivalent part-time. (The first year of this course may be studied at Wangaratta TAFE.)

Monash University — Berwick and Gippsland campuses:

- Bachelor of Business (Hospitality Management), 4 years full time or 8 years part time.

RMIT:

- Bachelor of Applied Science (Hospitality Studies), 3 years full time plus 1 year of industry experience.

University of Ballarat:

- Bachelor of Management (Tourism), 3 years full time or equivalent part time.

Victoria University of Technology — Footscray Campus:

- Bachelor of Business (Catering and Hotel Management), 4 years full time.

http://jobguide.thegoodguides.com.au

Chapter 8

MANAGING A BUSINESS

LEARNING outcomes

- Examine organisation structures of business enterprises.
- Understand and apply financial management skills.
- Identify management skills.
- Investigate how e-commerce is changing businesses.
- Identify enterprise attributes and skills in small business.
- Describe how innovation and enterprise affect the economy and society.
- Plan and conduct a small-scale project that applies enterprise skills and attributes.

INTRODUCTION

Any successful business activity requires a great deal of planning and an understanding of customers and their needs. Running a successful business means that you must stay ahead of your competition and be constantly monitoring your own business performance.

To assess business performance, it is important to understand how financial transactions are recorded and reported upon. The key to long-term survival in business is the ability to generate profit (make a surplus) and the capacity to meet financial obligations or repay debts (maintain healthy ***liquidity****).*

In this chapter you will be introduced to the basics of marketing, which will help you to understand how a business can more accurately plan for success.

You will also learn about the basic process that businesses use to record and report on financial transactions. Finally, you will find out how to use financial information to assess a business's two vital performance signs: profit and liquidity.

Glossary

assets: items of value owned by a business and which are used to earn income in the future

balance sheet: a statement of the financial position of a business at a given time. It shows a company's assets, liabilities and owner's equity (assets minus liabilities).

brand awareness: a buyer's knowledge of a certain brand product, achieved by marketing campaigns such as lowering the price of a product

capital: the amount of money deposited by the owner (proprietor) of a business when it commences; the amount of money borrowed *from* the owner *by* the business

cash payment: cash outflow (such as paying wages or buying supplies) which decreases the cash balance of the business

cash receipt: cash inflow (such as cash sales or contributions made by the owner) which increases the cash balance of the business

cheque: a document that authorises the bankers of a business to pay an amount to the payee, or the person whose name is written on the cheque.

contribution margin: the difference between the selling price and the variable costs per unit; the amount of money left over after a sale and used to offset the fixed costs of a business

corporation: a company that has been registered and incorporated according to relevant laws

cost of goods sold expense: the amount of money spent by a business on buying its stock

creditors: people or companies that a business owes money to as a result of purchasing goods or services on credit

e-commerce: the buying and selling of goods and services electronically

enterprise: a company organised for commercial purposes

expenses: costs incurred by a business in order to earn income or revenue

fixed costs: costs which will not change with output; also referred to as sunken costs because they are money spent before trading commences

foot traffic: the number of customers and potential customers that come through a store

franchise: permission given by a manufacturer to a distributor or retailer to sell the manufacturer's products

gross profit: the difference between the value of total sales and cost of goods sold

invoice: a document used by a business to record the credit transactions of its customers

liabilities: amounts owed by a business to others

liquidity: the cash position of a business and its ability to meet its financial obligations

marketing mix: the right strategy to market your product to suit the needs of your customers. It addresses the four Ps: product, price, place and promotion.

market segment: a section of the market such as a particular age group or a geographical location

net profit: occurs when the income earned by a business in a given period is greater than the expenses incurred

niche marketing: a type of marketing that concentrates on a small section of the market in an attempt to satisfy its particular needs, and to personalise its service

partnership: a legal entity in which between two and 20 people carry on a business together with the aim of making a profit

private company: business organisation that has two to 50 shareholders and is not listed on the stock exchange

private sector: the part of the economy where production is generated by privately owned resources

profit report: a report that indicates how successful a business is at trading

proprietorship: the net worth of the business to the owner; the amount left over after deducting liabilities from assets

public company: a company that is listed on the stock exchange and has an unlimited number of shareholders

public sector: the part of the economy where production is generated by government-owned resources

shareholder: an individual or a firm that owns shares in a company

sole trader: an individual who owns and operates a business alone and is not in partnership or incorporated into a company

target market: the group of buyers and potential buyers a business will aim its marketing strategy towards

variable costs: costs which increase as the level of output increases, for example wages, cost of supplies and electricity

TYPES OF BUSINESS

Each week we are involved with a range of **enterprises** which exist to provide us with goods and services. Some of these businesses, such as the local supermarket or music store, are fairly obvious but remember that each time you receive mail, turn on a tap, ride on a train or watch television you are involved in a business transaction.

In Australia about 75 per cent of all business is under private ownership; that is, the **assets**, or resources, of the business are owned by individuals or other businesses. They are thus part of the **private sector**. The remainder of businesses (approximately 25 per cent) are owned by the government, which makes them part of the **public sector**. This means that the assets of the business are owned collectively by the people of the nation or State but come under direct control of the government. The table below lists different kinds of business and the sectors to which they belong. These are explained in the following sections.

Examples of private and public sector businesses

Private sector	Public sector
Sole trader Partnership Public corporation (Ltd) Private corporation (Pty Ltd)	Government department Government enterprise

PUBLIC SECTOR BUSINESSES

A government department is a form of business activity since it provides goods or services to the community. Under this form of ownership, the business does not generally raise revenue or income in the course of its activity.

For example, if your house was being burgled you would immediately call the police, who would provide a service of protection to your home without any direct charge to you or your family. In a similar way our roads and highways are built and maintained without a direct fee being charged each time we drive along them.

A government enterprise on the other hand, earns revenue by charging fees or making sales. Australia Post is an example of a government enterprise because it is not privately owned yet it charges consumers directly by selling postage stamps.

PRIVATE SECTOR BUSINESSES

A **sole trader** is a business owned and operated by one person. This form of business structure is common among small businesses. Self-employed tradespeople such as plumbers, carpenters and shopkeepers may typically use this form of business structure.

As a business grows and requires more funds for expansion, sole traders may not have enough money, time or even expertise to run a business on their own. A **partnership**, which can include up to 20 people, allows for some of the business responsibilities to be shared. If a business expands even further and needs additional financing, business owners may choose to form a **corporation**. Under law, a corporation is separate from the owners of the business and can be sued or prosecuted in its own right.

A **public company** is generally listed on the stock exchange, where the public can become part owners of the company through buying shares in it. In theory, the number of owners or **shareholders** is unlimited. A public company is usually recognised by the abbreviation Ltd (Limited).

A **private company**, on the other hand, generally restricts the number of owners, and shares in the company are not made available to the public to purchase. Private companies typically grow from a family business, where the family members seek to keep control of the business as it grows. A private company is usually recognised by the abbreviation Pty Ltd (Proprietary Limited).

FRANCHISING

Most of us are familiar with McDonald's, Pizza Hut, Hungry Jack's and Sizzlers. What all these businesses have in common, apart from food, is that they are all **franchises**. A franchise exists when the original owners of the business sell the rights to use their name, product and systems of operation to other business owners In return for the use of the business name and product, the franchisor (the one selling the rights to the name) expects to receive a certain percentage of the sales.

Your local McDonald's store is owned and operated by a private individual or company who has entered into an agreement with McDonald's to use their name and to sell and manufacture their product according to strict guidelines. The local store pays a certain proportion of their sales income to McDonald's who, in return, provide support in advertising, technical knowledge and staff training.

Activities

Investigation: *Exploring different business types*

1. Refer to the photographs on this page and match up the business with the appropriate business structure, listed below:
   (a) franchise
   (b) sole trader
   (c) government enterprise
   (d) public company.
2. In what way are McDonald's and Australia Post similar? How are they different?
3. Peter Simpson is currently operating a sports store as a sole trader. He asks your advice on whether he should change his business into a partnership. List and explain two advantages and two disadvantages of a partnership over a sole trader.
4. The state police force delivers a service to the community free of charge. It is considered a government department. Imagine what our world would be like if there was a charge involved for calling upon the police to protect you and your property. Write a humorous short story or cartoon which would show how our lives might change.
5. Determine what is the most appropriate form of business structure for the following businesses:
   (a) hairdresser
   (b) mineral exploration in outback Australia
   (c) doctor's surgery
   (d) film production for a national and international market
   (e) plumber
   (f) water catchment and distribution.

Businesses in a shopping centre

Working with a partner or by yourself, visit a large regional shopping centre. Record the information about the businesses you find there in a chart like the following one.

Name of business	Type of business activity	Form of business ownership
Crazy Bill's	Lighting store	Private company (Pty Ltd)

Collect data from at least 15 different businesses. Analyse your results to discover what is the most common form of business ownership. Can you give reasons to explain why this form of ownership is the most popular? Present your findings in a pie graph.

ESTABLISHING A SMALL BUSINESS

Owning and managing your own small business can be rewarding and satisfying. Whether a small business succeeds or fails depends largely on the owner's abilities, resources, enthusiasm, initiative and level of management expertise. Small businesses are a reflection of the character, skills and personality of their individual owners.

There are two main ways of going into business:

1. setting up a new business from scratch, including a franchise
2. purchasing an existing business.

The more common option is setting up a new business from scratch — approximately 70 per cent of all new businesses start this way. The purchasers of existing businesses accounted for approximately 26 per cent of all start-ups. The remaining four per cent were businesses that had been:

- inherited from a family member
- restarted from a previously failed business
- bought by the employees from the owners (buy-ins and buy-outs).

Choosing between the two main options is sometimes quite difficult; each has advantages and disadvantages. The ten essential steps in establishing a small business, as outlined in the figure below, apply equally to both options.

START NOW

10 Do I have a way of monitoring the business's performance?

9 What type of business training do I need?

8 What form of business structure should I choose?

7 Where will the money come from?

6 How much money will I need?

5 Have I prepared a comprehensive business plan?

4 Should I purchase an existing business or start a new one?

3 What is my financial position? (choose an adviser)

2 What type of business should I enter? (the prime function)

Step 1 Am I capable of starting and running a business?

The ten essential steps in establishing a small business

SUCCESS OF SMALL BUSINESS

All small business owners start off optimistically, believing that their business venture will lead to financial success and security. They will most probably have read a few of the many books that have been written about being successful in small business. These books often highlight five common 'keys' to small business success.

1. *Entrepreneurial abilities*. The people in small businesses are crucial to the success of the enterprise. Attitudes and personalities of owners will vary enormously. Some will have drive and enthusiasm, many will set targets and some will take big risks. Some will thrive on the challenge of a potential failure, enjoying the process of solving the problem. The majority will be highly motivated and optimistic.
2. *Access to information*. It is always difficult for a small business owner to choose relevant information and to gauge the quantity of information needed. As a bare minimum, the small business operator must have information regarding profitability, the quality of products and services and the performance of employees. Accurate and up-to-date information will allow the small business owner to make better decisions.
3. *Flexibility*. The small size of the business allows the owner to adapt quickly to changes in the external environment. Because there are fewer levels of management, decisions can be made quickly. In addition, the close contact between owners and their customers allows the establishment of personal relationships, helping owners to respond quickly to clients' changing tastes and preferences.
4. *Focus on market niche*. Small businesses can concentrate their efforts on a few key customers or a specific segment of the market. This provides the opportunity for the small business to become more specialised and able to deliver a high level of service.
5. *Reputation*. Because the small business is servicing a narrow market niche, it can develop an enviable reputation for quality and service.

Establishing a new business

by Cyndi Kaplan

In just four years, Petals Network has become a thriving business with an international network and 20 per cent of the floral distribution market in Australia. Based in Armidale NSW, Petals receives orders for the delivery of flowers from florists around Australia and the world and relays them to an appropriate florist to supply the order.

Petals was the 1996 recipient of the Telstra Small Business Award for an Australian business with fewer than ten employees. The business was established by Scott Williams and Bobbi Ballas who met when they were studying and working at the University of New England, Armidale.

When Bobbi, who had owned a florist shop in the US, began discussing a business plan for opening a florist shop in Armidale, Scott saw an opportunity. Although he'd never even bought flowers before, Scott believed a smart company could easily take some market share from Interflora, which had dominated the relay flower market for 40 years. His expertise was in accounting, communications, computers and networking.

The main thrust of this success is the concept that information and communications businesses can operate from anywhere in Australia by using a 1800 telephone number.

As one of Telstra's biggest customers in NSW, Petals' phone bill is bigger than its wages cheque. The business has established a strong alliance with Telstra, using a Telstra consultant to benchmark its phone system. Orders are received by phone, fax, email and the Internet.

'We planned our attack carefully before we took on the giants in the international florist distribution network,' Scott said. 'Petals now has more than 750 of Australia's 3500 florists on its books.' The relay business comprises 10 per cent of the florist industry in Australia which is worth $380 million a year.

Interflora had been established internationally for 40 years. Bobbi and Scott realised early on that they could not compete head-on with Interflora in terms of public awareness. Instead, they decided to focus their marketing activities to the florists and not to the general public.

Scott uses data banks to create records of all the florists, showing the size of their businesses, marketing histories and how frequently they use Petals Network. There are incentives which encourage florists to use their service and feedback is encouraged so that the service can be constantly improved.

Customer satisfaction is the key to their success. 'Our staff are trained to listen to customer requests and to ensure that people get value for money,' Bobbi said.

Petals is conscious of floral design but its main focus is business management and personalised service. They're currently connected to the world by fifty phone lines. Scott has also created a website on the Internet. Although this might not be a major source of orders yet, he believes that by the year 2001 up to 35 per cent of sales will be through the Internet . . .

Petals is an excellent example of what can be achieved from a regional area with two people at the helm who have a clear concept of what they want to accomplish. They have been innovative in their use of technology, built solid relationships with their customers and close alliances with their suppliers.

Petals Network has succeeded through careful marketing and superior customer service.

Dynamic Small Business, April/May 1997.

Activities

Check your understanding

1. What are the two main ways of getting into business?
2. Which is the most common option?
3. Provide an example of a franchise.
4. What are the advantages of becoming involved in a franchise?
5. What are the five keys to small business success?
6. List five keys to business failure.
7. What is market niche and why are they important to small businesses?
8. In your own words, explain the ten essential steps in establishing a small business.

Investigation: *Innovation and enterprise*

Look carefully at the article on Petals Network.

(a) What is the main function of Petals Network?
(b) When it began was it a new business, a franchise or did it take over an existing business?
(c) Which enterprise was the leader in this market niche?
(d) What innovations did Petals Network introduce?
(e) Which other Australian business has been important in the success of Petals Network?
(f) What are the key enterprise skills required for Petals Network to be successful?
(g) In what ways do enterprises such as Petals Network affect Australia's economy and society?

8.3

CHOOSING THE RIGHT PRODUCT AND LOCATION

Choosing the right product and location allows your business to have the right exposure before you even begin to market it. Some key factors in the location of an enterprise are:

- exposure of product
- location of customers
- availability of factory for production
- room for expansion
- reputation of the area
- costs of location.

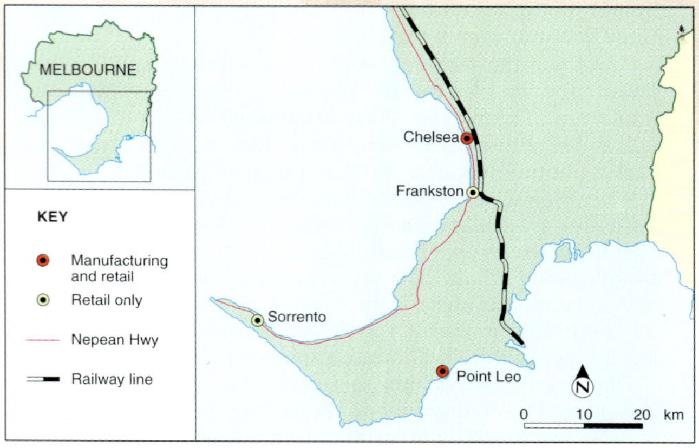

Location of Trigger Brothers Surfboards businesses

TRIGGER BROTHERS SURFBOARDS

Many manufacturing firms are small in their factory size and output. Trigger Brothers Surfboards is an example of a small manufacturing business in the surfboard-making industry.

Paul and Phil Trigger began making surfboards in 1968 in the backyard of their home. As their product became more popular, a shop site was purchased in 1971. This was at Chelsea in Melbourne, Victoria. The site was chosen because of its location on the coast, access to the Nepean Highway and because it was close to the surfing population.

In 1976, a second retail outlet and factory was opened at Point Leo, a popular surfing location on the Mornington Peninsula near Melbourne. The site is quite a distance from major roads and population centres, but was favoured by the owners because of the proximity to the beach. Since then, two more retail shops have been opened — one at Sorrento and one at Frankston.

Employee numbers increased from two in 1976 to 15 permanent staff in 1996. Six of these are involved in the manufacturing process while the rest operate the retail shops.

While some manufacturing occurs at the Chelsea location, most of the surfboards are made at Point Leo. The manufacture of these surfboards begins in Queensland. Boards are made from a polyurethane foam in a factory in Currumbin, Queensland. At this stage of the process, the boards are called *blanks* and are made in moulds of various lengths and thicknesses. The Currumbin blanks are chosen because of their high quality.

The blanks are transported to the Chelsea store by truck and stored there. The next process is called *shaping*. There, Garry Taylor uses a template, or pattern, to cut and sand the boards to a required shape. The shape is determined by the surfer's ability and by the popularity of certain boards. About five per cent of the shaping occurs at the Chelsea location and five per cent at Point Leo. Ninety per cent of this process is contracted out to a professional shaper.

All the shaped boards now move to the Point Leo site. The next process involves covering the board with fibreglass. One layer is used for the bottom, and two for the top of the board. Any stickers (prepared at a printing factory) or colour paints are added to the board at this stage.

The fins are then placed on the underside of the board. Most fins are moulded in factories in Maroochydore, Queensland and transported by truck to the Chelsea site and then to the factory. Resins, synthetic substances, are now applied over the fibreglass to make it adhere to the foam board. One layer of laminate resin is applied followed by a layer of filler resin. The worker must take care to avoid the toxic fumes given off by the resin. The board is now ready for sanding.

At this stage, the boards have a resin cover, but are not smooth. They have many lumps and distortions. Sanding is required to remove these distortions. Sanders are used to smooth most of the board, progressing from rough to smooth sandpaper. The final sanding is completed by hand. Workers must wear protective clothes as much dust is generated during the sanding process.

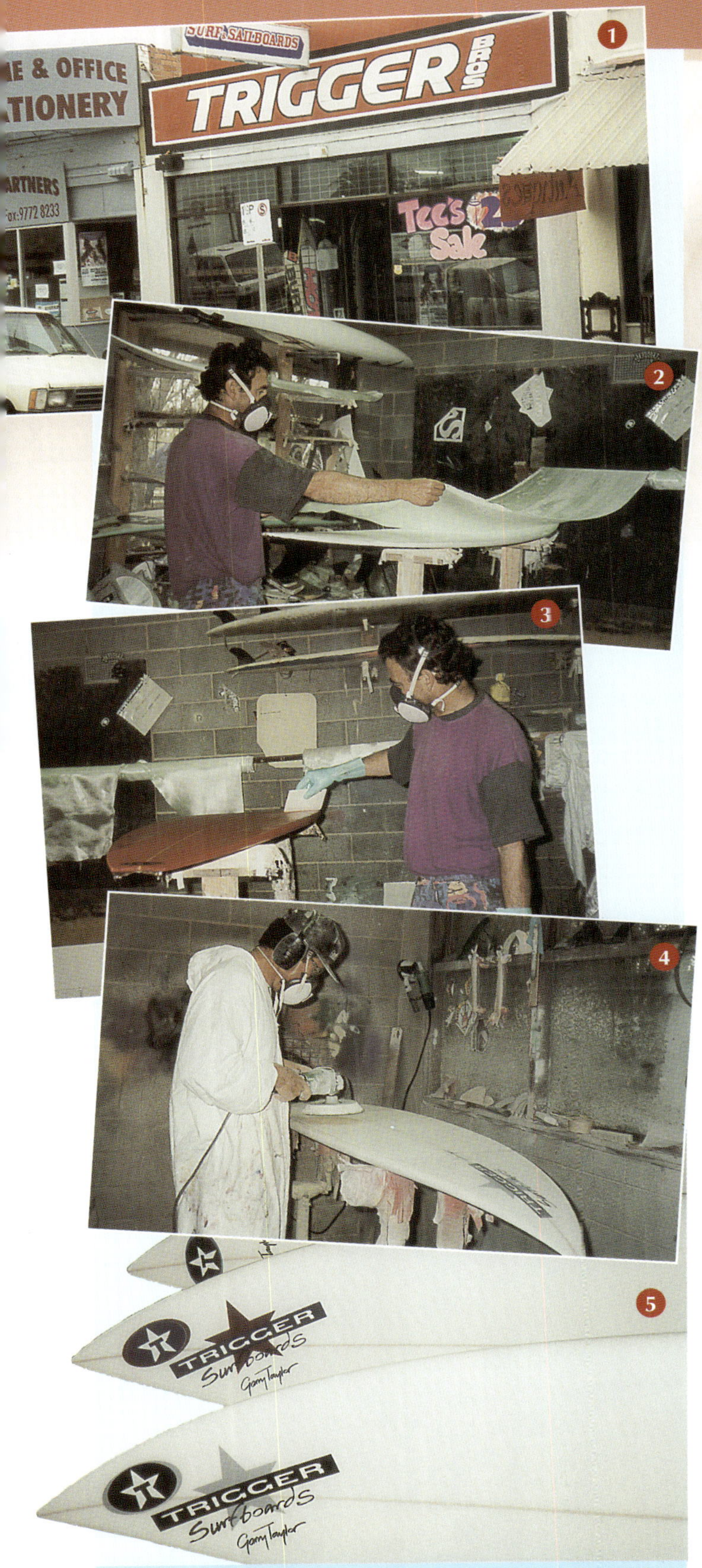

1. The Chelsea site — a shop front with the factory at the back
2. Fibreglass is placed over the shaped board.
3. The surfboard is being covered with resin.
4. The surfboard is sanded after the resin has dried.
5. The final product

The final process involves spraying a clear lacquer over the entire board.

Trigger Brothers manufacture approximately six boards per week. Over the year approximately 60 per cent of boards are made to specific customer requirements and 40 per cent made to stock the retail outlets. Trigger Brothers try to stock a wide range of board sizes and styles to suit many needs. A basic board sells for $550 with cost increasing when intricate colours and design work are added.

This type of manufacturing is labour intensive. This means people complete many hours of work to make the surfboards with little use of machinery. Some factories in New South Wales have begun to use computer technology to complete most of the first stage of surfboard manufacturing — the shaping.

Trigger Brothers surfboards are sold in a very specific area. Only the four retail shops sell the boards and the majority of buyers are from south-eastern Melbourne. In the surfboard industry most manufacturers sell to people within their local area.

Activities

Investigation: *Product and location*

1. List the raw materials used to make a Trigger Brothers surfboard. Where do these raw materials come from?
2. Describe the factors which helped to determine the location of the two factory sites.
3. How important are individual orders to this business?
4. What does the term 'labour intensive' mean? Why might products from a labour intensive industry cost more than ones which use more machinery and technology? What might prevent a small business like Trigger Brothers setting up computer-operated machines?
5. List the factors for consideration, when deciding the location of the following businesses:
   (a) a car manufacturer
   (b) a restaurant
   (c) a supermarket
   (d) a specialist food store
   (e) an importer of exotic plants.
6. Select a site in your local area that has shops (businesses), houses and perhaps industrial areas, and complete the following:
   (a) draw the site plan, detailing traffic flows and locations of shops and houses
   (b) explain the reasons for the location of each business
   (c) if you were to open a restaurant, where would you locate your business? Give reasons for your answer.

SETTING UP SHOP: INTERNAL LAYOUT AND DESIGN

While a good location is important for business success, care must also be given to the internal layout and design of a shop so that customers come into the store and create **foot traffic**.

A business can choose to use one of three basic designs in setting out its store.

1. Grid layout. This is suited to self-service stores and is used particularly by supermarkets because it encourages customers to cover the entire store. The grid formation is efficient in moving large numbers of customers.

Supermarkets use the grid layout to encourage customers to shop the entire store.

2. Open-plan layout. This is designed to create more relaxed shopping. Customers can move in a more haphazard fashion through the store and the traffic flow is less directed. Large variety stores like Kmart and Target tend to use this design.

Variety stores often have an open-plan layout.

3. Boutique layout (or shop layout). This creates mini-shops within a larger store by placing products that appeal to certain customers in a certain section of the store. A bookstore might use this design, with one corner for sporting books and another corner for children's books. David Jones, Daimaru and Myer uses this type of layout. The boutique layout encourages people to wander through each section of the store.

While there are many variations on these three basic designs, most layouts are influenced by buyer behaviour and the traffic patterns they create. There are three main traffic types.

1. Destination traffic consists of those shoppers who enter the store knowing what they intend to buy. These customers move purposefully through the store, avoid other customers, and usually move in a clockwise direction.
2. Browsing traffic consists of those shoppers who are uncertain about their purchase and move slowly through the store. Browsing shoppers tend to move right after entering the store and move in an anti-clockwise direction.
3. Impulse buyers make unplanned purchases, which are often 'one-off' purchases.

By understanding the traffic patterns of buyers, goods can be placed strategically throughout the store. Consider the illustration below. This shows how more profitable goods can be positioned in a way that attracts browsing customers, while less profitable, high-turnover goods can be placed for the convenience of destination shoppers.

Necessities placed at rear encourage customers to shop the whole store

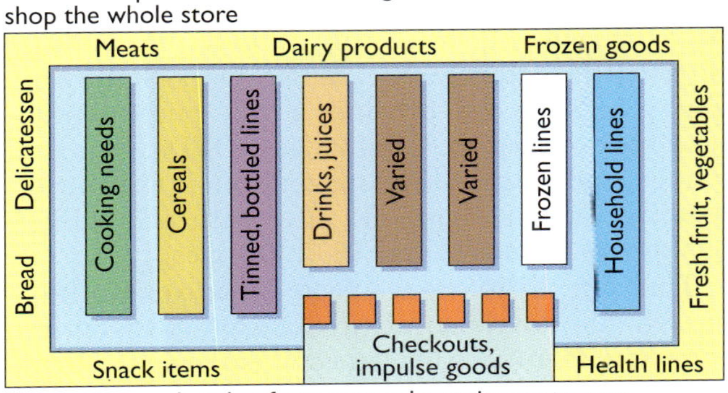

Impulse items placed at front attract browsing customers

Grid layout

Most traffic flow occurs at the front of a store because this is where all customers enter and exit, so goods that are likely to attract impulse buying should be displayed here. Supermarkets employ these tactics by displaying certain goods at the checkouts and placing basic, low-cost items at the rear of the store.

Activities

Investigation: *Shop design*

1. What is foot traffic and why is it important for the success of a business?
2. Why do supermarkets tend to have dairy products, meat and bread at the back of the store?
3. Jennifer has just become manager of an electrical appliance store and wants to place her more profitable and expensive stock items at the back of the store because she is concerned about theft. Is this a good strategy to adopt? Why or why not?
4. For each of the following, indicate what type of shopper he or she represents. Give reasons to support your answer.
   (a) Sophia has just finished the grocery shopping and, while waiting in a queue at the checkout, chooses a chocolate bar from the display.
   (b) Bill enters the hardware store and moves immediately to the fastener section to buy some nails he needs in order to finish building a shelf in the workshop at home.
   (c) Cameron is not sure what his father would like for his birthday and starts in the sports section of the bookshop. He quickly becomes distracted by the number of books on display about computers.

Communication : *Designing shops*

1. Congratulations! You have just been appointed manager of Sportzmania, which sells a large range of sporting equipment, accessories and clothes. Use the following information about buyer behaviour to design the most appropriate layout for your store.

Stock item	Number of units sold last year	Cost price of stock item	Selling price of stock item
Tennis racquets	3570	$50	$70
Golf clubs	345	$150	$285
Footballs	5790	$18	$25
Basketballs	6830	$15	$23
Exercise bikes	72	$95	$175
Football jumpers	4360	$12	$20
Running shoes	5920	$28	$45
Bicycles	720	$175	$310
Cycling clothing	1375	$25	$45
Sports drinks	8350	$0.75	$1.50

2. In pairs or on your own, visit a large shopping complex or centre near your school or home. Choose one large and one small shop and make a sketch of the internal layout of each. Mark on your diagram the traffic flows and patterns created in the store. Comment on the effectiveness of the design, particularly regarding congestion for shoppers. By observing shoppers, and the way they move through the store, try to establish whether they are destination or browsing shoppers.
3. Visit your local supermarket and sketch the internal layout. Make a note of where basic food items are displayed and whether the design encourages customers to shop the entire store. Observe how the supermarket encourages impulse buying. Write up your findings in a report that can be presented to the class.

E-COMMERCE

Internet-based businesses are flourishing as the influence of the Internet has a large impact on commerce throughout the world. The shop fronts are the web pages on the Internet where these businesses conduct electronic commerce — known as **e-commerce**. The term e-commerce describes business-to-consumer transactions that are conducted electronically via the Internet.

Internet trading systems can be accessed by anyone in the world at any time, as long as the customer has access to a computer and an Internet link. Forecasters have predicted that e-commerce transactions will grow from a global total of $12 billion dollars in 1998 to more than $160 billion by 2003.

Trading electronically will bring about great change to the way business is conducted. In the past, personal shopping has advantaged those businesses that were able to afford a strong presence in the marketplace. Coles Myer, for example, has a presence in most suburbs with Coles supermarkets and Myer and KMart department stores. When using the Internet, however, consumers don't even have to leave home, and can quickly and easily choose from a range of suppliers.

Online sales by transaction type – 1998

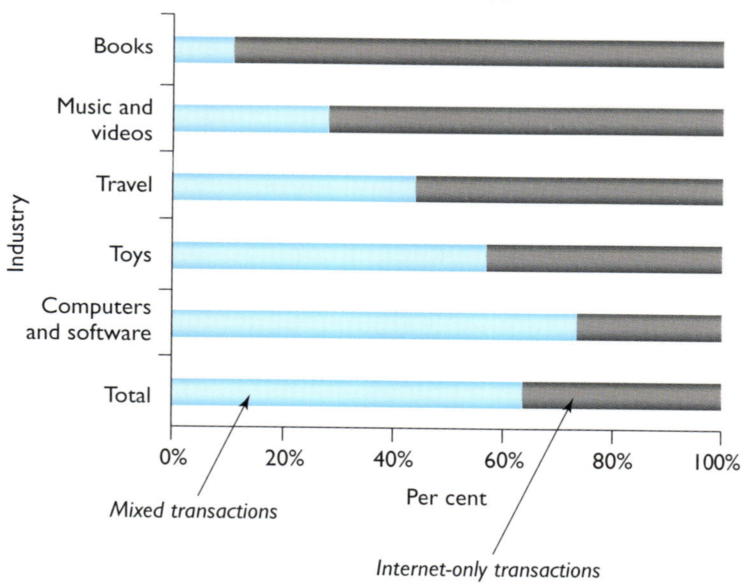

Source: The *Economist*, 21 August 1999, p. 54. Originally work done by the Boston Consulting Group.

E-commerce is unlikely to replace traditional shops and shopping centres, particularly where the customer needs to try or fit the goods before buying. However, it is making great inroads into other industries such as music, videos, DVDs, software, books and travel. Success by on-line stores such as Amazon.com have bred a large number of competitors in Internet trading. Business is done on an international scale, forcing local companies to become competitive or lose business.

AMAZON.COM

Amazon.com opened in July 1995 with a mission to use the Internet to transform book buying. Today, Amazon.com provides a wide range of products such as books, CDs, videos, DVDs, toys and games, and electronics. Amazon.com is the world's leading online shopping site with 17 million customers in more than 160 countries.

The core of the Amazon.com business is a huge searchable database of products and an on-line ordering facility. Amazon.com is designed as a virtual store with the products organised to allow customers to quickly and easily find the product they are looking for. The web site also gives customers the opportunity to browse through categories, providing a similar experience to the traditional shop.

Activities

Investigation: *Electronic commerce*

1. How will the innovation of e-commerce affect:
   (a) large businesses such as Coles Myer?
   (b) the Australian economy?
   (c) Australian society?
2. List three advantages of enterprises offering e-commerce.
3. List one disadvantage of e-commerce for the provider and the consumer.
4. In traditional transactions there are a number of people in the supply chain: Producer > Warehouse > Wholesaler > Distributor > Consumer. Draw a flow chart to show how an e-commerce transaction could take place.

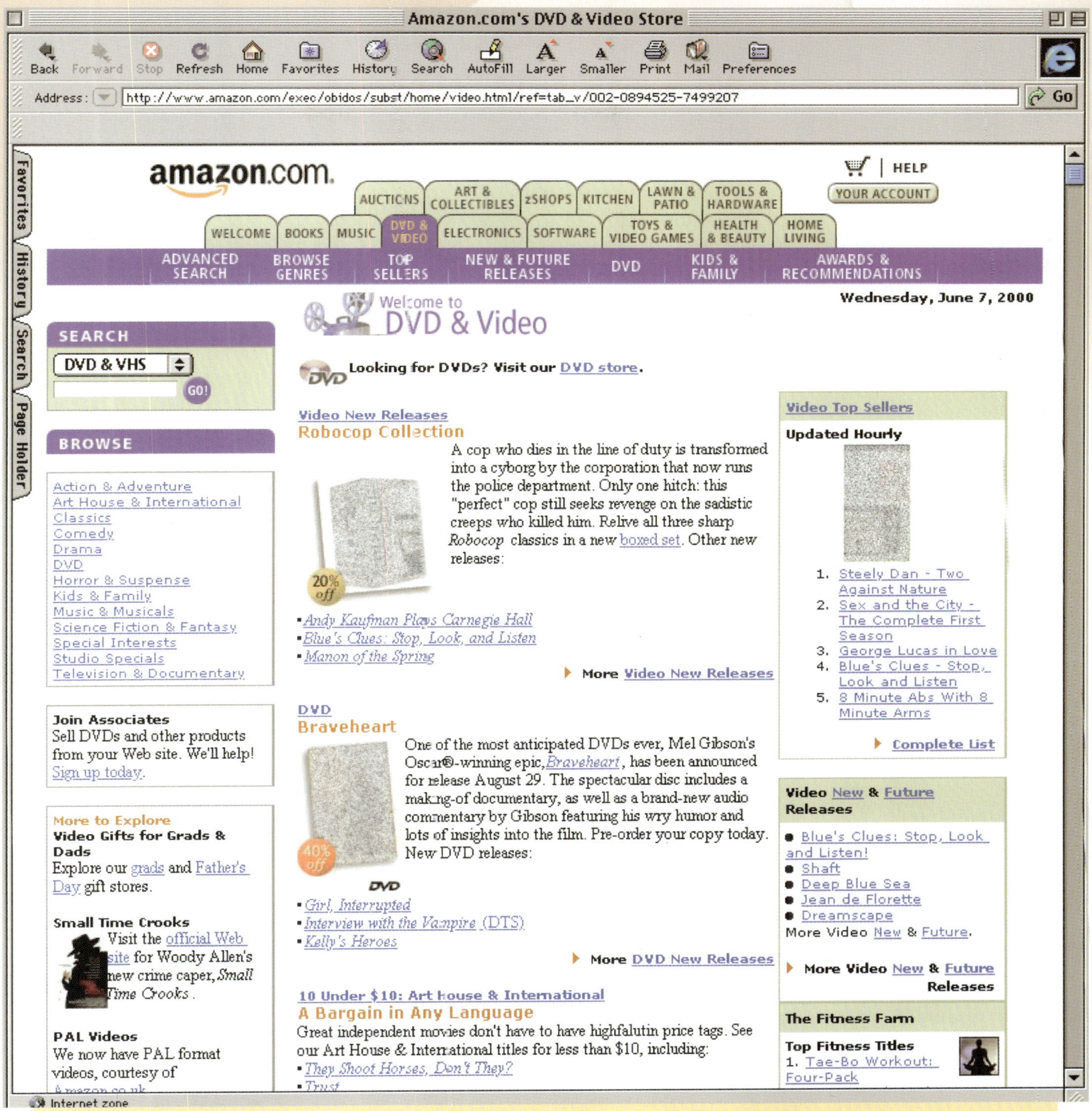

5. Visit the following Web sites and describe the type of e-commerce that takes place:
   www.sony.com
   www.woolworths.com.au
   www.commbank.com.au
   www.express.com

Communication: *Using a Web site*

Examine the pictured page from the Amazon.com Web site.

1. List the tabs at the top of the Amazon.com Web site.
2. Which of these sites has the user selected in the example shown?
3. What are the features of this web page?
4. In what way is this web page similar to going into a shop that sells videos and DVDs?
5. How is shopping on the Internet different from traditional shopping?

8.6

MANAGING AN ENTERPRISE

Management involves the creation of an environment that harnesses specialist skills to achieve the objectives of the business. To ensure that all employees are committed and working towards the common goal, effective managers generally promote a structured, controlled and uniform environment. Ideas about the managerial qualities needed to achieve this kind of stable and efficient environment have been actively promoted for a large part of the twentieth century.

As well as demonstrating effective and efficient management, today's business leaders must have:

- a vision of where they want the company to be at some point in the future
- the ability to impart that vision to everyone in the organisation.

FUNCTIONS OF MANAGEMENT

Effective and efficient management requires the achievement of four crucial functions.

Planning

A plan is an outline of the actions by which a business intends to achieve its goals. The process involved in developing the plans is referred to as 'planning'. For successful business outcomes, short-term and long-term planning are critical. To achieve business goals, management must:

- establish the mission statement and determine organisational objectives
- make plans and decisions about inputs, work in progress and output through strategic, tactical and operational planning.

Phantom Zone

Phantom Zone is the largest comic collectable chain store in Australia. It specialises in selling comics, trading cards, games and paraphernalia associated with the Phantom and other superhero characters. The first store was opened in Parramatta in 1989. Parramatta was chosen because it had an established retail market and research indicated that it was the geographic centre for their customers. Additional stores have since been opened in Wollongong, Chatswood and Canberra. The chain also has three franchises in Liverpool, Gosford and Newcastle.

According to its directors, Phantom Zone's niche in the marketplace is in their specialised items, often 'one-offs'. None of their items is mass produced. Ninety per cent of their items are imported from the US and UK.

The directors stress the importance of establishing goals for their business. Planning involves important questions, such as: Where do we want to take the company? Into what areas do we want to move? What new lines of products do we want to introduce? They emphasise that financial plans are always in place and are crucial to the strength of the business. Ongoing and regular meetings between the owners, the store and franchise managers and staff ensure that organisational objectives are set, understood and worked towards.

Currently their strategic plans include consolidating their position in the marketplace and looking for further opportunities in the retail sector. They do not have any plans for new stores because of the current difficulties in retail trade. Their short-term (twelve months) plans include consolidating their operations, 'making what we have strong' and diversifying their product lines. As each of the stores offers different products reflecting the different clientele, planning is essential for each store.

The directors of Phantom Zone, Xanthea Boardman, Glenn Ford and Harry Brady

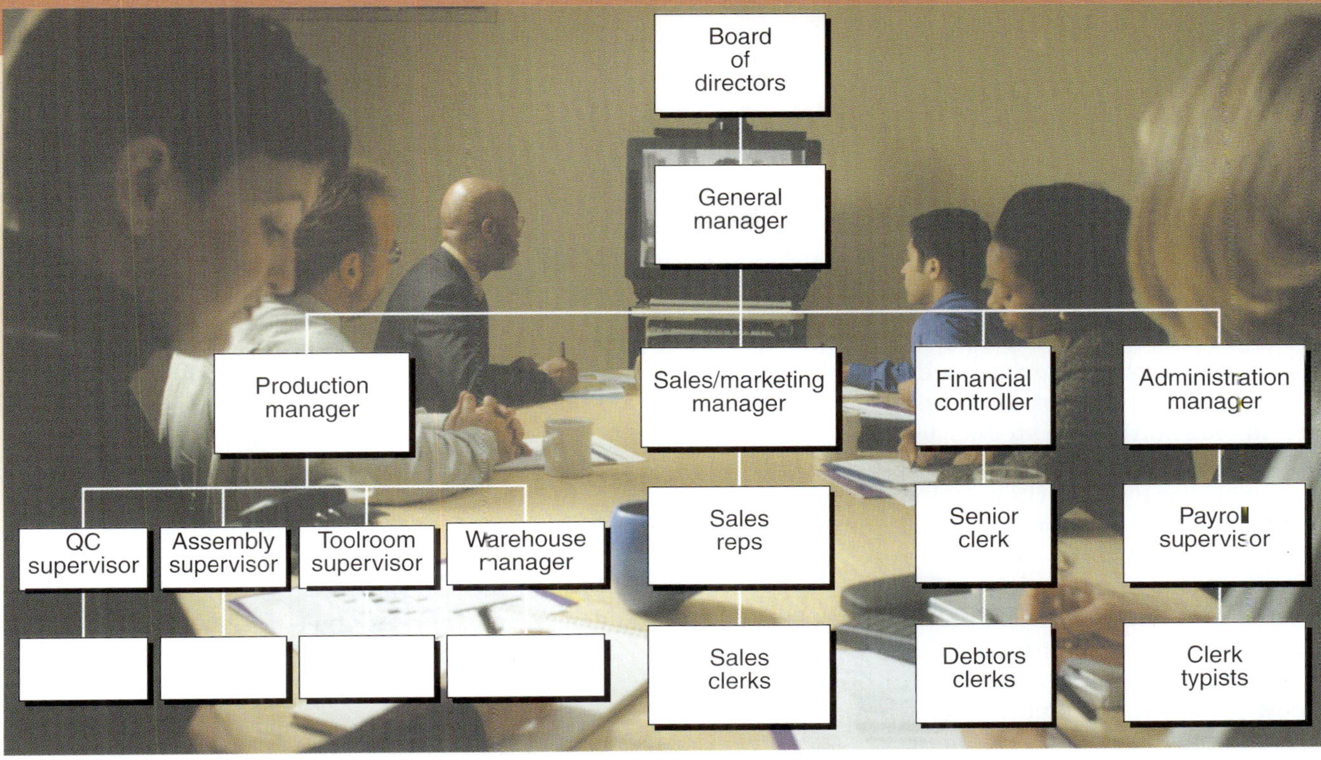

Typical pyramid-shaped, hierarchical organisational chart

Organising

Organising is the structuring of the organisation to translate plans and business objectives into action — that is, organising the financial, human and material resources to achieve the organisation's objectives. This includes coordinating activities and determining responsibilities for individuals in the organisation. It also involves managing the flow of funds and working **capital**.

Leading

Leading is the process of directing, guiding, developing and motivating others. Increasingly, managers in Australia are taking on the role of 'change leaders' to guide businesses through turbulent change. Successful leadership in the twenty-first century will require leaders who can embrace and manage change, with the ability to lead teams and encourage a teamwork approach to solving problems in the workplace.

Controlling

Controlling involves evaluating and monitoring performance against predetermined plans and objectives, as well as taking corrective action when performance does not meet the required standards.

Production lines such as this were considered to be the most efficient method of production in the early twentieth century.

Activities

Investigation: *Managing an enterprise*

1. What skills does a modern manager require?
2. Look at the case study of The Phantom Zone stores.
   (a) What planning questions do the managers (directors in this case) ask of the business?
   (b) What type of business structure does The Phantom Zone use?
   (c) What strategic plans do the managers have in mind for the business?
   (d) What are the short-term plans for the business?
   (e) Draw a diagram to show the management structure of The Phantom Zone.
3. List three different resources that require organisation by a manager.
4. Observe the organisation chart.
   (a) What type of business resource is shown on the chart?
   (b) What type of managers are at the top of this business?
   (c) Which managers report to the general manager?
   (d) Is the payroll supervisor a manager? Explain.
   (e) What are the responsibilities of the production manager?
   (f) Explain why many larger businesses have this model of organisation.

MARKETING YOUR BUSINESS

What do home-delivered pizza, a sample tube of shampoo in your letterbox and a competition on the side of a cereal box all have in common? They are all marketing strategies used by a business in order to respond to the needs of the customer.

Marketing is more than just selling. It involves a careful study of your existing and potential customers and delivering the right product, at the right time, at the right price.

In today's business world it is a buyer's market because there are many products available and competition is fierce. A successful business must know who its customers are, what their needs are and how best to reach them.

In the 1950s, businesses employed mass marketing techniques, where one product would be made to suit everyone. In the 2000s a business will tend to focus on a small portion of the market, or a **market segment**. For example, The Coca-Cola Company does not market its product to all ages but tends to focus on young people. By personalising their approach to customers, businesses can refine their products and offer better service. This intense concentration on a small portion of a larger market is often known as **niche marketing**. For example, Mercedes-Benz operates in the car market but tries to attract only those buyers who have a high income and will respond to images of luxury and status.

BULLSEYE!

The first and most important step in successful marketing is to define your **target market**. This means determining the type of people who will be your customers. Your target market can be determined by age, gender, geographical location, educational background or level of income. Unless the market is clearly defined, the marketing strategy will miss the mark. Successful marketing involves the use of the **marketing mix**, or what is often referred to as the four Ps:

- *Product* — developing a good or service that meets the needs of your target market; for example, a low-fat food product for a target market of health-conscious people
- *Place* — placing your business in a location that will capture your target market; for example, setting up an exclusive clothing boutique in a high income suburb
- *Price* — attracting clients through setting a price that reflects value ahead of your competition
- *Promotion* — creating the awareness and the desire for your product; for example, using a hot air balloon at major sporting events to create interest and desire for your product.

The soft drink 'Coca-Cola' has been expertly marketed.

Businesses use different techniques in the marketing mix.

Activities

Investigation: *Types of marketing*

1. Look at the advertisements (left). For each one, identify which of the four Ps they correspond to.
2. Explain what is meant by a market segment.
3. Give reasons why mass marketing techniques are no longer as effective in the 2000s.
4. Describe the market segment that would best suit the following products:
   (a) low-alcohol beer
   (b) white-water rafting adventure
   (c) low-calorie soft drink
   (d) rock'n'roll greatest hits CD
   (e) private school education.
5. For each of the target groups listed below, think of a product or a business that would cater for their needs. Compare your answers with a classmate.
   (a) people who are health conscious
   (b) people who are young and active
   (c) people who are interested in personal fitness
   (d) parents
   (e) people who are well educated
   (f) high income earners.
6. Identify the marketing techniques employed by Coca-Cola. It has survived for decades as the leading soft drink around the world. How do these companies differentiate the product from its competitors?
7. Design a survey that tests the two most popular cola drinks among your classmates. In your questioning, try to establish whether it is taste, price, fizziness, promotion or advertising which most appeals to them in their favourite cola.
8. Conduct a taste test. Collect a range of cola drinks and pour them into unmarked cups. Invite the people you survey to choose their preferred cola by taste. Record your answers in the form of a chart. Write a short report about your findings and draw some conclusion about the way careful use of the marketing mix can appeal to a target market.

Communication: *Design a poster*

Design a promotion letter to advertise the opening of a new music store in the local neighbourhood. Be sure to include the following details:

- name and address of the store
- date of opening
- hours of trading
- details of opening specials or other promotional activity.

8.8

CHARGING THE RIGHT PRICE

Once you begin business operations cash will be one of the most motivating factors of staying in business. If you ask for too much, no-one will buy your product. Price your product too low and you will sell it, but you won't make a profit.

Before you place your product on the market, it is important that you decide its price. Whatever the price is, it must cover the costs involved in making the product and provide a profit margin.

Costs can either be fixed or variable. **Fixed costs** are costs which do not vary with the number of the product made. These costs are sometimes referred to as sunken costs, or establishment costs, because the business incurs them before it produces anything. Examples of fixed costs include equipment, buildings or premises, furniture and fittings. For a takeaway food store, fixed costs would include the grill, refrigerator, serving counter and cash register.

Variable costs are those which do vary with the number of the product made. As the volume of output increases, so does the total of variable costs. Variable costs are sometimes referred to as operating costs, examples of which are electricity, telephone, wages, and inventory (supplies). For a takeaway food shop, variable costs include potatoes, bread rolls, meat patties and cans of drink.

When setting a price for a product, it is important to cover variable costs. The difference between the selling price and the variable costs is the **contribution margin** which is calculated as:

Sales revenue – Variable costs.

This margin is then used to offset fixed costs. Once fixed costs have been recovered, the break-even point has been reached. This is the point where total costs equal the total amount made from sales (total revenue); that is:

Total costs = Total revenue (Price × Quantity).

Let's say Ashan and Courtney set up a hamburger stall and must pay fixed costs of \$50: licence fee \$15, advertising \$10, and hire of equipment \$25. Making a hamburger costs \$0.80: bread roll \$0.35, meat patty \$0.15, lettuce, tomato and sauce \$0.10, napkins and packaging \$0.05, and gas \$0.05. They sell their hamburgers for \$1.00.

Each time they sell a hamburger, the contribution margin (sales revenue – variable costs) is \$0.20 (\$1.00 – \$0.80). To break even, they must sell enough hamburgers to cover their fixed costs. In other words, how many hamburgers at \$1.00 each must they sell to cover their costs?

$$\text{Quantity sold} = \frac{\text{Fixed costs}}{\text{Contribution margin}} = \frac{\$50}{\$0.20}$$

$$= 250 \text{ hamburgers}$$

The running of a takeaway food shop involves both fixed and variable costs.

Reaching break-even point allows a business to keep its head above water.

WHAT THE MARKET CAN BEAR

While it is important that a business can adequately cover all costs, it must still charge a price for a product that is affordable for the target market, and is consistent with the price charged by its competitors. There are different approaches to pricing, two of which are listed below.

- Discount pricing. With this approach, a business lowers its price and suffers a reduced profit margin but by doing so, it attracts more sales and takes customers away from its competitors. By lowering prices even for a short time, a business can create **brand awareness** and loyalty from new and existing customers.
- Premium pricing. When the price of a product is set quite high, it can actually attract customers by creating an image of quality or prestige. Premium pricing is used, for example, to sell clothes at the start of a season, with the new styles and colours attracting greater interest among buyers. Premium pricing is a way of conveying to buyers that a product is of superior quality.

Products must be priced to meet consumers' expectations.

Activities

Investigation: *The right price*

1. Study the photograph of the takeaway food shop and identify at least two examples of a fixed cost and two examples of a variable cost for this business.
2. (a) List four fixed costs that a hairdresser would face when establishing a business.
   (b) If you were starting a restaurant, what are five fixed costs you would have that would be different from those of a hairdresser?
3. Complete the following table by calculating the correct amount for each blank cell.

Variable costs	Selling price	Contribution margin
$1.50	$1.75	$0.25
$12.60		$1.60
$25.75	$38.50	
$18.95	$29.50	
$35.80		$12.75
	$119.20	$15.90
	$299.95	$89.50

4. Jodie wants to know what price to charge in order to break even. She is running a cake stall and has worked out that her operating costs are $1.25 per cake and her fixed costs are $250. Jodie expects to sell 300 cakes.
5. What profit could Michael expect to make from operating his small lawn-mowing business? He charges clients $10 to mow their lawns; the cost of purchasing the mower was $600; his fuel costs have been $250 and advertising was $80. In the past three months Michael has mowed 120 lawns.
6. Complete the following table.

Selling price	Discount offered	New price
$3.65	$0.50	$3.15
$4.85	$1.20	
$12.75		$10.50
$18.50	15%	
$27.80	20%	
$80.50	%	$71.95
$146.20	%	$117.56

7. Explain why summer clothing attracts a premium price at the start of the season but a discount at the end of the season.
8. Working with a partner, undertake some research on a range of fresh food items such as tomatoes, oranges and bananas, and collect their prices over a period of three weeks. Plot your findings on a graph. Describe the trend you notice in the price. Calculate the percentage change in the price from week to week. Present your findings in a written report.

THE BODY SHOP: AN INNOVATIVE ENTERPRISE

Every two seconds, somewhere in the world, somebody buys something — a soap, a shampoo, a massage oil or a moisturiser — from The Body Shop. Since its humble beginnings in 1976, when Anita Roddick opened the first store, The Body Shop has grown to be a worldwide organisation, with over 1700 branches in 48 countries, including 66 stores throughout Australia, a mail order and Internet sales service and The Body Shop at Home direct selling network.

The Body Shop manufactures and sells naturally based skin-care and hair-care products. While this in itself may seem unremarkable, The Body Shop has gained international prominence and growth by advocating the pursuit of social and environmental change.

The Body Shop is committed to awareness and education in the course of running its business. It shows its commitment by: caring about environmental protection; not using animals to test its cosmetics; promoting community action; insisting on fair trade; respecting the values of people rather than just pursuing profits; and maintaining that business is centred on relationships.

Anita Roddick, since opening the first shop in Brighton, England, has received countless awards in recognition not only of her business ability but also of her commitment to the core values which underpin the way The Body Shop operates. In 1988 Ms Roddick was awarded the Order of the British Empire for Services to Industry. In 1991 she received the World Vision Award from the Centre for World Development Education and the Midwest Academy Award, USA, for vision, courage and integrity in working for social change.

THE MARKETING PROCESS AT THE BODY SHOP

Like most businesses, The Body Shop has a defined marketing strategy which centres around four key elements: product, price, promotion and place.

- *Product*. The Body Shop sells over 500 products that aim to meet the needs of women, men and children. Ingredients are natural and not tested on animals, and the packaging is simple, with a strong emphasis on recycling. Most bottled products are refillable and discounts are offered to customers to encourage the practice of 'return and reuse'.
- *Price*. The Body Shop attempts to provide value for money. Most bottled products come in a range of sizes, so that customers have a choice of price relative to the quantity they want to buy. The Body Shop customer also benefits from the no-advertising and no-excess-packaging policies, which help to keep prices to a minimum. The Body Shop estimates that up to 70 per cent of the price of cosmetics made by its competitors is created by advertising and packaging.
- *Promotion*. The Body Shop believes that the best promotion is a quality product. It uses no formal advertising and the idealised beauty presented by the rest of the cosmetic industry is ignored.

The Body Shop's style of promotion is not about image but about information. In-store promotion includes displays and product presentations while posters, leaflets and shelf cards are all used to give information to customers. Messages on T-shirts, badges, bags and postcards all take the message of natural beauty products and social change to the community at large.

Word of mouth generates interest and repeat business while editorial coverage in magazines, radio and television all assist in raising the profile of the organisation.

- *Place*. The Body Shop is to be found throughout the world in locations where it is visible and accessible to the public. Since no advertising is used, the store location is crucial, and busy shopping malls are a common site for The Body Shop. Throughout the world, all its stores reflect a strong corporate identity: the identical logo, the use of green paint, identical products with their distinctive smell make The Body Shop immediately recognisable to its customers.

THE BODY SHOP AND SOCIAL CHANGE

In the first issue of *Full Voice* (The Body Shop publication that is freely available in its stores) Anita Roddick attacked the view that beauty is culturally conditioned and said that the beauty industry seems 'hellbent on promoting unattainable ideals'. She points out that the narrow definition of 'ideal', stereotypical beauty is not possible for the majority of women, yet this does not make them less beautiful. However, the continual striving for youth and perfection undermines the celebration of diversity among women and leads to a genuine loss of self-esteem.

Activities

Investigation: *Looking at innovation in an enterprise*

1. Indicate whether the following statements are true or false.
   (a) The Body Shop sells beauty products.
   (b) Animals are used to test hair and skin products sold by The Body Shop.
   (c) The Body Shop is found only in Australia.
   (d) The Body Shop advertises on television and radio.
   (e) Recycling is encouraged by the sale of refillable bottles.
   (f) Promotion costs account for 70 per cent of the price of products sold at The Body Shop.
   (g) Word of mouth is an important means of advertising for The Body Shop.
2. Divide your page into four columns and head them Product, Price, Place and Promotion. Under each heading fill in a summary of the marketing strategy used by The Body Shop.
3. Look at the in-store poster for The Body Shop (opposite page) and explain its message.
4. In not more than 60 words, identify and explain the chief reasons for The Body Shop's success.
5. The Body Shop aims to reduce the impact on the environment and empower local communities to share knowledge and trade equally. Complete the following table using information from The Body Shop Web site: www.the-body-shop.com/products/index.html

Product	Key ingredient	Community producer
Brazil Nut Oil Damage Care Shampoo		Kayapo Indians, Brazil
Cocoa butter hand and body lotion		
Fake it! Self tan lotion		
Blue corn scrub mask		
Ananya body lotion	Babussu oil	
Honey lip care		

Communication: *Collect information*

1. Visit The Body Shop in your area. Collect evidence of the values that the organisation holds by: examining products; checking ingredients and packaging; observing evidence of environmental concerns; and reading any information which challenges traditional views. Then make a presentation to your class by way of a talk, a computer application or a poster.
2. Research the life of Anita Roddick, the founder of The Body Shop. Present your findings to the class.
3. Visit your local shopping centre to observe business practices that promote recycling and protection of the environment. Record any examples of recycling being practised. Identify a business you believe is not environmentally aware and write a letter suggesting some ways that it can promote recycling or other environmentally sound practices.

8.10

BUSINESS DOCUMENTS: CASH AND CREDIT TRANSACTIONS

Every day, a business completes many transactions which involve the buying and selling of goods and services in exchange for cash. For any business, cash transactions mean the exchange of currency (notes and coins), or a ready substitute for cash (**cheques**, electronic funds transfer and credit cards).

When a business *sells* goods or services, cash flows into the business and is called a **cash receipt**. When a business *buys* goods and services, cash flows out of the business and is called a **cash payment**.

Each time a transaction occurs, a business document is written. Cash receipts are recognised by the business through issuing one of three documents:

1. a cash receipt
2. a cash register roll
3. a credit card voucher.

These documents record the date and the amount of cash received by the business, and generally give details about the nature of the transaction. A cash receipt is issued by a business when cash is received.

Bogong Secondary College
P.O. Box 6943 Bogong 3946
Tel: 9479 9426 Fax: 9479 9430

RECEIPT Date: 5th Feb. 1997

Received from: J. Barlinson

The sum of: Thirty-five dollars

For: School excursion $35.00

Signed: J. Nolan

A cash receipt

The cash register roll used by Sureway Supermarkets details the grocery items purchased, and shows that the customer paid using electronic funds transfer.

When a person uses a credit card, it suggests they do not have enough cash at the time of the transaction. However, when a business accepts a credit card transaction, the money is guaranteed to the business from that date, provided the card is not stolen, invalid, or used without proper authority.

Consider this example. When Paul Chao uses Bankcard to purchase a new stereo from Brashs, he is being offered credit by the credit company which issues Bankcard. Any business which has a formal arrangement with a credit company can accept credit cards from customers and be guaranteed payment by the credit providers. So it is like getting cash: funds are received without much delay. In this case, when Paul Chao uses his credit card, Brashs is guaranteed funds almost straight away.

Sureway Supermarkets
379 High St.
Newtown
Telephone: 9862 1003
'Service and quality at the right price'

Qty	Item	Amount
1	Cornflakes 500 g	4.89
3	White sandwich bread 680 g	4.95
1	Family block chocolate 300 g	3.86
1	2 litre tomato sauce	3.72
2	Lite milk – 1litre	1.86
1	Chocolate biscuits	2.25
3	2 litre softdrink	4.59
		26.12
	Less rounding benefit	26.10
	Total	26.10

E.F.T. – AN2 4564192738247
Transaction approved
8/2/97 3.50 pm

Part of a cash register roll — the 'docket'

4564-2100-0061-3146
04/97 04/99
P.CHAO

5536629

B'Card ☑ M'Card ☐ VISA ☐

Authorisation No. 278031		Date 19/02/97	
Qty	Description	Dollars	Cents
1	Sony hi-fi system XT10865F	450	–

1262937
BRASHS LTD
MELBOURNE

Validity date checked ✓
Sales person initial JS

SALES VOUCHER Total $A $450 –

CARDHOLDER'S SIGNATURE: Paul Chao

A credit card sales voucher

CASH PAYMENTS

Cash paid by a business to another business or individual is usually done using a document called a cheque. A cheque is filled out and signed in order to instruct the bank to pay the payee (the person or business whose name appears after 'Pay ...' on the cheque). The cheque itself is torn out of the cheque book and sent or given to the payee, while the details of the cash payment transaction are kept on the cheque butt. Note that the cheque and cheque butt are both numbered to assist with the task of checking cash records.

As cheques can be converted to cash, proper care must be taken to ensure that business funds are directed to the right people. Crossing a cheque with double parallel lines and inserting the phrase 'not negotiable' means that the cheque can only be paid into the payee's account. Therefore, if someone steals the cheque, that person cannot cash it.

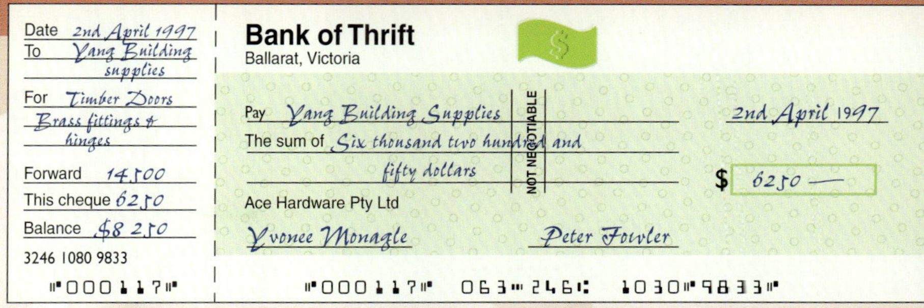
Date 2nd April 1997
To Yang Building supplies
For Timber Doors Brass fittings & hinges
Forward 14 500
This cheque 6250
Balance $8 250
3246 1080 9833
⑈000117⑈

Bank of Thrift
Ballarat, Victoria
Pay Yang Building Supplies 2nd April 1997
The sum of Six thousand two hundred and fifty dollars $ 6250 —
NOT NEGOTIABLE
Ace Hardware Pty Ltd
Yvonee Monagle Peter Fowler
⑈000117⑈ 063⑉246⑆ 1030⑉9833⑈

A cheque and cheque butt

CREDIT TRANSACTIONS

A business may offer its customers the opportunity to buy goods on credit. This means customers have the opportunity to buy goods now with the promise of paying the business (as opposed to a credit company) later. An **invoice** is used to record credit transactions. By examining the invoice illustrated below, you can see the type of information recorded on this document.

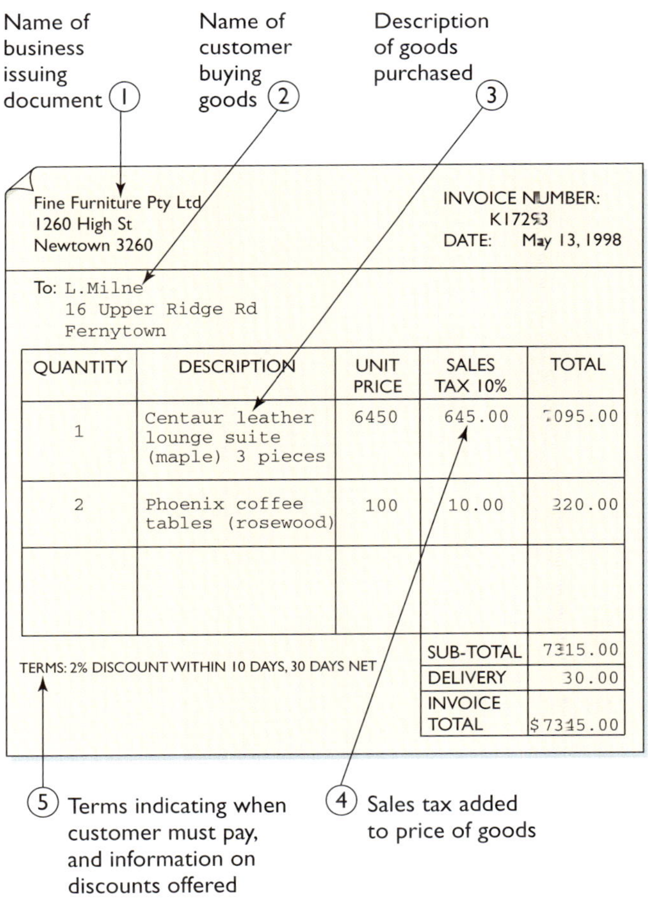

Fine Furniture Pty Ltd
1260 High St
Newtown 3260

INVOICE NUMBER: K17293
DATE: May 13, 1998

To: L.Milne
16 Upper Ridge Rd
Fernytown

QUANTITY	DESCRIPTION	UNIT PRICE	SALES TAX 10%	TOTAL
1	Centaur leather lounge suite (maple) 3 pieces	6450	645.00	7095.00
2	Phoenix coffee tables (rosewood)	100	10.00	220.00
			SUB-TOTAL	7315.00
			DELIVERY	30.00
			INVOICE TOTAL	$7345.00

TERMS: 2% DISCOUNT WITHIN 10 DAYS, 30 DAYS NET

An invoice

Activities

Investigation: *Cash and credit transactions*

1. What is the difference between a cash transaction and a credit transaction?
2. Why is it important to record transaction details on the cheque butt?
3. Why is a business cheque crossed with the words 'not negotiable'?
4. In your workbook, write out each of the following transactions that occurred at Ramsey Clothing, and indicate whether the transaction is a cash payment or a cash receipt by placing the letters P or R at the end of each transaction.
   (a) Catherine paid $25 for a windcheater.
   (b) Wages of $150 were paid to staff.
   (c) Rendi purchased a new suit for $375 and used his Mastercard to settle the transaction.
   (d) Lieng bought ten netball skirts for the players in the junior school team. She agreed to pay within a month, after the girls brought their money from home.
   (e) Mrs Singh bought a new tie for her father for Father's Day, paying $30.
5. Study the invoice (left). Who is the customer and what did they buy? How long have they got to pay and can they reduce the amount they owe? Explain your answer.

Communication: *Business forms*

Copy the forms found on this spread, and enter the following transactions for Top Clothing in the appropriate documents.

(a) Mr Doherty, on 2 July 1993, bought goods to the value of $56 and paid cash.
(b) A shirt, tie and shoes to the value of $225 were sold to John Jackson on 3 August 1995. He has promised to pay for these goods within 30 days.
(c) The manager of Top Clothing paid the business's electricity account of $176.58 to United Energy on 16 September 1997.
(d) Paula Macintosh bought a new dress for $255 on 27 October 1997. She paid using her Visa card, which expires on 6 May 1999. The card number is 4564 0078 9523 8.

8.11

RECORDING AND REPORTING CASH TRANSACTIONS

Cash is one of the most important resources a business owns. Tight control and monitoring of a business's cash position is vital for business survival. Information about cash transactions found on business documents is recorded in the cash book. The cash book stores transactions as either cash receipts (cash inflow) or cash payments (cash outflow) and enables a cash balance to be calculated.

A business's cash book is divided into two sections, with cash receipts generally recorded on the left-hand side and cash payments recorded on the right. Transactions which occur often are grouped together and recorded in separate columns, which allows a clear breakdown of cash transactions. In the example of a cash book shown below, note that on April 2 and 5 the business earned cash fees of $500 and $350 respectively. By recording the transaction under Cash Fees and under Total Receipts, at the end of the month the business can identify what proportion of total cash receipts is represented by cash fees. Likewise, on April 7 and 21 the business paid wages to its employees. By recording this information under Wages and under Total Payments, at the end of the month the business can see at a glance the proportion of cash payments that was used on wages.

At the end of the month the cash balance can be discovered by subtracting the total cash payments from the total cash receipts. As the cash book below shows, there is a balance of $145 brought forward at the start of May.

STATEMENT OF CASH FLOWS

From time to time, a business will report to owners, managers and other interested parties about its performance. The information contained in the cash book is used to complete a statement of cash flows.

Date	Details	Cash Fees	Other	Total Receipts	Total Payments	Wages	Suppliers	Rent	Other
April 2	Cash Fees	500		500					
3	Rent				120			120	
4	Interest on loan				35				35
5	Cash Fees	350		350					
7	Wages				200	200			
10	Owner, P. Smyth		1000	1000					
12	Cash Fees	300		300					
17	Equipment				850				850
19	Supplies				450		450		
20	Advertising				200				200
21	Wages				300	300			
25	Supplies				550		550		
27	Cash Fees	700		700					
		1850	1000	2850	2705	500	1000	120	1085
30	Closing Balance				145				
				2850	2850				
May 1	Opening Balance			145					

Transactions recorded in a cash book

For example, consider the Statement of Cash Flows for High Country Riding School, shown below. The cash receipts section shows that High Country Riding School has received a total of $15 800 in cash during May, with most of the money coming from cash fees charged for riding lessons, and some received from customers renting stables for their own horses. The cash payments section shows that the largest payments were for instructors' wages and feed for the horses.

In the third section (starting at excess receipts over payments) the statement shows whether there has been a cash surplus or cash deficit for the period. In July the cash balance of High Country Riding School increased by $500 as a result of cash receipts being greater than cash payments.

HIGH COUNTRY RIDING SCHOOL
Statement of Cash Flows
for month ended 31 May 1997

	$	$
Cash receipts		
Fees — riding lessons	12 200	
Rent received	3 600	
Total receipts		15 800
Cash payments		
Instructors' wages	9 600	
Feed for horses	2 700	
Cleaning	1 800	
Advertising	700	
Bridles and stirrups	500	
Total payments		15 300
Excess receipts over payments		500
Opening cash balance		1 200
Cash balance at 31 May		1 700

Activities

Investigation: *Cash flow*

Study the cash book (page 214) and the statement of cash flows (above) and answer the following questions.

1. Describe the transactions that occurred on the following dates.
   - April 3
   - April 10
   - April 17
   - April 20
   - April 25
   - April 27
2. What is the total of cash fees for April? Calculate this as a percentage of total receipts. How might a manager use this information?
3. What is the total of wages for April? Calculate this as a percentage of total cash payments. How might a manager use this information?
4. Explain the difference between the opening balance and the closing balance on the statement of cash flows.

Communication: *Cash flow statements*

Peter Agricola is the manager of The Mane Event Beauty Salon. He is concerned about the amount of cash he has been spending in the business and asks for your help to clarify his situation. Use the information below to construct and complete a statement of cash flows.

- On 31 May the business had $5750 in the bank.
- During June the business received cash fees for haircuts of $3600, of which $1750 was for perms and tints. The business also received $650 for waxing and facials.
- Wages paid for the month totalled $1780 and advertising was $350.
- The business purchased cash supplies worth $2400, of which $1800 was for hairdressing supplies, with the remainder being for wax and facial supplies.
- The business paid $360 interest on its loan.
- A new hair dryer was bought for $95 and a steriliser unit was bought for $1350.

8.12

MAKING A PROFIT

By selling a good or providing a service to its customers, a business earns income or makes money. This activity of selling goods or providing a service is known as trading. To measure how successful a business is at trading, a **profit report** is drawn up.

First, details about the type of income and the amount of income earned by the business are recorded. For a service firm, the income is earned by charging fees. For example, a hairdresser earns fees by cutting and styling hair. A merchandising firm, on the other hand, sells goods to earn revenue and the value of sales is recorded on the profit report. For example, a newsagency sells books, magazines and newspapers.

To earn revenue, a business must pay some costs or **expenses**. Expenses are amounts that must be paid by the business in order to earn revenue. For example, before earning a fee for styling hair, a hairdressing business needs to pay wages, and pay for supplies such as hairspray and gel, and for power to run lighting and the hairdryer.

The final section of a profit report shows the difference between income earned and expenses paid. A **net profit** is recorded when income earned is greater than expenses, while a net loss means expenses have been greater than income.

A profit earned by a business is used in one of two ways. It is either distributed to the owner of the business for his or her own use or it is used to buy more equipment or other things the business may need in the future.

An example of a profit report is shown below right.

The pie graph above shows how a graph can be used to explain how each dollar of income earned by Jodie's Screen Printing is distributed. This is important information for managers and owners because it can help them make decisions about the business.

A merchandising firm is different from a service firm because its expenses relate directly to the goods it sells to its customers. Before the newsagency can sell its books, magazines and newspapers, it must first buy them from its suppliers.

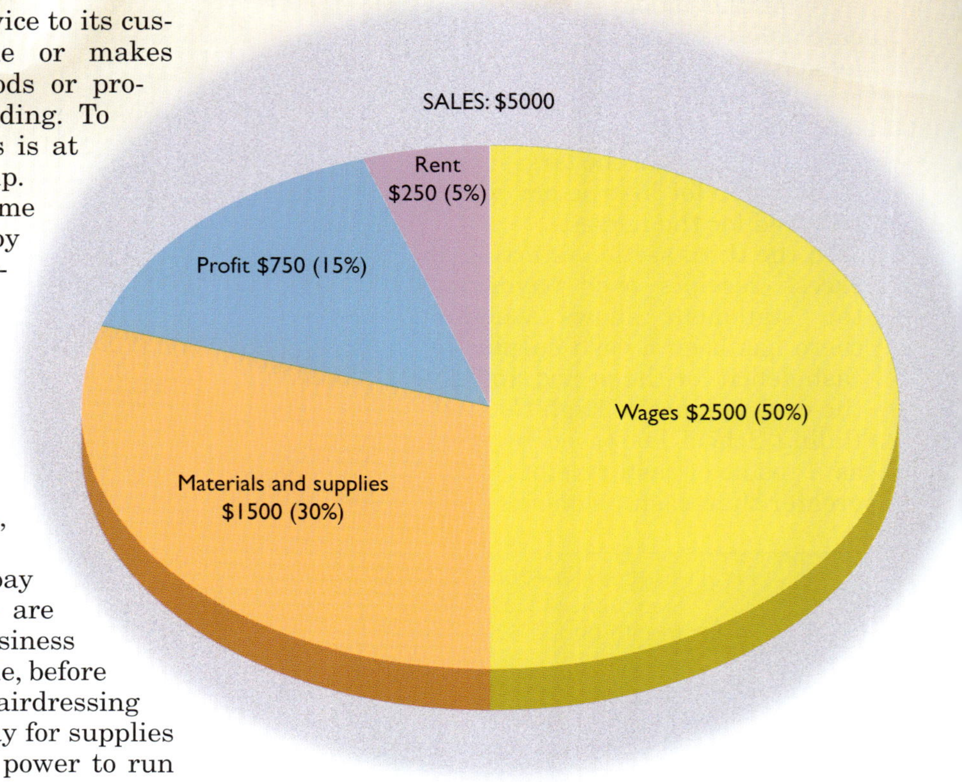

Distribution of sales income — Jodie's Screen Printing

The cost of buying goods which are then sold to customers for a higher price is known as the **cost of goods sold expense**. The difference between income earned and the cost of goods sold is known as gross profit. When all other expenses are taken from **gross profit**, the net profit figure is found.

JODIE'S SCREEN PRINTING
Profit Report
for month ending 30 September 1998

Income		
Fees		$5000
Less expenses		
Materials and supplies	$1500	
Wages	2500	
Rent	250	
Total expenses		4250
Net profit		$ 750

Profit report for Jodie's Screen Printing

Activities

Investigation: *Profit reports*

1. Using the information in the profit report for Jodie's Screen Printing, answer the following questions.

(a) Jodie's Screen Printing earned an income of $9600 for the month of October. Assuming expenses remain unchanged, prepare the profit report for the business.

(b) During September the following expenses were omitted from the profit report. Rent $350, vehicle costs $370, and packaging expenses $120. Rewrite the profit report for September to include this information. What is the new profit figure?

(c) Using the expenses in (b), and the income in (a), what would the profit figure be for Jodie's Screen Printing business now?

2. Prepare two profit reports using the following information.

Riteway Driving School

Figures for November
Income: fees from driving lessons $8250.
Expenses: advertising $340, fuel $785, wages $4200, telephone $75, office rent $175, other vehicle expenses $975.

Figures for December
Income: fees from driving lessons $9050.
Expenses: advertising $340, fuel $895, wages $4550, telephone $90, office expenses $175, other vehicle expenses $1855.

(a) Compare the two statements for November and December. What has happened to the net profit over the two months?

(b) Which item of the profit report is most responsible for the change?

(c) Can you give some explanation of why the change has occurred?

(d) How could the owner of the business use the information gained from the profit report to help improve the business?

(e) What is the difference between gross profit and net profit?

(f) What is the cost of goods sold expense?

(g) If Yurike's Bicycles sold 600 bicycles for the month, what must the selling price per bicycle be?

(h) If 600 bicycles were sold for the month, calculate how much it costs Yurike's Bicycles to buy bicycles from the manufacturer.

(i) What is the gross profit per bike for the business?

(j) Yurike has been informed that the manufacturer will raise the cost of bikes to $175 next month. If Yurike wants to maintain the same profit, what will be the new selling price of the bikes?

(k) Rent for the shop will rise to $1200 next month. How will this affect the profits of the business if the price of bikes remains the same?

(l) If Yurike plans to make the same profit in April, how many more bikes will she need to sell if the selling price remains the same but the cost of bikes and the rent increases?

3. Study the profit report for Yurike's Bicycles, shown below.

YURIKE'S BICYCLES
Profit Report
for month ending 31 March 1998

Income		
Sales		$132 000
Less cost of goods sold		90 000
Gross profit		$ 42 000
Less expenses		
Rent	$ 1 100	
Wages	12 000	
Advertising	7 500	
Electricity	1 250	
Interest on loan	1 800	
Distribution expenses	9 500	
Total expenses		33 150
Net profit		$ 8 850

8.13

BALANCE SHEETS: VALUE OWNED AND VALUE OWED

CASE STUDY: MARIA AND THE SILVER LINING CAFÉ

When Maria Vespucci finished school, she enrolled in a diploma course in catering and hospitality. While completing her studies, she decided her goal was to own her own café.

Having unexpectedly inherited a significant sum of money, Maria purchased an existing café in Lygon Street, Carlton and, as a tribute to her grandmother, she renamed the business the Silver Lining Café.

Maria had a hectic time trying to refurnish the café and get it ready for trading. In the middle of these preparations, she met with her business adviser, George, to ask how much the business was worth to her as the owner. She handed George the following list of information.

- Building worth $65 000.
- Equipment worth $20 000.
- Furniture and fittings worth $12 000.
- Owed $2500 by previous customers.
- Owe the bank $30 000 — used to buy the building.
- Owe $5200 to Caterers' Friend Pty Ltd for food and drinks to be used and sold in the café.
- Have $7200 worth of supplies on hand, which includes some supplies from the previous owners.
- Owe J. S. Interiors $3800, which is the final instalment on the café renovations.
- Have tablecloths and napkins worth $850.
- Have $3000 left in the bank.

'You need to draw up a **balance sheet**', said George. 'First of all, we need to gather together all your assets — the items of value owned by the business.'

George prepared the following list.

THE SILVER LINING CAFÉ

Current assets			
Cash at bank	$ 3 000		
Debtors	2 500		
Tablecloths and napkins	850		
Stock of supplies on hand	7 200		
Total current assets		$13 550	
Non-current assets			
Building	65 000		
Equipment	20 000		
Furniture and fittings	12 000		
Total non-current assets		97 000	
Total assets			$110 550

'So you see, Maria, the Silver Lining Café is worth $110 550', said George.

'I'm beginning to understand', said Maria, 'but what is the difference between a current asset and a non-current asset?'

'Current assets will be used up by the business usually in the course of one year, while non-current assets of the business will last for longer than a year', said George.

'We must now subtract from your assets the amount of money the business owes to others. This is known as **liabilities**.'

George then produced another list of items.

THE SILVER LINING CAFÉ

Current liabilities			
Owing to Caterers' Friend	$ 5 200		
Owing to J. S. Interiors	3 800		
Total current liabilities		$ 9 000	
Non-current liabilities			
Loan to bank	30 000		
Total non-current liabilities		30 000	
Total liabilities			$39 000

'Current liabilities are amounts that must be paid within a year, and would include **creditors**', explained George. 'Non-current liabilities can be paid back over a longer period.'

'So the business is worth $71 550 to me as the owner, which is the difference between my total assets [$110 550] and my total liabilities [$39 000]', said Maria.

'Precisely', said George. 'On a balance sheet this would be known as **proprietorship**. This amount is also called capital, and it represents the amount of money you have invested in the business as the owner.'

George was then able to produce a final balance sheet for Maria as follows.

Activities

Investigation: *Assets and liabilities*

1. What is the difference between an asset and a liability?
2. What is meant by the term 'net assets'?
3. What is meant by the term 'debtor'? Explain why it is a current asset.
4. Explain the difference between a current and a non-current liability.
5. Study the photograph on the opposite page. Divide a page of your workbook into two columns, with the headings of current assets and non-current assets. Find three examples of each.
6. Consider the following information and fill in the missing amounts.

Assets	=	Liabilities	+	Proprietorship
$75 000	=	$40 000	+	?
?	=	$105 000	+	$245 000
$165 000	=	?	+	$95 500

7. Copy the following list of balance sheet items into your workbook and indicate whether they are assets or liabilities:
   - loan to bank
   - stock on hand
   - debtor
   - cash at bank
   - equipment
   - building
   - furniture and fittings
   - loan from a relative.
8. Prepare a balance sheet for Top Cut Hairdressing Salon from the following information. (Use the format shown in The Silver Lining Café case study.) Loan to bank $60 000; building $85 000; equipment $30 000; stock of supplies on hand $15 000; amounts owing to suppliers $17 000; cash in bank $2500; amounts owing by customers $2400; proprietorship $?

THE SILVER LINING CAFÉ
Balance Sheet at the start of trading

Current assets			**Current liabilities**		
Cash at bank	$ 3 000		Owing to Caterers' Friend	$5 200	
Debtors	2 500		Owing to J. S. Interiors	3 800	$ 9 000
Tablecloths and napkins	850				
Stock of supplies on hand	$ 7 200	$ 13 550	**Non-current liability**		
			Loan to bank		30 000
Non-current assets					
Building	$65 000		**Proprietorship**		
Equipment	20 000				
Furniture and fittings	12 000	97 000	M. Vespucci, Capital		71 550
		$110 550			$110 550

8.14 Meeting the outcomes

DEMONSTRATE AN UNDERSTANDING OF PERSONAL AND BUSINESS FINANCIAL MANAGEMENT, AND IDENTIFY AND APPLY ENTERPRISE SKILLS AND ATTRIBUTES.

Examine the structures and financial management processes of business enterprises, including the identification of management skills.

Questions 1 to 4 relate to the study of JMS Hairdressing, below.

1. Identify and define the three types of business structures.
2. What are the management skills required of a business owner?
3. In a table format, like the one on the right, list the faults of James's management style and how he could improve on these areas.
4. Devise some management strategies for JMS to deal with their stock of hair products, and for their cash in the till.
5. 'Location is crucial for the success of some kinds of businesses, but not others.' Discuss.
6. Visit your local shopping centre. Identify some shops in a prime position and explain why you think they have the best location.
7. In pairs, discuss the following:
   (a) three products that offer value for money
   (b) three products that reach their target market successfully
   (c) three products that have a price advantage over others in the market.
8. With a partner, design the layout of a shop of your choice. Create a name for your shop and list the products sold in it. Mark on your diagram the traffic flows and patterns created in the store. Make sure your layout is effective.

Management skill	Faults	Ways to improve
e.g. Human resources	Relationships with staff	Human resource company to hire
	Rumours	Probation
	Poor hiring and firing skills	Properly train staff

JMS Hairdressing

My name is James and I have been on a very successful journey through the business world. I, along with two other directors, Serge and Mikey, own a hairdressing company known as JMS. We have five stores in the Melbourne district and inner suburbs.

The journey began some 10 years ago when I opened a store called James' in Collins Street, Melbourne. I was the owner and the manager of the business and I found this work extremely busy. Being responsible for the staff and trying to satisfy my customers, along with cash management issues were really too much.

I found myself having to juggle the demands of what was proving to be a successful business. While satisfying my regular customers with the latest hair designs and colours, I also had to hire new staff as my business expanded. This was really a difficult area. One time, I had employed this young gentleman called David, who despite being a lovely person was doing some terrible things with people's hair. There were so many complaints, that finally I decided that I just had to sack David. Well, I called him into my office and I just didn't know how to approach this. I mean, what do you say?

'Knock. Knock. Who's there? You're fired!' Or, 'Why did the chicken cross the road? To tell you you're fired!'

Although rumours were floating around the salon, by the time I spoke to David, I had promoted him to personal assistant. This really wasn't my intention, but I am just way too soft.

I'm just terrible with money. We have an enormous amount of cash that is put into the till every day. I find that I am often low on money by the end of the month, sometimes the staff ask for a loan, after that I have no idea where it goes.

Finally, everyone thinks I am way too generous with the shampoo. I like to please my regular customers, so I often give them free shampoo and conditioner to keep them coming back.

I employed Serge after three years, and he proved to be a very capable employee. After a few years I asked Serge if he would like to become a partner of my business. We changed my business from a sole proprietorship where I the owner was totally responsible for the day-to-day running of the business, to a partnership and called this new business Partners Hair. Now Serg and I share the responsibilities of the business. We are both responsible for haircare of our customers and for the management of the business. Serge is particularly talented with cash issues, so I leave these to him, and I might say we have cash to splash!

Well the business just continued to get better and better. We expanded into Toorak, Carlton and Port Melbourne. Things were just wonderful; however, Serge and I were finding it way too much. We hired a wonderful accountant who looked after the finances, and assigned a manager of stocks of all haircare products. Finally, we looked for another person to go into business with us.

Mikey was a competitor. He had a successful salon in Queen Street, Melbourne. Serge and I approached him and asked him if he would like to go into business with us. He agreed, provided we changed the business structure to a company, and we were all equal owners, known as directors.

Each of us work at different locations, but we meet regularly to discuss the overall performance of our company. We discuss all issues, including the hiring and firing of staff (thank goodness Mikey looks after this), finances and hair competitions, etc.

I am very pleased about the way my business has grown into this successful three-way venture. It has taken some pressure off my time and my own resources and talent.

I can now concentrate more on what I like — hair.

Plan and conduct a small-scale project that applies enterprise skills and attributes.

1. What does it mean to be enterprising?
2. In groups, list some other enterprising ideas that your class could conduct.
3. Identify management issues involved in an enterprise and discuss how you would allocate roles.
4. As a class, plan and conduct a small-scale project, and include the following items:
   - business plan
   - organisation chart
   - target market
   - marketing and advertising strategy
   - price and accounting issues such as cash control
   - accounting reports
   - analysis of performance.

Identify enterprise attributes and skills, and describe how innovation and enterprise affect the economy and society.

Read the article entitled 'Quick and cheap way to get the facts'.

(a) What do you think about this innovative idea?
(b) How does it change the research practices of business?
(c) Explain the impact that innovative technological practices are having on business, society and the economy.

Quick and cheap way to get the facts

by Alex Kennedy

One of the problems facing small business owners is the avalanche of information that arrives on the desk each day. Proprietors say they regularly miss important information because there is no time to sort out the diamonds from the dross, and most of the mail ends up in the bin.

The problem has prompted the Sydney-based Australian Business Ltd (formerly known as the Chamber of Manufactures of New South Wales) to develop a national business information service called ChamberNet. The service provides information on a wide range of subjects, and all that is needed is a personal computer and a modem. (About 75 per cent of small businesses in Australia already have a computer, and a modem can be bought for less than $200.) The service is available on the Internet or as a software package, costing $17–20 a month, which includes four hours' use.

ChamberNet has been developed so companies can quickly find information directly related to the type and size of the business they operate. This is a big advantage in areas such as industrial relations, occupational health and safety, exporting and award conditions.

The head of new business strategies at Australian Business, John Murgatroyd, says: 'What we are doing is taking all the hard work out of getting to the right information. Our research told us that small business wanted all the information that would help their business to grow, and to run smoothly. And we know that it can be hard and time-consuming work tracking down what you need, especially in areas where there are so many variables. A lot of time people don't know where to start. We also know that they are often unaware of government programs which could help their company, and of the targeted training courses available — the how, why, when and where of improving their business. We know a lot of that material is mailed out, but it gets lost in the daily pile.'

Using ChamberNet, small business owners will be able to tap into regularly updated market intelligence, such as which countries are looking for their products and who to contact. They will be able to see which products government and local companies are trying to track down in their import-replacement purchasing programs. Also on line are basic support systems relating to Austrade, Customs and tariffs, exchange rates and benchmarking.

John Murgatroyd, head of new business strategies at Australian Business Ltd

Business Review Weekly, 11 March 1996.

Chapter

9

AUSTRALIA AND THE GLOBAL ECONOMY

INTRODUCTION

A day does not go by without reference made to globalisation in the media. In economic terms, globalisation has something to do with:

- *increasing international trade of goods and services*
- *increasing production undertaken by transnational corporations like McDonald's, Nike and BHP*
- *increasing international financial transactions — the growth of international credit and debt.*

What does this mean for the Australian economy? How can the Australian economy maximise the benefits and limit the costs of globalisation? There is a debate over whether globalisation makes national boundaries redundant — that more goods, services, investments, credit and labour will move without regard to national boundaries. These are important issues for students as they contemplate working in the twenty-first century. Local businesses face more competition from imports, many companies need to export to stay profitable, companies compete for funds in international financial markets and all companies face the possibility of an international takeover.

This chapter will help students develop an understanding of the Australian economy in a global or international context.

Glossary

bonds: sold by many governments worldwide to finance some of their spending. They are also bought by companies and individuals as an investment as they pay interest.

capital: wealth, in money or property, owned by a person or business and used to create more wealth

commodities: articles of trade or commerce

current account deficit: occurs when the cost of the import of goods and services into Australia has exceeded the revenue obtained from the export of goods and services

customs union: a group of countries where there are no barriers to the free movement of goods, services, capital and labour between them

direct investment: as when an overseas company establishes a new enterprise, such as a factory, hotel or shopping centre in Australia

economic development: occurs when a nation's GDP grows faster than its population

economic growth: occurs when a nation lifts the quantity of goods and services it produces this year as compared with the previous year

elaborately transformed manufactures (ETMs): goods such as pharmaceuticals, office machinery, telecommunications equipment and road vehicles

endorsement: approval or sanction

equities: shares in companies that are traded in stock exchanges

exchange rate: the current value of a currency in relation to another; the price of a currency when buying it with another currency

footloose industries: industries that move around the globe seeking the most favourable places to locate, generally in cheap labour countries to minimise labour costs

foreign aid: the transfer of money and other types of assistance by governments and private individuals from high income to low income countries

foreign debt: the net amount of money a country owes to all other countries

foreign exchange market: part of the money market that deals with the trading of one currency for another

globalisation: the breaking down of traditional barriers between nation states allowing movement of goods, capital, people and information

gross domestic product: the total value of all goods and services produced each year by a country

import: the bringing in of commodities or articles from abroad for sale or for use in processing

loan: amount of money borrowed from a bank or other lender

mass media: the means of communication, as radio, television, newspapers, magazines, etc. that reach large numbers of people

material living standards: the amount of goods and services available for use in the community per head of population; mainly concerned with food, clothing, housing, education and health

nation state: people living in a defined territory who are sufficiently united to possess a government of their own

productivity: a measure of the efficiency of production which compares the level of input with the level of output

research and development: scientific research and product development aimed at producing new or better quality goods and services

subsidy: a payment made to a producer to enable it to sell at a lower price on local or overseas markets

sustainability: the ability of a nation to increase the production of goods and services from one year to the next without jeopardising other economic targets, including external stability, resource maintenance and a clean environment

tariff: a tax on imports designed to protect local industries from more competitive imports that come from overseas

trade weighted index (TWI): a measure of the value of the Australian dollar against a 'basket' of currencies of our trading partners

transnational corporation (TNC): a large business organisation that operates in more than one country

value-added: the extent to which the value of a finished product exceeds the cost of its raw material components

LEARNING *outcomes*

- Discuss the ways in which the government influences the development of the Australian economy.
- Discuss and investigate how global issues affect the Australian economy.
- Analyse the relationship between international economics and the Australian economy.

ECONOMIC GROWTH AND DEVELOPMENT

Nearly all of us enjoy going to the cinema to see the latest film. Most of us would like to have some new clothes, a CD or a holiday. Initially, you may be excused for thinking that all your problems would be solved if a generous government printed lots of money and gave it to us so that we could purchase all these things and enjoy better **material living standards**. Unfortunately, having heaps of money by itself cannot make people better off. A country can only enjoy better material living conditions or standards if it increases the amount of goods and services it produces each year from the natural, human and capital resources at its disposal. It is only by producing more goods and services that people can gain higher incomes and become better off economically. For this reason, nearly every country tries to increase its national production fairly quickly between one year and the next.

The people in this photograph enjoy a high material living standard.

ECONOMIC GROWTH

For a country, **economic growth** occurs when a nation lifts the quantity of goods and services it produces this year as compared with how much it produced last year. Put another way, economic growth causes the size of the economy to grow. Economic growth is measured using **gross domestic product** (GDP). GDP represents the total value (in dollars) of all goods and services produced each year by a country. Two sets of factors can contribute to a country's economic growth.

- Firstly and most importantly, economic growth is helped by a country having access to extra quantities of natural, human and capital resources, or perhaps the existing resources could be used more efficiently.
- Secondly, economic growth can be helped up to a point by increased sales or spending by households, businesses and governments on locally made products.

Economic development and material living standards

Economic development occurs when a nation's GDP grows faster than its population. This means that, on average, there are more goods and services for each person to share so we say that general material living standards should rise, making people better off economically.

$$\text{Economic development (material living standards)} = \frac{\text{a country's GDP (\$ millions)}}{\text{a country's population size (millions of people)}}$$

In this case, economic growth has led to economic development and higher material living standards (higher GDP per person) assuming that people equally shared the benefits of increased production. However, if a country's GDP grows more slowly than its population, it is likely that economic development or material living standards would fall (falling GDP per person). In order to illustrate these principles, take a look at the figure below. It shows the developments in a country between 1950 and 2002.

Notice that, over these years, the country's GDP has grown to 50 times the original value, while population has risen to four times its original size. Clearly, rapid economic growth has enabled the country's people to enjoy better living conditions than previously, provided that the increase in production has been divided fairly evenly. Normally, we would expect that economic development should not only mean more adequate food, shelter and clothing, but also better health care, education, life expectancy, transport and economic security.

In addition to material living standards, people's overall wellbeing is also affected by non-economic considerations such as the crime rate, level of personal freedom and political democracy, the state of the natural environment and the amount of leisure time relative to hours of work.

LEVELS OF ECONOMIC DEVELOPMENT

When examining the level of economic development, it is a good idea not to look just at figures for GDP per person per year, but also to check out other indicators such as:

- average nutrition levels (average intake of food calories per day per person)
- average life expectancy (in years)
- average literacy rate (as a percentage of population)
- average proportion of the population with access to safe drinking water (as a percentage).

In addition, as already mentioned, we must also have information relating to how evenly or unevenly production is shared among people. One indicator of the level of inequality is the proportion of the nation's total income received by the poorest 20 per cent of the country's households as compared with that for the richest 20 per cent of households. Another indicator is the proportion of people living in poverty without access to basic goods and services.

	1950	2002
Yearly GDP	$1 000 000	$50 000 000
Population size	500	2 000
Average GDP/person/year (indicator of general economic development)	$2 000	$25 000

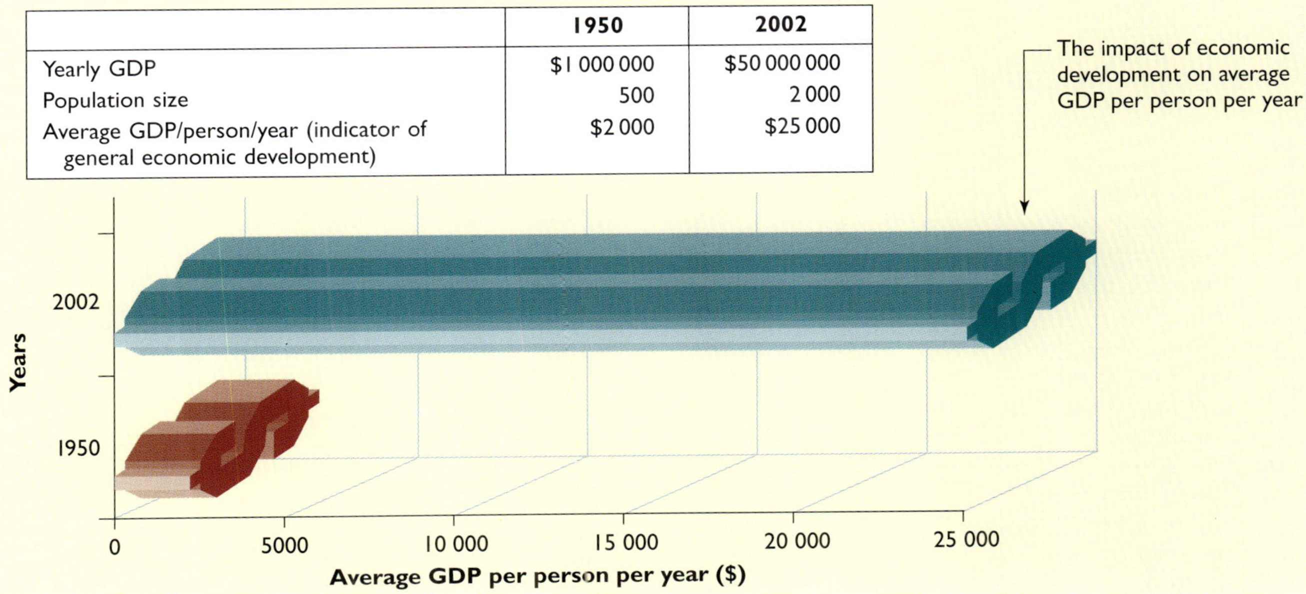

The relationship between GDP, population and economic development

Activities

Investigation: *Discussing economic growth*

1. Discuss the key difference between economic growth and economic development (i.e., material living standards).
2. In groups, discuss how each of the following events might affect the rate of economic growth in a country like Australia. Be prepared to defend or justify your answer in class discussion.

Event	Likely impact on the rate of economic growth and development
1. There was a massive new discovery of oil and gas in the Timor Sea.	
2. The level of business investment spending on capital resources fell.	
3. Fifteen-year-olds increase their spending on Coke and pizzas.	
4. Sales of Australian commodities (e.g., wool, minerals) to Asia fall.	
5. There is an increase in the general level of education and research.	
6. Over-clearing of farming land leads to soil erosion and a rise in salt levels that ruin soils.	
7. There is a rise in the unemployment rate of the labour force.	
8. There is an increased use of new technology by businesses.	

3. What would each of the following indicators suggest about the level of economic development in a country?

Indicator of the level of economic development	Likely change in the level of economic development
1. Average GDP/capita/year rose from $350 to $495 (without a rise in inflation).	
2. There was a fall in the percentage of people with access to safe drinking water.	
3. The illiteracy rate fell from 30% of adults to 20%.	
4. Infant mortality rates for children aged 5 or under were up from 5% to 18%.	
5. Enrolments in secondary education fell from 85 to 75% of children.	
6. Access to sanitation rose from 80% to 85% of all households.	
7. The total value of rural production in a poor country fell 10% due to a drought.	
8. Average daily intake of food calories per person rose from 1200 to 2600.	

Communication: *Using tables of data*

1. Using the table below right, your task is to prepare an attractive wall chart or poster that contrasts the level of economic development in

Australia with that of one other country. Your poster should:

- have an appropriate title
- include sub-headings that focus on different indicators of economic development (e.g., 'A comparison of GDP/head', 'A comparison of the proportion of national income received by the poorest 20 per cent of households', 'A comparison of literacy rates')
- include a range of graphs comparing statistics for each country
- contain brief point form explanations of the differences shown by statistical or graphical data
- include appropriate illustrations or cartoons
- have an overall conclusion about economic living standards in the two countries.

2. For China, the United States and India, calculate average GDP per person per year and per day by completing the data provided in the table on the right.

(a) Which country has the highest average level of economic development or material living standards? How much money per day does the average person receive in this country?

(b) Which country has the lowest average level of economic development or material living standards? How much money per day does the average person receive in this country?

(c) How would low material living standards be likely to affect levels of food consumption, ownership of televisions, access to safe drinking water, education levels and life expectancy?

Information relating to economic development in three countries

Economic data	China	United States	India
• Annual GDP ($US billions, 1997)	1055	7690	374
• Population size (billions)	1.2	0.2	0.9
• Average GDP/ person/year ($US)	$.........	$.........	$........
• Average GDP/ person/day ($US)	$.........	$.........	$........

Source: Data derived from various tables contained in the World Development Report, 1998-99 (OUP, 1999).

Some indicators of economic development in selected countries

Indicator of economic development	Australia	Russia	Indonesia	Nigeria
1. Average GDP/person/ year	20 500	2700	1110	260
2. Average annual growth rate in GDP/person (latest %)	3.6 (1998)	–4.0 (1997)	2.8 (1997)	1.2 (1996)
3. Percentage of national income received by poorest 20% of households	7.0	7.4	8.4	7.5
4. Proportion of the population living below the accepted international poverty line (%)	na	31	40	43
5. Life expectancy at birth for males (years)	75	60	63	51
6. Prevalence of child malnutrition (% children <5 years old)	<1	3	40	35
7. Adult illiteracy rate for females (%)	<1	na	22	53
8. Access to safe drinking water, urban areas (%)	>99	na	78	63
9. Government health spending (% of GDP)	6	4.1	0.7	0.3

Source: Data derived from various tables contained in the World Development Report, 1998–99 (OUP, 1999).

AN UNEQUAL WORLD

Perhaps one of the saddest observations in the world today is the extreme level of income inequality between countries. This means that there are around five billion people struggling to survive in low income and middle income countries, while the remaining one billion lucky residents of high income countries sit back and enjoy a life of comparative luxury. This reflects the very obvious fact that, over the past 500 years or more, some countries have enjoyed far more rapid economic development than others.

LOW INCOME COUNTRIES

Over two billion people out of the world's population of six billion residents subsist in low income countries. Here they have an average income of between $110 and $785 per person per year, or up to $2 per person per day. Nations in this category include Bangladesh, Cambodia, Chad, Ghana, Ethiopia, India, Mongolia, Nepal, Nigeria, Uganda and Vietnam. For people in these countries, low income means constant hunger, poverty, disease, a short life expectancy, hopelessness and poor services in areas such as sanitation, health and education.

Street scene in India, a low income country

How low income countries might raise their incomes

In the last 50 years there have been many examples of low income nations that have successfully made it up the world's economic ladder. Here we think of Japan, South Korea, Singapore, Malaysia and Taiwan. Clearly, if conditions in countries are sufficiently favourable, strong economic growth can accelerate economic development. Unfortunately, there is no single magical solution that will help all countries enjoy an economic miracle. However, there is some agreement that the following policies are important because they improve the quantity or efficiency of the country's resources so that the economy can grow more quickly.

- *Human resources and population*: There is a need to slow down the often rapid rate of population growth by reducing infant mortality and improving health standards, by means of clean water, medical attention and vaccination, for example. In addition, there is a desperate need to improve the education and skills of the labour force.
- *Capital resources*: Capital resources (machines, road systems, power and water supplies) are used for making all goods and services. These are also vital because they help to lift the efficiency of labour and natural resources. Higher efficiency means that more production can be made from the same resources, thereby increasing incomes and living standards. Many low income countries will not have the financial capacity and saving needed to lift investment in new plant and equipment. They will be forced to rely in part on foreign aid and other assistance.
- *Natural resources*: In many low income countries, the majority of people are subsistence farmers. Often good land for agriculture is scarce, so there is a need to make the best use of it. The challenge is to raise efficiency through better farming techniques, use of improved capital resources and high yield crops (possibly genetically modified breeds of animals or crops).

In addition, mineral exploration may be helpful for some countries in helping to raise national production and income.

- *Improved government*: Governments in some low income countries are unstable, corrupt and incompetent in their administration of the economy. In such cases, limited finances are often wasted on projects (such as military ones) that do not help ordinary people become more economically self-sufficient. Alternatively, money may be siphoned off by corrupt officials. This environment also discourages foreign assistance. Often, what is most needed is improved levels of democracy or open government, where, during free elections, the people can remove administrations that perform poorly.
- *Involvement in international trade*: The expansion of exports is one important way for low income countries to increase incomes and promote economic development. If producers can become involved in trade, this can help them expand their market size. The recent move towards 'free trade' (lower tariffs or taxes on imports) between most Asian countries represents one attempt to accelerate trade and economic development in the region.

Australia's foreign aid to low income countries

Foreign aid represents the transfer of money and other types of assistance by governments and private individuals from high income to low income countries. It can take the form of gifts, loans (involving the payment of an interest rate to the donor country) and technical assistance. Australia is a fairly generous giver of aid. For instance, we contribute around 0.27 per cent of our GDP in foreign aid, which in 1997–98, amounted to $1440 million. This assistance is administered by AusAID or the Australian Agency for International Development. Help includes:

- country assistance (the training of students, development projects, technical assistance, the supply of equipment and food aid) designed to reduce poverty
- government and private contributions to the work of the United Nations (for example, the World Food Program and the Children's Fund), help for refugees and assistance for the victims of war and other disasters.

HIGH INCOME COUNTRIES

Less than one billion of the world's population live in high income countries where average GDP or income per person ranges between $9656 and $44 320 per year, or up to about $70 per person per day. These people are found in nations such as Australia, Canada, France, Germany, Italy, Japan, South Korea, New Zealand, Singapore, Sweden, Switzerland, the United Kingdom and the United States. For most, high incomes mean adequate food, shelter, clothing, clean water, excellent community services such as health and education and long life expectancy.

Singapore is a high income country.

Activities

Investigation: *Looking at foreign aid*

1. Working in groups, research Australia's foreign aid programs to poor countries. Case studies of particular aid projects can also provide information on the role of foreign aid. References for your investigation might include:
   - the latest Australian Yearbook (ABS No1301.0)
   - web sites
     - www.dfat.gov.au
     - www.ausaid.gov.au
     - www.dfat.gov.au/int/wp.html
   - publications and web sites of private international agencies involved in foreign aid including
     - the Red Cross
     - CARE
     - World Vision.

   Following your research and the preparation of a brief report, have one member of your group present your findings.
2. Examine the photograph below showing rural production in a low income country.

Cultivation on the Ganges flood plain

   (a) What economic activities are shown in the photograph?
   (b) What are the main differences between the way production is taking place in the photograph and the way similar production would take place here in Australia?

Communication: *Preparing a report*

1. The following exercise could be submitted as a written report, a class presentation (for example, a talk illustrated with overhead projector transparencies, a PowerPoint data show) or a wall chart.
   (a) Using an enlarged version of the world map on the right, classify (as low or high income), locate, shade in and name the following countries.

Australia	Nigeria	United States	Germany
South Korea	Indonesia	Russia	Ethiopia
China	India	Italy	Sweden
Vietnam	Cambodia	Switzerland	Chad
Mongolia	Singapore	Malaysia	Japan
United Kingdom	France	Canada	New Zealand
Brazil	Afghanistan	Austria	Bangladesh

   Use two colours, one for all the low income countries and one for all the high income countries. Include a key on the map to show which of the two colours represents which group of countries.
   (b) What do you notice about the geographic location of most low income countries?
   (c) What do you notice about the geographic location of most high income countries?
   (d) List five common differences between living conditions in low income countries and those for most people here in Australia.
   (e) Briefly explain three important ways whereby some low income countries may be able to increase their income during the next decade.

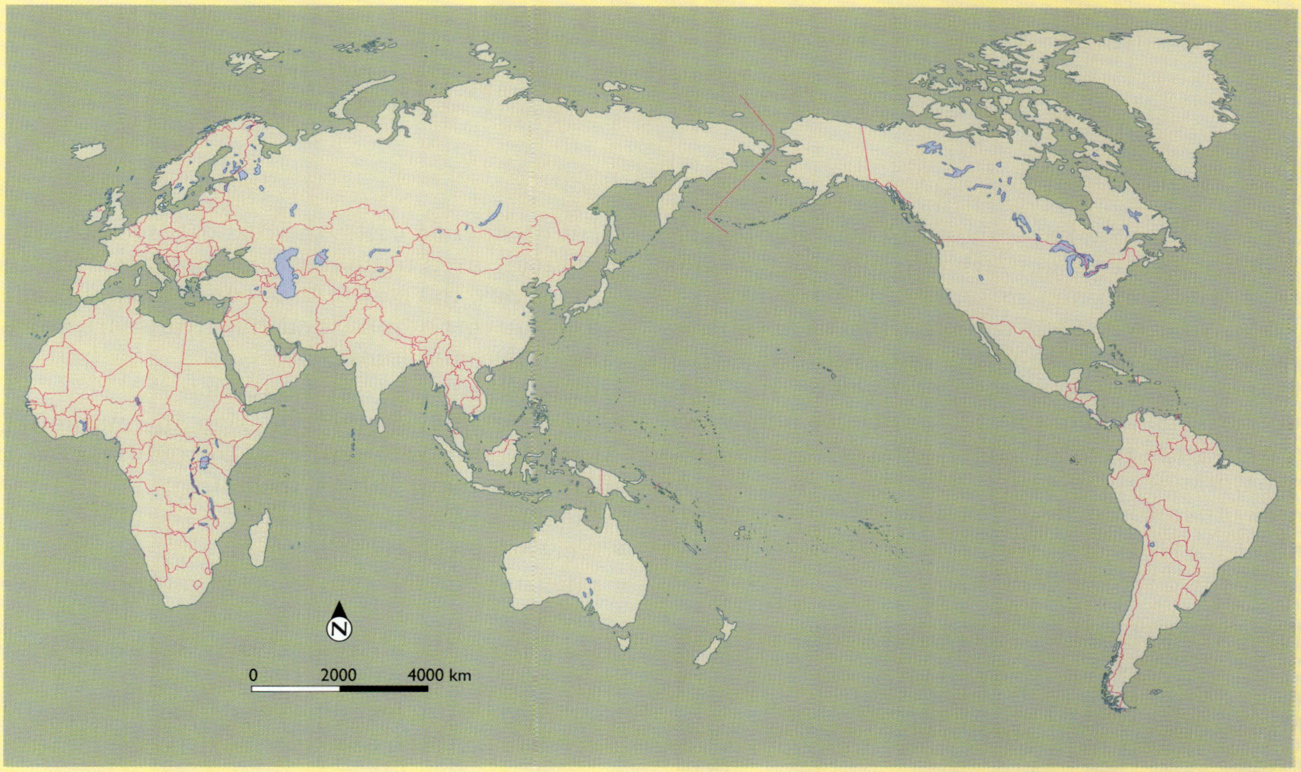

2. Examine the figure below showing the main countries receiving Australian foreign aid.
   (a) Explain what is meant by 'foreign aid'.
   (b) Name the two countries to receive most Australian foreign aid.
   (c) Suggest two important reasons why these countries were singled out for favoured treatment.
   (d) Since its destruction by civil unrest, violence and, finally, independence in 1999, East Timor has received considerable foreign aid from Australia. Assume that you are in charge of deciding how this foreign aid is to be used. Prepare a brief report that lists and justifies your three most important development projects to be financed by foreign aid.

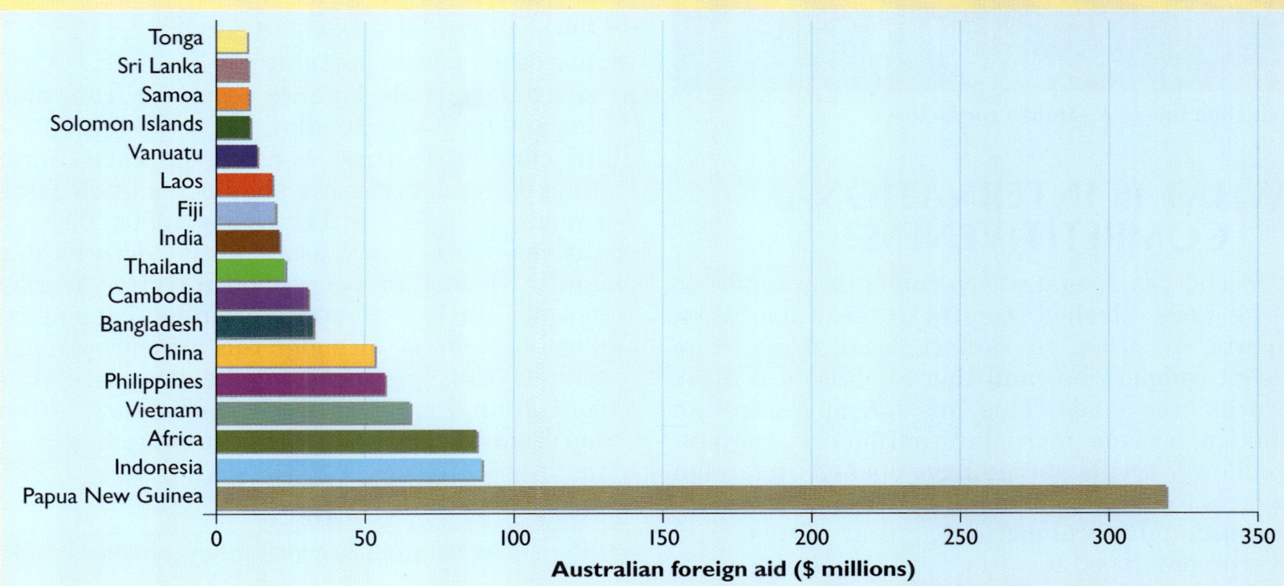

Source: Data derived from ABS 1301.0, Yearbook Australia.

9.3

AUSTRALIA – A COMPETITIVE NATION

Those of you who have played in sporting teams probably already know what competition is all about. The main aim in competitive activities is to beat your opponent using all the tricks of the trade. Sometimes you are successful but, on other occasions, even your best efforts are not enough. The same sort of principles apply in international trade, where a country's local firms and workers compete for survival against those from other countries. Sometimes we even hear reports of a 'trade war' as countries battle to dominate their opponents.

Production line in Australian car factory

WHAT IS INTERNATIONAL COMPETITIVENESS?

In recent years, many governments around the world have slashed **tariffs** (taxes placed on imports in order to protect local firms from foreign competition) and there has been a move towards free trade. This has forced Australian firms to become more internationally competitive. Lower tariffs abroad have opened up foreign markets to local exporting firms. To become more internationally competitive, local firms and governments need to:

- sell goods and services at prices equal to or below their foreign rivals
- cut production costs (the cost of wages, the cost of credit used to finance the purchase of better machines, the cost of taxes on company profits and the cost of inputs such as transport, power and telecommunications)
- increase efficiency in production
- improve product quality, design and marketing.

Clearly our international competitiveness is affected by many things, including:

- business efficiency
- worker efficiency
- efficiency in the provision of government services
- the strength of competition between firms operating in Australian industries
- the level of taxes imposed on local companies relative to those abroad.

It is rather sad that in most Australian industries, efficiency levels have been only around 60 per cent of those in the USA. Improving the situation depends on solutions developed by businesses, governments, unions and other institutions.

The effects of international competitiveness

There are many advantages for Australia if our firms and workers can become more competitive and efficient. These include:

- lower prices for goods and services
- increased jobs opportunities
- a stronger trade balance resulting from more income from export sales.

In addition to these benefits, improved international competitiveness should result in faster economic growth. Until the early 1990s, the competitiveness of our local firms deteriorated, mainly because of poor **productivity**. 'Worker' efficiency can be estimated very roughly using the following formula (although this measure wrongly assumes that productivity changes only come about from improved worker efficiency, rather than from better organisation or equipment).

$$\text{Worker productivity} = \frac{\text{GDP (\$)}}{\text{The number of workers employed}}$$

Low efficiency results in higher costs and prices for local products. This slows economic

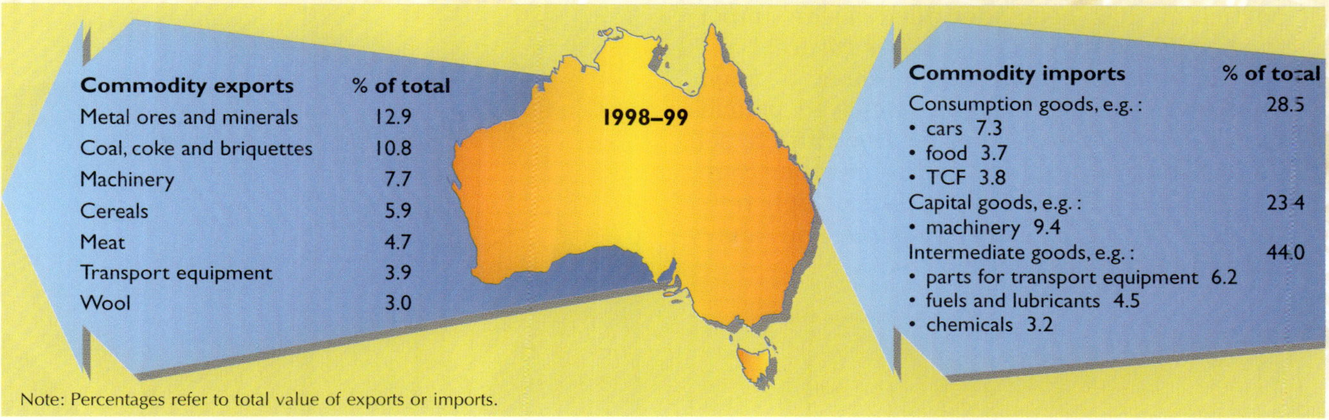

Australia's main exports and imports, 1998–99

Source: ABS Australian Economic Indicators 1350.0 March 2000.

AUSTRALIA'S FOREIGN DEBT

For many years Australia has had a **current account deficit**. This means that the cost of the import of goods and services into Australia has exceeded the revenue obtained from the exports of goods and services. To pay for these goods and services, Australia has borrowed money overseas (capital inflow). Over time, Australia has built up **foreign debt**. At the end of 1999 Australia's foreign debt was over $250 billion.

1998–99 merchandise trade shares by selected countries and country groups

	Annual exports (%)	Annual imports (%)
ASEAN[(a)]	12.1	12.7
China	4.6	6.3
European Union[(b)]	13.5	23.9
Hong Kong	3.6	1.3
Japan	19.3	13.9
New Zealand	6.8	4.0
Republic of Korea	7.3	4.0
Taiwan	4.9	3.1
USA	9.3	21.4

(a) Association of nine South-East Asian Nations: Brunei, Indonesia, Laos, Malaysia, Myanmar, Philippines, Singapore, Thailand and Vietnam.

(b) The European Union is made up of 14 countries and includes the United Kingdom.

Source: ABS Australian Economic Indicators 1350.0 March 2000.

GROWTH OF WORLD TRADE

During the last 50 years there has been a rapid growth in world trade — it is now increasing at an annual rate of around six per cent, which is faster than the growth of the world's economy. Much of this growth has been associated with:

- the decrease in barriers to trade, such as tariffs
- the rapid growth of transnational corporations (TNCs) which dominate world trade.

The rapid growth in trade has resulted in a more global allocation of resources. For example, the energy-poor countries, such as Germany and Japan, import much of their fossil fuel energy needs (coal and petroleum) from other parts of the world. Australia is a major exporter of coal to these countries while the oil-rich Middle Eastern countries such as Saudi Arabia and Kuwait are major exporters of petroleum.

REGIONAL TRADE LINKS — CHANGING DIRECTIONS

In 1902, around 50.4 per cent of Australia's exports went to the United Kingdom. By 1998, this figure had fallen to 6.3 per cent. From the 1950s, when Australia signed a trade agreement with Japan, the Asia–Pacific region has grown in importance as a destination for Australian exports and the UK and Europe has become less important. The two main reasons for this are as follows.

1. The Asia–Pacific has enjoyed a long period of economic growth, and countries such as Japan, Korea, Taiwan and China have bought large quantities of Australian energy, minerals and agricultural products. China, in

particular, has been identified as an important trade partner in Australia's future.

2. The European Union has become a major **customs union** which has followed policies that have made it difficult for Australia to sell its agricultural products to the member countries. These policies have included high tariff barriers for agricultural imports and heavy **subsidies** for local agriculture.

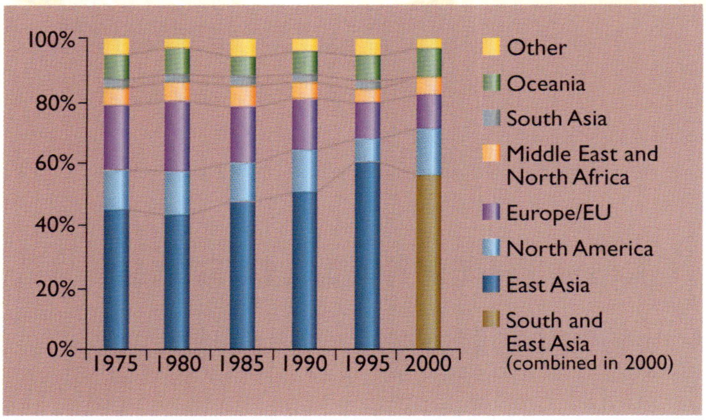

Changes in the direction of Australia's merchandise exports

New Zealand: closer economic relations

During the 1960s, the Australian and New Zealand governments began moves to establish a customs union between the two countries. By the end of the 1990s, the closer economic relations (CER) links were firmly established and there is almost free movement of goods, services, capital and people between the two countries. New Zealand is now Australia's fifth largest export market and the main market for Australia's **elaborately transformed manufactures (ETMs)** — goods such as pharmaceuticals, office machinery, telecommunications equipment and road vehicles.

Chinese President Jiang Zemin and the Prime Minister, John Howard discussed future economic and trade links between the two countries when President Zemin visited Australia in September 1999.

SAMPLE STUDY

Strengthening links through APEC

The Asia–Pacific Economic Cooperation (APEC) forum was established in Canberra in 1989. It allows leaders of Asia–Pacific nations — including the US, China and Japan — to meet regularly for discussions on economic and trade policies for the region. The nations are strengthening links towards developing an Asia–Pacific economic community and working towards free trade and open market policies in the Pacific Rim. There is a wide economic diversity among the countries represented, and political and cultural differences must be put aside to enable talks to focus on mutual trade and the economy of the region.

Another grouping that was formed to foster stability and cooperation in the region is the Association of South-East Asian Nations (ASEAN). Its nine member countries are Indonesia, Malaysia, Myanmar, the Philippines, Singapore, Thailand, Brunei, Vietnam and Laos. Australia does not have membership of the group but is a 'dialogue partner'.

Activities

Investigation: *Looking at trade*

1. Explain reasons why countries engage in international trade.
2. Distinguish between and give examples to illustrate:
   (a) export of goods/import of goods
   (b) export of services/import of services.
3. Explain what happens if the cost of importing goods and services exceeds revenue obtained from the exports of goods and services.
4. Refer to the diagram on page 235 which shows Australia's main exports and imports from 1998–99.
   (a) Explain why the type of commodities imported are different from those exported.
   (b) Should Australia be concerned about its reliance on primary export goods? Explain your view.
5. Refer to the table on page 235 which shows Australia's merchandise trade shares by selected countries and country groups, and answer the following:
   (a) Identify our most important trading partner in terms of our exports. Give a reason why this country would demand/buy so many exports from Australia.
   (b) Identify the major source for Australia's imports. What might be a reason for this?
6. Explain the aims of each of the following trading unions/policies and comment on whether these developments have been positive or negative for Australian trade:
   - APEC
   - ASEAN
   - European Union (EU)
   - CER (closer economic relations).

   (You may wish to use the Internet to help answer these questions by visiting each of these unions' Web sites.)
7. (a) Identify three products that Australian businesses are able to make competitively and export because of certain resources in Australia.
   (b) Other than a favourable allocation of resources, list other factors that may be important in creating a successful product for export.
   (c) Identify three products that are imported into Australia because the resources needed to make these products efficiently are not available in Australia.
8. (a) Distinguish between imports that are consumption goods, capital goods and intermediate goods. Provide examples of each category.
   (b) Suggest a reason why imports have been categorised in this way.
9. Using the resources in your library and/or the Internet, investigate how the direction and composition of Australia's trade has changed over the last 30 years. Identify major changes and give reasons for this changing pattern.
10. Predict how the composition and direction of Australia's trade may change in the next 10–20 years. Give reasons for your prediction.

Communication: *Presenting information in different ways*

1. Draw pie charts to represent information about the direction and composition of Australia's trade shown in the tables for 1998–99.
2. 'Tourism is one of Australia's main service exports.' Explain the meaning of this statement.
3. Explain why the government is prepared to spend money overseas on advertising tourism in Australia.
4. Suggest reasons why tourists are attracted to Australia as a destination. Arrange your thoughts by completing the following web diagram.

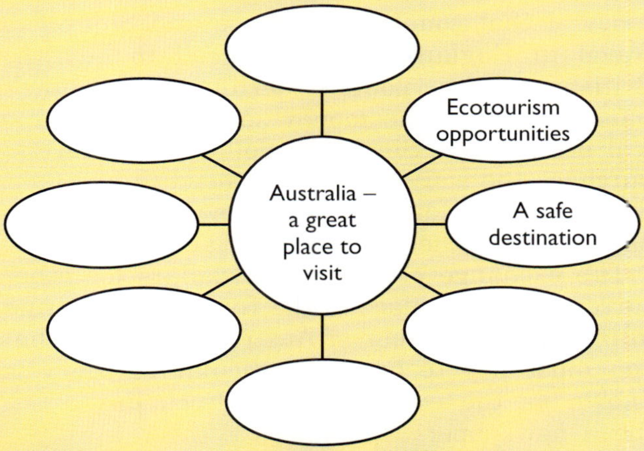

5. In small groups, prepare an advertising campaign selling Australia as a great tourist destination. Present your campaign as a PowerPoint presentation, a Web page, a series of posters, or a brochure.
6. Visit the ABS Web site and view tourist data over recent years. Prepare a short report which discusses trends in tourism in Australia in recent years. Comment on whether numbers of tourists are increasing or decreasing, where the majority of tourists come from and draw up a list of the most popular places visited in Australia.
7. One way to help reduce Australia's foreign debt is to reduce the number of goods and services Australia imports. One campaign that focused on achieving this was the 'Buy Australian' campaign.
   (a) Explain how the 'Buy Australian' campaign hoped to lower Australians' import demand.
   (b) Create a pamphlet or poster supporting the Buy Australian promotion.

FOREIGN CURRENCY

Marc wants to buy a computer software package he discovered on the Internet from a company in Switzerland; Bonnie wants to send money to her cousin in Singapore for her birthday; and Steve and Sharon want to go on a holiday to England. All these people have one thing in common — they need to buy foreign currency to fulfil their ideas.

Every country has its own form of money, or currency. Australia and America both have dollars but there are many other currencies around the world, including drachmas, francs, marks, lire and rupees.

To engage in financial transactions with other countries a person needs to purchase the currency of that country. For Steve and Sharon to travel in England they will need to buy the British currency, pounds sterling. For Bonnie's cousin to spend the money sent to her, Bonnie will need to buy Singapore dollars. For Marc to purchase the software, he will need to purchase Swiss francs. How do they know how much to pay for these other currencies? **Exchange rates**.

The exchange of Australian dollars for other currencies takes place in the **foreign exchange market**. The number of Australian dollars that you must pay to buy a particular currency is known as the exchange rate. Each day the newspaper publishes the exchange rates for the major currencies. Two rates are published — a bank's buy rate and a bank's sell rate. In all of our examples above, the bank's sell rate would be used. If, upon their return from overseas, Steve and Sharon still held some British pounds and wanted to exchange them for Australian dollars, the bank's buy rate would be used.

Consider the following example. Troy wants to send \$500 to his uncle in New Zealand. He needs to buy New Zealand dollars. The sell rate for that day is 1.2221 which means that one Australian dollar buys 1.2221 New Zealand dollars. How many New Zealand dollars will Troy's uncle receive?

A\$1 = NZ\$1.2221
A\$500 = 500 × NZ\$1.2221
= NZ\$611.05

As you can see, Troy receives more New Zealand dollars for his Australian dollar. Therefore, at the time of purchase, we say that the Australian dollar was worth more than the New Zealand dollar.

TRADE WEIGHTED INDEX

In its trade with the rest of the world Australia buys and sells goods from several countries which each have their own currency. It is useful to know whether, over time, the Australian dollar is gaining or losing value against other currencies. The **trade weighted index** (TWI) shows the change in the average value of the Australian dollar against a 'basket' (or representative sample) of currencies of our major trading partners. The currencies in this basket are weighted according to their importance in our export and import transactions. While the Japanese yen and the Singapore dollar are both included in the basket of currencies considered for the TWI, the yen is given a higher weighting because Australia trades more with Japan.

When the trade weighted index is falling, the average value of the Australian dollar is falling. This means that our exports earn less, and that more dollars are needed to buy the same amount of imports. A fall in the TWI is not a good thing for Australia because our living standards fall compared with the countries we trade with.

Activities

Investigation: *Exchange rates*

1. For each of the countries listed, match the correct currency.

Country	Currency
Australia	Rupee
Italy	Yen
Germany	Drachma
South Africa	Pesos
India	Deutschmark
Greece	Rand
England	Lire
Thailand	Pound
Mexico	Dollar
Japan	Baht

2. Consider the following table of Australian dollar currency conversions. For each of the situations listed below the table, calculate the value of the transaction.

Currency	Bank's buy rate	Bank's sell rate
US$	0.7986	0.7933
Yen	90.68	90.10
NZ$	1.2385	1.2221
Swiss franc	1.1002	1.0584
Deutschmark	1.2307	1.2286

(a) Jenny is travelling to the United States on holiday and wants to change the A$500 she has saved as spending money for her trip.

(b) Jai wants to buy a rare book on Japanese bonsai he has discovered through a mail order catalogue. The book is priced at ¥5000 (5000 yen). What will the book cost in Australian dollars?

(c) Khanh wants to send the equivalent of A$100 to her cousin in New Zealand as a birthday present. How many New Zealand dollars will her cousin receive as a present?

(d) Claudia has arrived in Australia from Germany for a six-week student exchange. She has 1000 marks that she wishes to exchange for Australian dollars. Calculate for her, using the appropriate rate, the number of dollars she will receive.

(e) Kim needs to place 2000 Swiss francs in her bank account in Geneva. How many Australian dollars does she require?

(f) Tony has just returned from a 14-day holiday in Hawaii and is left with US$75. Calculate how many Australian dollars he will receive in exchange.

(g) Kumiko, who lives in Tokyo, is travelling in Australia during her school vacation. She has a ¥100 000 travellers cheque she wishes to convert to Australian dollars so she can buy souvenirs. How many Australian dollars will she receive?

(h) Matthew and Michelle are discussing their travel plans to Singapore over the summer vacation. Matthew thinks they don't need to worry about purchasing any currency because both Australia and Singapore use dollars. Is Matthew correct in his thoughts about purchasing currency? Explain to him why the currencies are different and outline the process he and Michelle must go through in order to purchase Singapore dollars.

3. In the currency table in the previous question currencies were quoted at a buy rate and a sell rate. Explain the difference between the rates and comment on why these differences occur.

Communication: *Drawing graphs*

1. Over a week, collect daily exchange rates for the following countries by looking in the newspaper or contacting a bank. Plot the movement of the currency every day on a graph and describe the trend you see emerging. The countries for which you need to find exchange rates are:

Germany	Japan
Switzerland	Singapore
Italy	United States.

2. Use the data in the table below to draw a line graph showing the change in the TWI between December 1998 and February 2000.

(a) What was the highest and lowest value of the TWI between December 1998 and February 2000?

(b) Describe the trend you notice in the trade weighted index.

(c) Is this trend favourable or unfavourable for Australia? Explain.

Trade weighted index of value of the Australian dollar (May 1970 = 100)

	1998 Dec.	1999 Jan.	Feb.	Mar.	Apr.	May	June	July	Aug.	Sept.	Oct.	Nov.	Dec.	2000 Jan.	Feb.
Period average	53.0	54.8	55.4	56.1	58.3	58.0	58.4	57.1	56.0	57.0	55.7	55.3	56.4	56.0	54.5

9.6

TALKING TRADE — TREATIES AND COOPERATION

Australia has global interests that require a broad approach to trade policy. Australia is a significant economy — the fourteenth largest in the world. It is among the world's most important commodity exporters and a crucial supplier of industrial raw materials, energy and food to East Asia. Australia is also rich in its languages spoken and other skills that are a significant advantage in doing business in a global economy. Yet Australia is not one of the major trading countries in terms of goods and services traded. Australia accounts for less than one per cent of total world trade and is dwarfed by the trading giants — the United States, Japan, Germany, France and the United Kingdom.

In the twenty-first century, Australia will look to improve its foreign trade performance, focusing on:

- continued bilateral agreements and treaties, such as Closer Economic Relations (CER) with New Zealand and those with Japan, China and the United States
- Asia–Pacific Economic Cooperation (APEC) as the major regional agreement
- the World Trade Organisation (WTO) as the major global agreement.

Australia must also develop its mix of exports into the rapidly growing **value-added** industries, particularly information technology and telecommunications (IT&T), and high-tech industries and services. This has been difficult in the past due to low levels of spending on **research and development** compared with other developed countries. Also the manufacturing sector has tended to rely mainly on imported technology. Strategies for the future include:

- training more engineers, scientists and managers
- encouraging new businesses and entrepreneurs through government incentives
- 'clustering' information technology industries and related services.

The latter part of the twentieth century has seen a trend towards a much greater degree of interdependence or integration between economies. People increasingly refer to the global economy. Governments have recognised this trend and have reacted by creating a number of international economic organisations and forming international economic agreements or treaties. Some examples follow.

APEC

Asia–Pacific Economic Cooperation (APEC) is one of the region's most prominent and important international forums for cooperation on economic matters, particularly trade. In 1996, the member countries agreed on the following goals for APEC and these were reinforced at the 1999 forum:

- to attain sustainable growth and equitable development in the Asia–Pacific region
- to reduce economic disparities among APEC economies
- to improve the economic and social wellbeing of the people
- to deepen the spirit of community in the Asia–Pacific.

APEC's member countries, 1999

Australia strongly supports APEC as the major regional economic agreement and has much to gain by its continued development in the twenty-first century.

WORLD TRADE ORGANISATION

The World Trade Organisation (WTO) had its origins in the General Agreement on Tariffs and Trade (GATT). The GATT was signed at the Geneva Convention in 1947 and came into effect in 1948 when 23 countries, including Australia, became signatories. This multilateral trade agreement set out rules of conduct for international trade relations. It also provided a forum for multilateral negotiations to solve trade problems and to work towards the removal of tariffs and other barriers to trade.

In 1994, the World Trade Organisation emerged after a prolonged period of trade negotiations known as the Uruguay Round. It incorporates the General Agreement on Tariffs and Trade made in 1994, which superseded the earlier GATT. Around 120 countries, including Australia, are members.

The WTO is important to Australia because it is the major forum for global trade liberalisation, that is, freer international trade and, through its rules and disciplines, provides a positive environment for business and for resolving disputes. In the future, Australia will be working within the WTO to provide a fairer deal for agricultural exporters in world markets. Visit its Web site at www.wto.org/.

Activities

Investigation: *Trade and treaties*

1. What are the main types of products that Australia sells on world markets?
2. What will be the main focus of Australia's trade strategies in the future? Why?
3. (a) What is APEC and what are its main goals?
   (b) Observe the map of APEC member countries.
      (i) List the member countries.
      (ii) What do you think are the advantages and disadvantages for Australia in being a member of APEC?
4. (a) What was the GATT? What was its main aim?
   (b) Write a paragraph explaining why the WTO is important to Australia.
5. Why do you think many countries protect their agricultural products from imports? Explain.
6. Read the article below.
   (a) What was the reason for conflict between the US and Australia?
   (b) Why did the US want to place quotas and tariffs on Australian lamb?
   (c) A short time after this article was written, the US government announced that it would impose heavy tariffs on Australian and New Zealand lamb imports. Write a paragraph outlining the effects of this decision on: (a) US lamb producers
   (b) Australian and New Zealand lamb producers.

Fischer takes aim at US lamb tariffs

by Wayne Adams

Trade Minister Tim Fischer is not happy with a US recommendation for tariffs and quotas on Australian lamb imports and is expected to convey his objections in talks with key US politicians and officials in Canberra today. The US International Trade Commission recommendation, which also applies to New Zealand, could still be resonating later in the year, with the Cairns Group of countries, including Australia, pushing for trade to be opened up under multinational trade talks.

The issue arose last year when the US Sheep Industry Association approached the ITC, claiming a 'flood' of imported lower cost lamb was causing serious injury to the domestic industry. Evidence from Australia and New Zealand identified marketing, rather than import competition, as the main problem behind the US lamb industry.

'The Australian Government and industry have established very clearly in evidence to the ITC that imports are not the cause of the problems of the domestic industry,' Mr Fischer said yesterday. 'It is quite clear that, without imports, the steady decline in this industry will continue — the US industry has shown that it produces a product that US consumers don't want.'

The six ITC commissioners were split on the issue with half backing a quota at existing levels of trade (about 35 000 tonnes) and a 20 per cent tariff on levels above that. Two commissioners wanted a 22 per cent tariff on all imports and the other commissioner recommended setting a quota at two-thirds of existing levels.

The ITC decision now goes to the Administration, with US President Bill Clinton to make a decision within 60 days about what action should be taken …

[A] spokesman for Mr Fischer said yesterday 'it is not the end of the matter … Australia will be making absolutely clear to the US that we do not accept that there should be any restraint on our trade, that any restraint would be against the interests of the US lamb market, and that what we expect from the US at this time is leadership, not pandering to protectionist pressures. Imposing restraints is not the trade policy signal we expect now from the US as we draw closer to a new round of trade negotiations to be launched in Seattle.'

The ITC suggestion also got a cool reception across the Tasman. Trade Minister Lockwood Smith said New Zealand would 'object strongly' to the introduction of 'safeguard measures' to protect the US sheep-meat industry proposed by the ITC …

Mr Smith said the US was a leading proponent of free markets and trade liberalisation and that New Zealand had worked closely with the Americans in pursuit of these goals in many forums.

'The US will be aware of the importance of this case to New Zealand and its potential to send signals to other nations with a commitment to fair and efficient trade,' he said.

Australian, 29 March 1999.

LIVING IN A GLOBAL WORLD — THE 'GLOBAL VILLAGE'

During the latter part of the twentieth century there was a growing trend towards **globalisation**. Globalisation is the breaking down of barriers that have historically separated countries or **nation states** from each other. Through globalisation, the economies and cultures of communities around the world are becoming increasingly integrated. For example, did you know that you can eat a McDonald's meal in 101 countries around the world? Some of the forces that are leading the world towards economic and cultural integration are the growth of transnational corporations, the movement of people and capital between countries and the influence of global media networks. Within these processes, resources are not always evenly or fairly distributed. While the countries with most wealth, resources and technology are growing richer, many of the world's poorer countries are being left behind.

GROWTH OF TRANSNATIONAL CORPORATIONS

A **transnational corporation (TNC)** sometimes known as a multinational corporation is a large organisation that operates in more than one country. The major TNCs are based in the United States, Europe and Japan and have established many subsidiary companies in other countries. Examples include: General Motors (Holden), Ford, Toyota, Shell, IBM, Nestle, Sony, McDonald's, Pizza Hut, National Panasonic and Nike (see pages 246–9). Australian TNCs include National Bank, News Limited, BHP, Westfield and Qantas. Not all TNCs are huge companies. Many are small by world standards and operate in only one other country outside their home country.

TNCs have played a major role in economic and cultural integration. For example:

- Around two-thirds of all international trade is accounted for by just over 500 corporations.
- Around 40 per cent of world trade is intra-company trade, that is, between the parent company and its subsidiaries. An example of this could be Toyota in Japan providing Japanese-built six-cylinder engines for Australian-made Toyotas.
- There is a significant flow of information between TNC parent companies and their subsidiaries. These information flows are often of major importance to countries in which subsidiaries are located as they provide access to technology and 'knowhow'.
- There is a significant flow of highly skilled labour between various parts of TNCs. For example, highly trained executives move freely between the different countries in which a TNC is located.
- TNCs often provide highly standardised products sold all over the world. For example, a family in Sweden could be watching an American 'sitcom' on a National Panasonic Japanese-designed television made by a subsidiary in Malaysia.

TNCs are sometimes criticised with accusations of exploiting cheap labour in poor countries and making excessive profits. The other perspective is that they often bring much needed technology and create jobs for local workers. Singapore, for example, has become a highly prosperous country through its policy of encouraging TNCs to locate in that country.

FACT*file*

- McDonald's and other fast-food outlets have done much to spread American 'fast-food culture' around the world. In the 1950s, the founder of McDonald's Corp, Mr Ray Kroc, estimated that one day there might be 1000 of the hamburger stands. In June 1999, McDonald's opened its 25 000th store, making it the retailer with the largest number of outlets worldwide. McDonald's sells food in 115 countries and is recognised everywhere for its all-American image.
- The bulk of the world's recorded music industry is in the hands of only six corporations. In order from greatest to smallest market share, they are: Polygram (19 per cent market share); Time Warner (18 per cent); Sony (17 per cent); EMI (15 per cent); Bertelsmann (13 per cent); and Universal (9 per cent). The remaining 9 per cent of market share is with a range of smaller companies.

In terms of their sales, some of the larger TNCs have a greater income than many entire countries (see the table below). The ten largest TNCs have a total income greater than 100 of the world's poorest countries. Taken together, the world's largest two hundred companies control almost 30 per cent of world economic activity, but they only employ about one per cent of the world's workers. Of the 100 biggest economies globally, 51 are corporations and 49 are countries.

Transnationals are particularly powerful in five sectors — cars, banking, trading, retailing and electronics. Transnational companies have the power to move goods, money and jobs across national borders. They tend to set up where the wages are lowest, they move their operations to minimise taxes and maximise profits and they have the power to obtain concessions from governments eager to create jobs.

Country or corporation	Total GDP or corporate sale ($billions) 1994	Country or corporation	Total GDP or corporate sale ($billions) 1994
Indonesia	174.6	Portugal	91.6
General Motors	168.8	IBM	72.0
Turkey	149.8	Malaysia	68.5
Denmark	146.1	Venezuela	59.0
Ford	137.1	Pakistan	57.1
South Africa	123.3	Unilever	49.7
Toyota	111.1	Nestle	47.8
Exxon	110.0	Sony	47.6
Shell	109.8	Egypt	43.9
Norway	109.6	Nigeria	30.4
Poland	92.8		

Source: adapted from *New Internationalist,* November 1997.

MOBILITY OF EMPLOYMENT

Along with the major global role of TNCs in world trade there has been a trend for employment to be more mobile. This can be seen in three major areas.

1. ***Footloose industries.*** These are industries such as clothing and footwear that are mainly controlled by TNCs and move around the globe seeking the most favourable places to locate. They seek to minimise labour costs and locate in cheap labour countries, such as Indonesia, Thailand, Philippines, Sri Lanka, Egypt, China and India.
2. *Low skilled labour.* The movement of low skilled labour is usually for a limited period of time and these workers are rarely offered citizenship in their host countries. Filipino women are often recruited as maids and shop assistants in oil-rich Middle East countries and high income areas with shortages of cheap labour, such as Hong Kong.
3. *Highly skilled labour.* These are highly trained workers who have skills that are specialised and in short supply. They move around the globe where their special skills are needed. They often work in different subsidiaries or branches of TNCs.

As globalisation continues and barriers between countries break down, we can expect a greater mobility of highly skilled labour. Some professionals and executives are required to settle for several years in foreign countries and need to understand the benefits of cultural diversity, as the article below argues.

Good ideas in the race for business

By Fiona Carruthers, Ethnic affairs writer

A multicultural group of managers is more likely to come up with a good idea than a group from the same ethnic background, says one the the world's top executives.

Companies should aim to have at least three different nationalities on any management team, according to Goran Lindahl, chief executive of global engineering giant ASEA Brown Boveri (ABB), in a paper published by Monash University.

Managers should also be rotated around different counties so cultural differences can be overcome, allowing companies to benefit from cultural diversity.

'A group of people from several different cultural backgrounds is more likely to come up with an innovative idea than a group from a single culture,' Dr Lindahl writes in the current issue of the Monash Mt Eliza Business School's management journal.

'They must respect others and respect differences. They must lead by example. They must cultivate the trust of their people by involving them in decision processes.'

Dr Lindahl said the increased need for companies to send managers to work in Asia, South America and the Middle East meant it was critical that corporations embraced cultural diversity.

Forty per cent of the workforce at ABB — which employs more than 200 000 people in 140 countries — now works in emerging markets, compared with 20 per cent a decade ago.

The company employs psychologists to help managers confront their prejudices.

Australian, 17 November 1998.

MOBILITY OF CAPITAL

Capital is accumulated wealth that is used to finance production, and it is given a monetary value. When capital moves from one place to another it is usually as a flow of money. Every day, well over $US1500 billion flows around the world. This flow from one country to another is made easy through the electronic transfer of money. It takes less than a second for money to flow from Sydney to London.

The main movement of capital is to buy foreign exchange. For example, if a Sydney-based importing company wanted to purchase computer software from the United States, it would need US dollars for the transaction. The company's bank would buy the US dollars in foreign exchange markets. These markets are all around the world. London is the largest financial centre for foreign exchange transactions but many other cities, such as Paris, Hong Kong and Sydney, are also important.

Other capital flows are in the form of:

- **bonds** — these are sold by many governments around the world to finance some of their spending. Companies and individuals buy bonds as an investment as they pay interest. The largest bond market in the world is New York.
- **equities** —these are shares in companies that are traded in stock exchanges. The largest stock exchange is Wall Street in New York.
- **loans** — obtained by companies by borrowing from international banks, most of which are American based
- **direct investment** — as when an overseas company establishes a new enterprise, such as a factory, hotel or shopping centre.

New York is the most important city in the world for international capital flows. Other major cities include London, Paris, Zurich, Tokyo, Hong Kong and Sydney.

New York is the most important city in the world for international capital flows.

GLOBAL MEDIA NETWORKS

The **mass media** play an important part in our lives — they entertain us, inform us and have a great influence on us. Each mass medium in most parts of the world has the following characteristics:

- many people read, listen or view the one message simultaneously
- advertising provides most of the revenue for the media, although some are state owned such as the ABC in Australia and the BBC in the United Kingdom
- audiences have few means of direct feedback to the various corporations and institutions that own and control the mass media.

Media networks that are significant on a global scale include: the British-based radio network, the BBC; the Australian-based newspaper, television and movie network News Limited; and the American-based television news network CNN. Such networks have an enormous influence on the information people receive. This in turn can influence the attitudes people develop towards major issues and affect their cultural values and perspectives. Global media networks are also largely responsible for the creation of global 'superstars'. Through the networks' huge publicity and merchandising machines, entertainers, athletes and even cartoon characters become household names and children all over the world model themselves on these heroes.

There is much debate about the effects of global media on culture. In Australia, broadcasting networks must abide by rules covering the amount of 'local content' — that is, Australian-made productions — shown on television. The aim as stated in the *Broadcasting Services Act* is to 'promote the role of broadcasting services in developing and reflecting a sense of Australian identity, character and cultural diversity'. Some fear that without these content rules the local film and broadcasting industry would collapse and Australian culture would be overwhelmed by Americanisms. Others claim that the public wants more of the Hollywood products and that the free exchange of culture through global media channels helps in improving cultural tolerance and understanding.

RESOURCE ALLOCATION

The trends of globalisation have the potential to bring about the free exchange of goods, services and ideas among all the people in the world. However, there is a serious gap between the 'haves' and the 'have-nots'. For example, in 24 of the world's developing countries, one-fifth of primary school-age children are not receiving any education. In many African countries, more than half the population cannot read and write. For a person in Bangladesh, the cost of buying a computer is equivalent to eight years' wages. Even if the poorer nations were given access to the resources of the new 'information technology age', such as the Internet, they would find that more than 75 per cent of web sites are in English, a language understood by only one in 10 people.

The developing countries are also losing their valuable resources overseas. In trade, for example, there has been a growing trend for the high income developed economies, such as the United States, France, Germany and Japan, to import large quantities of natural resources from the low income developing economies. There is a huge world trade in oil and other fossil fuels. Even though fossil fuels are non-renewable resources, there appears to be little world concern about future shortages. In the case of timber, the trade has put great pressure on natural forests and caused concern over the rapid depletion of world forests. The world's forests are being consumed at an accelerating rate, far beyond **sustainability**.

Activities

Investigation: *The global village*

1. Explain the meaning of the term 'globalisation'. Comment on how it affects economies and cultures.
2. Draw up a table which summarises the forces that have influenced economic and cultural integration, such as globalisation.
3. What is a TNC?
4. Observe the table of selected countries' GDP or corporate sales.
   (a) List all the countries shown that have a GDP less than the value of the corporate sales of General Motors and Shell.
   (b) Why do you think Australia is not shown in the table?
5. Working with a partner or team, make a list of the parts of our culture that can be clearly recognised as: (a) American; (b) British; (c) Australian; (d) any other country that has a major influence on our culture.
6. In which three areas is there a global mobility of employment?
7. Read the article 'Good ideas in the race for business'.
   (a) Draw a mind map showing the issues that a person working overseas would have to deal with, such as food, language, and so on.
   (b) Summarise the article's main points about the benefits to the business and its people of mobility and multiculturalism for increasing cultural understanding.
8. In Australia, around fruit-picking time, there is often a shortage of labour to pick the fruit. Sometimes part of the crop perishes because it cannot be picked in time. Working with your partner or team, brainstorm arguments for and against allowing cheap labour from nearby countries to enter Australia with temporary work visas to pick the fruit. Report, either for or against, to the class.
9. What are the five main forms of international capital flows?
10. Prepare an argument for or against the case that 'global entertainment is highly Americanised and is affecting our own culture'.
11. In which sorts of industries do TNCs dominate? List examples of the industries and examples of the corporations; for example, cars — GM.
12. Conduct a class debate on the following topic: 'Globalisation is good for the Australian economy.'

Communication: *Writing reports and articles*

1. Using the resources in your library and/or the Internet, select a TNC to research, then write a report on the corporation. Include information about:
   - the size and structure of the corporation
   - the countries in which it operates
   - the strategies (including marketing and advertising) that have helped the TNC to grow
   - its mission (aims and objectives)
   - any stated policies about industrial relations, the environment, etc.
2. Write a short newspaper article which discusses the factors that have facilitated the growth of globalisation.
3. Examine the positive and negative effects of globalisation on:
   - consumers
   - labour markets (workers)
   - financial markets
   - the Australian economy
   - the environment
   - government.

NIKE — A CASE STUDY OF A TNC

A GLOBAL COMPANY

Nike is a US-based sports and fitness company and the largest supplier of athletic footwear in the world. It designs and produces high quality footwear, apparel, and accessories such as sports bags.

Nike products were sold in over 100 countries around the world in 1999. Nike became an international company when it opened an office in Taiwan in 1975. The countries in which its branch offices are located are shown below.

The location of Nike manufacturing sites has changed over time. The map opposite shows the location of its footwear manufacturing plants in 1975 and in 2000. A company such as Nike, which manufactures and sells its products in many locations around the world, is a transnational corporation (TNC).

By 1996, virtually all Nike products were manufactured by independent factories which were contracted to Nike. All their footwear is manufactured outside the United States.

Approximately 40 per cent of the Nike apparel which was for sale in the United States in 2000 was manufactured in the United States. The remainder was manufactured in Asia, Europe and South America. Almost all the clothing for Nike's international market was produced outside the United States. Nike's main clothing factories are located in the United States, Thailand, China, Taiwan, Korea, Mexico and Turkey.

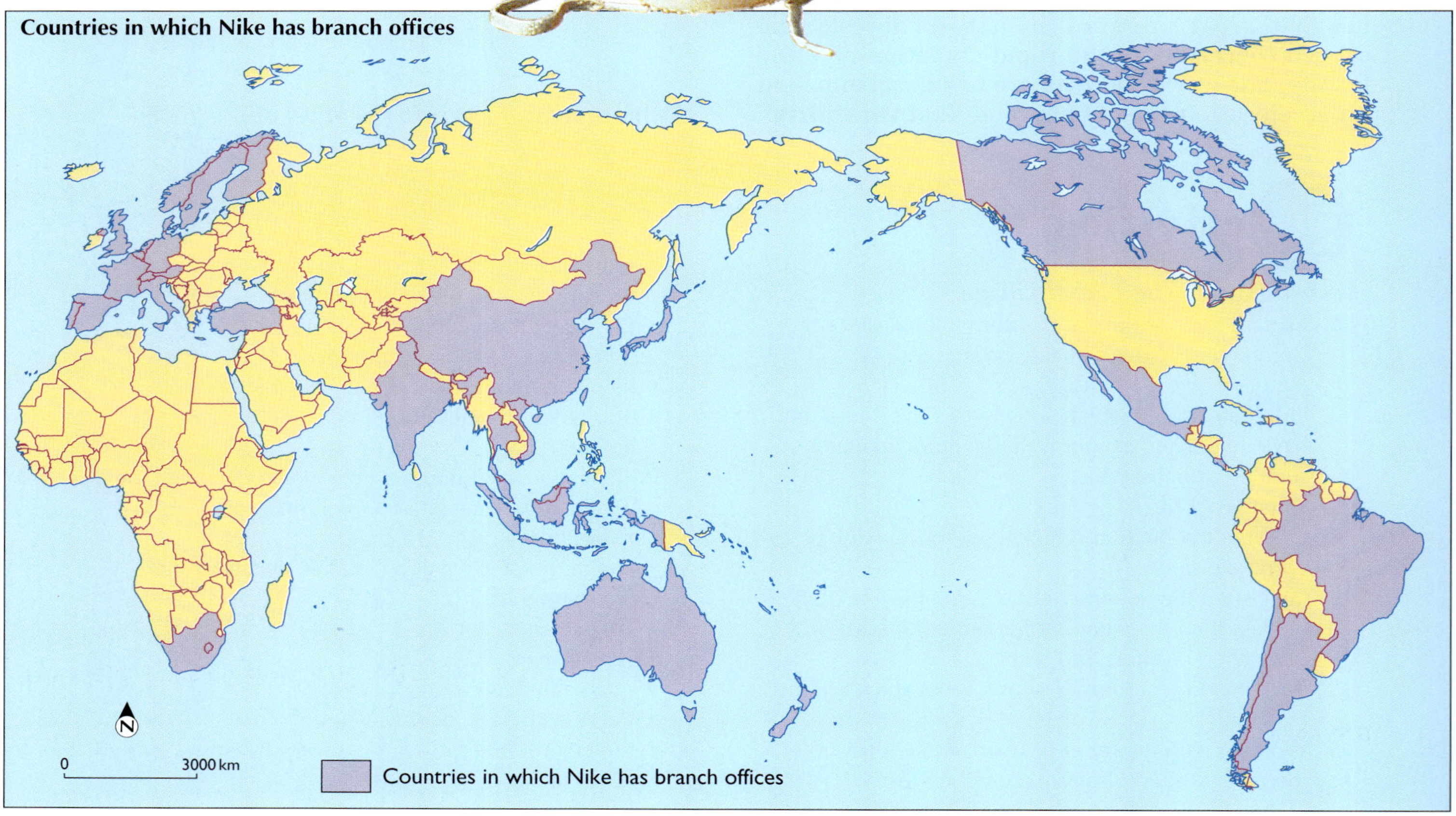

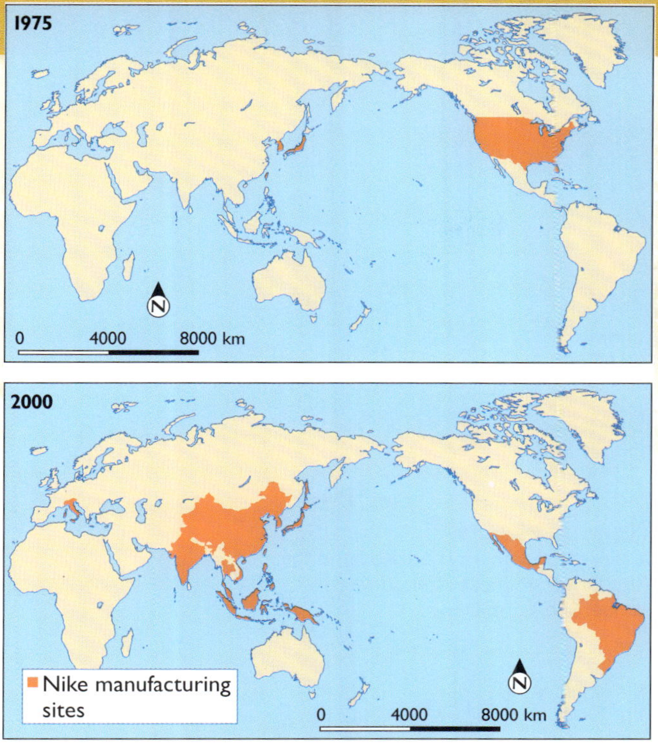

Location of Nike footwear manufacturing sites in 1975 and 2000

The pie graph below shows a breakdown of Nike footwear production for export in 1999. Most companies in the industry produce footwear in Asia because of ready access to materials and low-cost labour.

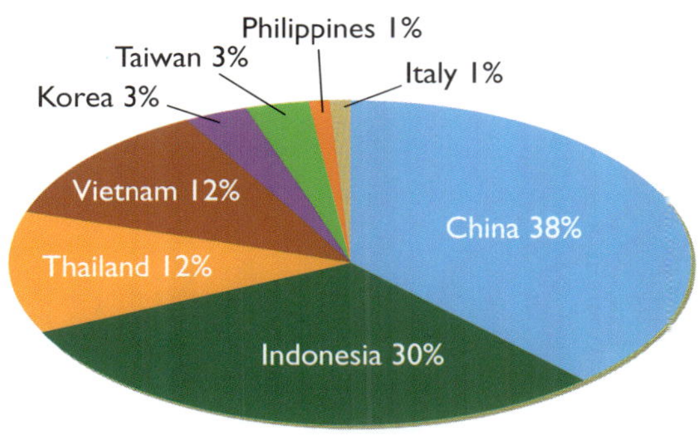

Country of manufacture of Nike export footwear, 1999

Manufacturing sports footwear is labour intensive and involves cutting, stitching, shaping and packaging of up to 200 components per pair. The more complicated the shoe, the greater the labour input. The main raw materials used to make Nike shoes are natural and synthetic rubber, vinyl and plastic compounds, foam cushioning materials, nylon, leather and canvas. Some raw materials are available in the countries where manufacturing takes place. However, most of the development technology for the products occurs in the United States.

The timeline on page 248 is a summary of the growth of Nike between 1964 and 2000.

NIKE MARKETING

One of the main reasons for Nike's success is the **endorsement** of many successful athletes. These include Michael Jordan, Shane Warne, Wayne Carey, Cathy Freeman, Tiger Woods, Andre Agassi and Pete Sampras.

Nike's marketing strategies seem to work.

- By the end of 1979, one out of every three Americans owned a pair of running shoes and nearly all running shoes sold were Nike.
- In 1981, 150 junior high school students in Dallas, Texas, were asked to name their favourite athletic shoe. All of them said Nike.
- In 1993, results of a survey indicated that in the perfect world, the shoes that 77 per cent of American boys aged between 15 and 25 wanted (as opposed to the ones they actually had or could afford) were Nike.

*The company's overall net income after taxes in 1999/2000 was about 6%.

Breakdown of the costs of Air Skylon Triax — retail price, US$70.00

Timeline showing the development of Nike

1964 Phil Knight and Bill Bowerman form the Blue Ribbon Sports (BRS) company and begin selling sports shoes made in Japan. Revenue: $US8000

1967 The first lightweight, durable running shoe is developed. Employees: 3. Revenue: $US150 000

1971 The 'Swoosh' design trademark is created and the word Nike (the Greek goddess of victory) is adopted. Revenue: $US1.5 million

1974 BRS begins manufacturing in the United States and expands its operations to include Australia. BRS spreads manufacturing to Taiwan and Korea. There are 250 employees. Revenue: $US4.8 million

1977 Nike shoes are sold in Asia. Revenue: $US28.7 million

1978 BRS changes its corporate name to Nike. Successful athletes begin to win competitions wearing Nike shoes. Revenue: $US71 million

1979 Nike begins to manufacture apparel. Nike is the most popular running shoe company in the United States with nearly 50 per cent of the market. Revenue: $US149 million

1980 Shoes begin to be produced in China. Employees worldwide: 2700. Revenue: $US269 million

1985 Employees: 4200 Revenue: $US991.4 million

1987 Nike is now manufacturing athletic, golf, tennis, walking and cross-training shoes. Revenue: $US877 million

1989 The 'Just do it' campaign begins. Revenue: $US1.6 billion

1991 Nike becomes the first sport and fitness company in the world to earn more than three billion dollars in revenue. Employees: 5300. Revenue: $US3 billion

2000 Nike's main product is still footwear but its apparel division is worth $US3 billion. Its fastest growth area is equipment — sports watches, sunglasses etc. Nike has 700 contract factories in 50 countries. Employees: 22 000. Revenue: $US9 billion.

Activities

Investigation: *Nike*

1. Refer to the maps on pages 246 and 247.
   (a) Describe the location and distribution of Nike offices.
   (b) Compare the distribution of Nike footwear manufacturing in 1975 with 2000.
   (c) Give some reasons for the differences you observe in part (b).
2. Apparel is a term used by Nike to describe clothing items other than shoes.
   (a) Make a list of Nike accessories and apparel you may have seen in some shops.
   (b) How does the manufacture of these products show how Nike has changed since its beginnings?
   (c) Explain why Nike clothing for the US market might be produced in the United States while other Nike clothing is produced elsewhere.
3. Study the pie graph on page 247.
   (a) Which location factors do you think Nike considered when deciding to set up factories in these countries?
   (b) How might manufacturing costs change if Nike produced all its footwear in the United States?
   (c) Describe how you think contracting companies might gain from making Nike products.
4. Identify and explain the features of Nike that make it a transnational company.
5. Study the diagram showing the cost breakdown of Air Skylon Triax on page 247.
   (a) Who makes the most money from the sale of a pair of Air Skylon Triax?
   (b) What percentage of the costs went to:
   - labour?
   - Nike?
   - taxes and duties?

   (c) How might these figures change if Nike shoes were manufactured in the United States or Australia?
   (d) What effect would there be on the factory locations if Nike stopped producing its shoes overseas?
6. Study the timeline opposite.
   (a) Describe the changes in employment at Nike from 1964 to 2000.
   (b) Compare the types of work employees would perform in:
   - the manufacturing factories
   - Nike headquarters
   - retail stores.
7. Obtain a copy of a world map. Using different colours for each country shown in the pie graph on page 247, shade the countries that manufactured Nike footwear in 2000. Describe the changes that have taken place since 1975.
8. Study the timeline opposite.
   (a) Draw a graph to show the increase in revenue of Nike over time.
   (b) To what extent might the advertising of products by prominent sports people increase the success and, therefore, revenue of Nike?

Communication: *Conducting a survey*

1. Form groups to design a questionnaire to survey students about the popularity of different sports shoe brands and about their awareness of the people who endorse them.
   (a) Conduct a class discussion to decide on the appropriate questions for your questionnaire.
   (b) Each student should survey 10 people.
   (c) Conduct the survey among students at your school and pool your results with the rest of the class. Convert the raw numbers to a percentage and tabulate the results on the blackboard.
   (d) Use these figures to draw bar graphs or pie charts showing the results of the survey. Display the results on the wall for the whole class to see.
   (e) Write descriptions of the graphs to summarise students' awareness of different sports shoe brands
   (f) Are students representative of the general population? How might results change if other people were included in the survey?
   (g) Were the most popular brands imported or made in Australia?
2. Visit the Nike web site at www.nike.com. Nike is very concerned that it builds a positive image and is seen to tackle the negatives. Its mission statement is all about responsibility. Provide case study examples from the web site to show whether Nike is a 'good' global corporate citizen.

9.9 Meeting the outcomes

DESCRIBE THE MANAGEMENT OF THE AUSTRALIAN ECONOMY IN AN INTERNATIONAL CONTEXT.

Identify examples of how international economic transactions, decisions and agreements affect the Australian economy.

1. Complete the following statements in your workbook to compile a summary of this chapter. The missing words can be found in the list below.
   (a) __________ occurs when there has been an increase in the value of goods and services produced in the economy over a given period of time.
   (b) Land, labour and capital are examples of __________.
   (c) __________ is an indicator of economic growth or economic expansion.
   (d) __________ is associated with increases in the standard of living and welfare of citizens in an economy.
   (e) __________ are goods and services purchased by overseas economies which add to Australia's national income.
   (f) A tax placed on imports is known as a __________.
   (g) The number of Australian dollars needed to buy a particular currency is known as the __________.
   (h) The __________ shows the change in the average value of the Australian dollar against a representative sample or 'basket' of currencies of our major trading partners.
   (i) A large business organisation that operates in more than one country is known as __________.
   (j) When an overseas company establishes a new branch or subsidiary enterprise in another country, this is known as __________.

Word list

factors of production
gross domestic product
tariff
trade weighted index
direct investment
economic growth
exports
transnational corporation
economic development
exchange rate

2. Draw a mind map using key words or concepts explained in this chapter.
   - international trade
   - exports
   - imports
   - current account deficit
   - foreign debt
   - exchange rates
   - consumption goods
   - capital goods
   - intermediate goods
   - globalisation
   - transnational corporations
   - ASEAN
   - APEC
   - EU
   - WTO
   - trade weighted index
   - tariffs
   - trade liberalisation
   - international capital investment flows
   - bonds
   - equities
   - loans
   - direct investment

   Once you have drawn your mind map, describe its meanings and its links to the class in an oral presentation.

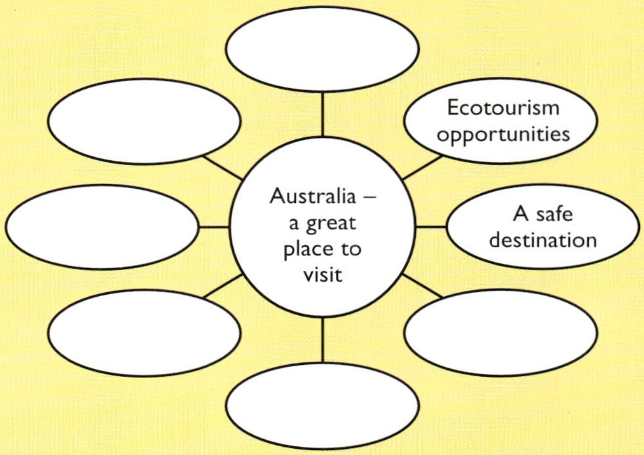

3. Visit web sites that deal with exchange rates (such as www.bloomberg.com). Track changes in the Australian exchange rate in relation to our major trading partners. Draw a line graph to illustrate. (9.5)
4. Identify any reasons for changes in the Australian exchange rate. (9.5)
5. Explain how the changes are likely to affect:
   - tourists
   - exporters
   - importers
   - consumers
   - businesses.

6. Imagine you are working as an economic adviser in the Department of Trade. Prepare a report which shows how the direction and composition of Australia's trade has changed over the last 30 years. You may be able to find statistical and other information if you visit the ABS web site, the Reserve Bank of Australia web site or the Department of Foreign Affairs and Trade web site — www.dfat.gov.au. In your report discuss the sorts of commodities Australia tends to export and import, explain whether this poses any dilemmas for the Australian economy, highlight the changes in direction of Australia's trade and suggest reasons for the change in the direction of Australia's trade. Finally, predict how the direction and composition of Australian trade may change in the future and give reasons for your predictions.
7. Aside from APEC and WTO, there are other global organisations and agreements. For example, ASEAN, OECD (www.oecd.org/), United Nations, World Bank (www.worldbank.org/), IMF (www.imf.org/), EU, etc.
   In small groups, choose one of the above and investigate the main role or purpose of the organisation. Explain the extent to which you think these organisations are relevant or important to Australia. Present your findings to the class.

DESCRIBE THE MANAGEMENT OF THE AUSTRALIAN ECONOMY IN AN INTERNATIONAL CONTEXT.

Discuss ways in which the government influences the development of the Australian economy.

1. The Australian government continues to push for greater trade liberalisation. Australia has reduced or removed tariffs from a large number of goods over the last decade or so. This policy has supported the Australian government's view that protectionism is wrong because it generates less efficient business in Australia. (9.3)
   (a) Define the underlined terms.
   (b) Describe how the removal of tariffs would impact on:
   - consumers
   - importers
   - exporters
   - the government.

   (c) The reduction and removal of tariffs has generated a large amount of debate. Summarise the arguments for and against lowering tariffs. You may find it useful to consult the Department of Foreign Affairs and Trade web site www.dfat.gov.au.
   (d) Conduct a class debate on this topic: 'The lowering and removal of tariffs has been good for the Australian economy.'
2. Invite a speaker from Austrade to address the class on how the Australian government is helping exporters, or write to Austrade seeking information, or visit www.dfat.gov.au in order to investigate:
   (a) the types of government assistance available for exporters, for example tax concessions
   (b) current government economic policies aimed at boosting Australia's trade performance
   (c) current government alliances
   (d) the role of Australian trade commissions overseas.
   Create a brochure for potential Australian exporters that provides advice on how to become a successful exporter based on your investigations above.

DESCRIBE THE MANAGEMENT OF THE AUSTRALIAN ECONOMY IN AN INTERNATIONAL CONTEXT.

Examine how different types of economic systems achieve economic development.

1. Choose a country in Asia that is experiencing relatively high rates of economic growth. Write a report or prepare a PowerPoint presentation, describing aspects of economic growth and economic development in your chosen country. This report/presentation should include:
   (a) statistics about growth rates and standard of living (draw suitable graphs/tables/diagrams)
   (b) discussion of strategies used to achieve economic growth and economic development
   (c) a list and assessment of economic strengths
   (d) a list and assessment of economic weaknesses or factors causing problems with growth
   (e) the political situation in the country and its relevance to economic growth
   (f) any other special features relevant to the country's economic growth including its trade performance, its population policy, etc.
   Resources could include:
   - case studies in textbooks
   - *Far Eastern Economic Review*
   - *Economist* magazine
   - *Economist* country reports
   - *New Internationalist*
   - Internet — for example, do a country search, or go to www.dfat.gov.au
   - www.worldbank.org/
   - www.envista.com/
   - www.odci.gov/cia/publications/factbook/.
2. Australia is considered a high income, developed economy. Outline reasons why Australia would be categorised in this way.
3. Visit www.worldbank.org/data and draw up a table of countries that may be classified as having high income or low income economies. Prepare a visual display that represents global income distribution. Your display could include:
   - tables of statistics
   - map of the world highlighting countries in each category
   - size of population and other comparative data.
4. Australia provides foreign aid to assist with the reduction of poverty. Visit www.globaled.audaid.gov.au. Explore the web site and find examples of actual case studies of Australian aid assistance. Choose one of these cases and prepare a report on how this aid can assist in achieving a reduction in poverty and higher economic growth.

Chapter 10

THE AIR THAT WE BREATHE

LEARNING outcomes

- Analyse the impact of human activities on the atmosphere.
- Understand key issues such as global warming, ozone destruction and acid rain.
- Describe the likely impact of fossil fuel burning on the environment.
- Understand how the management of resources affects the quality of the environment.
- Identify strategies to halt global warming.

INTRODUCTION

Ozone depletion, acid rain, global warming . . . we seem to be constantly reminded of the environmental problems facing our planet. The ways and demands of consumers have resulted in rapid production and industrial growth. While no-one will deny that industrial growth has brought advances in medicine and an easier way of life, there seems to be uncertainty about how to halt or control the environmental consequences of providing these things. This is particularly important given the global nature of some of the problems.

This chapter presents the facts about Earth's atmosphere and how it operates. It raises the problems of air pollution and ozone depletion and presents case studies for you to analyse. The activities at the end of the chapter enable you to put into practice some suggestions for change that will improve your environment and the air you breathe.

GLOSSARY

acid rain: rain in which acidic oxides, such as sulfur and nitrogen oxides, are dissolved

atmosphere: a layer of gases which completely surrounds the Earth. It is denser close to the Earth.

biofuel: fuel produced from plant and animal wastes, such as sewage

carbon dioxide: a common atmospheric gas which absorbs heat

carbon monoxide: a poisonous gas formed when fossil fuels are not completely burnt

catalytic converter: a filter fitted to car exhausts to help minimise pollution

chlorofluorocarbons: CFCs; artificial gases previously used in many products such as aerosol sprays, refrigerators and airconditioners, and gradually being phased out

fossil fuels: fuels such as coal, oil and natural gas, which have been formed in the ground over millions of years from the decay of organic (once living) matter, such as animals and vegetation

global warming: a rise in temperature of the Earth's atmosphere

greenhouse effect: a natural process whereby the Earth's atmosphere conserves heat

greenhouse gases: a number of gases in the atmosphere that contribute to the greenhouse effect

methane gas: gas formed from any decaying matter and by bacteria in the gut of a ruminant animal

monsoon: the seasonal wind of the Indian Ocean and Indonesia, blowing from the south-east in winter and the north-west in summer

nitrogen oxides: polluting gases formed from nitrogen in the air. They are produced when fossil fuels are burnt.

ozone: a colourless gas present in the stratosphere which stops harmful ultraviolet radiation from reaching the lower parts of the atmosphere

ozone hole: a thinning of the ozone layer above Antarctica and the Arctic, especially in the southern springtime, caused by destruction of ozone

pH: the unit for measuring acidity

pollution: harmful substances in the atmosphere, soil or water

precipitation: moisture that falls to Earth in the form of rain, snow, sleet or mist

renewable energy: energy that cannot be used up, no matter how much it is used. Sun, wind and water are the main sources of renewable energy.

smog: a mixture of particles of pollutants and fog (water droplets) suspended in the air

stratosphere: part of the atmosphere which contains the ozone layer

sulfur dioxide: a polluting gas formed from sulfur, produced when fossil fuels are burnt

temperature inversion: a situation in which a cold layer of air settles under a warmer layer and cannot move; occurs under certain weather conditions

trade winds: winds that prevail over oceans between the latitudes of 30° north to 30° south, and blow from south-east to north-west in the southern hemisphere, towards the Equator

troposphere: the lowest layer of the atmosphere; where we live.

ultraviolet radiation: short-wave energy from the sun which can be blocked by the ozone layer

AIR AND ATMOSPHERE

OUR ATMOSPHERE

The Earth is surrounded by a layer of gases called the **atmosphere**. The atmosphere continually moves and churns like a transparent ocean. It has different temperatures and pressures. We live at the bottom of the atmosphere in a region known as the **troposphere** where the continual changes in the atmosphere are referred to as the weather. Atmospheric gases, which become thinner the further they are from the Earth, are mostly made up of nitrogen (78 per cent) and oxygen (21 per cent). The remaining one per cent is made up of argon (0.9 per cent), **carbon dioxide** (0.03 per cent), varying amounts of water vapour, and trace amounts of hydrogen, **ozone**, methane, **carbon monoxide**, helium and neon.

The illustration at right shows that the atmosphere can be divided into several layers. The troposphere is the lowest layer. Above this layer is the **stratosphere** where ozone gases are found. The next layer is called the mesosphere. The thermosphere extends from 80 kilometres to an altitude of 640 kilometres from the Earth. The region beyond this is called the exosphere, which extends to about 9600 kilometres — the outer limit of the atmosphere. Most of the atmosphere's gas is in the troposphere.

The blanket of gases in the troposphere allows the sun's rays through and traps some of the heat. If this heat, instead of being trapped, was radiated back into space, the Earth's climate would be up to 30°C cooler. Life as we know it would not exist. Carbon dioxide is the main **greenhouse gas** involved in trapping this heat, and it helps determine the Earth's climate. The process that allows Earth's temperature to be regulated in this way is sometimes called the **greenhouse effect**.

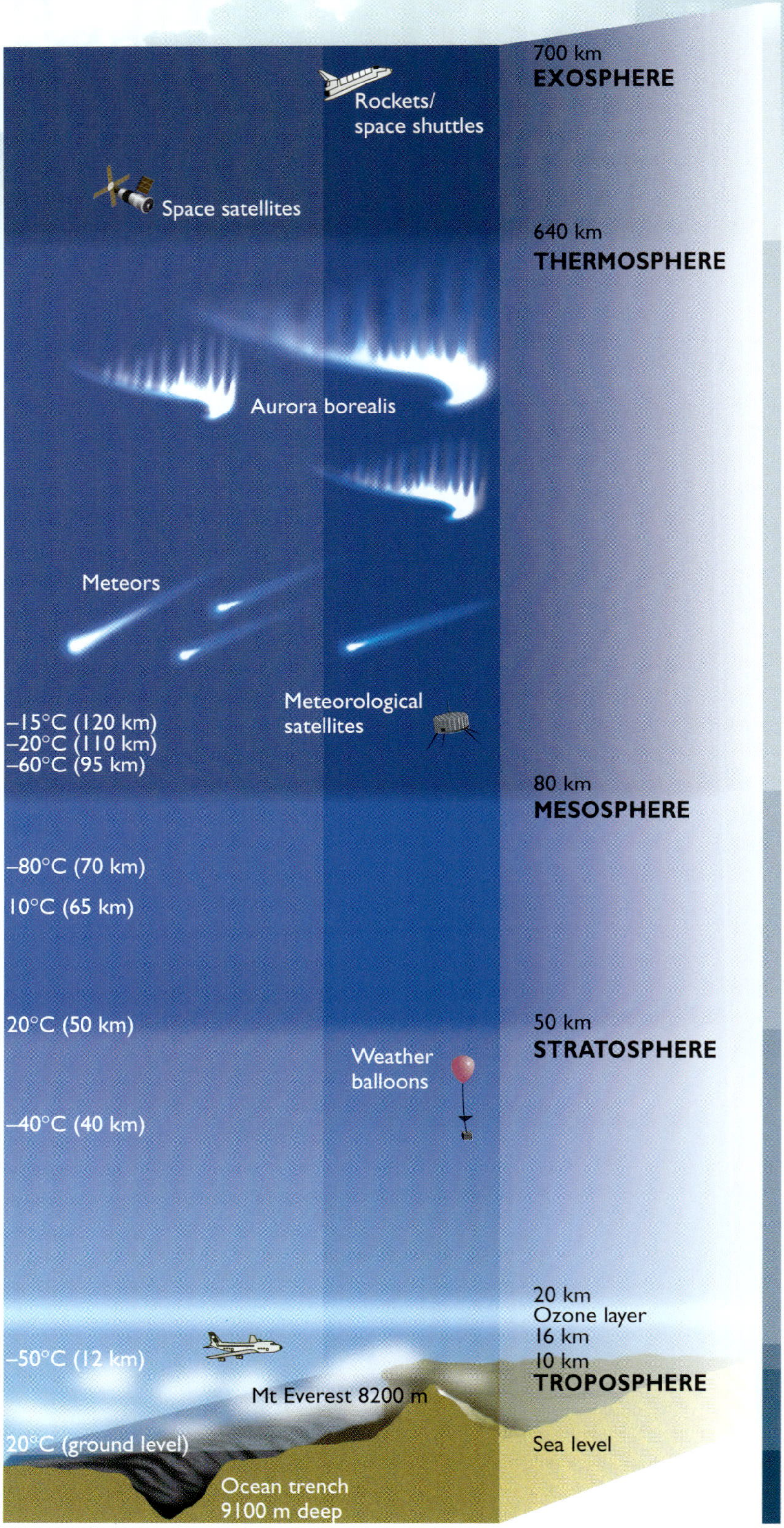

Structure of the atmosphere (not to scale)

CIRCULATION OF THE ATMOSPHERE

The air around the Earth is constantly circulating. Hot air from the equatorial regions rises and moves towards the poles. At around 30 degrees of latitude, some cold air descends and moves back towards the Equator while the rest continues towards the poles. At around 60 degrees of latitude, the warm air meets the cold polar air. Both are forced into the higher atmosphere and the warmer air moves back towards the Equator while the cold air moves back towards the poles. The diagrams opposite show the circulation of the world's atmosphere and the general air circulation around Australia and part of South-East Asia.

AIR DEGRADATION

Air degradation is linked to atmospheric circulation. It refers to the contamination of the atmosphere by products that can cause health problems to humans, plants and animals. Large-scale changes in the Earth's temperature and atmosphere have far-reaching effects on people and the environment. Main concerns are the depletion of the ozone layer, **global warming** and the incidence of **acid rain**.

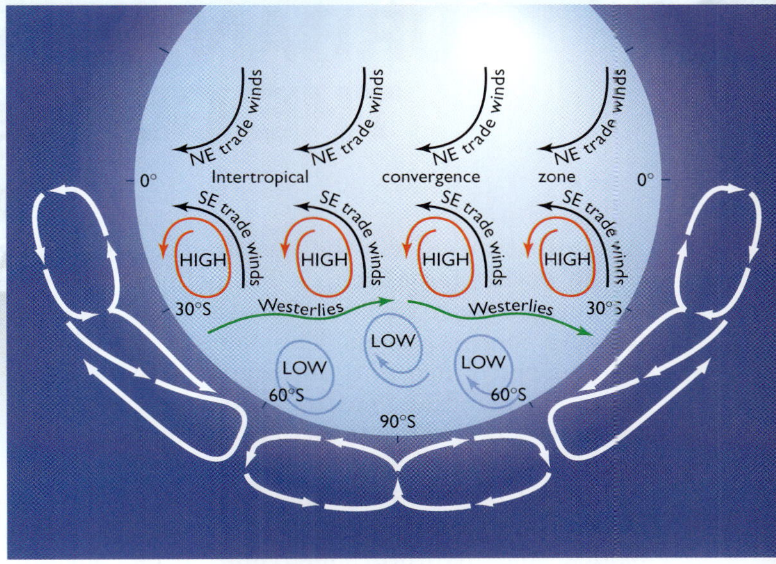

Circulation of the atmosphere

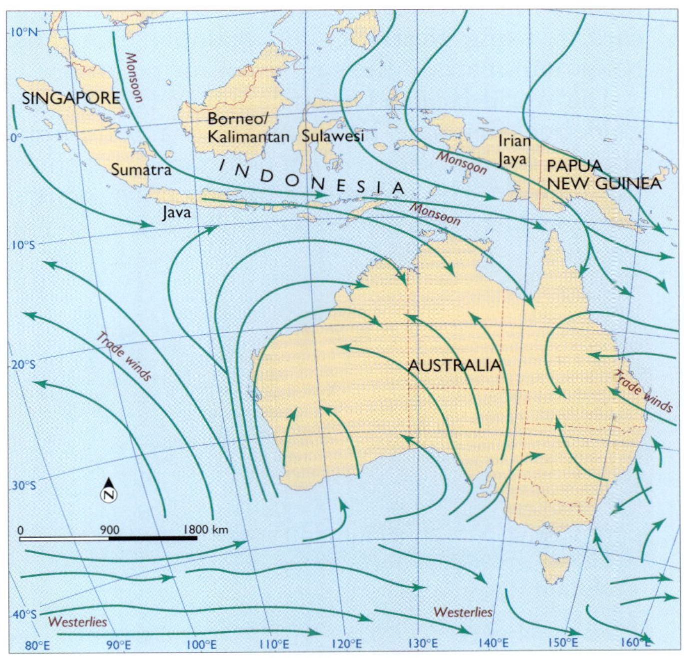

Australia's atmospheric circulation — January

Activities

Investigation: *Atmospheric conditions*

1. Study the illustration showing structure of the atmosphere.
   (a) For how many kilometres do the following extend above the Earth's surface?
   - troposphere
   - stratosphere
   - mesosphere

   (b) For how many kilometres does the ozone layer extend?
2. Explain why the air over cities and industrial areas can become so polluted.
3. Study the illustration showing circulation of the atmosphere. Describe this atmospheric circulation in your own words. In which atmospheric layer does this take place?
4. Study the illustration showing Australia's atmosphere circulation in January.
   (a) Identify where you live. What is the general atmospheric circulation experienced in January in your area?
   (b) Turn to the glossary on page 253 to find out the meaning of the following terms in the map above.
   - **monsoon**
   - **trade winds**

   (c) Describe how the general circulation in the atmosphere in Australia differs in the following locations in January.
   Melbourne
   Darwin
   Perth
   Broome
   Cairns
5. Use other sources to find information about the aurora borealis.

10.2

URBAN AIR POLLUTION — THE GLOBAL PICTURE

Air **pollution** affects the health of many people in the world's largest cities. The pollutants in our air come from a variety of sources and occur in varying concentrations. The combustion of coal, oil and petrol accounts for many of the air pollutants, including **sulfur dioxide**, **nitrogen oxides** and airborne particles. These are produced by fossil-fuel-fired electric power plants, industrial boilers and home heating appliances. Most of the carbon monoxide and many nitrogen oxides and hydrocarbons come from burning petrol and diesel in cars and trucks. We are all involved in producing pollution, by travelling in cars or using electricity for example. The table below summarises the sources of air pollution.

The World Health Organisation (WHO) has set guidelines for safe levels of various pollutants. Human health suffers when pollutants rise above these levels. The pollution in many cities around the world exceeds the WHO guidelines — for the inhabitants of those cities, simply breathing the air is a health hazard at certain times of year. Nitrogen dioxide, for example, exceeded WHO guidelines in Cordoba, Argentina, for 70 days in 1991; in Capetown for 160 days in 1994; and in Athens for 31 days in 1995. Sulfur dioxide levels exceeded WHO guidelines for five days in Athens in 1995 and 11 days in London in 1995.

In 1952, severe pollution in London caused the deaths of nearly 4000 people and another 700 in 1962. In Indonesia in 1997 the health of thousands of people was affected by prolonged air pollution as a result of forest fires in the region.

The first table on the opposite page shows the pollution levels in some cities in the world and compares them with WHO guidelines. The second table summarises major urban air pollutants from transport on a per capita basis. It compares average Australian, US and European cities with other specific cities around the world.

The air in Los Angeles has very high levels of nitrogen oxide.

Sources of major air pollutants

Pollutant	Sources of pollutant
Carbon dioxide	All types of combustion
Carbon monoxide	Car exhaust, some industrial processes
Lead	Car exhaust, batteries, lead smelters
Sulfur dioxide	Power and heat generation processes that use coal or oil containing sulfur; sulfuric acid plants
Airborne particles (particulate matter)	Car exhaust, industrial processes, domestic wood and coal fires, rubbish incineration, power and heat generation, reaction of pollutant gases in the atmosphere
Nitrogen oxides	Car exhaust, power and heat generation, explosives, fertiliser plants, nitric acid
Photochemical oxidants (mostly ozone)	Formed in the atmosphere by reaction of sunlight, nitrogen oxides and hydrocarbons. (While ozone in the upper atmosphere is essential, it is a poison in the lower atmosphere.)
Non-methane hydrocarbons (including acetylene, butane, ethane, ethylene, pentanes, propane)	Car emissions, evaporation of solvents, industrial processes, fuel combustion, disposal of solid wastes

Pollution levels — selected cities

City	Country	Sulfur dioxide annual mean (micrograms per cubic metre)	Nitrogen oxide annual mean (micrograms per cubic metre)
Cordoba	Argentina	na	87
Mendoza	Argentina	26	43
Sao Paulo	Brazil	20	86
Santiago	Chile	29	81
Quito	Ecuador	31	na
Mexico City	Mexico	39	48
Caracas	Venezuela	34	59
Melbourne	Australia	1	30
Beijing	China	84	na
Shanghai	China	60	na
Calcutta	India	34	29
New Delhi	India	30	72
Osaka	Japan	19	63
Tokyo	Japan	18	68
Johannesburg	South Africa	19	32
Durban	South Africa	31	na
Capetown	South Africa	21	72
Los Angeles	United States	3	92
Toronto	Canada	13	46
Montreal	Canada	11	40
Vancouver	Canada	17	52
Vienna	Austria	13	34
Brussels	Belgium	17	44
Sofia	Bulgaria	39	122
Zagreb	Croatia	40	30
Copenhagen	Denmark	11	69
Helsinki	Finland	5	38
Frankfurt	Germany	45	na
Munich	Germany	7	41
Athens	Greece	34	64
Bucharest	Romania	10	72
Madrid	Spain	10	25
Geneva	Switzerland	13	58
London	England	25	77
Edinburgh	Scotland	25	49

WHO guidelines are: nitrogen oxide, 40 to 50 micrograms per cubic metre per year; sulfur dioxide, 50 micrograms per cubic metre per year.

Activities

Investigation: *Major sources of pollution*

1. Study the table showing the sources of major air pollutants.
   (a) What are the most common sources of all air pollution?
   (b) Describe actions that could be taken to reduce the air pollution emissions.
2. Study the table showing transport emissions per capita in selected cities.
   (a) Which country has cities with the highest transport emissions per capita?
   (b) In Australia, which transport emissions are among the highest per capita in the world?
   (c) How do the Australian levels compare with the US, European and Asian cities?
   (d) Kuala Lumpur, Bangkok and Manila are developing cities, whereas Tokyo and Hong Kong are developed cities. Compare their transport emissions. Outline factors that might help explain any pattern you observe.

Communication: *Drawing a pollution map*

Study the data in the table showing pollution in selected cities. Using a blank outline map of the world and your atlas, complete the following activities.

1. Devise symbols to show sulfur dioxide and nitrogen oxide. Use two colours to show cities with emissions below and above the WHO guidelines.
2. Use the data in the table to map levels of sulfur dioxide and nitrogen oxide emissions in selected cities. Give your map a title and legend.
3. Describe the location of polluted cities in the world.
4. Does any one region have a greater concentration of polluted cities than another?
5. Is your map conclusive? What other data would you like to add to it? You may like to search the Internet to find the data you need.

Transport emissions per capita in selected cities (kilograms per capita)

Cities	Carbon dioxide	Nitrogen oxides	Sulfur dioxide	Carbon monoxide	Volatile organic compounds	Fine particles
Australia (average)*	2788.9	21.9	0.6	185.8	23	1.4
USA (average)*	4541.0	22.3	1.6	204.5	22.3	1.0
Europe (average)*	1887.9	13.0	2.0	72.6	11.6	0.8
Toronto (metro)	2434.3	27.0	2.3	160.6	21.7	3.9
Tokyo	1397.4	4.4	0.8	14.3	2.0	na
Hong Kong	760.4	8.0	1.7	25.2	2.4	1.1
Kuala Lumpur	1424.0	11.2	1.0	90.0	22.8	1.0
Bangkok	1304.4	3.6	1.8	84.6	23.2	9.1
Manila	610.0	9.2	1.5	67.5	11.2	1.5

* Represents the average of all cities in that country

SMOG ALERT

Days of heavy **smog** are common in many cities and occur each summer in Melbourne and Sydney. However, neither of these can compare with Mexico City. In 1988, smog exceeded recommended levels there on 312 days out of 365. In January 1989 the smog was so bad that children did not attend school for a month. It is said that breathing the air in Mexico City is equivalent to smoking two packets of cigarettes per day. This amount of pollution is obviously very hazardous to health and to the environment.

Smog in Mexico City

The amount of pollution occurring in urban areas depends on temperature, wind speed, the movement of pressure systems, local topography (such as mountains and valleys) and the amount of pollution produced in the city. In the troposphere, temperature normally decreases with altitude: the higher you go, the cooler it gets. But under certain weather conditions and in certain terrains the reverse is true. A colder layer of air settles under a warm layer, which is known as a **temperature inversion**. The cold layer of air cannot rise; it traps pollutants, which then gather near the ground.

The geography of Los Angeles, for example, causes such inversions and smog conditions. The city is surrounded by the San Gabriel mountains and experiences low average wind speeds. It receives a lot of sunlight, which acts on certain pollutants to create photochemical smog. Los Angeles has also experienced rapid population growth. In 1950 the regional population was 4.8 million. This grew to 14 million by the early 1990s. In the same period, car numbers went from 2.3 million to 10.6 million.

An incident such as the forest fires in Indonesia in 1997 coupled with extreme weather conditions causes severe air pollution problems. The article on page 259 outlines the impact of such an event.

To control air pollution, hazardous material must be removed before it is used or after it is formed. Ideally, the pollution should not be formed in the first place. However, car exhaust pollutants can be controlled by: burning the fuel as completely as possible; recirculating fumes from fuel tank, carburettor and crankcase; and using **catalytic converters** to turn the engine exhaust into harmless substances. In industrial processes, electrostatic precipitators can trap particles produced.

In Mexico City cars can be driven into the city on only four days of the working week and public transport is extensively promoted. All cars must now pass an emissions test to enable access to the city.

Activities

Investigation: *Pollution*

1. Find out how many smog alert days were announced in your nearest capital city last year. Research some of the causes of pollution in this city.
2. Read the news article on the following page. Why were such high pollution levels recorded in this region? Is this a normal event? Explain.

Pollution levels go off the scale

By MARK BAKER — South-East Asia correspondent, Bangkok, Friday

Early on Tuesday afternoon an unofficial world record was created in the east Malaysian city of Kuching, a statistic that represents environmental damage out of control.

Under Malaysia's Pollution Standard Index, a reading above 100 points is regarded as unhealthy, above 300 is hazardous and anything beyond 400 is deemed life-threatening to the sick and elderly. The scale stops at 500.

On Tuesday afternoon in Kuching, a normally bustling but now crippled port city on the coast of Sarawak, Government authorities recorded a PSI level of 851 points — what is believed to be the highest level of air pollution recorded. Anywhere. Ever.

As the dense blanket of smog fed by thousands of unchecked forest fires spreads across a vast swathe of equatorial South-East Asia, the Governments of six nations are being forced to confront the most serious environmental crisis in the region's history. . . .

[The crisis includes] devastated forests, damaged plantations and crops, idle factories and offices, closed airports and cancelled tourist bookings, and a potential public health bill of incalculable dimensions.

Two deaths have already been reported and tens of thousands of people have been treated for lung and throat infections, eye problems and diarrhoea caused by severe air and water pollution. 'This is certainly by far the worst episode that's ever been experienced in this region,' said Mr Steve Tamplin, a World Health Organisation spokesman based in Manila.

In Sarawak, where a state of emergency is in force, schools, offices and factories have been shut and mass evacuations are being considered. In the southern Philippines, fishermen have been unable to leave port because of poor visibility. In the tourist resorts of southern Thailand, hotels are emptying. And in Kuala Lumpur, embassies and foreign companies are sending non-essential families and staff on leave, and fears are mounting about the viability of next year's Commonwealth Games . . .

The explanation for the crisis is apparently simple. A severe drought and the late onset of the annual monsoon has trapped smoke from thousands of forest fires in a toxic pall that has spread across a 2500-kilometre span of South-East Asia, enveloping most of Indonesia, Malaysia, Singapore and Brunei, and now drifting northward into Thailand and the Philippines.

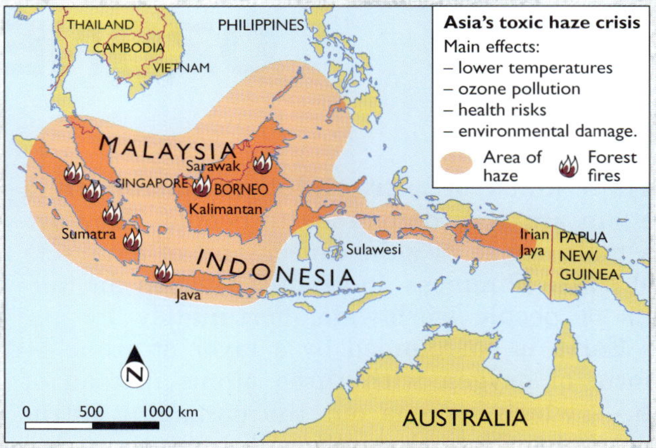

But while Indonesia has accepted primary responsibility and apologised for the effects of fires deliberately lit by logging companies and traditional slash-and-burn farmers, the real problem runs much deeper and is one for which Governments throughout the region must share the blame.

The freak weather conditions have also trapped toxic emissions from poorly regulated industries and the exhaust fumes of millions of vehicles that choke cities across the region. And the crisis is being compounded by the wholesale destruction of millions of hectares of natural forest, not just in Indonesia but also in Malaysia, Thailand and the Philippines.

The outcry from Malaysia, which has been hardest hit by the crisis, has been tempered by the knowledge that their own urban pollution levels are among the worst in the region, and that Malaysian companies have played a substantial role in the destruction of forests in Indonesia.

Malaysia's own record for forest destruction is lamentable. In Sarawak, some of the world's richest remaining rainforests are being rapidly destroyed by logging companies with powerful political connections.

Age, 27 September 1997.

Communication: *Using photographs and maps*

1. Look at the photograph of smog in Mexico City. Imagine you live in Mexico City, and a smog alert day has been announced. How would you respond and what would you do that day if you were:
   (a) a school-age child?
   (b) an elderly person?
   (c) a city office worker?
   (d) a person with children?
   (e) an industrial worker?
   (f) a health worker?
2. Study the map accompanying the news article above.
   (a) In which direction were the prevailing winds blowing in September 1997?
   (b) How far did smoke from the forest fires carry?
3. During November 1997, smoke from these fires began to descend on Darwin. Use the map on page 255 to explain how the atmospheric circulation caused such pollution movement.

Investigation: *Toxic haze crisis*

1. Form groups of six. Read the news article above and write down the main events outlined. Each group member should take one of the following roles:
   - a Malaysian government official
   - an airline pilot
   - a tourist hotel owner
   - a Malaysian doctor
   - a Malaysian logging company representative
   - an Indonesian government official.
2. Each student will need to write a role-play card for the person allocated. Include the following information in your card.
   (a) What is the main issue for that person?
   (b) Outline the person's view (immediate, medium and long term) about pollution from the fires.
   (c) Describe the management strategies this person might suggest for dealing with the pollution.
3. Perform your role play to the class, and discuss the diversity of opinions.

THE OZONE LAYER

Certain kinds of **ultraviolet radiation** from the sun are very dangerous to people. They are the main cause of skin cancer and of cataracts that cause blindness and reduced vision for millions of people worldwide. Fortunately for us, the Earth is surrounded by a layer of ozone — a form of oxygen with three atoms instead of two — which screens out the damaging ultraviolet light. (Note that although ozone is necessary in the upper atmosphere, in the lower atmosphere it is highly toxic and poisonous to humans. Here, it is a dangerous pollutant found in smog and is produced by the interaction of hydrocarbons and nitrogen oxides under the influence of sunlight. It can cause extensive crop damage.)

In October 1982, scientists found that much of the ozone layer in the upper atmosphere over Antarctica had completely disappeared. This was an unexpected and dramatic discovery, which has been of concern ever since because of the danger of ultraviolet radiation to people and to the environment. The diagram below shows the depletion of ozone over time. The greatest decrease in ozone has been in southern Australia and southern South America.

The ozone layer has been damaged by **chlorofluorocarbons**, or CFCs. These are very stable chemicals in the lower atmosphere. They have wide industry application and are easy to store and cheap to produce. They have mainly been used as coolants in refrigeration and airconditioning and as propellants in aerosol sprays.

CFCs can survive for up to 100 years in the atmosphere. When they are released they drift upwards, taking about eight years to reach the ozone in the stratosphere. Here they are exposed to high levels of ultraviolet radiation, which causes them to break down and to release chlorine. The chlorine reacts with the ozone and converts it to oxygen. Thus the amount of ozone is depleted. The chlorine itself does not change and is therefore available to destroy many more ozone molecules.

As a result of the depletion of the ozone layer, there has been international agreement to phase out the use of CFCs. In many cases, the CFCs in aerosols, refrigerators and airconditioners have been replaced with alternative propellants and coolants. Despite coordinated worldwide action, damage to the ozone layer continues faster than expected. The ozone layer is predicted to be at its most vulnerable in the next decade, and so far there has been no reduction in the size of the **ozone hole**.

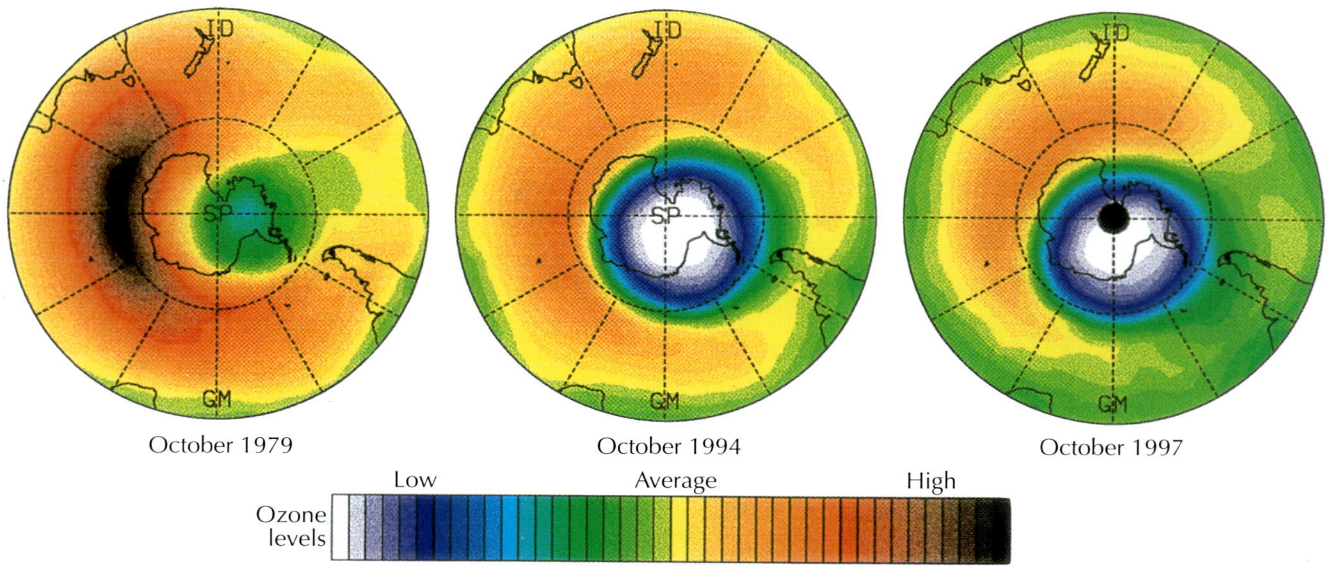

Increase in the size of the ozone hole over Antarctica — 1979, 1994 and 1997

Which of these products contain CFCs?

Ozone hole back as big as ever

Washington

The ozone 'hole' over the South Pole is back and it's as big as ever.

The United States' National Oceanic and Atmospheric Administration reported yesterday that satellite measurements show the area of thinned ozone covers nearly 22 million square kilometres, about the same as in 1995 and 1996.

The hole is actually an area of thinned ozone, where the gas is depleted by chemical reactions in air trapped over the South Pole during the Antarctic winter.

Ozone helps block damaging ultraviolet rays from the sun, and scientists have been concerned that, if it becomes depleted, there could be an increase in skin cancer and cataracts.

Certain chemicals believed to damage the ozone layer have been banned, including the chlorofluorocarbons widely used as aerosol propellants and in refrigerators and air conditioners.

The area of reduced ozone expands at this time of year, as sunlight returns to the Antarctic region.

The area covers most of Antarctica and, on 2 October, just touched the tip of South America. The region has a measure of 220 Dobson units of ozone or less, an amount scientists consider low.

Ozone can range from 250 units to more than 500 units over various parts of the world. One Dobson unit means that if all the ozone in the atmosphere directly overhead were squashed down to the surface level it would amount to a thickness of 0.01 millimetre. At that rate 220 units would be about as thick as two thin coins.

The hole, first observed in the 1980s, has reappeared each September and October when cold temperatures combine with the sun's rays to create the conditions for maximum ozone depletion.

Associated Press/AAP, November 1997.

Activities

Investigation: *Ozone depletion*

1. It is thought that people in southern Australia and southern South America will be more exposed to the effects of damaging ultraviolet radiation than people living elsewhere. Use evidence on these pages to explain why this might be the case.
2. Study the diagram showing the size of the ozone hole. Describe how the hole has changed over time. Which areas were more affected by ultraviolet radiation in 1997 than they were in 1979 and 1994?
3. Read the newspaper article on the right.
   (a) What does one Dobson unit measure?
   (b) Why did the ozone hole first appear over Antarctica?
   (c) Chemicals causing ozone depletion were banned in Australia in the early 1990s. Why is the ozone hole still as large as it was in 1995 and 1996?

Communication: *Drawing a flow diagram*

Carefully re-read the text about the effect that CFCs have on ozone. Using different coloured pencils to represent CFCs, ozone, chlorine and oxygen, draw a flow diagram that shows the processes which destroy and deplete the ozone layer. Provide a title and key for your diagram. You might like to display your completed flow diagram on the classroom wall.

Preparing a speech

Working with another student, imagine a United Nations meeting is being held to discuss the problem of ozone depletion. Write a speech that you will deliver to the UN assembly (the class), describing the action that needs to be taken to reduce the size of the ozone hole in the atmosphere. Describe how the strategies for developed countries, developing countries, local government and individuals will each need to be different. When you present your speech to the class, you may like to make use of the flow diagram you drew in the first part of the Communication activity.

ACID RAIN

Acid rain is produced when pollutants from industry combine with water vapour, oxygen and sunlight to produce dilute forms of sulfuric and nitric acids, which fall back to Earth as a form of **precipitation**. In some heavily polluted areas, large amounts of hydrogen chloride gas released into the atmosphere can form hydrochloric acid. The scale below shows how acid is measured. Acid rain has a **pH** value of five or less.

The pH scale

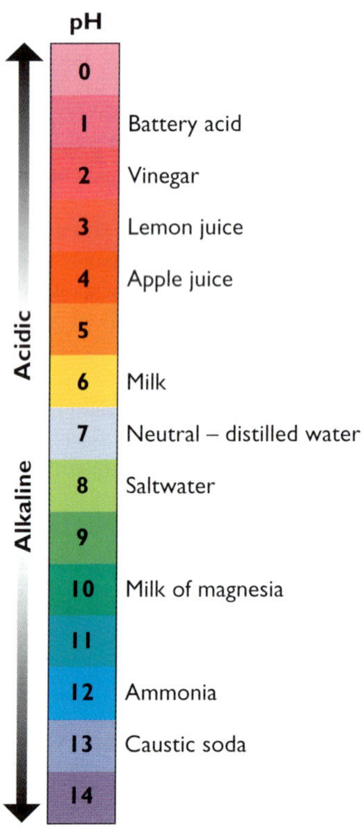

Measuring acidity

> The lower the number on the pH scale the higher the acidity; the higher the number, the lower the acidity. Healthy lakes and rivers should have a pH between 5.6 and 8.
>
> The pH scale goes from 0 to 14, but it is logarithmic. This means that a change of one unit indicates a tenfold increase or decrease in pH. A solution at pH 2, for example, is 10 times as acidic as one at pH 3 and 1000 times as acidic as pH 5.
>
> Acid rain has a pH value of 5 or less.

Acid rain can form naturally in areas where volcanic eruptions occur. The gases produced by the eruptions form acids that return to Earth in rain, snow and sleet. These natural amounts, though, are not significant in comparison with the acid rain produced as a result of pollution emissions from industrial areas. In attempting to reduce the concentration of pollutants at ground level, industries build tall smoke stacks that discharge pollution high into the atmosphere. Winds then transport the pollution away from the area where it is produced to areas far from the industrial site.

Data collected in Australia shows that the main contributors to SO_2 emissions vary between cities: in Adelaide, it is the sulfuric acid plants and cement works; in Brisbane, it is the burning of coal for power generation; in Perth, it is the petroleum refinery industry. Motor vehicles are the main sources of NO (nitrous oxide) emissions in all cities.

Some areas are more sensitive than others to the effects of acid rain. Alkaline soils, as found in areas such as the US Midwest and south-east England, neutralise the acids. In contrast, regions with thin soils, such as Scandinavia, Scotland and central Europe, have little protection and are badly affected by acid rain.

Forest destroyed by acid rain

One problem with acid rain is that the pollutants from which it is formed can be created in one country yet fall in another. The UK, for example, has large reserves of coal and has traditionally used this coal in power generation. Sulfur dioxide and nitrogen oxide emissions from the UK are causing acid rain to fall in Norway and Sweden. The pH level, or relative acidity, of many freshwater lakes in Scandinavia has been changed so much by acid rain that entire fish populations have been destroyed. Sulfur dioxide emissions and the subsequent formation of sulfuric acid in the air can also be responsible for destroying limestone and marble hundreds of kilometres from the source of the pollution.

Solutions to the acid rain problem include:

- adding lime to lakes and forest soils to neutralise the effects of acid rain
- reducing sulfur dioxide and nitrogen oxide emissions at the industrial source
- fitting cars with catalytic converters which reduce the emissions of nitrogen oxides and other pollutants.

The formation of acid rain

Adding lime to a lake to reduce acidity

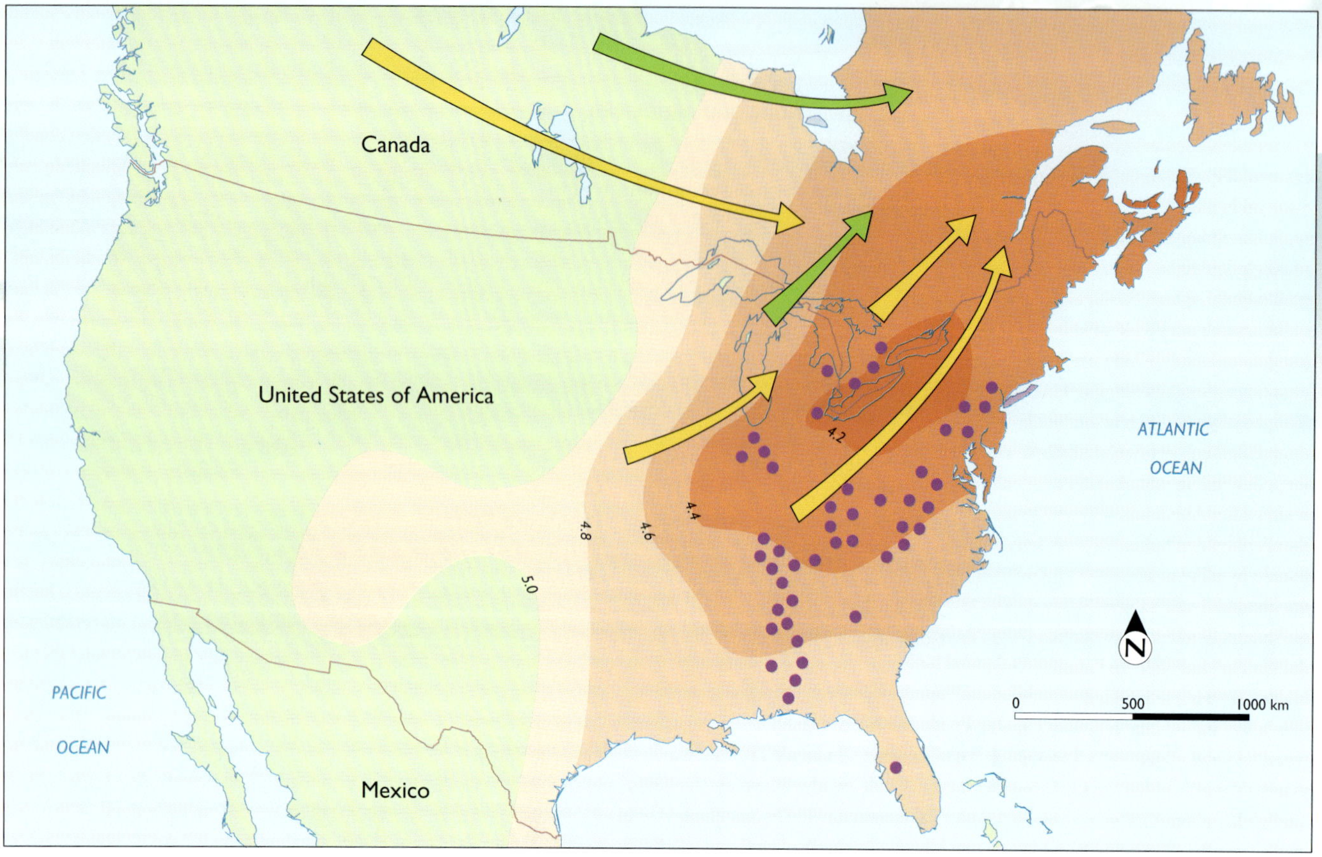

Acid rain in North America

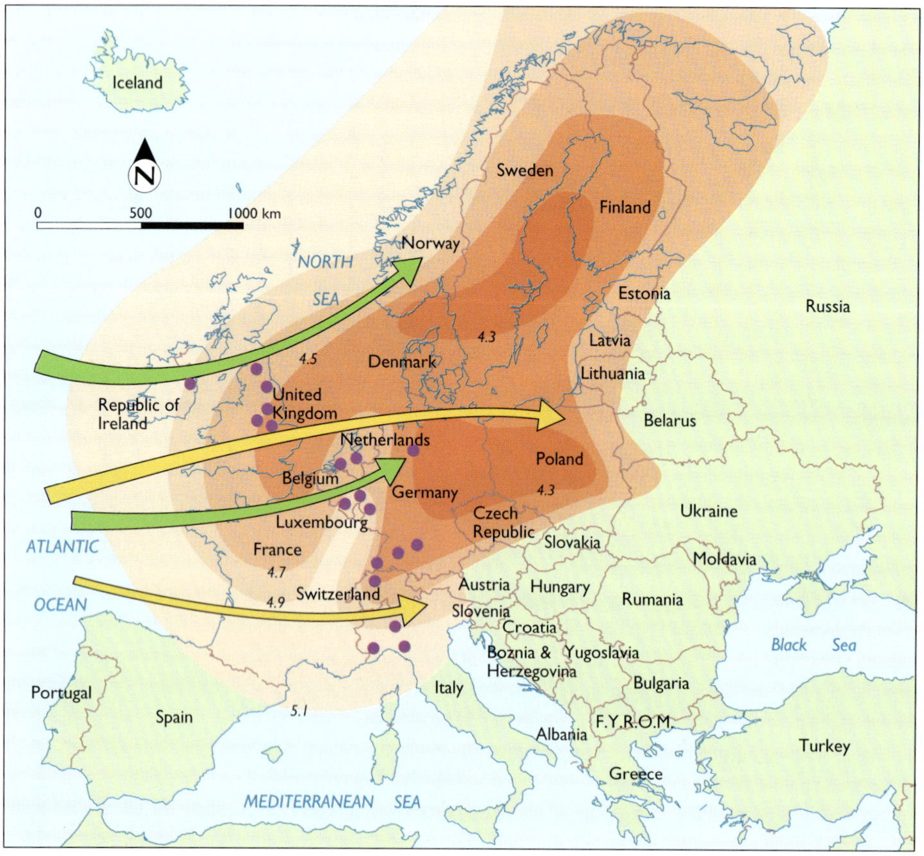

Acid rain in Europe

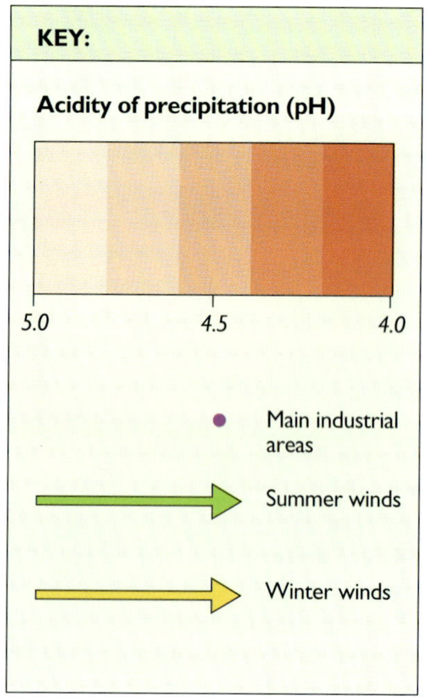

Activities

Check your understanding

Use the word list below to complete the following paragraph.

The lower the pH number, the __________ the __________. The __________ the pH number the lower the acidity. Healthy lakes and __________ have a pH ranging from 5.6 to __________. The pH scale ranges from 0 to __________. A change of one unit means an increase or __________ in pH by 10 times. Therefore a pH of 2 is __________ times as acidic as a pH of __________, and __________ times as acidic as a pH of 4.

Word list: decrease, higher, 10, 8, greater, 100, acidity, 14, rivers, 3.

Communication: *Using diagrams and maps*

1. Study the diagram showing the formation of acid rain on page 263 and explain the process in your own words.
2. Study the maps of North America and Europe opposite.
   (a) Describe the relationship between prevailing winds and acid rain deposition.
   (b) Why are some areas more sensitive to acid rain than others?

Investigation: *Conducting research*

1. Investigate the sources of acid rain pollution and the countries and regions most affected.
   (a) Use an atlas to describe the country or region that contains the main industrial areas.
   (b) In which direction are the summer and winter prevailing winds?
   (c) Which countries are most affected by acid rain in summer? Which countries are most affected in winter?
2. The countries producing pollution are sometimes different from those affected by acid rain. A solution to the problem therefore requires international cooperation. Imagine you are attending a meeting in Geneva at the headquarters of the United Nations. Six students will be chosen as representatives of each of the following countries: United Kingdom, Norway, Sweden, Canada and the USA. Each representative should prepare a presentation for the meeting regarding the acid rain problem. Include discussion of the following:
   - your government's view of the acid rain problem
   - action that could be taken to overcome or reduce the problem
   - difficulties that may be encountered when implementing your solution
   - any other action that might be relevant.

   Use the maps and diagrams from the Communication activity to support your stance. You may like to use overhead projections in the presentation to the class.
3. Work in groups of four to produce a 'futures line' about the acid rain problem. A futures line allows you to predict what might happen in the future, based on past and present events. Copy the diagram below onto a poster-sized sheet of paper. Make notes about what is occurring in the present. For the optimistic future, describe the changes and actions that will reduce acid rain and what will happen in each of the countries listed. For the pessimistic future, describe continuation or increases in the levels of acid rain. Display your completed posters on the classroom wall.

   Compare your futures line with the others on display. What similarities and differences do you observe?
4. 'Acid rain is trans-boundary pollution'. Write an extended response of 500 words, with diagrams, to explain this statement.

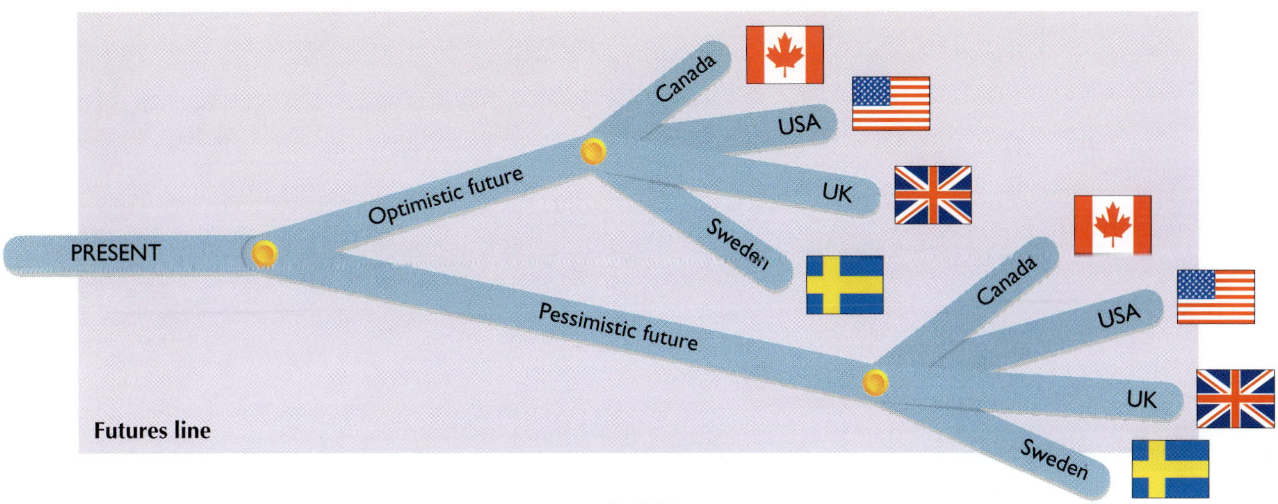

Futures line

FEELING THE HEAT

The world is now warming faster than at any time since the last Ice Age. Nine of the ten warmest years have occurred since 1980, confirming worldwide concern that the Earth's atmosphere is heating up. The increased concentration of carbon dioxide in the atmosphere from the burning of **fossil fuels** such as coal and oil is considered to be a major cause of global warming.

Over a number of decades, scientists have observed a steady increase in carbon dioxide levels in the atmosphere. We know from section 10.1 that carbon dioxide traps heat and warms the atmosphere, so the increase in carbon dioxide levels, according to many scientists, may be causing an enhanced greenhouse effect, also known as global warming. The illustration below shows this process in more detail.

There has also been an increase over the years in emissions of **methane gas**, which, like carbon dioxide, is a greenhouse gas. Increases in methane are therefore believed to also contribute to global warming. Most methane is produced by decomposition in rice paddies, swamps and in the intestines of grazing animals. Nevertheless, carbon dioxide is the gas that has increased the most over time, as we can see from the graph opposite. The table opposite shows the current and future production of greenhouse gases by countries and regions.

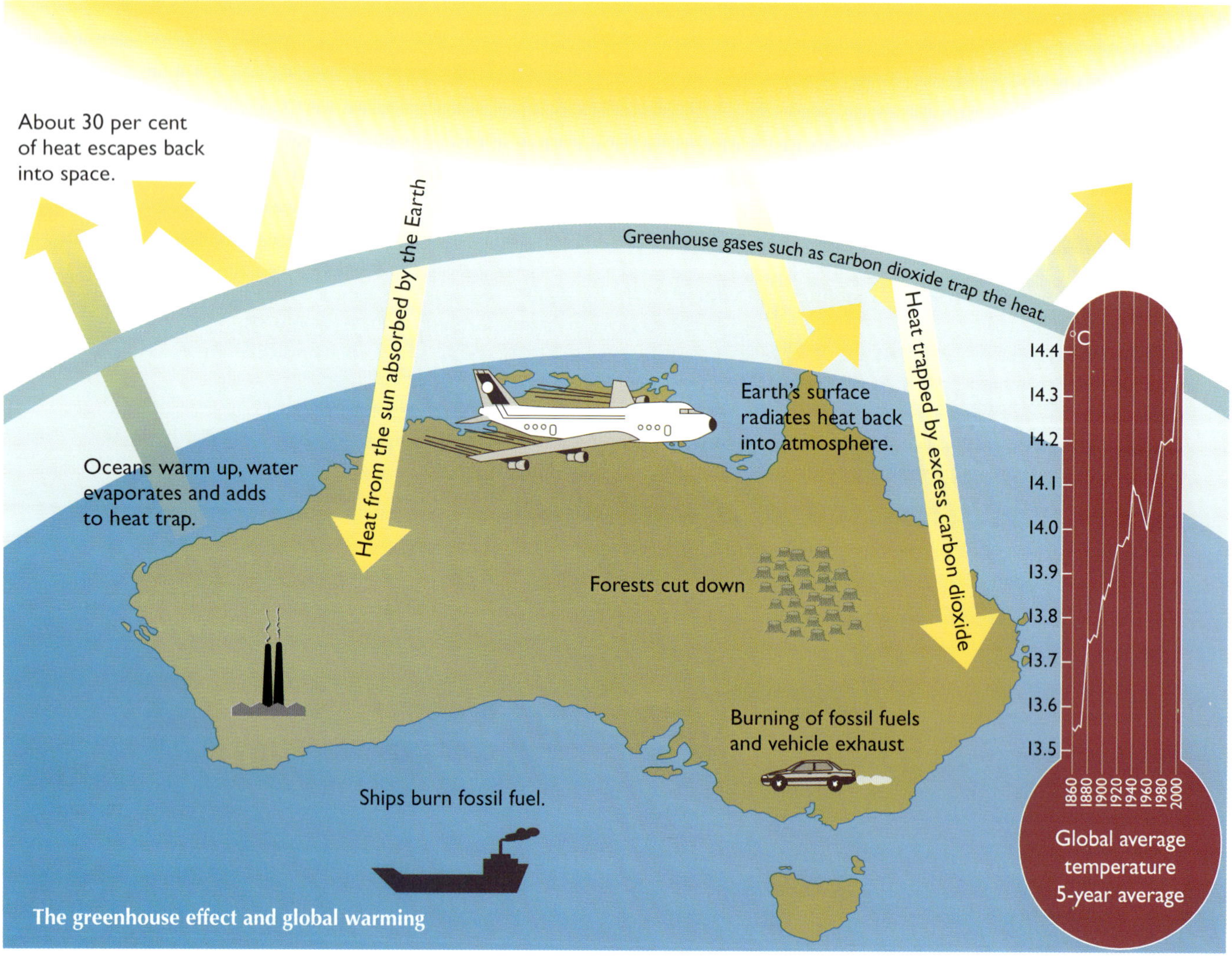

The greenhouse effect and global warming

World CO_2 production — 1995 and 2035 (predicted)

Country or region	1995 emissions (%)	Predicted 2035 emissions (%)
USA	22	15
Western Europe	17	12
Eastern Europe	27	19
Asia	7	4
China	11	17
Other Asia	6	14
Middle East	3	5
Africa	3	8
Latin America	4	6

It is estimated that 38 billion tonnes of greenhouse gas emissions are released annually. Australia, which produces 1.4 per cent of this amount, is about the fifteenth largest emitter. Importantly, though, we produced the greatest levels of greenhouse gases per capita. In Australia, most of these gases are produced as a result of energy production, when coal, gas and oil are burnt. Land clearing is the second largest contributor to greenhouse gases. When forests, woodland and scrub are cleared, carbon stored in the trees and soil is released as carbon dioxide into the atmosphere. The pie graph on the right shows a summary of the sources of greenhouse gases.

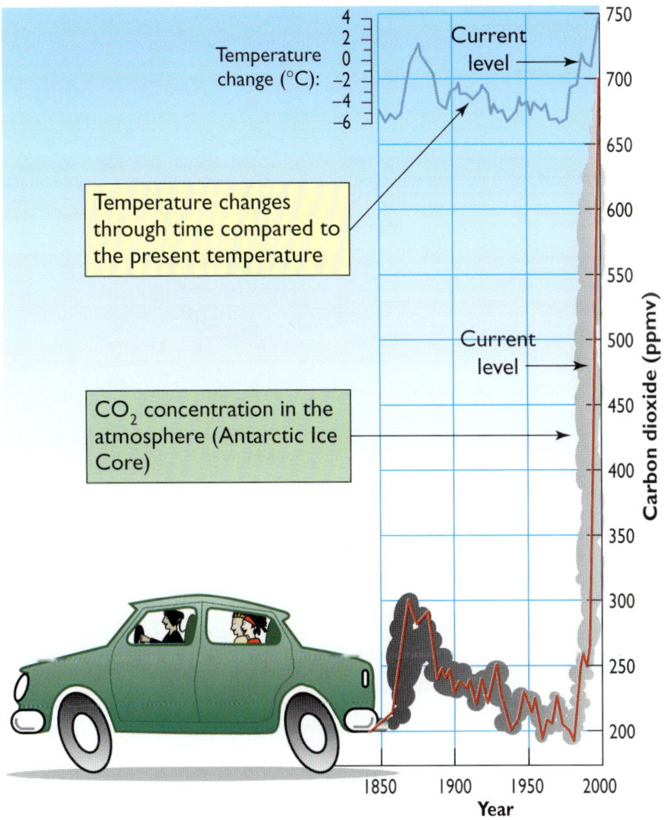

Increase in carbon dioxide over time

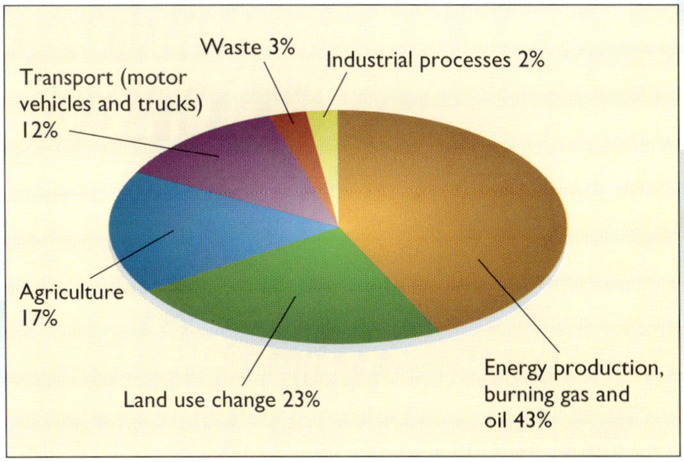

Major sources of Australia's greenhouse gas emissions, 1996

Activities

Investigation: *Interpreting graphs*

1. Study the diagram opposite showing the greenhouse effect.
   (a) Describe the greenhouse effect in your own words.
   (b) How has the average global temperature changed over time?
2. Study the graph on the left showing the changes in carbon dioxide levels over time.
   (a) Describe the changes in carbon dioxide levels.
   (b) What might have caused the increase in carbon dioxide 130 to 140 years ago?
   (c) What has caused such large increases in the last 20 years?
   (d) Compare the increase in carbon dioxide with the change in temperature over time. Explain the correlation between these factors.
3. Study the pie graph above.
   (a) Which activities account for the greatest amount of greenhouse gas emissions in Australia?
   (b) Draw a table with six columns. List the six main emission sources at the top of each column. Under each source, list the actions government, industry and individuals can take to reduce the amount of greenhouse gases produced.

Communication: *Drawing graphs*

Use the data in the table (top left) to draw two pie graphs showing world CO_2 emissions in 1995 and emissions predicted for 2035. Provide an appropriate title and legend for your graphs. Study your completed graphs and answer the following questions.

1. Which regions or countries are predicted to reduce or increase their greenhouse gas emissions?
2. Outline the social and economic reasons that might exist for some countries reducing greenhouse gas emissions while others increase them.

IMPACTS OF GLOBAL WARMING

Scientists use models to predict the degree of global warming. Although most scientists agree that greenhouse gases are increasing, there is debate about the future impact of this increase. All predictions are based on computer modelling, and scientists do not all agree on whether any long-term global warming has yet occurred and, if it has, what the impacts of it will be. The table on page 270 shows some changes that have been observed and are thought to be a result of global warming.

THE EFFECTS ON CROPS AND SOILS

If the Earth is warming up, then crop growing around the world is likely to be affected. Plants are very sensitive to changes in temperature and levels of rainfall. Some areas will experience drier weather, other areas will be wetter, which will affect where crops can be grown. The map below provides a global picture of what might occur.

With global warming, agricultural production could be reduced because of shortened growing seasons and water loss. If the growing season became short enough, some crops might fail altogether and not be able to be grown in the future. The impact of land degradation would be prominent in areas where increased rainfall occurred. Soil loss in those areas would affect both soil fertility and its ability to store water during the drier parts of the year.

RISING WATERS AROUND THE WORLD

The global average sea level has increased by 10 to 25 centimetres over the last 100 years. Sea levels are expected to rise by 15 to 95 centimetres

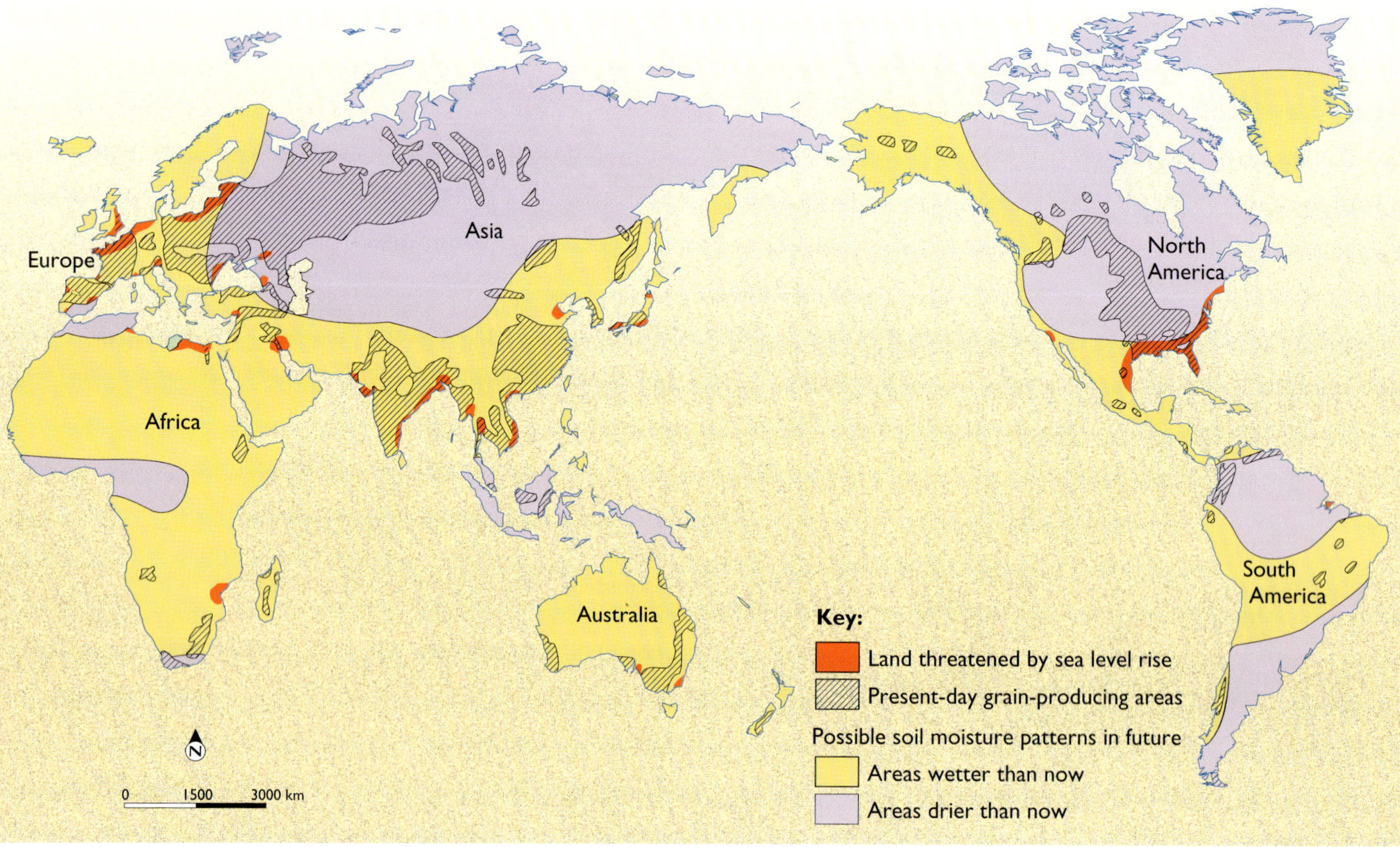

Distribution of potential changes thought to be caused by global warming

Key:

Present area of the corn belt

Possible corn belt area if there is a 3°C temperature increase and 8 cm precipitation increase:

Dryland corn

Irrigated corn

N

0 500 1000 km

Predicted effect of climate change on the North American corn belt

by 2100, with a best estimate of 50 centimetres. These rising sea levels are thought to be caused by partial melting of mountain glaciers, ice caps and the expansion of sea water as it heats. One major concern about this is the effect on small island states and low-lying coastal regions. The Maldives, for example, are made up of over 1100 islands, most of which are less than three metres high. On these islands, most people live less than two metres above the sea level. Other coral atolls facing a similar problem are the Cocos Islands, Tuvalu, Kiribati, the Marshall Islands and the Line Islands. If sea levels continue to rise, then according to some predictions around 300 small Pacific islands may disappear. Many are already experiencing storm damage from high seas and contamination of fresh water by salt.

The Nile delta in northern Africa is a densely populated area that is heavily cultivated. This area is also sinking because the Aswan Dam traps much of the sediment that would normally be transported to the floodplain and deposited there. Rising sea levels would have a great impact on agricultural land in this region and on the lives of its inhabitants.

Bangladesh is a country that occupies the world's largest river delta the mouths of the Ganges and Brahmaputra rivers. One half of the country is less than 4.5 metres above sea level. Bangladesh already faces severe problems from flooding and some of the land is sinking due to the thousands of wells being dug to obtain freshwater supplies. Bangladesh's flooding problems could be made even worse by global warming.

THE EFFECT ON AUSTRALIA

There are also predictions of local impacts in Australia as a result of global warming. Some of these are listed in the following table.

POSSIBLE IMPACT OF GLOBAL WARMING ON AUSTRALIA

- Sea water contaminating freshwater aquifers on the central Queensland coast
- Beach erosion in Port Phillip Bay, the Gippsland Lakes and to the west of Cape Otway in Victoria
- Storms and flooding on the New South Wales coast
- More intense cyclones in northern Australia
- Tropical cyclones further south
- Stronger monsoon westerlies in northern Australia
- Global average sea level rise of 3 to 10 centimetres per decade
- Weaker trade winds
- Increased damage to agricultural land due to floods and erosion
- The potential for increased drought in wheat and barley areas
- Temperatures up by 1 to 2°C in northern coastal areas; 1 to 3°C in southern coastal areas; 2 to 4°C inland
- An increase in crop diseases such as mildew on grapevines and rust on wheat
- Higher yields for some crops due to more carbon dioxide, others lower
- Some tropical livestock diseases decrease while others increase
- Apricot, peach, nectarine, cherry and plum crops in Forbes, Griffith and Narrandera in New South Wales may not flower or set fruit as well if normal winter chilling decreases.
- Increased number of cattle deaths as the cattle tick, currently contained at the New South Wales border, spreads south
- Increased distribution of diseases such as Murray Valley encephalitis and Ross River fever
- The possibility of malaria in the Northern Territory

Apparent impact of global warming

Location	Observed biological and physical changes
Antarctic Peninsula	Antarctic ice sheets are melting. Two thirds of the Wordie Ice Sheet (2500 km^2) has disappeared.
Antarctic Peninsula	Adelie penguin numbers are decreasing and krill is disappearing.
Barrow, Alaska, USA	Ancestral Inuit ice cellars in permafrost areas are melting.
Belize	In 1995, warm waters bleach (cause colour loss to) the world's largest reef system off the Belize coast.
Britain	Hot, dry summers result in forest fires in southern England in 1997.
Costa Rica	There has been local extinction of 40 per cent of all frog and toad species.
California, USA	Eighty per cent of the zooplankton in the Pacific Ocean west of California has disappeared. This has also caused the collapse of the local anchovy fishery.
Chesapeake Bay, USA	Wildlife habitat is disappearing due to rising sea levels.
European Alps	Half the volume of alpine glaciers has been lost in 140 years.
Galapagos Islands	These islands have experienced extremes of weather which have caused fires and bleaching of the coral reefs.
Greece	Decreased river flows in the Mediterranean region have been caused by low rainfall and high evaporation rates.
Indian Ocean	Warming has been detected in the Indian Ocean to a depth of 800 metres below sea level.
Japan	Warmer winter waters have melted ice flows near the island of Hokkaido. This has resulted in the disappearance of Steller's sea eagles from the region.
Kenai Peninsula, Alaska, USA	Plague of spruce bark beetle killed 20 million trees.
Kenya	The volume of ice on Mount Kenya has decreased by 40 per cent since 1963.
Mexico	Colonies of a butterfly species (Edith's Checkerspot butterfly) have moved north to Canada and are disappearing from Mexico and southern California
Minnesota, USA	Over 30 years, soils at a research plot have warmed by 1.1° to a depth of 13 metres.
North America	Rainfall downpours have been 25 per cent more severe during this century, causing more floods.
Northeastern USA	The frost-free season begins around 11 days earlier than it did in the 1950s.
North Atlantic	Oil rigs have had to be redesigned as wave heights in intense storms have increased by 50 per cent in the last 30 years.
Peru	Since the early 1980s glaciers in the Peruvian Andes have been melting seven times faster than in previous decades.
Siberia	Thawing permafrost is causing ground collapse and creating sinkholes affecting trees and buildings.
Spain	An estimated 400 km^2 of wetlands has been lost due to long droughts and pressure on water resources by people.
Svalbard, Norway	Flowering plants are colonising and spreading in areas where they have never before existed.
Wadden Sea, Germany	Red toxic algae have returned to this sea after their disappearance 300 years ago.
Western Samoa	This country suffered three violent cyclones in four years during the late 1980s. Prior to this it had experienced only one violent cyclone in 100 years.
Yellowstone National Park, USA	There is great risk of summer fires in the northern summer as severe drought continues.

Activities

Investigation: *The impact of global warming*

1. Study the map on page 268 showing the potential changes caused by global warming.
   (a) Which areas are more likely to be threatened by sea level rises?
   (b) What might happen to the people living in these areas if they become flooded?
   (c) Would responses be different in developed and developing countries?
   (d) Describe the location of areas that would be wetter or drier than now. How would this affect:
   - people?
   - economies?
   - the environment?
   - governments?

   Would such an impact be felt more in Australia or the UK? Explain.
2. Why are coral atolls at risk from the effects of global warming?
3. Study the map showing predicted changes to the North American corn belt and the cartoon below.
   (a) Describe the predicted change in distribution of corn-growing areas in the United States.
   (b) How might this change affect the agricultural economy?
   (c) Will more or less irrigation be needed? Describe possible effects on the environment.
   (d) Imagine you are a corn grower in the south-west of the current corn belt area. What action would you take if you were forewarned of the possible changes?
   (e) Will this impact be gradual or sudden? How will people know what is occurring?
4. Search in newspapers, scientific journals and on the Internet for research that says we are not experiencing global warming. Summarise the arguments against global warming.

Communication: *Mapping global warming*

1. You will need a sheet of poster paper, a blank outline map of the world and an atlas to complete this activity. If possible, enlarge the map to A3 size.
   (a) Study the table opposite showing the apparent impact of global warming. Classify each observed change as physical (changes to the climate or landscape) or biological (changes to plants or animals). Choose two colours to represent each classification.
   (b) Use the information in the table to map the changes. Provide a legend and title for your map.
   (c) Attach your map to the centre of the poster paper. Use the margins of the poster to make annotations (brief notes) to describe the change at each location. Use the information in the table to do this.
   (d) Study your completed poster.
   - Which regions of the world have shown the greatest changes?
   - Do you think the physical or biological factors will have the greatest effect on people and the environment? Justify your choice.

   (e) Read the environmental news reported in your newspaper and add information to your map over time.
2. You will need a blank outline map of Australia and an atlas to complete this activity.
   (a) Use the instructions in Communication question 1 to create a map showing the predicted impacts of global warming in Australia. Make sure your annotations are clear. Provide an appropriate title and legend for your map.
   (b) Study your completed map and answer the following questions.
   - Which areas might be most affected by global warming?
   - What will be the main effects in these areas?
   - What will be the effect on agriculture?
   - Describe the predicted changes in your region.

Drawing a cartoon

The cartoon below depicts one possible consequence of global warming. Draw your own cartoon about global warming.

10.8

HALT THE WARMING!

WHAT ARE THE ALTERNATIVES?

There are a number of strategies that can be adopted to reduce the production of greenhouse gases. Some of these include:

- developing **renewable** and sustainable **energy** sources such as solar and wind power and harvesting **biofuel**
- electricity companies giving customers the choice of having their energy supplied from renewable sources
- supporting the production of appliances, equipment and buildings that are energy efficient
- governments setting fuel efficiency standards for all new motor vehicles
- improving urban public transport systems to attract people away from using cars
- controlling land clearing and encouraging the planting of native vegetation.

In Australia, some electricity is produced from renewable sources. These include hydro-electricity, biomass-landfill plants, wind and solar-generated power. Consumers in some States can opt to buy their electricity from these sources.

At the Sydney Olympic village in Homebush, Sydney, between 500 and 665 homes will be built using rooftop solar voltaic power plants. Along with passive solar design, the houses will make use of gas-boosted solar water heating, gas cooking appliances and energy efficient lighting. Greenhouse gas emissions from each house will be reduced by 3990 tonnes per year and will be 75 per cent lower than from typical homes.

A wind farm in the USA

Sydney Olympic village, Homebush

A solar power station in California

Solar-powered vehicle

ACTION BY GOVERNMENTS

Various countries and governments have adopted different measures to deal with greenhouse gas emissions. Emission standards specify a limit to the discharge of atmospheric pollutants so that we can breathe cleaner air. The nature of the global warming problem, though, requires international environmental treaties.

In December 1997 representatives of many countries met in Kyoto, Japan, to discuss ways to reduce the production of greenhouse gases. The European Union proposed that all developed countries reduce gas emissions to 15 per cent below 1990 levels by the year 2010. There were many reactions to this proposal. The United States (the highest greenhouse gas polluter in the world, producing 24 per cent of world emissions) wanted just to stabilise emissions by 2012. In contrast, the South Pacific islands wanted global emissions to be reduced to 20 per cent below 1990 levels by 2005, because of their fear of rising sea levels.

The Australian Government began its negotiation with an offer to cut emissions growth between 1990 and 2010 from 28 per cent to 18 per cent. Any further reduction, it argued, would damage the economy, which is heavily dependent on fossil fuels. The final outcome and its implications are summarised in the article on page 274.

A glimmer of green from Kyoto

Binding greenhouse targets *But the Kyoto protocol is only the beginning of a sustainable global economy*

What is radical in one era becomes accepted in another. At least the leaders of the nations of the world now accept that global warming is real, and that it is beginning to affect humanity in dangerous ways. But reaching agreement on how it is to be solved and who should bear most responsibility for solving it has been as hard as it was to admit there was a problem in the first place. For 11 days, representatives of 160 countries made speeches in public and squabbled behind closed doors, trying to come to an agreement on binding targets to cut greenhouse gas emissions.

The Kyoto climate treaty commits developed countries to cut six greenhouse gases by an average 5.2 per cent by 2012, using 1990 levels as a baseline. It is a far cry from the European Union's ambitious target for a 15 per cent reduction, and even further from the 60 per cent reduction during the next century that many scientists believe is necessary to seriously slow global warming. The agreement is not perfect. Developing countries such as China, which are becoming major polluters, are exempt. While in one way this is fair — after all, rich countries caused the problem — this should be a temporary exemption. As well, getting the treaty ratified by every country may be even more difficult than reaching consensus at the conference. One American senator has already vowed the treaty will be 'killed' by the Republican-controlled US Congress. And while the targets are supposed to be binding, the conference did not decide on what, if any, penalties should be imposed for breaches.

Even so, the achievement in getting all the countries of the world to agree on binding targets for the first time should not be underestimated. The Australian Government, which as recently as last July was still disputing the scientific evidence on the dangers of global warming, found itself isolated among developed countries for much of the conference and accorded pariah status by environmental groups. The Prime Minister, Mr John Howard, has hailed the treaty, which allows Australia to increase its emissions by 8 per cent, as 'a splendid result'. Whether it is a splendid result for the environment is a matter of dispute. However, it is a considerable amelioration of Australia's starting position, which, according to the Prime Minister, was that our emissions would need to be increased by 18 per cent. Mr Howard had long argued for 'differentiation' in the targets allocated to countries, and has achieved a significant victory in having this argument eventually accepted by the conference. Another considerable victory for Australia was to have land clearing, which releases carbon into the atmosphere, accepted in its 1990 baseline figure — even if this seems like arguing that the more polluting we have been in the past, the fewer sacrifices we will need to make to achieve the required reduction.

It is true that Australia would have been put at a disadvantage among other developed countries because of our dependency on fossil fuels. However, our unwillingness to compromise from the outset did little credit to our international reputation and gave no comfort to the majority of Australians who have said in surveys that protection of the environment is more important than the economy.

Much of the resistance to realistic reduction targets, from Australia and other countries, comes from a fear of change. But, as the US President, Mr Bill Clinton, said, 'Every time we tried to improve the American environment in the past 25 or 30 years, somehow it was predicted that it would wreck the economy.' Yet, as a result of America's attempts to clean up its industries, it has cleaner air and water, and the lowest unemployment rate in 24 years. Worldwide, governments are beginning to discover that efforts to create a cleaner atmosphere can lead to new industries and create jobs.

There is reason to hope that the Kyoto protocol is the beginning of a long process towards a more environmentally sustainable global economy. It appeared at times during the conference that Australia was not going to be part of that agreement. Now that Australia has been treated so generously by the world community, we should strive to achieve, or better, the 8 per cent increase in emissions that we have accepted. In any case, the fact that European nations and Japan, the major importers of our coal, have accepted 8 per cent and 6 per cent cuts respectively, means our dependency on fossil-fuel industries will have to be reconsidered. We will need to foster other industries. But ordinary Australians will also have to be more mindful of the way we live and do our part to share the burden.

Age, 13 December 1997.

Each nation's commitment to emission targets

The Kyoto protocol covers emissions of six greenhouse gases. Carbon dioxide, nitrous oxide and methane levels are based on 1990 levels, and hydrofluorocarbon gases, perfluorocarbons and sulfur hexafluoride are based on 1995 levels. There should be an overall reduction in greenhouse gases by 2008–2012.

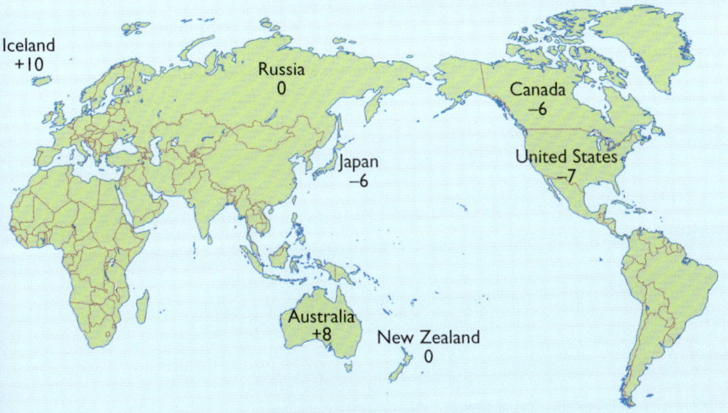

Percentage change from 1990 level

European Union countries	–8	Bulgaria	–8	Monaco	–8
Norway	+1	Czech Republic	–8	Rumania	–8
Ukraine	0	Estonia	–8	Slovakia	–8
Croatia	–5	Latvia	–8	Slovenia	–8
Poland	–6	Liechtenstein	–8	Switzerland	–8
Hungary	–6	Lithuania	–8		

World emission targets, Kyoto 1997

WHAT CAN BE DONE BY GOVERNMENTS?

- Enforce laws on CFCs.
- Improve public transport so it is efficient, safe and cheap.
- Encourage transport of goods by train which is more energy efficient than road trucks.
- Protect forests by logging very selectively.
- Initiate massive tree-planting programs in forests, farms and parks.
- Provide money and incentives for research into renewable energy technologies.
- Support industries that produce environmentally safe products.
- Encourage people to use less energy.
- Provide monetary incentives for all households to install solar heaters.
- Ban the import of rainforest timbers from other countries.
- Prevent the export of Australian rainforest timber.
- Use some petrol taxes to subsidise efforts to improve public transport.
- Use the 'polluter pays' principle, whereby people pay for the pollution and waste they produce.

Activities

Investigation: *Looking for alternatives*

1. What is renewable energy?
2. Study the photographs in this section. Describe how the landscape may change in the future if more energy supply is from renewable sources rather than non-renewable sources. You may like to draw your impressions of what a future landscape may look like.
3. What strategies have been adopted to reduce greenhouse emissions from the Sydney Olympic Village at Homebush?
4. An example of the polluter pays principle is where people are charged a garbage disposal rate according to the weight of their rubbish. List two other ways such a system could be applied.
5. Study the article opposite about the Kyoto conference and the map of emission targets.
   (a) Which countries make up the European Union? What target did this group of countries want to reach?
   (b) What reasons are given for exempting developing countries from signing the treaty? Describe the future impact this might have on global warming.
   (c) By reducing land clearing, Australia is able to gain greenhouse gas credits without necessarily reducing greenhouse gas emissions. Explain the impact of allowing Australia to include land clearing in its 1990 baseline figure. How does Australia benefit from this?
   (d) Describe the outcome for emission targets shown in the map. Why was Australia allowed to increase emissions so much?
6. Conduct some research into alternative energies and how they operate. Choose from solar, geothermal, wind, biofuel and wave power. Use diagrams and notes to explain how energy is produced and how expensive the power is to buy.
7. Working in groups of four, imagine that the Kyoto conference had a different outcome. This may have been one of the following:
   - All countries agree to stringent reductions in greenhouse gas emissions; or
   - No agreement is reached about emission targets.

   Now draw a diagram that shows the consequences of each of these possible outcomes. Consider changes in employment, atmosphere, research and development, environment, and decline and growth of different industries.

Communication: *Design a house*

Design an energy smart home. Think about energy efficient technology and practices such as insulation, house orientation, efficient water and space heating, efficient lighting and appliances. Draw a diagram of your house and list the appliances you would use.

10.9 Meeting the outcomes

EXPLAIN THE PROCESSES AND INTERACTIONS BETWEEN PEOPLE AND MAJOR NATURAL SYSTEMS.

Analyse the impact of human activities on natural systems.

1. How do pollutants become trapped in the basin?
2. Why does polluted air flow inland in the early afternoon?
3. How does the cool morning air become polluted?

SAMPLE STUDY

Sydney's smog problem

The air flows between the Sydney Basin, the Hunter Valley and the Illawarra region are all interconnected. Pollutants produced in one area can be carried by air flows to other areas. On some days, pollutants from smokestacks at Newcastle and from power stations in the Hunter Valley flow south to Sydney and then down the south coast. Air quality also varies throughout the year. Brown haze is more common in winter and photochemical smog occurs more often in summer.

The topography of the Sydney region consists of a large basin, bounded by steep, sandstone ridges to the north, south and west and the ocean to the east. During calm nights, cold air flows into the basin from surrounding ridges and areas to the south. In the early morning hours, this cold air drains towards the sea following the river valleys. As the sun warms the air above, the cooler air is trapped underneath forming a temperature inversion. Under normal atmospheric conditions warm air rises. As it rises it takes the pollution with it and fresh cool air moves in to replace it. A temperature inversion means the air near the ground cannot rise because it is cooler than the air above it. Air pollutants are trapped in the layer near the ground and Sydneysiders wake to see a dirty brown or whitish haze in the sky.

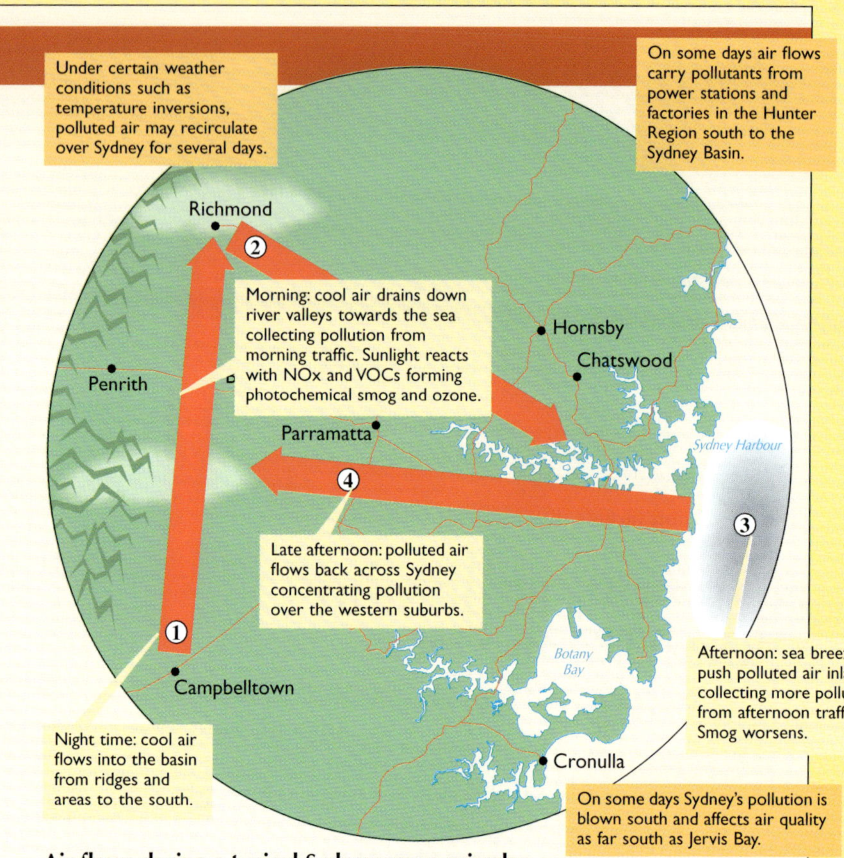

Air flows during a typical Sydney smog episode

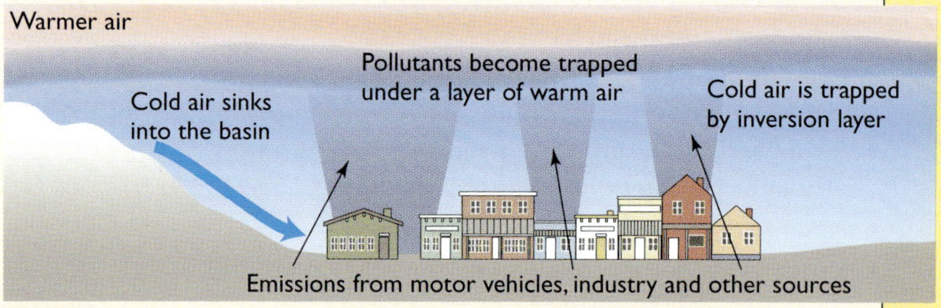

Temperature inversions can contribute to Sydney's air pollution.

PREDICT THE EFFECTS OF RESOURCE DEVELOPMENT AND USE ON A SELECTED NATURAL AND HUMAN ENVIRONMENT.

Describe the likely impact of resource development and use on a natural environment.

Examine the graph of Australian and global mean temperatures since 1910.

(a) Describe the trends in global and Australian temperatures from 1910 to 1997.
(b) State the years when Australia's temperature was more than 0.5°C above or below the average temperature.
(c) What interesting trends can be noted from 1980–1997?
(d) Suggest reasons to explain the trend in global and Australian temperatures from 1980 to 1997.

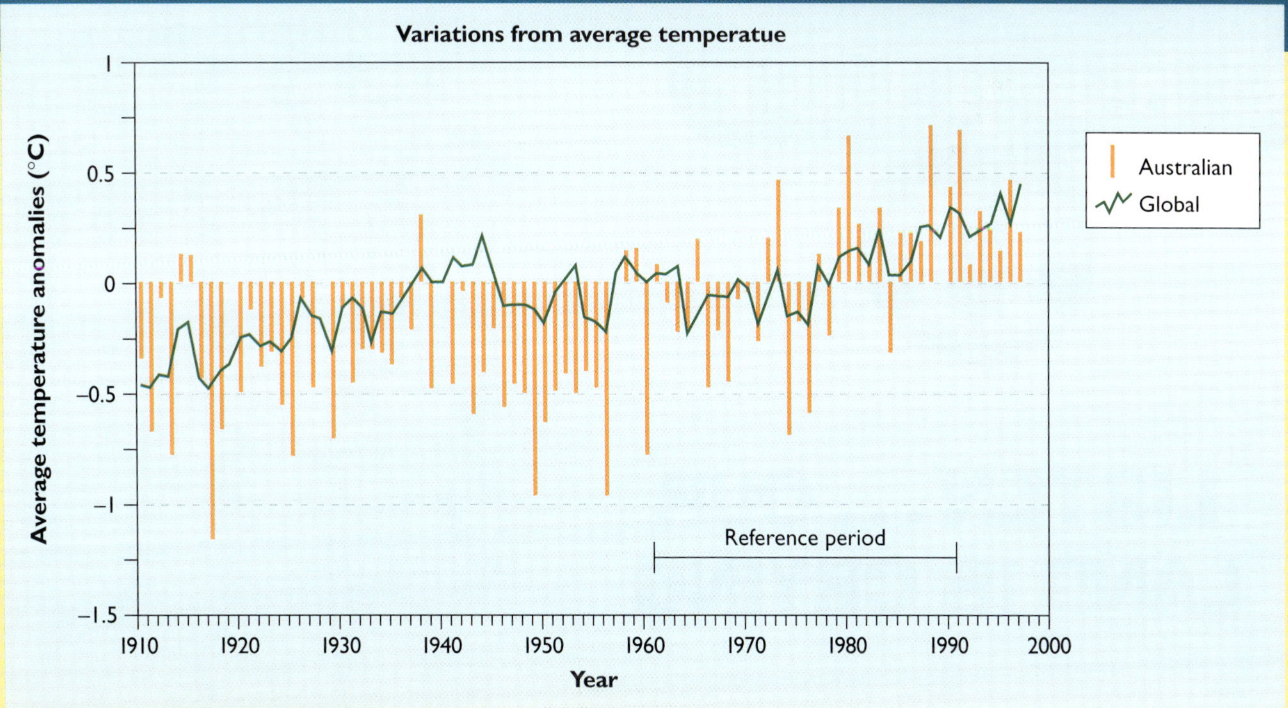

DEVELOP A COMPREHENSIVE STRATEGY TO RESOLVE AN ISSUE RELATED TO THE USE AND MANAGEMENT OF AN ENVIRONMENT.

Evaluate the factors contributing to the development of an issue relating to the use and management of an environment.

Refer to the graphs of carbon emissions below.

(a) How many million tons of carbon were emitted per person by Australia in 1996?

(b) How does this output compare to other countries?

(c) Calculate the increase in total carbon emissions from 1950 to 1996.

(d) Which economic region burned the most fossil fuel in 1950?

(e) What was the trend for fossil fuel useage in developing countries between 1950 and 1006?

(f) What environmental impact does the burning of fossil fuels have?

Identify strategies formulated to address the issue.

1. List three alternative power resources that would help reduce our reliance on fossil fuel. (10.8)

2. Which groups might be opposed to a reduction in the use of fossil fuels? (10.8)

3. What proposal did the European Union put to the Kyoto climate conference in 1997? (10.8)

(a) How did Australia respond to this proposal?

(b) How does Australia compare to other countries of the world on this issue? (10.8)

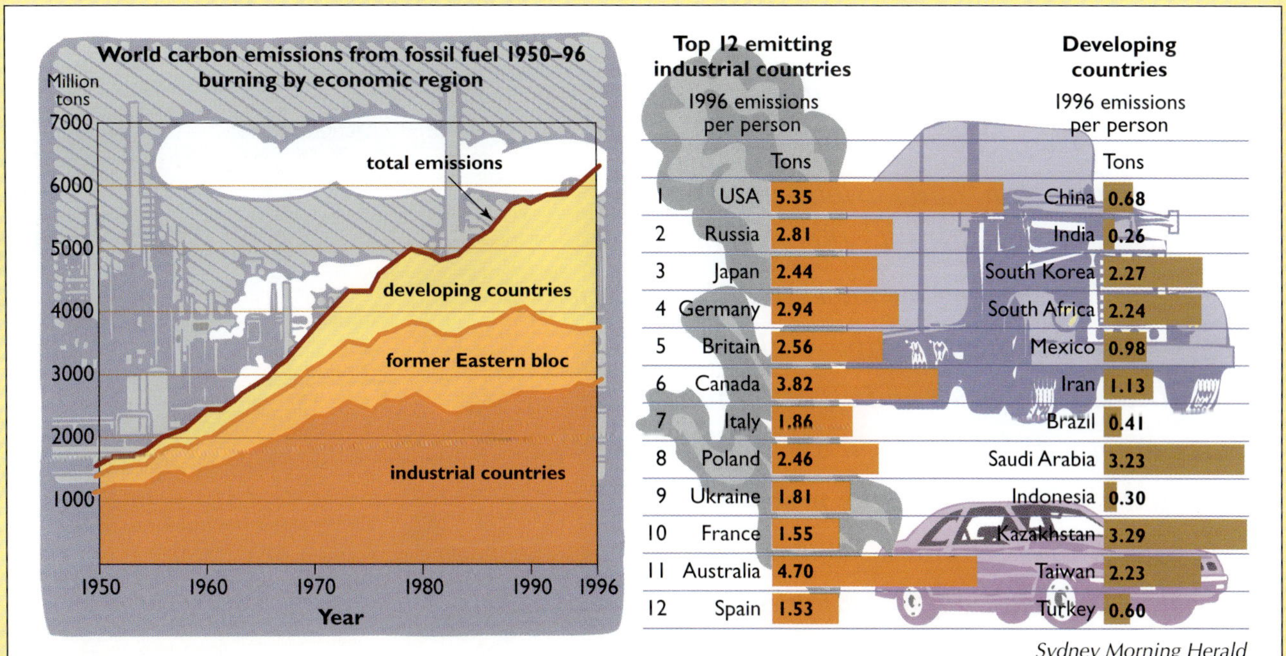

Sydney Morning Herald

Chapter

11

LISTEN . . . OUR LAND IS CRYING

INTRODUCTION

Everyone on Earth relies on the land. We live on it, we work and play on it and we grow our food on it. In fact, it is the ***topsoil*** *on which we rely and this topsoil is spread very thinly over the Earth's surface. Some soils are naturally fertile, some need chemicals added to them to become fertile and some are infertile.*

Across the globe, humans use the soil in numerous ways and they have not always taken good care of it. The land has suffered degradation — its ability to be productive has been diminished. There are many different types of ***land degradation****, and various causes of and solutions to this problem. In this chapter, you will learn that the way we have used the land in the past has been incompatible with the land's capabilities. The causes and effects of land degradation will be discussed and you will investigate how to prevent the problem from occurring in the first place. The responsibility of improving the health of our land lies with everyone in the community.*

This grazing land in New South Wales is suffering from severe gully erosion caused by excess water discharge from a nearby mine.

GLOSSARY

capillary zone: the zone of soil above a watertable through which water moves upwards towards drier soil
carrying capacity: the absolute maximum number of animals an area of land can support
contour ploughing: ploughing the land in a direction consistent with the lie or shape of the land
dryland salting: occurs in all areas of salting where irrigation is not present
EC: electrical conductivity, a measurement of salinity based on the capacity of a solution to pass an electric current
erosion: wearing away of the soil by wind or water
extensive farming: a system of farming which involves the use or cultivation of a large area of land with a minimum of labour
ground water: water combined in and saturating the subsoil
intensive farming: a system of farming which involves using the land as effectively as possible. Usually, it involves smaller farms and the application of labour, fertilisers, etc.
irrigation: the addition of water to crops or pasture in order to promote growth. Water may be added by way of channels, sprays or drip systems.
irrigation salting: salting which occurs in areas under irrigation
Landcare: the name given to the movement charged with improving and maintaining the quality of Australia's land resources
land degradation: the loss in quality of land
low tillage: ploughing or harvesting with minimal damage to the soil surface
salinity: the saltiness of a solution or substance
soil salting: soil degraded by the presence of salt, rendering it useless for agriculture
sustainable farming: methods of farming which ensure the economic and ecological long-term viability of the farm
topsoil: the surface layer of soil
water table: the upper level of the ground water
whole-farm planning: a strategy which takes into account all of the variables and constraints on a farm to ensure that the farm is sustainable

LEARNING *outcomes*

- Describe how farming has impacted on soils in Australia.
- Describe the location and distribution of degraded land in Australia.
- Analyse the impact of human activities on farmland.
- Identify strategies to manage degraded land.

A RESOURCE DEGRADED

Land is a resource; it is something we all use in one way or another, as you can see from the photographs below. In your local area, you can see land being used in many ways. Some land may be used for housing, some will be taken up by parks, some for factories, office blocks or shopping centres, some even used for farming. The value of land varies according to many factors. A housing block of land might be valuable because it is located near a big city. Land set aside for a factory might be valuable because it is located near a freeway. An area set aside as a national park is valuable for environmental, rather than economic, reasons. Often, the value of farming land is stated in terms of how productive the land can be; that is, how large a crop can be harvested or how many cows can be grazed on the piece of land.

One very productive farming area in Australia is the Murray–Darling region which spans Queensland, New South Wales, Victoria and South Australia. Many people in Australia rely on the farming of this land resource. It provides one-third of Australia's total rural production, including one-quarter of the country's cattle and dairy farms and one-half of the sheep, lambs and croplands in Australia.

However, much of the value of the land in the Murray–Darling basin and in other farming areas around the country is being lost because of land degradation. Land degradation is the decline in quality of the land. In terms of agriculture, this means that the land is not as productive as it used to be. Land is said to be degraded when:

- the soil becomes too acidic
- the soil loses its structure
- the soil becomes eroded
- the soil becomes too salty
- the land is mined and not rehabilitated
- the land turns into desert
- plant or animal pests have overtaken the land.

Australian soils can be easily degraded. They tend to be naturally deficient in nutrients. There are highly fertile, well-structured soils in river valley flood plains but most of our soil is shallow and infertile. Australian soils have an average depth of only 50 millimetres and 90 per cent of the soil is too poor or too dry to support the **intensive farming** we need to produce our food. In addition, much of the water that lies under the ground is very salty because the land in southern Australia was once covered by the sea.

Two types of land use

EARLY HISTORY

Past generations of settlers who arrived in Australia did not realise the land had previously been covered by sea. European pioneers were hard-working, courageous people. They endured extremes of climate and isolation. They did not know that the farming methods they used to conquer this foreign land could easily damage and destroy the soil. Naturally, they used the farming methods they had used in their homelands. They cleared the land of all vegetation, ploughed the land with hard-hoofed animals and introduced species of plants and animals that were damaging Australia's environment.

When the land had been cleared, it was often left bare and open to **erosion** by the wind and water. The hard hooves of the animals churned up the soil and broke down its already fragile structure. Over the years, farming with heavy equipment did little to help the problem. Some farmers also used every single centimetre of their property and added irrigation and chemicals to make their land more fertile. It is easy to understand why farmers did this: they had to feed their families and try to make enough to sell at the market.

Two hundred years later we can see the error of these ways. Although Australia's soils took hundreds of years to produce, it has taken only a short time to degrade them. The way in which past generations have used the land has not been compatible with the capabilities of the soil.

Activities

Investigation: *Land use*

1. (a) Use the photographs on the left to complete the table below.

Photograph	Description of land use	How land use might degrade the land
1		
2		

   (b) Which land use do you think has the least impact? Give reasons for your choice.

   (c) Which land use do you think would have the greatest impact? Why?

2. Make a summary list of farming methods that have resulted in damage to the topsoil.
3. Describe what life might have been like for the early settlers of rural Australia and explain why you think it is unfair to blame them for all of our soil problems today.
4. Look at the photographs below showing land degradation. Describe the damage you see. Describe how you feel about this damage to a resource that you rely on to produce your food.
5. Name four resources, besides land, on which we all rely. Is any one of the Earth's resources more important than another? Explain your answer.
6. Australians seem to be well aware of issues such as the greenhouse effect. Why are we perhaps less knowledgeable about the state of our land?
7. You will need an atlas for this activity and an outline map of Australia. Using the information in the text and your general knowledge, predict the regions in each State of Australia that you think might be subject to land degradation. Shade these regions on your map. Give reasons for your choices.

Logging in Tasmania

Severe creek erosion

Dryland salinity

11.2

LAND DEGRADATION IN AUSTRALIA

Useable land is being lost or poisoned by land degradation. This is a broad term used to describe the loss of soil productivity through erosion, salinity, compaction or desertification. Clearance of trees and removal of vegetation leaves the soil vulnerable to being blown or washed away. Tree clearance also allows groundwater to rise bringing salts from the subsoil closer to the surface. Salt kills most plants, so the land degradation cycle begins again.

The map on the right shows where land degradation is of serious concern, since land degradation does not occur evenly throughout Australia.

In the panel below, you will find more facts which should alert us all to the seriousness of this problem.

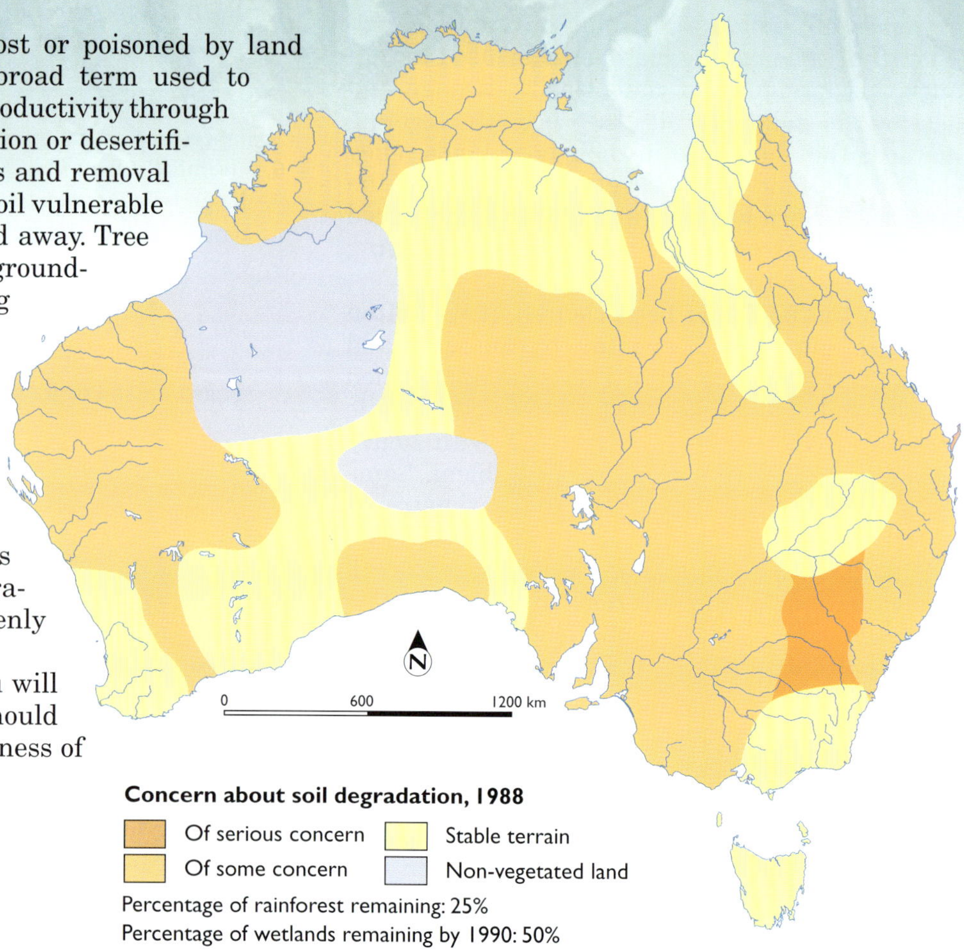

Concern about soil degradation, 1988

- Of serious concern
- Of some concern
- Stable terrain
- Non-vegetated land

Percentage of rainforest remaining: 25%
Percentage of wetlands remaining by 1990: 50%

Australia's land degradation

- In Australia six tonnes of topsoil are lost for every tonne of produce grown.
- The intensity of land use has an effect on the type of degradation that will occur.
- In those parts of Australia where natural vegetation has been cleared on sloping land, there is a major soil erosion problem.
- Some forms of degradation are continuing to increase rapidly as a result of current poor farming practices.
- In the Murray–Darling region alone it is estimated that land degradation costs more than $260 million each year.
- The area used for agriculture in Australia has steadily increased over the last 200 years. Sometimes this has involved movement into marginal areas that are ecologically fragile and/or less suitable to agriculture.
- In Australia solving the problem of land degradation is so important (economically and environmentally) that the Federal Government declared the 1990s the 'Decade of **Landcare**'.
- Drought is a recurring feature of the Australian farming scene and puts a great deal of pressure on the health of the soil. We have had nine major droughts since the 1860s. Drought makes the soil more susceptible to degradation because farmers tend to use land more heavily. More soil becomes exposed to the effects of wind and water.
- Some of Australia's most productive land areas — the wheat areas in Western Australia, the rice fields in New South Wales and fruit and dairying regions in central and northern Victoria — are all affected by salt. This costs a great deal of money in lost production and in controlling the problem.

Activities

Investigation: *Australia's land degradation*

1. (a) Study the map showing land degradation in Australia. Copy the table below into your workbook and complete it by ticking the appropriate box.

	Percentage of land in Australia				
	0–20	**21–40**	**41–60**	**61–80**	**81–100**
Of serious concern					
Of some concern					
Stable terrain					
Non-vegetated land					

(b) In which State of Australia is there the greatest concern about land degradation?

(c) Name one State where there is little or no concern about land degradation. What do you think might be found in the non-vegetated areas? Check an atlas map to provide evidence for your answer.

2. (a) Study the map below showing Australian agricultural land use. Describe the location of types of farming that could be described as **extensive farming**. Describe the location of intensive farming types in Australia.

(b) Which method of farming do you think would have a greater ability to cause damage to the soil? Give two examples of this farming method and explain how each could cause damage to the soil.

Communication: *Comparing maps*

(a) For the State in which you live, describe the correlation between farming type and land degradation type. Use a map of your State to give the names of the regions in which soil damage is occurring.

(b) Which of your State's soil damaged regions have you visited? Did you notice any evidence of the agricultural land being degraded? If your answer is 'Yes', describe what you saw that alerted you to the problem. If your answer is 'No', explain why you might not have noticed anything wrong.

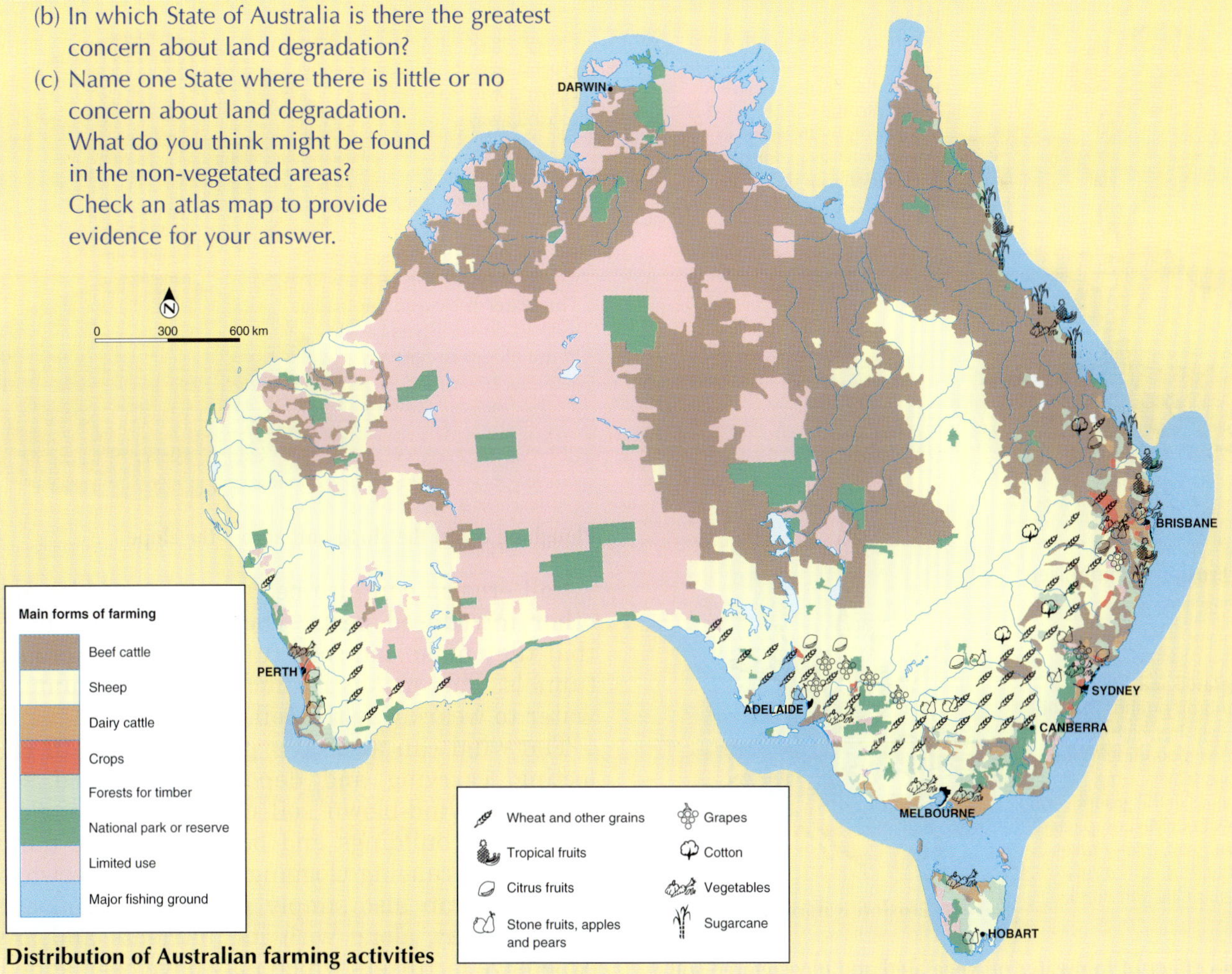

Distribution of Australian farming activities

WIND AND WATER

SOIL EROSION

One type of land degradation is soil erosion. The process involves the wearing away of topsoil by wind and water. Usually soil particles are held together by the roots of vegetation. Once the protection of natural shrubs and trees has been removed (to make space for crops and livestock), there is nothing but grass to bind the soil particles together. When hard-hoofed animals or heavy machinery are allowed on the soil, it is worn away even further. Over a period of time, the soil is broken into smaller pieces, causing a loss of soil structure. During wind or rain, the soil is picked up and moved elsewhere.

The effect of rainwater on vegetated and unvegetated soil

Apart from clearing the native vegetation, there are some other farming practices which can result in soil erosion. When there are more animals on a piece of land than the soil can tolerate, the land is said to be overstocked. Another way of saying this is that the **carrying capacity** of the land has been exceeded. The result is that the animals eat and trample all of the grass available. Once again, the bare soil is vulnerable to wind and water.

When a farmer ploughs down a slope, water is more easily able to flow down the furrows made by the tractor. As water flows away, it takes valuable topsoil with it. An appropriate remedy for this is **contour ploughing**, whereby the farmer ploughs in a direction consistent with the contour or shape of the land. You can see this in the diagram below.

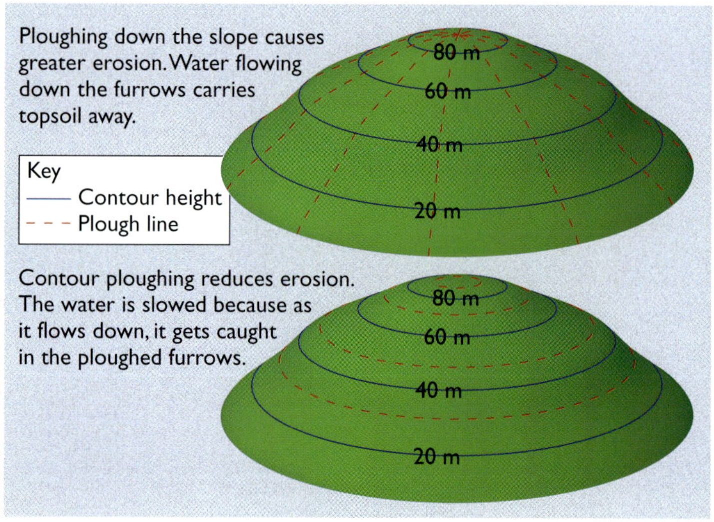

Ploughing down the slope and across the slope

Soil erosion can also be caused by rabbits and other introduced pests. The burrows and holes that they make can soon turn into deeply eroded tunnels. This makes it much easier for running water to wear away the soil.

The wind can also be a powerful force in collecting, carrying and depositing loosened soil particles. Wind-blown soil can build up against fences and buildings and be dropped into dams and rivers, causing clogging of those waterways. The wind can also simply pick up the soil and blow it away, along with its nutrients and any expensive fertilisers which may have been added.

Badly eroded farmland

Activities

Communication: *Comparing maps*

Use the maps at right to answer the following questions.

(a) Describe the extent and location of water and wind erosion in Victoria.

(b) Is water erosion in Victoria evenly or unevenly distributed? Can the same be said for wind erosion?

(c) Compare this map with those showing rainfall and elevation in Victoria. Write a paragraph which accurately describes the connection between the occurrence of water erosion, the elevation of the land and the amount of rainfall.

(d) Answer true or false to the following statements:

- Water erosion is always found in areas which experience high rainfall.
- Water erosion is most severe in areas where the elevation is highest.
- There seems to be a high degree of spatial association (the degree to which two or more things are similarly arranged over space) between no water erosion and low lying land.
- Elevation has little to do with erosion.

(e) Are there any other patterns that you can see? Describe them and then compare your findings with other class members.

Investigation: *Soil erosion*

1. Look at the photograph above which shows a badly eroded gully.
   (a) What do you think has caused this to happen?
   (b) What effect would this loss of land have on the farmer economically and ecologically?
   (c) Explain why filling in this gully with a huge pile of dirt will not fix the problem.
   (d) Suggest three solutions that the farmer could undertake.
2. Choose a partner to work with for this activity. Make a list of places where you have seen evidence of soil erosion. You may have seen land being degraded near your home or at a holiday location. You may have noticed road cuttings, erosion in the school grounds, on vacant blocks or in a local park. Describe what these areas look like, how you think the erosion occurred and how you think the problem could be fixed.

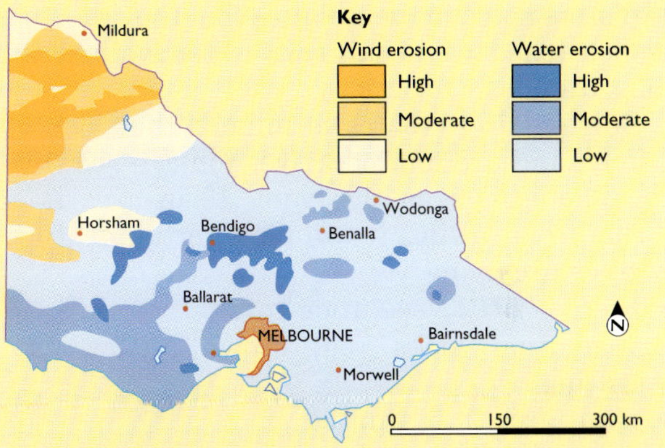

Type and degree of erosion in Victoria

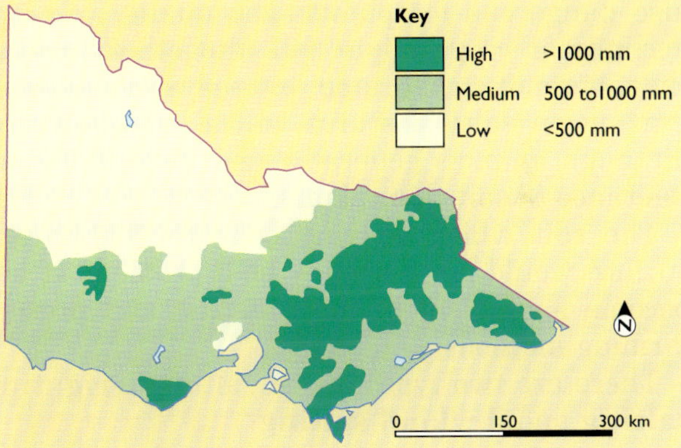

Rainfall in Victoria

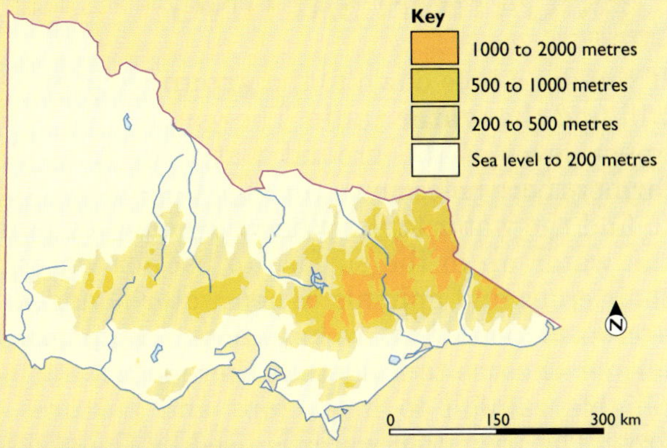

Elevation in Victoria

SALTY SOIL

Salinity is yet another form of land degradation. We have both saline soil and saline water in Australia. These terms mean that there is a concentration of salt in both the soil and the water. The salt has been around for a very long time (remember, much of southern Australia was once a sea bed and the salt was deposited during that time). Even our early explorers noted in their diaries that they were often disheartened to find only salty water available after long, arduous journeys.

Soil salting creates farmlands that look very barren and are unproductive. You can see this in the photograph on the right. If an area is suffering from salting, it will have certain features:

- trees are dying
- there is little vegetation cover
- vegetation looks red, brown, yellow or is wilting
- plant growth is stunted
- only salt-tolerant plants are growing.

Just as too much salt is bad for humans, it is also dangerous for plants. The quality of crops declines or crops might fail altogether because they become dehydrated by the salt. Animals grazing on salty pastures will also be affected, although animals generally have a much higher tolerance to salt than plants.

The salt which is lying beneath the Earth's surface would not normally be a problem. It has become a problem because of past and present farming methods.

There are two types of soil salting: **irrigation salting** and **dryland salting**.

IRRIGATION SALTING

If you dig a hole down to the **ground water**, you will find the **water table**. The water table is the upper level of the ground water. In Australia, farmers bore holes down through the soil and rock to find the water table. When they do, they pump the water up to the surface to use for watering their crops and animals. When water is added to a crop or pasture it is known as **irrigation**. A farmer chooses to irrigate if there is not enough reliable rainfall to help crops and pastures to grow. The irrigation water is used by the grasses (on grazing land) and plants (on crop land). Any excess water either seeps down through the soil to be added to the ground water or it runs off the surface. The water that seeps downward raises the water table in the subsoil layers. These subsoil layers are often high in natural salt (remember those ancient sea beds!). In areas that have been irrigated for many years, the salty water table has risen to very near the surface and now lies within the reach of plant roots. The salty water is sucked to the surface by the plants and is then evaporated by the sun and the plants themselves. Salt is left behind, lying on the wasted ground.

Salt-affected farmland

DRYLAND SALTING

Another process of salting happens in farming areas that are not irrigated. Once again, it begins with the clearing of trees from the land, thus disrupting the natural water balance. When deep-rooted native trees and shrubs are replaced by shallow-rooted crop and pasture plants, much more rainwater is able to filter down to add to the ground water. The ground water rises through the underground soil and rocks. As it does this, it collects any salt held in the rocks. The water table rises often to within two metres of the surface and into the **capillary zone**. In this zone, water is sucked upwards by surface tension and is attracted to the soil particles surrounding the air spaces in the soil. This process is just like sucking water through a straw: the thinner the straw, the higher the rise of the liquid. Again the salt finds its way to the surface, where it can severely affect crops and pastures. The diagram on the opposite page shows this process of dryland salting.

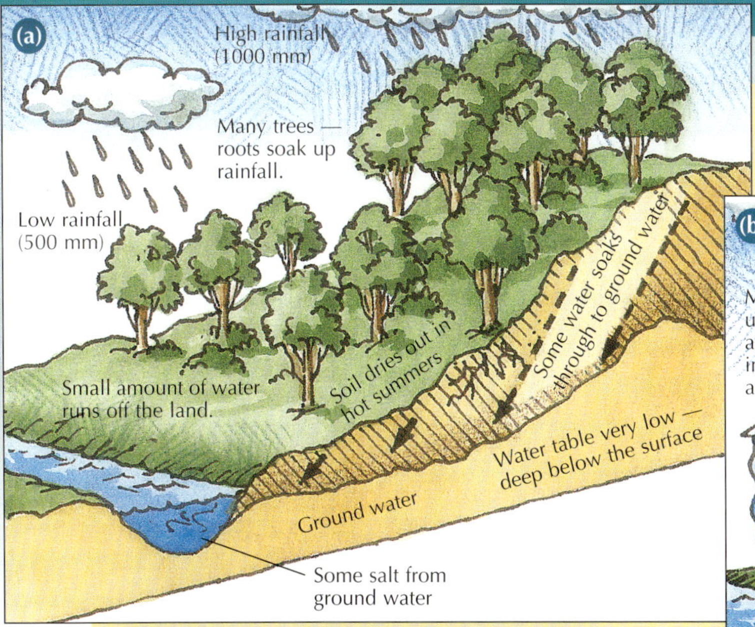

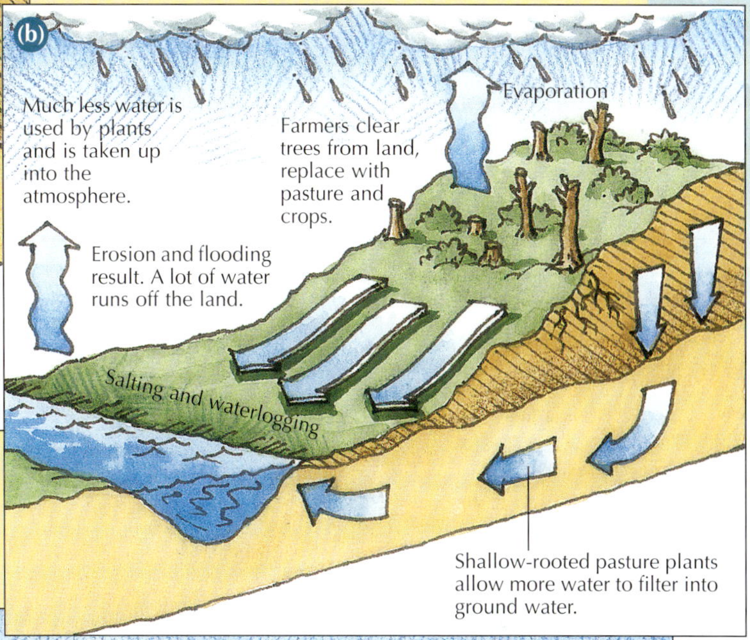

(a) A natural system
(b) What happens when the land is cleared of vegetation
(c) What happens when irrigation water is added — irrigation salting

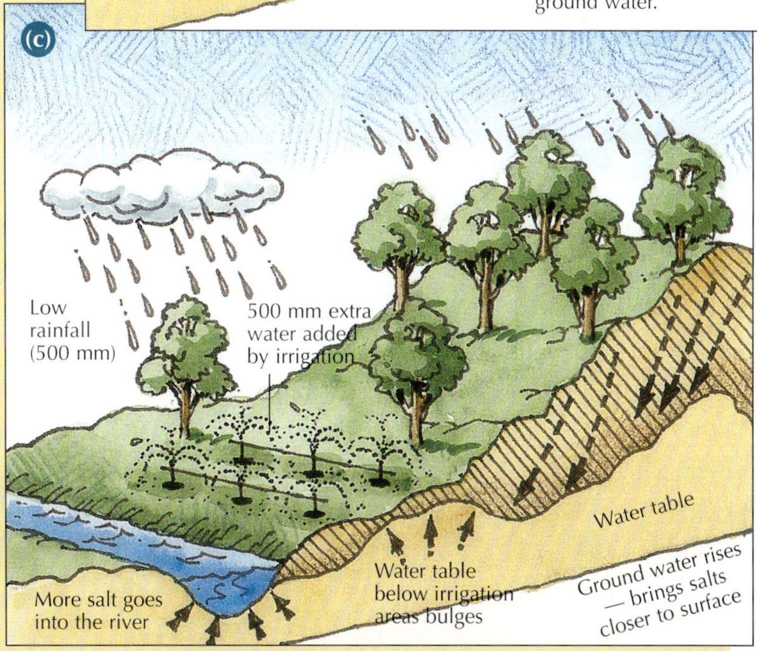

Activities

Investigation: *Why and where salting occurs*

1. Look at the series of diagrams on this page.
   (a) What happens to the water table when trees are cleared?
   (b) What happens to the water table when irrigation water is added to the land?
   (c) What problems can occur when ground water is closer to the surface?
2. When land has been poorly managed, there are more than just the obvious consequences of plants dying or soil being washed away. Below is a brief overview of these consequences in point form. Categorise each point as either an economic, social, environmental, physical or political consequence. In some cases you may need to select two categories.
   The consequences of soil erosion include:
   - a loss of valuable and irreplaceable soil
   - a loss of nutrients in the soil
   - costly and time-consuming repair work on slopes
   - a loss of seed and fertiliser
   - a decline in the number of animals the land can carry (carrying capacity)
   - drifting soil covering fences, buildings, roads and fertile crop and grazing land
   - the soil from one area choking irrigation channels, dams and rivers at another location.

   The consequences of soil salting include:
   - the death of plants and sick animals
   - a decline in the productive capacity of the land
   - a degraded environment, and loss of habitat for native plants and animals
   - a loss of water quality
   - a disrupted natural water balance
   - soil left bare and wasted
   - saline water flowing downstream to affect other farmers and consumers.
3. Obviously the economic and physical consequences affect a farmer immediately. Explain how the two are related.

4. Explain why simply providing billions of dollars to prevent land degradation will not fix the problem. What other ways can you suggest?
5. Draw up a flow chart which explains the causes of soil salting. You may draw up separate charts for each type of salting or one chart that links the two types of salting with a common cause.
6. Soil salting has often been described as 'underground flooding' or 'flooding from below'. Explain what is meant by these statements.
7. Explain the role of deep-rooted plants in preventing dryland salting.
8. Use the map below to briefly describe the distribution of dryland and irrigation salting in Victoria.

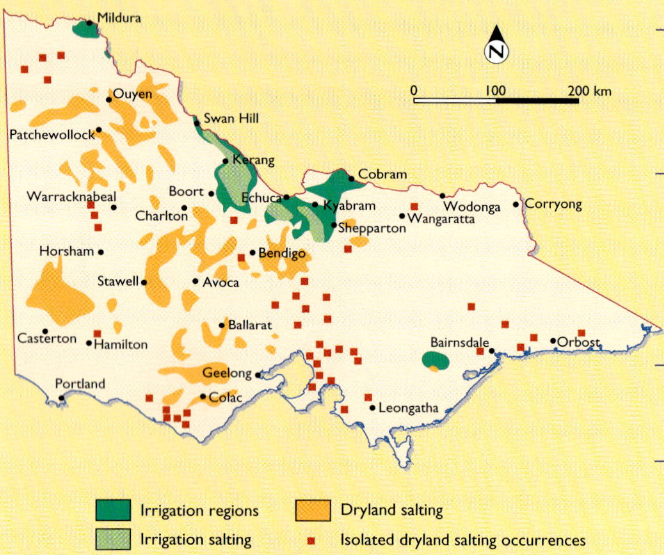

Distribution of salt-affected areas in Victoria

Victoria's agricultural regions

9. Using the map that shows Victoria's agricultural regions and the map below left, complete the following table.

Region	Town	Type of agriculture in that area	Type of salting
Mallee	Mildura		
	Ouyen		
	Patchewollock		
Wimmera	Warracknabeal		
	Horsham		
	Stawell		
Glenelg	Portland		
	Hamilton		
	Casterton		
Loddon/ Avoca	Swan Hill		
	Kerang		
	Boort		
	Avoca		
Campaspe	Bendigo		
	Echuca		
Goulburn	Shepparton		
	Kyabram		
	Cobram		
North-east	Wodonga		
	Corryong		
	Wangaratta		
South-east	Leongatha		
	Bairnsdale		
	Orbost		
Corangamite	Ballarat		
	Colac		
	Geelong		

10. Using the information on these pages and other research, write an extended response of 500 words describing the salting problem in one of these regions. You must include the extent and type of salting, the crops and animals likely to be affected and how you think the individual farmer would be affected.

Communication: *Write a letter*

Farmer Gaye in Kyabram, Victoria, has been growing pears and milking cows for a number of years. The pears are sent to the local cannery in Shepparton and the milk goes to the local dairy. Rainfall over the last few years has been unreliable and so the farmer increased the number of irrigation channels on the farm. Despite this, pear production has been declining. The cows do not seem to be affected.

Write a letter to Farmer Gaye explaining why pear production is down and why the cows are still producing well. Use all of the data in this section to outline what the problem might be, how it occurred and how it affects production. Inform Farmer Gaye that you will write again as soon as you have learnt about some suitable solutions.

Conduct an experiment

1. You will need a partner for this activity. You will be tasting six different types of salty water. You may need to enlist the help of your school's laboratory technician. Arrange to have six jugs of distilled water (water that has no salt) available. The technician can help you to carefully weigh and then add varying amounts of salt to each jug. The table below shows you the quantity of salt to add.

Jug	Amount of salt	Type of water
1	0 mg	Control
2	0.15 mg	Fresh water
3	1 mg	Marginal water
4	3 mg	Brackish water
5	35 mg	Sea water
6	130 mg	Recorded in a creek feeding into the Murray River

(a) Taste each of the solutions in turn, carefully rinsing your cup each time.

(b) What did each of the solutions taste like? Did you have a higher salt tolerance than your partner? Compare your results with those of other class members. Describe the reactions of your class to this salt taste test.

2. Look at the table below showing the salt tolerance of some plants and animals. Now that you've tasted some salty water, can you imagine why sheep tend to prefer salty pastures? Compare the solutions you tasted with the tolerance levels shown in the table.

Salt tolerance limits for humans and selected plants and animals

	Upper limits of salt tolerance (ECs)*
Crops under irrigation	
Tobacco	80
Citrus, legumes, garden plants	1 660
Vines, grass, cabbages	2 500
Cotton, lucerne	4 160
Lettuce	1 100–1 600
Peas	1 500
Apricot	1 500
Grape	1 500
Apple	2 500–3 000
Pear	3 000
Tomato	3 000
Date palm	7 500
Stock	
Poultry	5 800
Pigs	7 500
Horses	10 000
Milking cows and ewes	10 000
Beef cattle	16 700
Dry sheep	23 000
Human consumption	
Highest desirable level for humans (WHO)	800
Maximum permissible level for humans (WHO)	2 500

* Electrical conductivity

MANAGING LAND USE

There are many things that can be done to prevent and manage land that has suffered from erosion. Here are some of these techniques.

First, a farmer needs to repair any existing damage. For example, a badly eroded gully, such as the one shown on page 285, could be filled in with rocks and soil, fenced and then revegetated. Sometimes, school or community groups can help with these tasks.

Next, the farmer needs to slow down moving water and break the force of the wind. If the farm is on flat land, the farmer can plant the crops in strips across the slope. This helps to slow down the water because the crops force the water to spread out over the land and it is therefore less likely to become an erosive force. This is called strip cropping. If the farm is on sloping land, contour ploughing can be undertaken. Farmers can even try **low tillage** farming. This is done by using machinery which causes the least disruption to the soil. At all costs, a farmer should not leave the land bare and vulnerable to the elements.

Fenced area shows the effect of rabbits on pasture growth

Finally, soil erosion can be repaired by making sure that strong plant cover is maintained. Some ways in which this can be done are by:

- preserving any native forested areas currently on the farm
- replanting any areas that have been cleared
- rotating crops
- not burning off stubble and roots from plants so that they bind the soil together
- trying not to overload the land with too many animals in one area
- getting rid of rabbits and other pests
- building windbreaks using suitable trees (that is, local native species).

Grain farm before land conservation methods were used

Grain farm after land conservation methods were used

Communication: *Write a letter*

Farmer Gaye in Kyabram, Victoria, has been growing pears and milking cows for a number of years. The pears are sent to the local cannery in Shepparton and the milk goes to the local dairy. Rainfall over the last few years has been unreliable and so the farmer increased the number of irrigation channels on the farm. Despite this, pear production has been declining. The cows do not seem to be affected.

Write a letter to Farmer Gaye explaining why pear production is down and why the cows are still producing well. Use all of the data in this section to outline what the problem might be, how it occurred and how it affects production. Inform Farmer Gaye that you will write again as soon as you have learnt about some suitable solutions.

Conduct an experiment

1. You will need a partner for this activity. You will be tasting six different types of salty water. You may need to enlist the help of your school's laboratory technician. Arrange to have six jugs of distilled water (water that has no salt) available. The technician can help you to carefully weigh and then add varying amounts of salt to each jug. The table below shows you the quantity of salt to add.

Jug	Amount of salt	Type of water
1	0 mg	Control
2	0.15 mg	Fresh water
3	1 mg	Marginal water
4	3 mg	Brackish water
5	35 mg	Sea water
6	130 mg	Recorded in a creek feeding into the Murray River

   (a) Taste each of the solutions in turn, carefully rinsing your cup each time.

   (b) What did each of the solutions taste like? Did you have a higher salt tolerance than your partner? Compare your results with those of other class members. Describe the reactions of your class to this salt taste test.

2. Look at the table below showing the salt tolerance of some plants and animals. Now that you've tasted some salty water, can you imagine why sheep tend to prefer salty pastures? Compare the solutions you tasted with the tolerance levels shown in the table.

Salt tolerance limits for humans and selected plants and animals

	Upper limits of salt tolerance (ECs)*
Crops under irrigation	
Tobacco	80
Citrus, legumes, garden	1 660
plants	2 500
Vines, grass, cabbages	4 160
Cotton, lucerne	1 100–1 600
Lettuce	1 500
Peas	1 500
Apricot	1 500
Grape	2 500–3 000
Apple	3 000
Pear	3 000
Tomato	7 500
Date palm	
Stock	
Poultry	5 800
Pigs	7 500
Horses	10 000
Milking cows and ewes	10 000
Beef cattle	16 700
Dry sheep	23 000
Human consumption	
Highest desirable level for humans (WHO)	800
Maximum permissible level for humans (WHO)	2 500

* Electrical conductivity

MANAGING LAND USE

There are many things that can be done to prevent and manage land that has suffered from erosion. Here are some of these techniques.

First, a farmer needs to repair any existing damage. For example, a badly eroded gully, such as the one shown on page 285, could be filled in with rocks and soil, fenced and then revegetated. Sometimes, school or community groups can help with these tasks.

Next, the farmer needs to slow down moving water and break the force of the wind. If the farm is on flat land, the farmer can plant the crops in strips across the slope. This helps to slow down the water because the crops force the water to spread out over the land and it is therefore less likely to become an erosive force. This is called strip cropping. If the farm is on sloping land, contour ploughing can be undertaken. Farmers can even try **low tillage** farming. This is done by using machinery which causes the least disruption to the soil. At all costs, a farmer should not leave the land bare and vulnerable to the elements.

Fenced area shows the effect of rabbits on pasture growth

Finally, soil erosion can be repaired by making sure that strong plant cover is maintained. Some ways in which this can be done are by:

- preserving any native forested areas currently on the farm
- replanting any areas that have been cleared
- rotating crops
- not burning off stubble and roots from plants so that they bind the soil together
- trying not to overload the land with too many animals in one area
- getting rid of rabbits and other pests
- building windbreaks using suitable trees (that is, local native species).

Grain farm before land conservation methods were used

Grain farm after land conservation methods were used

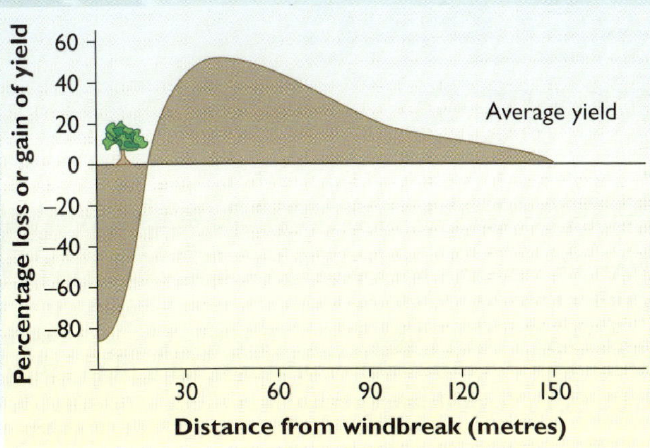

The effect of shelter on crop and pasture yields

FIXING SOIL SALINITY

Believe it or not, land that is suffering from salt can become productive again! The main way to achieve this is to lower the water table. Listed below are some ways to do this.

- Use more water where it falls. Plant trees and deep-rooted pasture plants which use up a lot of water.
- Fence off areas that are salted and don't let cattle graze there.
- Use low tillage farming when cropping.
- Irrigate more effectively. Grass over irrigation channels, reduce the amount of machinery entering the irrigation area, change from channels to spray and drip systems where appropriate.
- Provide proper drainage from irrigated areas so that excess water is drained away. One type is tile drainage, where agricultural pipes are placed beneath the soil surface. The pipes have to be deep enough to lower the water table and placed very carefully, depending on the type of soil.
- Pump water away from underground sources to evaporation ponds. The company that operates the evaporation ponds in the photograph below exports two million tonnes of salt per year.
- Mulch areas to reduce salting by capillary action and then plant salt-tolerant species.

Activities

Investigation: *Improving the land*

1. Explain why fencing off areas is often described as the 'first line of defence' in rehabilitating the land.
2. Look at the pair of photographs on the opposite page. What land use approach has this farmer used?
3. Planting trees is also vital to helping the land to improve, but this is an expensive and time-consuming exercise. How can the community help individual farmers with this?
4. Many of the suggestions here could be seen as 'radical'. Why might this be so?
5. Explain, in your own words, why it makes good economic sense to spend money on improving eroded or salted land.
6. Look at the photograph below. What do you think is meant by 'farming salt'? Why is this a good idea, both economically and environmentally?
7. 'The real villain is not irrigation water but the lack of drainage for excess irrigation water.' Do you agree or disagree with this statement? Explain your reasons.

Communication: *Methods of communicating*

1. Armed with the information you've learnt in this section, write again to Farmer Gaye in Kyabram. Explain how pear production could be increased by rehabilitating land on the farm. Be very specific in the methods you choose and suggest how they could be implemented.
2. With a partner, create a talk show radio program about the ways to rehabilitate a farm suffering from soil erosion or soil salting. Assume that your broadcast will be heard all over Australia by both rural and urban dwellers. Remember that your listeners will not be able to see diagrams or photographs, so you will need to explain the problems and solutions in a clear, concise manner.

Salt stockpile and evaporating pond at Port Hedland in Western Australia

FARMERS HELPING THEMSELVES

The unplanned clearing of native trees that occurred when Australia was being developed has had negative results for farm production and the environment in general. Problems increased with the use of large machinery in the 1950s to 1970s. The land became more exposed to damage. Soil loss was made worse by tree removal and **salinity** increased in the lower areas of properties. Land degradation costs Australia over $700 million per year.

There are many land owners across Australia who have taken up the challenge of improving their degraded land. Often they have been regarded as radical by their neighbours, who can't understand why someone would want to turn farming land back into treed bushland. But the results have been rewarding. The greatest successes have been made when a land owner has practised **sustainable farming**, or **whole-farm planning**, as it is also known. This is a way of farming that ensures that the land is productive for years to come.

A whole-farm plan is a plan that balances economic and environmental factors. The plan must take into account the specific farm features such as:

- climate (for example, the amount and reliability of rainfall, number of frost-free days, etc.)
- drainage patterns on the farm
- location and extent of existing treed areas
- type and depth of soil
- current land use and future land uses.

These plans involve preparing ahead in order to:

- save and improve the soil
- protect and improve supplies of water
- protect or improve the diversity of plants and animals.

The following articles describe how individual farmers and groups of farmers have worked to improve their land.

Caring for land spans generations

Article by JOH-ANNE GOODE

Landcare is a family affair for the three Fagg brothers of Mt Mercer in Victoria, who aim to leave their land in better condition for the next generation.

At 63, Les is the middle brother. 'Dad was always keen to improve the property. He had soil conservation people in to look at the salt scalding back in the mid-1940s,' he said.

Land care methods have changed since then. 'Dad put contour banks around the salt pans — that's how they tackled it in those days. It diverted the water, but it didn't help much.

'They just didn't know what to do. It's a learning process — you learn something new every day,' he said.

In 1942, after a lot of bad years growing wheat in West Wyalong in NSW, the family moved to Mt Mercer, 30 minutes south of Ballarat, to take advantage of the area's reliable rainfall.

These days, Keith, Les and Don Fagg also manage to plant 1500 trees and hundreds of hectares of deep rooted pasture annually, and are founding members of the Woady Yallock Catchment Project.

The project has created much local and international interest with its treatment of land and water degradation over a whole river catchment.

Salinity in the 120 000 hectare catchment is a major problem with 900 hectares of land salt affected, 80 kilometres of gully erosion, severe rabbit infestation and 35 000 tonnes of salt leaving the catchment annually and draining into Lake Corangamite, Victoria's biggest inland lake.

If salinity is not stopped, it also threatens the catchment's agricultural production of $20 million a year, and the livelihood of 220 farmers.

The project started in 1992 as a team effort between catchment farmers and the project's major sponsor, Alcoa Australia. Since then, 135 000 trees and several thousand hectares of deep-rooted perennial pasture have been planted to soak up excess rainwater and stop salinity spreading.

Keith said being a member of the Woady Yallock Catchment Group has provided the encouragement he needed.

'The help they've given us is good. I don't mind putting in the labour, but it helps a lot when you get financial and technical assistance. Otherwise, I might not have been bothered,' he said.

Les said conservation is the key. 'We are always trying to increase our carrying capacity because we've only got 1000 acres each. You'd slowly disappear if you didn't improve pastures, because you'd be non-competitive,' he said.

'I can take you to an area where nothing grew when we first got here. It was completely scalded, and the topsoil was eroded away. Now it's grassed over completely.'

Don said it feels good when the results start to be seen. 'We've been trying to control salt on the property most of our lives. Since pastures have improved and trees were planted, the salt pans have decreased,' he said.

All three brothers share confidence about their future.

'I've got five children. One son, Steven, works with me, and you know the old saying about leaving the place in better condition than what you found it. That's exactly what we're trying to do,' Les said.

Conservation Gazette, March 1997.

FARMING THE NATURAL WAY

W. Twigg

My family farm is at Bears Lagoon, 60 km north of Bendigo on the Loddon Plains. It is a mixed farm — sheep, grains and cattle. The soils are naturally poorly structured red duplex type (average 5.5 pH) with shallow top soil and dense clay.

The Loddon Plains were originally savannah woodlands. The area has been heavily cleared, and we have been left with a harsh environment and some areas of dryland salinity. In 1970 we had 1500 acres and were farming with traditional methods. But we began to notice that although yields were good, our expenses were high in comparison to our gross income.

We decided to set about reducing our expenses while trying to maintain yield. After many years we have been able to develop a system of farming in sympathy with the environment and nature that has enabled us to achieve this aim. The biggest obstacle I had to overcome in developing this system and understanding my land was with myself — ingrained beliefs and attitudes to the land that all my life I had accepted from other people, farming books and farming traditions.

Farm like a drug addict

When we were farming traditionally, our farm became like a drug addict — the more we put in, the more the land demanded to achieve a satisfactory yield. We felt we were using most of the fertility in our soil to pay the cost of the inputs. We concluded that a smaller yield per acre with less expenses would be almost as profitable and, considering the reduced demand on soil fertility, much more profitable in the long-term. Over the last 25 years we have rarely needed to use inputs such as fertilisers, drenches, supplementary feeding, and dips.

The secret of this system is in the development of lucerne, a deep-rooted perennial plant, as our major pasture species. Lucerne has similar root growth to much of the original vegetation of our area and it has the ability to recycle nutrients and moisture to the soil surface. With our whole farm sown to lucerne we are able to double the dry sheep equivalent per acre compared to traditional annual pasture. The lucerne also uses rainfall more efficiently which helps eliminate dryland salinity.

Imitating nature on the farm

We try to imitate nature on the farm by establishing lucerne at a density of one to three plants per square metre, which is similar to the density of the original native vegetation in this area. It allows annuals to thrive in winter and spring and provide a balanced pasture for livestock. Clovers and rye grass are also sown to improve soil fertility and structure. In contrast to most other farming systems where watertables are rising, in our system the sinking of test bores has shown that the watertable is receding.

With the introduction of lucerne we have moved to spring lambing, which is after all nature's time to reproduce. Spring lambing has increased our lambing percentages by at least 20%. As the feed requirements of the stock follow the pasture production more closely than in autumn lambing, no supplementary feeding is needed. We sell the prime lambs in the higher priced markets of February and March.

Our lucerne pastures are rotational grazed and for this reason we do not need to drench livestock. Rotational grazing imitates the cycles of native animals, they graze and pollute one area and move to another, reducing the spread of worms and disease.

Our approach to weeds also tries to imitate what happens in nature. When weeds appear in certain areas of our farm, this is telling us something about soil conditions — nature is trying to balance her system. If a particular weed is causing a problem it is because the land really needs what that plant has to give or that the land is badly in need of a rest. It is the same with sick and unhealthy plants, nature responds to imbalance by sending in insects to destroy them.

In nature we find that the sick and unhealthy individuals are culled out — this keeps the species strong and continually evolving and improving over time. Instead of spraying unwanted weeds we use heavy stocking to manipulate the weeds to our advantage and correct the imbalance of the pasture or soil.

The next major change occurred on our farm in the mid-1980s. We came to the realisation that, as farmers, all we sell is our fertility to produce our income. Cereals extract massive amounts of fertility but bring in only 20 cents per kg. Meat brings in around $2 per kg and wool $4–$5 per kg. Since we have reduced our cereal production our fertility has increased and so has our profitability.

Trees are an integral part of our farming system. We plant 5000 indigenous trees each year to improve the landscape and soften the environment. The trees are planted in irregular clumps of 5–10 acres (100 trees/acre planted). We plant a large percentage of acacias, which put nitrogen back into the soil for eucalypts and other species to feed from. When most of the acacias are dead, (in 10–15 years) the area is burnt to promote regeneration, as in a forest fire where the eucalypts survive. The trees have brought an increase in bird activity and we encourage the birds to breed and become part of our work force. All native species, plant, animal and insect are needed to create a balanced system.

Along with the changes on the farm I have also changed my approach with people. I used to argue and debate and try to convert people to my way of thinking and feel disheartened and depressed when they didn't change. Now I'm much more interested in doing it myself and showing it can be done.

I get a great deal of personal satisfaction from seeing the ways of nature and adapting them to our farming system. Our farm has increased from 1500 acres in 1970 to 10 000 acres now. It is a profitable and sustainable enterprise. I am happy to share my ideas and experience with people who are interested but don't judge anyone for what they do on their own properties.

Source: Landcare: Best Practice, Department of Primary Industries, South Australia, September 1997, pp. 38–9.

Activities

Investigation: *Looking at case studies*

1. Read the articles in this section and summarise them by answering the following questions.
   (a) What is the location of the area/farm?
   (b) What is the nature of the land degradation?
   (c) Who instigated the improvements?
   (d) How are the improvements being funded?
   (e) What other support/advice did the person/group need?
   (f) By 1997 what improvements had taken place?
   (g) How were these improvements measured?
   (h) What future plans do the land owners have?
2. What do you think is meant by 'best practice'? Name some examples of best practice described in the articles above and left.
3. What is your opinion of these farmers who have helped themselves? Should they be entirely responsible for fixing up their farms? Why might some believe that other people in the community (such as urban dwellers) should be called upon to help out?

CARING FOR THE LAND

The majority of Australians live in the city and have little idea about the extent or importance of land degradation. They may not be aware that it does impact on their lives. A dairy farmer in Victoria puts it like this: 'There's no hope for those of us who live off the land unless we have empathy from those we sell to in the cities'. As mentioned at the beginning of this chapter, we all rely on the land for our food. We can't just leave it up to the rural land owners to correct the problems. There are many ways in which governments, farm agencies, businesses, community groups, school groups, individuals, and rural and urban dwellers can band together to make a difference.

Volunteer groups from the community can help with tree planting.

What can I do to help?

You don't have to be a farmer or live in a rural area to help with Landcare. You don't even have to join a Landcare group. By using a little forethought, every Australian can do their little bit for Landcare.

- Be careful what you put down the sink — old milk, cooking oil, household paints, chemicals and food scraps should go in the bin. Food scraps can also be composted. Use low phosphorous or phosphorous free detergent in the kitchen and laundry.
- Buy recycled products and those which use less packaging. Re-use things when you can and recycle household waste. A compost bin or heap will greatly reduce the amount of rubbish that goes to the tip.
- In your garden, plant Australian native trees and shrubs that are already adapted to local conditions. They usually require less water and fertiliser and provide habitats for wild life including pest-eating birds.
- Don't overuse fertiliser — it will wash into waterways and feed blue–green algae and weeds.
- Put mulch on the garden to reduce run-off and extremes of temperature. Reduced temperature on the surface will assist plant growth.
- Encourage your local school to get involved in a landcare project. There are plenty of projects specifically designed for the school environment such as Stream Watch, where children monitor the water quality, and other monitoring programs including Frog Watch, Bug Watch, Salt Watch and Pasture Watch.
- When walking on beaches or in bushland, be sure to keep to the paths and don't trample the native vegetation.
- Don't dump your garden clippings and rubbish in bushland areas. Weeds can easily take over and smother native bushland, driving away native birds and animals and creating fire hazards.

Conservation Gazette, March 1997.

The wider community pays for land degradation too!

THE DECADE OF LANDCARE

A scheme that exhibits successful cooperation between many people is Landcare. You have probably heard or read about Landcare in the media. It is a community program involving groups of landholders and other volunteers working together to tackle the land protection issues in their local area. The articles on these pages explain some more about the work of Landcare groups. A Landcare group doesn't just have to be focused in a rural area. Urban areas also have land degradation, especially on the land around urban creeks and parklands.

Wetlands saved in Sydney

For city dwellers, the image of Landcare may well be one of farmers and others in rural areas working to preserve the land.

But urban areas can benefit as much from the hard work of committed people, as rural places.

Recently, one of the country's remaining urban wetlands was given a reprieve with the launch of a Landcare project at Dee Why Wetland, on Sydney's northern beaches.

The wetland area has been reduced by more than 90 per cent since the mid-1940s.

Dee Why Wetland C.A.R.E. project co-ordinator, Ms Sue Lennox, said the reduction was due to the area being drained and filled for developments like housing, soccer fields, car parks and an industrial estate.

'There was no appreciation of the vital role that wetlands play in coastal ecosystems,' she said.

'The wetland is also under threat from sewage leaks and overflows, storm water pollution, weeds and industrial runoff.'

Landcare Australia chief executive, Mr Brian Scarsbrick, said 95 per cent of the country's wetlands have been destroyed, and Dee Why is one of the few in an urban area with bush surrounding it.

'It has the largest and one of the few remaining stands of swamp mahogany on the east coast, and is a resting place for endangered migratory birds, like Latham's Snipe from Japan and the Double Banded Plover from New Zealand,' Mr Scarsbrick said.

Last year the wetland was given a National Heritage listing as an important remnant area needing protection.

The project is being funded by photographic company Hanimex over the next three years and will bring in schools, businesses and the local community to work on solutions to problems facing the whole catchment. Other organisations involved are Oz Green and the Warringah Council.

Water quality monitoring, weeding and replanting native species are among the activities planned, with a strong educational focus about how locals can help.

Conservation Gazette, March 1997.

Office landcare

Landcare is a national cause in which all individuals, businesses and companies, no matter how large or small, have an important role to play. Even in the office, you can play your part, simply by conserving resources. Here are a few examples:

- Help stop the great Australian paperchase. You can often use both sides of the paper and some copiers and laser printers have double-sided options.
- Buy recycled paper in your office and arrange to have the used paper collected for recycling.
- Turning your PC off at night rather than leaving it on can help save hundreds of dollars each year in power bills. This goes for lights and other electrical equipment such as photocopiers too.

Conservation Gazette, March 1997.

Activities

Investigation: *Becoming an active campaigner*

1. Read the articles on the left. What do these articles tell you about Landcare as a national issue?
2. Which of the actions listed do you do?
3. Survey five people you know who work in an office. List the ways their office acts to ensure that paper, power and water resources are conserved. Which office would you judge as exhibiting best practice in helping the environment?
4. What evidence is there in the information presented here that people of all ages can be involved in Landcare?

Communication: *Spreading the message*

1. Present a poster that shows people in your local area how they can help protect the land against degradation. If you are able to, write it in another language.
2. Write a letter to your local newspaper explaining why the whole community needs to take up the challenge of Landcare.
3. Imagine that you are in charge of organising a local plant-out day, similar to the Clean Up Australia Day. Write a strategy for action for the day. You will need to consider the following questions.
   - Where in your local area are plantings needed?
   - Which local businesses could provide trees and shrubs?
   - Which types of plants would be suitable for your local area?
   - Which local community groups could you approach to provide volunteer labour?
   - How would you advertise and market it as an event that local people would want to support?
   - Would you need the support of some businesses to provide support financially or 'in kind'? (That is, a local milk bar might provide advertising space, a local supermarket might provide cups, tea and coffee or soft drinks.)
   - How would you coordinate the planning prior to and on the day?
4. Is there a local Landcare group already operating in your area? Find out where the nearest group is based. Arrange a group of friends from school or a club to which you belong to offer your help on the next day of action.

11.8 Meeting the outcomes

DEVELOP A COMPREHENSIVE STRATEGY TO RESOLVE AN ISSUE RELATED TO THE USE AND MANAGEMENT OF AN ENVIRONMENT.

Use a range of geographical media to describe the environment.

Fieldwork

Aim: To find out if there is land degradation in your local area.

Prior preparation

1. Gather the following equipment from your school science department:
   - one **EC** meter, to measure the level of salt in water
   - six clean collection bottles and lids
   - six sticky labels
   - pens, clipboard, etc.
   - map of the area to be investigated.
2. Look at the map of your local area and identify, with the help of your teacher, an appropriate local creek, stream, dam or river. Choose six sites from which you will collect water samples, keeping in mind ease of access and the distance between each site. Number each site on the map.
3. Test out the EC meter. (EC means electrical conductivity.) The more salt in the water sample, the higher the EC reading will be. Try it using water samples in the classroom. Ensure that you are very familiar with how it works and how to read it.
4. Arrange suitable dates to visit your sites. This may be arranged jointly with other class members.

In the field

1. Make detailed notes of each site before you collect the water sample. Note things such as evidence of erosion on the banks, type and amount of vegetation on and near the banks, evidence of land use in the vicinity (for example, urban settlement, farms, industry). Are there any indications of salting? (Refer to pages 288–9.)
2. Note the slope of the bank at your access point. Grade it as steep, moderate or flat if you have no other way of measuring it. Note any evidence of silt or pollution in the water.
3. Mark on the map exactly where you collect the sample from. Collect your water sample, noting on the label the time and day of collection and the collection point. For example: Monday, 20 March 2000, 12.30 p.m. Site 1 Fitzroy Creek. Sample taken in middle of creek.
4. Move away from the collection site to more stable ground. Use the EC meter to measure the salt level.
5. Repeat this procedure for all six sites.
6. If possible, repeat the full set of tests a week later, to check the accuracy of your results.

Back in the classroom

1. Tabulate your data as follows:

Site	EC reading in week 1	EC reading in week 2
1		
2		

2. Mark your readings on your map.
3. Provide annotated (labelled) site sketches using the details in your notes.
4. (a) What do your results show?
   (b) Describe the changes in salt levels over the space of the six sites. How did your results vary over time? What reasons might explain the similarities or differences between these results?
   (c) What do you think of the water quality in the creek you studied? Refer to the table of water quality standards below to support your findings.

Water quality standards

EC units	Use
0–800	Good drinking water for humans, irrigation and livestock
800–2500	Tastes salty to humans, but can be drunk. Can be used to irrigate some plants. Livestock can drink it.
2500–10 000	Humans cannot drink this. Not suitable for irrigation. Livestock can still drink this.
Over 10 000	Not suitable for livestock, irrigation or humans
50 000	Sea water

5. Write a detailed conclusion to the question originally posed: Is there evidence of land degradation in your local area? Provide this evidence from the primary data you have collected.

Identify strategies formulated to address the issue.

1. In 1997 Australian biologist and author Dr Mary E. White published a book called *Listen . . . Our Land is Crying*. This chapter is named after that book. What have you learned in this chapter that explains this title? What images of care and concern for the Australian land come to your mind? What do you plan to do with this knowledge?

2. Use the facts in this chapter to create an interesting, stimulating and educational board game for younger geography students. Your game might take the form of snakes and ladders or bingo and should be suitable for students in years 5–6.
3. You will need to work in a group for this activity. Create a puppet show for year 2–3 students that depicts one aspect of land degradation. You will need:
   - various players or characters
   - a decorated 'front-of-house' scene
   - a set of puppets
   - a script expressing information about soil erosion or soil salinity in a very simple manner.
4. Read the articles below and make a list of the actions that the groups described have taken. Once you have made this list, highlight those actions that a group in your school could undertake.
5. Some types of land degradation that have been dealt with only lightly in this chapter are:
   - soil acidity
   - infestation by exotic weeds (for example, bitou bush, ragwort, blackberry)
   - loss of soil structure
   - desertification, as a result of farming fragile, marginal lands
   - litter control on public lands
   - infestation by exotic/pest animal species (for example, rabbits, donkeys and brumbies).

   Conduct some research on the occurrence of one of these problems in your State or Territory. Write a report on the location and extent of the problem and the solutions that are being put in place.

Junior Landcare

Junior Landcare has developed in response to schools and children's groups taking an active interest in land degradation issues. Teaching materials have been developed to assist teachers incorporate Landcare activities in their curriculum.

There are also many opportunities for Junior Landcarers to help out practically. They often support rural Landcare groups and organise activities to raise money, grow trees from seed they have collected themselves, help plant trees and shrubs and prepare displays for their school or library. They also carry out Landcare projects in their own school grounds and surrounds. Many Junior Landcarers are involved in environmental monitoring projects such as Salt Watch and Water Watch, which provide valuable information on the quality of soil and water resources.

Source: Landcare: Best Practice, Department of Primary Industries, South Australia, September 1997, p. 17.

Clyde Fenton Landcare Group

Abstract

Clyde Fenton Landcare Group is a school community-based group made up of students, parents and teachers. Students studying river bank erosion along the Katherine River inspired the formalisation of the Landcare group, which established in late 1996. The group has since presented a management plan for part of the river to the Katherine River Advisory Committee. The management plan includes measures to control erosion along the river bank.

The beginnings

The desire by the Clyde Fenton School Community to establish a Landcare group dates back to September 1994 when a parent suggested that this would be a good community project for the school to undertake. An informal group formed and was involved in the development of the Katherine River Plan of Management. The Clyde Fenton School still has representation on the Katherine River Advisory Committee to this day.

Objective three of the current school action plan states:

'To promote and enhance the teaching and learning of science at Clyde Fenton School 1996–98'

'An active Landcare group be formed early in 1996 comprising students, parents and staff'

During 1996, students in the year five/six class undertook a year-long project comparing two sites along the Katherine River. The two sites were:

- site 1 — a low-use area at the Katherine Gorge; and
- site 2— an uncontrolled high human-use area, at the mouth of Two Mile Creek (opposite the school).

The students then devised their own plan of management for the river bank at the Two Mile Creek junction. The long-term plan was to form a Landcare group that would work with the Katherine Town Council to adopt and manage the river bank area opposite the school.

Management plan for river bank erosion control

Early in 1997, the Landcare group met with a delegation from the Katherine River Advisory Committee. They toured the project site and discussed their proposals for the area. A management plan was developed and presented to the Katherine River Advisory Committee. If endorsed by the River Committee, the plan will be forwarded to the Katherine Town Council for approval.

The management plan will include measures to control erosion along the river bank where numerous active gullies are eroding into the bank. The plan involves minor earthworks to formalise drainage lines that will divert water into an existing drop structure. Run-off water from the open areas will be diverted into a single, rock drop structure that will be armoured to handle the increased water flow. With water no longer entering numerous small gullies, they [the small gullies] will stabilise naturally or, where needed, native plants will be established.

The open area between Gorge Road and the top of the river bank will be revegetated using trees and shrubs native to the area. The plan will also identify areas for car parking, better alignment of the bike track and formalised pedestrian access down the bank to a popular swimming hole.

The project is planned to commence later this year and will run for three years. The management plan will be implemented in three stages commencing with the area in front of the school and expanding annually to take in the area of river upstream as far as the cemetery, near the town boundary.

Source: Landcare, Best Practice, Department of Primary Industries, South Australia, September 1997, p. 17.

Chapter

12

FORESTS – OUR GREEN MANSIONS

INTRODUCTION

People's concepts of forests vary tremendously. Some have described forests as 'living dinosaurs' or 'green dinosaurs', making us think of them as very old and worthy of conservation. Some people see forests as a resource to be harvested — the timber sawn or chipped for different uses — then a new forest replanted. Others refer to our forests as the 'lungs of the Earth' because of their ability to produce oxygen and soak up excesses of carbon dioxide. For the innumerable plants and animals that live in them, forests are their habitat. For a forester, the treasure lies within the trees themselves; for a conservationist, the treasures lie within the entire forest. This is the source of the current environmental controversy.

In this chapter you will learn about the many ways of 'seeing' a forest. You will discover that although there are varying views on how to use and manage our forests, there is general agreement on the need to ensure their long-term economic and ecological lives.

LEARNING*outcomes*

- Understand how forests are used.
- Describe different ways of viewing a forest as a resource.
- Compare the current use of forests and future availability of resources.
- Describe the likely impact of logging on a natural environment.
- Evaluate ways of sustainably developing our forests.
- Suggest strategies for managing timber harvesting.

GLOSSARY

coupe: groups of trees in a forest chosen for harvesting

emergent: a tall tree with a crown (top) that stands above all other vegetation in a forest

hardwood: trees belonging to the group of plants known as angiosperms, or flowering plants; also known as broad-leaved plants. Examples include eucalypts and deciduous trees.

native forest: forest composed of a variety of native trees and shrubs; can include old growth or regrowth forest from fire or from timber harvesting

old growth forest: very old and largely undisturbed region of forest usually containing diverse plant and animal life and many mature trees; suitable as habitats for animals and desirable as timber

plantation forest: forest established by planting either native or exotic trees and managed intensively for timber harvesting; generally contains only one species (monoculture) and no understorey of competing plants

pulp: the mushy mixture of water and chipped wood used to make paper products

pulp logs: logs taken from weak or diseased trees and pulped to make paper

regrowth forest: native forest containing a substantial proportion of trees that are actively growing in height and diameter; may contain some old growth trees

resource security: the guarantee of the long-term availability of a resource

sawlogs: logs taken from tall, straight, healthy trees that can be cut at a sawmill to create timber for building frames and furniture

sclerophyll: (pronounced 'sklerrofill') trees and other plants that have leathery leaves; forests composed of such trees. Eucalypt forests are described as 'wet sclerophyll' or 'dry sclerophyll', depending on the amount of rain the forest receives.

softwood: trees belonging to the group known as gymnosperms, or conifers; evergreens such as pine, spruce and fir trees

sustainable levels of harvesting: the use of a forest at a level or rate which will not reduce the overall amount of forest in the specified area, or significantly damage its quality

trade deficit in forest products: the amount of money Australia earns exporting forest products being less than the amount it pays to import forest products, creating a trade deficit

value adding: increasing the value of a product by changing and improving the product. For example, a log sawn into timber planks is worth more than a log that has not been sawn.

woodchipping: where areas of natural forest are felled and the trees cut into chips. Australian woodchips highly sought after because when pulped they make high quality paper.

AUSTRALIA'S REMAINING VEGETATION

A forest can be defined as a group of trees and associated organisms that covers a fairly large area and in which the trees are close together. This means that a forest is much more than trees — it is a complex mix of plants, animals and microorganisms that depend on each other for survival. The amount and diversity of life in a forest is influenced by several factors, as shown in the figure below.

In just 200 years, we have cleared half of the continent's total forest cover — two-thirds of our rainforest and one-third of our woodlands. More than 4000 species of plants and animals are under threat and more Australian mammals have become extinct than on any other continent on Earth. Less than five per cent of Australia has been preserved as National Park or World Heritage area; most of the country has given way to urban settlement, agriculture and mining.

In the debate over the loss of forest, some people argue that logging of **native forests** decreases the number of trees remaining, while others claim that with **plantation forests** being established, tree cover will actually increase by the start of the new century.

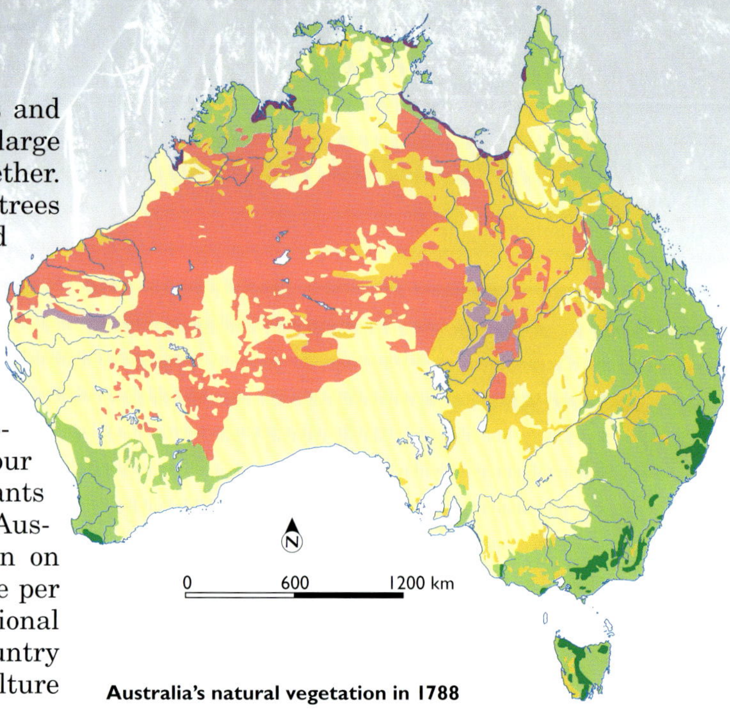

Australia's natural vegetation in 1788

- Tall forest — trees over 30 metres, dominated by eucalypts
- Medium forest — trees 10–30 metres, rainforest where rainfall exceeds 1200 mm
- Scrub — low trees and woody shrubs under 10 metres
- Tussock grasses and graminoids — grasses and grass-like plants
- Hummock grasses — mound grasses, typically spinifex
- Forbs — non-woody non-grass species
- Mangroves and salt flats — areas subject to tidal influence

Influences on the forest environment

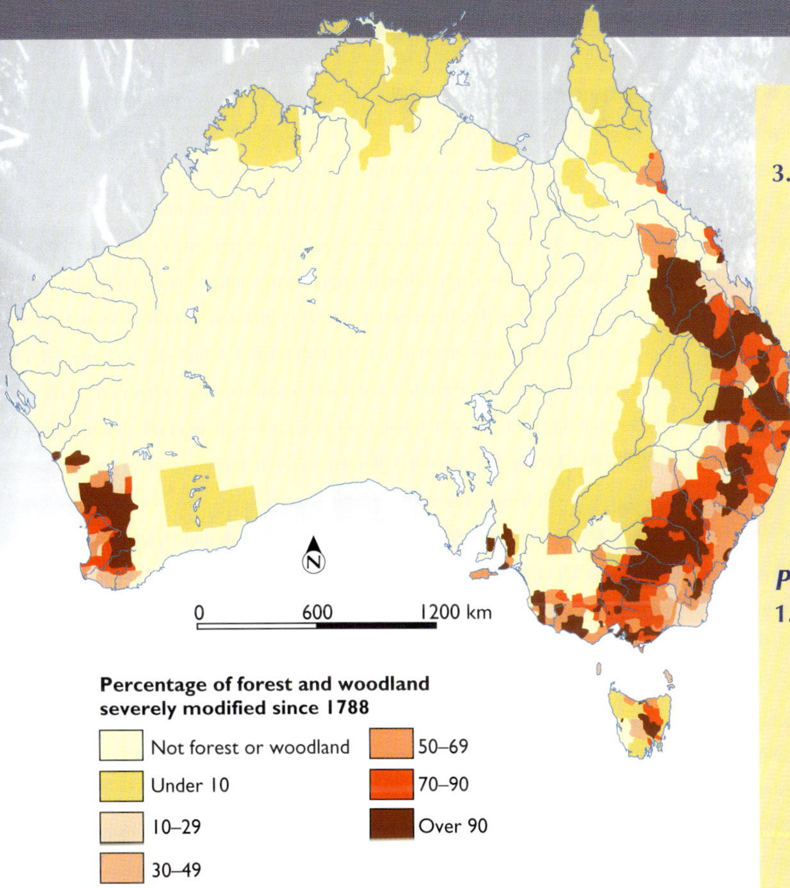

Activities

Communication: *Using a range of data*

1. Refer to the maps on these pages. Describe the changes to forest cover between 1788 and 1998. Use an atlas to refer to actual locations of the remaining forests.
2. Describe the current extent of vegetation cover for the State in which you live. Repeat this for the other States and then rank them according to which has most vegetation cover and which has least vegetation cover.
3. Refer to the table below. Explain why New South Wales, Victoria and South Australia have had forest loss of 70 per cent, 67 per cent and 66 per cent respectively, while other States have not experienced such losses.
4. Which State or Territory in Australia has the best record for the least percentage of forest and woodland loss? What reasons can you give to explain this?
5. The data for South Australia and Western Australia is incomplete. How do you think the percentage of loss figure was arrived at for these States?

Preparing a map

1. Conduct research to find a map of your State or Territory which shows the amount of forest cover. This must include native forest regions and plantation forest areas. Enlarge and trace this map onto poster paper. Label your map according to the forest's type, location (use nearby towns) and distance and direction from your capital city. Provide a brief written description titled 'The location of forests in (your State or Territory)'. You might acquire information from:
   - your State or Territory's Department of Environment/Resources
   - your State or Territory's Forestry Association
   - National Association of Forest Industries (NAFI), Web address: www.nafi.com.au
   - your school and local library.
2. Write a paragraph explaining why some people think there will be more tree cover in your State or Territory by 2000, while some argue that there will be less. (*Hint*: Is tree cover different from native forest cover?)

Tree cover throughout Australia since European settlement

	Forest cover			Percentage of woodland cover		
State	**Before settlement (%)**	**1986 (%)**	**Loss (%)**	**Before settlement (%)**	**1986 (%)**	**Loss (%)**
ACT	59	26	56	38	13	67
NSW	20	6	70	57	31	46
NT	4	4	—	22	22	—
Qld	21	11	47	28	20	28
SA	—	—	66	6	3	45
Tas.	47	25	47	31	20	36
Vic.	38	13	67	34	8	76
WA	1	—	48	14	9	37
Total	**9**	**4**	**56**	**23**	**15**	**33**

(*Source*: *State of the Environment in Australia: Source Book*, AGPS, Canberra, 1986)

TYPES OF FOREST IN AUSTRALIA

Apart from Antarctica — which has no trees — Australia is the world's least forested continent. The prevailing vegetation in Australia is woodland and shrubland. Before European settlement only about nine per cent of Australia was forested. Today, about five per cent of the country is forested. Even though Australia exports timber and timber products, large amounts of timber, particularly softwoods, have to be imported.

There are many ways of classifying forests. One classification distinguishes between:

- native forests, which contain plants that are unique to Australia and are growing in their natural state, and
- plantation forests, which are grown like a crop, often planted in rows, can be either pines or eucalypts, but generally lack any other plant life.

Some other names that you might read about are: **regrowth**, **hardwood**, **softwood** and **old growth forests**. These terms are explained in the glossary.

NATIVE VEGETATION

Native forests are classified in many ways, but one system classifies them as either open, closed or woodland. These names refer to the density of the canopy (tops of trees) and the structure or make-up of the forest. Other sub-groups of these forests are defined by the main type of tree, the climate of the area and the amount of rainfall the forest receives. The information on the opposite page describes the groups and sub-groups of native vegetation.

PLANTATION FORESTS

A plantation forest is full of trees of the same type. A site is chosen and a crop of trees is planted. While the trees are growing, chemicals may be added to enhance growth or prevent disease. Mature trees are then harvested and taken to a sawmill to be processed. Today, both eucalypt (hardwood) and pine (softwood) plantations play an important role in supplying Australia's forest product needs.

Activities

Investigation: *Classifying forests*

1. Name a forest that you have visited and describe its location in relation to where you live. Then:
   (a) Classify it according to the categories opposite. Explain what you liked about the forest.
   (b) What did you do there?
   (c) What other land uses surround the forest?
   (d) Is the forest in an area of high or low rainfall? What evidence in the forest supports your conclusion?
2. 'A forest is more than just trees.' Explain what is meant by this, using evidence from a forest you have visited.

Communication: *Creating a labelled diagram*

You will need tracing paper for this activity.

1. Use the photographs on the opposite page, or a photograph from a forest you have visited, to sketch or trace the different layers of vegetation that you see.
2. Label your drawings using the following terms:
   - lower understorey — the seedlings of larger trees, bushes, ferns
   - upper understorey — taller trees, not quite as tall as the canopy
   - canopy — the tops of trees, which form the 'roof' of the forest. The canopy can be 'closed' or 'open'.
   - **emergents** — the very tallest trees, which stand out, or emerge, from the canopy.
3. Name the different types of vegetation using the terms 'shrubs', 'trees', 'ferns', 'grasses', 'mosses'.
4. Are there different levels in the forest you have drawn? What climatic factors might explain this?
5. Compare your drawings with those of other class members. What differences and similarities do you notice? Do all forest types have the same levels?
6. For this activity, you will need to interview someone who was born or who has lived in another country. Write the person's responses to these questions.
   (a) What memories do you have of forests in that country?
   (b) Describe the vegetation. What type of trees grew there? Was the forest thick and lush?
   (c) What was the forest used for?
   (d) Who managed or owned the forest?

Open forests

Sunlight reaches forest floor. Mainly eucalypts. Trees further apart than in a closed forest. Amount of rainfall determines height of trees. Tall open forest (also known as wet **sclerophyll** forest) has trees over 30 m, canopy cover greater than 70%, moist forest floor, eucalypts susceptible to fire. Low open forest has trees under 30 m. Open forest sub-groups are:

Mixed eucalypt
- Trees vary in height.
- Found in drier areas.

Examples are Victorian stringybark, WA jarrah, NSW and Qld spotted gum forests.

Dry eucalypt
- Has low rainfall.
- Has dry forest floor, slow decomposition.
- Eucalypts are generally fire insensitive.
- Also known as dry sclerophyll forest.

Examples are Victorian and NSW red gum forest, WA mallee forest, Victorian ironbark and box forests.

Woodland

Found in drier regions where rainfall is 400–900 mL per year. Canopy is usually very open (up to 20%) but denser stands are sometimes classified as open forest.
- Usually has only a grass understorey between short, stunted trees.
- Consists mainly of eucalypts and acacias (gums and wattles).
- When annual rainfall is less than 400 mL, the area turns to shrubs and grassland or open woodland.

Note: Some scientists would not class woodland as a forest because it has less than 30% canopy cover.

Examples are cypress pine areas in Qld and mallee woodland in NSW and Victoria.

Closed forests

Tops of trees (crowns) touch each other, creating a dense canopy. Only 2% sunlight reaches the forest floor. Major type of closed forest is rainforest.

Rainforest

Forest that receives more than 1000 mL of rain per year.

1. Tropical rainforest
- Rain falls relatively evenly through the year.
- Contains large range of plants and animals.
- Soil is deep and fertile.
- Extends from Mackay to far north Qld.

2. Sub-tropical rainforest
- Has lower annual temperatures than tropical rainforest.
- Extends from Wollongong, NSW to Mackay, Qld.

3. Temperate rainforest
- Patches in south-eastern NSW, Victoria and Tasmania

Wet eucalypt
- Has high rainfall, but less than rainforests.
- Trees grow rapidly.
- Some need a fire every 100 years or so to create an ash bed for new seed germination.

WA's karri forests and Victoria's mountain ash forests are examples.

HOW ARE OUR FORESTS USED?

Forests can be said to have *intrinsic* value. This means that they are important simply because they are part of the natural world. They have *aesthetic* value in that we enjoy being in them and we appreciate their natural beauty. Forests also have *ecological* value because they provide a habitat for plants, animals and micro-organisms; they give out oxygen, which humans need for survival; they soak up the carbon dioxide which humans create; and they clean our air and our water. Finally, our forests provide *economic* value, mainly by providing wood for all sorts of purposes, including the manufacturing of paper. The photographs and captions in this section show you most of these uses.

MEDICINAL

Ground tea-tree leaves are used in cosmetics; eucalyptus and tea-tree oils are widely used in the home.

WATER CATCHMENT

Forests help to filter and purify our drinking water. Tree-covered slopes allow clean water to flow into streams.

HOW WE USE AUSTRALIAN FORESTS

FRUITS AND NUTS

Bush tucker is still gathered by some Aboriginal people, and has potential use as commercial food.

ANIMAL HABITAT

Forests provide habitat for possums and other animals.

RECREATION

Bushwalking and other recreations

SOIL CONSERVATION

Forests help to conserve soil. After the trees were cut down in this formerly forested area, the soil washed away.

Native seeds are exported for use overseas.

Forest honey supplies about one-third of the honey produced in Australia.

Tall, straight trees are sawn into timber for use in housing, flooring, furniture and other building products.

Imperfect trees are cut into woodchips and then pulped to make paper, cardboard, tissues etc.

Forests provide a great classroom in which to learn about our flora and fauna.

Activities

Investigation: *Forest use compatability*

1. Some forest uses are compatible, which means that they can occur together in a forest without one use affecting the other. For example, passive recreation such as bushwalking is usually compatible with having an undisturbed habitat for wildlife. With a partner, complete the table (below) of forest use compatibility. Use a tick for uses that are compatible and a cross for uses that are incompatible. For example, at the point where the 'soil conservation' column meets the 'trail bike riding' row, a cross has been placed, indicating that these two things are not thought to be compatible. (You may not agree with this, of course.)
2. Compare your results with another pair in the class. Note down up to five differences in the two sets of results. For each of these differences, give reasons why you classed certain uses as compatible while others classed them as incompatible.
3. List five compatible uses on which you all agree.
4. Choose two uses that you nominated as incompatible. Can you think of any way in which this could be overcome?
5. Some forests in Australia are managed as 'multiple-use forests'. What do you think this means? Name some uses that could be included in a multiple-use forest. Under what circumstances would multiple-use forest management be a good idea?

Forest use compatibility

	Bushwalking	Canoeing	Picnicking	Horse riding	Trail bike riding	Animal habitat	Soil conservation	Water catchment	Medicinal
Bushwalking			✓						
Canoeing									
Picnicking									
Horse riding									
Trail bike riding							✗		
Animal habitat									
Soil conservation									
Water catchment									
Medicinal									
Seed collection									
Beekeeping									
Timber harvesting									
Education/Research									
Gums and resins									
Mining									
Agriculture									

✓ Mark with a tick the forest uses you think are compatible.
✗ Mark with a cross the forest uses you think are incompatible.

TWO WAYS OF SEEING

'I am an old, old tree. I live in a forest that has not been touched since white people came here. I am surrounded by many old gums who live in this tranquillity with me. In my forest, birth and death surround me. While I am alive, birds and animals live in the hollows in my trunk. But when an old tree dies, it crashes to the forest floor, cushioned by the grasses and ferns there. At the same time, a tiny new tree is struggling for life, sending roots into the moist, rich soil and reaching upwards to catch the sunlight. The slow dying of one of us is not the end. Lying on the forest floor, an old tree is invaded by insects, birds, snakes and spiders, all trying to carve out new homes. Some animals use the old tree as a hunting ground or as a daytime resting place before they hunt at night. Beetles, grubs and cockroaches move in to demolish the log. Fungi and other tiny organisms grow on the tree. This is good . . . there will be young trees to replace us and they need nutrition returned to the soil. Soon the earthworms arrive, to munch the whole lot down. I know all this to be true because I have lived here for so long. I know that I too will be useful to others in the forest long after I have become diseased and can no longer stand. I rejoice in being able to provide a home, a hunting ground, a food store and a nursery. I may be old, but I am still able to bring new life to the forest.'

'I am an old, old tree. I live in a forest that has not been touched since white people came here. I am surrounded by other old trees and because we are very mature, the wood within us is of a very high quality. It is dense and strong and it will make the very best timber available. Our timber will provide homes for people and beautiful furniture. Some of the trees around me are diseased and weak. When people come into the forest to collect me, they might also cut down the weaker trees. They can be chipped into small pieces at the local sawmill, mixed with water and made into pulp. Eventually, this pulp will become paper. Some pulp becomes fine writing paper, other pulp becomes cardboard and tissue paper.

Together, our sawlogs and pulp logs provide jobs and income for the people who live near the forest and when we are improved upon by, say, being dried in a kiln, we are even more valuable to the wood industry. We even get shipped overseas as sawn timber or woodchips, thereby creating export dollars for the whole country.

When I am removed from the forest, new trees will be planted in my place. Then, in 80 years or so, other old trees will be available to help people by providing wood. I may be old, but I am still able to bring new life to the forest.'

Top left: Cocoon hidden on the underside of a leaf

Above: Only very old trees have hollows large enough to provide a safe home for animals such as this feathertail glider.

Left: A moist forest floor, rich in decaying material, provides exactly the right conditions for a new seedling to grow.

Above left: Logs ready to be mulched to supply our paper requirements.

Above: Logs with deformities such as knots cannot easily be sawn, so they are cut into small pieces and may then be pulped for paper production.

Left: Planted all together, these eucalypt seedlings are monitored to ensure their growth in years to come.

Activities

Investigation: *Different points of view*

1. Read through the two viewpoints on pages 306 and 307.
   (a) Make a list of the ways an old growth forest can be used.
   (b) Categorise each of these according to whether it is an ecological use.
   (c) Write a brief paragraph explaining how you view these forests.
   (d) Compare your answers with a partner. Together, draw up a flow chart to explain the two ways of seeing the fate of an old growth forest.
2. Forests can be seen as:
   - a biodegradable, renewable, recyclable resource that uses solar power (forest industry view)
   - having value in their own right, providing habitat for wildlife, necessary for maintaining biodiversity and the cycle of life (conservationists' view).

   What do *you* think? Write your views in the form of a letter of support to either the forest industry or the conservation movement.
3. In 1997 about 11 per cent of our **sawlogs** and 23 per cent of our **pulp logs** came from old growth forests. However, 18 per cent of old growth eucalypt forest and 38 per cent of old growth rainforest remained untouched. The timber industry sees old growth forests as essential to their economic livelihood and would like access to more areas. The government could choose to allow them greater access, or they could act to prevent this.

   Work in small groups to complete a futures wheel for one of these possibilities. Place the possible change at the centre of the wheel (for example, government allows greater access to old growth forests). From the centre, you should write the first, second and third consequences of this outcome. Fill in the successive boxes until you have anticipated a full range of consequences.

Futures wheel

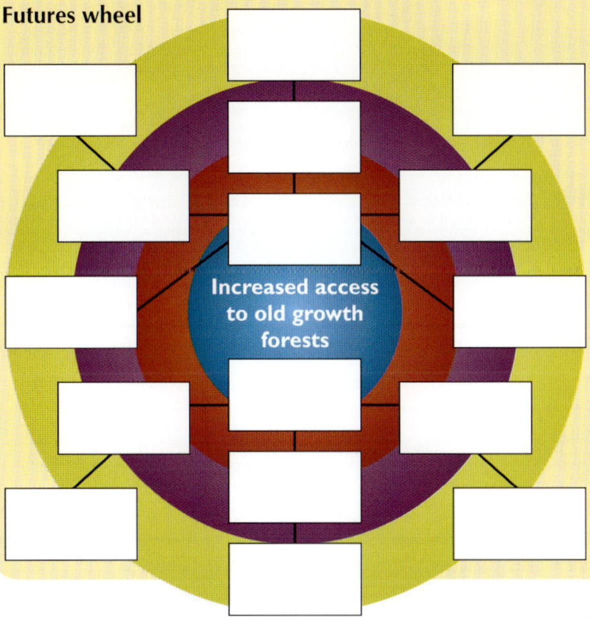

4. Your whole class will need to work together on this activity. Researchers and speakers will be needed. Present a debate on the issue:

   'You can put back the trees, but you can never replace the forest'.

   To help your team to prepare, see the list below of the arguments that could be presented. You will need to research each point more thoroughly, providing real evidence in the form of up-to-date data.

Arguments for woodchipping and logging native forests

- Woodchipping makes use of waste material.
- Native forest harvesting is good for the economy.
- Woodchipping is a potential growth industry.
- Wood is environmentally friendly.
- Native forests can continue to supply timber and woodchips.
- Timber harvesting is carefully managed.
- Most native forest is off limits.
- Australia leads the world in forest conservation.
- Wildlife conservation is not threatened by woodchipping.
- Bushfire control is enhanced by the native forest industry.
- Timber harvesting is a tradition.

Arguments against woodchipping and logging native forests

- Woodchipping is not simply a use of waste material.
- Harvesting of native forests is subsidised by taxpayers.
- Woodchipping is not good for the economy.
- Harvesting of native forests is not environmentally sustainable.
- Harvesting of native forests is not confined to a small area.
- Harvesting of native forests causes the loss of species.
- Sooty owls and other species are threatened.
- Animals die during timber harvesting.
- Tree ferns are destroyed.
- Timber harvesting rotations are too short for wildlife survival.
- Timber harvesting is not a natural process.
- Timber harvesting increases the risk of weed invasion and decreases water quality and quantity.
- Timber harvesting increases carbon dioxide gas production.
- Harvesting old growth forests is unethical.

12.5

DOES SUSTAINING OUR FORESTS MAKE CENTS?

Sustaining our forests means that instead of using them up until there is nothing left, we carefully use and manage them so that they can be constantly replenished. People who work in the forestry industry point out that forests and forest products are a $10 billion industry in Australia and create about 85 000 jobs. The forest industry is one of Australia's largest resource industries and Australia's second largest manufacturing industry. About 74 000 jobs are in the wood products manufacturing sector (sawmilling, paper and paper products, veneers and so on) and about 10 000 are in the logging operations sector. Much of this employment is in rural areas, where there are fewer opportunities for skilled work. The Australian community has a strong demand for forest products. This demand exceeds what we produce ourselves. We have to import about one-third of our annual needs. Because we import more than we export, Australia has a **trade deficit in forest products**. The table below shows this.

The forest industry says that there are three things that could be done in order to decrease the trade deficit.

1. If the government ensured **resource security**, then more businesses would be prepared to invest in making improvements and updating technology in the industry.
2. If we built more pulp and paper mills, we could make more paper products within Australia. Instead, we currently send the pulp overseas, only to buy it back as paper at a much higher price.
3. If we continued with **value adding** to our wood before it was sold overseas, we would gain more export dollars; for example, woodchips earn about $80 a tonne and sawn timber can earn about $200 a tonne.

Value of trade in paper and paperboard — 1996–97

Product	Imports $m	Exports $m
Newsprint	204.5	4.9
Printing and writing	740.6	55.7
Household and sanitary	40.2	60.0
Packaging and industrial	276.5	249.9
Total	1347.4	370.5

(*Source*: ABARE, *Australian Forest Product Statistics*, December quarter 1997, Canberra)

Should Australia have more paper mills like this one?

Australia's balance of trade in forest products

	1987–88 $m	1988–89 $m	1989–90 $m	1990–91 $m	1991–92 $m	1992–93 $m	1993–94 $m	1994–95 $m	1995–96 $m	1996–97 $m
Imports	1990	2262	2001	1990	2208	2437	2642	3001	2899.0	2547.1
Exports	481	537	541	649	702	777	854	1008	1018.1	1104.6
Trade deficit	1509	1752	1460	1341	1506	1660	1788	1993	1880.9	1442.5

(*Source*: ABARE, *Australian Forest Product Statistics*, June quarter 1995 and previous issues, Canberra)

Conservationists, on the other hand, do not agree that **woodchipping** is good for the economy. They argue that jobs in the forest industry are declining not because native forests are being 'locked away' but because the industry itself has become more mechanised. For example, a sawmill might have invested in a faster, more efficient saw, which could mean that fewer workers are needed.

> *The timber industry was shedding jobs long before the woodchip licence debate began. Future forest employment is clouded more from the industry running out of its own resource, continuing mechanisation and short term value added products such as woodchips, rather than any environmental restrictions.*
>
> Dr John French, convenor
> United Scientists for Environmental Responsibility and Protection, *Sydney Morning Herald*, 1995

Conservationists also argue that although the timber industry pays the government royalties for the timber they take from native forests (an agreed amount for every tonne of timber), the government, via the taxpayer, pays for access roads to the forests and for the overall management of the forests. A 1995 study in Victoria (Dr Andrew Dragun's *The Subsidisation of Logging in Victoria*, 1995) found that for every dollar the Victorian Government received in royalties from forest companies, it spent $2.25 supporting them.

Activities

Investigation: *Patterns in the timber industry*

1. Explain why, in economic terms, it doesn't make sense to woodchip sawlogs.
2. Using evidence from the table showing Australia's balance of trade in forest products, describe the imbalance. Is the situation getting better or worse? What do you think might happen if:
   - Australia was able to charge more for the forest products it sells overseas?
   - consumer demand for imported forest goods decreased?
   - Australia was able to make the products it currently buys overseas?
   - Australia banned the export of native forest products?
   - Australia banned the import of forest products native to other countries?
3. The table below names some people who are dependent on our forests. Copy the table and tick the appropriate column according to whether you think they are directly dependent or indirectly dependent on the forest.

	Direct	Indirect
Loggers		
Mill workers		
Paper-factory workers		
Timber merchants		
Builders		
Cabinet makers		
Local shopkeepers		
Furniture shop owners in cities		
Scientists		
Tourist operators		
Park rangers		
Consumers such as you		

4. Refer to the table opposite showing the value of trade in paper products. Describe the imbalances evident in the table. Suggest five reasons why Australia does not make enough of these paper products to meet its own demands.
5. An issue that the forest industry and the conservationists agree on is that a major way of reducing the imports of paper and paper products is to encourage consumers to *reduce*, *re-use* and *recycle*.
   (a) Make a list of the things that you already do at home and at school to help this cause, then compare your list with those of other class members.
   (b) With a partner, prepare a series of six mini-posters on this theme. Make sure that your message is simple, clear and eye-catching.
   (c) If appropriate to your school, write your messages in languages other than English. When the whole class has completed its posters, arrange with your teacher to post the 'reminders' around the school.
6. Some councils are threatening to stop collecting recyclable paper because the price they receive for it has become very low. In a group, discuss what you think about this, and what would happen if councils stopped collecting paper for recycling.

12.6

MANAGING A FOREST FOR TIMBER HARVESTING

You have learned that Australia's forests are not only an important part of our environment but also a vital economic resource. A number of industries are based on the harvesting of natural resources. They include fishing, forestry and industries using wildlife and wildflowers. If sustainably managed, harvesting is not necessarily detrimental but problems can arise when the resource is overexploited or when harvesting methods damage or cause destruction of habitat. Forest management involves making decisions about how to protect native plants and animals, cater for recreation, protect soil and water quality, allow for timber harvesting, and protect the environment for future generations.

REGIONAL FOREST AGREEMENTS

The Commonwealth and State governments have been working together to outline how, when and where forests may be logged and used for various purposes. First the governments find out as much as possible about a forest in a region. They ask groups of people living and working in the region, people who care for the forest and any other interested people to assess the value of the forest. This is called a comprehensive regional assessment (CRA). When all points of view have been considered, the premier of a State or Territory and the Prime Minister sign a Regional Forest Agreement for that forest. Some forests in a region are 'reserved' or set aside because of the very special plants, animals and habitats there. Others are not reserved and are managed for a range of uses such as recreation and timber harvesting.

MANAGING A HARVEST

A logging operator is issued with a licence to harvest timber. The logger and a local forestry officer then visit the forest to be logged and select a **coupe**. This is a group of trees chosen for harvesting. The size and shape of the coupe depends on the type of trees represented, the steepness of the slope, the location of the access roads and other factors. There are very specific rules about the use of a coupe, as you will see from the illustration on page 314. In Victoria, a coupe is generally not bigger than 40 hectares.

After selection of the coupe, the logger is then ready to cut the timber. This can be done in one of three ways, depending on the characteristics of the forest:

- *Clearfelling*. All trees are cut down except for those used to collect seed for the replanting of the coupe. In some cases, the coupe is then burnt, providing a warm ash bed for the new seeds to germinate in. The coupe will then be harvested again in about 80 years.
- *Selective logging*. Under this system, only the most mature trees are removed every few years. As regrowth of new trees occurs, trees of different ages grow in the forest. Seeds fall naturally to the ground, where they will later regenerate. Open forests can be harvested with minimal damage to other vegetation, with less visual impact and with less degradation of soil and water quality. However, there is more frequent disturbance in the forest by logging operators, because they move in to harvest the trees more regularly. Selective logging is used in all Queensland forests.
- *Shelterwood logging*. This technique is used in drier, more open forests. Mature trees are harvested in two or three stages. This helps to establish a new forest, with trees of about the same age, under the shelter of trees retained from the first harvest. The next mature trees are then harvested after about 20 years.

The main aims of all methods of timber harvesting are to:

- maximise the amount of sawlog timber from a tree
- ensure that the forest is regenerated after harvesting.

One final management strategy

Once the logger has cut the timber, it is carted by trucks to a local sawmill. The logs are stripped of their bark, left to dry in a yard or dried in a kiln. They may be sawn into planks or cut into woodchips. The Value Adding Utilisation Scheme (VAUS) ensures that the sawmiller obtains the maximum economic return for the logs. Good logs should not be wasted on woodchipping. The diagram opposite shows that with further processing, the product can have value added to it.

A recently clearfelled and burnt coupe showing ash beds and retained seed trees

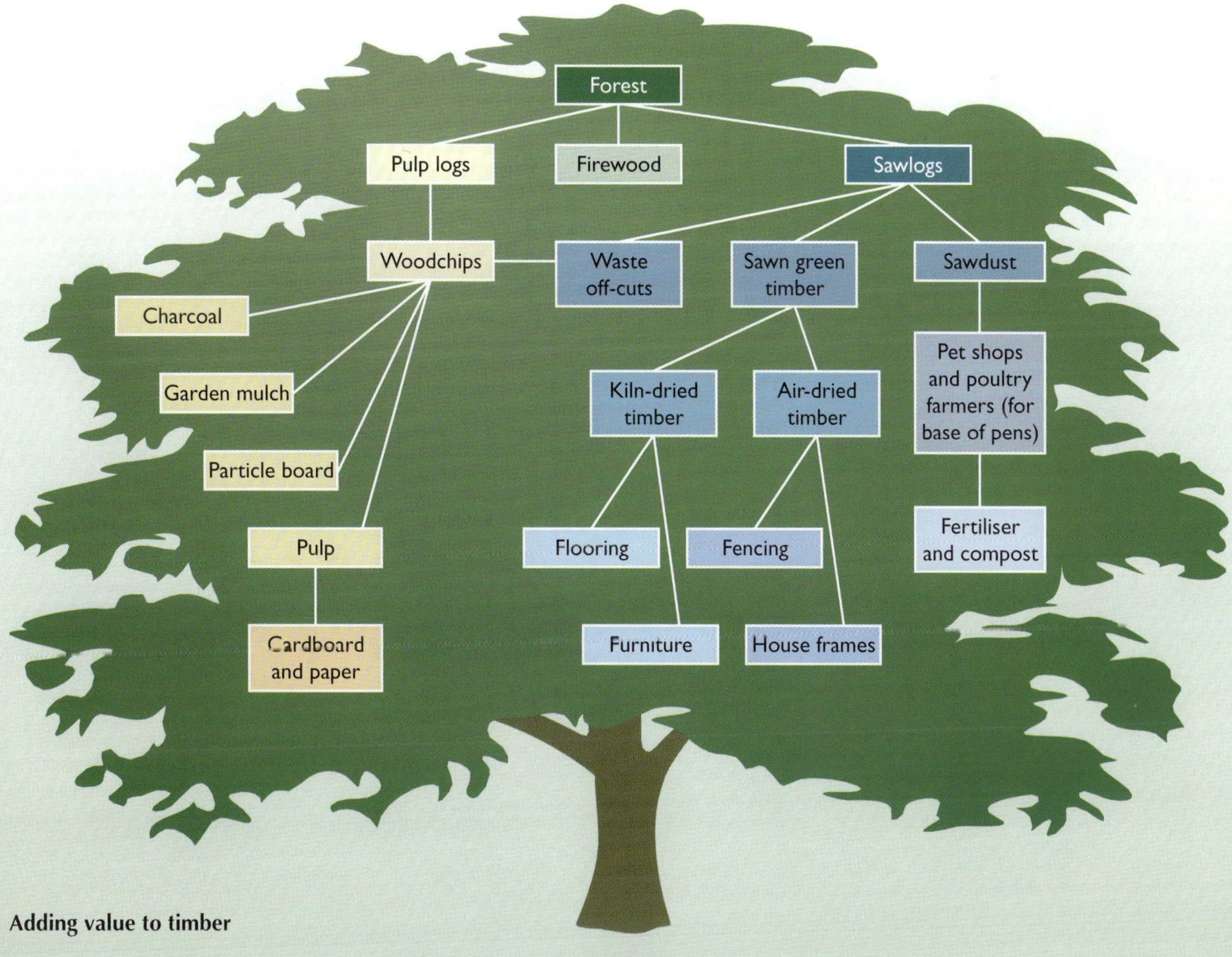

Adding value to timber

The code of forest practice for timber production

Some of the rules are:

- There should be no harvesting within at least 20 metres of a stream, in order to protect water quality.
- The area must be surveyed before approval of harvesting so that any significant animals or plants requiring protection can be identified.
- Before harvesting, several trees must be identified and marked as habitat and seed trees, then left unharvested.
- There must be maintenance of wildlife corridors that link areas of existing forest.
- No harvesting is allowed during wet weather because of the potential erosion and the effect on water quality.
- Damage done by heavy machinery during harvesting must be repaired afterwards, and the area must be reseeded or allowed to regenerate naturally.

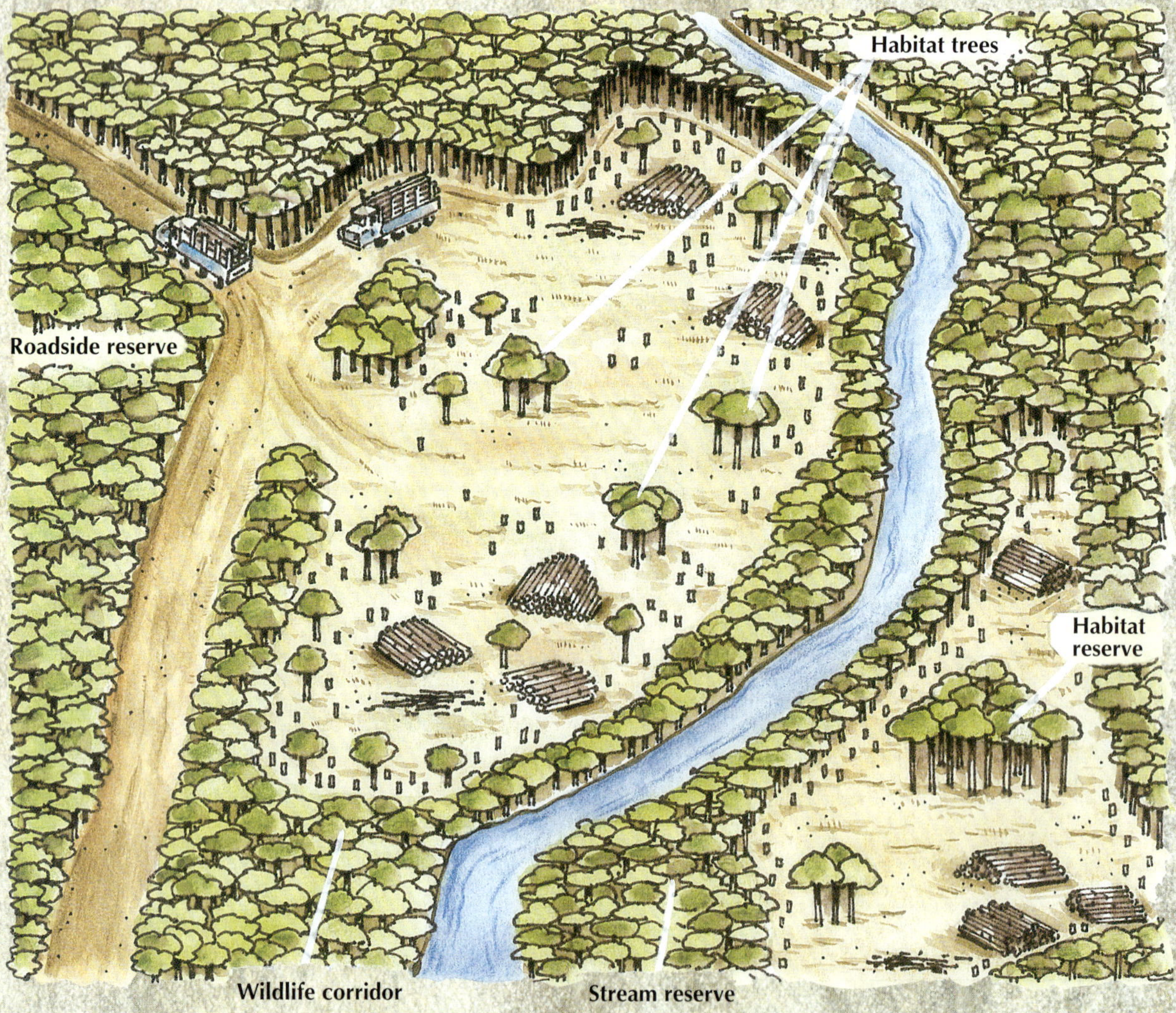

Activities

Investigation: *Towards sustainable management*

1. In your own words, outline the several ways in which timber harvesting is managed.
2. Trace the diagram shown below.
   (a) Label the parts of the tree that you think would be used as a sawlog (straight sections) and those parts that would be used for woodchipping or pulp logs (crooked, knotty, defective sections and those that are too small).
   (b) Draw an example of a tree that would be excellent for sawlogs.
3. Write the following stages of clearfelling in the correct order.
   - Break up the compacted soil with a bulldozer.
   - Remove all trees except those needed to protect water, soil and habitat.
   - Harvest again in 80 years.
   - Visit coupe to decide on coupe design.
   - Collect seeds from felled trees.
   - Reseed the coupe.
   - Burn forest debris.
4. Which of the following ensure **sustainable levels of harvesting**?
   (a) harvesting every tree in a forest
   (b) harvesting 50 000 cubic metres of timber when there is 50 000 cubic metres of wood growth in a year
   (c) harvesting 50 000 cubic metres of timber when there is 40 000 cubic metres of wood growth in a year
   (d) harvesting 75 000 cubic metres of timber when only 50 000 cubic metres has grown that year
5. How would each of the following events affect timber harvest yields?
   (a) a bushfire
   (b) a very wet year when the loggers could not always access the coupe
   (c) protesters in the forest preventing operations from continuing
   (d) the discovery by researchers of a rare plant species in the coupe
6. If you were in charge of managing a forest, what level of timber harvesting would you allow in each of the five years following a bushfire? Explain your reasons.
7. In pairs or small groups, research the timber industry strategy in your State. Find out about the guidelines for coupe plans and how value is added to logs. Does your information indicate that your State's strategy is in line with the national forest protection strategy?
8. With a partner, look through newspapers and magazines to find pictures of various value added wood products. Glue each of these onto a tracing of the diagram 'Adding value to timber', to show the variety of ways that value can be added to wood and wood products.

MANAGING A WHOLE FOREST

Most countries now recognise that almost all environmental problems, at a local, national and global scale, arise from unsustainable use of the resources of the physical environment. This has resulted in many countries, including Australia, developing comprehensive planning systems for managing the environment. We can expect that, in the twenty-first century, environmental management will become an even more important issue.

Timber harvesting is only one use of a forest. There are many other uses that are important, as you learned in section 12.3. Unless a forest has been specially reserved for its ecological worth, it is usually managed with these many uses in mind. This is called 'multiple use management'. Compatible uses are planned for, so that one use does not impose on another.

In this section you will have an opportunity to plan the multiple use management of a forest, based on what you have learned in previous sections.

YOUR FOREST: BACKGROUND BRIEFING

Fernybush Forest is located approximately 100 kilometres from a major city and five kilometres from a small township of 1000 people. The forest contains some small pockets of temperate rainforest, which have been nominated as 'reserved' in the Regional Forest Agreement. The main vegetation in the rest of the forest consists of eucalypts, with an understorey of wattles, ferns, grasses and mosses. The streams running through the forest eventually feed into the city's water supply. There have been several studies of the oldest trees in the forest, showing that their hollows are well used as habitat by animals, especially birds.

A local farmer has applied to establish some beehives in the forest so that the production of local honey can begin. People from the city often arrive at Fernybush Forest wanting to picnic, swim, bushwalk and take photographs of the beautiful views. Others want to go horse riding and trail bike riding or participate in other activities they cannot undertake in the city.

Activities

Communication: *Planning, negotiating, creating*

1. Now it is your turn to manage a forest. Since forest management plans are never done by one person working in isolation, you will need to form a group of four. Nominate the following roles.
   - *Forestry planner.* You would like to ensure that the loggers who apply for licences can harvest timber for many years to come.
   - *Environment planner.* You want to protect the ecological value of the forest (plant and animal habitat, water and soil quality).
   - *Recreation planner.* You are interested in providing a range of passive and active recreational pursuits for people who come from the local area and from further away.
   - *Local planner.* You want to ensure that the aesthetic quality of the local area is maintained. You are concerned that the traffic from increased visitors and logging trucks will affect the area, but you realise that the forest is there for everyone.

   You will each have to research your own role so that you can have genuine input.
2. Consider the background information given earlier and study the map carefully. The map shows the elevation and slope of the land, the location of major transport routes and some of the key features of the forest.
3. Refer back to the table of forest use compatibility that you developed in section 12.3. As a group of planners, decide which uses are going to be allowed in your plan.
4. Copy the map shown opposite. After discussions with all the planners in your group, use your copied map to draft out your ideas. Use rough notes, colour and symbols to create this draft.
5. When you are sure that all possible uses have been catered for, transfer the groups' ideas to an enlarged, fresh copy of the map. Remember to also change the scale when you do this. Use the scale when deciding the size of an area nominated for a certain use. Finally, write some explanatory notes to accompany the visual and oral presentation.

   Alternatively, your group may wish to video your presentation and then present this to the class. You could film 'on site' in a local park, create a background display within an office setting, or arrange an interview between the planners concerned.

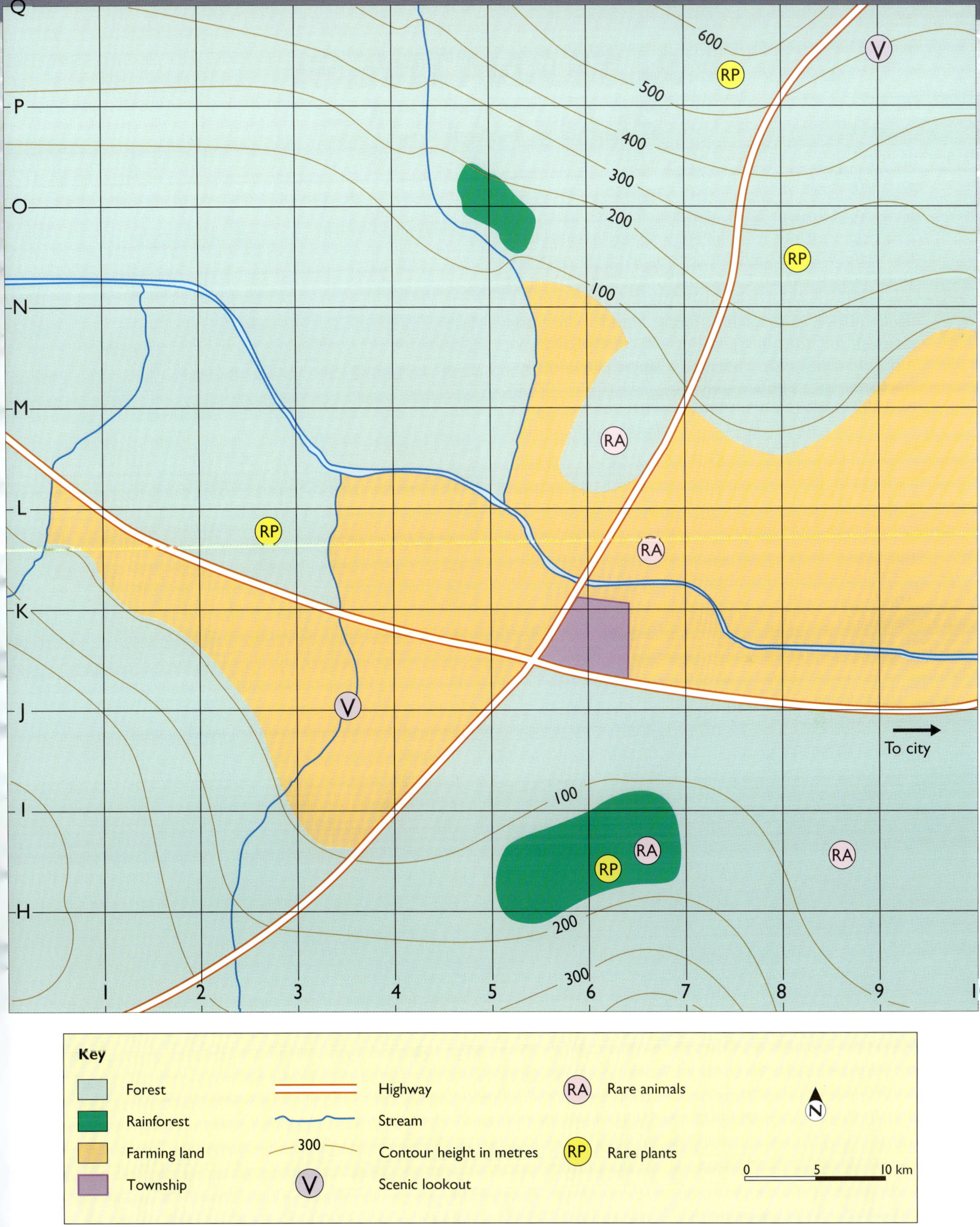

Map of Fernybrook Forest

12.8

ALTERNATIVES: PLANTATIONS

Growing timber in a plantation is just like growing any other crop on a farm, except that the crop takes much longer to bring to harvest. Both hardwood and softwood trees are grown in Australia in this way. Such plantations are created either on native forest land especially cleared for that purpose or on less productive agricultural land. There are about one million hectares of plantations in Australia. About 850 000 hectares are planted with softwood pine trees and about 150 000 hectares are planted with hardwood eucalypts.

Compared with a native forest, plantation forests grow very quickly. A softwood tree in a plantation can become a high quality sawlog in 40 years, whereas it would take a eucalypt in a natural native forest 60 to 80 years. Trees in a softwood plantation are grown close together and are cared for like a crop; pests, fires, water and fertilisers are all controlled.

Softwood plantation

Hardwood plantation

Naturally, eucalypt plantations take longer to mature. The timber industry argues that it may not always be economic to grow hardwood in plantations because of the time it takes for the trees to be ready to harvest. Conservationists see plantations as the great hope of the future. They argue that if eucalypts are grown in plantations, then eventually there will be less need to use native forests, particularly old growth forests.

The estimated future production of timber from Australia's plantations is shown in the table below.

Future yield from Australian forest plantations — all products ('000 m^3 per year, roundwood equivalent (RWE))

	1996–2000	2001–05	2006–10	2011–15
Softwood	11 800	12 500	12 200	12 200
Hardwood	500	1 900	4 000	6 100
Total	**12 300**	**14 400**	**16 200**	**18 300**

(*Source*: R. N. James et al., *Forest Plantations of Australia: their role in providing current and future wood supplies*, Department of Forestry, Australian National University, Canberra, 1995)

Current levels of production from plantations are much less than Australia's consumption of forest products. This will probably continue for at least the next decade.

The common uses for plantation and native forest timbers in 2000 are shown below.

Type of forest and timber	Uses
Plantation softwood	Building construction Paper production (mainly newsprint, tissues, cardboard) Fencing Panels, particleboard Furniture
Plantation hardwood	Paper production Panels, particleboard
Native forest hardwood	Furniture Flooring Building construction Panels, particleboard Paper production (high quality printing paper) Fencing

There is great debate about whether plantation timbers can be an adequate substitute for native forest timbers. Below are three responses, from three different groups, to the question: 'To what extent should production from plantations be expanded and production from native forests be reduced?'

The question implies that there is a relationship between expanding timber production from plantations and reducing production from native forests. There is no such relationship and the question is misleading. Any decision to expand plantations must meet appropriate environmental and financial criteria. Such decisions should not be contingent on decreasing timber production from native forests and there is no compelling reasons for such a course of action [in Victoria].

Victorian Association of Forest Industries, *Forest Education Project Opinion Series*, no. 1, paper 2

Internationally, many of the world's native forests (notably in tropical areas) are being depleted. World shortages in high quality timbers loom.

Those native forests in Victoria that are available for carefully managed timber production (following the process of scientific review and community consultation) can make an on-going contribution to our economic well-being and to our quality of life.

Victoria's forest management practices are, by international standards, very sophisticated. For the foreseeable future ... our approach should see an expanding area of both hardwood and softwood plantations being managed to meet a range of community needs, and the continuing sustainable use of available native forests to produce increasingly high quality timber products for both the domestic and export markets.

Victorian Department of Natural Resources and Environment, *Forest Education Project Opinion Series*, no. 1, paper 4

Our community has a variety of needs for timber. As far as practicable, those needs should be met from plantations. This may take time to achieve. However, over time, there should be a shift towards plantations as the source of our timber to the maximum possible extent. Native forests should only be used as a last resort and we should not be producing timber beyond our means.

Victorian National Parks Association *Forest Education Project Opinion Series*, no. 1, paper 3

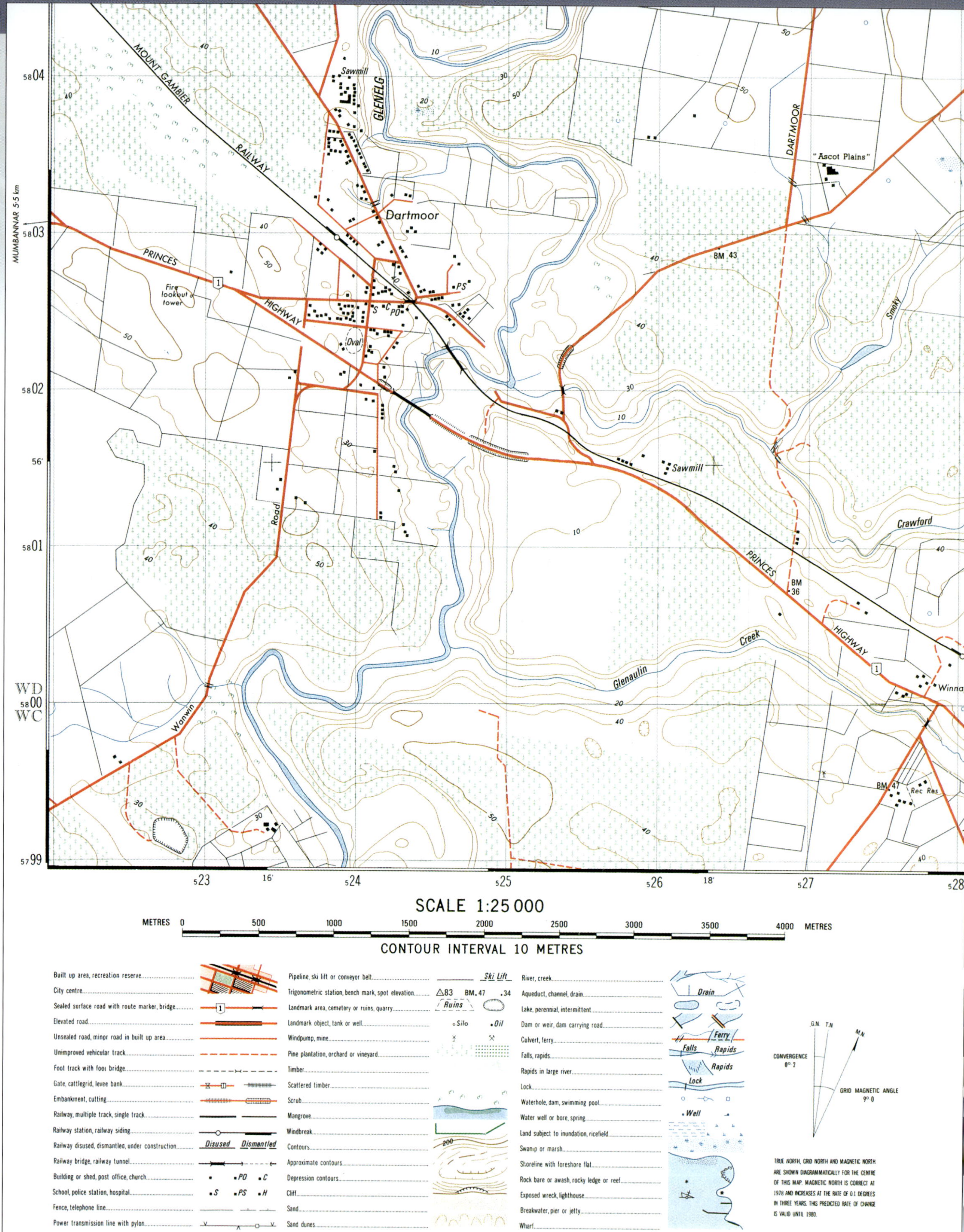

Topographic map of Winnap

Activities

Communication: *Using topographic maps*

Refer to the topographic map opposite.

1. What is the dominant forest type represented in this area?
2. Using the scale, estimate the area of land taken up by:
   - pine plantation
   - timber
   - cleared land.
3. What can you say about the slope of the land on which pines are planted?
4. What services are provided in Dartmoor that indicate this town relies on the plantations?
5. Complete the following table for the two sawmills in the area.

Sawmill	Grid reference	Distance from post office (km)	Advantages of this location
1			
2			

6. Suggest why the fire lookout tower is located where it is.
7. This map was produced in 1966. Since then, plantation forestry has increased in the Dartmoor area. Trace the areas of pine plantations in 1966 in one colour. Using another colour, draw in the regions that you think would probably be used for plantations today. Consider the factors mentioned earlier: proximity to transport, proximity to the sawmills and slope of the land.
8. Imagine that you are a sawmill owner. You have chosen this region to set up a new sawmill in 2001. Where would you locate your mill? Give reasons for your choice.

Investigation: *Plantation forests*

1. Look at the two photographs of hardwood and softwood plantations on page 318.
   (a) Compare them with the other photographs in this chapter. What differences do you notice between the structure of the native and plantation forests?
   (b) What do you notice about the variety of species and density of tall trees?
2. Pine plantations require weeding and fertilising. Why might this be so? What effect could this have on nearby rivers?
3. Read the three opinions presented on page 319. Use your own words to summarise them. Is there any common ground between these points of view? Which view do you agree with? Explain your reasons.
4. Look at the following information, found on the back of some greeting cards.

   What personal action can you take to support the plantation industry?
5. Find out about 'Plantations for Australia. The 2020 Vision'.
   (a) What is it?
   (b) Who is involved?
   (c) What are the aims of this group? The following Internet addresses will help you.
   www.dpie.gov.au
   www.nafi.com.au

INNOVATIONS IN THE TIMBER INDUSTRY

Timber for paper production doesn't always have to grow in natural forests — there are alternatives.

AGROFORESTRY

Agroforestry is the practice of grazing animals and growing trees for commercial timber on the same land. Private landowners may choose to plant trees as shelter for animals, as windbreaks, to protect crops from frost or to improve the quality of the soil. Plantations of trees can serve these purposes *and* earn the farmer extra income when the trees mature. Much research has been conducted to find out which trees are suitable, so that they can be matched to the farming type. For example, a farmer who plants rows of trees must ensure that the pasture grasses growing below the trees can still provide feed for the grazing animals. Farmers can grow trees for either paper or wood production.

TIMBER 2000

Timber 2000 is a group of Victorian farmers who have researched the growing of Tasmanian blue gum — *Eucalyptus globulus*. Operating in the traditional wool-growing region of the Western District, the venture promises income returns by harvesting the trees for woodchips. In 1996, the Timber 2000 farmers planted 1000 hectares of blue gum and they plan to have 80 000 hectares within 10 years. Blue gums are ready to be harvested after only eight years.

WATTLES FOR WOODCHIPS

Black wattle (*Acacia mearnsii*) is a small native tree that can be used for woodchips for fine paper production. It grows very quickly (seven metres in two years), is resistant to insects and has the special ability to increase the fertility of the soil. Its leaves can be used to feed cattle and, in South Africa, black wattle has been grown commercially for the tannin in its bark (used in leathermaking).

Agroforestry

HEMP

The plant known as Indian hemp (*Cannabis sativa*) can be used to make paper. Researchers, in trials under way in Victoria, are working on growing a 'non-drug' hemp variety for paper production. The benefits of cannabis grown for paper are that the plants mature in 100 days, can be irrigated with waste water and need few pesticides. Naturally, hemp will have far stricter controls than an ordinary crop. Other Australian States are waiting, before following the Victorian lead, to see if a viable industry can be established.

Cannabis sativa, **or hemp**

Activities

Check your understanding

1. Draw up a table that briefly states the advantages and disadvantages of each of the innovations mentioned here.
2. Which of these do you think has the greatest potential to provide material for paper production? Why?
3. Compare the methods and resources mentioned here with pine plantations. What type of government help would be needed to make these alternatives as viable and as large scale as pine plantations?
4. Do you believe that it is worthwhile to put money into these ventures? Explain your answer.

Communication: *Written responses*

1. Working in a small group, use all your answers from the Check your understanding questions above to write a letter to the editor of your local paper or one of the larger daily newspapers. Your letter must be brief and concise. Post your letter. What responses to your opinions were published in the newspaper?
2. Paste your letter in the middle of a large piece of cardboard. Paste on the responses so that they surround your letter. Write a summary of the views presented, and display this so that others can read about the issue (in the library, in corridors, in the classroom).

Hemp's new high

by Chip Le Grand

For 60 years hemp has been portrayed as a social demon. But, as Chip Le Grand reports, the plant has finally overcome its image problem.

When the United States government fired the first shots in its war on cannabis in the 1930s, industrial hemp, a non-toxic variety of the dreaded sex drug, became an early casualty.

Uprooted from the rich pastures of Kentucky and California, it was eventually eradicated by Western governments sympathetic to urgings from the US Bureau of Narcotics and banished to corners of the globe beyond Washington's influence.

With a view to history, it is perhaps fitting that following three years of State-sanctioned trials and tentative steps towards a hemp industry in Australia, it is technology developed behind the old Iron Curtain that is set to break Victorian producers free of the remnant shackles of prohibition.

Last week the Victorian Minister for Agriculture, Pat McNamara, revealed plans to introduce legislation in the current session of Parliament to loosen the laws prohibiting the farming and processing of industrial hemp.

Having signed off on a memorandum of understanding securing the use of technology developed by scientists in the former Soviet republic of Ukraine, McNamara predicted that within 18 months the northern Victorian town of Benalla would become the centre of a modern, economically viable hemp industry.

The technology, developed at the Ukrainian Academy of Agricultural Scientists, allows entire hemp bines to be processed into pulp, removing the expensive step of having to strip the fibres from the stem.

Daniel Tepavac, a Melbourne-based hemp wholesaler who beat US and United Nations interests in the race to secure exclusive rights to the technology, says it provides the key to a future paper pulp plant in Benalla capable of processing 8500 tonnes of raw hemp a year and undercuts the world market price of $1800 to $3000 per tonne by about half.

. . . Marketing consultant for Australian Hemp Industries, Martin Griffith, says the main producers of hemp are now India, China, Russia and Korea. The industry is well established in eastern and central Europe where, in places, hemp paper has been produced continually since the late eighteenth century.

Griffith says the global shortage in wood fibre for paper will sustain a world demand of about 124 000 tonnes of hemp for pulp, which can be used either as a supplement with timber pulp or for high-quality specialist paper. With the Ukrainian technology able to process about 65 per cent of the bine compared with the standard 25 per cent returned by other producers, Benalla will be able to supply about 5400 tonnes of pulp at a price well below even the Chinese, who have the benefit of cheaper labour.

With a potential return to farmers competitive with beef and wool and the lure of associated jobs for rural communities, the new hemp industrialists are no longer just blowing smoke.

Australian, 10 April 1997.

12.10 Meeting the outcomes

PREDICT THE EFFECTS OF RESOURCE DEVELOPMENT AND USE ON A SELECTED NATURAL AND HUMAN ENVIRONMENT.

Outline the relationship between current use of the environment and future availability of resources.

Look at the two forest regeneration methods shown below.

(a) What is the difference between the group selection and clear felling methods?

(b) Which method do you think would have the greatest impact on the following groups? (Explain your answer.)
  - (i) wildlife
  - (ii) profitability to the loggers
  - (iii) soil erosion
  - (iv) tourists and bushwalkers

(c) Which method of logging best ensures the future availability of forest resources?

Describe the likely impact of resource development and use on a natural environment.

1. Use the following cartoon to explain why Australia must make its forest use sustainable.

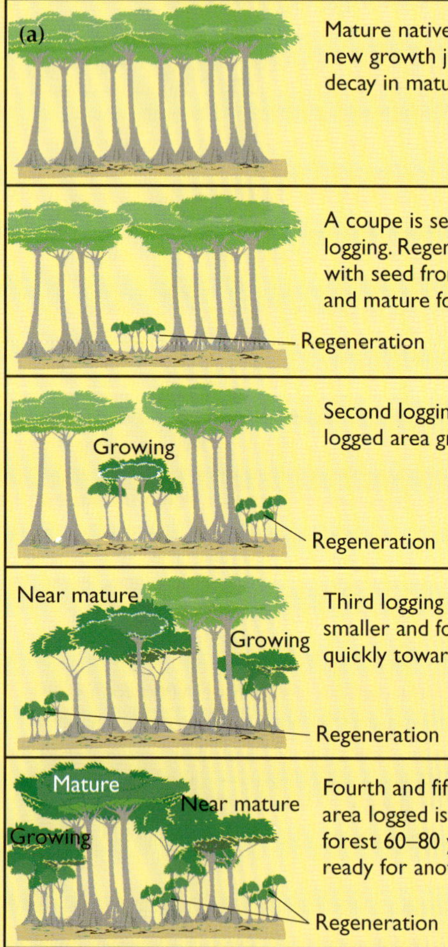

(a)
- Mature native forest — any new growth just equals the decay in mature trees.
- A coupe is selected for logging. Regeneration begins with seed from seed trees and mature forest.
- Second logging — previously logged area growing well.
- Third logging — mature areas smaller and forest growing quickly towards maturity.
- Fourth and fifth logging — first area logged is now a mature forest 60–80 years later, and ready for another logging.

(b)
- Mature native forest.
- Large coupe clearfelled. About five seed trees per hectare are left for regeneration. Post-logging burns aid regeneration.
- Mass regeneration of young seedlings follows burn-off.
- Older regeneration — forest is even-aged. Seed trees of mature forest often removed.
- Some trees removed to thin out forest. Forest ready for clearfelling again, often after 40 years, and before forest reaches maturity.

Forest management methods.
(a) Management of a native forest by group selection (or selective) felling methods. The pattern of logging over a 60 to 80 year period aims to create an uneven-aged forest that can sustain production over a very long period.
(b) Management of a native forest by clearfelling methods. This method ensures maximum use of the forest at one time, and leads to the development of an even-aged forest that can be clearfelled at a later date, usually before the forest reaches maturity.

2. Read the following opinion, expressed by Dr Patrick Moore, co-founder of Greenpeace. When asked to comment on Australian forests and forestry in 1996, he made the following comments.

'Somehow or other environmentalists have the public in Australia convinced that woodchips are tantamount to nuclear waste. I've never seen a case like this anywhere in the world — where people don't understand that woodchips are just chips of wood, which is a renewable resource, after all. It is too bad that the average Australian doesn't have to go down to the corner store every morning and buy their daily allotment of woodchips, because that's what they're doing when they buy the morning paper or a magazine.'

Dr Patrick Moore, 1996
in *Sustainable Forest Management: The Strength of Australia's Forest Industries*, National Association of Forest Industries

What does Dr Moore mean? Do you agree or disagree with his point of view?

DEVELOP A COMPREHENSIVE STRATEGY TO RESOLVE AN ISSUE RELATED TO THE USE AND MANAGEMENT OF AN ENVIRONMENT.

Evaluate the factors contributing to the development of an issue relating to the use and management of an environment.

Fieldwork

With your teacher, choose a forest to study that is not too far from your school. Your task is to answer the question: 'Is [your forest] being used in a sustainable way?' (Insert the name of the forest.)

In the classroom before you go

1. Obtain a location map and, if possible, a topographic map and a recent aerial photograph of the area.
2. Obtain a history of the forest and any other material that will help you to become familiar with the area.
3. Phone a forest ranger and a local sawmill owner to arrange help on the day of the field trip.
4. Learn and practise any field skills that you may need, such as sketching, counting species in a transect (a small area, two metres square), and taking good photographs.
5. Form groups of four. Check that you have all of the necessary equipment needed to maximise your data collection on the day.

In the field

1. You should visit a variety of areas in the forest. Conduct the following activities at each location.
   (a) Take a photograph.
   (b) Draw a sketch of the levels in the forest.
   (c) Take a transect, noting the amount and variety of plant species in each transect.
   Different groups could do different transects and then swap information.
2. Take extensive notes on the evidence of human impact, the presence of native animals and the evidence of multiple uses of the location. Some locations in the forest that will provide you with contrasts are:
   - an area reserved from human use (such as a rainforest, streamside, roadside reserve)
   - an area set aside for day trippers
   - an area that has been logged recently
   - an area of 10-year-old regrowth
   - an area of 30-year-old regrowth
   - an area that has never been logged.
3. If possible, visit a local sawmill. Find out the following information.
   (a) What happens once the logs are delivered there?
   (b) Name the various processes that the logs undergo.
   (c) What end products does the sawmill produce?
   (d) What value adding occurs here?
   (e) How many people does the mill employ?
   (f) How would the local town be affected if the logging operations were to cease?

Writing up the report — back in the classroom

1. Share all the data within your group and, where necessary, between groups.
2. Collate the data into a useable form. Choose appropriate ways to present your data. Your teacher will help you with this.
3. Decide on the format of your report. You could present a traditional written report, create an annotated visual display, or create an audiovisual presentation for other students.
4. Complete the presentation of your report. Remember that you have to respond to the question: 'Is [your forest] being used in a sustainable way?'

Chapter 13

FULL HOUSE? A LOOK AT GLOBAL POPULATION

Introduction

In 2000, the population of the world was about 6.1 billion people and growing rapidly. It is estimated that the world's population increases by an average of 236 000 people every day. This is the equivalent of the population of Switzerland every 30 days and the population of China every 14 years.

Such population growth is exponential. At first it took thousands of years for the population to double, then hundreds. Now it takes less than 40 years, although the rate has begun to slow.

There are many opposing views about the capacity of the Earth to withstand such growth in our numbers. Such views bring into focus the disparity between rich and poor countries, environmental and economic opinions, and the role of women and religious institutions.

In this chapter you will investigate many of these issues. By studying past and present population figures as well as predictions about the future, you will be able to discuss the issues involved.

LEARNING *outcomes*

- Identify factors such as death rates responsible for change to human populations.
- Explain the distribution pattern in human populations.
- Analyse human population change and its effects.
- Use a range of graphs to predict future patterns in the distribution of human populations.

GLOSSARY

age–sex pyramid: see population profile
birthrate: the number of people born for every 1000 people each year
birth potential: the potential number of babies which can be born, calculated on the number of women at child-bearing age
census: the counting of a population
contraceptive: an artificial means for preventing pregnancy
death rate: the number of people who die for every 1000 people each year
demographers: people who measure and study the human population by counting births, deaths and other population characteristics
developing country: a country with little industry and mainly rural economies. Average income per head is low and health and education provision is often poor, although conditions vary widely
doubling time: the number of years it takes for a population to double in size
exponential growth: growth which speeds up with time, starting slowly then getting faster and faster
fertility rate: the average number of children a woman is likely to have in her lifetime. A rate of just over two children, called the replacement level, keeps the population steady.
growth rate: (or annual rate of growth) the percentage increase in a population per year
industrialised country: a country with an economy based on industry, and where factories provide more jobs than agriculture. Usually the income per head is high and provision of health care, education and social services is good.
infant mortality: the annual number of deaths of children under one year of age for every 1000 live births; ranges from less than 10 in Western Europe to more than 100 in parts of Africa and Asia
life expectancy: the average number of years a person can be expected to live; affected by heredity, nutrition, occupation and other factors
literacy: the ability to read and write, providing access to education, skills and better jobs
pandemic: a disease that is widespread through an entire country, continent or the world
population density: the average number of people living in a certain area
population profile: a graph which shows the distribution of a population in terms of age and sex
population structure: the relative numbers of young and old people in the population. In developing countries with high birthrates, the young greatly outnumber the old.
replacement level: the number of births (two per couple) which keeps population numbers steady (ignoring migration)

THE RISING TIDE

Humans appeared on Earth about 100 000 years ago. In ancient times people lived in small isolated communities. The **birthrate** was high, but so was the **death rate** and population growth was slow and irregular. Agriculture was developing and food supplies were increasing. However, frequent wars, plagues and famines stemmed population growth.

By the birth of Christ 2000 years ago, there were about 250 million people; a **growth rate** of around 0.1 per cent per year. During the Middle Ages (AD 500 to AD 1500) increased knowledge in Europe of agriculture, hygiene and medicine resulted in people living longer, and world population increased more rapidly. World population growth was still contained by epidemics such as the Black Death, or bubonic plague. Infected fleas were carried in the fur of rats into every home and this contagious disease quickly spread. In the four-year period between 1347 and 1351, it is estimated that 30 million people died throughout Europe.

Around AD 1750, the world population began to experience **exponential growth**. The population doubled to one billion at around 1800 and two billion by 1925. Much of the world's population explosion is due to falling death rates because of:

- improvements in agricultural methods
- the introduction of machines on farms
- improvements in medicine
- improvements in hygiene.

This has also resulted in an increase in average **life expectancy**.

Since the early twentieth century the world's population has doubled about every 40 years, a growth rate of 1.6 per cent per year. Asia and Africa have the greatest population growth. In the last decade there have been signs that the global growth rate is slowing.

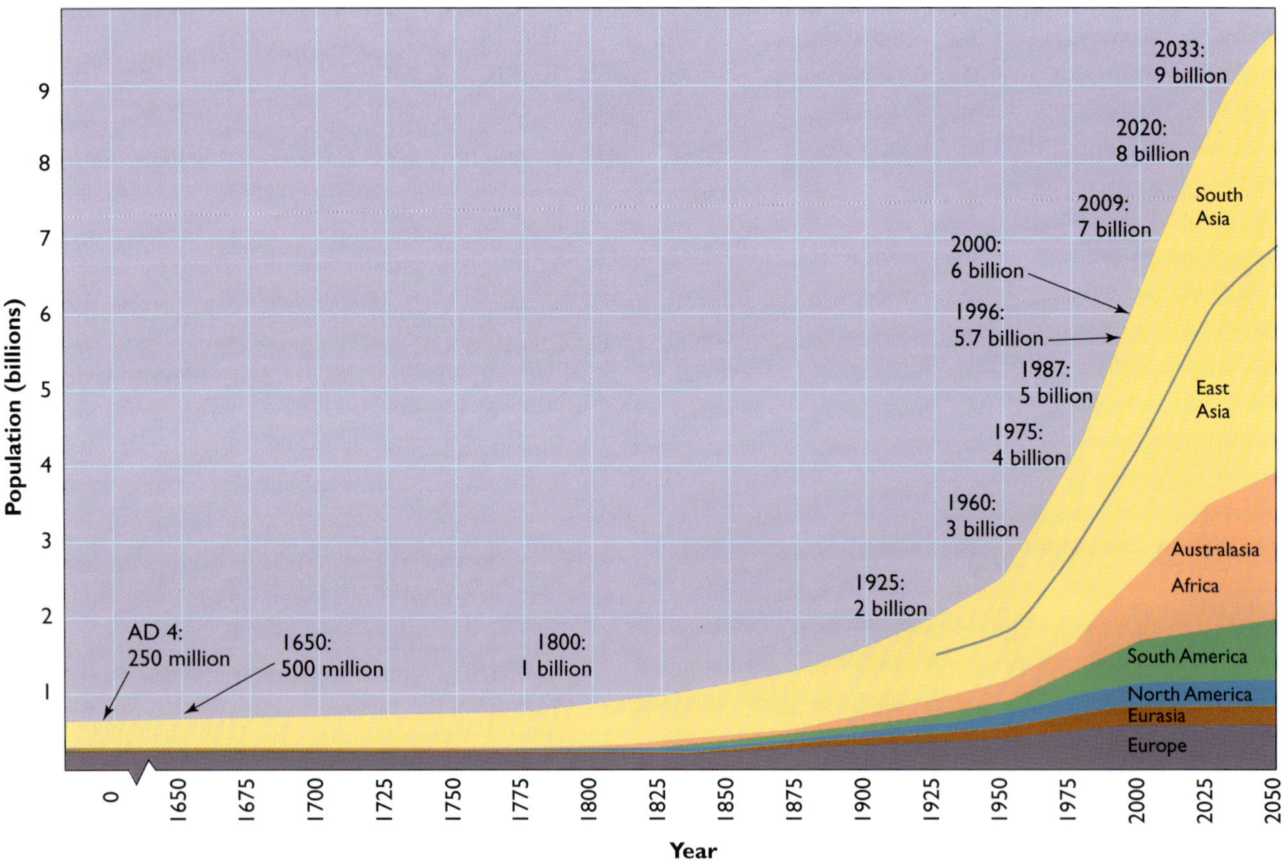

Exponential growth of the world's population — past and projected

(*Source*: Adapted from United Nations Population Fund, *The State of World Population*, p. 3 and PopNet, www.popnet.org/)

Population growth rate and doubling time

Growth rate (percentage increase per year)	Estimated doubling time (years)
0.1	693
0.5	139
1	69
1.5	46
2	35
2.5	28
3	23
4	17

Although the **doubling time** of the world population is around 40 years, variations exist in individual countries. Around the world, 80 countries will double their populations within 30 years or less. Of those, 43 are in Africa. The doubling time in Sweden is 99 years; Australia, 91 years; China, 62 years; Argentina, 55 years; Kuwait, 31 years and Ethiopia, 23 years.

Wars, disease and malnutrition do have an effect on local populations, but the enormous growth of the world's population seems unaffected by these events. The smooth population line in the graph opposite hides some dramatic falls and gains in local populations, as can be seen from the following graph.

Activities

Investigation: *Historical population growth*

1. Why was the world's population so slow to grow initially?
2. Outline the reasons given for the exponential growth of the world's population. For each reason, provide further detail to help explain why more people have survived.
3. Study the graph showing the exponential growth of the world's population.
   (a) Describe the growth in world population over time.
   (b) Which region has the largest population?
   (c) Study an atlas and compare each region by land mass and population total. To what extent is there a relationship between the amount of land a population inhabits and the population's numbers?
4. Study the table showing population growth rate and doubling time.
   (a) What is the relationship between growth rate and doubling time?
   (b) Describe the factors which might affect growth rate and doubling time.
5. Study the graph showing Egypt's population over time.
   (a) List three events which have caused the highest death rate in Egypt's history.
   (b) When was growth rate at its highest? What might be an explanation for this?

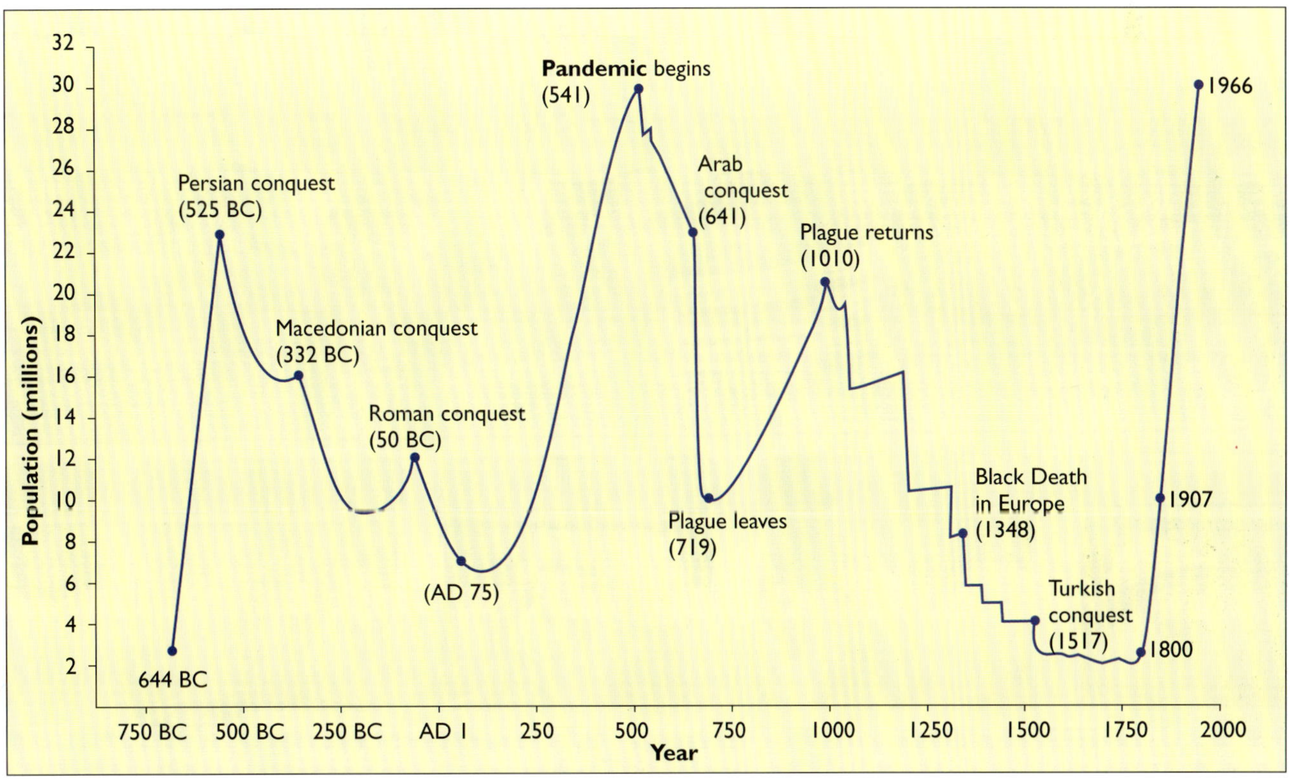

Egypt's population over time

WHERE ARE ALL THE PEOPLE?

Population statistics are very difficult to obtain with complete accuracy. Some countries are very precise in the way they count and maintain registers about people via a **census**. Others are not so exact and miscounts occur. In some countries, gathering statistics is easier because most people have an address, can read and write and there is a good postal service and transport. This may not be the case in other countries. Imagine the difficulties of trying to count where refugees from a war-torn area have gone or establish how many people have died in a conflict. In some countries and cities there are illegal immigrants who do not want to be counted and will not be included in final statistics.

Nonetheless, a lot of population information is accurate and regularly updated. **Demographers** are the people who count and work with these statistics. Demographers base future predictions about a population on the accuracy of statistics, resulting in two possibilities — a low number and a high number.

Population density shows where the world's population is concentrated. The world's population is not evenly spread. Some countries have many more people than others. At times, more land means larger numbers of people, but this is not always the case. Fertile parts of the world can support more people, but some countries have a lot of land and not many people because the land is unproductive. Antarctica, for example, is virtually uninhabited because it is the coldest, driest and windiest place in the world, with 98 per cent of its surface covered in ice. Similarly, the Sahara region of area supports very small and dispersed desert communities due to extremely high temperatures and low rainfall unable to support widespread agriculture.

In a densely populated country like Vietnam, services such as public transport are stretched almost to their limit.

The world's population density — people per square kilometre

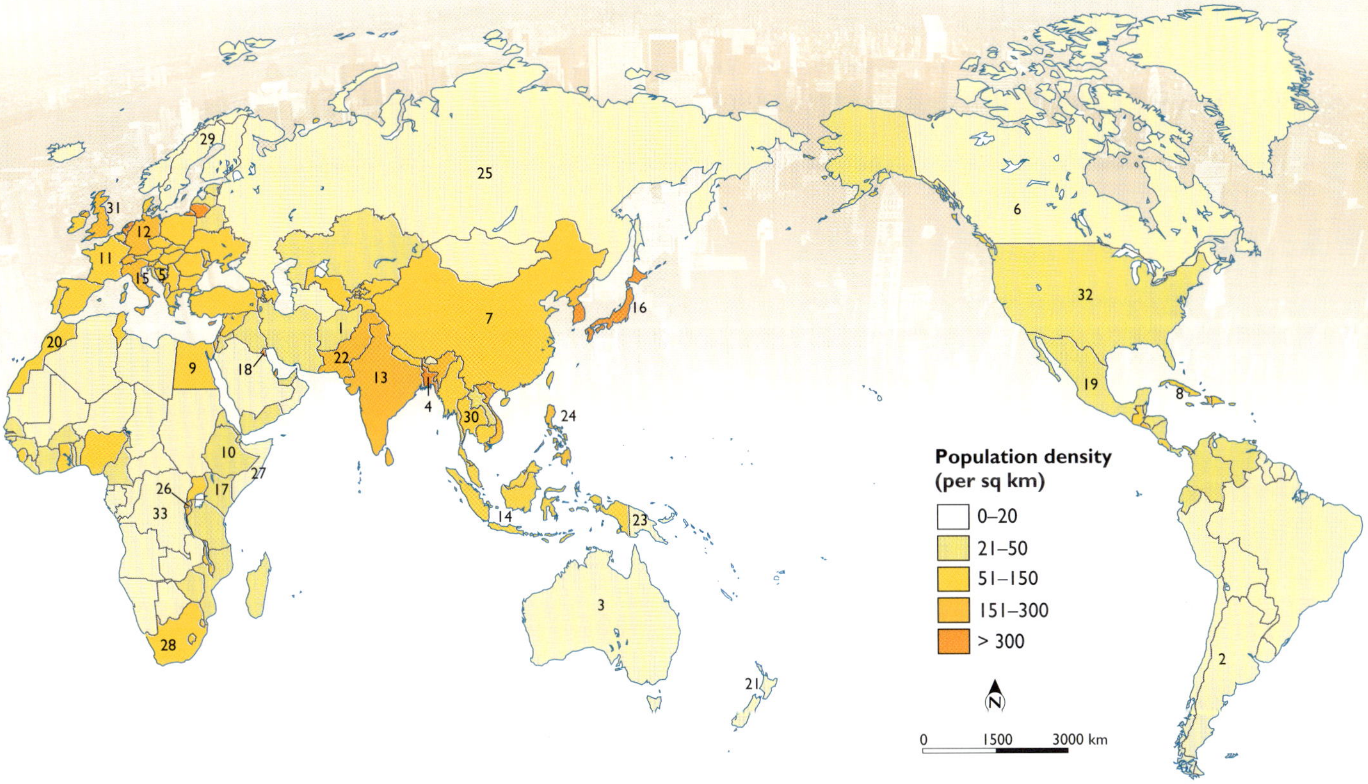

Population figures for countries numbered in above map, 1996 (in millions)

1. Afghanistan	22.3	9. Egypt	60.9	17. Kenya	29.1	25. Russia	148
2. Argentina	35	10. Ethiopia	56.7	18. Kuwait	2.0	26. Rwanda	6.8
3. Australia	18.3	11. France	58.3	19. Mexico	92.7	27. Somalia	6.8
4. Bangladesh	123	12. Germany	81.9	20. Myanmar	45.9	28. South Africa	41.7
5. Bosnia–Herzegovina	3.5	13. India	952.9	21. New Zealand	3.6	29. Sweden	8.8
6. Canada	28.7	14. Indonesia	198.1	22. Pakistan	133.5	30. Thailand	60
7. China	1218	15. Italy	57.5	23. Papua New Guinea	4.4	31. United Kingdom	58.7
8. Cuba	11.1	16. Japan	125.6	24. Philippines	71.7	32. United States	265.4
						33. The Democratic Republic of Congo	45.2

The main difference in world population is the concentration of people in poorer or **developing countries** compared to **industrialised countries**. More than 90 per cent of the world's population growth is taking place in the developing world. The bar graph below shows the actual and predicted population growth for the industrialised and developing countries.

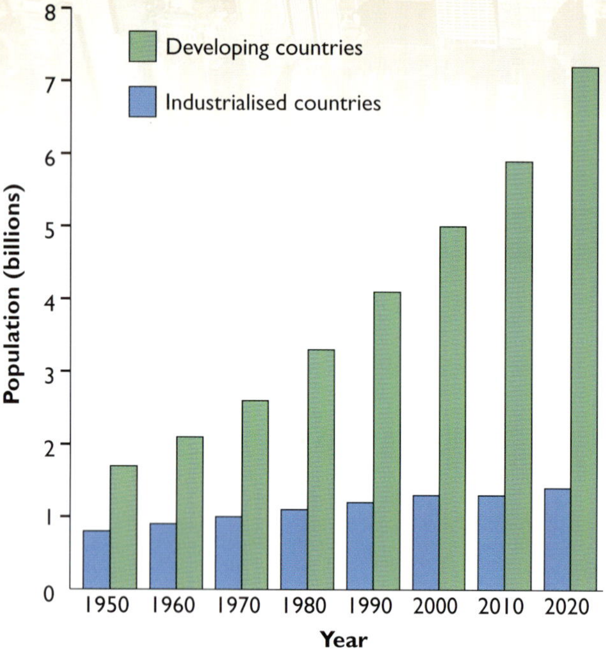

World population growth

An **age–sex pyramid** or **population profile** shows the age structure of a population. The population profiles on the right show the age structure of developing and industrialised countries. The broad base of the pyramid for developing countries is the result of high birthrates. A large percentage of the total population is less than 15 years old, containing many potential parents. This is called the **birth potential**. In the industrialised countries the percentage of young people is much lower, but the group over 65 years of age is relatively large. This group of older people is called the 'aged population' and relies on younger people to provide goods and services for them.

The **fertility rate** is also used to measure the potential size of a population and is the average number of children a woman is likely to have in her lifetime. A rate of just over two children per couple, called the **replacement level**, keeps the population stable. The average global fertility rate in 1997 was 2.9 children per woman. The table on page 333 compares the fertility rate and other data from selected countries.

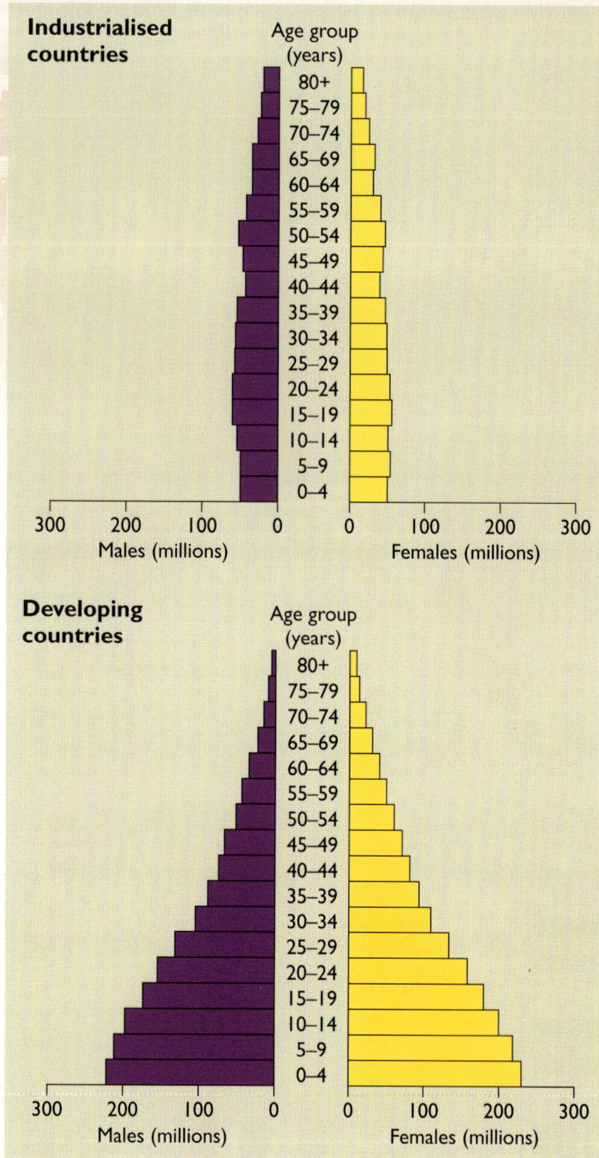

Population profiles for developing and industrialised countries

Activities

Investigation: *Analysing a range of sources*

1. Look at the map showing world population density on page 331.
   (a) Which continent has the greatest population density?
   (b) Which of the numbered countries has the highest population density?
   (c) Which of the numbered countries has the highest population? What population density does this country have? Why?
   (d) Suggest reasons why Japan has such a high population density. What problems might Japan face in the future?

Population statistics in selected countries, 1996

Country	Fertility rate	Infant mortality rate (child <5 dies)	Life expectancy (years) M	Life expectancy (years) F	Adult literacy (per cent)	Birthrate (births per 1000)	Death rate (deaths per 1000)
Afghanistan	6.2	153.0	44.0	43.0	26	42.7	18.5
Australia	1.8	5.7	74.4	81.1	100	14.1	6.9
Canada	1.7	6.2	74.7	81.7	99	13.2	7.2
China	2.0	26.0	69.1	72.4	19	17.1	6.6
Ethiopia	7.1	124.1	45.9	48.2	65	46.5	17.5
France	1.6	6.1	72.9	81.1	99	12.2	9.0
Germany	1.3	5.6	72.5	79.0	96	9.3	10.7
India	3.3	73.0	58.7	59.8	48	26.5	9.8
Italy	1.2	6.6	73.8	80.4	98	9.2	9.6
Kenya	4.6	55.4	56.9	56.8	22	34.3	9.8
Mexico	3.7	27.1	66.5	73.1	10	31.5	4.7
Philippines	3.7	38.0	66.0	70.0	5	28.7	5.9
Somalia	7.0	123.0	55.4	54.8	40	44.6	13.6
Sweden	1.9	3.7	75.3	80.8	100	11.7	10.6
United Kingdom	1.7	6.2	74.4	79.7	99	12.9	10.7
United States	2.0	8.0	72.0	78.9	99	15.2	0.7
Western Sahara	6.9	149.0	45.3	47.6	50	46.9	18.5

2. Study the graph that shows population growth in industrialised and developing countries.
   (a) Compare and contrast the population growth in developing and industrialised countries.
   (b) What does the graph indicate might happen after 2020?
3. Study the population profiles on page 332.
   (a) Describe the population profile for industrialised and developing countries. Which has the largest number of children? Which has the greatest birth potential? Which group has a higher proportion of older people?
   (b) Which group of people in a population looks after or indirectly supports the young and the aged? What is happening to the proportion of people in this group in both industrialised and developing countries?
4. Study the table above.
   (a) You can work out the rate of natural increase per thousand of a population by subtracting the death rate from the birthrate. Do this for the countries listed in the table.
   (b) Which countries have a high natural increase in population? Which have negative growth? What does this mean?
   (c) How does migration have an effect on the increase in a country's population?
   (d) How might refugees leaving a country affect these figures?

Communication: *Constructing and analysing maps*

You will need a blank outline map of the world to complete this activity.

1. Develop symbols for the data in the table. Draw a key on your map to show these symbols.
2. Now map the data in the table, using the symbols you have developed. Draw a border around the set of data for each country. If there is not enough space to draw this within the border of a country, draw it on the edge of the map with an arrow to show where it belongs.
3. Write a brief paragraph to describe the population pattern you have drawn.

Creating a table

Study the map showing the world's population density. Work with another student to complete this activity.

1. Draw a table with three columns in your workbook. Label the three columns 'Country', 'Population density' and 'Amount of productive land'.
2. Use an atlas to locate a map of the world which shows vegetation and land types. Study the atlas map and the world population map and record the population density and amount of productive land for the following places: United Kingdom, Germany, India, China, Egypt, Nigeria, Australia, Guatemala, El Salvador, Brazil, Indonesia, the Philippines and Japan.

13.3

POPULATION ON THE RISE

The world's population increases by 90 million people every year, putting further strain on our natural resources. Population growth in industrialised countries is low in percentage terms, but high in environmental impact. The United States of America will grow by 130 million people between 2000 and 2050, much less than the growth projected for most of the developing world. However, on average one American consumes as much energy as 2 Japanese, 6 Mexicans, 13 Chinese, 128 Bangladeshis or 370 Ethiopians.

In contrast, the populations in developing countries are growing quickly. Up to 95 per cent of all population growth between now and 2025 will occur in developing countries.

The populations of developing countries have doubled in a very short period of time. The death rate has dropped sharply, especially among mothers and young children. The average life expectancy has also increased. The lower death rates are due to improvements in general health and food production.

The desire for large families is the result of many factors, among them high **infant mortality** rates, agricultural methods based on labour, and the need for support in old age. The drawing below, and the following quote, show why many women or couples who would like smaller families do not actually try to reduce the number of children born.

> 'In a country like ours where the infant mortality rate is 140 per 1000 births, where infectious diseases kill so many children, where malnutrition affects 30–50 per cent of the people, where measles is a killer disease although it could be stopped by immunisation, how can you tell us to stop having children? When a mother has twelve children, only three or four may live.'
>
> A doctor in the Sudan

In countries such as Afghanistan and Ethiopia, medical advances have caused a rapid fall in the death rate. This will result in a fall in the birthrate, but there will be a large population before it begins to actually decline. This can be seen in the population pyramids. So, even though the fertility and birthrates of a population may decline, the population may continue to increase for many years.

Some of the reasons people have large families

Afghanistan's population in 1996 was 22.3 million people. The overall population density was 35 people per square kilometre. In 1993 the United Nations High Commission on Refugees reported that, in 1992, the world's largest refugee population came from Afghanistan. There were about 4.5 million Afghan refugees; 2.9 million of them were in Iran. By the end of 1992, 1.5 million Afghan refugees had returned to Afghanistan from Pakistan. More than 80 per cent of the people of Afghanistan live and work in rural areas, and approximately 2.6 million still lead a nomadic life.

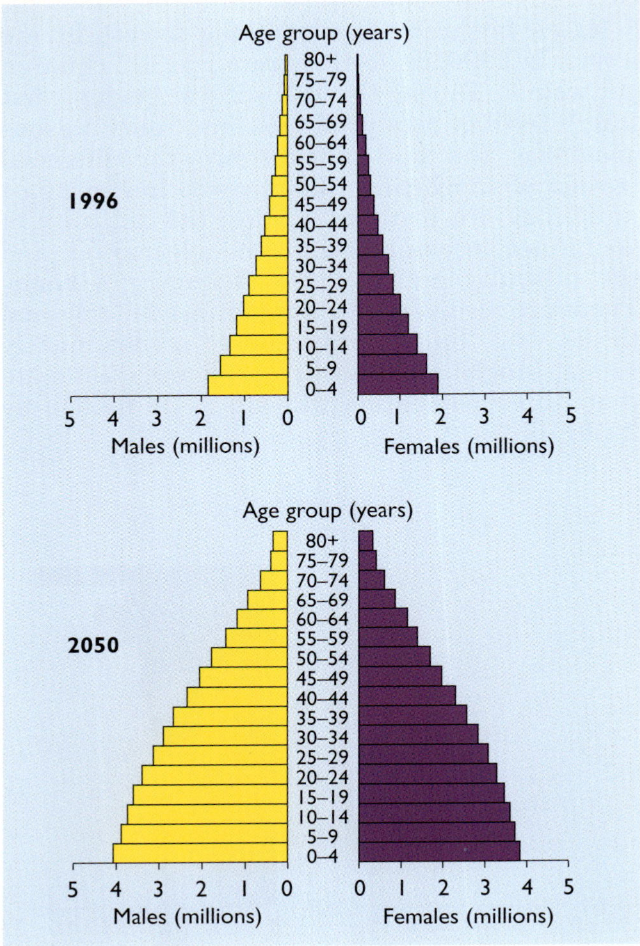

Population profiles for Afghanistan, 1996 and 2050

Comparison of population data for Afghanistan and Australia, 1996

Data	Afghanistan	Australia
Birthrate (per 1000)	43.0	14.0
Death rate (per 1000)	18.0	7.0
Annual rate of growth (per cent)	2.5	1.0
Life expectancy at birth (years)	46.3	79.6
Infant mortality rate (per 1000)	147.0	5.0
Total fertility rate	6.1	1.8

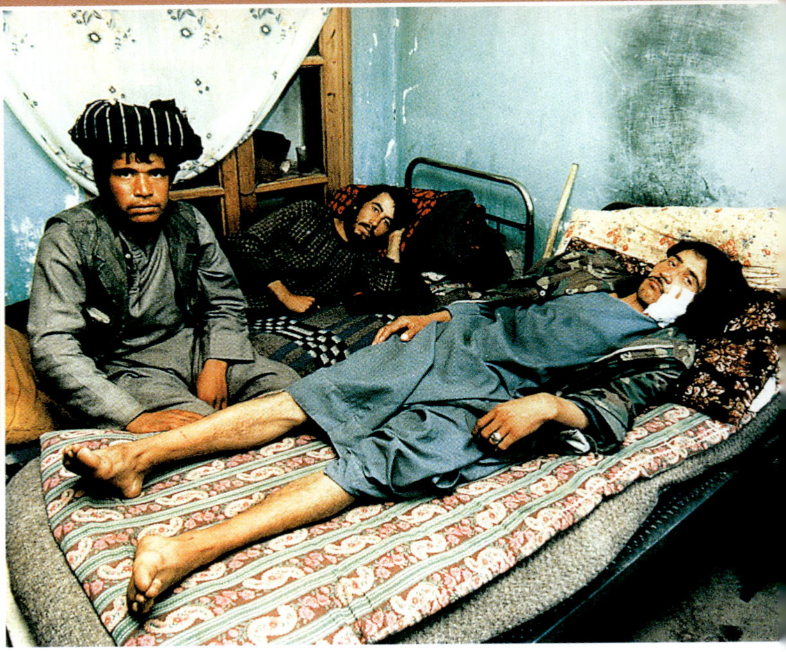

A hospital in Afghanistan

Activities

Investigation: *Examining growing populations*

1. Study the drawing of people discussing why they have large families.
   (a) Identify the strongest factors that result in people choosing to have more children.
   (b) Select two factors you have outlined. For each factor, develop some strategies to change the reasons for having a large family. Who would be responsible for such change?
2. Study the population profiles of Afghanistan.
   (a) Write sentences describing the population profile for Afghanistan in 1996 and the population predicted for 2050.
   (b) Why, do you think, is it predicted that Afghanistan's population will continue to grow for many years?
   (c) What do these profiles tell you about the number of aged people?
3. Study the photograph above. What effect might conditions in hospitals have on death rates?
4. Study the table comparing the Australian and Afghan populations.
   (a) Locate Afghanistan in an atlas. Describe its location, land capability and population density.
   (b) Write a summary paragraph comparing the population data for Afghanistan and Australia. Include the major differences and possible reasons for these.
5. In developing countries, there is often not enough money to pay for better education, health care, food and housing. Can they raise their standard of living while their populations continue to grow?

AN AGEING POPULATION

The populations of industrialised countries are increasing very slowly. As people become more affluent they want more comfort and fewer children. As life expectancy increases, birthrates fall. Urbanisation, industrialisation and improvements in education increase the cost of raising children and reduce their value as workers. Many people in industrialised countries prefer to have smaller families.

As the reasons for having large families have disappeared, the birthrate has fallen. Parents choose when to have children (if any), how many to have and when to have them. Birth control and education have played an important part in these decisions. Some people choose to have their families much later. Some women choose a career instead of children. Some people choose not to marry or marry at an older age. Sometimes the birthrates may fall below the level needed to maintain the size of a population. This is characteristic of Japan and Italy.

People who are 65 years or more are called 'aged'. Countries which have high numbers of aged people include North America, Japan, Australia, New Zealand and most of the European countries. An increase in the number of aged people in a population is related to two main factors — a fall in fertility and improvements in survival.

Japan is one of the most densely populated countries in the world and has an economy comparable to those of the European nations. It was the first developed country in modern times to initiate a birth-control program. In 1948 the Japanese Government formally instituted a policy using both contraception and abortion to limit family size. Japan's fertility rate is low at 1.4 children per woman.

Italy's birthrate is one of the lowest in the world. In 1996, its fertility rate was 1.2 children per woman. During the 1970s it was evident that Italy's fertility rate would decline. Some reasons given for the low fertility are the financial burden of supporting children who live at home until they are in their thirties; the difficulty of young people breaking into the job market; and the difficulty and expense of buying a home. There are also very few immigrants in Italy and those who have arrived are predominantly young, single males. Current figures estimate that Italy's population will fall to 38 million by 2050.

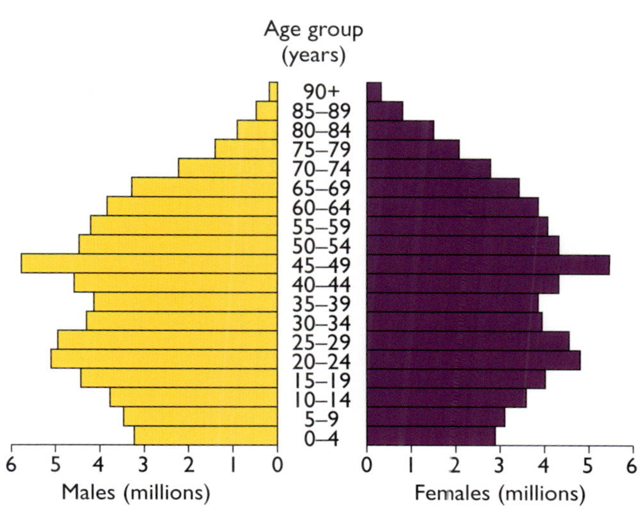

Population profile for Japan, 1996

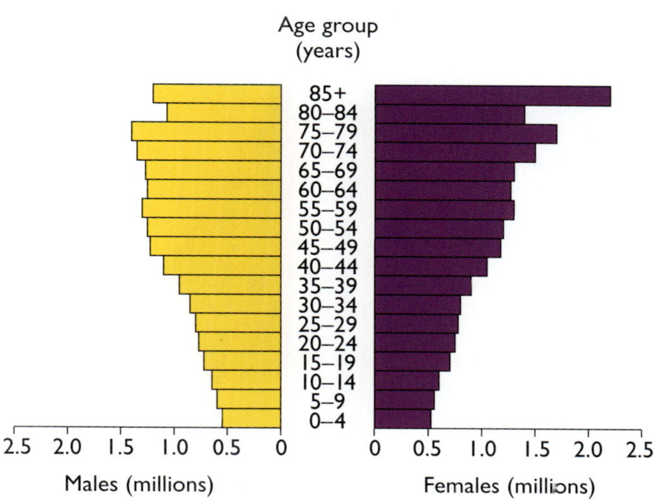

Predicted population profile for Italy, 2050

The consequences of an ageing population are numerous. The taxpayers will need to provide more funds for pensions, for not only are there going to be more people collecting a pension, but they will be collecting it for a longer time. The health and welfare of the elderly is also an issue. Hospitals and geriatric centres are expensive to establish and staff, and governments are faced with increasing expenditure in these areas as the population continues to age.

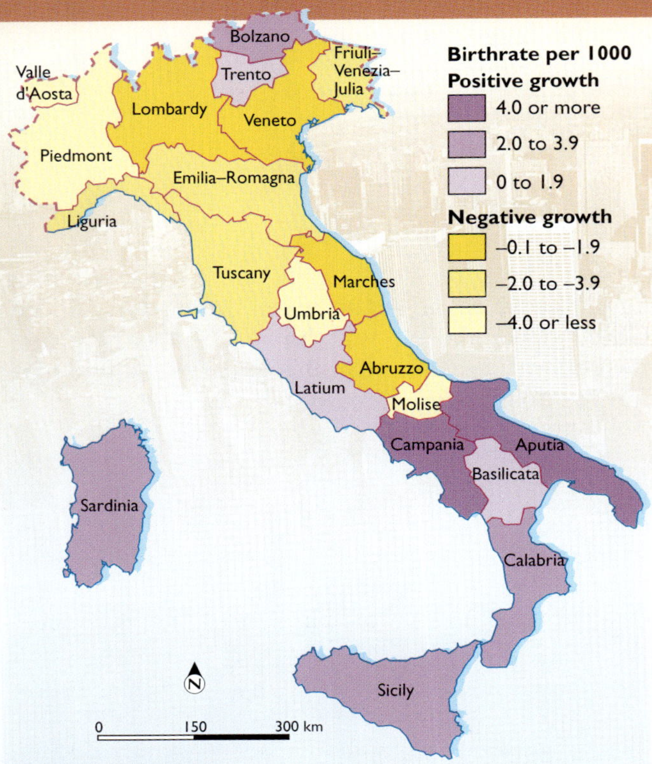

Birthrates in Italy

Comparison of population data for Italy and Japan, 1996

Data	Italy	Japan
Birthrate (per 1000)	9	10
Death rate (per 1000)	10	10
Annual rate of growth (per cent)	–0.1	0.2
Life expectancy at birth (years)	78.3	79.9
Infant mortality rate (per 1000)	6	4
Total fertility rate	1.2	1.4

In Australia an ageing population has also provided entrepreneurs with a new market. Housing villages for the elderly are a new idea. They usually consist of a number of individual units and common areas such as recreation halls and medical facilities that provide companionship and care for the elderly. Another trend is the number of media advertisements aimed at the elderly. Investments and trusts, gardening aids, and magazines are just a few of the products that are being developed specifically for the growing elderly market.

In some countries where the birthrate is so low the population is falling, people are being encouraged to have more children, so the country can look after its own population properly. This is occurring in Germany.

Activities

Investigation: *Factors of an ageing population*

1. List the lifestyle changes that have caused falling birthrates.

2. Describe the services that an aged population needs. Where does the money come from to pay for these services? What might happen in the future if the aged population increases?

3. Study the population pyramid for Japan in 1996. (Note that this is a similar profile to Italy in 1996.)
(a) Describe the 1996 population profile for Japan.
(b) How does this compare with Afghanistan's profile on page 335? What are the major differences?

4. Study the figure showing Italy's birthrates.
(a) Describe the pattern of birthrates in Italy.
(b) Explain why the following reasons help explain the birthrate pattern in Italy.
- Strong Catholic values and beliefs in the south
- The south has a more rural and agriculture-based economy.
- Elderly people are retiring to regions such as Liguria, Emilia-Romagna and Tuscany.

5. Study Italy's predicted population profile for 2050.
(a) Describe the population profile for Italy in 2050.
(b) Predict what will happen to Italy's population if it continues to fall.
(c) Italy's population in 1996 was 57.5 million. List the main impacts on the Italian economy and society if its population drops to 38 million, as predicted.
(d) What government action could be taken to overcome this population trend?

6. Study the comparison of Italy's and Japan's populations. How do these data compare with similar data for Afghanistan, on page 335?

7. Write a story describing the life of an elderly person or a young person in Japan in 2050.

8. A country which has a falling birthrate will have fewer children. The following describe some possible consequences of this.
- Young people become a scarce resource.
- Schools close due to the lack of students.
- The middle-aged and elderly determine society's priorities.
- There are fewer people to do the work and produce all the goods and services currently in demand.

Add further consequences to this list. Use a large sheet of paper to draw these ideas into a concept map where statements are linked with arrows. Add further consequences as you proceed.

IN CONTROL — CHINA'S POPULATION

The first national census in China took place in 1953 and showed a population of 582 600 000 people. A second census, taken in 1964, showed an increase to 694 580 000; the third, in 1982, revealed a population of 1 008 180 000. This made China the first nation to ever have a population of more than one billion people. Between 1953 and 1991, the death rate dropped from 22.5 to about 6.7 per 1000 population, while the birth-rate declined from about 45 per 1000 to 19.7. Life expectancy at birth in 1990 was 68 years for men and 71 years for women. At that rate China was still growing by 18 million people each year, the same as Australia's total population in 1997. Using these figures it was predicted there would be 1.3 billion Chinese people by 2000.

In 1972 China's leaders set a target to limit the population to less than 1.2 billion people by 2000. They began to educate the people and persuade them to have only one child per family. Contraception was, and still is, freely available, as are abortions and sterilisation. The legal age of marriage was raised to 22 for men and 20 for women. It is estimated that 70 per cent of Chinese couples use modern **contraceptives**. Huge numbers of unwanted pregnancies were ended by abortions. It is estimated that in 1984 there were 18 million births and 9 million legal abortions.

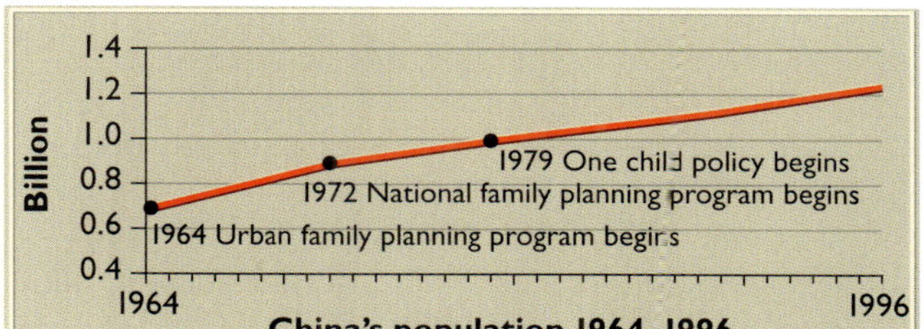

China's population 1964–1996

There were more than 1.2 billion people in China in 1996. In 1965 the fertility rate in China was 6.5. In 1996 it was 1.8, below replacement level. The Chinese have shown that governments can intervene to limit growth. The measures used would not be acceptable in many countries, but have been successful in slowing China's population growth.

In 1980 the government reported that 65 per cent of the population was less than 30 years of age. Therefore, a substantial proportion of the Chinese population will be of childbearing age for several decades. China's population will not fall for about four decades.

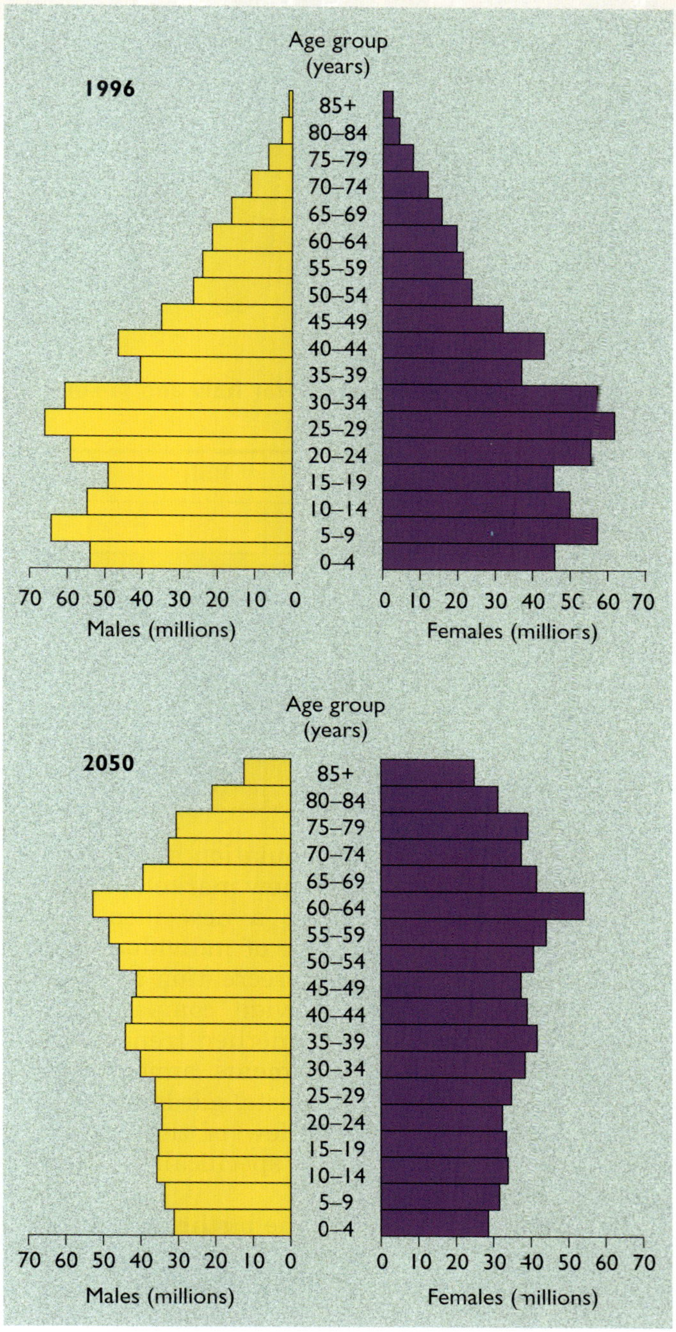

Population profiles of China, 1996 and 2050

Family planning poster in China

Activities

Investigation: *Controlling population growth*

1. Why did China's population increase so quickly?
2. Describe the social and environmental problems China would face if its population continued to grow by 18 million people per year.
3. What methods did the Chinese Government use to reduce its population?
4. Study the family planning poster. Huge posters such as these aim to convince people to have smaller families. What message might it give to people? Would this work in Australia? Why? Why not?
5. The birthrate in China is the same as Japan's. Why will it take longer for China's total population to fall?
6. Study the population profiles of China for 1996 and 2050.
   (a) Which population profile in previous sections of this chapter does China's 1996 profile most resemble? Which projected profile does China's projected 2050 profile most resemble?
   (b) Based on current predictions, the annual growth rate for China will be –0.5 per cent. What will this mean for the population?
   (c) Describe the problems which China may face if the projected 2050 profile is accurate. What action might the Chinese Government take to overcome these problems?
7. Some people in industrialised countries claim that China's method of birth control is an abuse of human rights. Discuss this with your class, carefully justifying your stance. You may like to consider the following:
   - Chinese society is rigidly organised, allowing the government to implement birth control steps which would be almost impossible in a democratic society.
   - China has limited resources and the highest population on Earth. Does it have any choice other than to control population growth?
   - The methods used by the government often reflect their fairness, that is, laws versus incentives. Which methods are used in China?

Communication: *Draw a diagram*

If only one child per family is born, there would eventually be no brothers, sisters, aunts, uncles or cousins in Chinese families. Draw a picture to show your family — grandparents, parents, uncles, aunts, etc. Now draw the same picture to show a Chinese family which has followed the one child policy for three generations. How would you feel being part of this Chinese family?

13.6

MORE PEOPLE, MORE PROBLEMS

Does the world have enough fertile land to feed twice as many people? Can productive employment be found for everyone? Can women everywhere gain access to the same opportunities for a full and healthy life as men? Can adequate health, housing and social services be provided for the billions more people expected to crowd the world's cities in the future? These are some of the questions being asked in relation to world population increase.

The population of the world's poorer countries is increasing very quickly. The number of people in poorer countries has risen by more than 3 billion in the past 100 years. In contrast, the number of people in rich, industrialised countries has increased by about 600 million over the same period of time.

The lowest-income countries are caught up in a phenomenon that has been called the 'poverty–population spiral'. This is illustrated in the diagram above right.

The more people there are on Earth, the faster resources are likely to be used up. Many people also argue that the increasing population causes large increases in pollution such as greenhouse gas emissions, acid rain and solid waste. But the countries which consume the most energy are the industrialised countries whose populations are not increasing as much as developing countries. Industrialised countries consume 80 per cent of world energy, but make up only 25 per cent of the world's population. It is the consumption by industrialised nations which is the biggest factor in the depletion of natural resources and environmental pollution.

The poverty–population spiral

Cairo — a densely populated, polluted city

It is estimated that by 2000 the world population will be 6.5 billion people. About two billion will be living in 400 very large cities. Large cities are greedy consumers of resources, producing vast amounts of waste and permanently damaging the environment.

The United Nations has suggested that the way of life of people in industrialised countries like Australia is too energy-expensive. For the poorer developing countries to become more industrialised and have a similar way of life would require five times as much energy as is used today. The answer must be for the developed countries to use less of the world's resources and for there to be a fairer distribution of these resources.

Activities

Investigation: *Problems of population growth*

1. Study the poverty–population spiral.
   (a) What is happening in each of the pictures? Why would the couple want more children?
   (b) How does this cycle perpetuate poverty?
   (c) List some strategies to help people break out of this cycle. Are the strategies acceptable to all people?
   (d) What impact does such a cycle have on the environment?
2. Why do people in industrialised countries cause more pollution than those in developing countries?
3. Study the photograph of Cairo.
   What will cities of the future be like? Would you like to live in one? Describe the impact of such places on people and the environment.
4. Study the following list.
   (a) Draw a table to identify which of the following you consider are luxury items and which are not.

   roads, fast food, medicine, CDs
   books, toasters, foot warmers, newspapers
   public transport, leaf blowers, televisions, computers

   (b) Add five more items to each column.
   (c) Share your ideas with another person. What are the similarities and differences in your list?
   (d) With your partner try to produce a common list. You must agree on the items to change and justify why each should go on one list or another.
   (e) Repeat this activity with another group.
   (f) Discuss the following questions with the class:
   - Was it easy to separate the luxury goods from the others?
   - Was it difficult to convince others to change their list?
   - Would you go without the luxury goods if other, less fortunate people could gain better lifestyles? Outline the difficulties of this suggestion.
   - Can education in your school and community change people's attitudes towards the consumption of goods? Explain.
5. Conduct a class debate on the following topic:
   'The damage to the world cannot be reduced while governments pursue growth of both population and per capita consumption.'
6. A just distribution of the Earth's resources would help lift the poor from misery and be a strong incentive to reduce population growth. But what comes first? Do you raise people's living standards so that they can choose not to have as many children? Or do you give people the means to stop having so many children so the living standards of the children they have can be raised? Conduct a class discussion on this question.

Communication: *Make a documentary*

The media presents many confusing images about the world's population and its possible impact on the environment.

Form groups of four students. You work for an independent film production company and are producing a short documentary to show what is happening to world population. Your documentary will explore the following broad themes:

- The world's population is increasing rapidly.
- The population in developing and industrialised countries is growing at very different rates, for quite specific reasons.
- Overpopulation in developing countries is often blamed for many local and global environmental problems, which is unfair in many cases.
- The lifestyles of people in many industrialised countries are causing the most environmental damage.
- There are enough resources and food for all the people in the world to live comfortable and healthy lifestyles.
- A reduction in consumption, especially of luxury goods, by people in industrialised countries is required to distribute resources more evenly.

For each segment, describe in detail the images which will be used and the facts which will be provided. You may like to use information and images from this chapter. Present your short documentary as a video or a play.

SOLUTIONS

Global overpopulation is seen by many as one of the world's greatest problems. The world at the moment does have the resources to support its inhabitants, however, access to these resources remains a problem. Issues in population control therefore must be directed to ensuring that resources are in place for future generations and that the division of resources between industrialised and developing countries is fairer.

Discussing solutions to the world's population problem is very difficult. Governments and religious groups have different views about family planning. It is also an emotional topic. People need to make their own decision after analysing the facts. Education is a key to understanding these facts.

Thomas Malthus, an Englishman born in 1766, wrote an essay about human population in 1798. He stated in this essay that the world would always produce a population which was too big for the food supplies and other resources needed for survival. From this he developed the theory that there would always be three checks on population numbers: war, famine and disease.

Some people still follow this view and believe there is no population problem because war, famine and disease will never be overcome. These disasters act as a natural control of population numbers.

Another view is that the Earth can actually support an even larger population than it does today and, if resources were shared more equally, the standard of living could increase for many of the poor in the world. The illustration opposite reflects some of the varying views about population control.

The difficulty of lowering fertility rates is related to cultural, social and economic conditions that have prevailed for generations. It is no coincidence that fertility rates are highest in developing countries where people are poor and have little education, and lowest in rich, industrialised countries with high levels of education and good social provisions.

Population control

ADRIENNE CLARKE

We're going to see the population of the earth almost double to about 10 billion people by 2050. Many of the other problems we face derive from the pressures of population — destruction of the atmosphere, forests, soils, water supplies and many animal and plant species.

One effective, two-pronged way of tackling the problem is to put population control in the hands of women and to reward them for limiting the size of families by giving them an economic advantage.

This isn't a novel idea. It was pioneered by Mechai Viravaidya, chairman of the Population and Community Development Association in Bangkok. There, he made condoms available where women congregate — at hairdressers, markets, sewing centres, etc. He also rewarded them for not being pregnant by granting them ownership of a pig.

The more years a woman avoided pregnancy, the more pigs she was granted. This gave her economic power over her own destiny. Viravaidya's strategy has been extremely successful: over a 25-year period the average number of children born per woman dropped from 6.14 to 2.2.

The experience of aid programs is this: if women are given some sort of economic independence through the provision of sewing machines, kilns or other tools, they will use them to gain benefits that will flow to the children, particularly food and education. The result is fewer, better-fed, better-educated children. In contrast, money controlled by men is too often diverted to buy guns and other weapons of destruction.

I would then extend this simple, but effective, idea to other groups where multiple pregnancies lead women — not only in developing countries, but in some parts of society in developed countries such as Australia and the United States — into a cycle of poor health, poverty, low education, lack of economic power and lack of choices, which persist for generations.

Rewards for not being pregnant could vary according to circumstances. In developing countries, it may well be ownership of animals or equipment for the manufacture of goods. In more developed societies it could again be equipment and training for the manufacture of goods or provision of services; or perhaps the opportunity to complete a tertiary education program or an apprenticeship, which could lead to better prospects of income earning than those available under a developed country's welfare system.

The long-term benefits would flow through the mothers to the children, who will be healthier and better-educated. Such an idea might even eventually lead to an enhanced participation of women in government in all countries.

Age, 19 January 1995.

Different views about population control

‘We are a small educational group that believes in the relationship between education, especially of women, and reduced birthrate . . . We move from one location to another and teach people reading and writing. We leave information about birth control and emphasise the benefit of having fewer children. As women become more literate, birthrates fall. Later marriages also lead to fewer children. Marriage is latest in countries that invest more in education. We need 50 units to train teachers to visit more people and spread the message.’

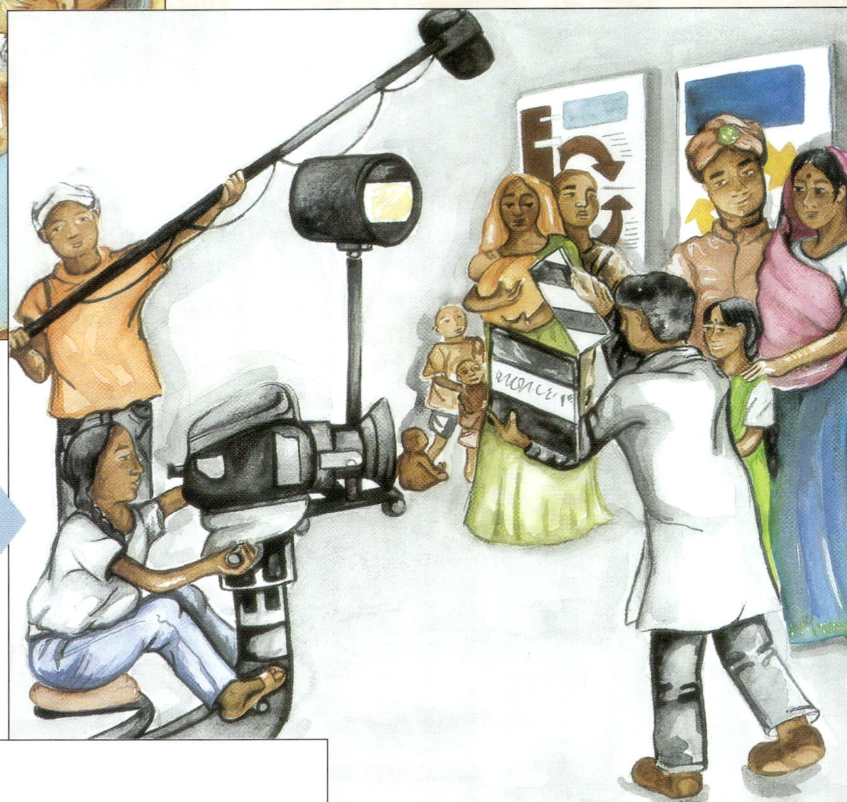

‘We are an advertising company employed by governments to teach people about birth control. Suddenly introducing birth control into societies where children have always been viewed as important is not easy. We produce posters and short films to help people understand birth control methods as well as explaining the benefits of having fewer children. We are making a film in which people talk about how having fewer children has increased their prosperity and chances of survival. We would like to make the same film in other languages. We have run out of money and need 30 units to complete it.’

‘We are a volunteer group which helps improve the living conditions in villages. We teach people from many villages how to build wells so they will have a good supply of clean water. These people return to their villages with their knowledge and the government provides them with materials to build wells. With a supply of clean water, health problems are reduced. As the children survive, there is a greater incentive to have fewer children and the birthrate falls. The villagers also have new skills to help in their community. We have broken a number of tools used to demonstrate well building. We need 35 units to replace them.’

Projects for population control

'We are a group of actors who travel around the country in a bus, teaching people about basic health care, which can help improve survival for them and their children. We give talks, sing, show films and perform plays at schools and offices. We believe that we are having an impact and improving health care. Many families are having fewer children as the ones they already have are surviving. Our bus is in urgent need of repair so we can continue our work. We need 45 units to fix it.'

Activities

Investigation: *Seeking solutions*

1. To what extent is Thomas Malthus's view about population control self-fulfilling? (that is, if nothing is done about war, famine and disease, they will always continue to happen). What other arguments might there be? What about over-consumption and ecologically unsound practices?
2. Some countries have developed solutions to lower population numbers, including:
   - tax relief and pensions designed to discourage big families (e.g. Colombia)
   - maternity provisions and school enrolment procedures that favour small families (e.g. Singapore).

   Explain how each of these strategies might work. Outline another strategy that could result in a smaller population.
3. Study the people presenting different views about population control (on page 343).
   (a) Do you agree or disagree with each of the views presented?
   (b) Rank the statements from one to seven. Rank the statement that you agree with most as number one and the statement you agree with least as number seven. Justify your choices.
   (c) Compare responses with another person, then with the class.
   (d) Did you have any difficulty coming to a decision about the ranking? What was most important when making your final decision?
4. Read the newspaper article about population control (on page 342).
   (a) Outline the main solution to overpopulation suggested by the author of this article.
   (b) Describe where this solution has been tried. How successful was this solution?
   (c) Is such a solution applicable for women in industrialised countries? Outline how this might operate.
   (d) Do you agree with the views outlined in this article? Justify your stance.
5. Work in groups of four to complete this activity. Study the information about projects for population control.
   (a) Each group has 100 units of money to allocate to the projects outlined. You will not be able to support all of the projects. Your group must decide which projects to support and provide reasons for your decision. You may decide to allocate less money to a project than has been requested, but must provide good reasons for doing so.
   (b) When you have allocated your money, report your decision to the rest of the class, clearly outlining your reasons.
   (c) Complete the following:
   - Which project was given the most support from the class? Why?
   - Which project was given the least support? Why?
   - Describe the difficulties encountered when making your decision.
   - Outline the factors which were taken into account when making your decision.
6. Conduct a class debate on the topic: 'Over-consumption in rich countries is, in terms of the Earth's habitability, more serious than rapid population growth in poor countries'.

THE FUTURE

Population numbers are still growing very quickly, but there are signs that growth is beginning to slow. From 1950 to 1955 the global fertility rate was 5.0. In 1997 it was 2.9 and falling. Other sections in this chapter have discussed regional differences in this change. Most of the falls have been in industrialised countries, but are also evident in developing countries such as India and Bangladesh. India's population should stabilise at 230 million in about 35 years. The total fertility rate in Bangladesh has nearly halved in 13 years and is now 3.4.

If current trends continue around the world, it is estimated that the global fertility rate will fall to 1.6 children per woman. This is the same as the average in industrialised countries in 1996. The reasons for the change in fertility rates are summarised on the right.

When parents know their children will survive, fertility rates fall. This results in an increase in the average age of people in society. In 1990 approximately six per cent of the world's population was more than 65 years of age. By 2050 it is estimated this figure will be between 15 and 19 per cent.

In 1990 appoximately 32 per cent of the world's population lived in the industrialised countries of Europe, North America and Japan. In 1996, 20 per cent of people did. By 2050 this figure may be down to 12 per cent. This may change global power and influence.

There have been many positive signs about population and people's quality of life. For example, average life expectancy in developing countries has increased from 40 years in 1950 to 63 years in the mid-1990s.

Also, despite population growth and high infant mortality rates in a few countries, the absolute number of child deaths worldwide is falling.

Moreover, from 1960 to 1995, education spending in the developing world rose from 2.2 per cent to 3.4 per cent of gross national product. Female **literacy** increased in all regions of the world, doubling from 18 to 36 per cent in the least developed countries between 1970 and 1995.

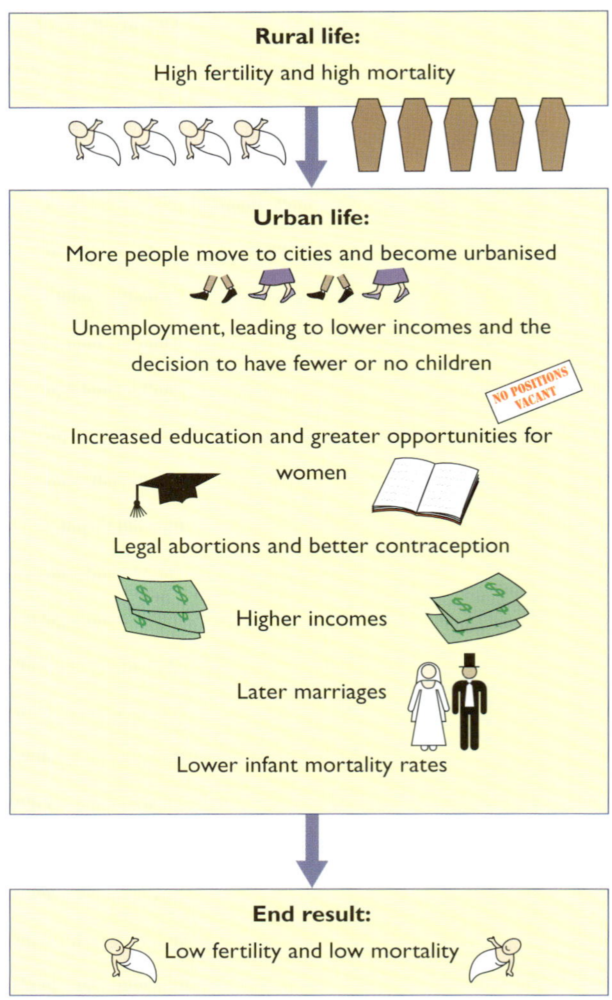

Demographic transition

Some people believe that a lower global population will be good for the environment. Others believe that if consumption increases despite falling population numbers, the environment will continue to suffer from pollution and degradation.

Even the smallest action by an individual can make a difference. Most often these actions result in reducing personal energy consumption, waste production and pollution. But how can we ensure the fair distribution of resources? The best answer is through reduced consumption.

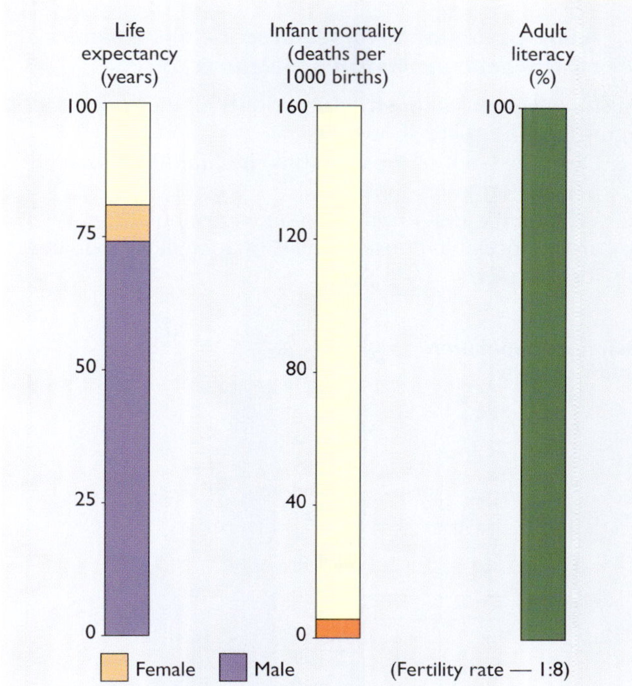

The physical quality of life index for Australia

Activities

Investigation: *Predicting future trends*

1. Outline the environmental, political, economic and social implications of a global fall in birthrates.
2. What will happen to domestic markets when population falls? For example, what will happen to the demand for new homes? What will happen to consumer demand in general? Who will produce the goods that are required by a society if a large portion of the population is aged?
3. If people in industrialised countries reduced their consumption, more resources would be available for the people in poorer countries. Complete the following activity to identify the things you could do without or use less of.
   (a) Imagine you are in your favourite room at home with many of your favourite possessions. Draw a picture of this room and label all the possessions.
   (b) Imagine there is a fire in your area and you must evacuate. Choose three things to take with you which will be saved from the fire.
4. Can you make do without the rest? Which other possessions would you have liked to keep?
5. Can you identify luxury possessions as opposed to those which are necessary?
6. Would your quality of life be reduced if you did not have all of your possessions?
7. How might your lifestyle compare to a person your age in a developing country? What might they choose to save?
8. Repeat this activity with other members of your family. What differences and similarities did you find?
9. Share your findings with others in your class.
10. Write an article in a futuristic newspaper describing what has happened to the world population. Give specific examples from a few countries.

Communication: *Creating a visual display*

You will need to refer to the population statistics in selected countries in 1996 (page 333) to complete this activity. You will also need a sheet of poster paper and a blank outline map of the world.

(a) The physical quality of life index (PQLI) is used to measure human progress. Infant mortality, adult literacy and life expectancy are given equal value and used to measure quality of life. The figure to the left shows the PQLI for Australia. A fertility rate is also provided to see if there is any correlation between it and a person's quality of life. A good PQLI has high life expectancy, low infant mortality and high adult literacy.

(b) Use sheets of graph paper to draw PQLI graphs for all the countries listed on page 333 (use the graph shown on this page as an example). Record the fertility rate as shown.

(c) Shade all the countries listed on page 333 on your blank world map. Now paste this map onto the centre of your sheet of poster paper.

(d) Cut all the graphs from the graph paper and paste them onto the poster around the world map. Draw lines to show the country to which each set of data refers. Provide an appropriate title for your completed poster.

(e) Answer the following questions:
- Which country has the best PQLI? Which has the lowest?
- Write a summary statement to describe the relationship between PQLI and fertility rates.
- Describe some of the cultural factors which might affect PQLI.
- What action might a government take to improve the PQLI of its people?
- Why is income not included in a PQLI?

13.9 Meeting the outcomes

EVALUATE HOW DIFFERENT FACTORS AFFECT THE DISTRIBUTION AND DYNAMICS OF HUMAN POPULATION.

Identify a range of factors responsible for change to human populations.

1. Write three summary paragraphs describing the factors responsible for population change. Use the following terms in your summary — birthrate, death rate, developing country, industrialised country, fertility rate, life expectancy, infant mortality, literacy.
2. Look at the photographs below. Sometimes images can be misleading and create stereotypes. For example, not all people in developing countries are poor and not all people in industrialised countries are rich. Study these photographs again and write a list of questions you would like to ask these families about where they live and what they do.

Apply relevant factors to explain the distribution pattern in human populations.

1. Why is there variation in the population density of the world? (13.2)
2. Explain why Australia has such a low population density. (13.2)
3. How can the United States have a high total population and relatively low population density? (13.2)

Analyse relevant factors to describe the dynamics of change affecting human populations.

Australia's **population structure** for 1996 and estimated figures for 2050 are shown below.

1. Describe each of these graphs, including the overall population trend shown.
2. What is the definition of an ageing population? What are the possible consequences of an ageing population for Australia?

Australia's population profile in 1996

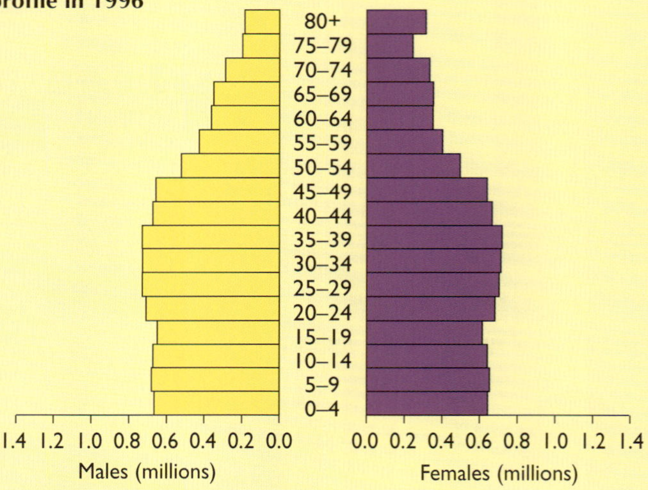

Australia's predicted population profile in 2050

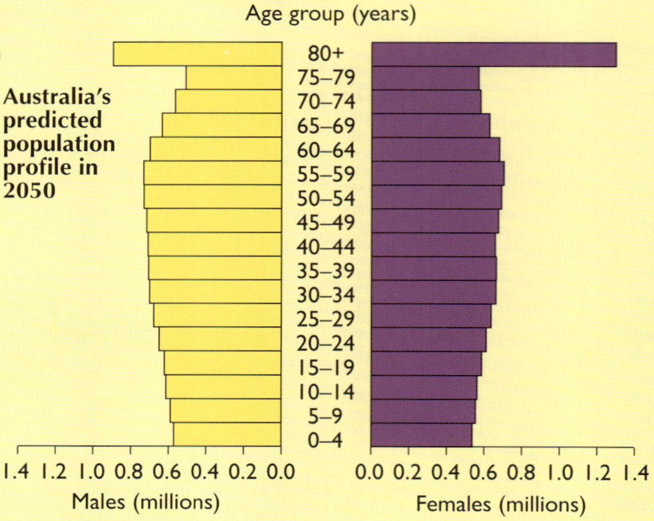

3. In 1996, Australia's fertility rate was 1.8 and growth rate was 1.1 per cent. What do these figures indicate about Australia's future population?
4. Use information in this chapter to describe the population differences between Australia and Italy.

Use current and historical data to predict future patterns in the distribution of human populations.

Study the newspaper article below.

1. Why do rural couples in China have more children than urban couples?
2. Poorer families in rural China have more children than those in a better financial situation. How does this reflect what is happening in developing and industrial countries?
3. Give examples from the article of using incentives and education rather than penalties to control population growth. In your opinion, which would work best? Which method might produce faster results? Explain your answers.
4. Why is it important to improve the status of women when considering action to reduce population numbers?
5. What are the reasons, do you think, for farmers and ethnic minorities in China being allowed to have more than one child?
6. What is the significance of having boys, as opposed to girls, in rural communities?
7. Construct a futures wheel which shows all possible consequences of a falling global population. (For an example of a completed futures wheel, see chapter 3, section 3.4.)
8. Write an essay which discusses the relative impacts of an increasing population in a developing country compared with continual growth in consumption by people in rich, industrialised countries.

China renews push to wean children from families

By STEPHEN HUTCHEON

China has launched a new nationwide campaign to stem the growth of its 1.2 billion population, offering rural couples economic incentives to bear fewer children.

The State Family Planning Commission will encourage farmers to have smaller families by offering those who practice birth control financial, material and technical incentives, the official Xinhua newsagency said.

Xinhua said the program will help farmers break free from the circle of 'poverty, more children, poverty' and in turn trigger 'a revolution in people's attitudes towards birth control through economic development'.

The focus on rural dwellers, who comprise 70 per cent of the population, highlights the problem facing family planners as they attempt to peg the population below 1.3 billion by 2000.

The birth rate is 24 per cent higher in rural areas than in cities. Most of the areas boasting the highest birth rates are also among its most impoverished.

Increasing wealth is therefore seen as the key to stemming the population tide. By raising incomes, the commission hopes to wean women off child-rearing and ease concerns about retirement.

In the countryside, farmers have needed children to help with the farm and to care for them in their old age. Boys are favoured as they are thought to be more capable of hard manual work. Tradition dictates that girls, when they marry, look after their husband's family.

According to Dr Huang Boashan of the State Family Planning Commission, the emphasis of the national policy over the past two years has changed from one that relies on penalties and administrative fiat to one that emphasises incentive and education.

'We want to improve the status of women in the family and in the society, but to do this we must first improve their economic situation,' he said.

Dr Huang said a pilot program combining income-generation programs for women with family planning classes had proven very successful in many regions, giving women opportunities to do more than raise children.

In addition, the commission is trying to raise standards of education in rural areas both to enhance employment prospects and to allow women to become more independent.

Dr Huang said such women would be more able to resist suggestions from their husbands and mothers-in-law to produce more children.

Beijing is also encouraging local governments to introduce a new social security system, allowing farmers to contribute to a state-run pension fund that would provide for them in retirement and diminish the need to produce offspring as insurance.

Although China's population is still increasing, the important fact is that the rate of growth has slowed, Dr Huang said.

Between 1964 and 1974 the population increased by 100 million every five years. It took six-and-a-half years to register the next 100 million increase and seven years to add the most recent 100 million additions.

The success in reducing the growth rate is due in part to the national family planning policy adopted in the early 1970s. This was refined in 1979 with the introduction of the one-child policy, an often coercive program which critics say forced many women to have abortions and undergo sterilisation.

The one-child policy has been a misnomer, according to a Western population expert who did not want to be named.

'Whilst the goal is for the Han community — China's predominant race comprising 92 per cent of [the] population — to have one child, provincial administrations are given considerable latitude for interpretation,' he said.

Under the policy couples in urban areas are allowed to have one child. Farm couples are allowed to have a second and try for a boy if the first child is a girl or is disabled. Couples among the nation's 80 million ethnic minorities can have up to three offspring.

Age, 15 February 1995.

Index